Manpower Planning and the Development of Human Resources

Manpower Planning and the Development of Human Resources

THOMAS H. PATTEN, JR.
Michigan State University

Wiley-Interscience
a Division of John Wiley & Sons, Inc.
New York · London · Sydney · Toronto

In memory of my father and mother

Preface

In the past fifty years, the industrial education function in America has evolved from an initial concentration upon the development of apprentices through the establishment of foreman training and later into executive development. In this period of time there has been a number of parallel developments such as improvements in methods for identifying training needs, the refinement of a variety of training techniques, greater sophistication in evaluation of the results of training, and considerable experimentation in deciding upon the most appropriate type of organizational pattern for carrying out industrial training activities.

The purpose of this book is to provide a framework for placing these developments in industrial education and training in perspective for the practitioner in industry as well as the social scientist and student, all of whom require a meaningful and convenient vantage point for understanding how these phenomena are interrelated.

Clearly, human development which takes place in industry must be seen in the context of the surrounding society, educational institutions, and socioeconomic change. In this context, manpower planning and the development of human resources can be viewed broadly as a cycle involving the determination of the numbers of people to be supplied by skill and/or educational level in either an organization, such as a business, or a total society; the establishment of specific educational and training programs of a wide variety of types; the identification and utilization of teaching, training, and instructional techniques necessary for carrying out human development; and, lastly, the identification and application of valid and reliable techniques for appraising the results of the educational and training programs. Policies, values, problems, and objectives are involved throughout the cycle. Obviously, at the completion of the cycle, the individual or organization that is concerned with administering the education and training is then in a position to plan anew in regard to recycling the entire process.

Each chapter of the book focuses upon what in my judgment is the key problem or cluster of central issues on a facet of the manpower field. This approach leads to an unpatterned format in the development of the different chapters, but it is deliberate. Different problems must be treated as is best for understanding them. Similarly, the book is written for practitioners who are not trained mathematicians, statisticians, or specialists in the analytical tools of econometrics and operations research. References to these topics as they relate to manpower planning and the development of human resources are made where appropriate.

I assume entirely the usual responsibility for errors of omission and commission, regretting any that may be discerned by readers more closely associated with the problem areas and emerging fields encompassed in the book.

THOMAS H. PATTEN, JR.

East Lansing, Michigan
November 1970

Acknowledgments

I wish to acknowledge assistance obtained from colleagues at the Ford Motor Company and the University of Detroit in the preparation of the book. Of the individuals with whom I was long associated at Ford, I would like to single out three as being sources of great personal stimulation and insight. Archie A. Pearson, Personnel Planning Manager of the Manufacturing Staff until his retirement in 1970, a perceptive and probing inquirer into training and industrial relations problems of all types, had an early influence on my thinking about the proper scope of manpower planning and its integration with training activities. He provided me with many opportunities to try out new ideas, supervise training materials development, and supervise and conduct personnel research and manpower planning studies. Dr. C. Hoyt Anderson, Director, Personnel Research and Recruitment Office, helped me get involved in a variety of projects and provided developmental experiences which have proven to be of inestimable value. Arthur W. Saltzman, Manager of the Personnel Research and Analysis Department in the Personnel and Organization Staff, an effervescent innovator and hard-charger against the forces of intellectual pusillanimity in all quarters, has been a constant influence and had a decided effect on my initial desire to write this book. Mr. Saltzman's high standards, broadranging intellectual interests, and search for significance in education suggested to me a decade ago that a broader look at industrial training and manpower than has prevailed in the past was warranted.

While serving on the faculty of the University of Detroit, I was given a reduced teaching load in the winter, 1967 trimester so that I could devote time to integrating my thoughts and starting this book. The late Professor Edward D. Wickersham had arranged for this load reduction before his death and had strongly encouraged me to go ahead with the book. We also collaborated in establishing a new graduate course on manpower planning and development, which I offered for the first time after his death. Most of the students in the course worked in various staff and line managerial positions in the automobile industry and had a wealth of experience to share both in the classroom and in term papers. I am indebted to many of them for ideas and examples which they provided me.

In addition, the University of Detroit made available the proficient and helpful typing of Mrs. Nell Hanks and Mrs. Erma Adams, who did much of the copy typing. Mrs. Dorothy Dudzinski did a yeoman job on typing first drafts.

The final draft and finishing touches in typing were covered by aid from the School of Labor and Industrial Relations, Michigan State University, whose faculty I joined on May 1, 1967.

Dr. Jack Stieber, Director of the School of Labor and Industrial Relations, gave me wide freedom and encouraged me to complete this book. Miss Emma Lee West did most of the final typing for me. She was at various times assisted by Mrs. Sharon Speck, Mrs. Jill Wood, and Miss Cheryl Green.

Robert Kempiak of the U-D and Ernest J. Richard of SLIR-MSU provided assistance to me, and the latter handled the final coordination of all the work needed to complete the manuscript and get it to the editor.

Contents

*Manpower Planning
and the Development
of Human Resources*

CHAPTER 1

Introduction to Manpower Problems in Industrial Society

True affluence should be measured by the quality of human beings living in a nation and working in organizations of all kinds. Enrichment of human life to the point where there is attainment of some ultimate Utopia will always be a noble objective; however, the ideal commonwealth will probably remain an elusive goal just beyond our grasp, although one toward which a society such as ours will always strive.

Judging by American social and economic history, concern for the quality of people and their well-being has heightened since the nation was founded. In recent years this concern has been shown in a spate of legislation on manpower, education, and welfare. It has also been reflected in changes in policies, plans, and programs administered by professional industrial relations and personnel managers and manpower specialists in pace-setting organizations of all kinds.

In this chapter we discuss the orientation of the book as a whole and also point out subjects with which it is not concerned or concerned only peripherally. We discuss some of the changing perspectives on education, personnel administration, and the public employment service in America. We then explain and define in a preliminary way some of the key concepts used throughout the book. These include organization, manpower planning, manpower policy, human resources, development, education, training, socialization, and learning. Next, we examine the central focus of the book and the conceptualization of manpower problems as a type of social problem. Finally, we discuss some of the more significant and dynamic aspects of change in contemporary American society, their possible implications for democracy, and then conclude the chapter.

ORIENTATION OF THE BOOK

This is a professional book addressed primarily to industrial relations and personnel managers and specialists in organizations of all kinds, including industrial, governmental, military, educational, and various others. In this sense the book focuses upon the establishment or micro level. It is not an economics book written for the professional economist and directed to economic analyses at the macro level.

The book is addressed to the "manpower specialist" in organizations, who is probably located organizationally in the industrial relations or personnel department. The author has taken the point of view that either someone or some organizational component in the firm, agency, or unit of a larger organization is responsible for the manpower-planning and human resource development function in the total organization. In a smaller industrial firm, this individual may have many other functions as well and be called the personnel manager, industrial relations manager, or training director. Probably he would most often have the title training director. However, we have eschewed use of the title "training director" because we do not wish to imply that our conception of the manpower specialist is limited to the duties which normally comprise the work of the typical training director. Our conception of the manpower specialism is considerably broader than training, as the reader will subsequently see.

In a large organization the manpower specialist's function is probably carried out by a multiplicity of persons, most of whom would organizationally be located in such functions as training, management development, organization planning, and personnel administration. In the very largest firms, the function would be split still further in its conduct. The administration of the manpower specialism would include the headquarters staff and counterpart managerial personnel in the decentralized locations, such as divisions, plants, branches, sales offices, subsidiaries, and affiliates, with all playing a part in the concerted effort. Therefore, the discussion in the book sometimes centers upon the person who carries out manpower planning and human resource development and at other times focuses upon the organizational component or components that have responsibility for this work. The point of reference in each case should be apparent from the context. For the sake of simplicity and to avoid discussing unnecessarily a variety of organizational arrangements, we have often used the term "manpower specialist" or "manpower function" in the book to refer to the person or the organizational component doing the work which we have in mind.

AN OVERVIEW OF THE MANPOWER SPECIALIST

Although in subsequent chapters we discuss the work of the manpower specialist in considerable detail, it should be helpful to provide here an indication of what the manpower specialist is supposed to know and to do. First, it is assumed that he has a good working knowledge of the organization in which he is employed, including its structure and policies. Second, he has knowledge of planning techniques, their control and implementation, and knowledge of ways to persuade managers and higher administrators to endorse and carry out these plans. Third, he has knowledge of educational and training program cycling. As a minimum, he knows how to conduct needs analyses, prepare training materials, present training sessions, and evaluate the results of programs. Inasmuch as educational and training programs are designed to meet the needs of organizations, and much of the content of education and training is concerned with organizational learning, the manpower specialist is necessarily a student not only of organizations in general but also of his employing organization in particular. At the same time, he is fully qualified to consult with managers and other employees and to provide advice concerning manpower planning, education, and training.

Fourth, the manpower specialist is also the company or organizational spokesman on internal manpower matters to various levels of government and colleges and universities. Fifth, he is, correspondingly, the interpreter to the employing company or organization of legislation and educational affairs. It can thus be seen that the fifth responsibility is the obverse of the fourth; the essential point is that the manpower specialist is the link in his sphere of competency between his employing organization and other outside organizations. Sixth, the manpower specialist formulates organizational policies on manpower, education, and training. These policies when formulated are referred to higher management for ultimate determination and approval.

To repeat, this brief sketch of the work of the manpower specialist indicates that our interest in manpower matters in this book is at the level of the organization, not at the level of the economy. This does not mean that we shall not be looking outward and upward to the surrounding economy and society from time to time. Indeed, we must do so in order to understand the manpower specialism in its proper context. Most education and training which is carried out in organizations is based upon the need for organizational learning and for solving organizational problems. But many of the problems that occur in organizations and the deficiencies in learning which people display are caused by inadequacies in society and in the socialization of people. Manpower specialists are often involved in remedying these imperfections through training and educational programs. For these and other reasons we must consider relationships between the organization and society.

We particularly lack a conceptualization of manpower planning and the development of human resources through teaching–learning processes in large-scale organizations. However, we cannot in this book accomplish a great deal more than provide some organized thoughts about manpower problems as social problems and to draw freely upon the conceptual corpus of sociology for useful analytical tools concerning the development of human resources. The result rules out a systematic analysis in terms of a general theory but provides a way of looking at the problems of manpower planning and development of people from an essentially sociological standpoint. This focus of attention is novel to the extent that the surface has only been scratched to date in the literature of a potential sociology of industrial education and manpower.

CHANGED CORE CONCEPTS IN PERSONNEL ADMINISTRATION

Concomitant with the changing social, political, and economic environment in America has been a shifting focus in the field of personnel administration. This is not an entirely new shift but probably a restatement of some of the traditional interests in personnel work which were lost sight of as other interests in the field ebbed and flowed.

Thirty years ago Chester I. Barnard made clear reference to the manpower–human resources area as being central in personnel administration:

"My own belief is strong that the capacity, development, and state of mind of employees as individuals must be the focal point of all policy and practice relating to personnel. . . . I suppose that the primary purpose in the minds of those who develop personnel policies and who manage businesses and organizations is generally not to develop individuals but to facilitate the working together of groups of people toward definite ends. In my view this purpose is secondary in point of order but equally important to that of developing the individual, and the two together constitute the entire legitimate purpose of management so far as the personnel is concerned."[1]

Other perceptive students of organization have reiterated this same thought from time to time. Writing in the early 1950s one of America's

[1] Chester I. Barnard, *Organization and Management*, Harvard University Press, Cambridge, 1948, pp. 6–8.

most insightful management consultants, Ewing W. Reilley, pointed out that personnel administration at that time presented one of the greatest untapped opportunities of any function in management—an opportunity that properly nurtured could give the function an almost explosive increase in its organizational importance. He noted that two functions (personnel and finance) cut across all others in organizations. The financial function provided the money, was responsible for its efficient utilization, and accounted for the results. Where the opportunities inherent in the finance function were fully developed, the chief financial officer had become the right arm of the president in many organizations. Personnel people were considered to have an opportunity to play a potentially even more important role as advisors to the president on the human resources of the organization, particularly regarding management employees. Personnel managers were perceived as standing at a crossroads: either they could go the way of treasurers and confine themselves to functions that, although important, were of no immediate or direct help to the president; or they could take the route of controllers and begin to look at the problems of the organization from the president's point of view, working on those of greatest concern to him. In the last twenty years controllers have attained a stature at least equal to that of their former bosses, the treasurers, because they have provided practical tools and analyses that help the president and operating managers to run the organization and solve important problems.[2] Personnel managers who were oriented toward the development of human resources, as opposed to those who were oriented toward such functions as placement, testing, recruitment, salary administration, employee services and benefits, and labor relations, could potentially become as important as controllers in the organization.

Typically, human-resources-oriented personnel managers would direct their attention to the top one percent, or even the top one tenth of one percent of employees whose decisions and leadership ordinarily shape the course of the organization. They would concern themselves primarily with answers to three important questions. What can be done to improve the ability of present executives in the organization? How can management people be motivated and rewarded to give them the greatest incentive for promoting the long-range profitability (or other objectives) of the organization? How can a better job be done in selecting individuals of high potential and developing them so that they can assume greater responsibilities created by retirements or by growth of the business?[3]

More recently it has been noted that in personnel work the pendulum has

[2] Ewing W. Reilley, "Bringing Personnel Administration Closer to the President," *Personnel,* Vol. 29, No. 5, March-April 1953, pp. 381–389.
[3] *Ibid.*

decidedly swung toward total organizational planning and manpower planning (i.e., beyond planning merely for the top one percent of employees). Many members of the old guard in personnel work have found great difficulty in adapting to this rediscovered field of human resources in personnel administration. The old-timers have continued to execute personnel functions as semiclerical, sterile activities and have contributed to the image of personnel work as a secondary "staff" function, whose key people have neither the authority nor the respect that a full-blown manpower management function requires and demands.[4] This image of personnel work is bound to change in the 1970s as younger men with an orientation toward planning replace the old-timers.

CHANGED CORE CONCEPTS OF THE PUBLIC EMPLOYMENT SERVICE

Parallel with changes in concepts in personnel administration have been others that are analogous in type for the public employment service. In both cases these were changes affecting the essentially narrow placement outlook associated for many years with the work of personnel departments and the public employment service. These changes had been building up for a number of years but were brought to a head in 1960.

President John F. Kennedy in his first State of the Union message emphasized that there were fundamental and long-range problems in the field of human resources in America that must be met and that immediate steps must be taken to strengthen and improve the public employment service. For the first time in American history the nation set out on a course to make job opportunity and skill development matters of planning and design rather than chance.[5]

The mobility and flexibility of the American labor force are almost

---

[4] Gerald G. Fisch, *Organization for Profit*, McGraw-Hill, New York, 1964, p. 137. See also such representative articles as Aileen L. Kyte, "The Personnel Man—In Transition?," *Business Management Record*, Vol. 25, No. 12, December 1963, pp. 7–10; Allen Janger, "Structuring the Corporate Personnel Staff," *Conference Board Record*, Vol. 2, No. 5, May 1965, pp. 34–42; S. Avery Raube et al., "The Changing Character of Personnel Administration," *Conference Board Record*, Vol. 1, No. 6, June 1964, pp. 7–15; Dale Yoder, "The Two Roads to Success in Industrial Relations," *Personnel Administration*, Vol. 27, No. 6, November-December 1964, pp. 3–5, 41–45; Robert Schaffer and Philip Woodyatt, "New Horizons for Personnel Management," *Personnel*, Vol. 39, No. 2, March-April 1962, pp. 42–51; Stanley M. Herman, "The Personnel Field—Techniques and Trivia," *Personnel*, Vol. 39, No. 4, July-August 1962, pp. 17–24; and Morton Adelberg, "The Challenge of Today's Personnel Administration," *Personnel*, Vol. 42, No. 5, September-October 1965, pp. 67–70.

[5] Louis Levine, "An Employment Service Equal to the Times," *Employment Security Review*, Vol. 30, No. 6, June 1963, pp. 3–13.

legendary, but by themselves they are not sufficient to keep up with the new forces that continuously upset the equilibrium between manpower supply and demand. For the employment service, this means that it should not operate merely as a system of labor exchanges but must take on expanded responsibilities as a manpower agency concerned with all aspects of manpower. The new concept here was to convert the essentially placement-oriented employment office into a local "community manpower center." [6] The latter term has perhaps been overworked since the early 1960s, but it is very meaningful and represents a mighty effort to shift directions as anyone associated closely with the employment service in recent years can attest.

In its more than 35 years of growth and development, the federal-state employment service system has been shaped and tempered by the economic climate of the times. Created in the depths of the Depression, it has since adapted and broadened its programs and changed its directions and emphasis to meet the needs of recessions and booms, war mobilization of manpower, and peacetime readjustments. Placement service, or "getting the best possible job for the worker and the best possible worker for the job," has been the core of its activity. To accomplish placement in a complex society such as ours the employment service has been required to change from a rudimentary labor exchange to a "community manpower center." This new concept means that the employment service must be concerned not only with accepting orders for workers and referring workers to jobs, but also with manpower research and planning to anticipate long-range labor market needs, manpower development through training and retraining programs, manpower distribution through an effective placement service, and manpower utilization to assure full use of the nation's human resources.[7] Each local office serves as the local community manpower center and, beyond that, functions in a strongly linked nationwide network of offices operating to meet national manpower purposes. At the same time, the public employment service continues, as its name implies, to be a service institution available to employer and job seeker alike on a voluntary basis. Once again the federal-state employment service system has modified and adapted operations to meet the changing needs of a changing labor market.[8]

As the nation has focused increasing attention in recent years on manpower problems, the question has repeatedly arisen: what is the contribution of the federal-state employment service to an "active and positive

[6] *Ibid.*

[7] "Organizing the Job Market, Placement," *Employment Security Review,* Vol. 30, No. 6, June 1963, p. 24.

[8] Levine, *op. cit.,* pp. 11–12.

manpower policy"? The latter term, like "community manpower center," is perhaps also one which has been overworked since the early 1960s, but it too is suggestive of new directions in thought. No consensus has yet been reached about its specific meaning and content. At the moment, an active and positive manpower policy is an aspiration rather than a set of ongoing programs carried out by existing institutions and agencies. However, the aim of an active and positive manpower policy is to contribute to the amplification of the general welfare of the people of the nation insofar as that general welfare is dependent on the fact of, the resources for, and the productiveness, security, and voluntary character of the employment relationship. It is, consequently, the function of the policy to increase the quantitative and qualitative adequacy and adaptability of (1) the labor force and of (2) employment opportunities, to (3) provide the labor market facilities essential to bring supply and demand together in a way which promotes the economic strength and growth of the nation and maximum self-realization in work for its people, and (4) to participate in the formulation and implementation of all aspects of general economic policy and practice at all points where they affect, or are affected by, manpower and employment factors.[9]

The community manpower center concept and active and positive manpower policy concept as they bear upon the total society seem to be very similar in basic thought to changed concepts of the goals of personnel administration in organizations. Indeed, leading scholars view the employment service as potentially capable of playing a major role in the well-being of the individual and organizations, such as business firms, provided changes are made in the service and in certain related institutional spheres.[10]

There is another link between manpower planning in society and organizations—job vacancy information. Some consider the availability of such information as basic to the effective operation of the employment service and are encouraged by the potential cooperativeness and availability of data from employers.[11] Others are more skeptical and see a host of conceptual, measurement, and institutional problems that require surmounting before job vacancy surveys can be made meaningful. However, the basic difficulty which confronts the development of job vacancy data by occupa-

[9] E. Wight Bakke, "Employment Service Role in an Active Labor Market Policy," *Employment Service Review,* Vol. 1, No. 1, January-February 1964, pp. 1–8.

[10] See Richard A. Lester, *Manpower Planning in a Free Society,* Princeton University Press, Princeton, 1966, pp. 209–212, 45–191; and E. Wight Bakke, *A Positive Labor Market Policy,* Merrill, Columbus, 1963, *passim.*

[11] Louis Levine, "The Role of Job Vacancy Data for an Active Manpower Policy," in National Bureau of Economic Research, *The Measurement and Interpretation of Job Vacancies,* Columbia University Press, New York, 1966, pp. 54–71.

tions is not so much detailed questions of definitions, sampling, and reporting, but rather the fact that job vacancy concepts and data today still play a relatively small role in the operations of business enterprises, governments, and other employers. Until these data are perfected and used for manpower planning in organizations, the regular completion of survey questionnaires for outsiders will have limited meaning.[12]

JOB VACANCIES AND PLACEMENT

The development of job vacancy data inside an enterprise or other organization is one step—perhaps the key one—in a larger process of manpower planning. There are only a limited number of organizations in the United States which now seek to project their demands for manpower forward a few months, a year, or, in a few cases, for longer periods. In some cases these projections are only for a few occupational categories, but in others a larger range of occupations is considered. Yet the concept of an internal labor market is essential to provide meaning to job vacancies. A job vacancy, by definition, can only be claimed or filled by a person exterior to the organization (or relevant administrative unit, such as a bargaining unit, plant, multiplant, or hiring hall unit). The strength of attachments to a job within an organization by a person on layoff or on temporary or permanent leave varies widely among organizations. A vast complex of organizational policies and rules and personnel practices govern the allocation of manpower within the internal labor market and relations to exterior markets. These rules may be more formalized under collective bargaining agreements, but they are extensive even in nonunion establishments, particularly among large-scale organizations. Internal labor markets, and their connection to the exterior, are also importantly shaped by technology and the scale of operations of an organization. In sum, greater knowledge is needed concerning manpower projections by organizations, internal labor markets, and occupational content in order to enhance the meaning and measurement of job vacancies.[13]

Placement is probably the oldest and, it is hypothesized, the most problematical of the personnel functions in organizations. Often it has been administered solely as a service activity for short-range staffing and probably has given more attention to the internal placement problems caused by poor or marginal-performing employees than to identifying highly talented persons and conducting career planning for them. In recent

[12] John T. Dunlop, "Job Vacancy Measures and Economic Analysis," in National Bureau of Economic Research, *The Measurement and Interpretation of Job Vacancies,* Columbia University Press, New York, 1966, p. 45.

[13] *Ibid.,* pp. 45–47.

years, of course, some of this has changed; and much has been written in the personnel literature about the need for manpower development and planning, especially for managerial employees. Similarly, the employment service has been required to expand its concepts beyond the staffing aspect of placement. If anything, the employment service has had to concentrate on workers with problems, such as the hard-core unemployed, illiterates, and the poorly skilled. The outreach aspects of the various programs of the employment service are geared specifically to these groups.[14]

The employment service has become largely identified over the years with blue-collar workers having significant employment problems and principally serves them. This group commands far less attention and interest from placement specialists in industry for obvious reasons. The similarities and differences between organizational placement and the employment service point up the growing realization in America that manpower problems have come to the forefront and that stronger linkages between organizations and the society to foster the development, utilization, and conservation of human resources should be established.

PRELIMINARY DEFINITION OF TERMS

Terms such as organization, manpower, manpower planning, manpower policy, human resources, development, learning, education, and training have been used repeatedly up to this point without being defined. Each of these terms has connotations for the reader because some of them are used in conversation in everyday life. For precision, it is now desirable that these terms be more specifically defined, beginning with the term, organization.

Organization

For the purposes of this book, organizations are defined simply as groups that have been established for the pursuit of relatively specific objectives on a more or less continuous basis. Organizations have distinctive features other than goal specificity and continuity. These include relatively fixed boundaries, a normative order, authority ranks, a communications system, and an incentive system which enables various participants to work together in the pursuit of common goals.[15] A business corporation, a plant, a government agency, a school, a military unit, and any other similar group is an organization.

---

[14] See "Manpower Tasks for 1966," *Employment Service Review,* Vol. 3, June 1966, pp. 8–12; and Frank H. Cassell, "A New Beginning," *Employment Service Review,* Vol. 3, No. 6, June 1966, pp. 1–5.

[15] W. Richard Scott, "Theory of Organizations," in Robert E. L. Faris, ed., *Handbook of Modern Sociology,* Rand-McNally, Chicago, 1964, p. 488.

In this book, most of the time when we use the word organization, we have a business firm in mind, although other organizations have also been considered. It should be noted that the definition of organization selected is one generally acceptable to students in the field. A recent volume suggests, however, that the meaning of the word organization is diverse.[16]

Manpower

Manpower was a very popular term during World War II, then apparently passed out of widespread usage, and reappeared about 1960.[17] The term has many different meanings today and has once again become quite popular.

Sometimes the word manpower is equivalent to the term *labor* when labor is understood to be a factor of production in the basic framework of analysis used by economists.[18] In this very broad sense manpower can also be understood to mean generically "personnel" or "employees." [19] Actually these usages of the term are virtually identical; the differences are less in substance than in point of view, one being that of the labor economist and the other that of the personnel student or practitioner.[20]

Looked at in still another manner, manpower can mean the total quantitative and qualitative human assets or people in a society. In this sense we are literally interpreting the word to mean the power of man, both in terms of the size of the population and the talents and educational levels in that population. Population can be said to determine the quantity, and education combined with experience, the quality, of manpower. During World War II, when there was a War Manpower Commission, manpower seemed to have the latter connotations. The author shares that view of the term.

Other possible contemporary meanings of the term manpower include the following: Manpower is that group of individuals designed to be served by the Manpower Development and Training Act of 1962. Manpower can

[16] James G. March, ed., *Handbook of Organizations,* Rand-McNally, Chicago, 1965, *passim.*

[17] See Donald Ghent et al., compilers, *Manpower, Wages and Labor Relations in World War II, An Annotated Bibliography,* New York State School of Industrial and Labor Relations, Cornell University, Ithaca, 1951, *passim.*

[18] For example, see Herbert G. Heneman, Jr., and Dale Yoder, *Labor Economics,* Second Edition, Southwestern, Cincinnati, 1965, pp. 1–56; and Allan M. Cartter and F. Ray Marshall, *Labor Economics: Wages, Employment, and Trade Unionism,* Irwin, Homewood, Illinois, 1967, pp. 529–550.

[19] Leon C. Megginson, *Personnel: A Behavioral Approach to Administration,* Irwin, Homewood, Illinois, 1967, pp. 251–267, 83–99.

[20] Peter F. Drucker, *The Practice of Management,* Harper, New York, 1954, pp. 282–353 and *passim.*

be equated with the labor force. Manpower can be considered tantamount to "human capital."

Manpower Policy

From the total societal point of view, manpower policy is concerned with the development and use of human labor as an economic resource and as a source of individual and family income. Because national manpower policy overlaps national employment and educational policies, a clear definition is difficult. Therefore, we can probably more usefully define national manpower policy in terms of its goals and the tools with which it pursues these goals, recognizing that these same goals are pursued simultaneously with other policy tools. The goals of manpower policy may be identified as follows: first, employment opportunities for all persons who want them, in jobs which balance free occupational choice and adequate income with the relative preferences of members of society for alternative goods and services; second, the provision of education and training capable of fully developing each individual's productive potential; third, the matching of men and jobs in the economy with a minimum of lost income and production.[21]

Manpower policy defined in this context includes the demand side of the national economic equation in the creation of jobs for specific individuals, groups, and locations. It covers the supply side of the equation in the development of skills and bridges the two in the matching process. To the extent it is concerned with the welfare of workers, it inevitably becomes involved in income distribution and wage issues. Manpower policy thus clearly involves individuals, employers, labor organizations, and state and local governments, but in recent years the most significant developments in this field have been occurring within the federal government.[22]

In summary, manpower policy may be regarded as a kind of three-legged national stool, with one leg each for job creation, manpower education and training, and the matching of men and jobs. But from the standpoint of the firm, this concept of manpower policy must be altered if it is to be meaningfully understood.

Industrial organizations do not deliberately create jobs, nor do they have the same manpower, employment, and similiar concerns of governments. The primary *raison d'être* for industrial firms is to earn a profit through the provision of goods and services. Jobs are customarily created as a part of the task-specialization process. In general, this process may be conceptualized as follows: (1) determination of organizational objectives;

---

[21] Garth L. Mangum, "The Development of Manpower Policy, 1961–65," in Sar A. Levitan and Irving H. Siegel, eds., *Dimensions of Manpower Policy: Programs and Research,* Johns Hopkins Press, Baltimore, 1966, pp. 29–30.

[22] *Ibid.,* p. 30.

(2) organizational planning, including organization and job design based on the tools, machines, and systems technology to be used in achieving enterprise objectives; (3) development of job or position descriptions reflecting the resulting tasks to be performed; (4) determination of human qualifications required on these jobs (job specifications); (5) development of performance standards for each job; and (6) establishment of work rules. There is considerable reciprocal interdependence between the component parts of the process, although each tends to stem from the preceding.[23]

Once jobs are designed and openings are authorized, it can be said that jobs are "created." Manpower education and training come into play when thought is given to required worker qualifications and required worker behavior. In this way, industrial organizations necessarily concern themselves with manpower development, and then through recruitment, selection, and placement policies and procedures, the matching of men and jobs. But given the purpose of industrial organizations to provide goods and services at a profit, it is difficult to conceive that they would view as their central mission such objectives as supplying jobs for people who cannot compete effectively in the labor market, raising the quality of jobs provided, and creating a satisfactory relationship of jobs to income. In essence, we are suggesting that the concept of manpower policy has hitherto been alien to business organizations and remains so today, although firms have been required to rethink this concept in the past decade.

Manpower Planning

Manpower planning, like manpower policy, may also be viewed from the public and private standpoints. This term is one that is very difficult to define because it involves a number of complicated processes.

In general, a plan of any type may be defined as a predetermined course of action. Every plan should have three characteristics. First, it should involve the future; second, it must involve action; and third, there should be an element of personal or organizational identification or causation, which means simply that the future course of action will be taken by the planner, or someone designated by him within an organization or within society.[24]

Essentially, then, planning is a process of thinking ahead, a method for anticipating difficulties and seeking, through reasoned action based upon foreknowledge, to guide the course of events toward desired goals. By this means, planning approaches the future with the aid of systematic analysis

---

[23] Wendell French, *The Personnel Management Process,* Houghton Mifflin, Boston, 1964, pp. 71–72.

[24] Preston P. LeBreton and Dale A. Henning, *Planning Theory,* Prentice-Hall, Englewood Cliffs, New Jersey, 1961, p. 7.

in order to minimize surprise and uncertainty and to eliminate mistakes and waste.[25]

At the level of the economy, manpower planning applies the processes of planning in general to the preparation and employment of people for productive purposes. Manpower planning may thus be viewed as a tool of manpower policy. In a free society such as ours, manpower planning aims to enlarge job opportunities and improve training and employment decisions through the power of informed personal choice and calculated adjustment to rapidly changing demand. By means of more intelligent training and career decisions and greater adaptability of the nation's labor force, manpower planning may enhance satisfaction in a job, raise the quality and utilization of manpower, reduce the cost of job search and industry staffing, and, thereby, increase the output of a nation. In our type of economy, manpower planning works with market forces. It does not attempt to restrict individual choice, but rather it enlarges choice and helps the market to operate more effectively by anticipating and arranging for early corrective measures to avoid serious manpower imbalances. It is thought that, when armed with the best obtainable information about future needs for trained manpower of various types, individuals, firms, and government agencies can make their plans with respect to training, location, and work careers more intelligently. In essence, manpower planning aids in the intelligent allocation and utilization of human resources in our society.[26]

Manpower planning in organizations is defined in a way that is rather consistent with its definition as applied to the economy. Put simply, it is the process by which a firm insures that it has the right number of people, and the right kind of people, in the right places, at the right time, doing things for which they are economically most useful. It is, therefore, a two-phased process, by which we anticipate the future through manpower projections and then develop and implement manpower action plans and programs to accommodate the implications of the projection.[27]

This conception, which repeats the word "right" several times, may seem to be question begging; however, what constitutes "right" in each instance can be supplied when the objectives of management have been specified and the supporting analytical work for implementing these objectives have been carried out. In another sense, the norms which define what is right may be viewed as comprising the organization's manpower policy. To the extent an organization lacks explicit norms, has expedient shifting norms, has no stated or generally believed convictions about human resources and

[25] Lester, *op. cit.*, pp. 4–5.
[26] *Ibid.*, pp. 5–6.
[27] Eric W. Vetter, "The Nature of Long Range Manpower Planning," *Management of Personnel Quarterly*, Vol. 3, No. 2, Summer 1964, pp. 20–27.

their utilization, or has norms which are ignored in practice, that organization may be said to lack or have an ineffective manpower policy, as the case may be.

The connection between the thinking-through processes in manpower planning and action programs for developing people is considered of key importance in this book.

Human Resources

This brings us to the concept of human resources. Similar to the concept of manpower, the concept of human resources has many different meanings. Stripped of subtleties, both manpower and human resources refer to and mean people. Human resources could be equated with "labor" in the sense of a factor of production, or simply population. Human resources may also be viewed as a kind of natural resource or a people resource just as we have mineral and forest resources.

Human resources are considered to develop in many different ways. One is by formal education, beginning with primary or first-level education, continuing through various forms of secondary education, and then culminating in higher education, including colleges, universities, and technical institutes. Second, human resources are developed on-the-job through systematic or informal training programs in employing institutions; in adult education programs; and through membership in various political, social, religious, and other groups. A third way is through self-development, as persons seek to acquire greater knowledge, skills, or capacities through preparation on their own initiative, such as taking formal or correspondence courses, reading, or learning from others in informal contacts. Motivation for self-development varies from society to society. It is directly related to the social values in a culture, to incentives for training and entering one occupation rather than another, and to incentives for learning new skills.[28]

Education

This now brings us to definitions of education and training. Development growth, learning, and education are among the most difficult words in the English language to define, primarily because we do not know a great deal about these processes.

We assume that education is concerned with teaching the members of society how they are expected to behave in a variety of situations. Education is thus a broad concept that is related to the development of and changes in human behavior. Among young people education involves trans-

[28] Frederick Harbison and Charles A. Myers, *Education, Manpower, and Economic Growth,* McGraw-Hill, New York, 1964, p. 2.

mitting skills, beliefs, attitudes, and other aspects of behavior which they have not previously acquired. Among older age groups education involves substituting new ideas, beliefs, and skills for previously acquired ones. In both instances education broadly conceived is the process of teaching and learning expected patterns of human conduct.[29]

It is assumed that human behavior is essentially social. Most behavior either is learned in direct association with others or is greatly influenced by previous associations. Of course, some behavior is learned with little or no social interaction with other persons, as, for example, when a person learns from studying with a teaching machine.[30] But only a minuscule proportion of the behavior of the individual human being represents action without reference to other persons.

It is assumed that societies and organizations are perpetuated through education, the passing on of the cultural heritage. In order to remain an on-going entity, a society must transmit its ideas, beliefs, values, skills, and other behavior expectations to its new members. Each society passes its culture on, with some changes, to successive generations, largely through social interaction. Therefore, in the broadest sense, education is synonymous with socialization itself. Education would thus include any social behavior by which the society perpetuates itself through the new generation. In this very broad sense, education begins for the individual when he first interacts with other members of society in such a way that he is conditioned by their behavior.[31]

The Development Concept

The concept of development may be defined broadly as all the formal and informal processes by which individuals learn.

Formal development takes place when individuals learn as a consequence of participating in an educational or training program, such as those offered in a school or other institution, or by means of a planned learning experience, such as job rotation, special assignments, a designated internship, and the like. Formality is involved because a social situation has been structured. That is, there is a definite "form" to it, such as the grouping of persons in a classroom to study economics or the planned rotation of a single employee in several jobs so that he acquires experiences which add to his existing knowledge.

Informal development takes place simply as a consequence of living. This is a type of learning everyone is exposed to, although some individuals seem more observant or capable than others in learning informally.

---

[29] Wilbur B. Brookover and David Gottlieb, *A Sociology of Education,* Second Edition, American Book Company, New York, 1964, pp. 15–16.

[30] *Ibid.*

[31] *Ibid.,* pp. 16–17.

It should be noted that informal development always involves some formality because social interaction between human beings is almost always structured and, therefore, has a form. Informal development is thus only relatively less structured than formal development.

It should be noted in passing that people also learn in relatively unstructured situations involving collective behavior. For example, persons who have participated in mob violence, abandoned a sinking ship, or exited from a smoke-filled theater undoubtedly learned something from the experience. However, these kinds of collective behavior obviously cannot be usefully formalized for the purposes of developing human resources.

For many reasons the term education is normally used to refer to formal development, as through a system of schools or system of industrial educational and training programs. As we have mentioned, education is concerned with teaching people how they are expected to behave in a variety of selected situations. But in teaching behavioral expectations to persons consideration is given to drawing out from the person his potential for learning rather than getting him to do something which has, so to speak, been "poured" into him by means of training. The distinction between these concepts hinges upon the origins of the words "educate" and "educe," which suggest "leading out of" or bringing out the capacities and potential of the individual rather than "schooling" him in a skill by getting the mind "disciplined" to learn it.

Training

Turning to training per se, this term at one time had the restricted meaning of "education in a narrow sense" or "to drill."[32] Etymologically, the verb to train is derived from the French word *trainer,* which means "to drag." It is not surprising that English definitions of the word may be found to include such thoughts as, to draw along, to allure, to cause to grow in the desired manner, to prepare for performance by instruction, to practice, and to exercise. We find, in fact, that effective training is both alluring and concerned essentially with problems of growth. The allurement may even be coupled with entertainment but too much divertissement would be thought to repel serious learning. An individual who is providing formal or informal training for another, like the manager, the doctor, or even the gardener in a certain sense, is occupied with living processes of growth. The word doctor itself is derived from the Latin word *docere,* to teach, and its original meaning was, as a matter of fact, teacher. Interestingly enough, even the verb to manage means "to train by exercise."[33]

[32] William McGehee and Paul W. Thayer, *Training in Business and Industry,* Wiley, New York, 1961, p. 2.

[33] David King, *Training Within the Organization,* Educational Methods, Chicago, 1964, p. 125.

In industry the term training has become much broader than the words "dragging" or "drilling" would connote. Training now encompasses activities ranging from the learning of a simple motor skill up to the acquisition of complex technical knowledge, learning elaborate administrative skills, and even developing attitudes toward intricate and controversial social issues. In fact, at some point the line is passed into propaganda-purveying and ultimately perhaps to "coercive persuasion" (or "brainwashing").

In spite of these facts, the term training in many quarters still has the emotional connotation of the earlier narrower meaning. It is commonly applied to such learning activities as training seals to perform tricks or teaching dogs obedience through "classes" or training sessions. The term training is applied also to the learning of skills such as marksmanship or seamanship in the armed forces. The word is used in the rudimentary education of the child, such as in toilet training. Still another loose use of the word training applies it to the acquisition of a professional or vocational skill. Sometimes physicians discuss their medical "training"; or even professors will sometimes slip and use the word graduate training to refer to their career educational preparation. In other words, training may often have a large element of skill included in it although it is quite likely that considerable intellectual and technical knowledge is also involved. The tendency to use education and training interchangeably suggests that in many instances the words are regarded as synonymous in everyday life. It is well to keep in mind that they can also be conceptually distinguished.

Training in industry, which is of specific interest to us in this book, has a definite purpose. As was suggested previously, education is concerned with teaching the members of society how they are expected to behave in a variety of situations. Learning refers to the process or processes which take place when an individual acquires a skill, knowledge, or attitude. Learning is treated in this book as largely a residual category.

Industrial training, therefore, refers to the efforts that are made to facilitate the processes we call learning and which result in on-the-job behavior required of a member or members of an industrial organization. To put it another way, training in an organization is the formal procedure which is used to facilitate employee learning so that their resultant behavior contributes to the organization's objectives.[34]

The proper utilization of training in modern industry and other large-scale organizations requires that it be put in an appropriate context. In this sense, training is not an end in itself, but a means to an end. The function of an industrial organization is to produce goods and services at a profit, not to train members of society. Government became increasingly con-

[34] McGehee and Thayer, *op. cit.,* p. 3.

cerned in the 1960s with training members of society, such as the chronically unemployed and the disadvantaged, and this, as previously discussed above in reference to manpower policy, is probably more properly its responsibility than that of industry. Firms, of course, make efforts to train their employees because training may be perceived as a necessary part of being in business. Training still will not be looked upon as a central activity but as a tool which assists in the production of goods and services at a profit. In this way an industrial organization can justify the costs of training because they contribute intermediately to the effective development and utilization of the human resources in an enterprise and ultimately to the achievement of organizational goals.[35]

The People Focus

This lengthy discussion of definitions of the concepts organization, manpower, manpower policy, manpower planning, human resources, development, education, and training has been designed to identify the meanings of these terms and to reduce them insofar as possible to a common denominator. The latter is found when we consider that in a simplified way "manpower" and "human resources" are synonyms for people. Yet if this book were entitled "people planning and the development of people" the title would probably be incomprehensible to most readers.

Rather than limit themselves to the very broad word "people," social scientists and other writers have tried to identify richer, more suggestive concepts and provide them with meaning for analytical purposes. Conceptualization is highly desirable, but it has the disadvantage of creating a certain amount of bewilderment over terminology. The use of terms becomes even more perplexing when added to them are such other concepts as policy and planning. Such compounds as "manpower planning" do not communicate very well to the nonspecialist (or even the specialist making a mighty effort to be abreast of a changing field) and must be carefully defined if understanding is to be achieved. We have tried to do this here and continue to strive for specificity in other chapters where these terms are used.

CENTRAL FOCUS OF THE BOOK

Education and training are regarded today more than ever as crucial types of investment for the exploitation of modern technology. It is quite clear that this fact underlies recent educational developments in all the major industrial societies in the world. In an advanced industrial society

[35] *Ibid.,* p. 4.

such as ours, it seems inevitable that the educational system should come into a very close relationship with the economy. Modern industrial technology, based upon the substitution of electrical and atomic power for other forms, and introducing new and more intricate divisions of labor, as well as the elimination of labor through automation and cybernation, transforms the scale of production, the economic setting of the enterprise, and the productive and social role of labor. At the same time, modern industrial technology is dependent to an unprecedented extent on the results of scientific research, on the supply of skills and highly talented manpower, and consequently on the efficiency of the educational system in a society.[36]

Education becomes a major form of investment for the economy as a whole, and old educational forms must cater to the new educational needs of the mass of population so that they can find their places in the modern economy. Secondary schools, technical institutions, colleges, and universities expand in number and in scope. The process of democratization affects educational institutions in the selection of students and recruitment of teachers, the curriculum, the schools' perception of themselves as institutions, their structure and functioning as going concerns, and the very learning process itself.[37] Beyond this universities become multiversities, and questions arise whether when they reach that state they are still the kind of institutions desired in a democratic society. Various kinds of institutes for advanced study, research foundations, and other ultra-specialized or ultra-advanced educational institutions also come into being. Complex organizations undertake educational and training ventures on their own because they feel that existing institutions in the society cannot meet their needs.

The effect of all this is a new tempo in which education becomes the key institution in society in the eyes of many people, although no one knows where it is headed. Like H. G. Wells, they believe "human history becomes more and more a race between education and catastrophe" but they take little comfort in the fact this relationship specifies the problem without pointing to social solutions.

There is considerable confusion today about the objectives of education and training in an urban-industrial society such as ours as well as in industrial organizations. Ever since the launching of the sputniks by the Soviet Union in 1957 the spotlight has been upon education and training in America. Many people believe that technical training has been insufficient in quality and quantity and too much attention has been given to liberal arts and other forms of nontechnical and nonscientific education. At the same time, there has been a persistent problem of relatively high unemployment partly attributable at least to the educational deficiencies of the unem-

[36] Jean Floud and A. H. Halsey, "Introduction," in A. H. Halsey et al., *Education, Economy, and Society,* Free Press of Glencoe, New York, 1961, p. 1.
[37] *Ibid.*

ployed (which tapered off after the war in Vietnam intensified in 1965–66 but may recur in future years when that war is terminated). There has also been considerable concern over the need for retraining the unemployed and providing educational and training opportunities for persons living in poverty. The increasing involvement of the federal government in education at all levels has also raised a number of questions concerning the objectives of education and training in American society.

CONCEPTUAL FRAMEWORK FOR SOCIAL PROBLEMS

Problems in manpower planning and in the development of human resources are one species of social problem having to do with people. Contemporary manpower problems, because they involve human values and the prevention of waste of human resources as well as the proper utilization of people in a profoundly altered environment, have been called "the manpower revolution." [38] This manpower revolution which is fully upon us allegedly shows no signs of abating and can no longer be ignored. Public policy in the past few years has been forced to respond to the technological changes, unemployment, and modifications in job requirements caused by the many factors operative in the manpower revolution. The actions taken to cushion the effects of this revolution have lagged behind the needs. [39]

Whether contemporary manpower problems are of the magnitude of a true social revolution is debatable. There is no doubt that they constitute a social problem of major importance. The spate of legislation enacted in the Great Society programs, as well as the adjustments made by firms, indicates there is a recognized social problem.

Social problems arise because human beings form value judgments about what conditions of life promote their collective welfare. Standards of group well-being serve as social norms for the approval or disapproval of certain situations. When these cherished collective values are threatened by some definable source of irritation, the group becomes aware of it and is confronted with a social problem. A problem thus may be defined as a discrepancy between the expected (in terms of desired objectives) and the experienced. Social problems may be difficult to solve for several reasons, but they can be removed or corrected only by collective action. [40]

[38] Joseph S. Clark, "Foreword" to Garth L. Mangum, ed., *The Manpower Revolution: Its Policy Consequences,* Doubleday Anchor Books, Garden City, 1966, pp. vii–viii.
[39] Garth L. Mangum, "Introduction" to Mangum, *op. cit.,* p. xix.
[40] Richard C. Fuller, "The Nature and Study of Social Problems," in Robert E. Park, ed., *An Outline of the Principles of Sociology,* Barnes and Noble, New York, 1939, p. 3.

Solutions to social problems are made difficult because causes are often difficult to determine. The web of cause and effect may be complicated or our knowledge incomplete. Or the cause may be known but cannot be removed without jeopardizing some other value. We often see social problems that contain inconsistencies within themselves and are more willing to live with the agonies of these problems than to solve them and in the process cause others. Thus the proposed solutions to many social problems are often short-range expedient actions which fall far short of the thoroughgoing reform which is rationally required but culturally unacceptable.[41]

Public attitudes on a social problem such as manpower usually focus on debate concerning the means by which necessary action can and should evolve. Several levels of discussion take place. First, there is discussion of the facts thought relevant to policy. People become concerned with solutions to social problems. The solutions, in turn, involve decisions about appropriate public policy or law. The discussion of policy is conditioned by a labyrinth of attitudes—ethical, moral, political, economic, and the like. Prejudices and stereotypes are applied and tested; vested interests must be considered. The function of public discussion is to bring forth an examination of a culturally defined dangerous social situation which must be changed, but in a manner that does not imperil values and norms.

Next, there is a discussion of facts which are relative to the efficiency of administration. Once a policy is decided upon, the social problem dissolves into a number of specific technical problems for the solution of which technical experts with specialized training are necessary. Certain agencies and institutions are established which are considered capable of dealing with the problem. Their administration becomes a focal point for controversy.

Lastly, there is discussion of facts relative to research. The social scientist who is interested in social problems is primarily concerned with analyzing the cause and effect sequences involved in the social problem. His conclusions, if they are made available to the public, may diffuse eventually into popular discussions of public policy. Research may also point the way to more efficient administration of policies already in operation. Yet, in the final analysis decisions about the policy selected for solving social problems will follow from choices in values and norms, although the facts that are obtained through research may guide these choices.[42]

This conceptualization of social problems can be usefully restated in a series of propositions to which we refer subsequently. First, a social problem arises when there is an awareness among a group that a particular situation is a threat to certain values and norms which they cherish and that this situation can be removed or corrected only by collective action.

[41] *Ibid.,* pp. 3–4.
[42] *Ibid.,* pp. 4–5.

Every social problem thus consists of an objective condition and a subjective definition. The objective condition is a verifiable situation which can be checked as to its existence and magnitude or proportions by impartial and trained observers. The subjective definition is the awareness of certain groups that the condition is a threat to cherished values and norms.

Second, the objective condition is a necessary, but not in itself sufficient, condition to constitute a social problem. A given social problem is relative in space and time. Although the objective conditions may be the same in two different localities, the situation under consideration may not be defined as a social problem in both of these areas. In other words, social problems are what people think they are. If conditions are not defined as social problems by the people involved in them, they are not problems to these people, although they may be to outsiders or to scientists.

Third, no social situation involving the interaction of many individuals has a single unilinear cause. Yet the "fallacy of the partial view" is most common in the discussion of social problems. Oversimplification seems to be a constant accompaniment of social problems. Single-factor explanations must be rejected as inadequate; instead inductive analyses of facts are required. Also, most social problems are so complex that no one discipline can offer a complete understanding or solution to a social problem. In this book we have a sociological orientation, but we recognize that social problems have a way of not fitting conveniently into any one field of knowledge.

Fourth, all social problems are interlocked. The attempted solution of any one problem may aggravate or become the genesis of another.

Fifth, cultural values play an important causal role in the objective conditions which are defined as the problem. The objective conditions are cited as causes of the problem because, at least in part, people cherish certain beliefs and maintain social institutions which gave rise to the conditions considered problematical. There is considerable cultural relativity in social problems because identical cultural circumstances may be used to define a problem in one society but not in another.

Sixth, cultural values obstruct solutions to conditions defined as social problems because people are unwilling to endorse programs of amelioration which prejudice or require abandonment of their cherished beliefs and institutions. Rarely will people approve of solutions which result in practices that, in themselves, are defined as violations of the norms.

Seventh, social problems thus involve a dual conflict of values. In regard to some conditions, people disagree whether the conditions are a threat to fundamental values. In respect to other conditions, although there is a basic dissidence that the condition is a threat to fundamental values because of a disparity of other values relative to means or policy, people disagree over programs of reform.

Eighth, and last, social problems arise and are sustained because people do not share the same common values and objectives.[43] The neutral observer must, therefore, study not only the objective conditions that are associated with the social problem but also the value judgments of the people involved in it that cause them to define the same conditions and means to its solution in different ways.

A general analytical framework can be constructed on these propositions because we can hypothetically attribute to all social problems certain common characteristics. These common characteristics imply a common order of development through which all social problems pass, consisting of temporal sequences in their emergence and maturation. Social problems do not arise as full-blown entities, commanding community attention and evoking adequate policies and machinery *de novo* for their solution. On the contrary, social problems exhibit a temporal course of development in which different phases or stages may be distinguished. Each stage anticipates its successor in time and each succeeding stage contains new elements which mark it off from its predecessor. A social problem thus conceived is always in a dynamic state of becoming and passes through the natural history stages of awareness, policy determination, and reform.[44]

The same social structures and cultures that make for conforming and organized behavior also generate tendencies toward distinctive kinds of deviant behavior and potentials for social disorganization. In this sense, the problems current in a society indicate the social costs of a particular organization of social life. To a substantial extent, then, social problems are the unwilled, largely indirect, and often unanticipated consequences of institutionalized patterns of social behavior. In order to study and understand disorganization in particular aspects of social life, it is necessary to study and understand the social framework of their organization. The two concepts (disorganization and organization) seemingly at odds with one another from a common sense view are theoretically inseparable. From these related premises it can be concluded that each society and culture will have its distinctive kinds and degrees of social problems.[45] In a certain sense, social problems are "natural."

Only in exceptional cases do people in all groups in a complex society agree that particular conditions are social problems requiring solution.

[43] Richard C. Fuller and Richard R. Myers, "The Natural History of a Social Problem," *American Sociological Review,* Vol. 6, No. 3, June 1941, pp. 320–328; and their "Some Aspects of a Theory of Social Problems," *American Sociological Review,* Vol. 6, No. 1, February 1941, pp. 24–32.

[44] Fuller, "The Nature and Study of Social Problems," in Park, *op. cit.,* pp. 7–9.

[45] Robert K. Merton and Robert A. Nisbet, "Preface" to the *Contemporary Social Problems,* Harcourt, Brace and World, New York, 1961, p. ix.

Insofar as people variously located in the social structure differ in their appraisal of a particular situation as a social problem, we find that the solutions proposed for coping with these problems also differ. In other words, solutions too are limited and partly shaped by the social structure. As a consequence, the changes represented by the solution or the proposed solutions will accord with the interests and values of some and run counter to the interests and values of others. This is the reason that it is often difficult to develop and put into effect public policies designed to solve social problems.[46]

Manpower problems in contemporary society may be viewed as practical and moral problems or as relative problems explainable by the analysis of institutions and associations; social groups; cultural norms and values; structure, function, and power, and processes such as conflict, social mobility, individual autonomy, and changes in norms and values.[47] Many manpower problems are best understood as problems reflecting some of the larger and more general processes of change in modern society. Development of persons to their maximum potential and the conservation of talent as social and organizational objectives are problems in American society because ours is a highly complex, rapidly changing, technological, urban-industrial society. Much of what we value in American society (such as freedom, democracy, and economic opportunity—clearly values enmeshed in manpower problems in society and industry) is inconceivable apart from the processes of conflict, mobility, individual autonomy, and changes in norms and values as they operate in the broad society.

Historians have pointed out that the great periods of human thought and achievement are also the periods characterized by social problems and conflict of values. However, the conflict of institutions and values and the mobility of individuals and groups can have negative consequences for a civilization. These processes can lead, and often have led, not to creative achievement but to alienated and pathological behavior, particularly the kinds of behavior that are regarded as social problems.[48]

Identifying with and coping with contrary values in a society such as ours are the day-to-day activities of public policy makers. Resolutions of problems are never final in a society and in organizations undergoing change. We have found, over historical eras, that achievements and problems are mutually dependent and, contingent upon the way that they are examined, may be simultaneously normal and pathological. Problems have been opportunities in disguise.

[46] *Ibid.*, pp. ix–x.
[47] Robert A. Nisbet, "The Study of Social Problems," in Merton and Nisbet, *op. cit.*, pp. 12–18.
[48] *Ibid.*, p. 18.

We know that work is a central activity in an industrial society such as ours and have no reason to expect that there will be *pari passu* an absence of manpower problems if people who need to work and want to work can obtain jobs at a given point in time. We require a greater understanding of the processes which enable individuals to develop the skills, abilities, knowledge, and attitudes to qualify for and remain effective in employment. All these poorly understood processes are connected not only with social problems but are a central focus of this book and topics to which we repeatedly return in our explication of manpower planning and the development of human resources.

DYNAMICS OF CHANGE AND DEMOCRACY

In this introduction to manpower problems in industrial society, we have been discussing the point of view of the book, the concept of a manpower specialist, various definitions of key terms, the central focus adopted, and the conceptual framework. In discussing all these matters, reference has been made to change in American society.

The causes and effects of change are inextricably bound together and complicate the discussion of manpower planning and the development of human resources. Technological change in the form of automation, computerization, numerical control, and allied factors have had a significant effect on skill and knowledge obsolescence among workers and managers. Population changes, particularly the rising population of young people, have put increasing pressure on existing educational institutions and their capacity for absorbing the number of persons desiring to enter them. The changes in the occupational structure have increased the demand for more highly educated people in technical, professional, and managerial positions and lessened the demands for lesser skilled blue-collar workers. These changes, in turn, have had the effect of encouraging more people to attend college, the proliferation of adult educational programs after working hours, and of course, the various programs of retraining for the unemployed. Population change has also had the effect of providing a larger number of older and retired people than ever before in our history. Retirees have problems with how to utilize their leisure time, and some of this has been devoted to educational pursuits as well as training in arts, crafts, and hobbies. Also, an increasing trend in recent years has been to provide preretirement training and counseling for employees.

Unemployment, in its contemporary setting, has also been a result of technological and other change. Closely tied in with unemployment have been governmental retraining programs, the civil rights revolution, and the War on Poverty all of which, in turn, have affected education, jobs, and the power structure in the local communities and in the nation.

Industrial organizations, in turn, have been asked to participate in the "Plans for Progress" to eliminate, on a voluntary basis, discrimination in employment, and employers covered by the Civil Rights Act of 1964 have been required to comply with a number of antidiscrimination provisions in that law. Similarly, large industrial organizations have been included under the "equal pay for equal work" amendments to the Fair Labor Standards Act of 1938 in which discrimination against women in employment and promotion was made unlawful. Firms have participated in providing retraining for the unemployed, and some companies have become involved in the War on Poverty to the extent that they have operated Job Corps centers or participated in the work of the National Alliance of Businessmen.

Technological change has also caused certain problems of defining the roles of universities and industry in educational and manpower planning. It is clear that universities have a leading role in contributing to technological change and must expect to be asked to cushion some of its effects through the operation of educational and training programs for the general population as well as for employees of industrial firms. Education has undoubtedly a very important role in the economic development of American society in the future and in the success of organizations of all kinds.

The evidence of the last decade, judging by the legislation and economic support given education, indicates that for America education has become more important than ever as both a stimulus and a response to social change. The question today is not whether manpower planning and the development of human resources are deserving of the support given them, but how they can be improved to contribute in their own way to attain the democratic goals of our society. Obviously, there are no answers that can be translated into a program or grand design. There will be an evolving patchwork quilt rather than a blanket, if educational, training, and manpower legislation follows the same evolutionary course as most previous American social legislation. The course of action that organizations will follow is not yet clear. There is little evidence available now on which speculation can be based. It is hypothesized that organizations will begin with a patchwork of policies evolving out of traditional personnel policy modifications.

Upon first reflection it may seem that in tying education and training with organizations the democratic goals of society are being confused with the economic goals of industry. There is an apparent hiatus here. How many companies justify the budget of the contemporary training department because of the latter's contribution to democracy? The gap can be bridged by the concept of the social responsibility of business. Many of the conditions under which industry operates are prescribed by legislation which fosters the public interest. Profitability is also in the public interest. As we see in later chapters, manpower planning and human resource development are as vital to the success of large-scale economic organizations as they are to the society.

There is always the possibility, of course, that some individual firms will become more economically successful than others if they can cut corners or flout the law with impunity and exploit people. Most firms cannot escape detection and must plan if they are to perpetuate themselves.

Increasingly the pace-setting firms have tried to think through the component parts of manpower planning and human resource development so that they can survive and be successful economically. They have found that their employees are carriers of a culture stressing democratic values. This has sometimes culminated in a demand for bilateralism in decision making (as when unions become certified bargaining agents) or an exodus of college graduate trainees and managers (when it was felt a firm stultified their potential contribution).

The pace-setting firms have started to reconcile in practical terms the confrontation of democracy and profit. In the meantime, society through extensive legislation and taxation has taken action to provide economic opportunity and educational assistance for the unemployed, minority group members, the poor, the unskilled, and others considered in need and deprived from the standpoint of democratic values.

CONCLUSIONS

This chapter has set the broad context in which manpower problems in industrial society and organizations are discussed in subsequent chapters. The next chapter provides an analysis of manpower planning. Following chapters discuss the formal means for developing people and organizational structure for manpower planning and the development of human resources in industrial firms. Subsequent chapters aim at applying these concepts to the development of people through specific educational and training programs and ultimately examine connections between public and private policy on manpower. We also, in the process, examine how manpower plans are carried out and persons are selected for development, educational, and training programs. The implications for social mobility are, in turn, analyzed. Attention is given to how education and training is conducted and to means for evaluating the results of education and training programs. In essence, the remainder of the book is an attempt to tread a path through this complex for the student and practitioner who is concerned with this melange of problems from the vantage point of manpower planning and human resource development in organizations.

The manpower function is new in American industry. In much the same way that the personnel department emerged from line management fifty years ago in America, a new function has appeared—except in this case, one which is an outgrowth of the personnel department rather than an off-spring of overall management. The function involves macro- and micro-economic and societal considerations, which are far from worked out in this book or anywhere in the literature. Only a bold seer would have the audacity to suggest the ultimate configuration and orientation of this new function. The sole prognostications offered here are that manpower plan-ning and the development of human resources are likely to remain matters of concern indefinitely and these subjects require extensive research, which will be forthcoming in the future.

Insofar as possible, we have relied upon existing significant research studies in the literature in presenting materials in the later chapters although many of the problems discussed have not as yet been identified or handled effectively in the literature. In fact, many of the problems covered are just starting to emerge as legitimate targets for scholarly study and being given serious attention in the literature. As a result, many of the ideas advanced in subsequent chapters are based upon possible approaches and require experimental use before we can have full confidence in their efficacy. Pro-grams designed to cope with manpower problems, whether at the level of the economy or the organization, are by no means cut and dry. The sug-gestions and approaches advanced in this book should, of course, not be accepted uncritically. They are merely beginning points for experimental utilization.

To experiment and evaluate requires that the manpower specialist have an analytical and planning outlook as opposed to a narrow administrative orientation. The nature of the kind of outlook and skills considered neces-sary are the subject of the next chapter.

CHAPTER 2

Objectives and Practices in Manpower Planning

"Time which would otherwise be wasted shall be used for planning." These words were used in a report by a former subordinate to the author as a kind of catchall explanation in justification for requested manpower in his organizational unit. The subordinate conceived of his position largely as administering training programs, and planning was relevant to this only to the extent that there was unfilled time available "which would otherwise be wasted."

His thinking is a classical case of the tail wagging the dog, but it is probably not atypical among action-oriented people who obtain their job satisfaction more from busy work and doing than from planning. The latter is irksome for many individuals and probably has most appeal for reflective, intellectually oriented persons. Also, planning is probably less easily learned and applied than simply sliding into and carrying out the requirements of an organizational position involving program administration, where the problems are either obvious or are brought to the administrator for immediate or short-run solutions.

The purpose of this chapter is to indicate the meaning of manpower planning and to describe how it can be carried out in large-scale organizations. Two illustrations are reviewed in considerable detail in the next chapter.

We shall find that the term manpower planning has many meanings, although a gradual crystalization of its meaning is taking place. We also discuss how manpower planning is related to other kinds of planning that are conducted by organizations. In this way, we try to illuminate one new area of planning in the context of all types of planning.

MEANINGS OF MANPOWER PLANNING

It is possible to define manpower planning from a narrow point of view or from a very broad one. We shall start with the narrowest and gradually enlarge it.

First, manpower planning may be viewed in the very narrow sense of replacement planning as that term is normally used in the conduct of industrial relations activities in organizations. From this standpoint, manpower planning encompasses the analysis of labor turnover, thinking through personnel recruitment policies, identifying approaches to the planning of careers for employees, developing models for planning recruitment and the promotion of employees, and analyzing the relationship between pay policies and recruitment. This point of view on manpower planning was stated several years ago in a symposium in Britain and may be the prevailing view of the concept in that country.[1]

Some American students of personnel administration have also defined manpower planning as roughly equivalent to staffing. However, by and large, Americans view recruitment, selection, and placement as closely tied together, largely administrative activities, while manpower planning is perceived as the thinking through and rationale for the conduct of staffing activities. For example, a recent personnel textbook, representative of pace-setting thinking in this field, focuses not so much on how manpower planning is carried out but rather on how it governs and provides bases for recruitment, selection, and placement of employees.[2] It should also be noted that those in the United States who view manpower planning as closely associated with placement also believe that it includes management development, replacement planning, and the use of performance appraisals. A common focus on career planning and replacement charts bridges the British and American point of view.

A second way of viewing manpower planning is to consider it tantamount to personnel planning, that is, the planning carried out by the staff personnel department as opposed to the administrative work. Per-

[1] D. T. Bryant, "A Survey of the Development of Manpower Planning Policies," *British Journal of Industrial Relations,* Vol. 3, No. 3, November 1965, pp. 279–290; S. Wood, "A Simple Arithmetical Approach to Career Planning and Recruitment," *British Journal of Industrial Relations,* Vol. 3, No. 3, November 1965, pp. 291–300; Andrew Young, "Models for Planning Recruitment and Promotion of Staff," *British Journal of Industrial Relations,* Vol. 3, No. 3, November 1965, pp. 301–310; and Michael P. Fogarty, "Wage and Salary Policies for Recruitment," *British Journal of Industrial Relations,* Vol. 3, No. 3, November 1965, pp. 311–325.

[2] Wendell French, *The Personnel Management Process,* Houghton Mifflin, Boston, 1964, 113 ff.

sonnel planning ranges over all activities of the department, includes recruitment, selection, placement, training, education, wage and salary administration, safety, labor relations, and the like. This definition is obviously considerably broader than viewing manpower planning as programming the staffing of the organization.

A third meaning of manpower planning applies to manpower and employment policy at the level of the economy. In this framework "manpower" is regarded as the quantitative and qualitative measurement of a nation's labor force, and "planning" is regarded as establishing objectives and programs to develop human resources in line with various other goals. Very often the focus in this type of manpower planning is primarily on highly educated manpower and its role in the development of an underdeveloped country. Or, conversely, it may be on the most poorly educated manpower in an urban-industrial society and what is required (in terms of education, training, health improvement, and the like) to bring these human resources into the mainstream of society. This point of view typically becomes involved with demography, the population composition in terms of educational levels, age and sex ratios, the skill mix, and present and future gross national product. Among other sources, many of the publications of the International Labour Office and of the United States Department of Labor emphasize these foci in respect to manpower planning. Typical studies relevant here would include those conducted by either the Bureau of Labor Statistics or the Bureau of Employment Security in the United States Department of Labor.[3] It should be apparent that manpower planning at the level of the economy thus involves a melange of activities including occupational, industrial, and total labor force projections as well as analyses of the displacement consequences of automation.[4]

[3] See, for example, *Aerospace Employment* (Industry Manpower Surveys, No. 112), U.S. Department of Labor, Washington, May 1965; *Technician Manpower: Requirements, Resources, and Training Needs* (Bulletin No. 1512), U.S. Department of Labor, Washington, 1966; and *The Current Employment Market for Engineers, Scientists, and Technicians,* U.S. Department of Labor, Washington, 1966. See also: Sofia Cooper and Denis F. Johnston, "Labor Force Projections for 1970–80," *Monthly Labor Review,* Vol. 88, No. 2, February 1965, pp. 129–140; Jack Alterman, "Interindustry Employment Requirements," *Monthly Labor Review,* Vol. 88, No. 7, July 1965, pp. 841–850; and Allan F. Salt, "Estimated Need for Skilled Workers," *Monthly Labor Review,* Vol. 89, No. 4, April 1966, pp. 364–372.

[4] This would be still another type of manpower planning study. For examples see *Manpower Planning to Adapt to New Technology at an Electric and Gas Utility* (BLS Report No. 293), U.S. Department of Labor, Washington, 1965; Audrey Friedman, *Manpower Planning for Technological Change: Case Studies of Telephone Operators* (Bulletin 1574), U.S. Department of Labor, Washington, 1968; and Gunter Friedrichs, "Planning Social Adjustment to Technological Change at the Level of the

To the extent that displacement is the reverse of placement, we can see that the term manpower planning can include both the accession and layoffs and termination of employees in organizations.

The fourth and last meaning of manpower planning is the one which is of primary concern in this book. In Chapter 1 we suggested that manpower planning can be defined as the process by which an organization ensures that it has the right number of people and the right kind of people, at the right places, at the right time doing things for which they are economically most useful. We shall want to sharpen this definition later because as it stands it is too broad. It should be noted, however, that our concept of manpower planning involves, on the one hand, anticipating the future by manpower projections, and then planning, developing, and implementing manpower action programs, largely in the form of education and training, to carry out the implications of the projection.[5]

In considering manpower planning and the development of human resources together in subsequent chapters, we will be focusing most of the time upon the formal processes of human development; in fact, we largely confine our focus to formal devices used by organizations, particularly business firms, in developing people. We have chosen this focus because formal processes set in operation for the development of human resources are the product (or, at least, should be) of manpower planning. Formal educational and training programs which are concrete, can be described in writing, and are sufficiently detailed so that they can be controlled, meet our criteria of manpower action programs which are designed to meet the implications of manpower projections. These kinds of programs can be made to interlock with other plans formulated in an organization that are designed to implement the organization's short- and long-run objectives (such as production, sales, financial, and similar plans).

POSTWAR ORIGINS OF INDUSTRIAL INTEREST IN MANPOWER PLANNING

Any plan is essentially today's design for tomorrow's action. Inasmuch as tomorrow's possibilities depend upon the circumstances prevailing then, planning is inevitably bound up with forecasting and projecting.[6] This

Undertaking," *International Labour Review,* Vol. 92, No. 2, August 1965, pp. 91–105. See also: Thomas H. Sebring, "Planning for a Personnel Reduction," *Personnel Journal,* Vol. 44, No. 4, April 1965, pp. 179–183.

[5] Eric W. Vetter, "The Nature of Long Range Manpower Planning," *Management of Personnel Quarterly,* Vol. 3, No. 2, Summer 1964, pp. 20–27.

[6] Ernest Dale, *Management: Theory and Practice,* McGraw-Hill, New York, 1965, p. 348.

generalization holds up not only for planning in general but also for man-power planning.

All organizations plan to some extent, even though the plans may consist of no more than a few general ideas carried around in the heads of top managers and based on an informal forecast derived from past experience, known facts, common sense, and a few hunches. Planning of this type needs no explanation because it is tantamount to rational thinking (perhaps mixed also with a dose of the irrational). Our interest is in formal planning in which definite techniques and procedures are used and written plans are produced.

Formal planning systems as viewed in the perspective of managing large-scale organizations are a relatively new arrival on the managerial scene. Overall "master planning" or "corporate planning" was given impetus principally by World War II when organizations engaged in war work realized that the end of hostilities would mean they could no longer sell a large proportion of their output to the government and they would have to find new customers, if not new products, if they hoped to stay in business. An incipient need for manpower planning was also evident at this time. After 1940, many organizations experienced manpower shortages as a conquence of production needs during the World War II period, which ran from late 1941 to almost the end of 1945, and the entry of millions of young men and women into the armed forces. This period was preceded by a long depression and marked the prewar defense mobilization period. In the depression manpower problems were considered essentially employment problems because of the large number of unemployed persons. In the defense period prior to Pearl Harbor, and particularly after the entry of the United States into the war, manpower shortages developed in various industries.[7]

The specter of a postwar manpower surplus bothered those who thought that an armistice would mean a return to the inordinately high rates of unemployment which had characterized the prewar period. Apparently, however, business firms gave less attention to the possibilities of unemployment than they did to the recognized need for postwar planning concerning other aspects of the business. The idea of "postwar planning," as it was then called, gradually spread from organizations concerned mainly with war production to companies producing entirely for civilian markets because it was evident that peace and the end of wartime shortages would change their environment drastically.[8] As a result, corporate planning was added to the list of important managerial functions for many organizations.

[7] Joel Seidman, *American Labor from Defense to Reconversion,* University of Chicago Press, Chicago, 1953, pp. 152–172.

[8] Dale, *op. cit.,* p. 349.

Even without this push it is likely that formal corporate planning would have developed rapidly at this time, primarily as a consequence of industrial growth, technological change, and social trends. Industry had grown and the labor force had correspondingly increased. Also, in the large and diversified companies that have become preeminent in our society since World War II with the thousands of mergers that have taken place, there are many more factors to be considered in judging business prospects and setting goals than was the case in the smaller firm of the prewar period. A comparatively small company with a single product line has few problems in allocating the funds that it may have set aside for reinvestment in the business. On the other hand, in large organizations where product lines and activities are numerous, arriving at the proper emphasis on each means considering many different markets, profit margins, and other factors and determining the optimum among a vast number of possibilities. Judging by what has happened since 1945, it is quite clear that large organizations have resorted to formal planning as *the* device for determining courses of action for the business.[9] The rise of conglomerate corporate structure has further stimulated planning.

Another cause of postwar planning was the increasing technical complexity of many products as well as their faster obsolescence. This meant that, before a company would go ahead with a product requiring expensive research and development, it wanted some assurance through planning and forecasting that sales would be large enough and continue over a long enough period of time to make the investment worthwhile. In turn, this led to profit planning in which objectives were set and plans were made to insure that all parts of the organization were geared toward the accomplishment of those objectives by means of specific plans. In small companies the objectives could perhaps be transmitted orally and progress toward them determined by relatively simple reports. But in larger organizations there were so many different activities, a number of which contributed only indirectly to primary company objectives, that no control was possible unless the goals of each department and division were spelled out in detail, dovetailed, and integrated in plans that were, in turn, interlocked with organizational objectives.[10]

Automation further increased the need for long-range planning. Since automatically operated and other sophisticated equipment is usually very expensive, an organization must be sure it can sell enough of its greatly increased output to justify the investment in various kinds of automatic,

[9] *Ibid.* See also George A. Steiner, ed., *Managerial Long-Range Planning,* McGraw-Hill, New York, 1963. In this book some 19 pace-setting corporations and governmental agencies discuss their approaches to long-range corporate planning.

[10] Dale, *op. cit.,* pp. 349–351.

electronic-hydraulic, cybernetic, and numerically controlled equipment. An automated plant is also a capital-intensive plant that has continuing expenses. Fixed costs that continue whether production is in process or not become of great concern. Labor costs, which are generally regarded as variable or semivariable, tend to become almost fixed costs where there is extensive use of automated equipment. Although the equipment will require fewer production workers, maintenance workers must be retained even if production drops off substantially in order to keep the plant from deteriorating. In a labor-intensive plant, the cost of depreciation is less important than the costs of labor and material, which may drop sharply or even cease in a plant shutdown. However, in recent years union contracts have contained provisions for the payment of supplementary unemployment benefits of various kinds, which require organizations to pay certain percentages of wages to laid-off workers for a given time period. These innovations in compensation have the effect of no longer making it possible to reduce the wage costs of direct production workers in proportion to the cut in production. All these considerations have highlighted the need for planning (including manpower planning).[11]

SOCIAL RESPONSIBILITY AND PROFIT PLANNING

The trend toward social responsibility on the part of management has also been associated with a rise in emphasis upon planning.[12] Companies may have such social objectives as developing a reputation for paying good wages, making their plants and offices good places to work in, providing useful products, and insuring that their operations do not detract from the appearance of the communities in which they are located. Sometimes these social objectives are forced upon a company by the threat of legislation, the possibility of unionization, stirrings of unrest which suggest an impending strike, or because sales will be lost if the company acts in a way inconsistent with or offensive to public opinion. Yet, in the long run, pursuit of social objectives may contribute to profit-making capacity. In specific instances, of course, profit and social objectives may dictate opposite courses of action, and the decision to compromise on one or the other is one of the planning tasks.[13] Yet, the doctrine of social responsibility and the building of a corresponding "image" or reputation have undoubtedly caused many organizations to plan in order to assure that their corporate visage shines through acceptably, if not brightly.

[11] *Ibid.*

[12] Peter F. Drucker, *The Practice of Management,* Harper, New York, 1954, pp. 6–17, 381–392; and his "Integration of People and Planning," *Harvard Business Review,* Vol. 31, No. 6, November-December 1955, pp. 35–40.

[13] Dale, *op. cit.,* p. 352.

Top management must necessarily concern itself with the organization's growth and expansion in the future as well as with providing a marketable service or product at a profit. To grow and expand, the organization must meet all its manpower needs. Increasingly manpower planning has come to be recognized as the new essential for achieving all other corporate goals. Companies have found that they must "grow" their own manpower.

As previously mentioned, probably the most important plan in an organization is the annual profit plan (or its equivalent in terms of budgets and objectives in a not-for-profit organization). The annual plan becomes the principal planning and control device for harnessing the diverse orientations, interests, and suborganizational objectives of managers so that they are directed in a way consistent with the objectives of the total organization.

A long-range plan may be defined as one that projects or forecasts needs one to five years ahead. Few organizations apparently look beyond five years, except in limited areas of concern. In fact, it would probably be found in many organizations that there is a great deal more talk about planning than there is of formulation and commitment to the plan as a guide to action for the future time period encompassed by it. The exception here would probably be the annual profit plan. Of all types of planning, probably manpower planning is given the most lip service and least serious consideration. This is unfortunate and is probably changing nowadays because it has been found that when manpower planning is ignored, or poorly conducted, organizations lack the human resources which they need at crucial times in the future. They then resort to hasty, poorly conceived programs of recruitment, selection, placement, and training. In the process they not only incur costs that could have been less (or avoided) if there had been planning, but also obtain a far less than optimum solution to their needs.

FAILURES IN PLANNING

The reasons for failure or inattention to planning are diverse. One deterrent is the reluctance of many individuals to attempt to predict the future. Persons feel that they cannot prophesy with much confidence because the world is rapidly changing. Yet, they are forced to make assumptions about the future because the passage of time is inevitable and assumptions must be made as to what the future holds. Only when there are reasonable assumptions made related to previously established organizational objectives is there a basis for either short- or long-range planning. Second, many people fail to make constant reference to long-range objectives in their day-to-day tactical decisions and to keep the latter in harmony with long-range plans. Third, many find difficulty in maintaining a proper balance between long-range planning and short-range "payoff." They want to look good today and thereby lay the groundwork for their own upward career mobility tomorrow. This is not surprising, of course, because the major rewards in money and promotion often go to those who show the best records of solving current problems in management, and there is seldom a direct reward for those whose foresight keeps problems from occurring.[14] Thus, in an industrial setting we typically find many executives operating under the traditional accounting concept of a period of twelve months. This in turn, goes back to the annual profit plan and budget which perhaps have a tendency to make longer-range planning appear to be "blue sky" or impracticable.[15]

In addition to the aforementioned, there are many other factors that account for ineffective long-range planning in general and ineffective organizational and manpower planning in particular. As suggested, long-range planning as an organized integrated effort is relatively new to most organizations. However, of all the aspects of long-range planning, there are probably none of greater importance nor more frequently ignored than those of planning for organizational structure and for manpower. A major reason for the incompetence of much contemporary manpower planning is the fact that it is not closely integrated organizationally with the overall planning of the firm. Put simply, practicing managers do not know how to do it. This condition is somewhat easy to explain since planning is new, and manpower planning is the newest of all forms of planning. Furthermore, when a firm has employed a competent specialist in manpower, quite often line managers fail to recognize the new manpower specialism and together with it their own relative ignorance in such matters. Even though manpower planning is ultimately a line responsibility, the task is so complex that the line must use the technical-professional knowledge of the manpower specialist if planning is to be adequately carried out. But there is evidence that pacesetting firms have been able to surmount some of the problems involved in fitting manpower planning into the mosaic of all corporate planning.[16]

[14] Charles H. Kepner and Benjamin B. Tregoe, *The Rational Manager,* McGraw-Hill, New York, 1965, p. 208.

[15] Allison V. MacCullough, "Long-Range Organization and Executive Manpower Planning," *Michigan Business Review,* Vol. 16, No. 2, March 1964, pp. 28–32.

[16] See A. Young and John H. Morse, Jr., "Long-Range Planning at Aerojet Corporation," in Steiner, *op. cit.,* pp. 80–97; and Fred G. Secrest, "The Process of Long-Range Planning at Ford Motor Company," in Steiner, *op. cit.,* pp. 222–241, especially 238 ff.

ORGANIZATIONAL DEVELOPMENT

Since World War II there has also been a very strong corresponding interest in organizational planning. Obviously, there is a very close connection between organizational planning and manpower planning. There are reportedly some firms which have identified manpower planning with organizational planning and, in fact, consider organizational planning as identical with manpower planning.[17]

There are still other organizations in which organizational planning and management development have been crossbred to form a new hybrid called "organizational development." [18] This commingling of two types of planning indicates their close relationship. It is probably useful to keep them conceptually distinct. Organization planning refers to analyzing the present organization and making plans for the design of the future organization, where organization is understood to mean the structure of positions for groups that have been established for the pursuit of relatively specific objectives on a more or less continuous basis. On the other hand, manpower planning is specifically concerned not with the structure of future positions, but with the people who will be occupying those positions. The distinction is not an overly subtle one, although it is surprising to see in the literature the confusion that exists in many quarters between planning organizations and planning for the human resources that will man those organizations.

INTEREST OF GOVERNMENT AND FOUNDATIONS
IN MANPOWER PLANNING

Turning from industrial interest in long-range or postwar planning and manpower planning, it should be noted that there has been an emerging interest for many years in manpower and human resources on the part of educational, governmental,[19] military, and other organizations. An early example of this interest was the National Manpower Council, established at Columbia University in 1951 under a grant from the Ford Foundation.[20] The Council, which was a body of private citizens, was founded to study

[17] Vetter, *op. cit.,* p. 21.

[18] See Warren G. Bennis, *Organization Development,* Addison-Wesley, Reading, 1969.

[19] See, for example, Municipal Manpower Commission, *Governmental Manpower for Tomorrow's Cities,* McGraw-Hill, New York, 1962.

[20] See for a discussion of concepts of human resources popular at this time: "Human Resources of the United States," *Scientific American,* Vol. 185, No. 3, September 1951, pp. 27–110.

manpower problems and to contribute to the more effective development
and utilization of the human resources of the United States. The members
of the Council were drawn from different fields of activity and parts of
the country and were animated by the conviction that the nation's most
critical resource was its people. In 1965 the National Manpower Council
issued its final statement.[21]

Throughout its life the Council concentrated its work upon the attainment of a handful of key objectives. The Council believed that it was of
the highest importance for the nation to make a deliberate effort to enhance
the knowledge, skills, competencies, abilities, and creative powers of its
people. It sought to identify means through which this aim could be realized that were compatible with the ideals and values of a free and
democratic society. It urged others, such as governmental agencies, employers, labor organizations, private groups, associations, and individuals,
to undertake the continuing but changing task of developing human resources. Throughout, the Council consistently emphasized the extent to
which the liberating ideas of equality of opportunity and individual freedom
can serve as powerful forces in a national effort to achieve a fuller realization of human potentialities and a better utilization of manpower skills
and abilities.

Pursuit of these key objectives led the Council to popularize the idea
of investment in human beings as a national goal, one which we have
heard so much about in the 1960s. The Council desired to encourage an
informed and responsible public concern with investment in human beings.
Finally, it was hoped by the Council that the results of its work would lead
to the formulation of longer-range manpower policies, both governmental
and nongovernmental.[22] The publications of the National Manpower Council (which are cited in the bibliography in the back of the book) include
statements ranging from student draft deferment, policy on scientific and
professional manpower, policy for skilled manpower, womanpower, and
the role of education and government in developing human resources.

Another important source of interest in long-range manpower planning
was the federal government. The Bureau of Labor Statistics and the Office
of Education have had an historically well-established interest in the field
of manpower and the development of human resources. In both cases their
interest in human resources extends back to the turn of the century. Also,
at the end of World War II the National Science Foundation was established by the federal government. By the early 1950s it was becoming in-

[21] Recently, the essence of its work has been summarized in one volume: Eli Ginzberg, *The Development of Human Resources*, McGraw-Hill, New York, 1966.
[22] National Manpower Council, *Manpower Policies for a Democratic Society*, Columbia University Press, New York, 1965, Chaps. VII to XIII.

volved in research in the social sciences, including studies of scientific personnel and manpower.[23] It goes without saying, that since the mid-fifties, and particularly since 1960, as we shall see in a later chapter, the extent of governmental interest in and support of manpower and educational planning has been truly phenomenal.

MANPOWER PLANNING AS A SOLUTION TO PEOPLE PROBLEMS

There were undoubtedly spillover effects of the work carried out by the National Manpower Council, various foundations, and the federal government which affected many other organizations. An Engineering Manpower Council was established in the early 1950s and devoted considerable attention to the alleged shortage of engineers and a number of the social, economic, and educational problems impeding their development. Much controversy raged over the proper utilization of engineers, and there were serious questions raised by many as to whether engineers were being malutilized by performing technicians' work or were being provided with truly professional work experiences. Debates on these issues continue to the present. Judging by the literature of personnel administration in the decade of the 1950s, industrial firms became acutely aware of a perceived executive shortage and hundreds of articles were written about manpower shortages in the executive ranks. The term "management development" became a watchword, if not an elusive phantom, and companies went on a great management development binge. This included the establishment of innumerable in-company training programs for executives as well as a proliferation and elaboration of the university in-residence-type management development programs (which we call management education programs in this book). The perceived shortage of executives coupled with the need for highly educated and talented manpower made the business community very much aware of its own type of manpower problems in quantitative terms. In addition to responses to the challenge in terms of management development programs and various educational training programs, industrial firms became more interested than ever in qualitative dimensions of the managerial manpower problem. This meant that considerable attention was to be given to executive appraisal programs, personnel testing, manpower inventories, and the establishment of formal replacement planning. All these activities became associated with the concepts of manpower planning stated by firms, with some organizations stressing one or two aspects rather than others.

[23] Harry Alpert, "The National Science Foundation and Social Science Research," *American Sociological Review,* Vol. 19, No. 2, April 1954, pp. 208–211.

In the latter part of 1957 when the Soviet Union launched its first sputnik, the American population became increasingly concerned about the quality of education being provided at all levels from grade school through the university. Education became a social problem. In many quarters questions were raised as to whether American education was too soft and had not been devoting sufficient attention to the hard scientific and technological education and training thought to be required by the times. Also, in the late 1950s and early 1960s computers became increasingly sophisticated and were having spillover effects in the educational sphere. Teaching machines became better known, and educational technology underwent a revolution that was considerably less than the information-processing revolution, but one which nevertheless aroused widespread discussion throughout American society. The changes in job requirements and the need for highly talented manpower in professional, managerial, and technical positions suggested to many individuals that the time was ripe to look at manpower planning and the development of human resources in American society from the broadest possible perspective.

Finally, there was the creeping prosperity unemployment and the rediscovery of the poor. Poverty was now viewed as a social problem. In a typical American response to a challenge of this kind, education was emphasized as the key to helping the unemployed to qualify for work and the alpha, if not the omega, in solving this social problem. The extensive educational and training legislation enacted since 1960 was wanted and supported by a population that perceived education and training as the greatest need of the era.

In the midst of all these forces and shifting interests was the long tradition of industrial training, the extensive in-service formal and informal training provided by employing organizations of all kinds. Students of manpower who took a long-range view recognized that the diverse education and training activities being carried out in the United States should be coordinated to eliminate overlap and duplication. Industry apparently conducted its programs without much cognizance given to governmental programs. Similarly, the federal government as well as the state and local governments carried out activities that were not closely coordinated in fact with educational and training activities inside organizations. Since the early 1960s there has been recognition of the connection between the two, and the different levels of government have tried to make greater use of industrial firms in the provision of education and training, such as using industrial training resources for programs under the Manpower Development and Training Act and Job Corps programs under the Economic Opportunity Act. By the same token, industrial firms have become better acquainted with educational activities outside the walls of their plants and offices. Nevertheless, there remained problems in integrating these different types of education and training, and particularly problems pertaining to the lack of congruence in manpower planning within the firm and by various levels of government. It is to this subject which we turn next.

RECENT CONCEPTS OF MANPOWER PLANNING IN THE ECONOMY OF THE UNITED STATES

Since the end of World War II, the development of active manpower policies in both industrial and developing countries has created a demand for advanced information about manpower changes. In the underdeveloped countries, which have an oversupply of unskilled labor and shortages of highly trained and educated manpower, the emphasis has been on the supply of high- and middle-level manpower. As was indicated in the preceding section, the nations of Western Europe which have been confronted with increasingly tight labor markets have also directed their attention to the supply of labor, but at all levels.[24]

Similarly, in the United States some of the first efforts in manpower projection were concerned with the supply of manpower. The development of national income accounts and their projection required that estimates be made of the available labor input. The Employment Act of 1946 stimulated interest in the size of the labor force for which jobs were to be provided. Interest then shifted to the demand side in the creeping prosperity unemployment environment of the late 1950s and early 1960s.[25]

The Council of Economic Advisors, together with many other prominent economists, argued consistently in the last decade that the upward drift in the unemployment rate to about 1965 was attributable primarily to a deficiency of aggregate demand, which was associated with the lagging growth rate of the American economy. The implication of this view was continually rising unemployment. The opposite school of thought, which included among its adherents a predominantly conservative group together with some well-known labor economists, held that structural changes in the economy led to a growing imbalance between the increasing demand for highly skilled and educated workers, on the one hand, and a rising surplus of relatively unskilled, uneducated workers, on the other.[26]

[24] Garth L. Mangum and Arnold L. Nemore, "The Nature and Functions of Manpower Projections," *Industrial Relations*, Vol. 5, No. 3, May 1966, p. 1.

[25] *Ibid.*

[26] Margaret S. Gordon, "U.S. Manpower and Employment Policy," *Monthly Labor Review*, Vol. 87, No. 11, November 1964, pp. 1315–1316. See also Eleanor G. Gilpatrick, *Structural Unemployment and Aggregate Demand,* Johns Hopkins Press, Baltimore 1966, in which adequate aggregate demand is viewed as an essential condition for effective full employment but not sufficient in itself to bring it about. Miss

Regardless of whether one considers the causes of unemployment in the recent past to be attributable to insufficient aggregate demand or to structural changes, many persons still have uneasy feelings regarding whether a steady period of full employment will ever again be possible in the United States or whether manpower redundancy has set in, absent military operations which drain manpower from the civilian labor force and open up job opportunities for persons who might otherwise be unemployed. In addition, many people have been concerned whether educational requirements are outstripping educational attainment. Still others have asked questions whether the skills that are being supplied are those which are really in demand now and will continue to be in the future. This fear and fascination with employment and manpower problems has created a renewed interest in predicting the future as well as caused considerable frustration with some of the existing indicators of what the state of manpower will be at that time. The effect of this interest in the future has been to tax the energies and intellectual limits of specialists in manpower planning and to have led those who wish information on manpower planning to make demands on manpower specialists which are unrealistic given the existing state of knowledge.[27]

Manpower planning in the United States needs to be viewed in the context of American society and our prevailing cultural values. In this way, we can obtain an appreciation of the direction which manpower planning has taken in the economy and understand the implications of this direction for industrial organizations. In this way, we shall obtain some insight into why manpower planning has become a relatively new activity in industrial relations and why its importance will undoubtedly grow in the future.

The remainder of this chapter probes generally the nature, uses, and evaluation of manpower projections. In the next chapter we relate these ideas to two examples. In one of these we discuss manpower-planning techniques which could be used in projecting certain manpower needs in a large industrial plant; and, in the second, manpower techniques specifically applied to projecting the needs for one type of occupation (apprentices in the skilled trades) in a multplant organization, such as a large division in a corporation.

Gilpatrick notes that the war in Vietnam has somewhat obscured the issue of the extent of structural unemployment and proposes significant innovations in American economic planning in the manpower area to make valid the pledge of the Employment Act of 1946. For authoritative statements on this controversy by such leading economists as Charles C. Killingsworth, Walter W. Heller, Otto Eckstein, and Leon H. Keyserling, see Garth L. Mangum, ed., *The Manpower Revolution,* Doubleday, Garden City, 1966, pp. 95–172.

[27] Mangum and Nemore, *op. cit.,* pp. 1–2.

PROJECTIONS VERSUS FORECASTS

In examining the nature of manpower projections, we should at the out-set distinguish between projections and forecasts and make other defini-tional distinctions which will foster our understanding of the key concepts involved. In reality the difference between the two terms, projections and forecasts, turns on the confidence of the person making the prognostication. As was suggested earlier in the chapter, people are reluctant to prophesy and really know nothing of the future except what has happened in the past and at present. The projector, after examining past trends and current developments, develops or sets forth a working model of the system or body of data which he is studying. He then states a series of assumptions about how the important variables are likely to behave in the future and uses these assumptions to modify extensions of the past performance of the variables. The projector will defend his product only to the extent that his assumptions may be expected to prove valid. The accuracy of his projec-tions depends on the realism of the assumptions and the identification of all the relevant variables. On the other hand, the forecaster is a projector who has the confidence and the institutional freedom to state his conclu-sions unconditionally and to stake his reputation upon them.[28]

In a world undergoing dynamic change, it is seldom possible to validate a projection. In the case of projections that are made for policy purposes, it may not even be appropriate to consider validation since a projection may be successful only to the extent that it is proven false. For example, if the purpose of the projection was to warn of impending problems, the warning may permit avoidance of the crisis and, therefore, invalidate the projection. Of course, a projection may be criticized for failure to identify the relevant variables; but it cannot be criticized for the failure of the assumptions to hold true. One of the most important failures a projector may make is to neglect the explicit statement of his assumptions. Among the errors made by users of projections are failure to note and appraise the underlying assumptions of the projector and a tendency to read into long-range projections an implied commitment to an imputed straight-line trend at intermediate points.[29]

[28] *Ibid.,* p. 2. We have leaned heavily upon the thinking of Mangum and Nemore in explicating the key concepts in this section. For an excellent discussion see also Adolph Sturmthal, *Current Manpower Problems,* Institute of Labor and Industrial Relations, University of Illinois, Urbana, 1964, pp. 47–60.

[29] Mangum and Nemore, *op. cit.,* pp. 2–3. For a discussion of forecasting which supplements what is discussed here, see Eric W. Vetter, *Manpower Planning for High Talent Personnel,* Bureau of Industrial Relations, University of Michigan, Ann Arbor, 1967, pp. 125–174. He stresses profit planning and labor productivity, which are

Descriptive and Normative Forecasts

A distinction also should be made between descriptive projections of what is likely to be and normative projections of what ought to be. Criticism of normative projections is justified only when their intent is not made clear. In the past few years the relative value of descriptive and normative projections has been of international interest. For example, in Western Europe and the developing countries, where planning and government action are more accepted features of economic life than is true in the United States, the tendency is to produce forecasts which are expressions of policy, that is, estimates of what should happen if certain goals are to be met. Most discussions of manpower forecasting by the Organization for Economic Cooperation and Development (OECD) and the International Labour Organization (ILO) adopt this approach. However, in the United States, where economic and governmental action are acceptable but are still viewed with suspicion by many individuals and groups, the emphasis has tended to be on projections which attempt to predict what will happen under certain assumptions. There is a vague and implicit hope that if the projection indicates serious imbalances, some action will be taken by somebody to bring about a more desirable situation. Rarely do the prognosticators attempt to set goals when they prepare projections. Instead the tendency is to use a currently acceptable ratio (such as student–teacher ratios, or population to position ratios), which is usually developed by a private group with special interest.[30]

It is thought that projectors and forecasters in the United States generally are more experienced and have more sophisticated methodologies than their counterparts in other parts of the world. However, many foreigners consider American projectors and policy makers less sophisticated in the uses to which projections are put. Projections made in other countries tend to be tools of long-term public planning whereas in the United States projection techniques emphasize describing the probably future environment in order to enable private decision makers to make more rational decisions. American projectors are unlikely to abandon descriptive projections in favor of policy targets. Nevertheless, the acceptance of various forms of public planning appears to be growing; and, if it does, a shift in emphasis is likely to occur. As long as the descriptive and normative nature of the

---

particularly relevant for private enterprise. See also such managerially oriented recent works as John R. Hinrichs, *High Talent Personnel*, American Management Association, New York, 1966; and Edwin B. Geisler, *Manpower Planning: An Emerging Staff Function*, Bulletin No. 101, American Management Association, New York, 1967.

[30] Mangum and Nemore, *op. cit.*, pp. 3–4.

projections are made explicit, the use of both could have real advantages. For example, the development of manpower forecasts which are expressions of policy would force policy makers to give more serious consideration to the manpower implications inherent in their policy deliberations and decisions. A dual approach using normative and descriptive projections might also lead to less centralization and broader participation in policy-making processes because objectives and their implications would be exposed to public view long before they became irreversible fact.[31]

Projecting Supply and Demand

Still another distinction which should be made is between projecting the labor supply and projecting the demand for labor. Confusion may arise if there is failure to differentiate among projections of supply, demand, employment, and unemployment at both the aggregate and disaggregate levels. Aggregate supply projections are the simplest and most commonly made. The size of the labor force in an economy is projected 10 to 15 years ahead, both in gross numbers and by age, sex, and race based essentially on demographic factors and tempered by judgments about changing labor-force participation rates. Labor-force projections of this type are limited almost exclusively to estimates of changes in the numbers of persons. There is no inventory of the supply of existing skills because the only data which are available are on employment by occupation and industry. There is no base from which to project supply by skill level or any qualitative consideration except educational attainment. Little attempt is made to project the supply of skills except where enrollment in specific courses in vocational schools, colleges, or apprenticeship provide a data base and some information on trends. Yet, the lack of projections of the supply of skills does not appear to be a serious loss in terms of policy. In the United States, at least, few jobs appear to have a fixed skill requirement; and employers seem able to vary their requirements over a wide range, depending upon the state of the labor market. This means that to a surprising extent the skills required tend to be determined by the skills available! For similar reasons, the occupa-

---

[31] *Ibid.* Various examples of projection techniques utilized in the United States can be obtained by consulting references in the bibliography. Some examples would be Harold Goldstein, "Projections of Manpower Requirements and Supply," *Industrial Relations,* Vol. 5, No. 3, May 1966, pp. 17–27; Joel Darmstadter, "Manpower in a Long-Term Economic Projection Model," *Industrial Relations,* Vol. 5, No. 3, May 1966, pp. 28–58; and Robert Ferber and Kyohei Sasaki, "Labor Force and Wage Projections in Hawaii," *Industrial Relations,* Vol. 5, No. 3, May 1966, pp. 72–85. Numerous other articles can be found in the *Monthly Labor Review, International Labour Review, Review of Economics and Statistics, Management of Personnel Quarterly,* and similar professional journals.

tional and industrial mobility of workers make projections of supply by occupation and industry of relatively little value.[32]

A classical case in which supply of skills has historically been inadequate and in which employers seem to have adequately coped with projected shortages is seen in skilled trades apprenticeship. Through a variety of devices, which we discuss in more detail in another chapter, persons have drifted into the skilled trades in large numbers without completing an apprenticeship.[33]

Turning to projecting the demand for labor, it should be noted that one of the questions that is most frequently asked about this dimension is: what will be the future levels of unemployment? However, this is a question that cannot be answered by manpower projections because employment levels in modern economies are largely the consequence of public policy, or in other words, judgments by policy makers, not projections made by planning technicians. This means that employment levels are subject to guess; and there are two approaches to such "guesstimates" with little practical difference between them. The first is to assume a level of unemployment, based either on a normative judgment of what it ought to be or a more descriptive judgment of what it is likely to be. The second is to project gross national product on the basis of an assumption about future growth rates, estimate the consequent employment, and subtract the employment from the projected labor force to obtain an estimate of the implied unemployment. However, if the resulting unemployment estimate appears higher than that likely to be acceptable to policy makers, two types of modifications are made. Either one is made in the estimated growth rate or in the productivity assumptions (which underlie the estimate of the change in employment associated with the projected change in GNP) until the estimate appears reasonable.[34]

To look a bit more deeply into this matter, it should be noted that projections of the structure of the demand for labor, rather than of total demand, are the more relevant of the two for manpower policy. In the United States, the projections in use are not actually projections of the demand for labor, but projections of employment. In the absence of job-vacancy data to supplement employment data, our knowledge of present and past demand is very deficient. Instead, the occupational and industrial structure of employment is projected, assuming there will be no impediments from a shortage of supply. "Manpower requirements," as that term is commonly

[32] Mangum and Nemore, op. cit., p. 4.
[33] See George Strauss, "Apprenticeship: An Evaluation of the Need," in Arthur M. Ross, ed., Employment Policy and the Labor Market, University of California Press, Berkeley, 1965, pp. 299–332.
[34] Mangum and Nemore, op. cit., pp. 5–6.

used, becomes an abbreviated way of referring to this surrogate for demand. It is believed that for normal periods in the United States, the difference represented by job vacancies is certainly smaller than the margin of error in the projections themselves.[35]

Manpower Requirements and Job Vacancies

The United States remains as one of the few Western industrial nations with no national measure of job vacancies. As a result there is no conclusive evidence to disprove the claims that job vacancies actually equal, exceed, or shortfall the number of idle workers. Even if job vacancy data were available, they would be no more likely to answer questions on where the vacant jobs are, what their requirements are, and what they pay than existing unemployment data are adequate for describing completely who is unemployed, why, and what kinds of jobs the unemployed are seeking. Employers in a job-vacancy survey are apt to be asked questions very much like those asked in present monthly surveys concerning unemployment, such as, "How many vacancies were you actively seeking to fill last week?" Although employers have shown a willingness to cooperate in answering this question in the past, they might not be if they thought it would be followed by a flood of referrals from the public employment service. On the other hand, job-vacancy data can serve as economic indicators, they can identify communities and occupations with a shortage of labor, and they may be useful in furnishing guidance for education and training. But only job orders that are placed with the public employment services can actually be used to refer the unemployed to job openings. The latter type of information is already obtainable except that employers do not furnish a complete listing of their position vacancies. For these and other reasons, job-vacancy data, even if available in some detail, cannot be viewed as a panacea in projecting the demand for labor.[36]

It is thus possible to see why the concept of "manpower requirements" is used instead of job-vacancy data in making manpower projections. To obtain estimates of manpower requirements total assumed gross national product is distributed among industries on the basis of additional assumptions concerning the behavior of consumption, investment, and government spending. Industry employment is regarded as that which would be associated with the GNP assigned to the industry. Industry employment is, in turn, distributed by occupation, so that what is projected is not manpower demand per se but employment by occupation and industry.[37]

[35] *Ibid.,* p. 6.
[36] Sar A. Levitan and Garth L. Mangum, "Coming to Grips with Unemployment," *The Reporter,* Vol. 35, No. 8, November 17, 1966, pp. 44–46.
[37] Mangum and Nemore, *op. cit.,* p. 6.

In the United States today, only two types of projections are, in reality, projections of demand, and neither of these is based upon the most dependable data. State employment services, in the area-skill surveys mentioned earlier in this chapter, project demand for two to five years ahead based upon employers' estimates of their future manpower needs. The validity of these projections depends upon the employers' ability to foresee the future. The differences among the capabilities of employers to envisage change probably varies greatly. The second type of projections are those made of demand for particular occupations based upon such factors as the ratio of workers in the occupation to the total population or to the labor force. Examples of projections of demand of this type would include those made for classroom teachers on the basis of student–teacher ratios and for scientists and engineers on the basis of an assumption of a fixed relationship to total employment.[38]

Uses Made of Projections

Turning to usage, it should be noted that projections of the supply and demand for manpower may be utilized for a variety of purposes. These include (1) planning educational programs and estimating what expansions in enrollment must be provided for in order to meet future needs for workers of all types, (2) evaluating the feasibility of launching new programs requiring skilled personnel, (3) the vocational guidance of individuals, (4) developing manpower programs and policies. Essentially, we are suggesting that manpower projections are useful for two prime purposes: to alert the government and other organizations to emerging manpower problems; and to provide a basis for educational planning, counseling, and guidance. Each of these shall be discussed briefly, beginning with foreseeing emerging manpower problems.

The major concern of governmental policy makers in recent years has been to avoid mismatches between demand and supply at either an aggregate or disaggregate level. At the present time, long-range projections of the total supply of labor are used primarily as determinants of economic growth potential and requirements. Disaggregated supply projections have been of little value until recently, but there are indications that these projections are likely to receive more attention. The objective of keeping unemployment at low levels can be pursued with one year's advance notice of the size of the labor force to be employed. However, the minimum level of unemployment attainable without inflation and the speed with which it can be achieved are effected by the degree to which the jobs created match the qualifications of available manpower. This requires detailed projections

[38] *Ibid.*

by age, sex, race, and skill. In order to influence the allocation of labor between and within the public and private sectors of the economy, longer lead time than one year is necessary in projecting the size and composition of the labor force.[39]

The need for foreseeing emerging manpower problems in the United States has been intensified by three new policy developments. First, the various programs of the Great Society, particularly those included under the Economic Opportunity Act of 1964, require assessments of manpower requirements as well as dollar costs. Second, the expanded role of the government in economic life has increased the need to foresee the impact of government decisions as, for example, in obtaining measures of the impact of research and development spending upon the distribution and utilization of the nation's scientists and engineers. Third, the popular belief that technological change, including automation, causes widespread displacement of employees has aroused interest in projections designed to predict employment crises at the regional, industrial, occupational, and organizational level in order to make possible advance planning to ease the adjustment change. Industrial organizations which have traditionally limited their manpower planning to avoiding shortages of key personnel have now started to expand their efforts to balance expected manpower needs with attrition rates. The purpose of these efforts is to minimize abrupt noncyclical employment reductions with their consequent displacement, disruption of employees' lives, bad publicity, and disturbed labor relations.[40] Also as industrial firms have become increasingly large they have realized that in order to perpetuate their existence in the future they must have adequate plans for the recruitment, selection, placement, development, compensation, and retention of key personnel as well as others who may be in short supply or possess high talent of a technical, scientific or professional type. The tendency for persons to "get lost" in large scale organizations because there are no internal mechanisms for identifying the quantity and quality of human resources has also led to inventorying the manpower assets of firms.

Projections for the purposes of educational planning have been strongly desired by educators at all levels. Insofar as much of education is designed as preparation for the future, educational planners are among those most persistently demanding projections of manpower. The projections required to assist most educational planners are not especially difficult to make. The educational system is, of course, through its policies, practices, and decisions a major determinant of the development of manpower. Involved here are decisions required of educators concerning physical facilities, finances,

[39] *Ibid.*, p. 7.
[40] *Ibid.*, pp. 7–9.

and curriculum. Buildings have a relatively long life, but they exercise little restraint on curriculum choices. Financial needs depend essentially on the number of students to be enrolled. Curriculum planning requires neither as much lead time nor detail as is generally supposed, particularly at the elementary- and secondary-school levels. The uniformity in educational curricula at lower levels extends to some extent even to the college where concentrations and majors are sufficiently broad to require comparatively little detailed anticipation of occupational choices, graduate education being an exception. Since the population of the United States has been steadily increasing, more funds are always needed for education. The projections offer indications of how much more would be warranted in terms of demographic change.[41]

The main problem hinges upon vocational education: the more specific the occupational training involved, the greater the need for projections. National projections by occupation and industry are available for these occupations, but these may not be pertinent to a particular labor market. Local projections are inadequate in number and frequently not reliable because of the questionable accuracy of employers' estimates of future prospects. These considerations suggest that there is a need for more and better local manpower projections to help educators concerned with the vocational fields.[42]

Projections are also needed for the counseling and guidance of youth. The high levels of unemployment of youth in recent years have caused dissatisfaction with the information available for counseling and making vocational choices. The standard source of this sort of information is the *Occupational Outlook Handbook*, published by the Bureau of Labor Statistics, which projects, in terms of general trends, employment in nearly seven hundred specific occupations for approximately one decade ahead. Unfortunately, most counselees are more interested in local or regional than national employment prospects and the local equivalent of the *Occupational Outlook Handbook* is rarely available.[43] Perhaps even more important is the basic problem, which is developing and preparing a sufficient number of qualified counselors who possess not only occupational information but also knowledge of the labor market, student assessment, interpersonal relations, and the gamut of skills needed to assist youth.[44]

[41] *Ibid.*, pp. 9–10.

[42] *Ibid.*

[43] *Ibid.*, pp. 10–11.

[44] For a discussion of these problems see Ruth Barry and Beverly Wolf, *An Epitaph for Vocational Guidance,* Bureau of Publications, Teachers College, Columbia University, New York, 1962; and Robert H. Mathewson, "Manpower or Persons: A Critical Issue, *Personnel and Guidance Journal,* Vol. 43, No. 4, December 1944, pp. 338–342.

SUMMARY AND CONCLUSION

In taking an overall view of what we have been discussing in respect to manpower projections, we should probably complete our comments by a summary statement or two evaluating the state of the art. In the United States the skills of manpower projectors and the supply of information about the manpower future are more adequate than criticism would indicate. The unwillingness of the federal government in the 1950s and early 1960s to pursue aggressive fiscal policies, the unrealistic expectations of projection users, and the inability or failure to use the projections available are more to blame for the criticisms leveled at projections than are the intrinsic inadequacies of the projections. Projections do not provide a blueprint of the future. They can point the directions and signal the warnings for policy changes or new policies. On the other hand, the rising general educational attainment of the American population is far more important to facilitating adjustment to change than is any warning system.[45]

It is unrealistic to expect long-run projections of general levels of employment and unemployment because they are affected more by the decisions of public policy makers than by those of individual employers. It is more difficult to predict the extent and structure of local and regional levels of employment than those on the national level because changes are less likely to be washed out by crosscurrents than in the case of national averages. This means the first need is for a consistent national policy of full employment to provide a solid base for local projections. The second need is to proceed with a program of making projections so that experience can be gained. Regional and local manpower projections are a relatively unexplored frontier. Manpower planning at the level of the firm is still another frontier and the development of a methodology for manpower planning in the firm is thought by some to be a pioneering step that holds great promise.[46] Manpower planning in the firm is next considered.

[45] Mangum and Nemore, *op. cit.*, pp. 11–12.
[46] *Ibid.*, pp. 11–15.

CHAPTER 3

Models of Manpower Planning
in the Firm

In industrial organizations planning has been focused on profit making, production, marketing, quality, inventory, and only most recently, manpower. Whenever labor was in short supply, organizations concerned themselves with what they would do to "staff up," but only recently have they turned to manpower planning as a preventive measure and sensible basis for administrative action. Estimating the needs for apprenticeship systematically (or by "guesstimates") has probably a relatively long history in some firms. The use of manning tables is not new. The planning for managerial progression and succession has been associated with some pace-setting companies for many years. These were clearly straws in the wind.

Since the early 1950s firms have realized that failures in planning for and in developing people become a limiting factor in attaining organizational objectives. During the early 1960s a strong interest in manpower planning at the level of the organization developed and companies who were not planning for manpower became curious as to how it could be carried out. They sought guidance not only in manpower projection techniques but also in the resulting actions involving the most effective education and training needed to implement the plans. Individuals who were hired to carry out manpower planning became concerned with the timing and the scheduling of the planning and from a practical standpoint persuading the administrative or managerial power structures in organizations to use the results of manpower planning studies in the conduct of the business.

Many manpower planners found that it was difficult to keep the results of manpower planning studies alive and used as an organizational and managerial tool. Typically, firms expressed interest and enthusiasm with the studies, but when problems of obtaining profit objectives arose and it appeared that reduction in the size of the work force would be a solution (at least in the short run) to reduce costs, manpower planners found that some of their chief problems were not methodological or technical but grew out of coping with budgets, headcount restrictions, and other expedient actions which were severely detrimental to reaping the fruits of their manpower planning efforts. Some other firms expended a considerable amount of effort in integrating manpower planning with other aspects of planning in organizations (such as with the development of human resources) and with various phases of personnel administration. In this way they became involved in identifying and resolving the many problems of human input and output in the manpower pipeline. Some even became concerned with retirement planning and preretirement programs, which, of course, are tied in most closely with the removal of manpower from the organizations. One might say they became involved in the transition from seniority on the job to senior citizenship.[1]

Manpower planning specialists in organizations have necessarily been concerned with the problems of updating manpower plans under changing conditions. They have also necessarily tried to integrate their manpower projections with the educational and training policies, programs and procedures of their employing organizations. They have started to carve out a new and important organizational role for themselves. In order to understand this role, we require an expanded conception of (1) organizations, (2) educational and training programs, and (3) knowledge of the techniques used for manpower planning and development of human resources.

In this chapter a model is developed to explain the conduct of manpower planning studies in organizations. In doing this we anticipate some of the subsequent chapters in the book. For example, in Chapter 4 we survey organization for manpower planning and developing people in sufficient detail so that exploration of the main concepts on organization are postponed for treatment in that chapter. Similarly, in subsequent chapters we discuss the concepts and techniques for conducting educational and training programs in organizations in detail and shall postpone the main thrust of our thinking on these topics until then. However, in this chapter some references must be made to organization and educational and training programs in order to develop a meaningful model for manpower planning because, as we shall see, planning is most easily translated into action when development programs exist and are designed for employees with similar needs, at similar organizational levels, or performing similar work assignments.

---

[1] Ida Russakoff Hoos, "Technology, Retraining, and the Training Director," *Business Topics,* Vol. 14, No. 1, Winter 1966, pp. 47–61, especially p. 61.

MODEL FOR A TOTAL COMPLEX ORGANIZATION

In order to explain the model for manpower planning we shall proceed by assuming that the planning will be carried out in an industrial organization comprised of three organizational levels: the corporate, divisional, and local (which would include plants and other decentralized components such as warehouses, sales offices, branches, subsidiaries, affiliates, and the like). This type of organization has been chosen because it is the most complex and the type with which the author is most familiar.[2] Smaller firms and those with simpler organizations also require manpower planning; however, what we have to say about larger organizations will be equally applicable to smaller ones although the scope and complexity of planning would be scaled down. Of course, in what might be called "tiny" businesses (corner grocery stores, restaurants, and the like), there is virtually no need to plan for people inasmuch as owner-managers in the organization rely on direct hires and on-the-job training for the handful of people needed to man the organization.

In analyzing educational and training programs, reference will be made to the kinds of programs which can be used to develop people. In making these references we also get ahead of ourselves but shall minimize any confusion for the reader by simply indicating the kinds of people that would be required to man the organization, such as, newly hired unskilled workers, skilled tradesmen (e.g., toolmakers, carpenters, electricians, and machine repairmen), foremen, recently recruited college graduate trainees, and executives. Although these types of employees are normally considered as distinctively different categories, we shall see that there is a certain degree of interchangeability in manpower planning. For example, a college graduate recruit who aspires to the position of plant production manager may very well spend time during his first few years in industry working as a foreman. This is particularly the case in the chemical industry. Thus when projecting needs for foremen we must consider how many will be college graduate trainees, how many will be promotions from the hourly rated rank-and-file, and how many will be new hires.

Insofar as we have explained our concept of planning previously, the stage has already been set for our analysis of a model for manpower planning. To a considerable extent, the approaches that are used in projecting manpower needs have considerable similarity for employees at all organizational levels, for example, in projecting the needs for foremen, technicians, professional

---

[2] For a brief up-to-date discussion of this type of organization see Harold Stieglitz, "Divisionalization and Work of Top-Level Management," *Conference Board Record,* Vol. 1, No. 3, March 1964, pp. 7–11.

employees, salesmen, college cooperative students, college graduate trainees, and, to some extent, managers and executives. However, we shall see that in projecting the needs for executives that consideration is given to factors in addition to the ones discussed for personnel at lower organizational levels.

In stressing techniques for planning in this chapter, we need not repeat the same thoughts subsequently in discussing the development of manpower at different organizational levels, which is the principal subject matter of later chapters. Mention will be made of manpower-planning methodology in those chapters only when there are significant departures from the model presented in this chapter (or other types of qualifications required to make the model more appropriate).

Assumptions and Purposes of the Model

In reviewing the model, there are several assumptions that are implicit in our thinking. It is assumed that there are basic employee records which provide information on the usual demographic and related employment background factors such as age, education, sex, work history, length of service in the organization, and the like. Second, it is assumed that in the organization there exists a system of wage and salary administration and job evaluation such that organizational tasks have been identified and structured in terms of jobs and pay. It is also assumed that there is a means for processing data. These means may be either manual or computerized.

To restate the purpose of developing this model, it should be recalled that the manpower planning specialist has as one of his primary functions the systematic projecting of manpower requirements for the future. In turn, the projection has implications for educational and training program planning, minimizing disruptions to the work place, and recruitment, selection, and placement activities as related to changing levels of employment in the organization. Manpower planning also has obvious effects upon morale in organizations and provides an opportunity to improve the quality and productivity of the work force. Needless to say, manpower planning has important implications for profit planning (or vice versa) and the control of costs. In essence, we might say that manpower planning provides the basis for determining manpower requirements in the light of anticipated developments affecting the operations of an organization. This in turn requires a system through which manpower changes in an organization can be reported and appraised on a systematic and recurring basis.

ANALYSIS BY MANPOWER LEVELS IN ORGANIZATIONS

The manpower planning system should provide information necessary for the determination of: recruiting needs; the effects of anticipated changes

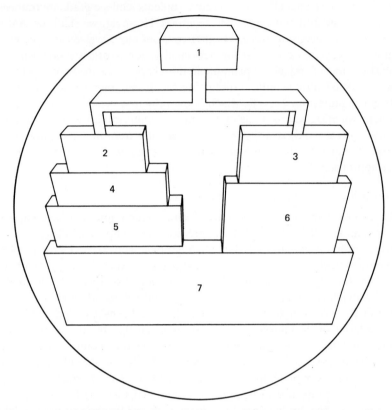

Figure 1   Levels of employees in a complex organization. (1) Top managers and executives; (2) staff supervisors; (3) line supervisors; (4) professional employees; (5) technical, clerical, and other salaried employees; (6) skilled-trades hourly employees; (7) semiskilled and unskilled hourly employees.

in technology, markets, and products on manpower requirements; and educational and training program requirements. The system should be applicable to a complex organization having levels of employees as reflected in Figure 1. Assuming that the organization is comprised of a corporate, divisional, and local level it can be seen that Figure 1 pertains to the local, and in this case, plant level primarily. Included are top managers and executives; staff supervisors; line supervisors (which would include foremen, general foremen, and superintendents); professional employees (which would include all persons filling positions requiring a degree from a four-year college as well as college graduate trainees); technical (by which is meant technician employees, that is, those whose educational background included one or two years of technical training in a community college, junior college, or technical institute or persons who have obtained technician skills in less formal ways, such as through the armed forces), clerical, and other salaried employees; skilled trades hourly employees (including journeymen, upgraders, and others who have acquired knowledge in depth of a craft); and semiskilled and unskilled hourly employees. In a typical manufacturing plant there may even be a distribution of employees of these types which roughly approximates the relative size of the boxes in Figure 1 depending, of course, on the industry, amount of automation utilized, size of the work force, and a number of obvious related considerations. For the sake of simplicity, sales personnel who are engaged in direct or indirect selling have not been included in Figure 1. If the organization is one in which outside salesmen are employed by it, such personnel would probably fit in categories 4 and 5 in the organizational levels reflected in Figure 1. On the other hand, if the salesmen are employed essentially in retail outlets, the nature of the organization would not include them in the manpower planning of the complex organization itself.[3]

Although Figure 1 applies primarily to the local or plant level in a manufacturing company, if levels 3, 6, and 7 are omitted, the remainder is the essential structure of the positions that exist at the level of a division and the level of a corporate staff in a large-scale organization. Therefore, the figure has relevance for manpower planning at all three levels in a complex organization.

Structural Considerations

Similar to long-range planning in general, particularly in industrial organizations, it is best for planning to start at the lowest organizational level then move up to the highest. A corporate plan may, of course, be developed by the chief executive officer with the assistance of headquarters or corporate staff planners. However, if personnel lower down in the organization start the planning process, among other things, the organization reaps the benefits of the thinking of persons who are more familiar with day-to-day problems and will be more interested in fulfilling the plans if they have had a hand in constructing them. It is, therefore, quite common, for example, to have small organizational components (departments) at low levels make up their own budgets which are submitted up the line for approvals and modifications. In many organizations a specialized planning group is then used to assist those down the line in drawing up plans for their segments of the organization and, later, to help top

---

[3] For discussion of some of these problems see Valentine F. Ridgway, "Administration of Manufacturer-Dealer Systems," *Administrative Science Quarterly,* Vol. 1, No. 4, March 1957, pp. 464–483.

management coordinate the various plans into a unified whole.[4] The same thinking is applicable to the conduct of manpower planning, namely, that it should begin at the lowest organizational level and be reviewed at successively higher organizational echelons. From the standpoint of the complex organizational model we have been discussing, this obviously means that manpower planning should begin at the plant level.

The manpower-planning system at the plant level would require the managerial group which operated the plant (often called the "operating committee") to review annually the previous year's manpower experience by comparing actual data with estimates that had been made in the prior year. They would then formulate a manpower plan or projection for the next year, including the numbers of employees required by level and the sources which could be utilized to meet these requirements. They would determine the numbers of promotable employees for the annual manpower plan. Finally, they would evaluate these plans in the light of expected changes of all kinds within the next five years and provide a supplementary statement indicating modifications that were made because of the anticipated changes. The manpower-planning specialist working at the plant level would do the staff work for the operating committee. In line with the principles of functional and administrative supervision, this planning would in turn be submitted to the next higher organizational level, which would be the divisional.

The parallel to the operating committee at the plant level ("divisional operating committee") would review the manpower plans submitted by all the plants in the division and formulate similar plans for the staff departments in the division (in other words, those divisional departments which would include employee levels 1, 2, 4, and 5 reflected in Figure 1). The divisional operating committee would then integrate all the manpower plans of its plants as well as those of its divisional staff departments into a comprehensive divisional manpower planning report, which in turn would be submitted to the corporate staff. The manpower planning specialist in the divisional staff would provide the services necessary for the divisional operating committee. These services would include the following: a detailed report of the previous twelve-month period for all the plants and the divisional staff departments, a consolidated manpower plan for each of the next two years, and a summary evaluation of the impact of anticipated changes in the future five-year period on needs for employees.

Reporting Relationships and Integration with All Planning

The last stage in the administration of this model system for manpower planning would be submission to the corporate headquarters of the divi-

[4] Ernest Dale, *Management: Theory and Practice,* McGraw-Hill, New York, 1965, p. 378.

sional manpower planning reports. At the level of the corporation, there is usually a counterpart of the plant and divisional operating committees called an "executive committee," "administration committee," or a similar committee designated by some other name. The manpower planning specialist at the corporate level would review all plans submitted by the divisions and develop similar manpower plans for the headquarters staffs. Again referring to Figure 1, in the headquarters or corporate staff, personnel identified as 1, 2, 4, and 5 would exist in such staffs as marketing, finance, engineering, personnel, and the various other functional fields of business. In organizations such as governments, hospitals, universities, foundations, and the military, departmentation would, of course, be different although the basic principles for administering manpower planning would be alike. The manpower-planning specialist at the headquarters level would act as the staff to the executive or administration committee of the total organization and consolidate the divisional and corporate staff plans, ultimately, in effect, formulating the organizational-wide manpower-planning report or manpower plan. (It may be appropriate for the manpower specialist at the corporate level to prepare, in addition, projections ahead for five to ten years in respect to overall organizational manpower needs which can be used as a crude logic check against the divisional projections. We return to this point later.)

As was previously postulated in the book, manpower planning must be closely integrated with all other planning in the organization if it is to make its proper contribution. This means that the manpower-planning specialist at the corporate level should be given all the information which he requires to make realistic projections of the organization's total manpower plans. He would need access to projections made of industry and national economic trends; projections made of long-range organizational changes; any assessments or special studies made of estimated technological change; and current information on estimates of the impact of any proposed new products or major business ventures, such as entering new markets, expansions of all types both in the United States and overseas; and any proposed plans for merger or absorption.

By and large, most planning would focus on a period running less than five years and in most instances would be limited only to one or two years. Because our society and technology change so rapidly, long-range plans beyond five years become similar to the long-range economic development plans of an underdeveloped country, that is, very broad, general, almost vague, targets toward which activity is directed by means of the more detailed specific short-range plans.

Figure 2 provides a visualization of the manner in which this process would operate, beginning at the plant level and moving upward through the divisional and, finally, into the corporate level. As can be seen, the man-

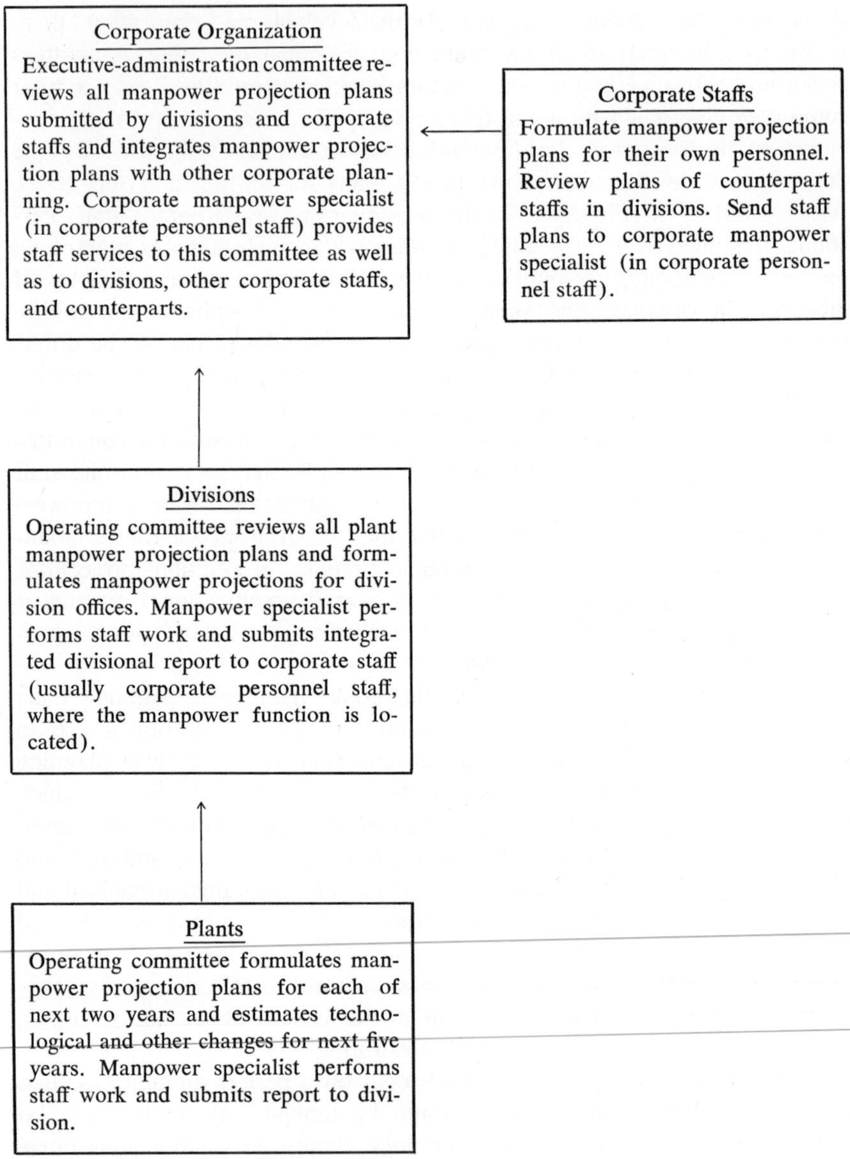

Corporate Organization
Executive-administration committee reviews all manpower projection plans submitted by divisions and corporate staffs and integrates manpower projection plans with other corporate planning. Corporate manpower specialist (in corporate personnel staff) provides staff services to this committee as well as to divisions, other corporate staffs, and counterparts.

Corporate Staffs
Formulate manpower projection plans for their own personnel. Review plans of counterpart staffs in divisions. Send staff plans to corporate manpower specialist (in corporate personnel staff).

Divisions
Operating committee reviews all plant manpower projection plans and formulates manpower projections for division offices. Manpower specialist performs staff work and submits integrated divisional report to corporate staff (usually corporate personnel staff, where the manpower function is located).

Plants
Operating committee formulates manpower projection plans for each of next two years and estimates technological and other changes for next five years. Manpower specialist performs staff work and submits report to division.

Figure 2 Flow chart of manpower planning system in a complex organization.

power specialist performs all the essential staff work at the plant, division, and corporate levels. As a rule, the manpower specialist would be located in the personnel or industrial relations department in the plant, division, and corporate organizational component.

Corporate staffs such as finance, marketing, engineering, personnel, or any other functional activity would probably have someone in their organization handling administrative matters who would be expected to have some competence in the areas of personnel administration and manpower. In the event that the staff was too small to have such an individual, the staff services required would be provided by the manpower specialist in the corporate personnel staff.

MECHANICS OF THE MANPOWER-PLANNING PROCESS

The flow chart depicted in Figure 2 indicates that manpower planning would essentially be carried out by the line organization (through administrative supervision) with the staff services provided at each level by the manpower specialist (through functional supervision). Obviously, in a large organization the various duties of a manpower specialist might be subdivided among several individuals. In a smaller organization where there were no divisions or other complexities in organization, the essential structure would be confined to what is depicted in Figure 2 as the plant level. Here the manpower specialist would carry out all the functions which in a larger organization would be subdivided to correspond with the various levels of organizational components.

Figures 1 and 2 indicate the levels of employees in a complex organization and the flow chart of a manpower planning system by which a manpower-planning scheme can be put into operation. In order to make the system work it is necessary that the approach suggested be specified in somewhat more detail. In order to do this a rational approach must be spelled out.

We proceed by explaining in Table 1 how the manpower projection plan for a division may be brought together. We have selected the divisional level for the purposes of illustration. Any organizational level could be used. In the next section of this chapter we examine in detail how manpower planning can be carried out in a large plant so that the system we are studying will be made clearer when applied to a realistic plant situation too.

In Table 1, the various rows correspond to the functions in the division, which in turn are subdivided according to managerial level. The number of functions shown, of course, is simply illustrative, for in any organization there may be many more functions than those indicated. Projections

Table 1 Manpower Projection Plan for a Division

Division	Current on Roll 9/15/70 (1)	Anticipate on Roll 9/15/71 (2)	Net Change (1)–(2) (3)	Total Employees Required (4)	Total Employees Made Available (5)	Promoted from Within (6)	Transferred from Inside the Organization (7)	To Be (8
A. Production 　　**Managers** 　　**Supervisors** 　　**Professional (exempt nonsupervisory)**								
B. Finance 　　**Managers** 　　**Supervisors** 　　**Professional (exempt nonsupervisory)**								
C. Marketing 　　**Managers** 　　**Supervisors** 　　**Professional (exempt nonsupervisory)**								
D. Engineering 　　**Managers** 　　**Supervisors** 　　**Professional (exempt nonsupervisory)**								
E. Total Management (A + B + C + D)								
F. Other salaried—nonexempt, nonsupervisory technical and clerical employees								
G. Hourly employees (skilled trades) (semiskilled and unskilled)								
H. Total (A + B + C + D + F + G)								

would begin with examination of the employees currently on the payroll as of September 15, 1970. The projection would be for one year after that date. In order to explain how the planning sheet would work, we should examine each of the separate columns.

Column 1. Current on roll 9/15/70. Numbers in this column would be obtained from the regular number of employees on the payroll for the business day closest to September 15, 1970.

Column 2. Anticipate on roll 9/15/71. Figures in this column would reflect the best estimate of numbers who will be employed in the division one year from the date of the projection, that is, September 15, 1971. In arriving at this estimate, the following factors would be taken into account:

(a) *Employment trends.* An examination of the numbers of employees on the payroll during the previous five years would indicate the trend within each employee group. It should then be possible to determine whether a particular group has been stable or unstable and whether it has been expanding or contracting.

(b) *Forward plans.* The plans of the various plants in the division would be carefully reviewed to assess their probable effect on the numbers of employees required in each group. Changes in the following would be particularly important:

(1) *The products to be manufactured or assembled.* Any significant change would probably affect the numbers and kinds of employees, not only in the plants, but also in divisional staff activities.

(2) *Financial planning volume.* Consideration would be given to the financial planning volume because manpower or staffing standards in complex organizations are frequently related directly or indirectly to anticipated volume as caused by sales.

(3) *Changes in technology and processes.* Any anticipated changes due to the introduction of automation or changes in processing should affect manpower needs in the plants as well as in the divisional offices. Attention would be given to automation both in the production and manufacturing activities as well as the office activities. Technological changes could be either obvious or subtle. They may involve not only changes in machinery and processing, but also sourcing as perhaps outside to a vendor. This means that manpower planning specialists should attempt to learn about such changes with sufficient time to appraise their possible impact on the numbers and kinds of employees required in the future.

(4) *Organizational change.* Any anticipated changes in the organization of the division would be evaluated from a manpower standpoint.

Column 3. Net change. If this number is negative, it means that the total number of employees within the group will be reduced. On the other hand, if the number is positive it signifies that the total number of employees will increase.

Column 4. Total employees required. This column includes net change (column 3) plus retirements anticipated during the projected period, plus other separations from employment (such as deaths, discharges, releases, quits), plus employees who are promoted or transferred out of the group.

(a) *Retirements.* This category would include all employees who will reach the normal retirement age during the projected year and will retire during that period in addition to those who are planning to retire early according to whatever provisions exist in organizational policy. The numbers who are likely to retire early can be estimated from a review of past experience.

(b) *Other separations.* This estimate should also be based upon past experience. An examination of the numbers of deaths, discharges, releases, and quits during each of the past five years should ordinarily provide a basis for projecting the next year's data. Any unusual situations, such as having a number of inadequate performers, should also be considered.

(c) *Employees promoted or transferred out of the group.* The numbers here can be estimated on the basis of a review of the numbers promoted or transferred during each of the prior five years.

Column 5. Total employees made available. The concept of being made available is one that is used in many but not all organizations. Availability simply indicates that either the employee on his own initiative or the organization employing him has indicated that the position which he is occupying is being relinquished by him. Commonly, this means the position is being eliminated and he is, therefore, "available" for placement elsewhere in the organization. Sometimes an employee makes himself "available" by voluntarily signifying that he desires a change of job assignment and that he would like to have his willingness to consider possible position vacancies publicized within the organization. If he does not obtain a new position in this manner, he is likely to quit since he has in the process cut his positional moorings. Obviously, it is rather difficult to estimate those who will voluntarily make themselves available although one could surmise from past experience.

The numbers in column 5 should also include more importantly the current employees who are performing satisfactorily, but will be made available involuntarily (i.e., laid off) during the forecast period. When availability is a consequence of reductions in work load, tighter staffing standards, reorganized work assignments, or various temporary fluctuations, advanced planning might assist in reducing the number who will leave the organization by seeking out other assignments for them well in advance of the scheduled layoff date.

Column 6. Promoted from within. Normally the employees within the division will be promoted into anticipated openings, although this is by no means universally the case. However, numbers reflected in this column should include only known and identified individuals, who, it is expected, will be promoted during the projected period. The boundaries of "within" are in this instance the division rather than the total corporation, of which the division is a part.

Column 7. Transferred from inside the organization. If openings are to be filled by employees from other parts of the organization, the names and numbers of such individuals should be known and available. The numbers in this column would refer only to these persons.

Column 8. To be recruited. This column would include all those who are to be hired into the organization. It would be possible to utilize the information in column 8 for the organization's establishing recruitment plans. Thus, when the manpower planning specialist at the corporate headquarters completes his staff work for the executive or administration committee of the corporation, they, in examining the staff work, could use the occasion to establish the recruitment authorizations for the organization for the ensuing one year. This authorization could then result in the follow-up preparation of requisitions for new personnel. In this way the manpower projection plan could be closely related to the next administrative step of actually formulating and carrying out recruitment.

In the final analysis, manpower planning can best be understood when the concepts, model, and systems are applied in a concrete situation. We shall use basically the approach described in this chapter and outlined in Table 1 in two additional examples of manpower planning.

MANPOWER PLANNING FOR A LARGE PLANT

We focus in the first example solely upon the male salaried work force required by a large plant in 1975 and include suggestions for programs for the development of human resources to assure that adequate manpower is obtained in an economical and educationally sound manner. Hourly employees are not included in the example; however, in the next section of the chapter we provide another example of projecting needs for skilled-trades hourly employees in a multiplant division. The two examples are intended to be supplementary illustrations. In this manner, we provide a meaningful example of manpower-planning techniques for one important category of hourly employees in terms which are easy to explain and understand. The results of these two examples, one of a plant male salaried manpower projection and the other of the skilled-trades work force in a division composed of a number of plants, should be adequate to illustrate properly the various techniques for manpower planning that are widely applicable. For illustrative convenience we assume that two studies are made in 1970.

The example may be viewed as a study designed to determine the male salaried manpower work force required by the large plant in 1975 and to recommend a program for the development of human resources based upon a procedure involving five phases. The first stage required developing a profile of changes in the characteristics of the plant's manpower during the past five years, that is, 1965–1969. This analysis included the numbers of employees, their educational attainment, training program participation, turnover experience, and accession characteristics. The second stage involved developing a profile of the work force in 1970, including data on age distribution, education, training, and work experience. The third stage was a projection of the current work force. From the data developed in stages one and two, a five-year projection of the plant's male salaried manpower requirements was made, assuming no changes in the work-force characteristics during the period which were not clearly identifiable from past experience. The fourth stage was a forecast for five years ahead of changes in technology and processes based upon interviews with persons in the plant as well as other people in the organization of which the plant was a part. An estimate was made of the future production volumes and technology of the plant. This information provided the basis for considering a future organizational structure, including the numbers and classifications of the people that would be required. The fifth and last stage was the establishment of an action plan to develop a qualified work force for 1975, five years ahead. This plan included information in respect to the hiring of personnel, plans for development of human resources, and the proper timing and setting-up of a time-phased approach to attaining the manpower objectives of the plant.

The approach to manpower planning requires intensive examination of the salaried personnel in the past five years, that is, 1965–1969, as a starting point, assuming we begin the manpower planning study during 1970. This examination would include an analysis of the total numbers, age and length of service, levels of education, prior training-program participation, and other pertinent personnel and organizational information which could affect the employment status of manpower included within the scope of the study. These statistical data would, in turn, be analyzed according to different organizational levels and fields of functional specialism in the plant. In addition, data regarding employees leaving the salaried payrolls for reasons other than retirement and those placed on the salaried payroll from recruitment and other sources would be analyzed.

Manpower and Production

In the example contrived here the basic environmental factor affecting plant operations during the ten-year period, 1960–1969 has been the decline in output of units produced. (The type of plant and units manufactured need not be discussed in the chapter; the approach is hopefully universal in its applicability and can be modified to accord with the realistic institutional considerations in any organization.) Table 2 indicates that there has been a decline from an annual rate of production of 417,593 units in 1960 to 271,450 units a decade later. This drop in production of 35 percent was accompanied by an even more dramatic decline in the total workforce in the plant. The decline in salaried employment was 41 percent and that of hourly employment more than 50 percent. It should be noted that the level of salaried employment remained relatively stable in the period 1966–1969, averaging about 515.

Table 2   Output and Employment in a Plant

| Year | Output (units) | Employment (daily average in a year) | | Total |
		Salaried Employees	Hourly Employees	
1960	417,593	891	8272	9163
1961	437,888	829	8466	9295
1962	405,760	853	7527	8380
1963	413,393	843	7533	8376
1964	384,793	790	6365	7155
1965	379,328	680	5102	5782
1966	353,796	529	5043	5572
1967	321,179	516	4307	4823
1968	263,031	496	3778	4274
1969	271,450	520	4090	4610

Age and Service

The data would next be examined from the standpoints of age and length of service of hourly and salaried employees. As can be discerned from Tables 3 and 4 and Figure 3 the average age of employees in this

Table 3   Age Distribution of Hourly Employees in a Plant

Age	Number	Percent	Cumulative Number	Cumulative Percent	Cumulative Number	Cumulative Percent
Under 20	8	0.2	4090	100.0	8	0.2
20–21	74	1.8	4082	99.8	82	2.0
25–29	163	4.0	4008	98.0	245	6.0
30–34	208	5.1	3845	94.0	453	11.1
35–39	286	7.0	3637	88.9	739	18.1
40–44	487	11.9	3351	81.9	1226	30.0
45–49	532	13.0	2864	70.0	1758	43.0
50–54	581	14.2	2332	57.0	2339	57.2
55–59	781	19.1	1751	42.8	3120	76.3
60–64	847	20.7	970	23.7	3967	97.0
65–69	123	3.0	123	3.0	4090	100.0
Total	4090	100.0				

Table 4   Age Distribution of Salaried Employees in a Plant

Age	General Foremen and Foremen	Staff Supervisors	Technical and Professional Employees	Factory Clerks	Managers	Totals
20–24			2			2
25–29	3		6			9
30–34	10	1	22			33
35–39	16	4	26	1		47
40–44	40	5	30	7	4	86
45–49	66	3	34	4	11	118
50–54	48	3	26	1	2	80
55–59	41		18		3	62
60–64	26	10	16	3	2	57
65–69	3		1			4
Totals	253	26	181	16	22	498 [a]

[a] Difference between 498 and 520 total salaried employees in the plant would be female salaried clerical employees arbitrarily excluded from the manpower projections.

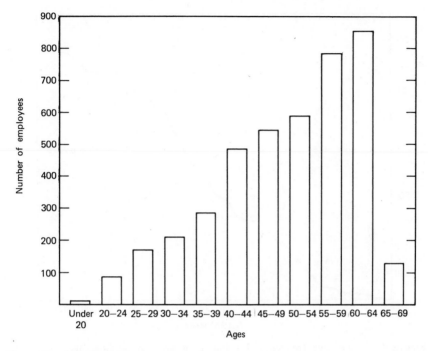

Figure 3   Age distribution of total number of employees in plant.

plant is very high from almost all points of view. The plant is known to be very old (first constructed in 1897), and production has been declining because many newer plants are more efficient and more favorably situated vis-à-vis the market. Yet management of the total organization has planned to keep the old plant in operation and renovate it once again. The circumstances are hardly unusual, although this plant may be much older than most still in operation. It has been modernized many times.

Figure 4 provides a cumulative frequency distribution of the years of service for salaried employees in the plant. As would be anticipated with an older work force, length of service is high. Average years of service is 23.4; nearly 43 percent of these employees have 25 years or more of seniority. (Greater detail could be shown if the manpower specialist desired to compute various statistics for subunits and functional specialisms in the plant.)

Educational Attainment

Table 5 shows by means of a percentage distribution of formal education completed the educational attainment or quality of one segment of the

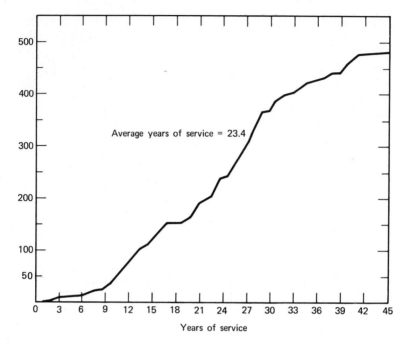

Figure 4 Cumulative frequency distribution of years of service for salaried employees in plant.

plant's human resources, key salaried employees (excluding, in effect, clerical and kindred personnel). More than one-half have completed high school and another 15 percent have gone beyond the secondary level. (These data could be further refined, if the organization desired a deeper analysis, by department, functional specialism, and the like. For example, one index of quality would be determining the percent of employees currently filling professional and managerial positions requiring a college degree who actually possess a degree.)

Training Program Participation

Another critical consideration regarding the quality of human resources is the extent of their training program participation, measured most easily by attendance, enrollments, completions of programs and courses, and similar statistics. In the example we are discussing, we are assuming that the organization maintains training programs for employees at various levels with differing needs. The kinds of programs used for illustrative purposes here are described more fully in subsequent chapters of the book. We are also assuming that there could be some dual enrollments in pro-

Table 5   Education Distribution of Key Salaried Employees
in the Plant by Highest Level of Attainment (percent)

Employee Group	Educational Level				
	Grade School	Some High School	12th Grade	Some College	College Graduate or More
General foremen and foremen	19.5	26.2	48.8	4.7	0.8
Staff supervisors	7.7	7.7	42.3	11.5	30.9
Technical and professional employees	5.0	16.1	57.2	8.9	12.8
Managers		4.6	41.0	18.1	36.3
Total	12.4	20.8	51.6	7.0	8.2

gram participation. For example, newly appointed foremen enrolled in
the Trainee Foreman Program could be attending a tuition-paid Adult
Education After-Hours Program course in a local community college.

Table 6 indicates many of the 520 salaried employees currently employed participated in the training programs listed during 1965–1969, and
64 (12 percent) are enrolled presently. In this plant the largest number
of enrollments in the past were in Adult Education courses after working
hours. No apprentices are currently on-program, although there have been
many apprentice participants in the past five years. Again, more detailed
analyses could be made to uncover such statistics as the percent of ap-

Table 6   Training Program Participation of Key Salaried Employees

	Number	Percent
Past participation, 1965–1969		
Apprentice Training Program	66	20.3
Trainee Foreman Program	54	17.2
Management Conference Program	36	11.3
Adult Education After-Hours Program	163	51.2
Total	319	100.0
Current participation, 1970		
Trainee Foreman Program	28	43.8
Management Conference Program	9	14.2
Adult Education After-Hours Program	19	29.6
College Graduate Training Program	2	3.1
College Cooperative Education Program	6	9.3
Total	64	100.0

prentice graduates among skilled trades employees, the percent of foremen and general foremen who are college graduates, the percent of managers who completed particular programs, and the like.

Terminations and Accessions: Turnover

Termination rates in the plant during 1965–1969 indicate that the rate
for the plant per year has been less than for the total organization of which
it is a part (except for one year). Let us assume that the total organization during the 1960s was experiencing a managerial reorganization,
sales decline, and effects of a corporate merger.

In view of the age distribution in the plant reflected in Table 3 and
Figure 3, differences in terminations between the plant and total organization (assuming data show lower average age-cohorts) could be expected.
The termination rates for 1966 shown in Table 7 could be explained by
a large layoff of salaried employees (assuming such was the case).

By analyzing terminations and accessions in more detail we could find
additional information required for manpower planning. For the sake of
brevity we will not provide additional tabular data; however, let us assume
the following information was uncovered. During the past five years, except for the mass layoff of salaried employees concentrated in 1966, the
largest single cause of termination was retirement, which accounted for
53 terminations or 14.3 percent of the total. The second most important
cause of termination was voluntary quits. There were 31 of these representing 8.3 percent of terminations. Further analysis may reveal that as
a percentage of the average salaried payroll, quits amounted to less than
1.1 percent per year, which in turn could be compared with rates for the
total organization. Other reasons for termination (all of lesser frequency
than the leading two reasons) would have included discharges, deaths,
and releases (for various reasons, including disability, entry into the armed
forces, completion of temporary summer replacement employment).

**Table 7   Termination Rates for Salaried Employees in the Total
Organization and the Plant by Year, 1965–1969**

Year	Total Organization (percent)	Plant (percent)
1965	16.2	12.0
1966	21.0	29.8
1967	12.1	6.1
1968	10.9	6.5
1969	11.4	7.3

Of 131 layoffs, releases, and quits during the period, it may be determined that 6.8 percent were subsequently reinstated in the plant and 11.4 percent were reinstated elsewhere in the organization.

Some employees probably experienced intraplant transfers. Analysis may reveal 109 employees transferred to the hourly rolls. Followup may show that 33.9 percent of these were reinstated to the salaried rolls and that 45.9 percent were currently on the hourly rolls as of 1970.

Further analysis of turnover may be fruitfully directed toward the characteristics of those who quit the plant. Let us assume it was found that the average age of quits was 36.3 years compared to the plant average age of 47.8 years. It may then be found that 95 percent of the quits had 12 or more years of schooling and an average of only 13 years of service. These easily obtained figures would suggest the quits were the younger, better-educated, shorter-service employees. The finding has important implications not only for future manpower projections and staffing plans but also perhaps for action in terms of the present managerial climate and personnel practices.

Turning to employee intake in the manpower pipeline, accession figures may show that 58 employees were added during the past five years. Let us assume 16 of them, or 27.6 percent, were hired from outside the plant. The remaining 42, or 72.4 percent, were obtained from the layoff list or from the ranks of hourly employees.

More detailed analysis of the accessions may reveal that the average age for this group was somewhat lower than that for the plant salaried payroll, that is, 41.7 years contrasted with 47.8 years. Looking at age-cohorts, 52 percent were in their forties; 28 percent, in their thirties; and 15 percent, in their twenties. Fifteen percent were more than 50 years of age. Inasmuch as a majority of the accessions were reinstated employees formerly in layoff status this rather high age for accessions can be understood.

Considered from the standpoint of their education and training, we may find the accessions were similar to the salaried employees in the plant. Except for the two newly hired persons shown in Table 6 as College Graduate Training Program participants, the typical accession was a high-school graduate. Twelve were Apprentice Program Graduates and 18 had completed the Trainee Foreman Program. Forty had taken one or more courses under the provisions of the Adult Education After-Hours Program.

To this point we have been considering external turnover. Turning to internal turnover among jobs and positions (what could be termed "career mobility"), we may find important facts that are needed in manpower planning, such as the following. Of the present line supervisory employees, 60 percent of the present foremen and general foremen have remained in their present classifications for the past 15 years. Because of fluctuations in production many general foremen and foremen have been required from time to time to revert to foremen and hourly rate jobs and have been subsequently reinstated to their former jobs when business improved. This may be called "status-level bouncing." Only 12 percent of all general foremen and foremen have not had to undergo "bouncing" from one status level to another in the past 15 years.

It may also be found that only 12 employees have been transferred out of the plant to jobs elsewhere in the total organization. On the other hand, 13 employees have been placed in the plant from elsewhere in the firm. Overall, 53.2 percent of the salaried personnel spent their entire working lives in the plant.

All these facts suggest that the plant offers limited opportunity for advancement and that mobility is very restricted.

After the examination of past patterns has been completed in sufficient detail so that the manpower specialist believes he is well-informed concerning pertinent manpower statistics, he would then evaluate the effects of changes in organization and technology on manpower. These changes may, of course, vary from plant to plant, organization to organization, and from time to time. They may be simple or complex. In view of the possible range of alternatives, let us take a middle road as to the complexity and extent of change and indicate how the manpower specialist may assess each.

Analysis of Organizational Change

In order to study organizational change, the manpower specialist probably should confine himself to changes in formal organizational structure as reflected in organizational charts. This limitation implies that there are organizational manuals, authorized positions, and statements of the functions of positions and that copies of prior organizational charts are available (or can be accurately reconstructed). Also implied is that informal structure will be ignored. Pragmatically, oversimplification of the study of organization is suggested but is justified because planning the future on the shifting sands of the informal organization cannot be seriously advocated.[5] Hopefully, there is sufficient concordance between formal and informal organization so that the planning of the former can be implemented administratively by appropriately adjusting the latter to it.

An analysis is made of organizational charts for the past five years. It is discovered that there were numerous changes in nomenclature during this period but the most important change of organizational relationships was the combining in 1967 of the two major product lines manufactured under

[5] For a discussion of the nature of staff work see *ibid.*, pp. 263–284.

one plant manager, responsible for both, whereas previously two managers were responsible for the lines, one for each product. (In effect, to simplify, it could be said two former "plants" were consequently consolidated into one.) This reorganization involved establishing two new staff departments reporting to the new plant manager which serviced both product lines. The quality control and financial controllership functions remained, as previously, departments reporting to the operations head of each separate product line. As a result of these changes and some minor ones, the plant management group was reduced by one plant manager and one department manager, but two production superintendents were added. Lastly, as a personnel improvement measure, all incumbent superintendents were replaced at the time of the reorganization.

Analysis of Technological Change

Turning to technological change, it is noted that several changes were introduced in processing, tools, machines, and equipment during the past five years. Technological change is, of course, a vast concept and is an accretion of many minor and major innovations. Technological change is defined here to mean any change in the types of, or methods of, producing and distributing goods and services which results from the direct application of scientific or engineering principles. The term defined in this way includes not only application of new labor-saving machinery (mechanization) and automatic controls (automation) but also changes in materials handling, the use of new and substitute products, changes in information handling and managerial control, and changes in production techniques and resources used.[6]

All estimations of the manpower impact of technological change must implicitly or explicitly include three basic steps: (1) an identification of expected technological developments; (2) a determination of the probable timing of introduction and rate of diffusion of these innovations; and (3) an evaluation of the probable manpower effects of these changes.[7] These steps would probably be equally applicable whether we are considering the level of the economy or that of the establishment, such as an industrial organization.

It is difficult to know where to begin to measure technological change in the practical situation. We assume the logical beginning point in a manufacturing plant is at the point of production. Manufacturing managers and unions must necessarily focus upon production, costs, and manpower when considering technological change in the context of collective bargaining.

---

[6] *Ibid.,* p. 322.
[7] Peter E. Haase, "Technological Change and Manpower Forecasts," *Industrial Relations,* Vol. 5, No. 3, May 1966, p. 60.

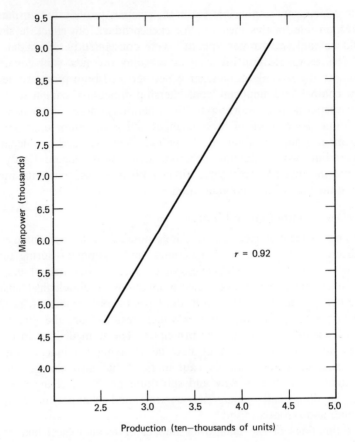

Figure 5   Correlation of manpower/production, 1960–1969.

Let us assume eight point-of-production technological changes were introduced and that by interviewing managers who were directly involved in these changes as well as by obtaining before and after data on costs, direct and indirect labor, production capability, materials savings, and similar matters we have a crude but better-than-guesswork estimate of what probably happened (at least formally and according to knowledgeable persons involved). Next, we would analyze productivity data for the plant over the five years during which these eight innovations were introduced. Let us assume that we found during the period that man-hours per unit produced varied only slightly for the plant. Using the data from Table 2, we could develop Figure 5 which shows this relationship. Statistical analysis of these data by means of the least-squares regression technique would produce a correlation coefficient greater than 0.90. This would suggest that the eight technological changes that we have studied had probably a minor effect upon manpower requirements, workforce characteristics, productivity, and organizational change.

Obviously, there is a red herring in an example such as this because one can easily point to complicated practical situations which do not admit of such a simplistic analysis. Yet there are many plant situations where output figures are available in abundance and workforce characteristics can be obtained. The manpower specialist can conduct research in the plant on before-and-after situations over a time span and clarify his understanding of technological change. Plant controllers, process engineers, maintenance managers, industrial relations specialists, and production foremen are human resources which can be drawn upon for factual information and informed opinion. More complicated situations can be researched through a similar methodology but will require more painstaking analysis in winnowing out meaningful correlates of technological change.

The Information-Gathering Process

The purpose of this manpower planning study in a large plant was to make a five-year projection. Organizations are not run backwards based upon historical data. The detailed projection of future requirements, including the identification of classifications and numbers of employees required as well as the time phasing, depends upon an assessment of some of the matters discussed at the outset of the last chapter, the long-range corporate plan and/or the annual profit plan. These involve the future. Manpower planning must be geared to them; the manpower planning of this particular plant is simply a part of overall corporate manpower planning.

In every complex organization, manpower planning needs to be systematic in order for continuous and proper staffing to be assured. Manpower planning obviously must be integrated with overall organization plans pertaining to sales and production, the purchase and use of equipment, research and engineering, the financial situation of the organization, and the planning of physical facilities. Manpower planning must be continuous on both a subunit and total organizational basis, with a central planning group assembling the overall information and coordinating the manpower plan.[8] In much the same way that budgeting begins at the subunit level and moves upward for approval and finalization, manpower planning is correspondingly implemented. Yet there must be a reciprocal exchange of information about the future.

---

[8] Wendell French, *The Personnel Management Process,* Houghton Mifflin, Boston, 1964, pp. 114–115.

Let us begin at the plant level and proceed with the model for manpower planning which was previously described. The manpower specialist may request information from all plant department managers about planned technological changes during the next five years and their estimate of how these changes are likely to affect manpower requirements. (He may also choose to obtain this information either in whole or in part from managers higher in the organization by working with his counterparts.) There is obviously an element of crystal-ball gazing at this juncture, but there also are objective bases that can be used. It may be hypothesized that failures to envisage the future based upon neglect can be less easily explained and accepted in industrial organizations than intelligent projections that go awry. The plant operating committee should be a starting point.

At this point, it is important to note that a forecast of presently unknown technological innovations is *not* required for this phase of planning. All innovations likely to have a significant effect for as much as ten years ahead are probably already known to the well-informed professional employee and manager. He need only identify and evaluate known developments. Although much additional research is needed to verify his generalization, it appears that the significant economic impact of a scientific or engineering discovery begins not when the discovery is first made, nor even when it is first commercially introduced, but only later when the resulting new product or process received widespread commercial acceptance.[9] Again, although research would be necessary to prove these generalizations, many competent managers in pace-setting firms keep abreast of changes in their fields and will be found to have thought about and to have decided upon what technological changes they will be able to use in the near future. It is hypothesized that they will also have thought about the cost-savings implications of these innovations (especially those costs attributable to manpower) and have decided upon an interpersonnel strategy to convince their organizational superiors to purchase, lease, or acquire the innovations. There will, of course, be variability among managers in organizations and industries as to the extent they are competent and have risen above day-to-day fire-fighting and crisis-oriented patterns of behavior to accomplish adequate planning. Where there is little or no management planning, it would obviously be fruitless to advocate manpower planning.

It is not practical or necessary to discuss fully how the manpower specialist should conduct himself here, except to observe that the objective is to secure the best information he can obtain based upon the best thinking of authoritative sources of information in the organization. Attention should

[9] Haase, *op. cit.*, p. 63. See also Kendrith M. Rowland, "The Certainty, Uncertainty Issue in Manpower Forecasting," *Management of Personnel Quarterly,* Vol. 7, No. 1, Spring 1968, pp. 21–25.

be focused upon the manpower and organizational aspects of this information. He will want to know such things as the following. What segments of the workforce will increase or decrease and by how many? Will there be an increase in numbers or requirements for new skills and/or management, technical, and professional knowledge for certain employees? What will the effects of the technological change be on the present departmental or other organizational structure? How many persons should be recruited outside the organization? What changes in job classifications will be requested and when? Because replies to these questions involve matters about which competent managers probably deliberate, the formal request for manpower planning information does not come as a surprise. Neither should the estimates received in response be regarded as definitive and unalterable. The important point is that this information is quite often obtainable on a scale perhaps seriously doubted by skeptics who have never experienced its attainment. To be sure, in many instances it may not be available.

Managers at the plant level probably know what the future plans of the organization are for their plant. However, it is wise for the manpower specialist to secure still more authoritative information on these plans (or to verify materials obtained) from executives at higher levels in the organization, such as at the division or corporate headquarters. Obtaining this information would involve coordination through the manpower specialists in the division and corporate offices as well as through line management. (Figure 2 illustrates how these organizational clearances would work.) Again, we must assume there are some plans involving either phasing out the plant, maintaining it at the same level, or expanding it in one way or another. If there are no such plans, there can be no meaningful manpower planning, only unguided guesswork.

In the example we have been analyzing, let us assume that top management has decided that this plant will remain at about the same level of production in 1971–1975 as it was during 1970 and that all financial, production, engineering, manpower, and other planning should be based upon this decision. If this decision is subsequently modified, lower levels of management will be notified of the change.

The Final Plan

A projection of manpower for the plant based upon this assumption would indicate that, on the basis of the past five years' experience, about 111 employees should be added during the next five years to maintain the number and composition of the present salaried work force. Of this number, 31 percent will be required to replace employees who are expected to die or to retire for disability; 41 percent will be needed to fill vacancies caused by retirement at normal retirement age (65); and 28 percent, to replace employees who may quit or be released from employment. No layoffs are anticipated. In terms of functional fields of work, approximately 49 new foremen and general foremen, 48 technical and professional employees, and 14 new staff supervisors would be required for replacement purposes. No managerial vacancies are foreseen above this level.

On an annual basis for the five years, an average of about 10 new foremen will be needed. It is assumed that line supervisory losses will be replenished through the existing Trainee Foreman Program; therefore, this aspect of manpower projection can be directly translated into the relevant program for developing the human resources required by the organization. As far as the remainder of the plant is concerned, by virtue of a policy of promotion-from-within and appropriate recruitment and selection standards, the source of staff supervisors would be the technical and professional group. Fifty-two persons would be required and fed into the non-supervisory technical and professional ranks at the rate of 10–11 individuals per year. If these are new recruits from the college campus, who tend to have higher quit rates than others filling technical and professional jobs, it is likely that perhaps five college graduates and eight persons from other sources should be hired annually. This decision also would have obvious training program implications for the College Graduate Training Program. If there are other judgments made as to sources of personnel, for example, a desire on the part of management to stimulate turnover, an interest in improving the quality of personnel, or a concern to reinstate a backlog of salaried employees on the layoff list, the annual timephasing of the five-year plan would require additional modification. In each case, the integration of the judgment with a determination as to training program utilization should be discerned.

Other decisions on the future status of the plant would require different types of manpower projections—more rapid additions, slower reductions using attrition, scheduled transfer of employees to other parts of the organization, and the like.

These alternatives underscore the need for manpower planning to be conducted and implemented at basically the lowest organizational echelon (i.e., at the plant or local level in a divisionalized corporation). Yet, at higher organizational echelons manpower specialists must be taking the overall view so that the separate manpower plans of the total organization are made to dovetail and function to attain organizational objectives. This involves another dimension of the manpower specialist's job, drawing upon broad analytical, administrative, and coordinative skills, but also implies intimate knowledge of the work of the manpower specialist at the grass-roots level. The higher-echelon manpower specialist may also make gross projections of manpower needs for the total corporation or division to determine if the parts add up to a whole, that is, whether the discrete plant manpower plans collectively are consistent with what a gross overall projection might suggest that they should be.

In discussing this manpower-planning example in a large plant we deliberately skimmed over the techniques used to move from an estimate of future needs to the actual development of specific figures. This was done to illustrate here the broad process without diverting to the minutiae of determining specific figures. However, this step cannot be overlooked by anyone seriously interested in how one of the most important problems in manpower planning is resolved in practice. We turn to it next in another example.

MANPOWER PLANNING FOR SKILLED TRADESMEN

Projecting the needs for manpower involves more than planning for the total manpower needs of a plant and requires the examination of needs in specific occupations. In many large organizations the needs for unskilled factory and clerical and other employees are not normally projected, except perhaps if consideration is being given to building a new plant in an area where the quantity and quality of the supply of manpower would be a factor. Projecting needs are extremely difficult for some levels of employees, such as managers and top executives. These employees may be relatively few in number, and planning for their replacement and development can be accommodated on different bases.

Planning for the number of apprentices needed provides an illustration of how projections can be carried out to ensure that an organization will have the right number of skilled-trades personnel at a future date. We shall examine how a manpower-planning study can be conducted and used to develop skilled tradesmen from apprentices.

In our example of manpower planning in a large plant we virtually ignored hourly rated personnel and simply indicated that an apprentice program had been used there in the past. Since skilled tradesmen were not salaried employees, we did not include them in the projection for salaried employees.

The number of apprentices required in a manufacturing plant would vary from plant to plant and from time to time, depending on the number of journeymen employed and the plant's needs. The knowledge, skill, and experience of skilled tradesmen are indisputably essential to cope with breakdown repairs, carry out preventive maintenance, and handle changeover or modernization. For these reasons apprentice programs are geared to manufacturing tempo, and planning for the numbers needed by given dates is fairly simple in concept (although meticulous in detail) even for as much as ten years ahead. Much less easy is convincing industrial management to hire apprentices and place them on-program (which we take up toward the end of the chapter). Also, practical problems regarding the availability of the data may impede projection making, as we shall subsequently see.

In 1966 a national manpower projection for skilled tradesmen indicated that more than 4 million skilled jobs will have to be filled throughout the United States during the period 1965–1975 because of the growth in the economy and the need to replace workers lost because of retirements and deaths.[10] Observations of this sort on the growth of skilled-trades jobs have been common for fifty years and have often been followed by dire warnings that there are nowhere near enough apprentices in training programs in the country to meet journeyman needs.[11] Yet amazingly, craftsmen do turn up one way or another and the predicted skilled-trades crisis is postponed.[12]

Today technological change is continuing to increase the need for highly trained skilled personnel who can install, operate, and repair complicated equipment. Industrial organizations have typically met their skilled-trades requirements with three types of employees: new hires (that is, hiring trained journeymen from outside sources); upgraders (giving employees a skilled-trades job classification because they are needed, available, and apparently qualified by experience but not by completion of an apprenticeship); and apprentices. (Sometimes "upgraders" are called "changeover employees.") If the demand for skilled tradesmen is high, the supply may become, *certeris paribus,* scant; and the number of qualified journeymen who can be obtained in the market is very small indeed. At the same time, the complexity of new equipment and technological change makes most upgraders underqualified, if not totally unqualified, to perform skilled work, and they are a mere last resort. Most lack the combination of theoretical and practical knowledge that gives the journeyman, who completed a proper apprenticeship, the versatility to adjust to change in his craft. But apprentices can be developed only over a four-year period (or longer if there are periods of discontinuous employment because of layoffs or if the prescribed program exceeds four years, which is the case in some trades). All this means that ideally the best source for journeymen is apprenticeship

[10] Allan F. Salt, "Estimated Need for Skilled Workers," *Monthly Labor Review,* Vol. 89, No. 4, April 1966, p. 365.

[11] See, for example, Paul H. Douglas, *American Apprenticeship and Industrial Education,* Columbia University Press, 1921, p. 83.

[12] George Strauss, "Apprenticeship: An Evaluation of the Need," in Arthur M. Ross, ed., *Employment Policy and the Labor Market,* University of California Press, Berkeley, 1965, pp. 320–332.

and that because of the long lead time needed for their development, a projection of at least five years, and preferably ten years, is warranted. Such lengthy projections as ten years are, however, often impracticable. Building an apprenticeship program then becomes a significant expense and commitment for an organization. The key question is: how many apprentices should be placed on the program? Too many would be cost-prohibitive; too few would cause problems of skilled-tradesmen replacement and eventually affect the quality and cost of work performed. Projection of the needs for skilled tradesmen thus becomes eminently rational.

It should be noted that to a considerable extent the techniques used to project the needs for journeymen are applicable to employees in other classifications also. Skilled-trades projections are perhaps easier to make than those for foremen, salesmen, accountants, and others because the training period and curricula are often set by a union-management agreement and the job being trained for is well identified in content and requirements (although, of course, it changes over time).

A Model

A simple model developed by the author and Henry P. Sims, Jr. (which we alter subsequently in the chapter to make it more realistic) can be constructed to simulate the manpower-planning process for skilled-trades jobs, as in Figure 6. The factors affecting the composition of the skilled-trades work force may be listed as follows:

A. Demand factors
   1. Retirements.
   2. Transfers to the salaried rolls.
   3. Terminations (deaths, discharges, releases, and quits).
   4. Expansions or contractions.
B. Supply factors
   1. New hires.
   2. Upgraders.
   3. Apprentice training program graduates.

Each key factor may be summarized as follows:

Retirements. Retirements may be easily predicted by examining the individual ages of the present work force. Historical records will show the percent who retired at normal retirement age, or earlier, or later.

Transfers to the salaried roll. Skilled tradesmen traditionally fill a certain number of line supervisory jobs in manufacturing plants. Requirements for the number to be transferred to the salaried rolls may be predicted by examining the individual ages of line supervisors, expansion plans, turnover

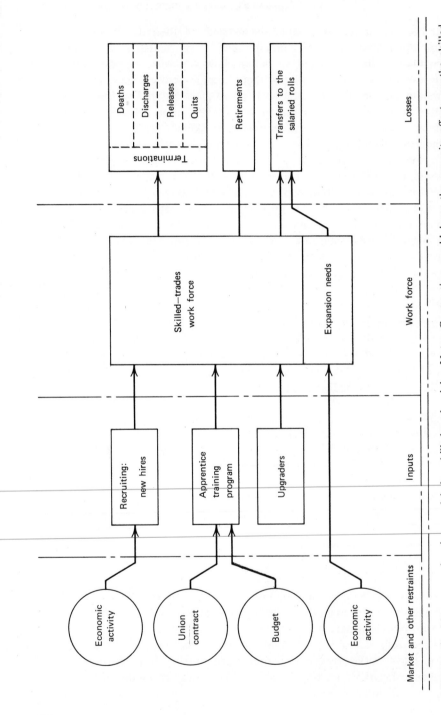

Figure 6 Manpower-planning model for skilled-trades jobs. Note: Contraction would have the opposite effects on the skilled-trades work force and could accelerate losses. Layoffs would be viewed as an aspect of manpower availability and require special planning, programs, and procedures.

records, and estimating the number of supervisory positions to be filled by college graduates.

Terminations. Historical records will indicate a certain percent of terminations for various reasons in the work force in each year.

Expansion or contraction. Historical growth rates and expansion and modernization plans are the basic sources consulted to predict needs due to increased volume. The estimated level of economic activity will also have significant effects and must be considered. Anticipated layoffs require special planning to cushion the effects of unemployment or relocation, which we do not discuss in this chapter.

New hires. If the level of economic activity is increasing, the number of journeymen in the labor market available for employment will probably decrease.

Upgraders. The qualifications of upgraders are limited. Therefore, use of upgraders should not be planned, but should be implemented only as a last resort, or as a "float" in the supply.

Apprentice graduates. The number of apprentices graduated is the unknown that is solved when data are analyzed by use of the model. It is desirable to fill as large a percentage of journeymen needs as possible from the apprentice training program. The number of apprentices to be hired is limited by the budget, which in turn is significantly affected by the level of economic activity. Lastly, the union-management agreement or "contract" may also impose limitations in the apprentice program.

The effective administration of an apprentice training program requires an adequate even flow of apprentices into the program annually over a period of time. This flow will, in turn, provide a regular annual stream of program graduates on completion of the four-year training schedule that will replace unavoidable journeyman losses. The extent of these unavoidable losses would vary from plant to plant and from time to time and would be primarily a consequence of the demographic characteristics of the work force.

In order to ascertain the inputs to start the flow, a method is needed to estimate quantitatively the different values for each factor over five years (assuming we want a five-year projection). Figure 7 is a sample worksheet which can be used to assemble the information needed for each of the future five years. The columns may be explained as follows:

Column A. The trades to be examined are listed. The list may be all-inclusive or limited to key trades as desired. (Twelve trades are listed in column A and subsequently discussed in the chapter in the example.)

A	B	C	D Terminations				E	F	G	H	I	J	K	L	M
Trade	Number of journeymen needed at beginning of 1970	Retirements	Deaths	Discharges	Quits	Releases	Transferred to salaried roll	Additions or contractions	Total new employees required 1970	New hires	Upgraders	New apprentices	Other	Additions (H–K)	Shortage
1. Toolmaking and diemaking															
2. Machine repair															
3. Millwright															
4. Electricity															
5. Plumbing–pipefitting															
6. Welding															
7. Automotive–truck mechanics															
8. Molding and coremaking															
9. Boilermaking															
10. Patternmaking															
11. Carpentry															
12. Blacksmithing															
Totals															

Plant _____

Division _____

Figure 7 Manpower-planning worksheet for skilled-trades jobs.

Column B.   The Numbers of Journeymen Needed in the work force at the *beginning* of the year are listed according to trade.

Column C.   Retirements can be estimated, by trade, from age records of those presently employed based upon previous experience with early, normal, and delayed retirements.

Column D.   Included in Terminations are the reasons shown: Deaths, Discharges, Quits, and Releases. It is always difficult to decide whether released employees will return after a leave of absence. Hence, they may be viewed as quits. Such cases are few in number, in any event.

Column E.   Transferred to Salaried Rolls may be estimated from historical records, the age structure of the present supervisory segment, and expansion requirements.

Column F.   Additions or Contractions may be estimated from expansion plans. Reductions would be listed as a negative number.

Column G.   Total New Employees Required are derived by summing items C through F, according to the various skilled trades.

Column H.   New Hires may be estimated from information about the local labor market. The quality of these data are not likely to be high in all instances.

Column I.   The number of Upgraders should be zero, or if absolutely necessary, kept to a minimum number. It can be estimated based upon knowledge of the organization's work force as reflected in records and information in personnel "jackets."

Column J.   New Apprentices may be estimated by the number that will be hired to meet manpower requirements. This number should be the "X," or unknown, in the problem that is to be "solved for."

Column K.   "Other" is a category included for any special circumstances at a particular plant. It is a judgmental factor.

Column L.   Total Additions is the summation of items H through K.

Column M.   Shortage is the difference between New Employees Required and Total Additions. Theoretically, if the estimates are correct and the planning is properly conducted, there will be no shortage.

Total row.   Each plant would total each column. Also, the reporting plant and division would be identified as a part of the total corporate manpower-planning effort.

The number needed at the beginning of each year will be: the number needed at the beginning of the previous year (column B) plus the additions to the workforce (column F).

Once the annual number of apprentices needed is determined in this way, the manpower planning for apprentices has only been started. What remains is planning for the development of these human resources through training programs, the subject of subsequent chapters in the book.

Subtleties in Apprentice Manpower Projections

However, in projecting the needs for apprentices, some subtleties have been skipped over that bear close-up analysis if we are to comprehend fully the nature of the projection. Let us consider some of these and then turn to an example for further clarification. The close-up allows us to experience the realistic nitty-gritty of planning and illustrates how the manpower specialist must make compromises down from the ideal in the conduct of his work, in solving for "x."

It is necessary to define carefully such concepts as "journeyman work force," "journeyman needs," "apprentice–journeyman ratio," "apprentices in training," "active apprentices," and "apprentice requirements" in order to make adequate projections. Some of these concepts are simple and clean-cut. The "journeyman work force" is the number of active (employed, not laid off) journeymen by trade, by plant, as of a given date. "Journeymen needs" are the numbers of journeymen needed annually to replace journeymen who are lost due to termination, retirement, and transfers to the salaried ranks. These needs may vary by trade, plant, and division. The "apprentice–journeyman ratio" is determined by dividing the number of journeymen by the number of apprentices and reducing the quotient to the nearest whole number.

"Apprentices in training" is a more difficult concept requiring computation based on experience in a plant or organization. Assume it is found that based upon historical statistics it is necessary that in order to graduate one apprentice to journeyman status annually on a continuing basis there must be 4.46 apprentices in training at all times. For example, if the annual need in any given trade is 6 journeymen, the number of apprentices in training at all times would equal $6 \times 4.46 = 26.76$ or 27 apprentices. "Active apprentices" would simply be the number of actively employed apprentices by trade, by plant, as of a given date. "Apprentice requirements" would refer to the additional apprentices required to satisfy the apprentice–journeyman ratio needed on a continuing basis to replace unavoidable journeyman losses. Meeting the requirements is a recruitment and selection task which should be administered on a planned basis over a reasonable time period consistent with the availability of training assignments. It goes without saying perhaps that the task should be carried out in accordance with the union-management agreement and orderly shop operations.

An example will illustrate how these concepts can be conjoined analytically for manpower-planning purposes. In order to obtain sufficiently large numbers so that the example is realistic, let us assume that we are interested initially in making in 1970 a ten-year projection covering 1971–1980 and have data from a division consisting of five plants which we can utilize. This time period would be double the length of the projection made in the example of manpower planning at the plant level, which we previously described. By viewing manpower planning at the divisional level of the organization in this case of apprentice needs, we are suggesting the kind of study previously mentioned which a divisional manpower specialist

Table 8 Divisional Apprentice–Journeyman Ratio by Plant and by Trade

In each plant cell the upper-left figure denotes the number of journeymen[a], the upper-right figure denotes the number of apprentices[b], and the lower figure is the apprentice–journeyman ratio.

Trade		A	B	C	D	E	Total (all plants)
Toolmaking and diemaking	J, A	162, 4	193, 7	127, 5	132, 11	206, 27	820, 54
	ratio	1:40	1:27	1:25	1:12	1:8	1:15.2
Machine repair	J, A	49, 0	87, 7	66, 6	85, 8	101, 23	388, 44
	ratio	None	1:12	1:11	1:10	1:4	1:8.8
Millwright	J, A	20, 1	80, 6	48, 4	87, 9	105, 21	340, 41
	ratio	1:20	1:13	1:12	1:10	1:5	1:8.3
Electricity	J, A	21, 0	73, 3	48, 4	83, 9	79, 14	304, 30
	ratio	None	1:24	1:12	1:9	1:6	1:10.1
Plumbing–pipefitting	J, A	17, 0	56, 3	22, 2	51, 6	53, 17	199, 28
	ratio	None	1:19	1:11	1:8	1:3	1:7.1
Welding	J, A	30, 0	17, 0	18, 0	19, 0	33, 5	117, 5
	ratio	None	None	None	None	1:6	1:23.4
Automotive–truck mechanics	J, A	NA[c]	NA	NA	23, 3	41, 5	64, 8
	ratio				1:8	1:8	1:8.0
Molding and coremaking	J, A	5, 0	NA	8, 0	10, 0	16, 1	39, 1
	ratio	None		None	None	1:16	1:39.0
Boilermaking	J, A	33, 0	NA	NA	NA	NA	33, 0
	ratio	None					None
Patternmaking	J, A	NA	NA	NA	NA	7, 1	7, 1
	ratio					1:7	1:7.0
Carpentry	J, A	NA	NA	NA	NA	5, 1	5, 1
	ratio					1:5	1:5.0
Blacksmithing	J, A	NA	NA	NA	NA	3, 1	3, 1
	ratio					1:3	1:3.0
Total	J, A	337, 5	506, 26	337, 21	490, 46	649, 116	2319, 214
	ratio	1:67.4	1:19.46	1:16.0	1:10.6	1:5.6	1:10.8

[a] Section denoting number of journeymen.

[b] Section denoting number of apprentices.

[c] NA — not applicable.

might want to conduct periodically to check on whether the separate plans of the plants make sense from a coordinated divisional standpoint. He may also want to take a longer-run perspective on events than would the plant manpower specialist looking ahead five years or less. In turn, the corporate manpower specialist might desire to assess in gross terms the manpower-planning studies of divisions and conduct an analogous study at the corporate level.

The divisional journeyman manpower-planning study is designed to determine unavoidable journeyman losses in order to determine the additional journeymen needs in relation to expanding manufacturing operations. This then would be a manpower-planning study intended to be implemented by the development of apprenticeable human resources to produce skilled tradesmen.

Table 8 displays the apprentice–journeyman ratio by trade for each plant as of the study date in 1970. Wide disparities in ratios can be quickly discerned among the trades and the plants. This initial overall view becomes the basis for further analysis to formulate ultimately a plan of action for developing and maintaining a qualified journeyman work force.

Similar to the example of manpower-planning analysis in a large plant,

Table 9   Age Distribution of Journeymen in All Trades for Five Plants

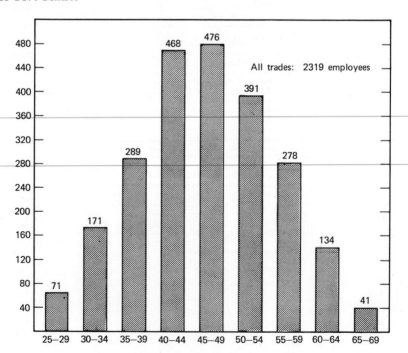

the steps which are taken next largely depend upon how much detail is wanted and needed. We proceed by setting forth illustrative data that lead to attainment of the objective of the study. For each table provided it should be obvious that many others could be structured for the various trades and plants.

Table 9 shows an age distribution in five-year intervals of the journeymen in all trades in the five plants. From this it can be seen that 412 journeymen are presently in the 55–59 and 60–64 age brackets and will reach normal retirement age (65) in 10 years. Forty-one others are already beyond the normal retirement age. An examination of Tables 8 and 9 would suggest to the manpower specialist that he should analyze further the distribution of journeymen by age and trade in each plant. This would be done next. (For the sake of convenience we have grouped the main trades in this organization into maintenance trades and toolmaking and diemaking, although in practice the manpower specialist may prefer a finer breakdown of the data.) Tables 10 to 14 indicate differences in age groupings among the different trades in the five plants. Yet the ten-year projection for losses for all trades due to retirement in the division is approximately 2 percent, as reflected in the simple calculations in the lower left corners of Tables 12 to 14. There are more differences among plants, as would be expected. For example, the projected annual journeyman loss in all trades due to retirement varies from 1.2 percent in Plant C to 2.5 percent in Plants D and E. But, by and large, it seems reasonable to estimate the annual loss due to normal retirement at 2 percent. (In reality, in an organization where there were other types of retirement such as late,

Table 10   Age Distribution of Journeymen in the Maintenance Trades for Five Plants

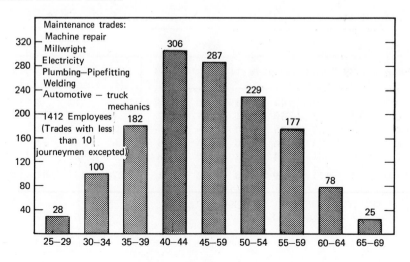

Table 11   Age Distribution of Journeymen in the Toolmaking and Diemaking Trades for Five Plants

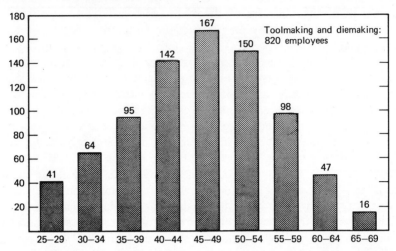

early, special early, or disability, the manpower specialist would be expected to derive a more sophisticated figure to reflect these considerations, especially when they may have an important bearing, as in the case of large numbers of employees.)

Turning to other causes of journeymen losses indicated in the model shown in Figure 6, we consider next the various types of "terminations" (deaths, discharges, releases, and quits). Deaths are perhaps the easiest of these to calculate. The manpower specialist requires data on total hourly employment termination due to death for a recent past time period (for example, 5 or 10 years), from which he could calculate an annual

Table 12   Age Distribution of Journeymen in All Trades by Plant

Plant	Age									Total
	25–29	30–34	35–39	40–44	45–49	50–54	55–59	60–64	65–69	
A	1	9	43	74	96	62	35	14	3	337
B	14	33	50	131	109	97	49	20	3	506
C	14	33	56	60	76	56	32	7	3	337
D	12	45	66	90	75	78	69	41	14	490
E	30	51	74	113	120	98	93	52	18	649
Total	71	171	289	468	476	391	278	134	41	2319

10-Year projection: normal retirement, 453
453/2319 = 0.195 or 19.5% (annually 2%)

Table 13   Age Distribution of Journeymen in the Maintenance Trades by Plant

	Age									
Plant	25–29	30–34	35–39	40–44	45–49	50–54	55–59	60–64	65–69	Total
A		5	15	34	33	27	17	5	1	137
B	5	16	36	90	67	58	34	6	1	313
C	4	14	30	41	52	29	23	7	2	202
D	7	31	51	69	50	58	43	29	10	348
E	12	34	50	72	85	57	60	31	11	412
Total	28	100	182	306	287	229	177	78	25	1412

10-Year projection: normal retirement, 280
$280/1412 = 0.198$ or 19.8% (annually 2%)

death rate for the total organization. He could then use this figure (or derive one for skilled-trades employees if there was a sufficiently large number of cases to provide a basis). Probably the difference in death rates between skilled trades and all hourly employees would be insignificant. Let us assume it is 0.3 percent, although obviously the figure found would have to be empirically derived and would reflect the demographic composition of the organization or division.

Discharges, quits, and releases are perhaps more difficult to project than deaths, although no more difficult to calculate if the raw data are available for analysis. In general, skilled tradesmen are distinguished from the rank-and-file hourly employee because they have a definite skill that

Table 14   Age Distribution of Journeymen in Toolmaking and Diemaking by Plant

	Age									
Plant	25–29	30–34	35–39	40–44	45–49	50–54	55–59	60–64	65–69	Total
A	1	4	23	31	49	28	17	7	2	162
B	9	17	14	41	42	39	15	14	2	193
C	9	17	23	19	24	26	8		1	127
D	5	14	14	20	23	18	25	9	4	132
E	17	12	21	31	29	39	33	17	7	206
Total	41	64	95	142	167	150	98	47	16	820

10-Year projection: normal retirement, 161
$161/820 = 0.196$ or 19.6% (annually 2%)

exceeds the quickly acquired veneer or "expertise" [13] of the typical semi-skilled factory employee. Although there is little research evidence to prove these hypothetical generalizations, it is likely that journeymen are less often discharged for inadequate performance or unsatisfactory behavioral patterns and far less often quit their employers than do the rank-and-file. Most who are released are young men who enter the armed forces and subsequently return to the employer upon completion of their military or naval service, at which time they are reinstated. Assuming wages, hours, and working conditions are competitive, an annual rate of loss of 0.7 percent would seem to be defensible. (Again the figure would vary in empirical situations.) Considering that pace-setting organizations which conduct apprentice training programs probably also look upon journeymen who take additional training and education work as candidates for supervisory and technical positions on the salaried employee rolls, there is an additional incentive for the journeyman to remain with his employer.

This brings us to the calculation of losses of journeymen due to transfers to the salaried employee rolls. This figure is determined empirically by conducting a follow-up study of graduated apprentices retained by the organization over a recent sufficiently long prior time period, such as 10–20 years, in order to have data for persons who have matured in the organization and had an opportunity to be promoted. Studies limited to young men with little experience will reveal nothing of value in this context to the manpower specialist. In many organizations these data may not be available, or, if available, only at a high cost and after monumental digging. Let us assume they are compiled, and it is found that 65 percent of all graduated journeymen who completed an apprenticeship in the past twenty years and are still employed remain classified as journeymen. Thirty-five percent of graduated journeymen have moved to the salaried employee rolls in various technical, professional, and managerial positions. Let us further assume that these data reveal that in the past ten years promotion to salaried classifications has accounted for an annual loss of approximately 2 percent. It would, therefore, seem reasonable to estimate that the annual projected loss due to this factor will continue at the rate of 2 percent (unless other data uncovered in the follow-up study suggest this figure should be changed).

Having analyzed the loss factors, we turn now to a consideration of expansion–contraction considerations. In the discussion of manpower planning for male salaried employees in a large plant, we assumed that corporate management had no plans to expand production in that plant.

[13] This concept was set forth in Edwin F. Beal and Edward D. Wickersham, *The Practice of Collective Bargaining*, Second Edition, Irwin, Homewood, Illinois, 1963, pp. 36–37.

In the example of skilled-trades manpower planning that we have been considering, let us assume that there are plans to expand production in these plants and that from a divisional standpoint there is a union-management agreement which allows the movement of skilled-trades employees from plant to plant with considerable flexibility, provided the employee is willing to move and management pays for household moving expenses and associated matters. Also, seniority is accommodated (but in ways which we need not go into here).

The manpower specialist would be required to obtain reasonable estimates of the effects of technological change on manpower and some detail on the plans for expansion. In realistic terms, let us consider what he may uncover. Presumably, he would go about this task in the same way that the manpower specialist in the plant did, that is, requesting information from authoritative sources in the organization who know the intent and details of the long-range plans. Realistically, the information would again be partly incomplete and require some crystal-ball gazing.

Let us assume the manpower specialist finds that he can secure only limited information covering 1971 and 1972 and nothing beyond this. This limitation means that the prospects for a strong, solid, ten-year projection are poor. Instead the manpower specialist may be forced to content himself with a partial projection of unavoidable losses, which has at least the value of shedding some light upon the rock-bottom minimum of apprentices needed.

Continuing, let us assume that the manpower specialist finds that additional unskilled and semiskilled "direct" labor and "indirect" labor (essentially the skilled tradesmen) will be needed to meet product changes and capacity expansion primarily at the D, E, and C plants, in that order of magnitude. The total of hourly employees to be added will be about 5400. Effects of expansion on plants A and B are considered minimal. He cannot obtain adequate information from managers relative to the number of skilled tradesmen to be added and is thus on his own to find a basis for projections.

Examination of data from past hiring reveals no consistent ratio between the addition of a total number of hourly employees and the portion of that total which will be skilled-trades employees. Other factors seem to have an effect, but the relationship is not entirely clear. These include additional machines and equipment, type of equipment, additional manufacturing and office floor space, and the number of shifts. An analysis of the current work force in the plants shows variances. In one plant, the number of skilled tradesmen involved amounts to 13 percent of the total hourly work force. In two others it is about 11 percent; and in the remaining two it is 9 percent. In consideration of the variance from 12 to 9 percent, the manpower specialist may conservatively estimate that skilled tradesmen will comprise at least 10 percent of the total number of hourly employees to be added during the expansion. Therefore, if it evolves over a two-year period, expansion will perhaps require an annual increase of 5 percent of the additional hourly employees in the skilled-trades classifications. (Five percent would be the figure used in the projection. However, the adequacy of this estimate should be repeatedly checked by the manpower specialist in future years as more information becomes available.)

To summarize, unavoidable annual journeymen losses when projected ten years and designed to maintain the current number of journeymen employed in all apprenticeable trades in all divisional plants (2319 journeymen) yields the following:

Retirements	2.0%
Deaths	0.3%
Discharges, quits, and releases	0.7%
Transfers to the salaried rolls	2.0%
Total	5.0%

5% of 2319=116 journeymen annually

As for expansion, 5400 hourly employees will be added in 1971 and 1972. Ten percent of these will be skilled tradesmen; this will yield a figure of 5 percent or 270 journeymen annually.

Table 15   Projected Annual Need for Journeymen in Five Plants Based on Estimated Losses

Trade	Number of Journeymen	Annual Need [a]
Toolmaking and diemaking	820	41
Machine repair	388	20
Millwright	340	17
Electricity	304	15
Plumbing–pipefitting	199	10
Welding	117	6
Automotive–truck mechanics	64	3
Molding and coremaking	39	2
Boilermaking	33	2
Patternmaking	7	0
Carpentry	5	0
Blacksmithing	3	0
Total	2319	116

[a] 5 percent per year, with some rounding.

Applying the annual loss rate to the skilled trades work force we would determine the facts reflected in Table 15. However, we have by this point merely gotten to the beginning of the analysis because we must scrutinize the data carefully in preparation for the next step. Also, we must have some historical benchmarks in order to proceed. Let us assume we have ascertained the following facts:

1. All apprenticeable trades cover the same term of apprenticeship, 4 years (or 8000 work hours per year).
2. Ten out of every 16.5 apprentices who start complete their training and graduate to journeyman status.
3. The average time required for an apprentice to complete his training is 3 years and 9.1 months (or 3.758 years) because of overtime work, credit given for past experience, and a few other factors that would have the effect of reducing the period below 4 years. (It could be longer in some organizations or at times when apprentices experience repeated but intermittent long layoffs.)
4. Of those apprentices who leave the program before completion, 57.48 percent drop out in the first year; 25.39 percent, in the second; 12 percent, in the third; and 5.13 percent, in the fourth year. (Dropouts taper off toward the upper end of the program.)

Considering these four facts, which would have been empirically determined, we may now estimate the number of apprentices needed in training at all times to provide 10 graduates annually. This can be illustrated by the flow chart in Figure 8. Let us assume, simply for the purposes of illustration, that we placed 66 apprentices on-program over a four-year period (or 16.5 per year). The apprentices starting each year are designated as Group A, Group B, Group C, and Group D. $\dfrac{(47.45 \times 3.7583)}{4}$

or 44.6 apprentices must be in training at all times to graduate 10 annually. More simply, it takes 4.46 apprentices in training at all times to graduate 1 annually. To attain the average number in training would require selection of 66 starting apprentices and the recruitment of a substantially larger number from which to choose apprentice candidates.

It can thus be seen that the recruitment, selection, and placement functions are given considerable direction as a consequence of a manpower-planning study. It can also be seen that the specificity involved requires considerable probing for historical guidelines and future estimates, which, if they cannot be obtained, make manpower planning impossible. At best, these guides and estimates are imperfect. All these complicating aspects probably explain why most organizations have not yet engaged in manpower planning and why upgraders and other poorly qualified persons

←———————————————	8000 Hours	————————————→	

Group A	First 2000 hours	Second 2000 hours	Third 2000 hours	Fourth 2000 hours
	Start Finish	Start Finish	Start Finish	Start Finish
	16.5 12.8	12.8 11.1	11.1 10.3	10.3 10.0

Group B		First 2000 hours	Second 2000 hours	Third 2000 hours
		Start Finish	Start Finish	Start Finish
		16.5 12.8	12.8 11.1	11.1 10.3

Group C			First 2000 hours	Second 2000 hours
			Start Finish	Start Finish
			16.5 12.8	12.8 11.1

Group D				First 2000 hours
				Start Finish
				16.5 12.8

Total   50.7   44.2
Average   47.45

Figure 8 Apprentice development, dropout, and program-completion flow chart.

have been employed in journeymen work—employers cannot or do not know how to estimate the number of apprentices needed. Moreover, the wage costs involved in hiring the numbers of apprentices needed on-program to graduate 10 annually (as in this example) may seem unjustifiably expensive to industrial management. Multiple employees are needed to assure the development and retention of fewer journeymen. Upgraders may thus be used preferably in order to curtail the expense of training apprentices. This insight and reasoning would also apply to estimating needs for other types of manpower and explain employer interest in learning more about manpower planning and its application.

To complete our discussion of the example, we next estimate the apprentices needed in training by trade to replace the losses of journeymen. Table 16 provides an indication of how this can be done, setting aside for the moment the accommodation of expansion needs. It can readily be determined that a sizeable number of apprentices is needed on-program simply to meet losses and compensate for program attrition (reflected respectively in columns A and C).

Turning back to the plants, Table 17 indicates, as could be expected, that the plants in the division show variance in the factors which contribute to annual journeyman losses. The various columns indicate the numbers of apprentices needed to replace losses and attain the staffing objective. This table serves to point up the need for practical manpower planning to be based upon grassroots considerations. The table also shows that the division

Table 16   Apprentices Needed in Training, by Trade to Replace Losses of Journeymen in Five Plants

Trade	Column A	Column B	Column C	Column D	Column E
Toolmaking and diemaking	41	4.46	183	820	1:4.4
Machine repair	20	4.46	89	388	1:4.3
Millwright	17	4.46	76	340	1:4.4
Electricity	15	4.46	67	304	1:4.5
Plumbing–pipefitting	10	4.46	45	199	1:4.4
Welding	6	4.46	26	117	1:4.5
Automotive–truck mechanics	3	4.46	13	64	1:4.9
Molding and coremaking	2	4.46	9	39	1:4.3
Boilermaking	2	4.46	9	33	1:3.6
Patternmaking	0	4.46	0	7	None
Carpentry	0	4.46	0	5	None
Blacksmithing	0	4.46	0	3	None
Total	116	4.46	517	2319	1:4.4

Column A. Journeymen needed to replace annual losses.

Column B. Apprentices needed in training at all times to graduate 1 journeyman annually.

Column C. Apprentices needed in training at all times to replace annual unavoidable loss (Column A multiplied by Column B)

Column D. Number of active journeymen as of the study date in 1970.

Column E. Apprentice–journeyman ratio needed to replace annual unavoidable loss.

is presently shortfalling its needs by about 20 percent (412 apprentices whereas 517 are needed) and has a recruitment task if it is to meet needs attributable to unavoidable losses alone.

The last task is to project the needs for apprentices caused by expansion. We have indicated that practical limitations require that the projection can now be made only for two years ahead. Table 18 indicates the manner in which these data can be handled. The information indicates there should be 539 apprentices on-program in 1971 and 565 in 1972 so that based upon known attrition rates for journeymen and apprentices there will be a sufficient number of apprentices to accommodate for losses and expansion. Of course, the apprenticeship requires more than two years to complete, and subsequent manpower planning will be needed beyond 1972 when information on other divisional or corporate plans becomes available. The number of apprentices currently on-program would be deducted from the projected needs to determine the recruitment task. In practice, the data would be further analyzed by trade to identify the numbers needed for each skilled field. Finally, the divisional manpower specialist could make

Table 17 Journeyman Losses and Apprentice Needs Statistics in Five Plants

Plant	Active Journeymen	Actual Annual Loss Percentage	Annual Needs (based on actual losses)	Apprentices Needed[a]	Ratio Needed	Apprentices Presently Active	Additional Apprentices Needed[b]
A	337	4.6	16	71	1:4.7	51	20
B	506	4.4	22	98	1:5.1	70	28
C	337	4.2	14	62	1:5.4	50	12
D	490	5.5	28	125	1:3.9	99	26
E	649	5.5	36	161	1:3.9	142	19
Total	2319	5.0	116	517	1:4.4	412	105

[a] This number is obtained by multiplying the annual needs by 4.46.

[b] The number of additional apprentices needed by plant is calculated on the basis of the plant total for all trades.

Table 18   Projection of Apprentices Needed by Plant for Expansion, 1971–1972

Plant	Active Journey- men	Gross Number of Projected Journeymen [a]		Actual An- nual Loss Percent- age	Journey- men Losses		Apprentices Needed On Program [b]	
	1970	1971	1972		1971	1972	1971	1972
A	337	354	371	4.6	16	17	71	75
B	506	531	556	4.4	23	24	103	107
C	337	354	371	4.2	15	16	67	71
D	490	515	540	5.5	29	30	129	134
E	649	681	712	5.5	38	40	169	178
Total	2319	2435	2550	5.0	121	127	539	565

[a] Five percent per year on the 1970 base.

[b] This number is obtained by multiplying the annual need by 4.46, rounding through-out to obtain arithmetically correct totals in the columns.

gross divisional calculations using these gross projections as a logic check against the meaningfulness of the plant projections.

In concluding, in this explication of manpower planning for skilled tradesmen, we have again taken, if not a red herring, a slightly pinkish one. We have found it necessary to assume the availability of considerable data and have simplified some of the stubborn facts that realistically impede projection making. It should be obvious that institutional considerations importantly affect projections because they virtually dictate how the model must be utilized if it is to have any practical value. Also, although we did not carry the projection forward for ten years, it should be obvious how this can be done when the basic figures are compiled. In the example there were a great many unknowns in the future, which would suggest that the ten-year figures when projected would be very tentative.

Finally, it can also be seen that there are intellectually many miles between the grubby fact gathering and analysis needed to carry out manpower planning at the level of the organization, and the sharp, overall but generalized thinking of manpower planning at the level of the economy. The summation of plant manpower plans do not necessarily add up to the divisional plan nor do the latter plans add up to the corporate plan. Indeed there is much rounding of data, crystal-ball gazing, and sheer judgment involved in manpower planning at the grass roots. These considerations lead the student of manpower planning to have a humble opinion of his efforts. Like all plans they provide a rational sense of direction, which is preferable to having no plan. Yet this is an area in which much more intellectual plumbing and bobbing could be used so that manpower planning may become increasingly refined in the years ahead.

SUMMARY AND CONCLUSION

Manpower planning has many different meanings. Interest in the subject has developed quite recently and may be explained as a part of the trend since the early 1940s for large-scale organizations to become interested in long-range planning of all kinds. Interest in manpower planning has its roots in labor-force shortages during critical time periods such as during World War II when semiskilled and unskilled laborers were not available. Since World War II, and continuing to the present time, manpower problems have been concerned with the alleged shortages of engineers, managers, and professional employees, and the general overabundance of unskilled and semiskilled workers.

Manpower planning at the level of the firm has become of increasing interest in the United States as students of manpower have become growingly concerned with employment policy and manpower policy in the society. Since the early 1960s American students of manpower have sharpened their concepts of manpower planning, projection techniques, and programs for the development of human resources. Considerable skill has been developed in projecting manpower needs at the level of the economy. Less attention has been given to regional, local, industrial, and organizational manpower-planning studies. At the level of the industrial firm or establishment, manpower planning is generally regarded as novel. Until very recently most industrial organizations equated manpower planning with staffing or even simplistic turnover analysis. In the future it would be desirable to study the nature of growth in firms and the means by which it is achieved. For example, it would be extremely worthwhile for the manpower specialist to know how much of growth is attributable to the added productivity of capital, how much is contributed by research and technical people, and how much comes through acquisition and merger.[14] Armed with this kind of knowledge the manpower specialist might be in a better position than he currently is to convince top management and administrators to set up reserves to replace human resources and provide the funds for these human resource reserves.[15] In any event, there is little doubt that the field of manpower planning as presently conceived presents many challenges to manpower specialists in organizations and universities.

[14] George S. Odiorne, "Company Growth and Personnel Administration," *Personnel,* Vol. 37, No. 1, January-February 1960, pp. 34–35.

[15] W. F. Rabe, "How to Forestall Depreciation of the Company's Human Assets," *Personnel,* Vol. 39, No. 5, September-October 1962, pp. 15–20.

An approach to manpower planning, a model, and some examples were described in this chapter. These were simple illustrations for a moderate-sized industrial organization and gave due attention to the main factors that effect causes for fluctuation in levels of manpower in a firm. The model and illustrations also provide room for including institutional factors in manpower planning.

The model and example of projecting needs for apprentices were intended to be useful for industrial management and industrial manpower specialists working in organizations. Although the model is somewhat unsophisticated, it probably goes far beyond the typical industrial "guesstimate" applied to manpower planning at the level of the establishment (at least according to the existing literature). This simplistic approach to manpower planning in an organization is offered here merely as a pioneering step which undoubtedly can be vastly improved upon in time. There is a great need for the development of an improved but relatively simple methodology which would be useful for manpower planners employed by organizations. Econometric projection techniques can probably for some time be left to BLS[16] and NPA[17] statisticians who are writing for more quantitatively oriented professional groups such as economists.

Another possible way of approaching manpower planning projections would be to view manpower replacement needs as a formal operations-research problem and express it in mathematical terms.[18] Most industrial training problems are probably what operations researchers would call "inventory" problems.[19] When viewed together, manpower planning and the development of human resources could be considered a mixed problem involving more than one formal category of operations research problem. For example, together they probably involve the inventory, allocation (particularly the assignment sub-type), and replacement (particularly the labor-wastage sub-type) problems. The field of manpower planning thus also offers a challenge to the operations researcher because it provides an opportunity for expanding the various concepts and techniques of modern management science. The manpower specialist we have been discussing in this book would not be expected to possess the skills of an operations researcher because the latter functions more generally in applying mathe-

[16] Harold Goldstein, "Projections of Manpower Requirements and Supply," *Industrial Relations,* Vol. 5, No. 3, May 1966, pp. 17–27.

[17] Joel Darmstadter, "Manpower in a Long-Term Economic Projection Model," *Industrial Relations,* Vol. 5, No. 3, May 1966, pp. 28–58.

[18] For an example, see George L. Newhauser and Henry L. W. Nuttle, "A Quantitative Approach to Employment Planning," *Management Science,* Vol. 11, No. 8, June 1965, pp. B-155–B-165.

[19] Russell L. Ackoff and Patrick Rivett, *A Manager's Guide to Operations Research,* Wiley, New York, 1963, p. 36 and pp. 12–17 for an illustration.

matical techniques to the solution of managerial and organizational problems of many different kinds. Nevertheless, to the extent that the operations researcher may be of assistance to the manpower specialist he should be called upon.

In conclusion, the literature (particularly that of industrial training and personnel work) indicates that while a great deal is stated about the advantages of manpower planning at the level of the firm few such apostles of manpower planning have indicated methodologies for its conduct. If this chapter induces others to make an effort to improve our knowledge of manpower planning, then it shall have had some value. In any event, the approach to manpower planning identified in this chapter is referred to in subsequent chapters as the basis for planning educational and training programs for the development of human resources.

CHAPTER 4

Formal Development of Human Resources in Industry

The stereotyped industrial-training man is in the eyes of many industrial managers a pitiable figure running around with a conference leader's guide while arranging ash trays in the training room and mumbling under his breath about how much he wishes he only had top management's support for his endeavors. He is not a planner but a responder to requests for service or orders from the plant manager.

Perhaps the training man is good old Joe from the plant—an ex-foreman or safety engineer who was kicked upstairs and is regarded as a "nice guy," albeit pathetic. Or maybe he is a former public school teacher who became disgruntled with his pay and thought he would make out better in industry but has not: he is regarded as schoolteacherish and impractical—with a weird nonindustrial vocabulary of such words as laboratory training, role playing, business games, heuristic problem solving, needs analysis, evaluative criteria, and the like.

The above are some training directors of the past. The reader can decide for himself whether they are caricatures or realistic characterizations.

In this chapter and the next we sketch the various tools, responsibilities, and organizational arrangements pertinent to human resource development in pace-setting organizations of the present and future. We have arbitrarily separated the tools from the normative and organizational contexts in which they are used merely for the sake of convenience in analysis. In practice both the tools and the contexts are part of the same reality: the formal approach used by industrial and other organizations for the development of human resources. Most plans for such development tend to concentrate upon the means to be employed rather than upon the end to be obtained.

As we consider the various methods for determining developmental needs, the techniques for meeting them through instruction and programs, and the ways of evaluating the results of programs, we can readily see that the complexity of each comprises professional subject matter which must be mastered by the manpower specialist.

We cannot cover in detail in this chapter all that the manpower specialist should know about the techniques pertinent to determining needs, conducting programs, and evaluating the results of developmental efforts. Each of these subjects is so broad that separate treatment of the details of each can best be found in the literature cited in the bibliography at the end of the book rather than here. Yet we do believe that the recurrent cycle of planning, programming, and evaluating efforts made to develop human resources should be covered as an overall process and its pertinence for manpower policy pointed out. The specific details of tools and techniques are ephemeral and heavily influenced by faddism but the recurring cycle is fundamental and of sufficient generality to be a focal point for the chapter.

In discussing the contents of this chapter it should be worthwhile to emphasize that our concern in manpower planning and the development of human resources is the socialization of the individual to work in organizations. Socialization involves change in the person; therefore, when we consider some of the techniques for developing human resources, we should be clear about the changes we have in mind. In the language of those interested in programmed instruction, we should concern ourselves with "terminal behavior(s)."

We are specifically concerned with five kinds of change. First are changes in skills (or, loosely, the abilities to perform some act). Next are changes in knowledge (or ideas about something). Third are changes in attitudes (or in the feelings, emotions, or beliefs people have). Fourth are changes in an awareness of self (or the present ways of seeing one's behavior, for which laboratory or sensitivity training is well known). Lastly are changes in motivation to perform (or the desire to act differently).[1] The various techniques used for development should be compatible with the type of change desired. Therefore, a repertoire of techniques needs to be discussed.

Our approach for the remainder of the chapter is to: set forth a comprehensive framework for needs analysis; describe some of the most useful techniques for analyzing education and training needs; examine the most important strengths and weaknesses of the various methods of instruction and programs for development; and review the concepts and techniques of program evaluation, the latter being one of the knottiest problems in social science, management, and education. The goal is to explain as clearly as possible methods for determining who needs what types of developmental opportunities and experiences for stipulated purposes in an organizational

[1] Allen A. Zoll, 3rd, *Dynamic Management Education,* Management Education Associates, Seattle, 1966, pp. 2–1.

setting. We stress that the basis for effective development is on-going research on needs and results. Research is the key to professionalization and destruction of the poor image of the stereotyped training man.

NEEDS ANALYSIS AND THE PROGRAMMING CYCLE

Manpower-planning projections indicate the quantitative need for people with various types of skill and education in a total society or organization. The analysis of human resources indicates the qualitative needs among people and logically leads to planning various types of developmental opportunities and experiences, especially educational and training programs.

The development of human resources, if it is to be effective, must be backed up by careful and continuous research. The research may be nothing more than the simple collection of existing data, arranging it in an orderly manner, and derivation of meaningful conclusions. Or it may be highly complex and technical experimentation concerning the investigation of the learning process itself in multidimensional situations in the production of goods and services.[2] The manpower specialist must know how to conduct research, evaluate the findings he obtains, and translate them into action. He need not be an expert on the intricacies of research; but if he is not, he should have access to a consultant who is. As a minimum, the manpower specialist should possess a research orientation to his job.

The manpower specialist must also acquire a systematic view of the cycle of activities that recur in the development of human resources so that the research which he conducts or has conducted can be used to optimum advantage.

His work or that of his staff is, or should be, on a continuous cycle. His work may conveniently be conceptualized as consisting of several identifiable elements which are interrelated in a simple repetitive cycle, depicted in Figure 1. The elements may be expressed as planning (based upon needs determination and goal setting), organizing (deciding what type of final program is needed and how it should be structured), implementing (making the program available and placing participants in it), reviewing (evaluating the results obtained in terms of the objectives set), and feedback (the overall assessment of what should be done next to recycling based upon the cycle just completed). Thus the development of human resources operates as a system and not as an open-end sequence.[3]

[2] William McGehee and Paul W. Thayer, *Training in Business and Industry,* Wiley, New York, 1961, p. 22.
[3] Jesse C. McKeon, "Training Records and Information Systems," in Robert L. Craig and Lester R. Bittel, eds., *Training and Development Handbook,* McGraw-Hill, New York, 1967, pp. 608–609.

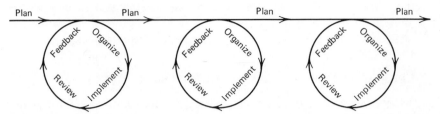

Figure 1   Human resource development planning and programming cycle. *Source.* Jesse C. McKeon, "Training Records and Information Systems," in Robert L. Craig and Lester R. Bittel, eds., *Training and Development Handbook,* McGraw-Hill, New York, 1967, p. 609.

The use of educational and training programs for developing human resources is not an end but a means to an end. It exists only to help achieve long-range and immediate organizational goals. Programs and approaches which are considered effective in one organization may be ineffective in another because of differences in the stage of organizational growth and the state of manpower policies.[4] As a consequence, the use of development programs to achieve organizational goals requires the careful assessment of needs within the organization: a determination of the goals that can be served by education and training, the people who need it and for what purposes, and the content of the programs.[5]

There are probably as many schemes and rationales for approaching the problem of determining development needs as there are persons who are concerned with planning and implementing the cycle displayed in Figure 1. McGehee and Thayer have devised a threefold approach which helps ordering of the complex problems connected with development planning in an organization or component of any organization. It consists essentially of the following:

1. Organizational analysis—determining where within the organization the education and training emphasis should be placed.

2. Operations analysis—determining what should be the contents of programs in terms of what an employee must do to perform a task, job, or assignment in an effective way.

3. Man analysis—determining what types of behavior change are required on the part of an employee if he is to perform the tasks which constitute his job in the organization.[6]

---

[4] *Ibid.,* p. 209.
[5] McGehee and Thayer, *op. cit.,* p. 24.
[6] *Ibid.,* p. 25.

ORGANIZATIONAL ANALYSIS

From the standpoint of the formulation by McGehee and Thayer, development needs can be viewed as equivalent to problems and can be identified by determining (1) the stated standards and behavior desired, (2) the standards inferred from and the behavior observed, and (3) the causes of discrepancies between the expected and the observed. Programs for the development of human resources (i.e., formalized chances to learn) are provided to remove the causes of failure to attain standards or the desired behavior.

The type of analysis for the organization, operations, and the man varies. Organizational analysis places an emphasis on a study of the entire organization, its objectives, its resources, and the allocation of those resources as they bear upon organizational objectives. To some extent it is an impersonal focus upon manpower quality. The concern is with discovering individuals who need training but is not initially directed toward the specific needs which they have. On the other hand, operational analysis and man analysis are concerned with the specific training needs of individuals.[7]

Operational analysis focuses upon the task or job regardless of the person performing the work. It includes a determination of what an employee must do on the job, the specific behavior required, if the work is to be carried out consistent with the standards set by management. Here again the focus is upon the task and not the man.[8]

Man analysis focuses upon the individual. It involves two considerations: (1) determining the behavior of the man on the job, and (2) deciding what behavior must be changed or developed if he is to fulfill the requirements as defined by management (or management and the union if there is a collectively bargained agreement containing such standards). Here the focus is on the individual in his present position and, to a lesser extent, possible future positions.[9]

The three types of analysis are closely related and are not performed in isolation of each other. For example, evidence of needs in terms of the entire organization may arise because of the structure of jobs in the organization or because of the performance of people who perform the jobs. Moreover, the tools for making these analyses are not yet fully developed. Much more research is needed to sharpen the tools before we can conduct the three types of analyses with the degree of precision that we would like.[10]

[7] *Ibid.*, pp. 25–26.
[8] *Ibid.*, p. 26.
[9] *Ibid.*
[10] *Ibid.*

Improvements continue to be made. Some elaboration on the state of the art for each type of analysis is worth discussion.

Organizational analysis is the initial step for the diagnosis of individual behavior. We must begin by determining whether there are organizational objectives and whether these are being achieved in order to obtain standards for individual behavior and performance. Of course, whether the organizational objectives are achieved is a function of many factors in addition to the development of human resources. Yet failure to attain objectives can be interpreted as a signal to ask, among other questions, whether the development of people has any causal connection with the failure.[11]

After this beginning, a second step is determining the adequacy of the human resources in the organization. Manpower inventories and performance appraisal systems (both of which are discussed in a subsequent chapter) can be used to this end. However, as jobs increase in complexity, the problem of man analysis, which is basic to human resource analysis, becomes increasingly complex. The initial analysis is often the most difficult one; subsequent analyses become easier with experience and the development of efficient procedures.[12]

A third step is considering deviations from managerial standards as shown by unacceptable ratios or scores on direct and indirect efficiency indices. Usually these indices are expressed by means of cost-accounting concepts. The exact nature of them varies from organization to organization but would include such factors as: costs of labor or materials to produce the goods or services; the quality of the same; the utilization of machinery and equipment to produce them; and the costs of distribution of the goods and services. To use these data properly the manpower specialist must investigate what they mean and should not launch remedial educational and training programs unless there are strong indications that deficiencies in human resources are a part of the cause of the problem. Similarly, in surveying employees' attitudes or broad organizational climate, manpower specialists should make a sophisticated appraisal of the data which they obtain to make sure that they are valid and reliable and should certainly not automatically jump to the conclusion that the results always require an educational or training program.[13]

Although the literature of the social sciences and management has been replete with references to organizations, organizational theory, organization planning, and organizational analysis in the past two decades, there

[11] *Ibid.,* pp. 27–31.
[12] *Ibid.,* pp. 32–36.
[13] *Ibid.,* pp. 36–60.

has been actually only a small part of this literature that has tied together organizational analysis and the development of human resources.[14]

A recent term "organizational development" has come into use, which is an abbreviated way of referring to organizational planning and management development, by simply combining the first and last words of a more cumbersome phrase. The assumption seems to be that organizations can be improved through the planned development of managers. Thus organizational development programs are really focused upon human resources rather than planned structural changes in organizations, which is perhaps what many persons think about when they see the term organizational development.

Perhaps the most provocative work on the use of organizational analysis for the planned development of managerial manpower is that of Fisch, particularly his OCA concept, standing for Organization Center Analysis. By this he means the thorough-going study of an organization by taking each position in turn as the center of investigation. OCA is thus a way of viewing an organization. The organization is studied and understood by taking each key position in turn, each man in his post, and every key individual's achievement pattern as the center of the organizational universe. Through analytical work too detailed to review here, the assembly and reconciliation of the sum total of all key organizational points of view is obtained to depict how the organization works and how it can be altered by planned change.[15]

OPERATIONS ANALYSIS

Whereas organizational analysis is concerned with determining where education and training are needed in an organization, operations analysis is concerned with the problem of what education and training should consist. An operations analysis is an orderly and systematic collection of data about an existing (or potential) task (or tasks). In distinction to job analysis, an operations analysis has as its purpose determining what an employee must be taught in order to perform the task or job so that he contributes maximally to the attainment of organizational goals. Failure to perform an adequate operations analysis of a job can result in unneeded

[14] For an imposing recent summary of the literature in organizations see James G. March, ed., *Handbook of Organizations*, Rand McNally, Chicago, 1965. The best recent book on organization planning in the pragmatic tradition is Ernest Dale, *Organization*, American Management Association, New York, 1967.

[15] Gerald G. Fisch, *Organization for Profit*, McGraw-Hill, New York, 1964, pp. 251–304.

effort in developing skills or inculcating knowledge which is not needed in the performance of the tasks in a job.[16]

An operations analysis will result in the following data concerning a task or task cluster: standards of performance for the task or job; if a task cluster or "job," an identification of the tasks that make up the job; how each task is to be performed if standards of performance are to be met; and the behaviors which are basic to the performance of each task in the required manner. Finding out standards of performance in operations analysis is analogous to stating organizational objectives in organizational analysis: the standards are benchmarks from which measurements can be made. If we know the standards by which results of performing a task or a job are measured, we can then determine if the task is being performed in a correct manner. This knowledge concerning tasks is a prerequisite for determining the behavior change required on the part of an employee if he is to perform the tasks adequately. Furthermore, without standards of performance we have no means of determining whether the education and training provided for the task or job is accomplishing its purpose.[17]

For many jobs in organizations, it is possible to set standards and measure work accomplishment. However, it is much more difficult to do this for high-level managerial jobs; and it is also difficult to measure the various individual skills, knowledge, and attitudes that affect and are inferred from behavior regardless of job level. Although research in operations analysis has grown apace in the last twenty years, little solid knowledge exists as a result of research investigation showing how valid and reliable work-sampling, interview-observation, critical-incident, and allied methods are in determining developmental needs.[18] Yet the studies that do exist [19] suggest operations analysis is a useful blueprint for organizing and implementing programs for manpower filling specific positions. Operations analysis is intended to be a controlled objective method for fact gathering and has great potential as a way of avoiding the subjective methods of needs assessment that depend upon individuals' reporting their perceptions of what they think they need, often being in error.

To this point we have discussed two steps in determining needs and planning for the economical use of the funds allocated for formal development programs. Organizational analysis and operations analysis are essential preliminary steps if we are to focus our efforts upon the individual who participates in a developmental program—the employee. He is the learner.

[16] Ibid., pp. 62–63.
[17] Ibid., pp. 63–64.
[18] Ibid., pp. 70–87.
[19] For example, see General Electric Company, The Effective Manufacturing Foreman, General Electric, New York, 1957.

It is he who will modify his behavior either to meet, or to circumvent, organizational requirements. The final step in determining needs, man analysis, is thus directed toward finding out whether the employee requires education or training and, if he does, what exactly he requires. The final step in needs determination is then focused directly on the individual employee.[20]

TECHNIQUES OF MAN ANALYSIS

Man analysis is concerned with how well a specific employee is carrying out the tasks which constitute his job. It is concerned too with the behavior change required to improve his job performance. The skills to be learned, the knowledge needed, and the attitudes to be developed would all be included under the concept of behavior change. Man analysis is thus the most difficult phase in determining developmental needs because not only are we interested in performance but also the cause of that performance. In addition, we are trying to determine the degree of skill possessed, the amount of knowledge available, and the specific attitudes involved. We want to know whether poor performance of a task is the result of insufficient skill or knowledge or some other factor which determines the quality of behavior. Merely securing a summary measure of job performance may seem to be a relatively simple task until we realize that we need to know the nature of job performance directly attributable to the individual and not contaminated by the many factors which are beyond his control. Underlying all these virtual imponderables is yet another complicating feature: the measurement of an individual's job behavior usually has to be made by another person. This feature leads to the injection of innumerable subjective or judgmental kinds of imprecision in measurement.[21] Although there are some steps that can be taken to reduce these possible biases, the crudeness of the various methods presently available cannot eliminate them.

The methods of man analysis can be classified in three major categories: objective records of job performance, devised situational measures, and observational measures. These methods for man analysis can also assist in organizational and operations analysis. For example, production records when secured from departments in an organization can indicate where education and training are needed, that is, organizational analysis. The same data when secured on individual employees can be a basis for man analysis. The techniques used for observing a job when directed toward discovering job content can be used for operations analysis. The identical

---

[20] *Ibid.*, p. 88.
[21] *Ibid.*, pp. 89–90.

techniques when focused on an individual employee to determine how he performs the tasks of his job can be used for a man analysis.[22]

Let us assume that any job which exists in an organization has been created to accomplish certain purposes which are, in turn, related to the attainment of organizational objectives. When a proper operations analysis has been made of jobs, these purposes may be stated in standards of performance. In industry these standards can usually be expressed in the amount of work done; the quality of completed work; the cost of the work finished as related to materials, machinery, equipment, and manpower; and the effect upon the continuing survival of the enterprise. When these results can be expressed in units produced which meet a given standard, in dollar costs, or in some other unit of numerical measure (hours of machine downtime or days lost due to absenteeism), the resulting figures can be called "objective records of performance." [23]

Objective records are usually not entirely relevant, reliable, or free from bias. Moreover, standards of performance are never static because organizations change their structures and goals. For example, changes in the national economy may affect a sales manager's gross sales; a foreman may experience a high number of grievances filed because contract expiration time is nearing; or reports on performance may be incomplete, out-of-date, or inaccurate. But as a general principle, when standards of job performance are established and where the standards are stated in terms of objective measures, consistent deviations below this standard should suggest to the manpower specialist that the situation deserves scrutiny to determine if education, training, or some other action is indicated.[24]

When an employee is responsible for a single outcome or a few relatively simple outcomes as a result of his job performance, one or more objective indices can be used in a man analysis:

1. Units produced in a given period of time.
2. Quality of units produced.
3. Costs of materials in producing a unit (by computing the expense of waste and scrappage).
4. Cost of the maintenance of equipment and machinery used by the employee.
5. Absenteeism and tardiness.
6. Grievances and complaints filed.
7. Accident frequency and severity.
8. Disciplinary actions.

[22] *Ibid.*, p. 91.
[23] *Ibid.*
[24] *Ibid.*, pp. 91–92.

Obviously, each of these items does not carry equal weight in determining the overall job performance of the employee. They do, however, provide a base for man analysis.[25] This is particularly true for manufacturing manpower.

Apparently standards are most easily set for employees at the lowest level in an organization, that is, those who carry out work requiring the lower-order skills or what may be called "expertise." What is meant by the latter term is expertness, deftness, ability in, or knowledge of some specialized task or group of tasks, such as can be acquired only through experience at that task, or on the job in which those tasks are grouped. An example would be an operative job composed essentially of semiskills, such as a truck driver.[26]

We have given very little attention in this book to how people should be trained to acquire expertise because most of them pick it up on the job by operating chain hoists, fixing looms, serving meals, and the like. Standards for these types of work can be set on an *ad hoc* basis. Likewise, we do not devote much attention to training clerk-typists, stenographers, or secretaries because the skills developed by persons in these jobs can be acquired through vocational courses in high schools, junior colleges, or business institutes. Measurement of such office work through work standards is possible but perilous because of the many difficult-to-judge aspects of the work, especially where the employees involved do not work in a stenographic pool or "bull pen" arrangement where there is a large unceasing volume of repetitive work. Skilled-trades apprentices and technicians require more than training on the job to be full-fledged practitioners in their fields, and standards for their performance can frequently be set, depending on the occupational content. For example, standards can be set in bricklaying or the number of engineering laboratory tests set up. Standards could readily be established for measuring the performance of graduates of government-sponsored retraining programs. In a sense these may be viewed as developmental programs for people who have lost expertise, or perhaps never had it, or need to learn new semiskills. The point is objective records of job performance could be used to a greater or lesser degree in all the aforementioned occupations and others as well.

The problems of securing objective performance records for a man analysis increase as the outcomes for which the employee is responsible multiply both in number and complexity. Yet it is this group of employees (technical, professional, and managerial manpower) who can and do influence the achievement of organizational goals in more significant ways

[25] *Ibid.*, p. 93.
[26] Edwin F. Beal and Edward D. Wickersham, *The Practice of Collective Bargaining,* Third Edition, Irwin, Homewood, Illinois, 1967, pp. 11–12.

than those of employees responsible for a single and comparatively simple outcome.[27]

The difficulty in obtaining objective performance records for technical, professional, and managerial manpower is accentuated by the time-span problem. For example, among production employees the performance record is available weekly, if not daily or hourly. Among managerial employees these data may not be available for months or sometimes for years. Profit-and-loss figures for major divisions of an organization usually are available on a monthly basis. But these figures must be used in terms of their trends over a reasonable period of time if they are to be an index of job performance of the persons who are held responsible for the profit performance of the organization.[28] In addition, it is difficult to measure exactly how much a given manager's performance contributed to profitability, particularly if we consider staff managerial manpower one or two organizational levels beneath the general manager of a divisional profit center yet undeniably in key positions. On the other hand, the time-span of discretion has been used as a basis for job evaluation and may ultimately prove to have advantages which can be related to the performance of specific job incumbents.[29]

TOOLS FOR ANALYSIS

The difficulties of securing a current objective job performance measure for managerial manpower usually have resulted in abandoning such measures in favor of ratings, observational techniques, and subjective reports. These kinds of measures present special problems in terms of relevance, reliability, and freedom from bias. In fact, there are many manpower and industrial relations specialists who hold the view that adequate objective or observational indices of managerial performance are impossible to obtain. Yet we know that organizational superiors constantly evaluate their subordinates and, on the basis of these appraisals, make decisions which affect the individual employee's career development. We need a great deal more research on better objective and observational instruments and methods. Specifically, man analysis will be strengthened in the future as we improve such tools as achievement tests of job knowledge, observation methods using work sampling, and behavioral rating schemes which steer clear of all the sources of contamination that have weakened them in the past.[30]

[27] McGehee and Thayer, *op. cit.,* p. 93.
[28] *Ibid.,* p. 94.
[29] See Elliott Jaques, *Equitable Payment,* Wiley, New York, 1961.
[30] McGehee and Thayer, *op. cit.,* pp. 98–122.

In practice, hunches and the crystal ball have probably been the most widely used ways of determining educational and training needs, particularly for managerial manpower. Interviews and questionnaires as means of securing information from an employee in regard to his developmental needs have been relatively neglected both in industrial practice and in the literature on training.[31]

The interview and the questionnaire have two unique advantages over other means of determining the developmental needs of an individual. These advantages exist only when the employee himself is asked about his own needs. First, the individual is the sole source of information as to what he believes he needs to learn to perform his job adequately. Only by asking through an interview or questionnaire can this subjective data be obtained. Second, self-insight can serve, in some instances, as a strong motivating device for modifying behavior. It is quite possible that an employee who recognizes and accepts defects in his behavior on the job will be more willing to make an effort to eliminate this defect than if the defect were merely pointed out to him by an instructor or supervisor.[32]

Interviews and questionnaires can be constructed quickly and tailored to the idiosyncrasies of a given organization. They can be administered by manpower and training specialists who have been familiarized with these methods. They may be easier to develop, use, and analyze than some of the testing, rating, and observational techniques previously discussed. However, it should not be concluded that anyone can construct, administer, and analyze questionnaires and interviews or that these techniques are a cheap and easy solution to the man analysis problem. They are merely two other methods that deserve greater attention than they have been given in the past.

We next turn to how they can be used and present some sample formats. We focus specifically on the use of questionnaires, checklists, interviews, self-reporting devices, and, to a lesser extent, performance data in determining for illustrative purposes the developmental needs of line and staff supervisors. It should be noted that as a result of using these methods we can categorize developmental needs in terms of those which:

1. An individual has.
2. A group has.
3. Must be met immediately.
4. Can be met in the future.
5. Require formal educational and training activities.
6. Require informal developmental activities.

---

[31] *Ibid.*, p. 124.
[32] *Ibid.*, pp. 123–124.

7. Require on-the-job instruction.
8. Require off-the-job instruction.
9. The organization can meet best within itself.
10. The organization can meet best through outside resources.
11. An individual can meet in a group session with others.
12. An individual can meet only by himself.[33]

One method which can be utilized in determining the developmental needs of both line and staff supervisors is to have them fill in a simple semistructured supervisory training-needs questionnaire, such as that shown

---

Part I

Directions

Please write below the subjects you would like to have developed and presented for discussion in future training conferences. Be specific. Consider first the functional areas which are listed below for your convenience. Make your suggestions under the proper heading. Feel free to recommend topics which do not fall under any of the listed categories. List as many subjects as you wish. Use the reverse side of the form to list subjects that would be most helpful to other supervisors.

Industrial Relations:
Quality Control:
Controller:
Manufacturing Engineering
   and/or Work Standards:
Production Control:
Plant Engineering:
Other:

Part II

Directions

What subjects do you think other supervisors would like to have developed and presented for discussion in future training conferences?

Industrial Relations:
Quality Control:
Controller:
Manufacturing Engineering
   and/or Work Standards:
Production Control:
Plant Engineering:
Other:

Figure 2   Supervisor training-needs questionnaire (for line and staff supervisors).

[33] Richard B. Johnson, "Determining Training Needs," in Craig and Bittel, eds., *op. cit.*, p. 17.

in Figure 2. (In each example of a technique discussed subsequently, in which a form is utilized, directions for completing the form are given in full. However, for the sake of brevity but without sacrificing sufficient descriptive information, the number of items comprising the body of a questionnaire or checklist has been held to a minimum.)

A review of the sample form in Figure 2 shows that the only restriction placed upon freedom of expression in suggesting subjects for discussion in a conference is the request to list suggestions under a few functional areas of a manufacturing business. Thus possible bias from more detailed structuring is held to a minimum.

The replies from a form such as that in Figure 2, being of the unstructured or essay type, make analysis of the returns somewhat laborious if a large number of supervisors is involved. Electronic data-processing equipment can be used if the raw data are coded and categorized.

A second form that can be utilized in needs determination is the staff supervisory training questionnaire shown in Figure 3. As the title indicates,

---

Part I

In carrying out your supervisory responsibility, you have probably encountered problems related to some of the following statements. After reading each statement, check the column on the left which indicates the frequency of your experience with the problem to which the statement refers. Then, check the column on the right which indicates the degree of difficulty you have in coping with or overcoming the problem. Make a check on the left and on the right for each statement:

Frequency of Occurrences   Degree of Difficulty

Frequently a Problem	Sometimes a Problem	Seldom or Never a Problem		Very Difficult to Overcome	Difficult to Overcome	Presents no Difficulty
			1. Handling requests for personal time off.			
			2. Making the decision about whom to select from a number of applicants.			
			3. Having capable employees resigning from the Company.			
			4. Applying Company policies regarding leaves of absence, etc.			
			5. Timing hiring of employees to correspond with availability of personnel, i.e., end			

Figure 3   Staff supervisory training questionnaire.

this form may best be used in determining the needs of staff supervisors. The forms may be filled in at regularly scheduled conference training sessions if they are used in an organization, or the forms may be distributed to supervisors to be filled in at their convenience and to be returned to the manpower specialist or training representative on or before a specified date.

Part II

A. Areas: Please check the areas listed below in which either you have experienced troublesome problems or have felt the need for more adequate information. (Check any that apply)

1. _____Administration of Personnel Policies
2. _____Communications
3. _____Employee Benefits
4. _____Organizational Relationships
5. _____Employee Motivation and Attitudes
6. _____Human Abilities
7. _____Group Behavior
8. _____Budgets and Costs
9. _____Business Outlook
10. _____Information about Company Products

11. _____Letters and Reports
12. _____Methods Improvement
13. _____Company Sales Activities
14. _____Engineering Developments
15. _____Company Expansion
16. _____Economics and Current Issues
17. _____Public Relations Activities
18. _____The Basis for Company Operations
19. _____Product Scheduling and Distribution
20. _____Other (Specify)_____

B. Description of Problems: Referring to the areas you checked above, describe in your own words, and in as much detail as possible, any significant problem(s) you have recently encountered as a supervisor. (Use space below and back of last sheet if necessary.)

Part III

List below any topics you would like to have discussed in future supervisory conferences.

Figure 3 (*Continued*).

Items listed in this type of questionnaire can be obtained by interviewing a selected sample of department managers in an organization. It is not advisable to dream up the items in the office armchair. The managers should be asked to identify problems and problem areas of their subordinate supervisors. The actual items to be included in the questionnaire can then be based upon information obtained in the interviews. Various parts of the questionnaire can be structured to attack needs analyses in different ways.

Data-processing equipment can be used in analyzing the items scored in the returned questionnaires. The remaining items requiring write-in information must be analyzed separately.

Part I

Consider each of the following topics and indicate your opinion as to whether or not additional training is needed. Check one response for each topic. (Supervisors should answer in terms of their own needs and those of other supervisors they know well. Managers should answer in terms of their own needs and those of supervisors reporting to them.)

Space is also provided for specific comments regarding the nature of the problem involved and/or the type of training that would be most appropriate. Such comments are particularly encouraged wherever the "Yes" column is checked. Indicate the number of the topic referred to.

Topic	Training Recommended		Comments
	Yes	No	
	(1)	(2)	
1. Organization and Functions of Major Company Components			
2. Functions of Plant and Division Staff Activities (Labor Relations, Controller, Plant Engineering, etc.)			
3. Line-Staff Relationships			
4. Interviewing Job Applicants			
5. Making the Selection Decision			
6. Position Classification System			
7. Salary Administration			

Figure 4 Staff supervisory training-needs survey.

Another form which can be used in determining supervisory training needs is the staff supervisory training-needs survey form shown in Figure 4. This form may be completed by staff supervisors at the end of supervisory development conferences or distributed to supervisors for later return to the office of the manpower specialist.

As shown in Figure 4, the form is composed of two parts. Items in the

Part II

Many specialized short courses and seminars of interest to management personnel are offered by various management and professional associations as well as colleges and universities. These courses are intensive and comprehensive programs of study and application in specific subject areas and generally involve eight to forty clock hours per topic.

1. The following list is a representative sample of possible topics for such specialized short courses. Review this list and check any you would be interested in attending, if offered by the Company. (Space is provided for suggesting additional topics.):

1_____ The Functions and Goals of Management: Trends and Problems
2_____ Data and Decision: The Use of Electronic Computers in Industry
3_____ Principles and Techniques of Interviewing
4_____ Understanding the Problems of Production Supervision
5_____ Application of Scientific Method in Solving Business Problems
6_____ Stimulating Employee Creativity
7_____ Market Research Activities
8_____ Effective Public Speaking
9_____ Supervising the Professional Employee
10_____ Operations Research Methods
11_____ Work Standards
12_____ Machine Capabilities
13_____ Labor-Management Relationships
14_____ The Decision Making Process
15_____ Recent Research Findings in Industrial Relations
16_____ Effective Report Writing
17_____ Manufacturing Automation
18_____ Human Relations in Industry
19_____ Company Research and Development Activities
20_____ Selection of Supervisory Personnel
21_____ Performance Appraisal
22_____ Information Theory Applied to Modern Physics and Engineering
23_____ Metal Processing: Recent Developments
24_____ Statistical Methods in Industry
25_____ The Design and Analysis of Industrial Experiments
26_____ Managing Product Engineering
27_____ The Future Growth of the National Economy
28_____ The Economic Challenge of the Soviet Union
29_____ Business Gaming: Simulating Managerial Decisions
30_____ Interpersonal Communications
31_____ Speed Reading

_____   _____
_____   _____
_____   _____
_____   _____

Figure 4   (*Continued*).

2. Review the topics you checked in Question 1 above, and rank in order of importance as follows:
   a) Write (1) in front of your first choice
   b) Write (2) in front of your second choice
   c) Write (3) in front of your third choice

32   3. Considering only the topic you ranked as number (1), would you regard it to be of sufficient importance and value to justify attendance during normal working hours?.................Yes____(1) No____(2)

59 Check your present classification.
(1)____Manager (Department Manager, Assistant Department Manager)
(2)____Supervisor (Section Supervisor, Assistant Section Supervisor, Unit Supervisor
(3)____Other (Specify)

Note: This questionnaire should <u>not</u> be answered by supervisors of production, i.e., Foremen, General Foremen, and Superintendents. (A separate form is available for the latter classifications.)

Figure 4   (*Continued*).

first part could be devised by reviewing the titles of supervisory development conferences previously presented in the organization (if there were any) and reviewing policies relating to salaried employees for which it was thought additional training might be needed.

Suggestions for items in the second part can be obtained by reviewing the titles of short courses, seminars, and meetings being utilized in the community for the development of the organization's manpower and of courses listed in university catalogs and the brochures of professional associations. These items could be included in the questionnaire to obtain an indication of the services that might be obtained from community educational institutions in meeting supervisory development needs.

A line supervisory checklist can be utilized in determining the training needs of line supervisors as shown in Figure 5. It can be constructed to include both objective and subjective data, if desired. Sometimes the line between the two is not always clear because factual situations may be perceived and evaluated differently.

For example, the items in the first part of this three-part form could be obtained through an intensive work-sampling observation-interview study of the actual plant activities of foremen, general foremen, and superintendents. The final checklist could, in turn, be composed of the items gathered through research and supplemented with problems selected from a previously used questionnaire or with items suggested by department managers. The last two parts of the form contain subjective requests for suggestions

Instructions: Circle the number in front of any item that you feel is an important problem or difficulty. There are no right or wrong answers. No one will have all of the problem items listed, but everyone will have some of them.

1. Truckers abuse their equipment.
2. It is difficult to discipline an employee for loafing when he fails to meet work standards.
3. Quality standards are changed without changing work standards.
4. Superiors sometimes forget other breakdowns may be more important than their own.
5. Other supervisors don't apply what is taught in training conferences.
6. Can't get my superiors to listen.
7. Foremen are willing to take credit but not blame.
8. Employees are uninterested or uncooperative.
9. Seniority prevails over merit when men are promoted.
10. The amount of work I have to do is excessive.
11. Some line supervisors lack aggressiveness or initiative necessary to do a good job.
12. Not enough opportunity to suggest changes in layout.
13. When the line-speed is changed, work standard problems arise.
14. Material Handling personnel frequently damage parts.
15. Paperwork interferes with more important duties.
16. Body-mix not as scheduled.
17. Too many departmental meetings.
18. My superiors don't take time to find out my problems or what causes them.
19. General Foremen or Superintendents bawl out men in front of other employees.
20. Seniority often keeps me from getting a job done in best way.
21. Employees do poor work just to be taken off the job.
22. Inability to give employees assignment outside of job classification interferes with getting the job done.
23. Some line supervisors don't always plan ahead.
24. Too many "complaints" end up as "grievances."
25. Inefficient equipment.
26. There are not enough work standards people.
27. Tools do not hold up.
28. Maintenance work is poorly done.
29. Production Control does not know where to find stock or does not keep enough on hand.
30. Superiors usually take the best men for transfers.
31. Staff departments usually ignore my opinions or suggestions.
32. Poor attitudes among high seniority employees.
33. Employees slow about reporting stock, tool, or maintenance needs.
34. Don't get the kind of employees needed.
35. Management proposals are rejected without good reason.

Figure 5 Line supervisory check list.

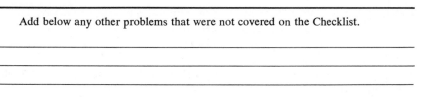

Add below any other problems that were not covered on the Checklist.

_____

_____

_____

_____

Describe in the space below three supervisory training conferences which you think would be of greatest value to you. Be as specific as possible. If your suggestions are related to conferences which have already been held, indicate how your suggestions are different.

Figure 5   (*Continued*).

of training needs from the supervisors. It is quite easy to use EDP equipment to analyze at least the first section of the checklist.

A final example of questionnaires used in ascertaining supervisory training needs is the production supervision training-needs survey form shown in Figure 6. The form may be filled in by supervisors of foremen, general foremen, and superintendents and returned to the manpower specialist. The governing concept is to obtain the perceived development needs of the trainee as seen by his organizational superior rather than by himself.

The terms in the questionnaire can be the officially approved statements (or condensed versions) of the responsibilities of line supervisors, assuming the organization has these identified and published in a supervisory handbook or manual.

Since these statements should tell the supervisor what his job is, they can form the basis for a major part of the topics presented at line supervisory development conferences. The conferences will then afford supervisors the opportunity to clarify their responsibilities and to discuss methods of effectively performing them.

ADDITIONAL TOOLS

Another approach which can be utilized in the determination of supervisory training needs is the application of the pass-card or card-sort system. This technique, which has many variations, may be used in the following manner. During the final five to ten minutes of a training conference session, the conference leader indicates to the supervisors that their help is needed in the planning of future supervisory development conferences. Since supervisors are often in the best position to judge what their most important problems are, their opinions as to topics that should be presented in conferences are desired. They may be informed that at the next training

Please check here to show the positions of the men that you supervise directly:

1. _____I supervise Superintendents
2. _____I supervise General Foremen
3. _____I supervise Foremen

This survey is intended to discover which job responsibilities present greatest difficulty to line supervisors.

We are asking that you do not sign your name to this form or identify yourself in any other way.

Consider all of the men whom you supervise directly. Now choose one of these men. Make your choice on any basis that you care to use. The important thing is to pick one man, to keep him clearly in your mind, and to answer all the questions in terms of this one man. Don't write his name on this survey form and don't identify him to anyone. Keep the same man in mind all the way through as you are answering.

Please note that this survey form is printed on both sides of the paper. You should answer every item. We believe that your judgment is important on each responsibility.

Instructions

Look at each of the responsibilities on the following pages. How difficult is each responsibility, in your judgment, for the man you have chosen? Use the boxes which follow each statement in order to show the degrees of difficulty. The boxes range from "very difficult" to "not difficult." Check in any one of the four boxes. If the responsibility does not apply in your area, indicate this.

Example 1   Does not apply in my area

1. Schedule Vacations   Very   1 2 3 4   Not   5
                         Difficult [|X| |]   Difficult   [ ]

In this example, box 2 has been checked. This would show that your subordinate tends to have difficulty in scheduling vacations.

Example 2   Does not apply in my area

2. Direct "-in-line" pack-
   aging of production   Very   1 2 3 4   Not   5
   materials.   Difficult [| | |]   Difficult   [X]

In this example, box 5 has been checked which shows that you cannot consider difficulty for your man since he is not responsible for packaging items directly from the production line. The item does not apply to him.

                                                                Does not apply in my area

1. Request repairs of machinery   Very   1 2 3 4   Not   5
   and equipment.   Difficult [| | |]   Difficult [ ]   (6)

2. Correct out-of-specification con-   [| | |]   [ ]
   dition when it does not involve
   change to tools and facilities.   (7)

Figure 6   Production supervision training-needs survey.

		Does not apply in my area

3. Schedule vacations.   Very   1 2 3 4   Not   5
Difficult   □□□□   Difficult   □   (8)

4. Make machine set-up changes.   □□□□   □   (9)

5. Comply with all applicable military security regulations.   □□□□   □   (10)

6. Get medical assistance for emergency illness or injury.   □□□□   □   (11)

7. Balance personnel to meet schedules.   □□□□   □   (12)

8. Enforce work standards.   □□□□   □   (13)

9. Refer employee for information on Unemployment Compensation to Hourly Personnel activity.   □□□□   □   (14)

10. Inform employee regarding Security and Fire Protection programs.   □□□□   □   (15)

Very   1 2 3 4   Not   5

11. Maintain daily report of time.   Difficult   □□□□   Difficult   □   (16)

12. Report suspicious conditions or actions of employees to proper authorities.   □□□□   □   (17)

13. Hold rejected items pending disposition.   □□□□   □   (18)

14. Direct "in-line" packaging of production materials.   □□□□   □   (19)

Do you have any comments on anything so far? What additional difficulties are your men running into in doing their jobs which have not been covered? Please use the following blank pages to provide any information which you believe will aid the Manpower Department in improving the job performance of your men.

Figure 6   (*Continued*)

session they will be requested to describe in writing three of their most difficult problems and subject matter they would like to have developed for conference presentations.

At a subsequent session, the conference leader brings three sets of 3×5 blank cards, each set of a different color. He first reviews for the conferees the need for their recommendations. He then passes out one set of cards (one card to each conferee) and requests each supervisor to write down the most prominent problem encountered in his work, or the subject he would most like to have discussed at a conference. The cards are then collected. This step is then repeated, using the remaining two sets of cards, to obtain the second- and third-most-important problems or second and third choices of desired conference subject matter. The three colors of cards are used to keep the rankings of problems and choice of topics segregated, thus facilitating the follow-up analytical work.

This technique has two advantages over a structured-questionnaire approach: answers are obtained spontaneously and stated freely within the frame of reference of the respondent; the process of collecting data consumes little time. On the other hand, analysis of the collected data is time-consuming since the answers are of the essay type and are of variable quality depending upon how well the responding supervisor can express himself in writing.

For each of the methods already described, it is possible to supplement the approach with interviews. For example, a sample can be drawn of the respondents, and they may be interviewed to obtain information which augments that obtained on the questionnaire. Of course, interviewing can be used independently too, although fewer people will ordinarily be reached this way. Their needs can be plumbed in greater depth using interviews that can be accomplished by a questionnaire.

The approaches to needs determination described to this point are, in reality, methods of obtaining opinions from a group of supervisors, or from their superiors, as to what the development requirements of supervisors are. Other approaches for determining needs, which are based upon more tangible or objective evidence of need, can be utilized either as substitutes for or supplements to these methods. A few of these approaches are described below.

The manpower specialist may attend meetings of the plant, sales office, hospital, or comparable operations committee in order to spot needs for programs. Usually such meetings are held in organizations weekly or on some regularly scheduled basis. The plant or divisional manager and his department managers are the regular attendants in industrial organizations. Problems and reports relating to costs, production schedules, quality control, and manpower are likely to be discussed at these meetings. Also many decisions involving the planning of plant, division, or corporate activities and the assigning of responsibilities are made in these meetings. The manpower specialist by observing the discussions of problems and reports often obtains first-hand knowledge of where programs for the development of human resources can make a valuable contribution to organizational goal attainment.

The manpower specialist may obtain requests for programs from individual managers and professional employees. Working closely with managers and professionals is one of the most fruitful ways for not only uncovering developmental needs but also building the stature of the manpower function. To develop supportive relations with these individuals, the manpower specialist must establish himself as an expert on developing human resources, which given the state of the art is difficult. It seems everyone has his own theory of development. Yet the servicing of requests for programs is a useful tool.

To attain the desired status, the manpower specialist should consistently follow certain basic principles in his on-the-job behavior. He should be a courteous and careful listener to each request for assistance on development problems. He should examine the conditions giving rise to a problem and carefully weigh the elements of a request in relationship to the functions of other departments before deciding that a bona fide development need is present. If based upon his analysis and research he decides that a development program is not the likely solution to a problem at a given time, he should be prepared to discuss to the satisfaction of the manager making the request approaches that may be taken to solve the problem. On the other hand, if a development program is to be applied to solving the problem, the manpower specialist should establish concise, specific objectives for the program, efficiently coordinate the creation and implementation of the program, and evaluate the results of the effort in terms of meeting the objectives of the program. In a word, he should carry out the cycling depicted earlier in the chapter in Figure 1.

As a logic check against these subjective means of assessing needs, the manpower specialist should constantly be juxtaposing data from organizational analyses and operations analyses against man analyses. His observations of unusual operating conditions, the introduction of new projects, processes, and techniques, and a review of customer complaints or guarantee claims may point to manpower deficiencies correctible through development programs. Certainly the manpower projections made by organizations are also basic for planning programs for developing human resources and should be mentioned here.

The examples of means for determining developmental needs which we have been discussing should not be considered inclusive of all possible approaches, although they cover most of the major ones.[34] They certainly are illustrative of the many devices which a manpower specialist has at his disposal to make manpower planning and the development of human resources effective for management.

It should be further pointed out that the methods used to determine the needs described above do not solely apply to supervisory development. These methods can be used to reveal needs for any or all groups of employees—or indeed that no formal development programs should be made

[34] See *ibid.*, pp. 16–33, for a more complete list.

available to anyone until basic organizational, operational, managerial, or manpower projection problems have first been resolved.

METHODS OF INSTRUCTION AND IMPLEMENTING PROGRAMS

Of equal importance to needs determination is deciding upon the methods of instruction and manner for implementing programs. No single type of presentation is "the" most effective one for all situations. The need itself, manpower to be developed, available physical facilities, costs and funds allocated, availability of instructional personnel, and urgency of the situation have a bearing on the selection of the type of presentation.

There is indeed an abundance of methods used for developing human resources. Some of them represent rather broad approaches to meeting developmental needs. Others are narrower in scope and have been developed to meet a special training need or to improve upon present methods. Still others should be distinguished by the amount of instruction received on- and off-the-job. Specific methods of teaching in on- and off-the-job programs may also vary widely.[35] The audio-visual aids and mechanical equipment available to enrich the teaching process are so diverse today that this field has become a specialism with which the manpower specialist should be familiar.

The administrative arrangements for the conduct of formal developmental activities are also important in discussing the methods of instruction and implementing programs. The impact of administration is not fully apparent until we see its consequences, which are worth examining.

Although the development of human resources in complex organizations in the United States has roots in medieval apprenticeship, the guilds, and the industrial education movement of the 19th and early 20th centuries, much of the impetus for establishing training department and training director positions in organizations was caused by the need for trained manpower in the defense mobilization period prior to World War II. Trained manpower was needed in war-production industry to replace young people entering the armed forces. But who could do the training? The supply of instructors from vocational schools was exhausted; and organizations realized that the line and staff supervisor had to carry out the manpower development function. Managements found that supervisors without skill in developing subordinates were unable to produce adequately for the defense or war effort. Yet with this skill, new production records were being established by the aged, minority group members, the handicapped, and industrially inexperienced women.[36]

---

[35] McGehee and Thayer, *op. cit.,* pp. 184–185.

[36] Cloyd S. Steinmetz, "The Evolution of Training," in Craig and Bittel, eds., *op. cit.,* p. 11.

Someone in the organization had to plan, direct, and coordinate all this new supervisory and operative employee training. Hence the training director became a necessity, and the title became common in large-scale organizations. The process of selecting training directors was often crude, arbitrary, and fortuitous, further demonstrating the imperative need for his services.[37]

TWI AND ITS INFLUENCE TODAY

Next came the massive efforts in training generated by the War Production Board and, within that organization, the Training Within Industry (TWI) group. Headed by five men who had faced the war-production manpower problems of World War I, TWI blossomed. Starting with the reformation of an on-the-job approach to training, the Job Instructor Training program (quickly shortened to JIT) was developed. It was a program oriented especially to the first- and second-level line supervisors whose need for skill in explaining their job know-how was essential to defense industry. Institutes were held throughout the country with 15–30 people in attendance. Initially the participants were given a three-day training program in how to train supervisors to use the JIT approach.[38]

JIT was all-inclusive and has left a strong imprint upon manpower development programs to this day. JIT not only taught how to instruct but also put emphasis upon the related problem of human relations between the supervisor and subordinate and the equally important matter of determining the best job methods. A spate of other programs, known to the present by their initials, followed. There was a Job Relations Training program (JRT). This was quickly followed by one known as Job Methods Training (JMT). Insofar as many workers were unfamiliar with the industrial environment (having been attracted into the labor force because of a manpower shortage), it was quite clear that a safety emphasis was needed. In response a Job Safety Training program (JST) was developed. A Program Development Training course (PDT) was developed for managers unfamiliar with training techniques. Each program was a specialized facet of the fundamentals expressed on the JIT card (shown in Figure 7), which had by the mid-1940s become famous. These ten-hour training programs were given to almost two million war production and essential-service managers.[39] They, in turn, trained some ten million war workers.[40]

Meanwhile, in order to meet the need for upgrading workers in college-

[37] *Ibid.*
[38] *Ibid.*
[39] *Ibid.*, pp. 11–12.
[40] "Training Manpower," in William M. Fox, ed., *Readings in Personnel Management from "Fortune"*, First Edition, Holt, New York, 1957, p. 43.

How To Instruct

1 PREPARE THE WORKER
 Put him at ease
 State the job and find out what he already
  knows about it.
 Get him interested in learning job.
 Place in correct position.

2 PRESENT THE OPERATION
 Tell, show and illustrate one IMPORTANT
  STEP at a time.
 Stress each KEY POINT.
 Instruct clearly, completely and patiently,
  but no more than he can master.

3 TRY OUT PERFORMANCE
 Have him do the job—correct errors.
 Have him explain each KEY POINT to you
  as he does the job again.
 Make sure he understands.
 Continue until YOU know he knows.

4 FOLLOW UP
 Put him on his own. Designate to whom
  he goes for help.
 Check frequently. Encourage questions.
 Taper off extra coaching and close follow-
  up.

 *If Worker Hasn't Learned,
 the Instructor Hasn't Taught.*

TRAINING WITHIN INDUSTRY FOUNDATION
1953

JOB INSTRUCTION

———

How To Get Ready To Instruct

HAVE A TIME TABLE—

how much skill you expect him to have,
by what date.

BREAK DOWN THE JOB—

list important steps
pick out the key points.
(Safety is always a key point.)

HAVE EVERYTHING READY—

the right equipment, materials and supplies.

HAVE THE WORKPLACE PROPERLY ARRANGED—

just as the worker will be expected to
keep it.

Figure 7   The JIT Card (front and back). Source. Training Within Industry Foundation, 1953.

level subjects, the Engineering, Science and Management War Training program (ESMWT) was started. These programs were conducted under the sponsorship and guidance of institutes of higher learning with competent academicians steering their progress. College-level courses in almost every phase of management and technology were offered.[41]

Manpower specialists today who have been directly influenced by the TWI concepts and approaches are likely to believe that one way of administering development programs is best. The foci of JRT, JMT, and JST lead them to see the foreman or supervisor as the best instructor and to consider conferences, clinics for problem solving, rough-and-ready formulas (see Figure 7), on-the-job training, vestibule training, apprenticeship, and the like as the proper methods of instruction. They believe that

---

[41] F. Steinmetz, *op. cit.*, p. 12. For other accounts of TWI see C. R. Dooley, "Training Within Industry in the United States," *International Labour Review*, Vol. 24, Nos. 3–4, September-October 1946, pp. 160–178; and Stuart Chase, *Men at Work*, Harcourt, Brace, New York, 1945, pp. 40–76.

programs should be implemented by a training coordinator. The content of programs should include a wide range of practical subjects, and the tools used for teaching should include movies, sound-slide films, cases (that have final answers), mock-ups, and perhaps some of the newer tools on a selective basis, such as programmed instruction. We posit that they would be very impressed with the orthodox learning theory that supposedly underlies operative, foreman, and certain types of other training.[42]

Manpower specialists who have backgrounds arising partly out of TWI and partly (or solely) out of company schools are likely to have a different point of view on methods of instruction and administrative arrangements for implementing development programs. Factory schools in the United States can be traced back to the 1870s and were established, of course, to meet the needs of the employer: machinists for the Hoe and Company's printing presses; apprentices for Westinghouse, General Electric, and Ford; salesmen for National Cash Register; and a wide range of employees for General Motors through the General Motors Institute. In recent decades we have seen executive development centers set up by such firms as IBM, GE, and AT & T. For the last dozen years various air transportation firms, led by American Airlines, Pan American Airways, United Airlines, and Trans World Airlines, have operated stewardess colleges or hostess training centers to meet the organization's needs for cabin womanpower, well known for short tenures of employment.[43]

There is no meaningful way to summarize what such manpower specialists advocate and administer. The institutions for education, training, and development which they operate have many unique features depending upon the type of firm, industry, and product or service. There is an emerging literature suggesting the beliefs about learning and instructional methods, but not enough to permit generalization.[44] In many instances the manpower specialists employed by these pace-setting firms are conversant with the gamut of methods of instruction and with implementing and evaluating programs. They keep up with the manpower field and are likely

[42] Such theory is found in McGehee and Thayer, op. cit., pp. 126–183; Frank A. De Phillips et al., Management of Training Programs, Irwin, Homewood, Illinois, 1960, pp. 67–128 ff; David S. King, Training within the Organization, Educational Methods, Chicago, 1964, pp. 109–124; D. H. Holding, Principles of Training, Pergamon, New York, 1965, pp. 1–119; and Bernard M. Bass and James A. Vaughan, Training in Industry: The Management of Learning, Wadsworth, Belmont, 1966, pp. 7–75.

[43] "Why Airlines Run a 'Bride School,'" Business Week, No. 1893, December 11, 1965, pp. 164–169; and Louis S. Bing, "Pan Am Stewardesses—Those 37-Day Wonders," Training in Business and Industry, Vol. 4, No. 9, September 1967, pp. 35–36.

[44] For some examples see Moorehead Wright, "Individual Growth The Basic Principles," Personnel, Vol. 37, No. 5, September-October 1960, pp. 8–17; Willard E. Bennett, Manager Selection, Education and Training, McGraw-Hill, New York, 1959; and George C. Houston, Manager Development, Irwin, Homewood, Illinois, 1961.

to engage in much action research and experimentation.[45] They have a repertoire of professional skills.

Lastly, there are manpower specialists who are serious students of behavioral change and are impressed particularly with the potential of applied behavioral science in organizations. They sometimes seem to believe that "training" is synonymous with laboratory or sensitivity training and apparently take very little interest in the broader concept of developing human resources which we have been discussing. Perhaps development to them is limited to self-development, the creation of self-awareness, and motivation to perform or change, where at least one of the basic goals is to assist individuals in learning how to learn.[46] Such a point of view turns partly away from the cognitive learning which is found in a great many formal development programs and leans toward existential learning. This difference, among many others equally fundamental, requires a method of instruction unique to laboratory training and usually a special kind of off-the-job learning environment.

Having now drawn some of the distinctions which are thought to bear upon methods of instruction, we can briefly analyze each of them. For convenience and clarity, we have grouped them according to their relevancy for on-the-job, off-the-job, and laboratory training.

Development On-the-Job

It is helpful for analytical purposes to distinguish between on-the-job and off-the-job methods, but the two are apiece. Some on-the-job learning must take place regardless of the nature and extent of training received off-the-job. If provision for transferring and reinforcing what has been learned during program participation to what must be done after training is terminated is not made, the training effort may well be wasted. Therefore, all formal development should provide for learning activities and the maintenance of acquired behavior.[47] Organizational socialization, of course, embraces both on-the-job and off-the-job development.

Distinctions can also be made between developmental methods in the degree to which the individual is expected to change his behavior through

---

[45] Among the books suggesting the sophistication, but written by academicians, are Rolf P. Lynton and Udai Pareek, *Training for Development,* Irwin, Homewood, Illinois, 1967; and Robert J. House et al., *Management Development: Design, Evaluation, and Implementation,* Bureau of Industrial Relations, University of Michigan, Ann Arbor, 1967.

[46] The general points of view suggested here can be found in Leland P. Bradford et al., eds., *T-Group Theory and Laboratory Method,* Wiley, New York, 1964; and Edgar H. Schein and Warren G. Bennis, *Personal and Organizational Change through Group Methods: The Laboratory Approach,* Wiley, New York, 1965.

[47] McGehee and Thayer, *op. cit.,* p. 185.

experiences other than actual job performance. Essentially, there is a continuum here, with one polar type being on-the-job and the other, off-the-job. Between these types are a number of intermediate methods that combine on- and off-the-job, such as in much foreman training, operative vestibule schools, and skilled-trades apprenticeship.[48]

Perhaps the most widely used method of development is on-the-job training. The learner, in acquiring job skills, knowledge, and attitudes, uses the tools, machines, equipment, materials, and other resources that he will use once his formal training is completed. He learns in the physical environment where he will ultimately be working at his regular tasks. He becomes acquainted with day-to-day operating procedures and interacts during his learning with his future organizational superiors and peers. On-the-job training can be varied from a method whereby the new employee is assigned to an experienced worker to be shown the job (the buddy system) to an arrangement whereby trained instructors are assigned to teach, guide, and evaluate the learning efforts of the trainee.[49]

On-the-job training using the buddy system, coaching by the supervisor (as in the TWI program), or more structured attempts to utilize directed work experience as the developmental vehicle have many advantages. The learner partly pays his own way by whatever he produces or does in the process of learning on the job. No special equipment needs to be set aside to instruct him because he uses job resources. From the point of view of learning theory, the method allows him to practice what he is expected to do later when his training is completed. Consequently, the problem of transfer of learning should be minimized.[50]

The disadvantages of relying solely on on-the-job training are numerous. The performance of learners, using production equipment and materials, may cause losses attendant from utilizing expensive equipment and materials to train novices. Some tasks, because of their complexity, pacing, or other pressures, may be more difficult to learn on-the-job than off-the-job, as in a vestibule school. Other methods can be less costly. Finally, the trainer used for developing the new man may be inadequate in job instruction.[51]

Well-qualified trainers may have difficulty in evaluating the success of their efforts because on-the-job effectiveness can be influenced by factors beyond the control of the trainee, such as machine breakdowns, poor stock, inadequate process engineering, and the like, depending on the job.[52]

While it is possible to create favorable circumstances for learning on-the-job, it is also very difficult. The main reason is that training on-the-job is made secondary to production on-the-job, the primary purpose in a work organization.[53] Pressures for organizational goal attainment will often override desires for manpower development, even in organizations that state they are committed to the development of human resources.

Vestibule Schools

Vestibule "school" training can be used sometimes to strengthen on-the-job training, it being the first cousin of the latter. In vestibule schools the trainee uses the same machines, tools, equipment, and materials and follows the same procedures which he would if he were learning the tasks in the actual work place. The training area is frequently removed from the actual work place (over the threshold of the shop floor and in the vestibule, as it were); and the usual pressures for production are diminished. A competent trainer should be in charge of the school. The primary purpose of the vestibule school is training, not production; therefore, the learning situation should be more favorable than on-the-job training.[54]

Despite some of the alleged advantages of the vestibule school method, it has some practical drawbacks. It may be uneconomical to use if only a small number of trainees is being developed at one time; if the machines, tools, equipment, and materials are expensive; or if the maintenance of the machines and equipment is costly. The method is not universally applicable and appears to have been used mostly to teach jobs involving machine operation, inspection, or packing. It could also be used as a method of instruction for less complex office tasks, as for example with mock-ups used in bank teller training or in getting retail clerks job-ready.[55] It is perhaps best known as a technique used to train people in plant start-ups or operation change-overs, as during the defense mobilization and war-production periods.

Vestibule training perhaps accentuates the problem of transfer of training from the learning situation to the actual workplace. The absence from the vestibule school of the pressures which make on-the-job training difficult may make it harder for the trainee to maintain behavior learned once the vestibule training is terminated. In addition, the learner must adjust to another supervisor and other peers once he completes the vestibule school. Careful planning of the activities of the trainee when he arrives on-the-job is required if the behavior learned in vestibule training is to be maintained.[56]

[53] *Ibid.*
[54] *Ibid.*, p. 188.
[55] *Ibid.*
[56] *Ibid.*

Apparently very little, if any, research has been published on the relative developmental value of on-the-job training and its cousin, vestibule school training. On-the-job training can be so loosely defined that it is tantamount to work experience; therefore, we might conclude that more hours are given to it than any other type of development experience available in American organizations. However, such an observation has little meaning and confuses the formal with the informal.

Much formal developmental activity which takes place in organizations builds upon on-the-job experience and adds such features as related instruction (as in skilled-trades apprenticeship), in-residence university-level courses (as in certain executive development programs), or classroom sessions (as in trainee foreman programs).

In general, integrated on-the-job and off-the-job programs have been used to develop manpower on jobs which require long learning periods and skills and knowledge which cannot be taught very well by sole resort to on-the-job instruction. Integrated on- and off-the-job development also has the supposed advantage of giving the learner an opportunity to practice on the job the things learned in the classroom. Correlatively, it facilitates classroom education through the interchange of ideas gained in experiences with practical day-to-day problems. Increased motivation is also claimed.[57]

Very little, if any, research has been published which demonstrates that integrated on- and off-the-job training is better than on-the-job or off-the-job used alone. The developmental value of integrated training has been accepted on faith or justified on the grounds of common sense, two unacceptable bases for manpower specialists inclined toward hard-rock empiricism. The planning of integrated programs should be based upon research and use organizational, operations, and man analyses in specific organizational contexts.

Development Off-the-Job

Off-the-job development programs are built upon learning in the classroom, laboratory, conference center, or some place other than on-the-job. Off-the-job training is usually supplemental rather than central to learning to perform the job tasks. This type of development is used more frequently in the United States in developing line and staff supervisors and other managerial manpower than it is for workers at lower levels in the organization. Yet there is no reason to think that manpower at all organizational levels cannot benefit from it, if programs are designed with their needs in mind.[58]

[57] *Ibid.*, p. 189.
[58] *Ibid.*, p. 190.

Perhaps the main reason off-the-job programs are not used very often for rank-and-file manpower is the belief that the expense of such programs (in possible lost production) is greater than the gain in improved human resources. Hard-nosed management is simply not convinced that off-the-job programs for the rank-and-file pay their way and often accepts such programs for higher-level manpower with reluctance. To this day, little experimental research has been published which demonstrates the value of off-the-job programs, particularly from the standpoint of behavioral change. Often it seems that organizations support the programs on the convoluted rationale: you cannot afford not to do it! Consistent with the argument we have made before, these programs should emanate from research studies, using organizational, operations, and man analyses.

The most impressive characteristic of off-the-job programs is their variation in substance and method. They can range from a one-hour course in "new plant safety rules," to a one-day course on "how to give a performance review," to six three-hour sessions after working hours on "rapid reading," to in-residence university-level executive development courses lasting several months or even one year, culminating in a master's degree. The programs may be organized and taught by company managers or professionals or they can be staffed by a variety of outside groups, ranging from colleges to consulting firms and employer or other associations. Programs may be conducted at locations inside the organization, on college campuses, or at distant resorts.[59] The costs of these efforts across the board are astronomical and could be up to $17 billion depending upon what factors one wished to include in his cost calculations.[60]

Off-the-job development is needed for manpower occupying positions for which formal education and training would be difficult if the trainees were not taken away from their jobs. Students of management have frequently made the point that day-to-day immersion in the details of a job, especially at higher organizational levels, makes it difficult to encourage changes in behavior associated with such activities as long-range planning, understanding complex subject matter (particularly if new), and learning how to relate broad principles to specific issues. In addition, an organization may not have the instructional or other resources to conduct such programs by itself.[61]

A major weakness of off-the-job programs is that they may fail to incorporate materials which will contribute to the transfer of learning.

[59] *Ibid.,* p. 191.

[60] Charles T. Schmidt, Jr., "Education: Can Business Do a Better Job?," *Management of Personnel Quarterly,* Vol. 7, No. 1, Spring 1968, p. 38. For lower estimates, see Lynton and Pareek, *op. cit.,* pp. vii and 3.

[61] McGehee and Thayer, *op. cit.,* p. 191.

Seldom are provisions explicitly made for the application of principles learned to the job or to follow-up to assist in such a transfer.[62] The proliferation of specific methods used to carry out off-the-job programs further complicates the measurement of results. For example, the novelty of the method may result in entertainment which is favorably reported on a testimonial-type questionnaire. However, in reality not only was the experience of no developmental value but also it never carried the potential of being transferrable to the work situation!

In order to meaningfully discuss off-the-job methods, we must step down to the plane of teaching or instructional techniques used. This plane is comprised of a bewildering thicket through which we cut a wide swath rather than get bogged down. We skip over descriptions of the obvious facets of the different instructional techniques and emphasize instead the salient features of each.

It is rarely possible to evaluate the off-the-job techniques in relationship to one another because little research evidence is available on which to formulate persuasive demonstrable reasoning. For the sake of convenience and clarity again, we discuss first all those techniques in which there is human interaction (such as the lecture, conference, case method, incident process, role playing, and management games and simulation); next those in which there is essentially personal study oriented toward skill improvement (such as reading programs of various kinds and correspondence courses); and last, those which use mechanical devices to an appreciable extent, such as programmed instruction with "hardware" and "software," and the most recent emergent, computer-assisted instruction.

Then, having completed our discussion of on-the-job and off-the-job techniques we turn to laboratory training, the third and last of the main methods that we have been stressing in this chapter.

TECHNIQUES INVOLVING HUMAN INTERACTION

Figure 8 shows the various teaching or instructional techniques used on a scale of relative concreteness–abstractness in human experience. In any given program it is possible to combine the use of various of these techniques. We thus begin our discussion with the method at the apex, the lecture. Yet, it should be kept in mind that the most popular techniques actually used by organizations with well-established development programs probably are on-the-job training, conferences and discussions, job rotation, special assignments to projects, and case analyses.[63]

[62] *Ibid.*, pp. 191–192.
[63] Wayne J. Foreman, "Management Training in Large Corporations," *Training and Development Journal,* Vol. 21, No. 5, May 1967, pp. 11–17.

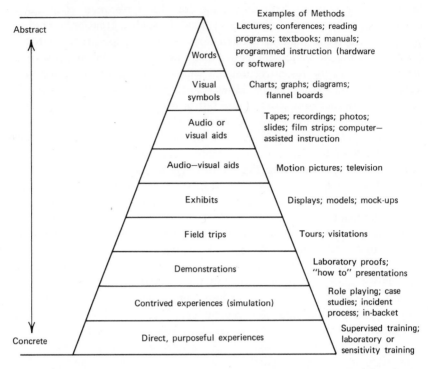

Figure 8   The pyramid of learning. *Source.* Louis S. Goodman, "Training Comes to Its Senses," *Journal of the American Society of Training Directors,* June 1959, p. 31, and Edgar Dale, *Audio-Visual Methods in Teaching,* The Dryden Press, New York, 1951, p. 39, as combined in Don R. Sheriff, *Guidelines for Employee Training,* Information Series No. 6, Bureau of Labor and Management, State University of Iowa, June 1963, p. 9, and published in Dalton E. McFarland, *Personnel Management Theory and Practice,* MacMillan, New York, 1968, p. 305, modified by the author.

    In general, the more the instructor knows about the subject and the less that the trainee group knows, the more the instructor and manpower specialist should consider using the lecture. Conversely, the more experience the group has with the subject, the more consideration should be given to the conference or some related group-participative method. If a group is large (more than 20 persons), the lecture may be the best and most economical initial method, which can then be followed by small group activity. If time is a factor, the lecture can be used to direct facts, principles, and concepts to the trainees' attention faster than such information can be drawn from them through case analyses, the incident process, or conference discussion. When the group is not knowledgeable on the subject, but adequate cases, incidents, films, or texts are available, then the group may be able to study these and become sufficiently informed in advance of the training session so that the conference-discussion method could be used. Research evidence suggests that straight, factual, descriptive, or explanatory material may best be learned by direct absorption by the learner. Programmed instruction would thus be appropriate in these circumstances and also because it provides learners the best opportunity to learn at their own speed. However, principles and concepts, such as those concerned with attitudinal and behavioral change, may best be learned by participation of the learner during the instruction period rather than through a lecture.[64] Although the deficiencies of the lecture have been well stated,[65] there are those who use it effectively in organizational settings by restricting its use to where it is appropriate and by using persons as lecturers who are skilled in presenting materials.[66] Unless a question-and-answer period follows the lecture, instructor–trainee interaction is obviously minimal.

Conferences and Conference Leadership

The conference method is widely used to supplement on-the-job development activities as well as to surmount the limitations of the lecture. When inadequately handled, the conference can become a conversational boat ride on unchartered seas to an unknown port.[67] If properly handled, a conference is a pooling of experiences and opinions among a group of people who have all had experience related to the problem or among people who are capable of analyzing the problem from information provided by the conference leader. Such a conference should promote definite constructive thinking by individuals and the group.

As a developmental technique, a conference is successful to the degree to which all participants contribute from their own experiences and comment upon the experiences and opinions of others and to the degree to which all come to understand the significance of group experience and opinion. The educational outcome of a conference is not dependent upon reaching an agreement. A conference that results in a disagreement which all clearly understand may be just as fruitful developmentally as one in which all agree.[68]

The effectiveness of the conference method depends largely upon the

[64] Harold P. Zelko, "The Lecture," in Craig and Bittel, eds., *op. cit.*, pp. 141–142.

[65] McGehee and Thayer, *op. cit.*, pp. 196–197.

[66] See Willard E. Bennett, "The Lecture as a Management Training Technique," *Personnel,* Vol. 32, No. 6, May 1959, pp. 497–507; and David S. Brown, "The Lecture . . . and How to Make It More Effective," *Journal of the American Society of Training Directors,* Vol. 14, No. 12, December 1960, pp. 17–22.

[67] Earl G. Planty et al., *Training Employees and Managers,* Ronald, New York, 1948, p. 182.

[68] Louis W. Lerda, "Conference Methods," in Craig and Bittel, eds., *op. cit.*, pp. 155–157.

competence and ability of the conference leader and his skill in eliciting interaction among the conferees. To accomplish maximum results in a given time, the typical conference group needs a leader to keep the discussion on the subject and thoroughly explore it. However, the conference leader's function is not to supply information or to do the thinking for the group. Since we have stated that in meaningful conference groups the conferees usually have all the information necessary for solving their problems and the conferees are expected to do their own thinking, the conference leader acts as a director and resource person rather than an instructor or lecturer. When the time comes, he helps to state the principle, rule, or explanation which seems to be the consensus of the group in analyzing the problem or the sum total of the information which they pooled. In providing this help, the conference leader assists group thinking.[69]

Conference leadership theory fits in nicely with organizations that attempt to solve problems and make decisions at the point of action. In highly centralized, hierarchical organizations the theory conflicts with the delegation of authority and cannot be meaningfully used.[70] Also, although conferences may theoretically be used in developing human resources at all organizational levels, they are most often used for supervisory and managerial personnel.

Lectures and conferences are useful in providing information about problems. But for supervisory and managerial work the real skill of the manager, in addition to acquiring knowledge and information, depends upon his attitudes, approaches, and actions in specific and complex situations where he must exercise problem-analysis and decision-making skills. Formal education is obviously unable to provide him with an answer to every situation with which he will be faced in his career. The case study method can be used to assist the learner in developing some skills in the self-sufficient use of analysis, clear reasoning, imagination, and judgment.[71]

Case Method

The case method (where cases are used exclusively) is quite different from the occasional use of cases in a training program. Using cases on an intermittent basis is perhaps the easiest way to make the transition from traditional cognitive styles of learning in orthodox training classrooms to more dynamic learner-involved participatory and existential styles of learning. Thus experimenting with the use of cases on a limited basis can

---

[69] *Ibid.,* pp. 157–158.
[70] Richard L. Dean, "The Conference Method: Panacea or Paradox?," *Journal of the American Society of Training Directors,* Vol. 13, No. 12, December 1959, p. 15.
[71] Zoll, *op. cit.,* p. 4–1.

gradually lead to the increasing use of cases and other dynamic techniques.[72]

The case method dates back to the 1880s when it was first used in the Harvard Law School. It has since been widely used in medical schools and business schools as well as in manpower development programs in organizations. Today there are numerous kinds of cases and varying concepts of the case study method.[73]

In its simplest form a case is a written slice of life used as a vehicle for discussion among trainees in a conference. They are given a chance to read the case (or see it on film or hear it on tape); and, through discussion and questions, they are expected to analyze the principles and practices integral to it. Rather than start as in a lecture with the principle and give illustrations of its application, the trainees are asked to study, discuss, and discover the underlying principles in the case and, usually, come to a conclusion. A basic assumption is that material so taught will be more meaningful than lectures and that the individual will learn and remember better those things which he discovers for himself. It is also usually assumed that the problem in a case does not have *a* solution but rather many, each of which is equally plausible depending upon the facts available for analysis and the premises considered.[74]

The lack of a definitive solution often irritates trainees when first exposed to learning through case analyses, and the conference leader's unwillingness to pose as the man with the final answers may heighten the irritation. A partial resolution of those difficulties is found in telling the conferees what really happened in the case (assuming it is not a contrived case) without implying the outcome is a recommended solution. With or without this feature, cases provide excellent practice in problem solving and decision making.

In practice, cases range from fabricated and abbreviated episodes to long chronicles of events in an organization. For example, the incident process is a shortened case which requires written analyses and quickly getting to the issues in an episode. The live case is a longer report of events that have just happened or are still taking place, often presented by a key person or people from the organization where the case situation developed. The British have made clever use of living case material in the residential Administrative Staff College at Henley-on-Thames. Here 66 participants are subdivided into "syndicates" of 10 members. They discuss cases from

[72] *Ibid.*, pp. 5–15.

[73] For excellent background see Kenneth B. Andrews, ed., *The Case Method of Teaching Human Relations and Administration: An Interim Statement,* Graduate School of Business Administration, Harvard University, Boston, 1953.

[74] McGehee and Thayer, *op. cit.,* pp. 201–202.

real life, break down the various problems raised into specific assignments given to individuals or teams to tackle, and later reconvene the syndicates to report to a plenary session of the 66 participants.[75]

Role Playing

Lectures, conferences, and case analyses all suffer from the grave disadvantage that they are confined to "talking about" rather than "doing."[76] Role playing involves action, doing, and dynamic practice. The technique makes it possible for individuals and groups to improve their effectiveness not by talking about problems and solutions but by actually doing something about them.

This action goal of role playing is accomplished by people playing parts or roles (their own or someone else's) in a hypothetical drama or real situation. Its origins can be traced back to the work of Dr. J. L. Moreno who developed psychodrama and sociodrama as well as other techniques useful in psychotherapy. Various specific techniques associated with acting are associated with role playing (such as soliloquy, role rotation and reversal, and alter ego doubling), but the basic process of interaction between people is the essence of the method. The enactment of situations, spontaneity, experimentation, practice, feedback, and analysis are the key ingredients of the technique.[77]

Role playing can be combined with the case method, thereby providing opportunities for trainees' using case studies to show how they would practice what they preach by acting out recommendations that might otherwise remain mere verbalizations.

Both role playing and the case method: provide a means for presenting a standard situation to all persons; enable a free exchange of views through discussion; cause a high degree of trainee interest through their personal involvement; offer stimulating ways of presenting problems; are taken from real-life situations; are oriented toward skill development; encourage the statement of multiple solutions to problems by the participants rather than the "best" solution by the instructor; and make it possible for participants to practice skills without anyone getting hurt in the process.[78]

[75] Paul Pigors, "Case Method," in Craig and Bittel, eds., op. cit., pp. 173–182. See also "It's Almost Like Working," Business Week, No. 1718, August 4, 1962, pp. 94–95; and "Bared by a B-School," Business Week, No. 1802, March 14, 1964, pp. 90–92.

[76] Alex Bavelas, "Role Playing and Management Training," Sociatry, Vol. 1, No. 2, June 1947, p. 184.

[77] Malcolm E. Shaw, "Role Playing," in Craig and Bittel, eds., op. cit., pp. 206–212.

[78] Pigors, op. cit., pp. 177–178, citing Allen R. Solem, "Human Relations Training: Comparison of Case Study and Role Playing," Personnel Administration, Vol. 23, No. 5, September-October 1960, pp. 29–37, 51.

Problem Solving, Decision Making, and Creativity

In the 1960s manpower specialists witnessed the combination of various methods of training in sophisticated packages to develop managerial skills in manpower in organizations. For example, reference is often made in management development to "the problem-solving process," "the decision-making process," or "the creative process" as if to suggest that problem solving, decision making, and creative thinking each involve a single process. We might even assume from the ideas of some experts that problem solving can be clearly distinguished from decision making or from creative thinking in terms of the processes involved. The view is also sometimes expressed that creativity should be defined in terms of some unique process.[79]

It now appears that, on the contrary, each of the processes involves a variety of sub-processes. Moreover, it seems that the processes important in problem solving are also often important in decision making or creative thinking. Therefore, distinctions in these activities may best be made not in terms of process but in reference to the product. Creativity may thus be defined as that thinking which results in the production of ideas (or other products) that are both novel and worthwhile. Decision making is that thinking which results in the choice among alternative courses of action. Problem solving is that thinking which results in the solution of problems. From this point of view, problem solving, decision making, and creativity are kinds of thinking. They would all be part of a general theory of thinking but the task of constructing such a theory is very complex and presently out of range.[80] It is therefore not surprising that attempts have been made to develop programs for developing competency in people in such presumably separate areas as problem solving, decision making, and creativity. Some of these should be mentioned by way of illustration of recent trends in combining instructional methods in sophisticated ways.

A widely used program originated by Kepner and Tregoe helps participants to develop skills in problem analysis and decision making.[81] Their basic one-week program is an ingenious combination of such methods as

[79] Donald W. Taylor, "Decision Making and Problem Solving," in March, ed., *op. cit.,* p. 48.

[80] *Ibid.,* pp. 48–49.

[81] See Charles H. Kepner and Benjamin B. Tregoe, "Developing Decision Makers," *Harvard Business Review,* Vol. 38, No. 5, September-October 1960, pp. 115–124; Perrin Stryker, "Can You Analyze This Problem?," *Harvard Business Review,* Vol. 43, No. 3, May-June 1965, pp. 73–78; and Perrin Stryker, "How to Analyze That Problem," *Harvard Business Review,* Vol. 43, No. 4, July-August 1965, pp. 99–110. See also Charles H. Kepner and Benjamin B. Tregoe, *The Rational Manager,* McGraw-Hill, New York, 1965, pp. 229–241.

the lecture, assigned outside reading material, role playing, case study, in-basket, and simulation (a business game). The program presents new ideas, new skills, or new ways of approaching old ideas and skills; an opportunity to put these innovations into practical action; and feedback as to (1) the results of the actions taken and (2) the relationship between what was done at each step of the way and the end result. Participants are given a chance to learn concepts, use them, and get an evaluation of how well they performed. In the process they learn much about their communications skills, ability to devise creative solutions to problems, and their collaborative skills in interpersonal relations.

More recently, still other work has been done on approaches to decision making which focus on decision "trees," essentially a new way of making the decision-making process more visible by showing how the subsystems leading to a decision may be elaborated into a physical configuration resembling the trunk, branches, and stems of a tree.[82]

Creativity has been approached various ways, and some of the classical questions about it remain unanswered, such as whether there is a difference between creativity in the arts, literature, science, management and the like and whether creativity is a function of the individual or the group, or both in some way.[83]

Under the designation "brainstorming" or "imagineering" organizational interest in the subject can be traced back to the thinking of a now deceased but well-known advertising agency executive.[84] Considerable research on brainstorming continues [85] and organizations report utilization of creativity programs.[86]

Synectics

In the last two decades a new operational concept of human creativity, called synectics, which is useful for finding and solving problems, has been

[82] John F. Magee, "Decision Trees for Decision Making," *Harvard Business Review,* Vol. 42, No. 4, July-August 1964, pp. 126–138; John F. Magee, "How to Use Decision Trees in Capital Investment," *Harvard Business Review,* Vol. 42, No. 5, September-October 1964, pp. 79–90; and John S. Hammond III, "Better Decisions with Preference Theory," *Harvard Business Review,* Vol. 45, No. 6, November-December 1967, pp. 123–141.

[83] Brewster Ghiselin, ed., *The Creative Process,* New American Library, New York, 1952.

[84] Alex F. Osborne, *Applied Imagination,* Third Revised Edition, Scribner's Sons, New York, 1963.

[85] See, for example, Marvin D. Dunnette et al., "The Effect of Group Participation on Brainstorming Effectiveness for Two Industrial Samples," *Journal of Applied Psychology,* Vol. 47, No. 1, February 1963, pp. 30–37.

[86] David L. Ward, "Creative Thinking," *Journal of the American Society of Training Directors,* Vol. 14, No. 10, October 1960, pp. 18–29.

formulated. It goes far beyond brainstorming and is a contribution to the theory of thinking.

The word synectics is a neologism coined by W. J. J. Gordon and means the fitting together of diverse elements. Synectics is particularly concerned with problems which require an innovative solution, problems whose solution cannot be derived by applying known formulas or available textbook knowledge. Instead synectics assumes that: creativity is latent in almost everyone to a greater degree than is usually suspected; when it comes to creativity and invention, the emotional and nonrational are as important as the intellectual and rational; and these emotional, nonrational elements can be methodically harnessed through training and practice— especially in metaphorical and analogical thinking which makes the familiar strange and thus a source for new insights. Using these assumptions, a special program is used involving two-week sessions in which techniques oscillate between the rational analysis of the real problem and the search for nonrational analogies, reported as like a psychedelic LSD party.[87]

Synectics thus takes a radically different tack from the Kepner-Tregoe programs. Both have been used by major corporate organizations in the United States. Both represent important combinations of developmental techniques involving interaction arrayed in different combinations but aimed at an apparently common complex subject matter close to the heart of organizational management.

Gaming

Mention has already been made of management games or exercises which utilize a model or simulation of a business situation for learning purposes. Gaming has been used by military organizations for centuries. Gaming has become popular in developing certain managerial skills among executives and business-school students in the past dozen years. The growth and popularity of gaming has paralleled the diffusion of computers, although there are many noncomputer games. Similarly, games may be oriented to the total organization or business (which is most common) or to only one functional field (such as marketing, personnel, or finance).

In the typical game, executives or students playing executive roles are grouped into teams representing the management of competing organizations and make the same type of operating and policy decisions that they do in real life. Using the set of mathematical relationships built into the model, the decisions are processed (often by computer) and result in a

[87] Tom Alexander, "Synectics: Inventing by the Madness Method," *Fortune,* Vol. 72, No. 2, August 1965, pp. 165–168, 190–194. See also W. J. J. Gordon, *Synectics,* Harper, New York, 1961; and George M. Prince, *The Practice of Creativity,* Harper and Row, New York, 1970.

series of performance reports. These decisions and reports pertain to a specific time period, which, depending upon the model, may range from one day to a month or year. Decisions are then made by the term for the next period. They too are processed, reports are returned, and the game proceeds. In this manner time is compressed, and many years of operations can be covered in one short play, such as a few hours in a day.[88]

Management games may be used for a variety of reasons. The primary one is the opportunity to learn from experience without paying the price that would result from the wrong decisions made in real life. This is, of course, the reason that war games have had a strong appeal to military planners over the centuries. Management games are used today for quite serious purposes. They can be exciting and powerful techniques for learning—with numerous applications for problem solving, decision making, research, and employee testing and selection.

However, the game player learns more about handling a large number of interacting variables simultaneously and the compounding effects of decisions over time than he does about the interpersonal process of decision making. The computer model's philosophy of expenditure is a key consideration in gaming and a constraint in the player's behavior.[89] For this and other reasons some managers might prefer simpler noncomputer games.[90] Yet games continue to be popular.[91]

Games can be combined with the in-basket method.[92] The in-basket is a simulation of the executive's in and out desk trays containing reports, memoranda, mail, and other typical items entering his office in-basket. In a game he is required to read these items, analyze the problems they present, perceive their interconnectedness, and determine a course of action much as he would in carrying out work in his organizational position back home.

Data input for games can be delivered to players in in-basket fashion to

[88] Clifford J. Craft, "Management Games," in Craig and Bittel, eds., *op. cit.,* pp. 267–268.

[89] Kepner and Tregoe, "Developing Decision Makers," *op. cit.,* p. 118.

[90] Lawrence L. Steinmetz, "Management Games—Computer Versus Non-Computer," *Journal of the American Society of Training Directors,* Vol. 16, No. 9, September 1962, pp. 38–45.

[91] Adair Smith et al., "General Motors Institute Experiences with Business Games," *Journal of the American Society of Training Directors,* Vol. 15, No. 4, April 1961, pp. 27–32; and Robert W. Dobles and Robert F. Zimmerman, "Management Training Using Business Games," *Training and Development Journal,* Vol. 20, No. 6, June 1966, pp. 28–34.

[92] Andrew A. Daly, "In-Basket Business Game," *Journal of the American Society of Training Directors,* Vol. 14, No. 8, August 1960, pp. 8–15; and George W. Gibson, "A New Dimension for 'In-Basket' Training," *Personnel,* Vol. 38, No. 4, July-August 1961, pp. 76–79.

simulate additionally the work situation. This procedure is used in the aforementioned Kepner-Tregoe program. The in-basket has also been used as a manpower selection device in employment, as previously mentioned.

TECHNIQUES STRESSING INDIVIDUAL STUDY AND SELF-IMPROVEMENT

Many of the developmental programs used today center upon ways to improve some facet of individual communication skill, such as speaking, listening, reading, writing, and, of course, getting along with people. Personal tickler systems for remembering and other techniques may even be included under the multitude of actions geared to self-improvement. Dale Carnegie courses and public-speaking courses are well known and widely available.

Communication is a broad concept whose meaning embraces a wide range of phenomena. It is inseparable from human interaction and organizations except for the purposes of analysis. It runs the gamut of organizational levels.[93] Much of the training needed to improve communications starts by making trainees aware of their habits and practices which block the sending and receiving of information.[94] In recent years a new interest has been shown in courses on listening and improving one's skills in this neglected aspect of communication.[95] Although these new communications programs stress individual improvement, they do not imply isolated individual study as the instructional method.

Reading

Reading courses of various types most closely approximate the technique of self-study. In this context, reading may be viewed as a way of learning, changing, and developing. The ideas and feelings aroused while reading become part of the person's total background of experience and can become integrated with it. Reading allows an individual to learn vicariously and permits the cumulative buildup of knowledge.[96]

[93] Robert N. McMurry, "Clear Communications for Chief Executives," *Harvard Business Review,* Vol. 43, No. 2, March-April 1965, pp. 131–147.

[94] Ralph G. Nichols, "Barriers to Communication," *Training Directors Journal,* Vol. 19, No. 8, August 1965, pp. 20–38.

[95] Walter S. Wikstrom, "Lessons in Listening," *Conference Board Record,* Vol. 2, No. 4, April 1965, pp. 17–20; Paul M. Hollingsworth, "Listening Training Course—A Must," *Training Directors Journal,* Vol. 20, No. 7, August 1966, pp. 46–47; and Nile W. Soik and Donald L. Kirkpatrick, "Effective Listening," *Training and Development Journal,* Vol. 22, No. 8, August 1968, pp. 31–35.

[96] J. E. Donald Hastie, "Related Reading," in Craig and Bittel, eds., *op. cit.,* pp. 285–286.

Many managers in organizations have little time to read and may be said to read with their ears, that is, by listening to the oral communications of others and interrogating them. For these managers skill in asking discerning questions is a prime tool. They are nonreaders but proficient interrogators.

Reading courses range from the planned reading of great books[97] to programs whereby readers get a chance to question the author.[98]

A different twist in reading programs is that aimed at improving the mature reader's speed and comprehension in reading. Although there are charlatans marketing inadequate rapid-reading programs, there is much evidence that professionally adequate programs can improve the reader's speed and comprehension. However, the exact nature of the change, its ultimate value in relation to the learner, and how long it will last are not known.[99]

Writing

Writing skill is equally important in many organizational positions. Yet, actually of the billions of dollars spent upon written communications, the amount of thinking and effort that goes into improving the effectiveness of business writing is very small.[100] There are a few novel programs,[101] but much more needs to be done. Many programs available seem to be at the level of sophistication of high-school texts which emphasize the formalities of business and social letter writing but actually do not address themselves to the skill components of successful written communications in organizations.

Correspondence Courses

Correspondence study is another type of self-study, often called home study. This method involves the instruction of an individual where the communication medium between the trainee and the source of instruction

[97] Ralph C. Hook, Jr., "Executive Development—A Different Approach," *Training Directors Journal,* Vol. 17, No. 11, November 1963, pp. 29–31.

[98] Robert V. Moore, "Meet the Author: Executive Training at Johnson & Johnson Takes a New Twist," *Personnel,* Vol. 43, No. 2, March-April 1966, pp. 46–50.

[99] William J. Underwood, "A Critique of Reading Improvement Training," *Training and Development Journal,* Vol. 21, No. 3, March 1967, pp. 14–21; Dan H. Jones and Theodore J. Carron, "Evaluation of a Reading Development Program for Scientists and Engineers," *Personnel Psychology,* Vol. 18, No. 3, Autumn 1965, pp. 281–296; and Dan H. Jones, "Training Industrial Executives in Reading: A Methodology Study," *Journal of Applied Psychology,* Vol. 49, No. 3, June 1965, pp. 202–204.

[100] John S. Fielden, " 'What Do You Mean I Can't Write?,' " *Harvard Business Review,* Vol. 42, No. 3, May-June 1964, pp. 144–157; and John S. Fielden, "For Better Business Writing," *Harvard Business Review,* Vol. 43, No. 1, January-February 1965, pp. 164–172.

[101] Robert Gunning, *New Guide to More Effective Writing in Business and Industry,* Industrial Education Institute, Boston, 1962.

is by mail. Correspondence study has been used extensively in more than 10,000 organizations where adults do not find it practical or possible to participate in conferences or classes. Communication between the trainee and the instructor takes place through the written rather than the spoken word. Correspondence study proceeds at the pace of the individual. Learning takes place when and where it is convenient for the individual and at his own pace. Slow learners and fast learners are not tied to the group pace, nor does the individual suffer gaps in his learning from being absent from a class. Correspondence courses can also be reduced to programmed texts.[102] The self-pacing and mail-out features render correspondence courses convenient and practicable in large organizations with far-flung operations.[103]

Tuition Refunds

Partaking of both self-study and formal classroom settings are tuition refund programs, which are becoming increasingly popular today. These programs provide partial or full financial reimbursement for employees of organizations after they complete the course, sometimes provided they attain a certain quality point average. Paid educational leaves of absence policies are becoming more common too.

Courses for which the tuition is refundable may be taken either on a correspondence study basis[104] or in universities, depending upon the organization's policies on the development of human resources.[105]

In conclusion, mention should be made of two other concepts in developing people that involve both self-study and formal classroom settings, depending upon the program being considered. These are the short courses for labor union members found in American universities[106] and unions[107] as well as those used contemporarily in Britain.[108] Most large unions have

[102] John E. Walsh, "PL-100 Programmed Instruction for Correspondence Courses," *Journal of the American Society of Training Directors,* Vol. 16, No. 8, August 1962, pp. 22–30.

[103] Hal V. Kelley, "Correspondence Study," in Craig and Bittel, eds., *op. cit.,* pp. 297–299.

[104] *Ibid.,* pp. 303–308.

[105] Ernest E. McMahon, "Universities and Their Extensions," pp. 440–458, and Patrick C. Farbro, "Scientific and Technical Personnel Development," pp. 474–492, in Craig and Bittel, eds., *op. cit.*

[106] Lois Gray, "The American Way in Labor Education," *Industrial Relations,* Vol. 5, No. 2, February 1966, pp. 53–66.

[107] Brendan Sexton, "Staff and Officer Training to Build Successful Unions," *Industrial Relations,* Vol. 5, No. 2, February 1966, pp. 83–96; and Herbert A. Levine, "Will Labor Educators Meet Today's Challenges?," *Industrial Relations,* Vol. 5, No. 2, February 1966, pp. 97–106.

[108] Robert F. Banks, "Labor Education's New Role in Britain," *Industrial Relations,* Vol. 5, No. 2, February 1966, pp. 67–82.

educational departments which offer training in techniques needed to be an effective citizen, union member, and union leader.

Preretirement Programs

Developing people for retirement from organizations is, lastly, a concept of growing importance.[109] The concept is a much newer one than labor education, which extends back a century.

Preretirement counseling and training programs would seem to be potentially important accompaniments of a well-rounded approach to manpower planning and the development of human resources. Such programs are logical outgrowths of plans for organizational egress to the same extent that manpower projections are useful in planned ingress. Postretirement programs may also have a place, as is now the case with some union senior citizen educational activities. Adult education programs of many types are growing rapidly in the United States and covering topics and clientele once considered beyond the pale of developmental activity.

Teaching Machines

In the last decade and one-half there has been a revolution in educational technology popularly known as the "teaching machine" revolution. It is worth a brief look.

Programmed instruction has evolved over the past forty years through two main channels: university research and development and military research and development. Professor Sidney L. Pressey while at the Ohio State University designed several devices in the 1920s for automatically testing and scoring students' progress in mastering material. Multiple-choice questions were presented to the student, and the machine would not advance until the student pressed the appropriate button. Pressey found that students who had been tested by his machine had, when they were tested again, learned significantly more than those who had not used the machines. Pressey predicted that teaching machines of his type would revolutionize education.[110] However, little interest was aroused in his work for several reasons. American educators had not yet been jarred by the post-sputnik revolution; there was little concern about a teacher shortage; research in the psychology of learning was not as advanced as it is today; and Pressey's early emphasis was on testing, not teaching.

---

[109] Alastair Heron, "Preparation for Retirement: A New Phase in Occupational Development," *Occupational Psychology,* Vol. 36, Nos. 1 and 2, January and April 1962, pp. 1–9.

[110] Sidney L. Pressey, "A Simple Apparatus Which Gives Tests and Scores and Teaches," *School and Society,* Vol. 23, No. 586, March 20, 1926, pp. 373–376; and "A Third and Fourth Contribution Toward the Coming 'Industrial Revolution in Education,' " *School and Society,* Vol. 36, No. 934, November 19, 1932, pp. 668–672.

Turning to military research and development, the training demands of World War II stimulated work on several devices which were quite similar to present-day teaching machines. But the programs were not as well developed because the emphasis was still on testing. In the early 1950s, however, Norman Crowder, who was engaged in training research for the Air Force, and Professor B. F. Skinner, the renowned Harvard psychologist, began independent development of the programming methods which underlie programmed instruction as we understand it today. Crowder developed the branching (intrinsic) method, and Skinner, the linear (extrinsic) method.

The Crowder method utilizes multiple-choice questions to test the student frequently. If a correct choice is always made, the student progresses through a program in the shortest sequence of programmed frames. If a wrong choice is made, he is given further instruction by "branching" out to other frames which contain more elementary material. The programming is called "intrinsic" because the actual sequence followed by the student is determined by his responses.

The Skinner extrinsic method requires the student to construct each response on-the-spot instead of choosing one alternative from a set of multiple-choice answers. The steps in a linear program follow what we might call a straight-line, catechetical approach rather than branching.

Today sophisticated programmers are mixing the Crowder and Skinner approaches to attain greater flexibility and to give students a change of pace. For example, there are linear-branching programs which may employ both constructed and choice responses or only choice responses.

In 1958 when Skinner described his method [111] the time was ripe for diffusion of this innovation. Shortages of teachers and demands for increased efforts to produce scientists and engineers "to keep up with the Russians" had created a climate receptive to programmed instruction. Interest spread rapidly in the military, schools, universities, government agencies, foundations, and industry. Within five years almost every major publisher either had published or planned to publish programs. Almost 900 programs were available from various sources. Several years ago, it was estimated that about 25 percent of the large companies were using programmed learning on a regular or experimental basis and many other organizations were keeping an eye on developments.[112] Programmed instruction is thus today an important field in educational technology.

[111] B. F. Skinner, "Teaching Machines," *Science,* Vol. 128, No. 3330, October 24, 1958, pp. 969–977.

[112] Harold L. Moon, "Progress Report on Programmed Instruction," in Jerome W. Blood, ed., *The Personnel Job in a Changing World,* AMA Report No. 80, American Management Association, New York, 1964, pp. 262–264.

"Hardware" or the machine itself is not needed to obtain favorable learning results. Indeed "software" programs carefully built to teach the terminal behaviors or goals of the program are equally acceptable and save the expense of machine purchase or lease.

Research results have been published indicating the value of programmed instruction as contrasted with conventional methods of instructing adults in industry. For example, in one industrial study at IBM it was found that there was a significant difference in only one of three measures of achievement in a course on electricity made available in "automated" instructional form and in conventional instructor-classroom form, although the group trained by the programmed device completed the course in 18 percent less time.[113] However, other nonindustrial studies have also suggested that differences in achievement among matched groups trained by conventional and programmed techniques have been slight.[114] Savings in training time by using programmed instruction have repeatedly been claimed.[115] Programmed instruction has been found useful in correspondence courses,[116] is a productive training tool,[117] and is well liked by users as a means for learning.[118] Finally, programmed learning and conventional

[113] W. Bruce Douglass and Warren Wong, "A Comparative Evaluation of Student Performance Under Automated and Nonautomated Learning Conditions," *American Psychologist*, Vol. 18, No. 7, July 1963, p. 428. Earlier research conducted at IBM also supports this conclusion.

[114] John L. Hughes, "Effect of Changes in Programmed Text Format and Reduction in Classroom Time on the Achievement and Attitude of Industrial Trainees," *Journal of Programmed Instruction*, Vol. 1, No. 1, Spring 1962, pp. 43–54; John E. Walsh, "Research of an Experiment Utilizing Programmed Instructional Material with Correspondence School Students," *AID*, Vol. 2, No. 9, December 1962, pp. 198–201; and Richard E. Ripple, "A Comparison of the Effectiveness of a Programmed Text with Three Other Methods of Presentation," *AID*, Vol. 2, No. 11, February 1963, pp. 218–220.

[115] Hughes, *op. cit.*; and John L. Hughes and Walter J. McNamara, "A Comparative Study of Programmed and Conventional Instruction in Industry," *Journal of Applied Psychology*, Vol. 45, No. 4, August 1961, pp. 225–231. See also such typical studies as Roger W. Christian, "Guides to Programmed Learning," *Harvard Business Review*, Vol. 40, No. 6, November-December 1962, pp. 36–44, 173–179; E. Gifford Burnap, "On-the-Job Instruction with Programmed Tapes," *Training Directors Journal*, Vol. 19, No. 10, October 1965, pp. 42–48; and George Douglas Mayo and Alexander A. Longo, "Training Time and Programmed Instruction," *Journal of Applied Psychology*, Vol. 50, No. 1, February 1966, pp. 1–4.

[116] Walsh, "PL-100 Programmed Instruction for Correspondence Courses," *op. cit.*, pp. 22–30.

[117] D. Wallis, "Experiments on the Use of Programmed Instruction to Increase the Productivity of Training," *Occupational Psychology*, Vol. 38, Nos. 3 and 4, July and October 1964, pp. 141–160.

[118] Charles O. Neidt and Terry F. Meredith, "Changes in Attitudes of Learners When Programmed Instruction Is Interpolated between Two Conventional Instruction Experiences," *Journal of Applied Psychology*, Vol. 50, No. 2, April 1966, pp. 130–137.

instruction have been viewed as equally worthwhile depending upon the needs of the learning group, their learning ability level, and their motivation to learn.[119]

Programmed instruction can thus preserve many of the advantages of the human instructor and, by the use of the printed page, provide economical and carefully presented material. In recent years there has been some exciting speculation concerning the future of teaching machines. Some experts envisage machines of greater complexity capable of performing in much the same manner as a human tutor.[120]

One futuristic concept that is already with us is CAI, Computer Assisted Instruction, a method of automating the teaching–learning process that probably has the greatest potential of all the tools of modern educational technology. In CAI instructional content is presented by a computer connected to terminal devices that lead the trainee through the program content and perform an evaluation of his level of achievement. Such "talking typewriters" or "interactive teaching devices" provide a "responsive environment" (to use the jargon of CAI) which has the greatest known potential for individualizing instruction mechanically. The computer can take into account the nature of the trainee and be able to modify its own functioning to work most effectively with him. In addition, CAI can free human instructors from the necessity of drilling students.[121]

CAI is the result of combining various technologies including: programmed instruction, which is most compatible with adjusting to individual differences in learners; audio-visual techniques leading to improved communications; electronic data processing, which provides computational speed, storage capability, and time-sharing capability; and data communications, which allows centralized computer installations to serve widely scattered points. The use of CAI is also compatible with teaching by discovery, which is not always possible with programmed instruction.[122] Crowder's branching perhaps does.

The most limiting aspect of the hardware teaching machine of the future will probably be the economics of its development and use. Elaborate machines will be costly. Another limit will be the requirement that they be easy to use. It is quite possible that cost and the need for simplicity will

---

[119] Albert B. Chalupsky and David D. Nelson, "Programmed Learning—Better than Regular Textbooks," *Personnel Journal*, Vol. 43, No. 10, November 1964, pp. 542–547. See also for a current overview Geary A. Rummler et al., eds., *Managing the Instructional Programming Effort*, Bureau of Industrial Relations, University of Michigan, Ann Arbor, 1967.

[120] William E. Hawley, "Programmed Instruction," in Craig and Bittel, eds., *op. cit.*, pp. 225–226, 248.

[121] *Ibid.*, pp. 248–249; and "Computers Find School Is Tough," *Business Week*, No. 1974, July 1, 1967, pp. 106–108.

[122] Hawley, *op. cit.*, p. 249.

determine the future development of teaching machines. If this is true, we can expect that the result will be low-cost, easy to use machines with features that will not dictate program style or format in the objectives of the program. We can also expect that program presentation techniques will become standardized so that programs from different sources can be used on any machine.[123]

In conclusion, the revolution in educational technology is very much with us and is shaping instructional methods. Closed-circuit television, videotape recording, educational television, greater sophistication in audiovisual aids,[124] and physical improvements in training facilities in organizations[125] should make a great difference in improved manpower development programs for employees at various organizational levels in the future.

BACKGROUND ON LABORATORY AND SENSITIVITY TRAINING

In distinction with such well-established means for industrial training as the on-the-job TWI approach, company schools, and apprenticeship is laboratory training (also called sensitivity training, group dynamics training, and human relations or leadership training). This method is an outgrowth of a leadership conference held in 1946 (intended to develop more effective local leaders in facilitating understanding of and compliance with a state fair employment practices act) and another conference in 1947 at Gould Academy, Bethel, Maine. An analysis of the results and the group dynamics of the 1946 conference convinced the training staff that they had inadvertently hit upon a potentially powerful educational medium and process of reeducation.[126]

Laboratory training may be defined as a type of human resource development which is based primarily on the experiences generated in various social encounters by the learners themselves and which aims to influence attitudes and develop competencies toward learning about human interaction. Essentially, laboratory training attempts to induce changes with

[123] *Ibid.* See also Harvey S. Long and Henry A. Schwartz, "The Potentials of CAI in Industry," *Training and Development Journal,* Vol. 20, No. 8, September 1966, pp. 6–17.

[124] Louis A. Goodman, "Training Aids," in Craig and Bittel, eds., *op. cit.,* pp. 310–337.

[125] R. R. Fuller, "Training Facilities," in Craig and Bittel, eds., *op. cit.,* pp. 410–427.

[126] Kenneth D. Benne, "History of the T-Group in the Laboratory Setting," in Leland P. Bradford et al., eds., *T-Group Theory and Laboratory Method,* Wiley, New York, 1964, pp. 81–83. The best short summary of this subject can be found in Leland P. Bradford and Dorothy J. Mial, "Human Relations Laboratory Training," in Craig and Bittel, eds., *op. cit.,* pp. 251–266.

regard to the learning process itself and to communicate a particular method of learning and inquiry. Often laboratory training is said therefore to be concerned with "learning how to learn." [127] Laboratory learning may thus be considered resocialization.

Laboratory training has been and remains difficult to explain for several reasons. It does not fit well into the conventional categories of education or therapy. It contains elements of both but maintains its uniqueness. The domain of laboratory training extends across the behavioral sciences and the helping professions. Yet, its borders with other disciplines are not clear.[128]

Laboratory training is distinguished, however, by its emphasis upon socially relevant aspects of behavior and the connections between the participant and those external reference groups which are most important to him. This means that a predicted change in behavior is more of a value in laboratory training than either the abstract cognitive functions of classroom education or the concrete emotional experiences of psychotherapy. Yet, laboratory training does encompass cognitive and affective functions (much as education and psychotherapy are related to social roles). There are unmistakable differences in emphasis, however. Although society is the ultimate benefactor in all cases, laboratory training is more concerned with society as the client than most educational methods.[129]

Laboratory training is far from being fully understood, either in terms of processes or outcomes. In the on-rush of experience-based learning in a laboratory, observers of a laboratory are likely to be impressed with the multitude of data generated rather than the lack of it; with the many levels and wide range of behavior, skills, emotions and intellect engaged in laboratory training rather than the narrowness of the experience; and with the simultaneity and immediacy of these compounding and interacting factors. The total experience is direct, immediate, dense, occasionally surprising, and engages many levels and many facets of interpersonal relations simultaneously.[130]

Lastly, laboratory training is new, rapidly growing, and ever-changing. It is not a monolith. Rather, it is composed of ideas and procedures practiced by social scientists and professionals who share certain beliefs and values, but who, on occasion, disagree on major issues. Because of its newness, laboratory training has not codified its concepts or practices, nor should it.[131] For example, some view the field as tantamount to the study

[127] Schein and Bennis, *op. cit.,* p. 4.
[128] *Ibid.*
[129] *Ibid.,* p. 30.
[130] *Ibid.,* p. 5.
[131] *Ibid.*

of psychological perception and consider the goal to be improving one's predictions about people.[132] Others view laboratory training (in the industrial context at least) as a tool of emotional reeducation for making the modern organizational executive "truly efficient" through understanding feelings as well as facts.[133] Still others view laboratory training as being the setting wherein "encounter groups" can use both verbal methods (such as fantasizing and psychodramatizing) and nonverbal techniques (such as acting out, mirroring, or pressing) to achieve personal growth and development. In this school of thought, much is made of the connection between emotional and behavioral states in personal and interpersonal functioning, the goal being expanding human awareness to achieve "joy" [134]

All these complications enveloping laboratory training hardly make it easy to understand or communicate to the "outside" world of potentially interested people. A review of its evolution helps one grasp its goals and meaning.

The Bethel Evolution

Early in the 1946 conference previously mentioned, Kurt Lewin, a renowned psychologist at MIT, had arranged for evening meetings of training staff members with research observers to pool and record on tape their process observations of each group, including the behaviors of members and leaders. It was found that group members, if they were confronted more or less objectively with data concerning their own behavior and its effects, and if they came to participate nondefensively in thinking about these data, might achieve highly meaningful learnings about themselves, about the responses of others to them, and about group behavior and group development in general. In considering future training sessions, no thought was given to the exclusion of content, whether in the form of uses suggested by the staff, situations reported by members from outside the group, or of role-played incidents. Initially, the notion was simply to supplement this "there-and-then" content with the collection and analysis of "here-and-now" data concerning the members' own behaviors.[135]

The training staff of the 1946 workshop involved other institutions in planning the sessions at Bethel in 1947. One of the features of this next session was a small continuing group, called the Basic Skills Training (BST) Group, in which an observer made the data gathered available for

[132] Henry Clay Smith, *Sensitivity to People*, McGraw-Hill, New York, 1966, pp. 12–20, 42, 57, 130–133, 165.

[133] Alfred J. Marrow, *Behind the Executive Mask*, AMA Management Report, No. 79, American Management Association, New York, 1964, p. 25.

[134] William C. Schutz, *Joy*, Grove Press, New York, 1967, pp. 15–23 ff. Joy is defined as the feeling that comes from the fulfillment of one's potential.

[135] Benne, in Bradford et al., eds., *op. cit.*, p. 83.

discussion and analysis by the group. One function of the training leader was to help the group in analyzing and evaluating these data, as well as supplementary data given by the participants and from the training leader. The BST group was intended, first, to be a place for learning "change-agent" skills and concepts. (A change-agent is a person—or persons—who alter(s) existing patterns of behavior or structures and cultures of organizations.) It was to be, second, a place for learning to understand and to help with group growth and development. To do this, it was necessary to "sensitize" the participants to the realization that groups very probably show a growth process (as do individuals), that a collection of mature adults will not necessarily make a mature group, and that many committee and staff-meeting failures result from expecting mature production from adolescent or infantile groups.[136]

The BST group was, thus, designed as a medium for many types of learning. First, it was to help members internalize certain conceptual schemes, one of which was a system of deliberate or planned change and the skills acquired by the agent of such change. Second was an expectation that the group would provide practice in diagnostic and action skills of the change agent and of the group member and leader.[137]

A third—and very important—expectation was that the behavioral content would run the gamut of "human organization" from the interpersonal level and the group level to the intergroup level (both in formal organizations and communities). The result was a competition between discussing here-and-now happenings (which of necessity focused on the personal, interpersonal, and group levels) and discussing outside case materials. Sometimes discussion of the latter resulted in the rejection of any serious consideration of the observer's report of behavioral data.[138]

A fourth expectation was that the BST group would help its members to plan the application of laboratory learning to back-home situations and to plan for continuing growth for themselves and their associates. A fifth hope was that members would gain a more objective and accurate view of themselves in their relations to others in the group and to the developing group as an entity.[139]

A sixth goal was that participants would develop a clearer understanding of democratic values. These values were to be operationalized in order to show persons' styles for functioning as a leader or member of a group and as an initiator and facilitator of change. The originators of the laboratory

---

[136] *Ibid.,* pp. 83–85, citing Leland P. Bradford, "Human Relations Training," *The Group,* Vol. 10, No. 2, January 1948, pp. 7–8.

[137] Benne, in Bradford et al., eds., *op. cit.,* pp. 85–86.

[138] *Ibid.,* p. 86.

[139] *Ibid.*

were convinced that the ethical commitments implicit in the scientific enterprise are consistent with the ethical commitments explicit in democratic patterns of social management and control. They believed that the BST-group experience would reinforce the democratic values held by trainees. How training was to be conducted to facilitate value reorientation by group members was a controversial point at that time and remains so to this day.[140]

The final expectation was that members of the BST group would not only acquire skills and understandings to help them function more adequately as change agents and as group members but that they would also acquire trainer skills and understandings required for communicating these to others. This expectation proved embarrassing to the laboratory-training staff because some trainees went home feeling that they were qualified to conduct human relations training in the laboratory style. Where their previous education did not warrant this claim, a few participants carried out inadequate training programs in the name of laboratory training. It was seen by the end of 1948 that both a background in one of the behavioral sciences and training beyond participation in one laboratory program were required as a minimum to produce adequate competence in a trainer. But it was not until 1955 that a special advanced program for the development of trainers was instituted at Bethel.[141]

The training staff of 1948 also was convinced that the training group was overlooked in terms of learning objectives. New groupings within the laboratory were seen as necessary to support at least some of the various objectives. This perception raised the question as to which should be assigned to the BST group or its equivalent and which should be sought through the use of other groupings and other training methodologies.[142] BST groups were modified and became T-groups.

In the following two decades the crystallization of T-groups and their place in laboratory designs has fallen into two periods. In the first, 1949 to 1955, there was a variety of experimental attempts to create training formats and technologies to serve learning objectives seen as extraneous to those peculiarly within the province of the T-Group. This experimentation led at times to virtual segregation of T-group activities. Separate groupings were formed for skill practice, for the application of laboratory learnings, and for the study of change. Sometimes separate staffs for handling T-group activities and non-T-group activities were recruited.[143]

The second period covers from 1955 to the present time and is marked

[140] *Ibid.*, pp. 86–87.
[141] *Ibid.*, p. 87.
[142] *Ibid.*
[143] *Ibid.*, pp. 87–88.

by efforts to reintegrate T-group experiences into the designs of laboratories. Experimentation with new designs and with innovative uses of T-groups continues to this day. There has been a proliferation in numbers and kinds of laboratories. Numerous occupational laboratories have developed, and the more traditional cross-occupational laboratories have continued.[144] New programs using T-groups as well as other approaches based on psychological and additional research have been devised, such as the managerial grid and the three-dimensional managerial grid. Criticism of laboratory training has mounted and defenders and critics have fired many a salvo at each other. Given the complexity of its goals and its relative newness, such criticism of laboratory training can be expected and should be useful to all people in the manpower field who are considering using it.

In the more than two decades of its evolution, laboratory training has been associated with the National Training Laboratories (NTL), a division of the National Education Association (NEA). In 1967 NTL separated itself from the NEA and became the NTL Institute for Applied Behavioral Science. It has plans for expanding its network of trainers and accommodating the growing demand for laboratory training.[145] Undoubtedly, the change in title and approach being used to develop trainers suggest that NTL-IABS will be making a significant contribution in the future to the development of human resources using available scientific knowledge. In essence, laboratory training may be said to be going the route of professionalization.

Self-Education and Social-Emotional Learning

In discussing laboratory training, we should point out the theoretical importance of the early contributions made by Charles Horton Cooley to social psychology, particularly the concept of the "looking-glass self," which is basic to T-groups. To be sure, contemporary theory concerning the nature and development of the self is the product of varied intellectual efforts, including psychoanalysis and psychiatry. Yet Cooley's importance lies in elaborating in a sociological context the thinking of earlier scholars, thus providing subsequent students with a point of departure which has proven most fruitful in understanding laboratory training.

He considered that the self arose in social experience and that it was on the same plane of awareness as that which led to the perception of others. The self-idea thus had three parts as he understood it: the imagination of

---

[144] *Ibid.*

[145] "National Training Laboratories Changes Name and Maps Major Expansion Program," *Business Week*, No. 1970, June 3, 1967, p. 152. See also Leland P. Bradford et al., "A Look to the Future," in Bradford et al., eds., *op. cit.*, pp. 477–486.

our appearance to the other person; the imagination of his judgment of that appearance; and some sort of self-feeling, such as pride or mortification.[146] Put another way, just as we can see our physical selves when we view ourselves in a mirror, we can see our social selves in others through imagining how we come across to them and how we think they perceive us. Verbal and nonverbal "feedback," the social reflection, from others gotten through social interaction with them provides the social mirror. Our feelings of this feedback comprise self-feelings and may be the basis for behavioral and other change.

The "Johari Window" model shown in Figure 9 has become a useful heuristic device for examining the looking-glass self and graphically explaining the goals of basic laboratory training, especially T-groups. The

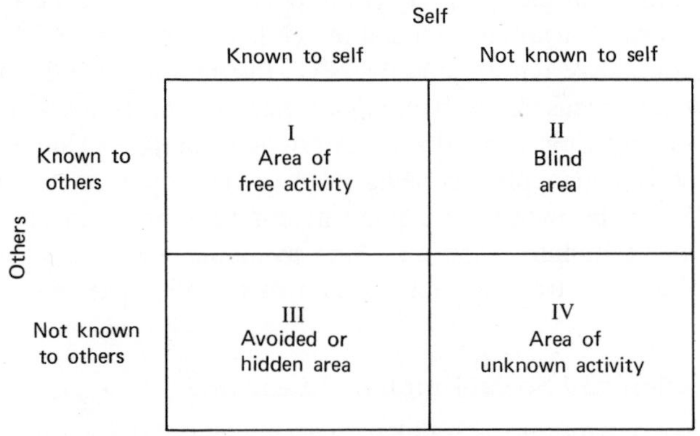

	Self	
	Known to self	Not known to self
Known to others	I Area of free activity	II Blind area
Not known to others	III Avoided or hidden area	IV Area of unknown activity

Figure 9   The Johari Window. *Source.* Joseph Luft, *Group Processes,* National Press, Palo Alto, 1963, p. 10.

window has four quadrants (shown in Roman numerals), each of which refers to aspects of self-awareness or self-education.

The first quadrant refers to behavior and motivation known both to self and others. It is free and open and on the surface. The second, or blind area quadrant, refers to behavior where others can see things in ourselves of which we are unaware. The third quadrant represents changes we know but do not reveal to others (such as well-masked feelings or hidden motives for action). The fourth quadrant refers to a sector of the self in which

[146] Richard Dewey, "Charles Horton Cooley: Pioneer in Psychosociology," in Harry Elmer Barnes, ed., *An Introduction to the History of Sociology,* University of Chicago Press, Chicago, 1948, pp. 837–848.

neither the individual nor others are aware of the person's behavior or motives. Yet we can assume their existence because eventually some of these things become known. It is then realized that these hitherto unknown behaviors and motives were influencing relationships all along.[147]

In a typical laboratory-training group meeting for the first time, quadrant I is very small. There is very little free and spontaneous interaction. As the group "grows" in openness and goes about its work as a laboratory for trying out and revealing more behavior, quadrant I gradually expands its size. (See Figure 10.) This enlargement usually means the participants are freer to be more like themselves and to perceive others as they really are.[148] Some of the ego defenses will be attacked and/or relaxed.

As quadrant I grows larger, quadrant III shrinks in area. People find it

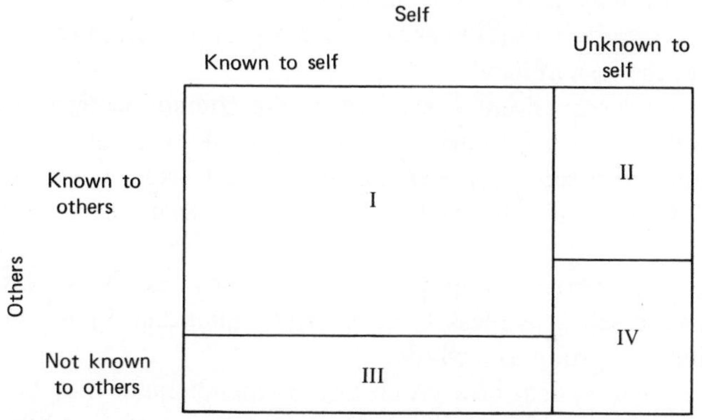

Figure 10 Laboratory goals shown as changing quadrants of self-knowledge. *Source.* Joseph Luft, *Group Processes,* National Press, Palo Alto, 1963, p. 13.

less necessary to hide or deny things they know or feel because with growth in a group, mutual trust is built. Quadrant II is slower to reduce in size because usually people have less of a grip on reasons or feelings as to why they blind themselves to the things which they feel or do. Quadrant IV is the slowest of all to change its size, although it probably changes to some extent in each laboratory.[149] Quadrant IV, of course, subsumes many aspects of the individual's personality growth and socialization, which comprise the virtually unknowable for persons who never take steps to probe it in depth.

[147] Joseph Luft, *Group Processes,* National Press, Palo Alto, 1963, pp. 10–11.
[148] *Ibid.,* p. 11.
[149] *Ibid.*

A number of useful propositions about learning can be set forth in reference to the Johari Window, which are summarized below.

1. A change in any one quadrant will affect all other quadrants.

2. It takes energy to hide, deny, or be blind to behavior which is involved in interaction. (A corollary is: one finds a new surge of energy when he finds he no longer must waste energy defensively on blind spots and hiding.)

3. A threatening situation tends to decrease awareness; mutual trust tends to increase awareness.

4. Forced awareness (exposure) is undesirable and usually ineffective.

5. Interpersonal learning means a change has taken place by making quadrant I larger and by reducing the size of one or more of the other quadrants.

6. Working with others is facilitated by developing a sufficiently large area of free activity so that everyone in the group can apply his resources and skills to the task at hand.

7. The smaller quadrant I, the poorer the communication.

8. There is a universal curiosity about the unknown, quadrant IV.

9. Sensitivity means appreciating the covert aspects of behavior in quadrants II, III, and IV and respecting the desire of others to keep them so.

10. Learning about group processes, as they are being experienced, helps to create self-awareness (i.e., enlarging quadrant 1) for the individual as well as the group as a whole.

11. The value system of a group and its membership may be discerned in the way unknowns in the life of the group are confronted.[150]

The Johari Window model may be further used to illustrate one of the key objectives of a basic human relations laboratory oriented toward personal growth experience, namely, to increase the area of free activity in quadrant I so that more of the relationships in the group are free and open. It follows, therefore, that the goal of the laboratory may be depicted as increasing the area of quadrant I while reducing the area of all other quadrants. In behavioral and social-emotional terms, an enlarged area of free activity (quadrant I) among the group members would immediately imply less threat or fear and greater probability that the skills and resources of group members could be brought to bear on the work of the

[150] *Ibid.*, pp. 11–12. In reference to item (9) a distinction should be made between healthy, desirable privacy and neurotic, compulsive controllable privacy. See Abraham H. Maslow, *Eupsychian Management: A Journal*, Irwin, Homewood, Illinois, 1965, pp. 179–180.

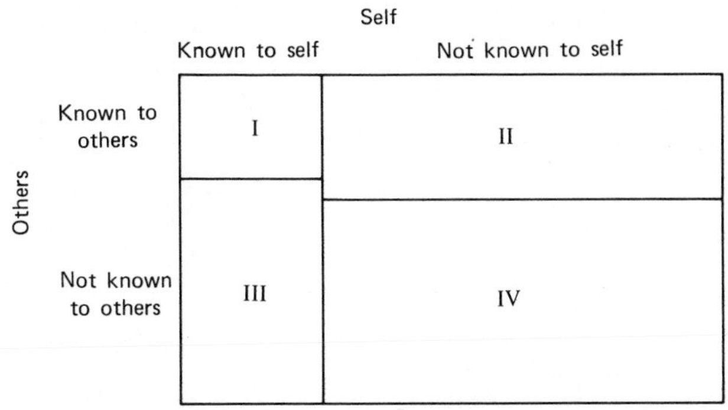

Figure 11   Beginning interaction in a new group shown as exposures of self. *Source.* Joseph Luft, *Group Processes,* National Press, Palo Alto, 1963, p. 13.

group. Enlargement of free activity suggests greater openness to information, opinions, and new ideas about oneself as well as about specific group processes. Inasmuch as the hidden or avoided area, quadrant III, is reduced, it implies that less energy is tied up in defending this area. Also, since more of one's needs are unbound, there is greater likelihood of satisfaction with the work and more involvement with what the group is doing.[151]

An interesting contrast conception to Figure 10 is Figure 11, which is applicable to a typical meeting of most groups. Interaction is relatively superficial and subdued. Anxiety or threat is fairly large. Interchanges among group members are stilted and unspontaneous. Ideas or suggestions are not followed through and are usually left undeveloped. Individuals seem to hear and see relatively little of what is really going on.[152]

The goal of basic laboratory training is thus as shown in Figure 12, to extend self-knowledge outward into the remaining quadrants. The dotted line suggests a possible outer boundary for a particular person in a given laboratory. The dotted-line pattern would vary for each individual and even for the same individual over time depending upon his readiness for and acceptance of self-education in a laboratory.

Laboratory training thus provides an opportunity for the participant to get feedback on himself, to learn about groups, and to learn how to learn. He can experiment with new styles of behavior in the relative safety of the laboratory and get feedback on them or return to laboratories periodically

[151] Luft, *op. cit.,* pp. 12–13.
[152] *Ibid.,* pp. 13–15.

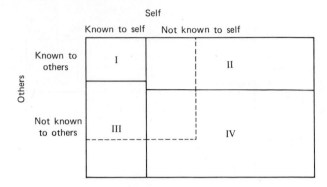

Figure 12 Expansion of self-knowledge. *Source.* Suggested by Professor Sheldon G. Lowry of the Department of Sociology, Michigan State University.

after sustained experimentation as a part of a plan to grow and become more effective in social situations. The process of learning in labs can thus be visualized as cyclical. (See Figure 13.) The person goes from step 1 through the next four, returning to 1A where the cycle resumes *ad seriatim*. Over a period of time, the learning cycle would be repeated, as shown at the bottom of Figure 13. If the laboratory training is effective, the spiral would move over time in the direction of favorable behavioral change.[153]

Depending upon the structure of the laboratory, the person may also learn about his hang-ups (on such subjects as power, conflict, authority, decision making, and risk taking), emotional style, change-agent abilities, and the like. He is likely to acquire some skill in listening, asking questions, accepting a wide range of behavior, being open, challenging stereotypes, confronting a person or group, dealing with the unexpected, coping with stress, taking risks, and building relationships with others. He becomes more sensitive—a more adequate perceiver—but not necessarily more soft or sentimental. He improves from a mental health standpoint. Indeed some laboratory participants may wish to become tougher through sensitivity training; or more objective; or to experiment with some new combination of soft, tough, and objective behavior, to use this typological oversimplification for the purposes of illustration. If we contrast an individual who has "growth" motivation with one who has "defensive" motivation, we would expect the former to be healthier from the mental standpoint and more competent in his organizational roles. The healthy individual can be expected to be realistic and flexible, that is, able to shift from growth to

[153] Matthew B. Miles, *Learning to Work in Groups,* Teachers College, Columbia University, New York, 1959, pp. 38–45. For a similar theory see also Schein and Bennis, *op. cit.,* pp. 272–276.

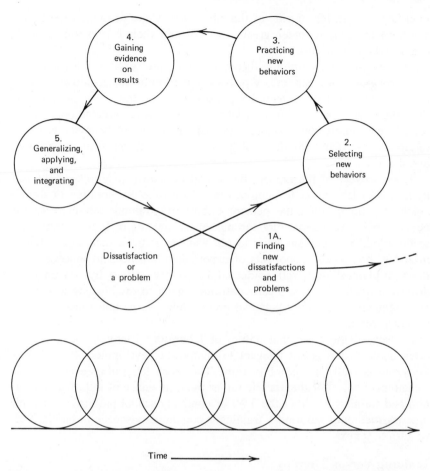

Figure 13   Steps in the training process. *Source.* Matthew B. Miles, *Learning to Work in Groups,* Teachers College, Columbia University, New York, 1959, p. 39.

defense as circumstances may dictate.[154] He has a repertoire of styles and skills which he draws upon from his real self.

Most of the time the participant in laboratories will be learning at the "gut" level, that is, emotionally rather than intellectually, existentially rather than cognitively. Through the nonverbal exercises that may be structured into the laboratory and by means of interaction with T-group members, he will naturally drift toward consideration of the emotional issues in learning and social relationships and get a better insight into them

[154] Maslow, *op. cit.,* pp. xi–xii.

than he would in life outside of the laboratory where emotional issues and emotions are placed under greater control and their expression carefully channeled by the norms.

The occasional lecturettes, theory sessions, and exercises involving all the participants in a laboratory provide some important cognitive learning and concepts that have potential applicability. Thus, there is some marriage of various types of learning in a laboratory, but a far greater opportunity for learning about the emotions and their influence on behavior is found in lab training than orthodox college classroom settings, company schools, and the like.

The discovery of the hidden, blind, and unknown quadrants of the self by means of laboratory training can be heady wine, exhilerating or threatening, depending upon the person. Laboratory training can increase the person's behavioral repertoire through experimentation. It is in this sense reeducation. Yet, persons who do not want to remove their ego defenses need not, nor do the opponents of experimentation need to innovate. But the well-planned and well-conducted laboratory staffed by a competent dean and qualified trainers can contribute much to establishing a learning environment for not only personal growth but also certain types of social skill acquisition.

In view of the emotional nature of laboratory training, the charge is often made that it is not relevant to manpower development in organizations and is really a type of therapy. The name laboratory even suggests something medical or therapeutic rather than the image of industrial education and training, in either the TWI or company-school patterns. Since this misconstruction of laboratory training is common and needs to be clarified, we turn to it next.

Training Versus Therapy

Figure 14 shows five different categories of developmental approaches that have been used in the United States, particularly in developing managers, but also used in other contexts. As we look from left to right, we can discern a number of organized ways to develop human resources ranging from information-providing lectures or films, with an essentially verbal and there-and-then intellectual message, shading off to laboratory training with its opportunity for learning at the here-and-now social-emotional and nonverbal levels. The line is provided merely for illustrative purposes and is considered only to suggest distinct tendencies. The intellectual and emotional dimensions are separate continua tied together here simply to illustrate a point.

Laboratory training provides a setting for self-education and possible experimentation in behavioral change which has more of the features of group psychotherapy than the other types of developmental approaches.

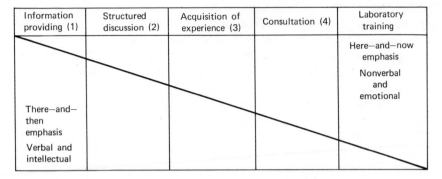

Information providing (1)	Structured discussion (2)	Acquisition of experience (3)	Consultation (4)	Laboratory training
				Here—and—now emphasis Nonverbal and emotional
There—and—then emphasis Verbal and intellectual				

Figure 14 Some categories of developmental approaches and their relative verbal-nonverbal and intellectual-emotional content. *Source.* Adapted from comments of Richard Allen Stull of Louis A. Allen Associates; and Warren G. Bennis, "Patterns and Vicissitudes of T-Group Development," in Leland P. Bradford *et al.*, eds., *T-Group Theory and Laboratory Method*, Wiley, New York, 1964, p. 274. (1) As in a classroom, lectures, movies, and the like. (2) As in case discussions, analysis of the incident process, and certain types of conferences. (3) As in systematic job rotation, role playing, and psychodrama. (4) Either individual or group consultation and counseling.

The similarities and differences can perhaps best be sharpened if we consider the T-group in laboratory training and the therapy group, recognizing that both types of groups are heterogeneous in practice.

Both the T-group and the therapy group used in psychotherapy are concerned with increasing the sensitivity of the members to their own functioning and to that of the other members and with correcting blind spots and distortions. For therapy groups the goal is to relieve the neurotically caused distress of the members. The theory of neurosis utilized here assumes that psychoneuroses are maladaptive processes resulting from disturbance in the normal processes of maturation. These disturbances arise from conditions, especially in the individual's formative years, which do not afford suitable opportunities for growth or produce chronically anxiety-producing situations with which the inadequately equipped person must deal. As a result of these early experiences, the person experiences conflicting urges and feelings which he cannot resolve effectively. These conflicts, and his futile efforts to deal with them, lead to distorted ways of perceiving himself and others, resulting in inappropriate responses in interpersonal situations. He carries over these early conflicts into his adult life, and while aware of the distress they cause him, is unaware of the sources of the conflict and the distortions to which they give rise.[155]

[155] Jerome D. Frank, "Training and Therapy," in Bradford et al., eds., *op. cit.*, pp. 442–451.

The crux of the psychotherapeutic problem is that the neurotic seems unable to learn from his life experiences and his self-respect is damaged from repeated failures in interacting with others. He carries areas of inadequately completed socialization into his later life. From this standpoint, the goal of all psychotherapy is to supply new interpersonal influences which help the patient find more satisfying ways to handle his conflicts. A group is used to help him unlearn faulty responses, loosen up old behavioral patterns, and learn more appropriate ones.[156]

The therapeutic effectiveness of a psychotherapeutic group depends upon how the phenomena of evocation, support, and implicit direction operate. The treatment must evoke neurotic responses because only a response which is operating can be changed. This evocation must be accompanied by emotion, which supplies the energy needed to disrupt old patterns and motivates the search for more adequate ones. The evoked response must be verbalized if the group member is to benefit.

The psychotherapeutic group, being without a formal structure, tolerates the expression of feelings, neurotic distortions, and conflicts among equals. People come to find that they are gradually being understood and that others care for them. They start to become clear about their feelings and behavior and to perceive alternative ways of reacting, thereby becoming amenable to implicit direction.

Some ways in which a therapeutic group offers implicit direction to each member are: supplying feedback from the other members and the leader as to the impression his behavior makes on them; exposing him to values and standards more adequate than those under which he is currently operating; and offering him models of different ways of behaving with which he can identify, imitate, or reject. This implicit direction occurs in a setting where there is a chance to experiment with and practice new behavior without serious penalties for failure.[157]

In the T-group the goal in increasing the member's sensitivity is not relief from neurotic distress but rather the provision of a personal growth experience so that the person can learn to function better as a group member or leader. (This assumes that a T-group member is not a neurotic, i.e., a patient in disguise.) Members of therapy groups are defined by themselves and others as patients; they are sick people seeking treatment to relieve suffering. The ultimate goal in a therapy group is thus change in the individual patient, and change in the functioning of the groups to which he belongs is subsidiary to this objective.[158]

Though both groups share the aim of improving the accuracy and

[156] *Ibid.*, p. 444.
[157] *Ibid.*, pp. 444–446.
[158] *Ibid.*, pp. 446–447.

sensitivity of members' perceptions of reactions to themselves and one another, this goal is an end in itself for the T-group. For a therapeutic group, it is a step toward the end of improved mental health. The T-group has served its purpose when the group has learned how to select a task and develop a social structure that enables it to work effectively. The usefulness of a therapeutic group increases as it approaches this state, but it can never completely achieve it because the members' dependence upon the clinical therapist cannot be fully resolved. To overstate the idea slightly, the therapeutic group reaches its maximum usefulness at the point where the T-group ceases to be useful.[159] Put another way: psychotherapists are more concerned with sensitivity as a process than as an outcome. They are essentially interested in understanding the immediate experiences of their clients during the therapeutic hour and in using their understanding to help their clients. They are not concerned with predicting how their clients behaved before the hour or how they will behave afterwards.[160]

There are also important differences between therapists and trainers. In therapeutic groups there is an irreducible gap between the leader and the members because the leader is in the role of a practitioner of a healing art from which the patients hope to benefit. The therapist may himself benefit from participation in a therapeutic group, and one of his objectives is to become a member of the group. But he can never become a patient and a group member on that status level. Similarly, patients do not expect to become therapists after treatment.[161]

The status of the therapist automatically gives him high prestige and the power to reassure or disturb the patients. It also causes them to depend heavily upon him at first. In all their activities, they are concerned with the effect of what they are doing on his evaluation of them and never develop a complete sense of self-reliance.[162]

The trainer in a T-group differs from the members only in the possession of superior knowledge and skill in a limited domain. If he successfully imparts this knowledge and skill, the gap between him and the group members progressively diminishes until, at the end of the laboratory of T-group and related experiences, there is no difference between the trainer and members. The latter may not be as interpersonally perceptive as the skilled trainer, but they should be keener than before the laboratory. The trainer must earn esteem because the prestige of a trainer in a T-group is ambiguous and he is not designated as group leader. The member's dependency on him is limited to looking to him occasionally for guidance as

---

[159] *Ibid.*, p. 448.
[160] Smith, *op. cit.*, pp. 4, 198–199.
[161] Frank, in Bradford et al., eds., *op. cit.*, p. 448.
[162] *Ibid.*

to how to proceed and for clarification of what is happening in the group. It is, in sum, relatively easy for a T-group to become genuinely self-reliant and eventually to absorb the trainer as merely another member.[163]

The functioning of the two groups is also quite different. For example, because T-groups have limited goals, these can be achieved in a relatively short time. A weekend laboratory of two days can be of value, and those of three weeks are a usual maximum. In this way, frequent T-group meetings and closed membership are both more necessary and easier to achieve.[164] Therapeutic groups can go on for months, if not years.

There is greater threat and more depth in the probing in a therapeutic group. Part of the threat arises from the limitless task in a therapeutic group, which is personal modification in its broadest sense. In T-groups the task is much more limited, and underlying motivations, if explored at all, are examined only to clarify the meaning of overt behavior. In therapeutic groups the process is reversed. Overt behavior is used to elucidate underlying motivations and to get at anxiety-provoking issues. Also, there is more anxiety in therapeutic groups because the members are emotionally ill and have their feelings under less firm control. The therapist may try to build up emotional tension, but he can also offer support. In a T-group there is less support offered, considerably less anxiety, and it is expected that members can handle and learn from exposures of their distorted perceptions.[165] The differences are those of group dynamics versus individual psychodynamics. Whereas group psychotherapy aims to make sick people well, laboratory-training T-groups aim to make well people better.[166]

In respect to conflicts among members, the T-group seeks resolutions. In the course of working through resolutions, light is cast upon the contributions of various members to the development of the struggle and its settlement. In therapeutic groups the occasion of conflict is seen as a means of evoking and clarifying the distortions and neurotic attitudes which are highlighted by the struggle whether the conflict is resolved or not.[167]

In conclusion, T-groups and therapy groups are very different in goals, types of members, types of leader–member patterns, duration, and functioning. Confusion of the two arises because of certain common features. Both are groups established for learning and have the goal of bringing about changes in their members. Both stress learning to communicate accurately with others. Both value mature, group-centered, altruistic, re-

[163] *Ibid.*, pp. 448–449.
[164] *Ibid.*, p. 449.
[165] *Ibid.*, pp. 449–450.
[166] Maslow, *op. cit.*, p. 178.
[167] *Ibid.*, p. 450.

sponsible functioning of members—in therapeutic groups because it is a sign of the improvement in individual patients and in T-groups because it improves group functioning. In neither group is there a sharp distinction between task and maintenance functions. In neither group is there an adaptive, instrumental function in respect to the outside world.[168]

Review of Selected Literature on Laboratory Training

Let us, next, look at the evidence from available research which provides some inkling of the value of laboratory training in terms of its goals. Obviously, we cannot be definitive at this time, primarily because the subject is volatile and becoming increasingly more complex.[169]

One of the earliest critiques of the subject by an eminent social scientist, Whyte, reflects his experiences at Bethel in 1950 and is characterized by his concern at the time with leadership, discussion groups, and the control of emotions. He noted groups (what were called A- rather than T-groups) as they were structured at Bethel in the early years would become deadlocked, confused, and frustrated when they tried to work through a course of action without a leader or to deal with interpersonal conflicts standing in the way of agreement on action. When such an impasse was met, there were two opposite schools of thought concerning what the group should do. One held that the deadlock could be resolved only if each member in turn described to the group how he felt about what had been transpiring. Critics of this school referred to the "feeling-draining" approach, also known as the "cesspool theory of group dynamics." They argued that the interpersonal conflicts could be resolved only when the members became actively involved in carrying through a course of action. In rebuttal, the feeling-drainers felt that members of the "work-through" school were afraid to make the emotional analyses necessary for effective group process.[170]

Neither school of thought was providing a solution to the problem, and the feeling-draining process was observed again and again. The Bethel experience suggested to Whyte that it was possible to drain a group's feelings every day and still have feelings left to drain. Bethel was an intense emotional experience for most people, but he wondered if it was not possible to provide an alternative experience in group participation that would be

[168] *Ibid.*, pp. 446–451. See also Roy M. Whitman, "Psychodynamic Principles Underlying T-Group Processes," in Bradford et al., eds., *op. cit.*, pp. 310–335.

[169] See Lewis E. Durham et al., *A Bibliography of Research* (Explorations, Human Relations Training and Research, No. 2, 1967), NTL Institute for Applied Behavioral Science, Washington, 1967, for a comprehensive annotated list of research studies.

[170] William Foote Whyte, *Leadership and Group Participation* (Bulletin 24), New York State School of Industrial and Labor Relations, Cornell University, Ithaca, 1953, p. 13. See also Benne, *op. cit.*, pp. 92–94.

at least as fruitful a learning experience while avoiding strife. He then went on to argue that, if there is no recognized leader and if the group is free to make any decision whatsoever, then there will be confusion, conflict, and frustration until a definite pattern of group organization arises. Unless such a pattern develops, people will be so preoccupied over problems of leadership and their relations with each other in general that they will be unable to act effectively upon the tasks which the group might undertake.[171]

Whyte's conclusions were: when an impasse is reached, the mere draining of personal feelings is of no use and may actually add to the confusion and frustration. Feelings should be expressed but in a context of explicit discussion of human relations problems. People must talk about the structure of their relations and about the interpersonal events of concern to the members, that is, what we have called above the here-and-now. If they talk in individual terms alone (the there-and-then), they will never talk their way out of the impasse. Only when they examine their relations to each other will it be possible for them to restructure those relations.[172]

He considered that groups needed a leader. To learn more effective ways of behaving, people need not only experience but also more effective ways of thinking about that experience. They may need knowledge and a framework of ideas before they can handle the analysis of experience. A leader can sum up the trend of a discussion, pointing to the steps that have been taken to analyze a problem and suggesting that the analysis might be advanced if people could think in terms of a framework that he can present. He can help the group focus upon task and emotional problems together. He can weave authority and participation together effectively.[173] Translated into laboratory training today, we might say that many of these leadership functions are provided in the lecturette and theory sessions of laboratories whereas experiences at the feeling level are handled mainly by T-groups. Some of Whyte's criticisms have thus been accommodated in recent approaches to laboratory training.[174]

Stock later reviewed most of the literature concerning T-groups up to about 1962 and stated some overall generalizations on what was being found out about them. She found that, as a T-group continues to meet, a definite structure emerges out of an initially more undifferentiated state. The group moves toward a balance among various kinds of affect and toward an effective interaction of work and emotionality. T-group members—because of self-selection as well as the standards of the NTL-IABS

[171] Whyte, *op. cit.*, pp. 15–25.
[172] *Ibid.*, p. 27.
[173] *Ibid.*, pp. 36–42.
[174] See also Warren G. Bennis, "Patterns and Vicissitudes in T-Group Development," in Bradford et al., eds., *op. cit.*, pp. 250–251.

—are likely to be quite homogeneous in regard to intelligence, job competency, and emotional stability. A trainer adapts his style to each particular T-group. He may be sensitive to missing functions in the group and may try to supply the missing element. He may provide a style of participation which members utilize as a model. Yet in respect to the basic questions, "How many people gain from a laboratory, and what do they learn?," Stock concludes research about T-groups suggests a checkerboard, incompletely and unevenly filled in. The questions are clear, but the methodology or theory are not yet fully developed.[175]

House in another more recent survey of the literature covered much of the work examined by Stock as well as other more up-to-date studies. In considering reported studies concerned with events taking place in T-groups, he concluded that people frequently experience high levels of anxiety in the T-group during the middle of the process and at the same time feel unsettled and uncomfortable about their own opinions and the comments made to them by others. As the T-group experience continues, anxiety tends to recede. T-groups may also have the intended effect of inducing more consideration for subordinates, less dependence upon others, less demand for subservience from others, more supportive behavior, and better communication through more adequate and objective listening. He concludes that there is ample evidence that the T-group is a powerful tool for changing behavior, which is differentially effective in a wide variety of situations with a wide variety of individuals.[176]

House notes that T-group participation has repeatedly been shown to result in changes in perception and opinions. Therefore, careful planning is required in preparation for laboratory training. Inasmuch as the T-group experience is a soul-searching process, it requires the individual to look at his own values and his own emotions, to ask himself whether and why he likes them, and whether he wishes to live the way he has. To prevent avoidable emotional disturbances, admission to T-groups should be based on a careful screening process designed to ensure that participants can withstand the benefit from the anxiety induced in the T-group process.

House believes that T-group trainers should have psychological training equivalent to that required for a clinical psychologist.[177] Some would broaden the training requirement to qualify psychiatrists and psychiatric social workers as trainers. However, perhaps the predominant view is that

---

[175] Dorothy Stock, "A Survey of Research on T-Groups," Bradford et al., eds., *op. cit.,* pp. 395–441.

[176] Robert J. House, "T-Group Education and Leadership Effectiveness: A Review of the Empiric Literature and a Critical Evaluation," *Personnel Psychology,* Vol. 20, No. 1, Spring 1967, pp. 6–7, 23, 29.

[177] *Ibid.,* pp. 25–26.

competent trainers vary in their theories of learning and intervention styles and that laboratory training should be as broad as the applied behavioral sciences, not limited to an aspect of one of them or any one of the helping professions.[178] Such persons can effectively deal with whatever comes up in a laboratory. Yet few would disagree that attendance at a laboratory should be voluntary and that when large organizations systematically install laboratory training programs, precautions are needed to prevent the actual or perceived coercion of participation. A trained professional should be available to laboratory participants who request or apparently need on-site individual counseling.

House concludes by setting forth certain guideposts for using laboratory training which should be valuable for manpower specialists in organizations. These proposals are offered by him as precautionary measures designed to insure maximum protection for the individual while allowing maximum freedom for the induction of needed changes in an organization:

1. An analysis of job performance requirements before deciding to use T-groups in order to ensure that changes brought about by the effective T-group are actually required for effective performance and are changes which the organization will support when the individual returns to the job.

2. Screening of possible program participants by means of adequate psychometric instruments to eliminate persons for whom the laboratory might prove overwhelming.

3. Explanation to persons selected for participation of the goals and the process of T-group training in order to allow withdrawal of any individual who prefers not to invest psychically in the program and to provide a mental framework which will facilitate the learning process of those who attend.

4. Careful selection of the T-group trainers and staff to ensure that they are qualified to conduct group emotional-learning sessions that deliberately induce anxiety, interpersonal feedback, intrapersonal introspection, and experimentation with new methods of behavior.

5. Continued research to elaborate further the relationships between individual characteristics and conditions for the use of T-groups which will result in greater refinement of the methodology and isolate those situations where the method can most effectively be used.

6. Provision of reserve precautionary procedures which can be installed if a laboratory program, once begun, fails to fulfill the expectations of either the organization or members of the T-groups. These precautions would include alternative methods for accomplishing the desired changes

---

[178] Schein and Bennis, *op. cit,* pp. 4, 16–17, 28–30.

as well as provisions for the safety and well being of individuals enrolled in an organization-sponsored program of behavioral retraining.[179]

In addition to the more general summaries of the evaluation literature on laboratory training, there is an abundance which focuses upon reaction appraisal. This literature is worth examining. For example, there are many articles on one man's feelings about a laboratory he attended or observed, with precautions expressed as to the conditions under which laboratory training should be used.[180]

THE EVALUATION CONTROVERSY

The most important interchange of reaction appraisals is that of Argyris and Odiorne, both of whom are experts in training, although Argyris undoubtedly has had more experience in laboratory training than Odiorne. The latter dislikes the cult-like defensiveness of some laboratory training adherents, particularly their rejection of orderly, rational, conscious criticism. He suggests that between 1948 and 1961 not a single conclusive piece of research was reported which proved that laboratory training changed on-the-job behavior of trainees. He then went on to explicate the weakness of laboratory training by citing a number of relevant anecdotes.[181]

Argyris' defense of laboratory training was equally effective, although he could not combat Odiorne's basic charge about evidence for on-the-job behavior change.[182] Argyris acknowledged that as of 1963 most of the evidence opponents and defendants of laboratory training could marshal was anecdotal, but in a more recent round of the "great debate" he has cited more solid data.[183] A stronger case could probably have been made in

[179] House, op. cit., pp. 29–30, not directly quoted. For similar ideas and precautions as to what to avoid see Leslie This and Gordon L. Lippitt, "Managerial Guidelines to Sensitivity Training," Training Directors Journal, Vol. 17, No. 4, April 1963, pp. 3–13.

[180] For example, see William F. Glueck, "Reflections on a T-Group Experience," Personnel Journal, Vol. 48, No. 7, July 1968, pp. 500–504; and John E. Drotning, "Sensitivity Training: Some Critical Questions," Personnel Journal, Vol. 45, No. 10, November 1966, pp. 605–606.

[181] George S. Odiorne, "The Trouble with Sensitivity Training," Training Directors Journal, Vol. 17, No. 10, October 1963, pp. 9–20.

[182] Chris Argyris, "In Defense of Laboratory Education," Training Directors Journal, Vol. 17, No. 10, October 1963, pp. 21–30.

[183] Chris Argyris, "A Comment on George Odiorne's Paper," Training Directors Journal, Vol. 17, No. 10, October 1963, pp. 31–32. See Marvin D. Dunnette and John P. Campbell, "Laboratory Education: Impact on People and Organizations," Industrial Relations, Vol. 8, No. 1, October 1968, pp. 1–27; Chris Argyris, "Issues in Evaluating Laboratory Education," ibid., pp. 28–40; Dunnette and Campbell, "A Response to Argyris," ibid., pp. 41–44; and Argyris, "A Rejoinder to Dunnette and Campbell," ibid., p. 45.

the first round of the great debate that laboratory training did make attitudinal not cognitive changes in the thinking of participants, rather than pivoting the debate on behavioral change back on the job.

Since the time of the Odiorne-Argyris debate, considering solely the studies made of laboratory training in industrial firms, quantitative and anecdotal evidence of behavior change attributable to laboratory training has piled up. For example, General Motors started laboratory training in 1962 and reported in 1965 that participants stated greater confidence, enhanced self-insight, and more productive ways of dealing with other people.[184] A major hotel chain with 26 properties started laboratory training and an organization development program in 1958 and by 1963 had improved communications among various parts of the organization, changed managerial styles from management-by-control to management-by-objectives, improved operating efficiency, increased the problem-solving skills of the total management, and established a systematic program of growth for executives.[185]

Well known as a progressive firm in management development, the Aluminum Company of Canada started laboratory training in 1961 and has been enrolling 200 or more participants from its managerial and professional ranks for basic human relations laboratories each year. There is some evidence that the value system, the norms, beliefs, and expectations of Alcan are consequently changing. The authoritarian managerial stance has given way, in some instances, to more participation in decision making, to freer and more open communication among subordinates with their superiors; the human side of enterprise is being talked about; and, perhaps what is most important, the expression of employees' feelings has been legitimized.[186]

TRW Systems Group of Thompson-Ramo-Wooldridge, Inc., has been involved since 1961 in an extensive organizational development program in which a heavy emphasis has been placed upon confrontation techniques and the use of laboratory training as a part of the effort to improve TRW Systems. Since the program started, more than 500 key people have attended laboratory training. The results have been most satisfactory in helping managerial manpower grow and function as managers.[187]

[184] Edwin C. Nevis et al., "Behavior and Attitude Changes Related to Laboratory Training," *Training Directors Journal*, Vol. 19, No. 2, February 1965, pp. 3–7.
[185] Richard Beckhard, "An Organization Improvement Program in a Decentralized Organization," *Journal of Applied Behavioral Science*, Vol. 2, No. 1, January-February-March, 1966, pp. 3–25.
[186] Alexander Winn, "Social Change in Industry: From Insight to Implementation," *Journal of the Behavioral Sciences*, Vol. 2, No. 2, April-May-June, 1966, pp. 170–184.
[187] Sheldon A. Davis, "An Organic Problem-Solving Method of Organizational Change," *Journal of Applied Behavioral Science*, Vol. 3, No. 1, January-February-March, 1967, pp. 3–21. On the confrontation meeting methodology see Richard Beck-

Also well known in California is the work in laboratory training completed at the Delta Design affiliate of Non-Linear Systems, Inc., where results in improving interpersonal relations have been reported.[188]

The grid organization development program has been successful at "Sigma" and affected productivity, profits, behavior, and attitudes in a manner that has been quantitatively documented.[189]

Manpower specialists in organizations who are necessarily concerned with the complicated social and psychological processes of human learning and change and the control of outcomes of the change process should give consideration to laboratory training and its proliferating variants. Guidance as to procedures for coordinating a laboratory [190] and handbooks providing more information on materials [191] are available. Several periodicals, such as the *Journal of Applied Behavioral Science, Journal of Humanistic Psychology,* and *Training and Development Journal,* are publishing articles on theoretical developments and empirical studies in the field.

The future of laboratory training seems bright. Already the spirit of experimentation has, for example, led to such innovations as the use of the managerial grid combined with confrontation techniques for organization development by Blake and Mouton,[192] the three dimensional grid by Reddin,[193] the use of non-groups for training in creative risk taking by Byrd,[194] and the development of a programmed instruction course on interpersonal relations taken by two persons at a time who interact by asking questions, playing roles, and conversing.[195]

---

hard, "The Confrontation Meeting," *Harvard Business Review,* Vol. 45, No. 2, March-April 1967, pp. 149–155.

[188] Arthur H. Kuriloff and Stuart Atkins, "The T-Group for a Work Team," *Journal of Applied Behavioral Science,* Vol. 2, No. 1, January-February-March 1966, pp. 63–93. See also Maslow, *op. cit.,* pp. 154–187 and *passim.*

[189] Robert R. Blake et al., "Breakthrough in Organization Development," *Harvard Business Review,* Vol. 42, No. 6, November-December, 1964, pp. 133–155.

[190] Schein and Bennis, *op. cit.,* pp. 339–356.

[191] Donald Nylen et al., *Handbook of Staff Development and Human Relations Training,* Revised and Expanded Edition, NTL Institute for Applied Behavioral Science, Washington, 1968.

[192] Robert R. Blake and Jane S. Mouton, *Corporate Excellence through Grid Organization Development,* Gulf, Houston, 1968.

[193] W. J. Reddin, "The Tri-Dimensional Grid," *Training Directors Journal,* Vol. 18, No. 7, July 1964, pp. 9–17; Robert R. Blake and Jane S. Mouton, "The Managerial Grid in Three Dimensions," *Training and Development Journal,* Vol. 21, No. 4, April 1967, pp. 8–17; and W. J. Reddin, "The 3-D Organizational Effectiveness Program," *Training and Development Journal,* Vol. 22, No. 3, March 1968, pp. 22–28.

[194] Richard E. Byrd, "Training in a Non-Group," *Journal of Humanistic Psychology,* Vol. 7, No. 1, Spring 1967, pp. 18–27.

[195] "Programming Harmony," *Business Week,* No. 1807, April 18, 1964, pp. 142–144.

Thus in the final analysis, what one makes of T-groups and laboratories depends upon a number of factors: on how one feels about the propriety of intimate conversations staged, as it were, under institutional auspices and with a tape recorder running; on one's tolerance for talk about helping and caring and adventures in growth; and on the degree to which one shares the assumption, shared by laboratory trainers, that improvement in self-knowledge and interpersonal relations is worthwhile for the individual and society.[196] It is an exciting new approach to learning, resulting at best in learning how to learn and resocialization.

Laboratory training has been controversial from its founding more than two decades ago. We have dwelled upon it at some length in this chapter because we regard it as an important innovation in the field of manpower development. It is as central to the subject as the concepts of socialization and apprenticeship and seems to open up new possibilities for the future in developing human resources.

CONCEPTS AND TECHNIQUES OF PROGRAM EVALUATION

The evaluation of development programs is made difficult because we must measure changes in human behavior and connect these causally with the achievement of program goals and organizational goals. Programs must always be evaluated so that cumulatively we can build up a better understanding of what has been accomplished.

Ideally, we would like adequate factor control so that we can have confidence that the experience intended to be developmental caused the behavioral change. It is entirely possible, of course, for an intended developmental experience to result in behavior that not only fails to contribute to organizational goals but actually impedes this achievement. The central problems of evaluation are, therefore, determining: (1) if the developmental program actually results in the modifications of the behavior of the employees concerned; (2) if the outcome of the program has any demonstrable relationship to the achievement of organizational goals.[197]

Program evaluation requires establishing a causal relationship between the program and the achievement of organizational goals, and the problems are basically the same as in establishing a causal relationship between any two classes of phenomena, whether physical or social. We begin by securing measures, representing the phenomena concerned, which have certain characteristics. These measures must be secured in such a way and

[196] Spencer Klaw, "Two Weeks in a T-Group," *Fortune,* Vol. 64, No. 2, August 1961, p. 160.
[197] McGehee and Thayer, *op. cit.,* p. 258.

under such circumstances that valid inferences can be made as to causal relations.[198]

Evaluative Concepts

The various measures which can be used in program evaluation may be categorized as follows: (1) objective-subjective, (2) direct-indirect, (3) intermediate-ultimate, and (4) specific-summary.[199] Obviously other possible classification schemes could be used. We discuss only the characteristics of measures, how they may be obtained under different designs, and then conclude by discussing a total of six subjective and objective tools for measuring the results of supervisory development programs. Although none of these tools is considered especially sophisticated, manpower specialists who use them in their organizations will have at least made a start on formal program evaluation which can later lead into more complex designs.

Turning to the objective-subjective dimension, it is obvious that the distinction between the two is a matter of source. A measure is objective if it is derived from overt behavior and does not require the expression of a judgment, belief, or opinion. If it expresses the latter internal states, it is subjective. However, the subjectivity-objectivity of a measure is not necessarily a measure of its worth in an evaluation.[200] Which is more valuable depends upon other matters subsequently discussed. Perhaps the bulk of program evaluation work undertaken in industry today is subjective.

Direct-indirect measures can easily be distinguished. A direct measure is one that measures the behavior of an individual or the results of his behavior. An indirect measure assesses the action of an individual whose behavior can be measured only by its influence on the behavior of others. The results of supervisory development programs are frequently measured indirectly. However, it is difficult to make causal inferences from indirect measures, and extreme care is required in securing these measures if the causal inferences are to be valid.[201]

Intermediate and ultimate measures differ most importantly in a temporal way. Manpower development programs that are designed to prepare an individual to perform his specific function in an organization should be evaluated in terms of how well he contributes, through his job, to organizational goal attainment. Inasmuch as this contribution is a temporal affair, seldom can we secure a measure of his ultimate value to an organization. Consequently, measures must be used that are available at various times

[198] *Ibid.*, p. 260.
[199] *Ibid.*, p. 261.
[200] *Ibid.*
[201] *Ibid.*, pp. 261–262.

over his work career. These are called "intermediate" as contrasted to "ultimate" measures. Most measures (such as test scores, performance ratings covering a recent work period, and learning time on a new job) are intermediate. The problem from an evaluation standpoint is establishing the relationship between the intermediate and the ultimate.[202]

Specific and summary measures refer in a sense to scope. For example, some measures may be used as an index of successful performance of a specific phase of a job. Others, summary measures, are indices of how well an individual performs all the critical aspects of his job. They are the most difficult to obtain.[203]

The categories of measures we have been discussing are not mutually exclusive. Regardless of their type, they must have certain additional characteristics, if they are to be used for causal analyses of the results of manpower development programs. These characteristics are: relevance, reliability, freedom from bias, and practicality. They refer to the quantity and quality of measures.[204] Each is worth a few words.

Relevance of the measure is largely a matter of judgment. In this chapter we have taken the position that development activities must be relevant to the performance requirements of the job and the attainment of organizational goals. Whether the goals attained are relevant should be decided by line management in an organization, for the line is the ultimate client. The manpower specialist can help objectify these judgments and indicate sources of irrelevance in the various possible measures of the outcomes of programs.[205] Goals should not be decided by him.

Reliability, the extent that repeated use of the measure with the same individual yields consistent results, is largely an application of certain accepted statistical techniques. In developmental activities we hope to bring about behavioral change. Measures used to describe these changes should change in amount during the period of education or training. They should be the type of measure that retains the individual in the same or nearly the same relative rank if no formal developmental activity takes place between the initial or later measurement. Measures that fluctuate from time to time and user to user would not be reliable measures of the actual performance of trainees.[206]

Freedom from bias is also important. Measures can be low in relevance or reliability because of contamination. Contamination can cause spuriously high reliability. Measures become biased (or contaminated) because

[202] *Ibid.*, pp. 262–263.
[203] *Ibid.*, pp. 263–264.
[204] *Ibid.*, p. 264.
[205] *Ibid.*, pp. 265–266.
[206] *Ibid.*, pp. 267–269.

they are not gathered under conditions completely independent of other variables or because they are unexpectedly affected by operating conditions.[207] The manpower specialist must be perceptive as to the operation of organizational and operational variables if he is to get sanitary measures.

Practicality is a major consideration in work organizations. Manpower development programs are an organizational tool; therefore, program evaluation must give ample consideration to economy and the convenience of employees.[208] Consequently, the researcher must often compromise with the ideal design if any evaluative work is to be done at all. Many of the measures that would be desirable are not found ready-made in industrial situations. In general, the measures available have probably been collected for purposes other than the evaluation of programs for the development of human resources. As a result, they may not permit causal inferences between program participation and the results of training, the core of the evaluation issue.[209] In view of these complexities, we turn next to general guides which are applicable to various designs for program evaluation, steering away from the shoals that have shipwrecked evaluative efforts in the past.

Principles of Evaluation

Although great disparities show up in the kinds of evaluation reported in the literature and also in the scientific rigor with which they are performed, general agreement exists concerning the following principles:

1. *Evaluation should be planned at the same time as the developmental program and should constitute an integral part of the total program from the beginning to the end.*[210] In other words, evaluation should not be perfunctory but rather a continual process. The selection of the criteria, controls, and statistics for the purposes of evaluation should be made with the same care used in identifying the needs and selecting the methods for development. Moreover, the more precisely the needs and objectives are defined, the easier it is to identify valid and reliable criteria for evaluation.[211]

2. *Evaluation should follow the most rigorous experimental design practicable.* Most of the program evaluations reported in the literature to date have been far removed from the ideal in experimental design. Most, in fact, would fall in the class of "after-only" evaluations—that is, the learner's behavior is observed or measured only after his exposure to

[207] *Ibid.,* pp. 269–271.

[208] *Ibid.,* p. 271.

[209] *Ibid.,* p. 276.

[210] These principles and their explication are from Bass and Vaughan, *op. cit.,* pp. 144–148.

[211] *Ibid.,* pp. 144–145.

training. An improvement over this single "after" measure of the training group is a comparable measure of a matched control group.[212]

A significantly higher level of scientific rigor is reached when evaluation includes "before-after" measures of the experimental or training group and a matched control group. The use of two or more control groups permits even more sophistication in design and allows the manpower specialist to isolate the effects of contemporary events, maturational processes, and the initial measurement. Practical problems often prevent the use of this design. An examination of the utility of the designs in Figure 15 is instructive.[213]

Design A requires that an "after" measurement be taken of both the experimental and the control group. The assumption is that both groups are exposed to the same external events and undergo similar maturational processes between the time of selection and the time at which the "after" program participation measurement is obtained. Thus, the difference (d) between X_2 and Y_2 may be taken as an indication of the effects of the program. This design also assumes that the groups do not differ on the "after" measurement prior to the program participation.[214]

In design B each subject serves as his own control and the difference between the "before" and "after" measurement is taken as the measure of the effect of the developmental experience. This design does not make it possible to separate the effects of contemporary events, maturation, and the initial measure from those of training. This design should be used, then, only if there is good reason to believe that the "before" measurement will not affect the trainee's response to program participation or the "after" measurement and that there are not likely to be any other influences, besides the program, that might affect the trainee's response at the time of the "after" measure.[215]

With design C both the experimental and the control group are measured before and after the training period, but only the experimental group, of course, receives the training. Because the control group, as well as the experimental group, is subjected to the initial measurement and to the contemporary influences, the difference between the two groups' scores should constitute a much more sanitary measure of the effects of training than that obtained in design A or B. The differences between the "after" scores (X_2 and Y_2) and the "change" scores (d and d') of the two groups can be compared when this design is used. Thus, the design safeguards

212 *Ibid.*, p. 145.
213 *Ibid.*
214 *Ibid.*
215 *Ibid.*

	A After-Only with One Control Group		B Before-After with Single Group	C Before-After with One Control Group		D Before-After with Two Control Groups		
	Experimental Group	Control Group	Experimental Group	Experimental Group	Control Group	Experimental Group	Control Group I	Control Group II
"Before" measurement	No	No	Yes (X_1)	Yes (X_1)	Yes (Y_1)	Yes (X_1)	Yes (Y_1)	No. $\left(Z_1 = \frac{X_1 + Y_1}{2}\right)$
Training	Yes	No	Yes	Yes	No	Yes	No	Yes
"After" measurement	Yes (X_2)	Yes (Y_2)	Yes (X_2)	Yes (X_2)	Yes (Y_2)	Yes (X_2)	Yes (Y_2)	Yes (Z_2)
Change	$d = X_2 - Y_2$		$d = X_2 - X_1$	$d = X_2 - X_1$ $d' = Y_2 - Y_1$			$d = X_2 - X_1$ $d' = Y_2 - Y_1$ $d'' = Z_2 - Z_1$	
Interaction							$I = d - (d' + d'')$	

Figure 15 Types of experimental designs. *Source:* Bernard M. Bass and James A. Vaughan, *Training in Industry: The Management of Learning,* Wadsworth, Belmont, 1966, p. 146, adapted from Claire Sellitz et al., *Research Methods in Social Relations,* Revised One-Volume Edition, Holt, Rinehart and Winston, New York, 1959, p. 110.

against attributing effects to training that may be due to other influences. This safeguard exists, however, only when there is no interaction between the "before" measure or external events and program participation. If an interaction effect seems likely between the "before" measure and the training, then design C should be used.[216]

Design D is similar to C except for the addition of a second control group that receives the training and the "after" measure but no "before" measure. Given an appropriate matching procedure and random selection of group members, we can assume that the "before" measurement for control group II would have been similar to those of the other two groups. We may infer a "before" score (Z_1) for control group II by averaging the "before" scores for the experimental group and control group I. We would now have a group that has received training and has "before" (assumed) and "after" scores but in which there is no possibility of an interaction between the training and the "before" measurement.[217]

The results of the design may be interpreted as follows: (1) the behavior change of members of control group II (d'') is due to the training alone; (2) the change of control group I (d') is due to the effects of the "before" measurement alone; (3) if the change score of the experimental group (d) is different from the sum of the change scores of the two control groups $(d'$ and $d'')$, this result is a reflection of the interaction between the training and the "before" measurement.[218]

An example of a still more powerful technique for evaluating training is the analysis of covariance as applied to a randomized groups design. Given a "before" and an "after" measure on the same variable or set of variables for any number of groups, the analysis of covariance makes it possible to subtract from the "after" measure only that portion of the "before" measure that correlates with it. This adjustment provides a more accurate test of the effects of a development program.[219]

The designs described above do not exhaust all the possibilities for evaluation; they merely illustrate conveniently the different kinds of inferences that may be drawn from different designs and therefore point up the importance of paying attention to design before beginning training.[220]

(3) *Program evaluation should be carried out at several levels and at several times.* Obtaining the trainees' immediate reactions when they complete a program is undoubtedly desirable; measuring their learning at the same time is perhaps also advisable. However, these same measurements

[216] *Ibid.*, pp. 145–147.
[217] *Ibid.*, p. 147.
[218] *Ibid.*
[219] *Ibid.*
[220] *Ibid.*

should be taken again after a lapse of time (six months to one year) together with a measurement of the change in the trainees' behaviors and an estimate of the results of training—that is, the effects of developmental programs on the organization.[221]

These three principles represent an ideal that we have not yet approached in the field of program evaluation. Although we are not likely to make massive breakthroughs in the near future, we should continue to improve evaluations in any way possible, realizing that a less than perfect evaluation is still better than none at all.[222]

Organizational Matters in Evaluation

Clearly, the final phase of any developmental program should be an evaluation of the overall effort itself despite the complications involved. When the effort culminates in a course presentation, this could mean ascertaining how well the course met the objective(s) for which it was developed and presented.

To assure that course objectives are consistently and well met, the factors influencing developmental efforts must also be identified and controlled. Such factors as the selection of manpower specialists, administrative and supervisory practices carried out by these specialists, and the quality of conference leadership and instruction have a strong bearing upon the outcome of program efforts. Therefore, the process of evaluating developmental programs should be directed toward organizational and managerial matters affecting programs as well as towards the end-products of programs, that is, learning as reflected in behavioral change. The state of the art of evaluation is still in its infancy and subjective reaction evaluations are probably still the most common.[223]

Methods of Evaluation

Six methods of evaluation are discussed next. Each method in itself enables the manpower specialist to evaluate and control a portion of the organization's total developmental effort. Taken as a whole, application of the six methods should give a satisfactory and balanced evaluation of the entire developmental activity. A brief description of each of the six methods follows.

One of the approaches to evaluation is to obtain the services of nationally

[221] *Ibid.*

[222] *Ibid.*, p. 148.

[223] Ralph F. Catalanello and Donald L. Kirkpatrick, "Evaluating Training Programs—The State of the Art," *Training and Development Journal,* Vol. 22, No. 5, May 1968, pp. 2–9. See also Donald L. Kirkpatrick, "Evaluation of Training," in Craig and Bittel, *op. cit.,* pp. 87–112.

recognized consulting authorities on conference leadership to appraise the quality of conference and formal classroom presentations. These consultants could observe a selected conference leader's presentations of two or more conferences. Following an observation, the observer should meet with the conference leader and provide him with direct criticism on the presentation. The consultant should also feedback his impressions of the general quality of conference leading in the organization. Included in the latter would be a write-up containing his general recommendations for improvement. Finally, the consultant or team of observers should meet with the manpower specialist for a group discussion on the overall quality of conference leadership. Subsequently, actions, based on the findings of the visiting observers, should be taken to make improvements in this field.

A second method of evaluating supervisory development conferences may be used by manpower specialists of decentralized operations to appraise conference leading at the plant level. A list of check-off items, relating to characteristics of conference leading, can be filled out by the manpower specialist while observing a conference. The list is then used as a basis for discussion in reviewing the conference with the leader. The sample conference leader evaluation checklist, a part of which is shown in Figure 16, is one of many such devices that can be utilized to evaluate conference leading.

In the first section of Figure 16, directions for using the checklist are shown. Following the directions, the first two of fifteen evaluation items relating directly to the conference are shown in full. The main categories of the other thirteen items may be: general participation of the group, promotion of group interaction, obtaining essential information from the group, encouraging various opinions and decisions, stimulating critical evaluation by the group, clarifying contributions when needed, maintaining a neutral role, handling troublesome participants, conference progress, rapport with the group, relating the conference to the local situation, attaining conference objectives, and summarizing and charting conference progress.

The second section of Figure 16 shows the part of the checklist which is utilized in evaluating physical factors that affect conferences.

A third technique, applicable for all types of supervisory training, is the use of survey questionnaires administered immediately following the completion of a course or program and again approximately six months after the completion date to obtain participants' opinions to various values of the training. Supervisors of participants may be surveyed to obtain explicit data on changes in performance that may have resulted from the training. This type of evaluation largely results in testimonials with some evidence regarding behavioral or attitudinal change. Negative evaluations obtained in this manner may actually be more instructive for improving developmental activities than positive evaluations. The latter simply confirm what

Conference Leader Evaluation
Checklist

Rate the leader on each item which is applicable and on which you have observed his work. Use a plus (+) to note an item definitely above average, a check (√) to show an average rating, and a minus (−) to show a below average rating. Use these ratings on the individual items as a guide in arriving at an overall rating for each major category. Indicate the overall rating by placing an "X" in the appropriate space.

1. Preparation for Conference
   Consider how well the leader planned and prepared his outlines, materials, equipment, and facilities.
   _____ Outline preparation
   _____ Organization of materials
   _____ Familiarity with subject
   _____ Local adaptation of material
   _____ Availability of equipment, materials, etc.
   _____ Room orderliness
   _____ _____
   _____ _____

   Overall Evaluation

Below Aver.	Average	Above Aver.

   Suggestions & Comments
   _____
   _____
   _____
   _____
   _____

2. Conference Introduction
   Consider the appropriateness and clarity of the introduction.
   _____ Opening statement
   _____ Statement of objectives
   _____ Clarification of participants' roles
   _____ Interest stimulation
   _____ Length of introduction
   _____ _____
   _____ _____

   Overall Evaluation

Below Aver.	Average	Above Aver.

   Suggestions & Comments
   _____
   _____
   _____

Physical Factors Affecting Conferences

I. Lighting
   _____ Adequacy
   _____ Arrangement
   _____ Working order
   _____ _____
   _____ _____

   Suggestions & Comments
   _____
   _____
   _____
   _____
   _____

II. Furniture
   _____ Arrangement of tables and chairs
   _____ Quantity of furniture
   _____ Condition of furniture
   _____ _____
   _____ _____

   _____
   _____
   _____
   _____
   _____

III. Ventilation
   _____ Smoke, fumes, dust
   _____ Humidity
   _____ Heat or coldness
   _____ _____
   _____ _____

   _____
   _____
   _____
   _____
   _____

Figure 16 Conference leader evaluation checklist.

we hope to obtain; we need not and should not regard such evidence as credible proof of perfection in manpower development programs.

The fourth method, the before and after comparison, may be used whenever tangible data relating to course objectives are available. This is a method that provides management with relatively incontrovertible results of a training effort and is one that developers of courses should be encouraged to build into a course wherever possible. An example of this would be comparing the amount of machine repair maintenance time required on gear-cutting machinery before a course on gear-cutting set-up procedures is presented with the time required after the training has been given. Examples from supervisory development programs would be more difficult to cite, but cost clinic programs might provide an example.

The fifth approach is to evaluate the effectiveness of terminal-type training programs (such as apprenticeship where the program runs for a given number of hours) on the basis of enrollees' completing programs and of the retention of graduates as employees of the sponsoring organization. At approximately two-year intervals a follow-up study should be made of the enrollees and graduates of each terminal-type developmental program in an organization. For any given program, such information as the following should be obtained: number of enrollees, program drop-outs, graduates, and graduate trainees; percent of enrollees completing program and of graduates retained in employment; and position classifications and salary grades of retained graduates. The data may be compiled to reflect the above items by year, by organizational component, and by functional field of business. Of course, if terminal-type programs are not in operation (as when programs are continuous, such as in on-going supervisory training), the above method cannot be used.

A sixth method of evaluating manpower development programs, especially in large-scale organizations, is that of auditing the conduct of developmental activities in decentralized organizational components. Supervisory training programs, as well as all training efforts at a decentralized location, may be assessed by this method. Briefly, the method can be described as follows. An evaluation checklist is developed which elicits pertinent information on all manpower development programs and on all training functions. The training representative at a location is sent copies of the checklist. He fills in the requested data which is analyzed by the manpower specialist at a centralized location. Aided with this analysis, an auditor (frequently the manpower specialist himself), during his visit to the location, obtains any supplementary information that is needed to obtain an understanding of the scope and operations of the local education and training activity. The auditor makes his criticisms and commendations of the activity to local management and counsels them in ways to make improvements. Following the visit, the auditor sends a written report of his findings to the appropriate division and local personnel. At the end of the year, a statistical report is sent to each division in the organization which informs them of how their component training activities rated in comparison to organizational averages.

CONCLUSIONS

In concluding this chapter, two points should be emphasized: first, the methods described herein of determining needs, of presenting programs, and of evaluating the results of developmental programs have been used with some success by various organizations; and second, experimentation with these and new methods in search of better approaches to effective development of human resources should be a continuing endeavor. Emphasis has been placed in the chapter upon formalities and technical instruments utilized to administer manpower development activities properly.

To provide some balance to the discussion, it should also be noted that a considerable amount of informal contact is needed between the various components of any large-scale organization through visits brought about as a consequence of requests for assistance or staff opinion on a local diagnosis of problems in manpower planning and the development of human resources. These types of informal face-to-face contacts provide a working basis for communicating manpower policy and philosophy and for resolving various administrative problems as they occur.

In meeting an organization's needs for supervisory manpower, terminal-type programs having selection phases may be used for the development of newly appointed supervisors. A series of on-going conferences can then be utilized to supplement the initial training provided in these programs. In addition to formal training, periodic performance reviews and contacts between the trainee, training coordinator, and the trainee's supervisor should be utilized for development. However, the guided experience of the learner which is carried out by his organizational supervisor is the principal mechanism used for much manpower development today.

The manpower specialist performs a staff service by seeing that developmental sessions are made available, but the training of the new supervisor is fundamentally the responsibility of his line organizational superior. Off-the-job development and laboratory training should be used to supplement on-the-job training in the integrated effort to provide socialization to the work organization. Manpower specialists should have knowledge in depth of off-the-job community educational resources and make a strong effort to keep abreast of the rapid developments taking place in the fields of applied behavioral science and organizational development.

CHAPTER 5

Organization for Manpower Planning and Developing People

We have already seen that organizations can be conceptualized as learning systems which can be used for developing people and as entities whose perpetuation as on-going systems can best be assured through manpower planning. It has also been shown that problems in organizations can often be resolved by educational and training programs of various types. Our goal in this chapter is to clarify how different models of organizational structure, organizational relationships, and manpower policy can be utilized for manpower planning and the development of human resources.

We begin by examining broadly the rationale for manpower development and training, the criteria for deciding the conditions under which training should be provided in an organization, and some fundamental considerations in organizational relationships. Next, we briefly consider the impact of organizational size as a practical limiting factor on the scope and type of developmental activities. Then we examine a schematic presentation of knowledge and skills required of manpower in a model complex organization and its particular relevance for business firms. Finally, we discuss in detail the organizational relationships and techniques for manpower policy formulation and implementation needed now and in the future.

RATIONALE FOR MANPOWER DEVELOPMENT

"Industrial training" as a manpower development activity is simply the name of a part of the broader learning process which affects a person continuously during his lifetime.[1] "Training" in this sense may be regarded

[1] Many of those ideas are expressed in Frank J. Fessenden, "Some Training Concepts," *Journal of the American Society of Training Directors,* Vol. 15, No. 10, October 1961, pp. 28–30.

as the sum total of one's learning experiences and tantamount to socialization. The question of the mission of training in complex organizations, therefore, resolves itself into two parts: whether it is better for individuals to learn in an unstructured way through trial and error (and where they may inadvertently acquire "bad" habits and less effective ways of carrying out their work), or whether individuals should learn under circumstances which are conducive to growth and development and integrated with the prevailing standards and norms of industry as stipulated by management. Thus, it can be said that an industrial firm or other organization never really faces the choice of whether it will have training or not. Training is inevitable; the only choice is whether or not the training, that is, the direction of experiences which cannot really be avoided, will be made effective in terms of management's standards.

Prior to entering the world of work, individuals learn primarily through associating with others of various ages and through a series of life experiences. As the individual associates and participates in activities, he takes on the values and attitudes which other people carry and learns (or fails to learn) a range of social and other skills. When an individual enters an industrial or other work situation, he must learn the values and attitudes that govern the work situation and work content. He does this by carrying out the requirements of a job or position. He acquires "experience."

The one person who is in the best position to direct the experiences of an employee is, of course, the employee's immediate supervisor. It, therefore, follows that the job or position must be utilized as the main vehicle for learning and the supervisor is by necessity an instructor. Inasmuch as the supervisor is responsible for the conduct of work assigned to him, he must assist employees in growing and developing on the job in a way consistent with the standards of management. This means that every supervisor must be trained in utilizing job resources for learning. If he cannot acquire this ability, he will probably be an ineffective supervisor.[2] The professionally qualified industrial trainer can help supervisors by showing them how job resources can be used for developing personnel. But, since most employees have 2000 hours per year which they spend on the job and most probably utilize no more than 30 or 40 hours after or during working hours annually in a college course or in formal training sessions (of course, many employees spend no time in these ways), it becomes apparent that training is inherent in the conduct and carrying out of work assignments and should be regarded as a prime responsibility of supervisors rather than

[2] See also Louis W. Lerda and Leslie W. Cross, "Training is a Joint Responsibility," *Journal of the American Society of Training Directors,* Vol. 16, No. 2, February 1962, pp. 3–8; and Karl G. Rahdert, "A Philosophy of Personnel Development," *Business Horizons,* Vol. 3, No. 4, Winter 1960, pp. 46–53.

of trainers, manpower specialists, or others not in a line relationship to the learner.

That is not to say, however, that every supervisor should do all of the training of all of his people. Many times the need for training is sufficiently common throughout a plant, a division, or total organization so that group meetings guided by a qualified trainer are desirable and can save individual supervisors a great deal of time. It is possible in these circumstances for an individual to absorb the cumulative knowledge of a group through sharing the experiences of each. The time normally required to gain the experiences of many years can presumably be condensed into a much shorter time span through formal training sessions. However, such meetings can, in the long run, be effective only if the supervisors themselves understand and enthusiastically support and endorse what is taking place in the formal training meetings. Under circumstances where formal training is required, an industrial trainer who is thoroughly conversant with learning theory and practice, the techniques of distilling and communicating information, and means for ascertaining that individuals acquire the norms and standards of the employing organization should be retained.[3]

CRITERIA TO BE USED TO DECIDE WHETHER TRAINING IS TO BE PROVIDED

As suggested above, the training function in an organization exists not for the purpose of training people but for helping managers manage. This means that the trainer's function is advisory and service in character. Management supplies the criteria regarding whether formal training should be offered or not because only management itself can certify that a need exists. In other words, the trainer can help managers manage, but he cannot manage for them.

Sometimes the trainer helps management by not agreeing to do some of the things that management requests him to do. Sometimes the trainer will be required to take the initiative and persuade management that it has problems which can best be resolved through training. We frequently see that when a staff man is willing to do what a manager should do for himself, the staff man will probably be allowed to do it. When the staff man takes this role, the manager does not develop as he should because he is really not doing the manager's job in its entirety. If the trainer takes the initiative totally and assumes people should be sent to him for training, many managers will be willing to go along with the concept. In all likelihood the training will be ineffective because the inherent learning possibilities of the principal training mechanism (the job) are not utilized.

[3] See Edgar H. Schein, "Forces Which Undermine Management Development," *California Management Review*, Vol. 5, No. 4, Summer 1963, pp. 23–34.

Inasmuch as the long-run objective of industrial firms is to obtain what may be considered a fair return on assets employed, it follows that training must assist management in producing products of the highest quality and at the lowest cost consistent with that quality. In order to secure this ultimate objective, formal training activities may be used to achieve the intermediate objectives of behavior change and improving the knowledge, skills, and abilities of employees in carrying out their present positions or positions in prospect. All such training should be approved by authorized personnel in the organization and be provided in as economically feasible a manner as possible. The decision as to the type, amount, and duration of training should be made by the training organization in consultation with and in concert with management. The latter has final authority for training.

ORGANIZATIONAL RELATIONSHIPS AND CRITERIA FOR ESTABLISHING RESPONSIBILITIES FOR TRAINING AT VARIOUS LEVELS

The function of a training department, if one is to be established, is, thus, to provide an organizational means whereby adults can learn most efficiently and effectively (informally or formally) what they need to know. This function is not and cannot be provided by any other component in an organization and constitutes the reason for having a training department. When this function is eliminated, the natural propensity for individuals to concentrate on meeting the immediate needs of the work situation in an idiosyncratic way to the exclusion of developing people to do the work in a manner consistent with generally accepted managerial principles and techniques becomes dominant. A successful, adaptable, and flexible organization probably cannot exist very long in a dynamic environment when the prevailing form of managerial behavior runs counter to the development of personnel. Organizational mechanisms are needed to reduce employees' bad work habits and poor work practices.

Unfortunately, we actually know very little about the development of human beings when they become adults. Good habits and acceptable practices must be defined by organizations. Because we lack sufficient scientific knowledge, it is necessary that personnel development activities engage in research to determine the best circumstances under which individuals having specific needs can have these needs met through a learning situation. University professors can probably be of only limited value in contributing to our knowledge of adult development since they often have limited access to and knowledge of industry and its impact upon the individual. This means that at the central staff level in a complex organization the training staff should focus upon analytical and exploratory work tied in closely with manpower planning. The results of this work should be translated into practical programs for the employing firm and ably administered by training representatives in decentralized locations. However, the divisional and field organization should also, on its own initiative, develop relationships with local management and apply the criteria for the provision of training previously mentioned. In addition, the field should conduct whatever analytical and exploratory work is required to assure it is operating effectively locally. Manpower and training specialists involved in the central headquarters activity should have a consultative and functional supervisory relationship with training personnel in the field and assist them in meeting management's needs.

More broadly, the training staff can serve an industrial firm or other organization in the same way that an educational institution can serve the total society. Inasmuch as the latter, in order to continue, must contribute to the development of members of society in a way consistent with the changing norms and standards of that society, industrial training must make provision for the development of members of an industrial organization in a way consistent with the changing norms and standards of the employing firm.

Academic educational institutions, such as institutions of higher learning, are centers for the discovery and dissemination of knowledge, some of which is acclaimed as highly valuable and some of which is considered recondite. Industrial-training activities cannot function as such centers, for they often must prove themselves to be valuable immediately to their employers. But excessive emphasis on the immediate to the detriment of soundly planned and conducted development activities must be avoided, particularly because much long-run manpower development can be destroyed by short-run expedients and deficiencies in practice.

SIZE OF MANPOWER IN ORGANIZATIONS

In discussing alternative ways of organizing for training and development, it is worthwhile to begin by considering the structure of American industry by employer size and employment. In doing so we would notice that although the large, *"Fortune* 500" corporate employers appear dominant in the economy from many standpoints, the vast number of small employers with relatively small-sized work forces is striking. These two contrasting observations set the limits on what needs to be said about organizing for training and development.[4]

[4] For ideas on this subject I am indebted to the late Edward D. Wickersham. See Edwin F. Beal and Edward D. Wickersham, *The Practice of Collective Bargaining*, Third Edition, Irwin, Homewood, Illinois, 1967, pp. 47–50.

Table 1   Percentage of Industry Receipts Generated by Corporate
Ownership, 1966

Industry Group	Percentage of Receipts Generated by Corporations
Manufacturing	97.7
Transportation, communication, gas, electric, and sanitary services	93.1
Finance, insurance, and real estate	88.9
Mining	87.4
Wholesale and retail trade	73.8
Construction	69.7
Services	47.4
Agriculture, forestry, and fisheries	16.8

Source. Statistical Abstract of the United States, Government Printing Office, Washington, 1969, p. 472.

If we were to look at manpower employed in various industries in the United States, we would find that the corporate form of ownership is predominant in certain industries and that manufacturing industry is the largest employer of nonagricultural manpower in the United States.

Data from Table 1 indicate quite clearly that the percent of industry receipts generated by corporate ownership in a recent year demonstrate that the predominance of corporate structure varies from industry to industry, ranging from manufacturing at the high end, to agriculture, forestry, and fisheries at the low end.

Tables 2 and 3 provide additional information about manpower in manufacturing industries. More recent data indicate that manufacturing enterprises are the larger ones and that 19 to 20 million persons in the American labor force are working in manufacturing industry. Scanning Table 2 we would find that very large enterprises are found in transportation equipment, electrical machinery, primary metals, textile mills, paper and allied products, and tobacco products. Some manufacturing industries are typified by small enterprises. For example, the printing and publishing; lumber and wood products; stone, clay, and glass; and furniture and fixtures industries rank on the low side in average enterprise employment. Accustomed as many of us are of thinking about the predominance and preponderance of large-scale organizations, it is perhaps a surprise to find that there are very significant differences in enterprise sizes in the various standard industrial classifications. When one examines average manpower per enterprise, he is likely to find a marked discrepancy between what he sees in the behemoths and the typical firm for that industry.

Table 2   The Structure of Manufacturing Employment, 1963

SIC	Industry	Average Manpower per Establishment	Total Industry Employment
20	Food and kindred products	44	1,643,111
37	Transportation equipment	217	1,601,158
36	Electrical machinery	152	1,511,819
35	Nonelectrical machinery	43	1,459,377
23	Apparel and related products	45	1,279,534
33	Primary metal industries	173	1,126,536
34	Fabricated metal products	38	1,082,102
27	Printing and publishing	24	913,243
22	Textile mill products	107	863,246
28	Chemicals and allied products	61	737,414
26	Paper and allied products	103	588,014
32	Stone, clay, and glass	36	573,859
24	Lumber and wood products	15	563,135
30	Rubber and plastic products (n.e.c.)	72	414,959
25	Furniture and fixtures	32	376,548
31	Leather and leather products	80	327,489
38	Instruments and related products	77	305,452
29	Petroleum and coal products	83	153,486
21	Tobacco products	201	77,330
	Average employment per establishment, all manufacturing	84	

Source. *Census of Manufacturers,* Government Printing Office, Washington, 1963, pp. 46–47.

In Table 3, data are provided on the prevalence of establishments by manpower size in manufacturing industries. These data show the numbers of employees according to different industries. The number of firms having 100 or more employees varies, but it can be seen that there are many such organizations. Unfortunately, data are not available in greater detail on this subject. However, one can only conclude for manufacturing industry as a whole that formal organization and full-blown programs of personnel administration, including manpower planning, should be very important. The relatively large size of employing enterprises makes it imperative that specific policies, systems, and procedures be formalized.[5]

Table 4 provides data on the structure of manpower in nonmanufacturing industry in the United States as of March 1969. It can readily be seen that retail and wholesale trade, government, and services combined provide more job opportunities than manufacturing industry. Large-employing establishments similar to those in manufacturing industry are prevalent in

[5] *Ibid.,* p. 49.

Table 3   Prevalence of Establishments by Manpower Size
in Manufacturing Industries, 1963

SIC	Industry	Industry Employment	1–19 Employees	20–99 Employees	100 or More Employees
20	Food and kindred products	1,643,111	23,408	10,224	3,889
37	Transportation equipment	1,601,158	4,328	1,672	1,196
35	Nonelectrical machinery	1,459,377	25,277	6,137	2,289
23	Apparel and related products	1,279,534	15,446	9,955	3,056
37	Electrical machinery	1,511,819	5,226	2,630	2,092
33	Primary metal industries	1,126,536	2,930	2,005	1,578
34	Fabricated metal products	1,082,102	17,765	6,931	2,279
22	Textile mill products	863,246	2,736	2,402	1,966
27	Printing and publishing	913,243	30,875	5,682	1,533
28	Chemicals and allied products	737,414	8,008	2,756	1,229
24	Lumber and wood products	563,135	30,385	4,785	2,455
32	Stone, clay, and glass products	573,859	11,183	3,481	1,174
26	Paper and allied products	588,014	2,161	2,019	1,533
31	Leather and leather products	327,489	1,974	1,135	938
30	Rubber and plastic products	414,959	3,279	1,695	754
25	Furniture and fixtures	376,548	7,165	2,455	858
38	Instruments and related products	305,452	2,606	868	475
29	Petroleum and coal products	153,486	1,150	425	264
21	Tobacco products	77,330	163	106	125
39	Miscellaneous manufacturing	390,760	11,104	2,832	786
	Total all manufacturing industry	16,234,506	207,265	70,243	29,109

Source. *Census of Manufacturers,* Government Printing Office, Washington, 1963,
pp. 69–71.

Table 4   Manpower in Nonmanufacturing Industry in the
United States (as of March 1969)

Industry	Manpower
Retail and wholesale trade	14,193,000
Government	12,752,000
Services and miscellaneous	10,741,000
Transportation and public utilities	4,390,000
Finance, insurance, and real estate	3,459,000
Contract construction	3,054,000
Mining	631,000
Total	49,220,000

Source. *Statistical Abstract of the United States,*
Government Printing Office, Washington, 1969, p.
215.

government, transportation, public utilities, and mining. For example,
consider the millions of employees that work for the federal government
itself. It seems reasonable to state that the manpower and organizational
problems confronting a government agency, a transportation enterprise
such as a railroad or an airline, a public utility, or a mine would be
equally as complex as those problems confronting a manufacturer of
transportation equipment, primary metals, or machinery. By the same
token, the principles and rules of thumb of organization and management
that are applicable in large manufacturing industry would seem to be
equally applicable in the larger-scale organizations found in nonmanufacturing industry.

It should also be noted that other very important segments of nonmanufacturing industry are confronted with problems similar to those
facing small-scale manufacturers. For example, small manufacturers in
food and kindred products, apparel, printing and publishing, and lumber
probably have a great deal in common from the manpower development
standpoint with much of wholesale and retail trade, services, and contract
construction. Smaller enterprises probably tend to rely on a less sophisticated technology than mass-production industry and have the potential
for retaining family-like employment relationships in the work setting.[6]

In Table 5, data are shown reflecting a distribution of manpower in the
500 largest industrial corporations as well as other business organizations
of the type designated in the United States in a recent year. It can readily
be seen that more than one-half of these 500 largest industrials have less
than 15,000 employees. The remainder of the top 500 include employees

[6] *Ibid.,* pp. 48–50.

Manpower (thousands)	500 Largest Industrials	Second 500 Largest Industrials	50 Largest Retailers	50 Largest Utilities	50 Largest Transportation Companies	50 Largest Life Insurance Companies	50 Largest Commercial Banks
Up to 4.9	47	406	3	10	12	32	30
5– 9.9	114	84	7	23	12	11	10
10– 14.9	96	10	8	10	6	1	6
15– 19.9	45		8	2	4	2	2
20– 24.9	38		4	3	3	1	
25– 29.9	24		4	1			
30– 34.9	27		3		2		1
35– 39.9	20		1		4		1
40– 44.9	16				1		
45– 49.9	10				3		
50– 54.9	10		2		1		
55– 59.9	2					2	
60– 64.9	8		1		1		
65– 69.9	4						
70– 74.9	4						
75– 79.9	1		2				
80– 84.9	1		1			1	
85– 89.9	3						
90– 94.9			2				
95– 99.9	1						
100–124.9	14		1		1		
125–149.9	6		2				
150–174.9	1						
175–199.9							
200–249.9	3						
250–299.9	1						
300–399.9	1		1				
400 and up	3			1			
Total employees	14,813,809	1,822,071	2,118,830	1,193,525	970,142	431,668	352,196

Source. "The *Fortune* Directory of the 500 Largest Industrial Corporations," and "The Fifty Largest Commercial Banks . . . Life Insurance Companies . . . Retailing Companies . . Transportation Companies . . Utilities," *Fortune*, Vol. 81, No. 5, May 1970, pp. 182–213; and "The *Fortune* Directory of the Second 500 Largest Industrial Corporations," *Fortune*, Vol. 81, No. 6, June 1970, pp. 98–117.

up to and exceeding 400,000. It is quite obvious that the *"Fortune"* employers should be the most concerned with manpower planning and the development of human resources. Employers with manpower in the ranges shown in Table 5 can ignore rational manpower planning and the development of human resources only at their peril as viable organizations.

Detailed statistics on manpower in the largest industrial firms outside the United States are not conveniently available. However, in Table 6 some overall data are shown, indicating manpower in industrial organiza-

Table 6 Manpower in the Largest Industrial and Commercial Banking Organizations Outside the United States

Manpower (thousands)	200 Largest Industrials	50 Largest Commercial Banks
Up to 4.9	2	7
5– 9.9	5	12
10– 14.9	10	13
15– 19.9	24	5
20– 24.9	17	3
25– 29.9	18	1
30– 34.9	19	3
35– 39.9	13	2
40– 44.9	10	2
45– 49.9	6	
50– 54.9	5	2
55– 59.9	3	
60– 64.9	10	
65– 69.9	6	
70– 74.9	7	
75– 79.9	4	
80– 84.9	4	
85– 89.9	2	
90– 94.9	6	
95– 99.9	2	
100–124.9	8	
125–149.9	5	
150–174.9	6	
175–199.9	2	
200–249.9	1	
250–299.9	2	
300–399.9	3	
400 and up	0	
Total:	11,511,433 employees	835,076

Source. "The *Fortune* Directory of the 200 Largest Industrials Outside the U.S." and "The Fifty Largest Commercial Banks Outside the U.S.," *Fortune,* Vol. 82, No. 2, August 1970, pp. 142–149.

tions outside of the United States. If we look back at Table 5, we would find that the United States has many organizations employing more than 50,000 persons. Yet, if one considers organizations outside the United States, there also are many which are employing 50,000.

At this point, it is not known how many foreign industrials engage in systematic manpower planning. Yet it is quite evident from their size that many should be giving manpower planning and the development of human resources their careful attention. Size itself will not, of course, dictate the immediate establishment of a manpower-planning activity or the foundation of a training department. The objective needs for these two activities may not be subjectively understood by organizational management. Moreover, the establishment of both of these activities involves considerable expense which organizations try to avoid if possible. Yet, if the long run success of the firm depends upon the human capital in it, wise managers should be willing to make the investment and back programs oriented toward the development of human resources.

TRAINING PROGRAMS IN THE UNITED STATES

In 1962 a survey was undertaken based upon a 1% sample of establishments in American industry. Approximately 9600 establishments were sent questionnaires by the United States Department of Labor, and more than 85% of these questionnaires were returned. This survey constituted the first time that information was gathered on the number of trainees and the types of formal employee training programs in operation in the nation's industries. The training programs, as defined in the survey, included any prearranged formal systems of instruction sponsored by the employer or by employer-union agreement and designed to develop employees to perform their current or future job duties. The survey covered instruction for employees both on and off the job site.[7] It is significant as a measure of training activities in the United States before the "manpower revolution" was well recognized.

In this nationwide survey in which data were gathered for 37 million workers in 711,000 establishments, it was found that a wide variety of formal training is being undertaken in American industry. However, only one of every five establishments in the survey sponsored some type of formal training. Of the 37 million workers employed in these establishments, only 2.7 million were actually enrolled in an employer-sponsored program. Inasmuch as some of these workers were enrolled in more than

[7] Manpower Administration, U.S. Department of Labor, *Training of Workers in American Industry* (Research Division Report No. 1), Government Printing Office, Washington, 1962.

one program, the number of trainees totaled 3.6 million. Therefore, workers in training, on the average, were enrolled in 1.3 programs.[8]

The proportion of establishments with training programs was directly related to establishment size. The larger the number of employees in an establishment, the greater was the probability that a training program was in operation. Of the 2.7 million workers in training, 1.5 million were employed in goods-producing industries and 1.2 million in service industries. Among establishments with training programs, the service industries tended to have a higher proportion of employees in training than did the goods-producing industries. Almost 17 percent of employees in the service industries, as compared with only 13 percent in the goods-producing industries, were receiving training. Larger and smaller establishments tended to emphasize different types of programs. Specifically, larger establishments emphasized training in the sciences, engineering, technology, and management. Smaller establishments emphasized training in the skilled crafts; in tool or machine operations; in mathematics; and in sales, office, and other office-related skills. Employer-subsidized training in educational institutions was heavily concentrated among the larger establishments.[9]

Regarding the type of trainees, it was found that 1.8 million trainees were enrolled in safety programs. Safety was by far the most prevalent type of training provided by employers. Most trainees were enrolled in short courses in which development of new skills or enhancement of existing skills was only incidental. For example, of the 3.6 million trainees, 1.8 million were enrolled in safety courses and 300,000 in orientation courses. Only 1.5 million trainees were enrolled in courses that were designed to provide substantive skills.[10]

Of the 1.5 million enrolled in some type of training other than safety or orientation, those enrolled in programs involving a specific industrial skill numbered fewer than 400,000. The largest groups of trainees were production workers (almost one-half million) followed by managers, supervisors, and foremen; skilled tradesmen; apprentices; and sales workers. More than 58,000 training programs in the skilled trades were conducted in 142,000 establishments which sponsored training. Almost one-third of all establishments which sponsored training included apprentices in their training programs. The largest number of apprentices were enrolled in plumber or pipe fitter, electrician, or machinist programs.[11]

Perhaps the significance of this survey can be appreciated if several considerations are emphasized. First, of the establishments surveyed only

[8] *Ibid.*, p. 1.
[9] *Ibid.*, pp. 1–2.
[10] *Ibid.*, p. 2.
[11] *Ibid.*, pp. 2–3.

20% sponsored one or more formal training programs for their workers. This indicates that 80% of private industry in the United States apparently has adopted no formalized program of training for its workers, relying instead on some informal system of training or perhaps obtaining trained workers from other sources. Secondly, it is the large organizations which are most heavily involved in education and training programs (see Table 7). Thirdly, of the 18.5 million employees in establishments with training programs, almost 2.7 million were receiving some type of training in 1962. This amounts to not quite 15 percent of the total. With the exception of large-sized organizations in contract construction and mining, the proportion of workers in training programs was relatively small in most industries, ranging from a low of 10 percent to a high of 30 percent. Overall, the service industries showed somewhat higher proportions of workers in training than the goods-producing industries. This difference was most noticeable in small-sized establishments, particularly those with less than 500 employees.[12] Table 7 provides an overall picture of the establishments by manpower size with training programs.

Table 7 Establishments by Manpower Size in a 1962 Survey of Training Programs

Establishment Size (in manpower)	Percent of Establishments with Training Programs
4–19	11
20–99	25
100–499	41
500–999	70
1000–2499	85
2500–4999	90
5000 or more	96

Source. Manpower Administration, U.S. Department of Labor, *Training of Workers in American Industry* (Research Division Report No. 1), Government Printing Office, Washington, 1964, p. 5.

Whether the information provided, regarding the extent of training program activities in the United States in 1962, is still applicable today remains doubtful. Since 1962, many companies have become involved with training programs because of the enactment of the Manpower Development and Training Act in 1962 and other government-initiated

[12] *Ibid.*, pp. 5–6.

Table 8   Membership in American Society for Training and Development by Manpower Size of Employing Organizations

Manpower Size	Percent of ASTD Members
Less than 25	0
25–100	2
101–500	9
501–1,000	10
1,001–5,000	40
5,001–10,000	18
10,0001–25,000	11
25,000 and over	10

Source. Patrick C. Farbro, "The ASTD Membership Survey," *Training Directors Journal,* Vol. 19, No. 9, September 1965, p. 30.

programs. As a consequence, we could expect to find differences from the participation rates reported in the survey made in 1962.

However, in trying to determine the extent to which training programs operate in the United States, it is instructive to look at data provided in a survey in 1965 of the members of the American Society for Training and Development. Each member was sent a questionnaire and 65 percent returned them. The data compiled in Table 8 indicate that the members of the ASTD are most numerous in organizations with more than 1000 employees. Smaller organizations have fewer members, and, strangely, fewer members are found on a percentage basis, at least, in organizations with more than 5000 employees. Although these data are probably inadequate and certainly are inconclusive, it does seem that the diffusion of training programs and the location of ASTD members, many of whom are training directors, seem to coincide and that in smaller organizations that there not only is less training but also fewer trainers and training directors. It is in the smaller organizations, undoubtedly, where training on the job is the primary mode of learning, and it is in these work environments where the bulk of American manpower is employed.

SETTING UP ORGANIZATIONS FOR DEVELOPING PEOPLE

Figure 1 is a useful device for considering the evolution of education and training programs in industrial and other complex organizations. The first stage of evolution from 1900 to 1930 shows a clear delineation between classroom instruction and work situation in an era when industrial training was coming into its own. Although there were formal training activities prior to 1900, training in industry was initiated in the 1900s

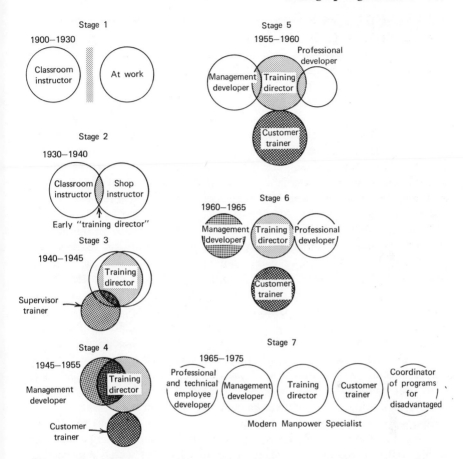

Figure 1 Evolution of the training director's job. *Source.* Adapted from Leonard C. Silvern, "Change in the Training Director's Job," *Journal of the American Society of Training Directors,* Vol. 15, No. 2, February 1961, pp. 24–25.

because the public and private schools did not accentuate the immediate employability of their graduates. Wartime periods gave another impetus to the need for establishing sound training programs outside of and beyond formal education. It was therefore quite natural that the industrial growth of the country led to a concentration of training in the trade and technical fields first.[13]

Stage 2 is shown in Figure 1 and covers the years between 1930 and 1940. This stage indicates that training grew out of education and for

[13] Leonard C. Silvern, "Change in the Training Director's Job," *Journal of the American Society of Training Directors,* Vol. 15, No. 2, February 1961, p. 24.

many years the content of training was classroom-oriented following a traditional pattern. Early signs of the training-director role were apparent. In other words, work skills were not learned so much by training as they were learned in the actual work situation. Gradually, however, the shop or laboratory influence was felt as shop schools and vestibule schools were instituted. Shop instruction and classroom instruction were thus coordinated.[14]

Stage 3 shows the situation in approximately 1940 and reflects the World War II period. By 1945 the civilian war training programs resulted in the creation of training directors who typically were persons with a satisfactory balance of experience in both the classroom and shop types of curricula and who were also becoming increasingly concerned with supervisory training.[15]

Stage 4 is shown as the period between 1945 and 1955. In this decade the training director, influenced by new organizational and management principles, found that supervisory training was really part of a larger whole, known as management development. Sometimes the latter was in the province of the training director but as often as not was located elsewhere in the organization. Quite often the thought apparently was that management development was too important to be left to the rather low-level training director and should be dignified by being called a new name and organizationally established in such a way that the function would have a new stature. In addition, complex product development and marketing competition resulted in the creation of formal customer training, usually in the marketing or field-engineering department.[16]

Stage 5 took place roughly between 1955 to 1960. In 1960 the typical training director of the pre-1945 days found management losing confidence in his ability to conduct the management development which was needed. Consequently, the management development specialist began to evolve and create new programs, shifting away from the training director and his sphere of influence. In the technical industries, particularly, the trend to develop technical or professional competence similar to but different from managerial competence was organizationally placed not in the traditional personnel department but in the technical staff itself. Finally, customer training can be seen as expanding, completely isolated from the training director's organization and evolving into a new entity of its own.[17]

Since the early 1960s we have seen the evolution into a sixth stage, particularly in the largest of organizations. The sixth stage indicates an impor-

[14] *Ibid.*
[15] *Ibid.*, pp. 24–25.
[16] *Ibid.*, p. 25.
[17] *Ibid.*

tant separation between management development, customer training, the traditional training director, and the professional developer. The splitting away of these functions obviously creates problems in the coordination of the development of human resources for the total organization. In many large companies important questions have been raised as to whether the gradual separation of functions concerned with the development of human resources is preferable to an alternative concept whereby they might be integrated and given concerted direction.

Many questions have been raised anew as the training function has increasingly become involved with national manpower policy. Thus, in many firms today we see a new stage already apparent concerned with integrating the disadvantaged group of Americans into the organizational structure of large firms. This might be considered Stage 7 although its existence is not yet as crystalized as those stages and spheres previously identified. If we were to look at the kinds of activities engaged in by the modern manpower specialist today in large-scale organizations, we would find him responsible for the planning and the development of five different kinds of manpower: professional and technical employees; management development; traditional training programs available to employees at diverse levels; some involvement in customer or dealer training; and, finally, coordinator of programs for the disadvantaged, including MDTA- and OEO-type programs, as well as other government- or industry-established programs studded with ephemeral acronymic titles (e.g., JOBS—Job Opportunities in the Business Sector).

In addition to the previously mentioned functions, the modern manpower specialist would also have responsibilities for the recruitment, selection, and placement of college graduate trainees and college cooperative trainees. Finally, he would in all likelihood have some responsibility for the development and improvement of relationships between institutions of higher learning and his employer, subjects of concern to us later in the book.

TOP-MANAGEMENT MANPOWER DEVELOPMENT COMMITTEES

Perhaps the early work by Morgan is still useful in obtaining organizational perspective on human resource development because in discussing the training department of the 1940s he differentiated between research, analytical, and standards sections in training departments, much as we would today. He was also quite aware of the differences between the conduct of training activities in a large and a small organization.[18] How-

[18] Howard K. Morgan, *Industrial Training and Testing*, McGraw-Hill, New York, 1945, pp. 55–64.

ever, most of his remarks apply to an era which has long since passed, at least among pace-setting large-scale organizations.

Today, as we have seen, industrial organizations have become very large and the corporate conglomerate is increasingly emerging as a prominent type of organizational structure. The essence of such an organization is decentralized decision-making, which can be greatly affected by the type of autonomy granted by the central or headquarters staff. As a consequence, there can be all sorts of variations in degree of autonomy from highly centralized at one extreme to local autonomy at the other. The advantages and disadvantages of each from the standpoint of manpower development tend to lessen as they approach a midpoint.[19] Let us examine this matter more closely.

Some large organizations which have practiced centralized autonomy find that their manpower development programs are announced, adopted, and mechanically implemented with dispatch and uniformity of procedure when directed from headquarters. The outward appearance suggests movement and progress. Desirable as it may seem, this type of program operation and administration can be superficial and cause subordinate levels of management to feel little real responsibility and, consequently, to participate less sincerely and less effectively in manpower development efforts.[20]

The other managerial alternative carried to an extreme would leave the origination of a program completely to the subordinate units. This can result in many programs of varying quality, diverse procedures and administrative practices, and a lack of coordination. However, the enthusiasm, participation, and accomplishment of objectives locally may be far greater than under rigid centralized control. Thus it appears that for each organization there is a balance point between these extremes that must be determined, that is, one which will provide the optimum conditions for manpower development in that particular organization.[21]

The kinds of policy that apply to building organizations for manpower planning and developing people vary considerably. The size itself of the organization can be a determining factor, as we have seen. In addition, some organizations believe that line management should be responsible for all functions necessary to conduct operations, with staff personnel providing only advice and assistance. Others hold staff departments responsible for the executions of their functions in the different line departments. In the latter case more responsibility for manpower development

[19] Robert B. Burr, "Management Development," in Robert L. Craig and Lester R. Bittel, eds., *Training and Development Handbook*, McGraw-Hill, New York, 1967, p. 379.
[20] *Ibid.*, pp. 379–380.
[21] *Ibid.*, p. 380.

would normally be placed in the training department. Developmental activity would tend to be more centrally conducted and less a part of experience obtained on the job.[22]

Again, depending upon the size of the organization, consultants may play a considerable role in implementing either concept, centralization or decentralization. The small firm without justification for a complete staff department may look to consultants exclusively in carrying out education and training activities. On the other hand, a large organization may find it desirable to augment its staff with consultants only in specific areas, relying upon its own staff to carry out the bulk of the education and training task.

Where there is a choice, we would be likely to find that development is regarded as primarily the result of daily work experience and primary emphasis is placed upon development in the present job rather than the job in prospect. These two ideas seem to be consonant with the idea of line responsibility for training. To be effective, it is necessary for a training department to have definite goals and policies as well as top-management support. The endorsement of training programs should start from the top of the organization down, or, at least, have the approval of the immediate organizational superiors of the trainees.[23] Without such endorsements the training activity may be wasted or even harmful. Where active opposition to the behavioral change intended by the training exists, the training will probably be useless and should be halted or postponed.[24] Therefore, in building an organizational arrangement for the conduct of the development of human resources, a realistic link must be made between the trainee, the training department, and higher management.

In order to be organizationally effective, a manpower-planning and development program must develop a linkage to top management in order to obtain its understanding, acceptance, and active support. This generally means that some type of manpower-planning and development committee is essential. The committee can usually be best established for an operational unit such as a plant or a division, but may be set up for a divisional function which cuts across a number of plants, such as in the accounting and financial control function. This committee should consist of persons most responsible for the success of the entire unit or profit center. At the plant level, for example, the committee would consist of the plant manager, production manager, industrial relations manager, and the head of any department during the time his employees are being evaluated and

[22] *Ibid.*

[23] See Robert J. House, "A Commitment Approach to Management Development," *California Management Review,* Vol. 7, No. 3, Spring 1965, pp. 15–28.

[24] George S. Odiorne, "A Systems Approach to Training," *Training Director's Journal,* Vol. 19, No. 10, October 1965, p. 19.

214 Organization for Manpower Development

discussed. A committee so constituted symbolizes and assures top management support.[25]

The manpower planning and development committee should serve the following functions:

1. Gives direction to the entire program by defining objectives, determining the scope, and deciding on the emphases of the program.

2. Guides the proper utilization of human resources by establishing broad, overall policies, advising with the manpower development staff, and evaluating present manpower resources.

3. Studies long-range manpower needs.

4. Evaluates available resources periodically and follows up on the status of individual and organizational developmental plans.[26]

A wide range of information is needed by the committee about the people in the organization, especially those having technical and managerial responsibilities, in order to assist the manpower-planning and development committee in carrying out its functions as enumerated above. Often the usual basic manpower data available from personnel jackets in the personnel department needs to be updated and supplemented by information regarding special skills, hobbies, leadership experiences, achievements, and aspirations. As a rule, improved job performance appraisal information is needed based upon how well the individual is doing those things he is supposed to do on his present job.

Usually it is necessary for staff people to help an organization to establish a means for obtaining these kinds of information. In order to aid in evaluating the range of talent and depth of human resource potential in an organization, a battery of psychological tests, covering various abilities, knowledge, and personal characteristics, helps to refine information obtained from other sources. Evaluative interviews, information about health, and developmental activities and plans complete the kinds of data which the manpower planning committee needs.[27]

It is also possible to have committees concerned with manpower planning and development which serve the entire corporation. Of course, if the organization is extremely large, it may be more realistic to have such committees operate only at the division or plant level. But in the many middle-sized and smaller organizations, which we discussed earlier in the chapter and were shown to be quite numerous in the United States, there

[25] Orlo L. Crissey, "The Industrial Psychologist in Manpower and Organizational Planning," paper read at the annual meeting of Division 14 of the American Psychological Association at St. Louis, Missouri, on September 4, 1962.
[26] *Ibid.*
[27] *Ibid.*

is every reason to believe that corporate manpower-planning and development committees can be successful and indeed are preferable. The staff work for these committees should be carried out by the manpower specialist or that part of the organization which is concerned with training and developmental activities. His goal should be to get the active involvement of top management in the manpower-planning and development effort.

ORGANIZATIONAL RELATIONSHIPS

Once a top-management committee has been established and maintained in the organizational power structure for such purposes as giving manpower, educational, and training plans and programs authenticity, to review research on manpower needs and developmental programs, and set pertinent policies, it becomes easy to demonstrate to the rest of the organization that manpower planning and human resource development are being carried out (or attempting to be carried out) in concert with organizational objectives set by top management. It then becomes necessary to build a model so that the organization can function to develop people while meeting its goals. If we take as the model of a large scale organization one which has a corporate level, division levels (based upon product, service, and/or geography), and a unit level (such as a plant, sales office, and district office), we can then proceed to describe in more detail the kinds of organizational relationships and responsibilities needed for human resource development.

At the corporate level, the manpower-planning and development activity would act in a staff capacity and perform such functions as the following. First, it should develop corporate policy on education, training, and developmental programs. Second, it should set standards for these activities throughout the organization. Standards would be established so that optimal learning takes place in an environment favorable to the development of people in economical circumstances. Third, the headquarters staff should provide advice within the organization to those who inquire about educational, training, and developmental resources that are available both inside and outside the organization. Fourth, this staff should provide information on developmental activities carried on inside the organization to those located in remote areas who wish such knowledge. This responsibility requires the staff to be *au courant* on a wide range of activities. Fifth, the staff should keep top management advised regarding developmental activities within the organization and do the necessary staff work for the top-management manpower-planning and development committee. Lastly, the headquarters staff should conduct research on new programs and techniques in development and experiment with new programs and techniques.

For most organizations such a manpower-planning and development staff would include only a small number of highly qualified professionals who had sufficient education and experience to constitute collectively an expert resource in a wide range of matters concerned with human development. Ideally, effective use would be made of their diversified capabilities in such activities as: program evaluation, the training of trainers, conference leadership and instructional methods, simulation exercises, programmed instruction, and the like. They would be required to be personally effective in conducting liaison and consulting work with divisions and staffs, highly competent in analytical work, and capable of producing high quality completed staff work with a minimum of direct supervision.

In a decentralized large-scale organization, the divisions would have several important responsibilities. First, they would be expected to diagnose their own needs for training, educational, and developmental programs. Second, they would be required to develop or obtain the necessary training materials to carry out these programs. Third, employees in the divisions would be expected to lead conferences and conduct various developmental programs. Fourth, divisional manpower staff members would be expected to coordinate all the internal training and educational activities within their division. Fifth, these same experts would be expected to evaluate their own programs. Sixth, the divisions would be expected to maintain whatever records are necessary concerning trainees and their progress and keep the corporate staff advised of their plans, policies, programs, and results. Seventh, and lastly, the divisions would be expected to develop their own manpower staff to perform the training and education activities.

In a decentralized organization the next lowest organizational level is that of the unit, such as a plant, district sales office, or similar organizational component. Whereas the division would be essentially responsible for augmenting and implementing the policies and plans of the corporate manpower-planning and development committee, at the unit level there would be a similar expectation for carrying out the developmental activities defined and designed by the division. However, these would be augmented and made relevant for local conditions. For example, it would be expected that at the local level manpower specialists would diagnose their own needs in the plant for training and education, develop or obtain necessary materials, lead conferences and conduct programs, coordinate all internal developmental activities, evaluate programs, maintain records as are necessary, and develop manpower specialists locally to perform manpower services, such as education and training programs.

In complex organizations there are innumerable functional staffs which exist. They have an important role to plan in educational and training activities. For example, there may be a marketing, purchasing, manufacturing, finance, engineering, or other staff, each of which has its own unique area of specialization. Each is usually very concerned with the development of technical and professional manpower within its own sphere. In fact, as we saw in Figure 1, the emergence of professional manpower development had a significant impact on traditional training activities and added a new dimension to the field about 1955.

It is therefore important that the functional staffs in a large-scale organization make their contribution to the development of human resources. This is best done when the following activities are carried out by the particular functional staff. First, such a staff should assist divisions in diagnosing their own training and education needs. Second, it should assist in developing materials. Third, it should assist in conducting programs. Fourth, it should assist in evaluating programs. It can thus be seen that the role of a functional staff is essentially to assist the separate staff primarily concerned with manpower in working with divisions to carry out the human resource development responsibility. The functional staff simply adds another specialized input to the training system. In this way, effective organizational relationships are established between a top management committee which focuses on manpower planning and the development of human resources, a manpower specialist staff, the various manpower specialists in the divisions of the organization, the local plants or sales offices or other components, and, lastly, the functional staffs which play a major role in many ways in the organization. As was suggested in Figure 1, one of the most important needs in large-scale organizations today is for coordination of these diverse organizational components. We are proposing that this be done by the specialist in manpower matters and that in the years ahead an increasing awareness will grow as to the need for such coordination.

In a large-scale organization, the importance of securing widespread organizational collaboration can never be underestimated. Indeed the prime problem in modern society is often effectively marshalling all the expertise available so that the organization can function most effectively and efficiently. It is very important that the relationship between policy making on manpower matters and policy research on the same subject be coordinated. Increasingly today, manpower policy is being used in large-scale organizations to promote the well being of society and to establish a new interface between, for example, business and the disadvantaged. The newly recognized responsibility of large-scale organizations in trying to solve some of the social problems associated with unemployment and minority groups have placed a new sphere of responsibility particularly within the business organization in America. We have been suggesting that this sphere belongs with all the others which have evolved over the decades in response to the need for developing manpower. Therefore, we have shown in Figure 1, where we would place the responsibility for developing disadvantaged individuals and helping them become job-ready, trained, and productive in work organizations.

The model which we have discussed under organizational relationships is primarily applicable to very large organizations. There is little doubt that much of it can be applied to medium and small organizations. Indeed, the difference between large, medium, and small organizations often hinges on what one wishes to focus upon. If it is simply a matter of manpower size, differences between the trichotomy of organizations might be not as great as would be expected. Perhaps the differences would be more of a quantitative rather than a qualitative type. Specifically, in any organization there is a need for manpower planning and development. The main question is how many individuals can be afforded by the organization to specialize in this function and conduct it. Another consideration would be the extent to which there are serious manpower and organizational problems in a particular organization. Organizations which have a minimum of these could perhaps do with fewer manpower specialists. Profitability would be still another consideration, although there are small, medium, and large organizations which may be profitable or unprofitable; size and profitability need not be associated.

In the final analysis, the difference would be perhaps one of scope. A well-managed small- or medium-sized organization could very well carry out all the manpower and organizational planning activities of larger organizations but would only need to do so in miniature and informal fashion. The kind of model of organizational relationships which would apply to medium-sized organizations would be essentially the same as that applicable to large-scale organizations except perhaps the corporate and divisional functions would be combined.

Small organizations are very diverse, and the model pattern for them could range from a miniature of a large-scale and medium-sized organization to one with virtually no formal structure at all, particularly in the latter case in organizations with less than 50 employees.[28]

[28] Those interested in manpower planning in smaller companies should consult Roger A. Golde, "Practical Planning for Small Business," *Harvard Business Review,* Vol. 42, No. 5, September-October 1964, pp. 147–163; Harold J. Baum, "Useful Job Training Criteria for Small Plants," *Training Director's Journal,* Vol. 19, No. 3, March 1965, pp. 20–28; James P. Dee, "Communications Training," *Training Director's Journal,* Vol. 17, No. 2, February 1963, pp. 42–48; and William H. Button and William J. Wasmuth, *Employee Training in Small Business Organizations* (Bulletin 52), New York State School of Industrial and Labor Relations, Cornell University, Ithaca, March 1964.

It should be noted that the trend in recent years toward corporate mergers and increasingly large-scale organizations suggests that the large-scale model has probably the greatest implications for the future and is perhaps the most important of all models.

AREAS OF COMPETENCY FOR MANPOWER IN ORGANIZATIONS

In the discussion to this point in the chapter we have been emphasizing organizational relationships and models which apply to large-scale organizations in the United States as we understand them. Figure 2 displays areas of competency for manpower in large-scale organizations. It can be seen that essentially the recognized areas of competency can be reduced to knowledge areas and skill areas. The knowledge areas may be further subdivided into the external which pertain to the relationship of the organization to the state (or industry), society, and economy. Internal knowledge pertains to the organization itself and its philosophy, policies and plans, procedures and records, and internal organizational relationships. The functional knowledge depends upon the number and kinds of functions in the organization and some of the more prominent functional fields in business are listed.

The areas of skill competency are shown on the right of Figure 2, again there are 3 subdivisions of skills. First, there are the administrative skills traditionally associated with the conduct of managerial work but not necessarily limited to management. Second, there are the interpersonal skills relevant to the work situation. Lastly, there are the various technical skills, ranging from reading, speaking, writing, and personal systems to specific crafts or trades. Using this type of schemata, we could probably categorize the education and training needs of most large scale organizations as they perceive themselves today.

However, we live in an era in which many are suggesting that bureaucratic large-scale organizations are on the decline and must be replaced with organizations in the future which are different in structure and character.[29] This shift may also change our prevailing concepts of manpower competency, and we should next consider how and why.

The general characteristics of on-going organizational change in growing, healthy organizations are shown in summary form in Figure 3. Stage 1 describes rudimentary organizational structures and the kinds of managerial patterns associated with the pioneering business enterprises in the United States. Many organizations in the United States are still of this type.

[29] Warren G. Bennis, *Changing Organizations*, McGraw-Hill, New York, 1966, pp. 1–15.

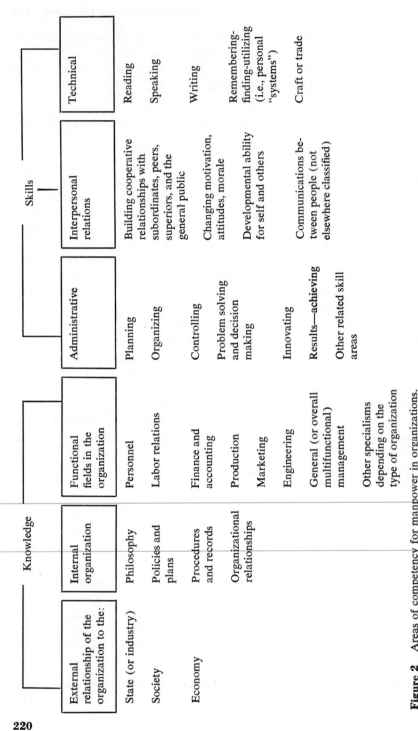

Figure 2 Areas of competency for manpower in organizations.

Note: There would be some variability in area and emphasis depending upon managerial level and whether the manager supervised others. Broad areas such as "attitudes" and "ability" or "capacity" are catagorized above under interpersonal relations and functional fields of

Stage 1	Stage 2	Stage 3
Charismatic domination (leadership)	Bureaucratic organization (professional leadership)	Task-oriented information systems and fluid organizations

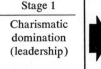

Strong top leader
Strong owner influence
Nonrational
Hierarchy with informality of roles, positions
Arbitrary succession in hierarchy
Loose functional units
Situation oriented
Emotional interpersonal relationships
Unstable; dependent on great leader
Resists specialization and routinization of decisions
No organization charts
Handles emergencies and new situations well
Arbitrary reward systems
No participation in planning or decisions
Strong discipline with arbitrary rules
Moderately legalistic
Loyalty and conformity to leader

Organizationally created leader
Indirect owner influence
Highly rational
Formal roles, offices, and positions; strong hierarchy
Planned succession;assured careers and merit appointments
Tight functional units
Institutionally oriented
Impersonal relationships
Stable and predictable
Promotes specialization and routinization of decisions
Strong dependence on charts
Less flexible in emergencies and new situations
Planned reward systems
Controlled participation
Strong discipline with fair rules
Strongly legalistic
Loyalty and conformity to system and institution

Group leadership and decision
Indirect owner influence
Highly rational
Fluid structures; deemphasizes hierarchy
Weak hierarchy and more informal offices, positions
Task forces, teams, projects, and interfunctional activity

Systems and computer oriented
Colleagueship and personal relationships
Stable, but less predictable
Deemphasizes specialization and routinization of decisions
Deemphasizes charts
Slower and more uncertain in emergencies and new situations
Rewards based on results
Meaningful participation in decisions and planning invited
Deemphasis on rules and discipline
Permissive
Loyalty and conformity to profession and peer groups

Figure 3 Emerging leadership and administrative patterns in business enterprises.

Source. Dalton E. McFarland, "Organizational Health and Company Efficiency," *Business Topics,* Vol. 13, No. 3, Summer 1965, p. 49.

The second column, Stage 2, summarizes the characteristics of the emerging large-scale bureaucratic structures in the period since about 1925.

The third column presents innovations in organizational culture designed to remedy the apparent defects in the typical bureaucratic structure.[30]

Most small organizations in the United States came into existence under charismatic leadership and were founded by highly motivated individualistic entrepreneurs. Over the years many of these charismatic organizations evolved into bureaucratic organizations. Those that remain probably are well characterized by the features listed in column 1 and the absence of formal manpower development activities.

Bureaucratic organizations are still considered by many students of management and organizations as the most productive arrangements possible for securing human effort. Their organizational superiority lies in their capacity to command and utilize technical and scientific knowledge. Their ability to accomplish objective organizational goals has led to very high productivity and the highest standards of living ever achieved by man. They are populated by specialists, and the bureaucratic form accommodates to the training, utilization, and proper status and economic rewards for the specialist so that his contribution to goals and sub-goals is rational, predictable, and controllable. If highly efficient productive effort is the main goal, then the bureaucratic form of organization is superbly designed for this purpose.[31]

However, efficiency is not the only demand we make of organizations, and it is in the sphere of human satisfactions that bureaucratic systems fall down. The indictment against bureaucratic models of organization is a growing one, and the criticism centers upon organizational health rather than upon the contribution of bureaucracy to productivity or efficiency. The essence of the charge is that bureaucratic systems are not particularly consonant with the fulfillment of human needs of their employees or with basic values espoused in our society other than those relating to production, success, and wealth. In addition, the implicit assumptions about people in bureaucracies are not congruent with scientific findings about human motivation.

Bureaucratic organizations provide ladders of upward mobility by which society at large defines success, and material rewards go to those who can succeed in this kind of a system. Yet we are suspicious of the system and accuse it of creating organizational men by valuing blind loyalty and rigid conformity. Increasing doubt is being cast upon the ability of

[30] Dalton E. McFarland, "Organizational Health and Company Efficiency," *Business Topics*, Vol. 13, No. 3, Summer 1965, p. 50.
[31] *Ibid.*, p. 53.

bureaucracy to fulfill the psychic, spiritual, and self-realizing needs of its members.[32]

On the basis of extensive research and experience in industry, behavioral scientists, such as Chris Argyris, have advanced an important hypothesis. They suggest that organizations based upon hierarchical structures and bureaucratic forms of management force their members into states of docility, submissiveness, and dependency that can lead only to severe frustration if the person behaves in a psychologically mature way. Psychological maturity is sacrificed in organizations that rely on strong controls, rigid rules, tight discipline, hard-boiled management, and the like. By the same token, creativity, innovation, involvement, and human dignity are sacrificed.[33]

Bureaucracies have fought back against these kinds of charges made by behavioral scientists and have tried to correct their defects in the human sphere with impressive lists of personnel administration techniques and with human relations policies and procedures. Training courses for supervisors and management development for higher-level executives have often been designed to get more mileage out of the bureaucratic system without fundamentally changing it. Organizations have literally spent millions of dollars on retreading the skills, beliefs, understandings, values, and communications of organizational members without examining their assumptions about people and organizations.[34]

The picture is not all gloom and despair, fortunately. There is increasing evidence that bureaucratic models are changing and that bureaucratic structures and concomitant assumptions are undergoing modifications. The character of these changes is still unclear but the main outlines are apparent. Some of these new patterns are shown in column three of Figure 3. The characteristic trend is toward loosening the structure through the creation of more fluid and informal organizational arrangements. These changes have the effect of reducing the impact of hierarchy, with its monocratic emphasis. Among the devices leading to such results are project management techniques, the use of task forces and management team concepts, and the management-by-results school of thought in administration. However, it should be noted that in some way these changes are reminiscent of the prebureaucratic period when businesses were run largely by the single owner-entrepreneur.

[32] *Ibid.*

[33] *Ibid.*, citing the various works of Chris Argyris including *Personality and Organization,* Harper, New York, 1957, and *Interpersonal Competence and Organizational Effectiveness,* Irwin, Homewood, Illinois, 1962.

[34] McFarland, *op. cit.,* p. 54.

The main strength of the classical enterpriser was his ability to maintain a fluidity and flexibility of organizational patterns. People were hired to get jobs done. People were far less specialized than they are considered to be today in large-scale organizations. Trouble-shooting, special projects, and rapidly changing assignments were characteristic of the managerial styles and *modus operandi* in these early organizations. Employees were kept off-base guessing about what was to be happening next, and this was thought to be good for them.[35]

The changes that we have described have grave implications for manpower and organizational planning in the bureaucratic setting. The education, training, and development of executives, supervisors, and other employees in the future cannot remain the same as in the past. The systems of rewards and punishments must adapt to these changes. Criteria for selecting new organizational members must shift from selection to fit specific jobs to the search for talented, creative, innovative people with the capacity to feel secure in more amorphous situations.

Perhaps the manpower and human relations concepts of the past 20 years have seemed so inadequate because they have been pitted against intractable problems inherent in bureaucracy itself rather than because of any inherent weaknesses in their logic or techniques. Thus, the challenge before organizational management today is to wrestle with the new problems of organizational change and manpower development even if this means discarding the ways of the past. For competent managers and executives, these changes will seem like opportunities for development rather than threats to their security and status.[36]

CONCLUSIONS

In this chapter we have clarified how different models of organizational structure, organizational relationships, and manpower policy can be utilized for manpower planning and the development of human resources. We considered various rationales applicable to manpower development and training and set forth some concepts that are useful for thinking in a general way about the development of human resources. It was suggested that such concepts are necessary so that we can grasp how the organization for developing people should be structured.

Consideration was also given to the gross number of employees in an organization as a conditioning factor in organizing for the development of human resources. Here we found that education and training activities are

[35] *Ibid.*, pp. 54–56.
[36] *Ibid.*, pp. 56–57.

more common in large- and medium-sized organizations than in smaller organizations.

The growth of organizations both in the United States and elsewhere in the world requires that formal efforts be given to the establishment of manpower planning and development programs. Specifically, when organizations attain 500 employees or more—and such organizations are numerous in the world today—they must give conscious attention to the devices they will use to perpetuate their existence. If they do not, the likelihood of their survival in a competitive business environment is substantially reduced.

We have seen the job of the training director in the large-scale organization evolve through at least 7 stages. Today he is likely to have an entirely different job from his counterpart of a decade ago—or certainly two decades ago. The modern manpower specialist in organizations today is (or should be) concerned with traditional training activities, management development, customer training, professional and technical employee development, and coordination of programs for disadvantaged Americans. The latter is a new emerging function which will be given more and more attention in the 1970s. At the present time, not many organizations have seen fit organizationally to combine the five spheres of the manpower specialism as it pertains to developing people within one functional area. It is predicted that such mergers will be forthcoming.

The focus in the chapter was on modern large-scale bureaucratic organizations and attention was given to the areas of competency required of manpower employed in such organizations. As would be expected, education, training, and developmental programs currently in operation in American industries focus upon the skills and knowledge required to carry out work in bureaucratic organizations. Yet there is a growing reaction against bureaucratic organizations and a rising sentiment that bureaucracies are inconsistent with motivating employees and in obtaining maximum advantages for organizational management. As a consequence, students of manpower and organizational planning are increasingly discussing the desirability of task oriented information systems and fluid organizational structure instead of the more rigid bureaucratic organizational structures typical of our age. In some respects these organizations of the future resemble the organizations of the immediate past in which there was charismatic domination of the organization by the traditional owner enterpriser of the 19th and early 20th century. Changes currently under way in thinking about manpower planning, the development of human resources, and organizational planning are typical of the times and indicate that in these fields turmoil is as apparent as it appears to be in other spheres of American life.

CHAPTER 6

Manpower Appraisals, Skills Inventories, and Human Resource Development

Personnel or manpower appraisal systems in organizations have a venerable history which has gone full cycle from an interest in measuring traits and assumed aspects of the human personality to jettisoning any such thoughts and installing rather free-and-easy, informal discussions about goals in their place. The appraisal situation in the newer perspective becomes a developmental interview involving planning, mutual goal setting, and subsequent review to determine how the plans are working out and if the goals have been met. There is a democratic sense of involvement in the interview. In a sense each interview becomes an occasion which has two objectives: development and control.

This new approach to appraisals is in marked contrast to earlier times when "merit rating" was the handmaiden of determining whether or not the rater would grant the ratee a merit increase. In fact, in recent years rating for pay purposes and for the development of human resources has been widely separated in many organizations. Today many manpower specialists believe that formal rating or appraisal is most appropriately used only to measure the progress of trainees on management development and other types of training programs and not for determining pay. For these reasons personnel appraisals may now be regarded as an integral part of manpower planning and the development of human resources.

Our purpose in this chapter is to discuss present thinking on how to utilize appraisals of human resources in manpower planning and to indicate the fundamental reasons for appraisals, describing some of the various methods currently in use. In order to do this, we give some attention to how electronic data processing has emerged in management and become established in the conduct of personnel administration in large-scale organizations. We next turn to management information systems as such by giving considerable attention to manpower skills inventories. Lastly, we take a critical look at performance appraisals per se and their role in planning for the development of people.

Performance appraisals are viewed essentially as the qualitative evaluation of the performance of individuals in organizations. In many respects they are the most strategic data available on an important dimension in manpower. When these qualitative evaluations are quantified and displayed together with certain basic demographic information about employees, the manpower specialist has potentially available a tool which may serve as a basic foundation for projecting manpower needs and planning for the development of human resources. Unfortunately, appraisals are conceptually weak and, as we shall see, leave much to be desired as measures of human performance in organizations.

In the remaining chapters we have referred to the use of performance appraisals in the development of manpower. For example, foremen, executives, college graduate trainees, cooperative trainees, and employees of almost all types make contributions to organizations which to a greater or lesser extent can be gauged by performance reviews. In evaluating the performance of salesmen, it is possible to focus upon a number of more objective measures such as the volume of sales, profit from sales, amount of returned goods, goodwill endeavors, the cultivation of new business, and the like. Performance reviews can also be used in evaluating how well skilled-trades apprentices acquire the skills of the craft which they are learning. Apprentices also have some aspects of their performance evaluated through the use of subject-matter examinations in courses of related instruction. Therefore, it can be said that performance reviews are useful for evaluating employees being developed in or for a number of different occupations in organizations.

Toward the end of the chapter we recommend a specific type of performance review which has wide applicability and is consistent with much contemporary thinking on appraisals. We furnish a form which can be used for performance reviews and state how it can be utilized in an effective manner.

The results of using a form and methods such as those advocated in the chapter are difficult to reduce to a computer input for the purposes of building a manpower information system. Thus, while the computer has much value in inventorying manpower, it is still subject to the problem of GIGO, that is, garbage in, garbage out. Unfortunately, the state of the art in performance reviews is such that much of what is inputted to computers is a poor qualitative measure of human performance. Until the behavioral sciences advance more and point to improved methods of human appraisal, this deficiency in knowledge of human performance measurement will plague the manpower planner.

Electronic data processing is a powerful tool for use in organizations, but it should not become the tail wagging the managerial dog. As has been suggested, we need better manpower information systems but not systems that fail to improve on existing approaches. Clearly, a word of caution is in order:

"Somewhat related to profit-performance, evaluation is the entire problem of personnel selection. Whom to hire, promote, discharge, or demote, as well as when these actions should be made, is critical to the successful operation of a decentralized company. Except for some convenience in the retrieval of personnel information, however, I do not see where the computer can even begin to solve management's personnel problems." [1]

There are also other views expressed in the hackneyed story of the new supercomputer that was being asked more and more difficult questions. After answering every one correctly, it was finally asked the ultimate question, "Is there a God?" The computer's high-speed printer rapidly spat out, "There is now!" If we are not careful with computers and EDP, we may become so impressed with this tool that we will keep doing things faster and better but perhaps trivial things that do not need doing at all.[2]

ELEMENTARY COMPUTER CONCEPTS

In considering the changes in concepts underlying personnel appraisal over the years, it should be noted that the advent of electronic data processing equipment has made it possible to compile manpower inventories of both a qualitative and quantitative nature. More specifically, the electronic computer enables management today to control its business and to assess its environment with incomparable effectiveness in two ways. First, it enables management to obtain relevant facts about manpower swiftly. In addition to supplying management with facts in historical time, or after they have happened, it supplies facts "on line," that is, as soon as they are born, and in "real time," that is, promptly and in sufficient abundance to control the circumstances they describe while those circumstances are evolving. Second, the computer helps management understand the changing relationships of facts chiefly by a technique known as simulation, or the imitation of experience with models. With the computer management needs only to translate an appropriate number of models into mathe-

[1] John Dearden, "Computers: No Impact on Divisional Control," *Harvard Business Review*, Vol. 45, No. 1, January-February 1967, p. 102.

[2] Howard C. Lockwood, "Data Processing and Personnel Research," in *Proceedings of a Conference on Electronic Data Processing and Personnel Management*, Institute of Industrial Relations and Graduate School of Business Administration, University of California at Los Angeles, 1965, p. 41.

matical formulas and instruct the computer to compare them and pick the likeliest. Also, management can simulate part or all of its organizational operations in the computer and test them in dozens of different situations. Simulation techniques grow in effectiveness when an organization can repeatedly inspect its past performance and gauge its objectives accordingly. In other words, after the business has become computerized, and the records of its transactions over the years have become stored in the computer's memory, the model can be refined by constant reexamination of its parts and reconstruction of components to accord better with experience. Thus a carefully constructed model enables management to know precisely what has happened and why, what should be happening and why, and what is likely to happen. All of this accessible information leaves management in a strong position to make decisions increasingly based upon analysis and less and less on guesses and hunches.[3]

The potential of the electronic computer may be harnessed to managerial desires to engage in manpower planning and the development of human resources. Today's administrator is in a position to transform organizational management so that it may never be the same again, if it is disposed to reap the advantages inherent in the new EDP and manpower projection tools. These tools provide a sounder base than has ever existed previously in the history of man for planning and carrying out programs for the development of human resources. For these reasons we consider in this chapter the explicit interconnections between computers, personnel appraisals, inventories, and human resource development. However, before proceeding further, other concepts need to be introduced and defined.

Turning back to real-time systems, it should be noted that there are both on-line and time-sharing kinds of real-time systems. On-line systems have been used by such organizations as airlines and banks for interrogating a computer by means of a remote console. The inquiry could, for example, go out over a telephone line to a centralized computer which would check the seat inventory, as on an airline, and transmit back the information to the inquirer. Thus, an airline ticket agent could use one program, looking up seat inventories and making reservations. With an on-line system there could be dozens or hundreds of agents actually operating off one system at the same time, but they would all be doing the same thing.[4]

[3] Gilbert Burck and the Editors of Fortune, *The Computer Age and Its Potential for Management,* Harper and Row, New York, 1965, pp. 27–28. See also Robert V. Head, *Real-Time Business Systems,* Holt, Rinehart and Winston, New York, 1964, pp. 1–26; and Frederic G. Withington, *The Use of Computers in Business Organizations,* Addison-Wesley, Reading, 1966, pp. 77–104.

[4] Roderick H. Bare, "Functional and Organizational Implications of Developments in Information Technology," in *Proceedings of a Conference on Electronic Data Processing and Personnel Management, op. cit.,* p. 57.

On the other hand, time-sharing allows many different users with completely different problems to operate on the same computer at the same time. For example, it would be possible under a time-sharing system to permit the simultaneous operation of a manpower information retrieval program, an automated teaching program, and up to two dozen or more different usages. However, it should be noted that the word "simultaneously" is only a convenient way of talking about an extremely rapid sequencing of users. Actually, what happens in time-sharing is that each user is given a short period of processing by the computer in turn or sequence. If the computer is a powerful one, a great deal of computing can be done on a problem each time the user's turn comes up. Furthermore, depending upon the number of users in the system, a chance to use it could come up as frequently as every couple of seconds.[5]

Turning back again to the previously mentioned use of computers in simulation, it should be noted that the term simulation has a broader meaning than that suggested in the linear programming or the mathematical model sense in which it is often used. Simulation may also mean putting into the computer's data base proposed item values for individuals and treating them as if they were "real" data. For example, it is possible to place in the data base an item with a future effective date such as a date for a planned promotion, executive development program enrollment, a scheduled retirement, a predetermined transfer, and the like. When such items are provided for all manpower in an organization it becomes possible, if desired, to process the information and see what will happen if the organization decides to go through with these various manpower transactions. The program on the computer would then prepare summary statistics for the total organization and process the data by showing the kinds of changes which would take place as scheduled. In other words, in such a computerized simulation, it would become possible to determine how existing organizational policies will work out prior to their actual implementation. In this way an organization is enabled to test out its policies before their implementation actually takes place. An opportunity is thereby provided to exercise various alternatives and make changes before time has elapsed. The effect of this is to maximize the use of the computer as a tool in manpower planning.[6]

SOME OVERVIEWS OF EDP IN MANPOWER PLANNING

Computerization in organizations is a relatively recent phenomenon. In less than twenty years, the electronic computer has become one of the

[5] *Ibid.*, p. 58.
[6] *Ibid.*, pp. 63–64.

greatest and most revolutionary tools of mankind. There are perhaps as many as 60,000 of these so-called "electronic brains" in use today in the world and 45,000 in the United States alone. Government, military, and industry together were spending a few years ago upwards of $4 billion per year on automatic data-processing equipment. Worldwide data-processing managers are operating about $20 billion worth of computer systems.[7] Technological advances by computers are rapidly creating a society that only decades ago would scarcely have existed in the wildest fantasies of science fiction. Today, computers predict the course of a spaceship orbiting the earth. Tomorrow, computer technology virtually will run the world in a certain sense. New developments are occurring so rapidly that a list of computer applications is outdated almost as it is being compiled.[8]

For a number of years, the major use of computers in organizations has been to handle routine calculations. Large, repetitive, numerical jobs such as payrolls, accounts receivable, and inventory control were among the first assigned to the computer. There has been a change since about 1960 and the applications of computerization have become increasingly diversified. Today, the number and uses of the computer seem to be growing almost geometrically.[9] The key managerial problem of an exploding technology is that it demands the most efficient employment of human talents and skills; therefore, this problem is appropriately assigned to the manpower specialist.

The uses of the computer vary from one organization to another depending on several factors. A firm that hires a large number of college graduates, for example, is likely to give highest priority to information relevant to recruiting. Another company which has a high percentage of unionized employees might find that labor-management negotiators were important consumers of the data spewed out by the computer. Figure 1 suggests how organizational components can make use of computerized manpower data.

In general, there are four consumer groups that seek manpower data provided by computers: the employee, line middle management, staff departments, and top management. The individual employee wants to know about his seniority, job classification, vacation eligibility, and accrued benefits. The line supervisor needs to know what skills and qualifications possessed by available employees are at his disposal, labor costs for various

[7] Russell J. Cooney, "Manpower Planning for Automation," *Public Personnel Review*, Vol. 26, No. 3, July 1965, pp. 151–155. See also J. Stanford Smith, "The Growing Maturity of the Computer Age," General Electric Company Executive Reprints, 1968, p. 1.

[8] James M. Elden, "Computer Technology and Public Personnel Administration," *Public Personnel Review*, Vol. 27, No. 4, October 1966, pp. 251–255.

[9] Barrie Austin, "The Role of EDP in Personnel," *Management of Personnel Quarterly*, Vol. 3, No. 4, Winter 1965, pp. 24–30.

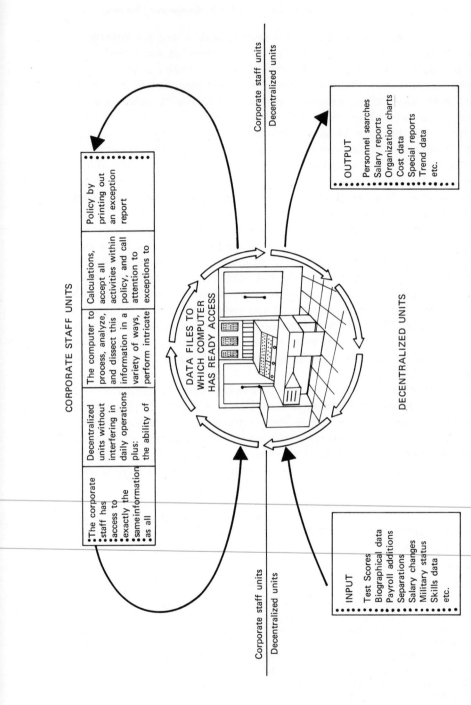

Figure 1 Corporate staff units and decentralization units use the same data files but for different purposes. *Source.* L. G. Wagner, "Computers, Decentralization, and Corporate Control," *California Management Review*, Vol. 9, No. 2, Winter 1966, p. 26.

Within the figure:

CORPORATE STAFF UNITS

| The corporate staff has access to exactly the same information as all | Decentralized units without interfering in daily operations plus: the ability of | The computer to process, analyze, and dissect this information in a variety of ways, perform intricate | Calculations, accept all activities within policy, and call attention to exceptions to | Policy by printing out an exception report |

DATA FILES TO WHICH COMPUTER HAS READY ACCESS

DECENTRALIZED UNITS

Corporate staff units
Decentralized units

Corporate staff units
Decentralized units

INPUT
Test Scores
Biographical data
Payroll additions
Separations
Salary changes
Military status
Skills data
etc.

OUTPUT
Personnel searches
Salary reports
Organization charts
Cost data
Special reports
Trend data
etc.

projects and time periods, absenteeism records, and individual employee work histories. Staff departments, such as manpower planning, seek skills inventories and other data that can be used in developing human resources for the organization. Staff employee benefits departments utilize actuarial information to establish adequate pensions and insurance funds. Medical departments must have records of treatment for job-related injuries. Top management wants to keep abreast of labor costs on a plant-by-plant basis in order to maintain budgetary controls, appraise plant-level managerial effectiveness, and anticipate future capital requirements.[10]

Computers can be used to make information rapidly accessible to all who need it. A personnel manager of one of Detroit's automobile firms reportedly made the following comment: "There's nothing new per se here for us. It [the computer] can only do the work we've been doing (or trying to do) infinitely faster than we could. That's where the real payoff lies; we're now about to do things we once only wished we could do—simply because we've now got the information at our fingertips." [11]

Theoretically, a computer can play an important part in administering a complete set of manpower-related programs from recruiting and hiring to promoting and retiring. The computer could be programmed to be fully aware of projected manpower requirements and the organization's ability to meet these needs. In terms of the manpower necessary to achieve organizational goals, the computer could have on file such data as coded job descriptions and an inventory of all the skills, training, and special abilities, including the performance level, of every employee.[12] Few organizations have as yet completely computerized their manpower planning function to that extent, but many have automated certain of these activities and others are rapidly following suit.

Computerized Manpower Records And Information Systems

The bane of every personnel manager's life seems to be paper work. Yet, current, accurate, and comprehensive information is essential to evaluate past activities, control present ones, and plan for future operations. In the past, the relentless flow of paper from the personnel office and manual processing of it have been accepted as an unavoidable cost of doing business. With the sustained pressure in recent years to reduce overhead and clerical costs, many organizations have taken a harder look at this paper-processing function.

Management is starting to ask if all of these manpower records are really necessary; and, even if so, are there not simpler and more efficient ways to

[10] *Ibid.*
[11] *Ibid.*
[12] Elden, *op. cit.*, pp. 253–255.

handle them? The conventional methods of handling these paper-processing jobs have been slow, laborious, and limited as to their value in providing a manpower information system. More and more, progressive personnel departments have consequently turned to the computer for help.[13]

Computerization aids in speeding the flow of manpower information and in providing a source of data which was previously impossible to obtain or available only through Herculean manual efforts at great cost in time and money. Many companies have used the computer to develop extensive records for specific purposes connected with manpower. By using the computer, a major automobile company maintains centralized information on the status of more than 50,000 salaried employees. This file includes salary, position code, age, educational level, date of hire, employment location, overall performance appraisal, and insurance data for each employee. One of the most interesting automated systems of a similar type is SPARTAN (Systems for Personnel Automated Reports, Transactions, and Notices) developed by the Bureau of the Census. This system provides a number of reports on employees and addresses memorandums to managers alerting them to the imminence of certain events.[14]

The use of EDP in manpower information systems has spawned a school of acronyms, such as Eastman Kodak's IRIS (Industrial Relations Information System), System Development Corporation's EPIC (Experimental Personnel Information Capability), North American Aviation's QIP (Qualifications Inventory Program), and Ford's EQIP (Employee Qualifications Inventory Program), all of which are designed for the same basic purposes: manpower information systems for management.

One advantage of automating manpower records is that all reports can be made from the same file since the data are recorded only once. Other advantages are the following: reduction in the size of the clerical work force, more timely data for decision making, a supply of broader information for salary comparisons and forecasts, and increased accuracy of manpower reports.

The future of manpower record simplification seems to be unlimited. The processing of records will undoubtedly become more and more simple. Manpower specialists in organizations must be willing to experiment with automated record-keeping systems. If they learn what constitutes good form design and achieve a basic understanding of the uses and limitations of data-processing equipment, they will be able to play an important part

[13] R. E. Mourglia, "Recruiting with the Aid of EDP," *Personnel,* Vol. 41, No. 6, November-December 1964, pp. 48–51.

[14] Richard T. Bueschel, "How EDP Is Improving the Personnel Function," *Personnel,* Vol. 41, No. 5, September-October 1964, pp. 59–64.

in making the manpower records more efficient, higher in quality, and lower in cost.[15]

Computerizing Manpower Recruiting

One manpower activity that particularly lends itself to the application of electronic data processing is recruiting. Recruiting is, as we have seen, by no means a simple matter of finding possible job candidates and hiring. Before the employment interview can even begin, there must be accurate job descriptions for the anticipated openings and an employee requisition from the supervisor who has a vacancy to fill. These are in many respects mechanical matters, but are the logical starting point of a recruitment campaign. In the recruitment process, all the information needed can be quickly and accurately provided by use of computers.[16]

In computerizing a recruiting operation, it is necessary to determine all the qualifications required for each position in the organization and to convert this information to punched cards or the equivalent. These records provide a master file of occupational requirements. Also, the file should include positions added by current manpower authorizations and budget plans for which the employment section has not received requisitions. The master file will then identify occupied positions, authorized requisitioned but unoccupied positions, and approved but unrequisitioned positions.

During the interviews, information should be gathered for a second computerized master file. This information may serve to establish whether the prospect has certain job qualifications that are usually difficult to obtain from the application blank. The second master file can also be used to validate the information on the application form.

After the data from the application blank is added to the second master file, the employment section will have a complete file showing all applicants available for hire. By comparing this file with the one containing all the manpower requirements and necessary qualifications, the computer will perform part of the actual selection process. When it is properly programmed, the computer will select the names of all applicants who meet the requirements of each vacant position, then all those who meet all but one requirement, and those who meet all but two requirements. This process will continue until a list of applicants without any qualifications has been compiled.

The usefulness of the computer in the hiring process need not end here. The possibility of promoting from within should not be overlooked. By adding the names of all employees who qualify for open positions to the

---

[15] Ibid.

[16] Mourglia, op. cit., pp. 60–64.

second master file, an exact and all-inclusive list of the skills already available in the organization is printed. A report listing all available employees qualified for a particular position would obviously save hours of laborious paper processing on the part of the recruiter. The recruiter would then be able to concentrate on weighing subjective factors that no machine can identify and to decide what applicants should be interviewed by the supervisor concerned.

The file of manpower information can be analyzed electronically in various ways useful to recruitment planning. For example, a report of the number of vacancies in each department will permit management to work out promotions and selling points about each vacancy in order to guide the interviewer. Computerized interview records are useful for compiling statistics concerning the number of interviews conducted by location and source and the proportion of suitable prospects obtained in relation to the total number of interviews. By analyzing these data, the employment department will be able to determine the effectiveness of the recruiting process.[17]

Computerized Manpower Skills Inventories

Many organizations coast along in the comfortable belief that all pertinent information about their employees' experiences and skills is on file somewhere. The trouble with this assumption is that the information that is only "somewhere" is nowhere when needed at short notice. It is unlikely that this information is available anywhere in the organization.[18]

A small company has little need for a formal computerized skills inventory because the study of manually compiled records is a simple task. But, as the organization grows, it is essential to consider setting up an elaborate computerized system. The manpower specialist is likely to find enthusiasm for this idea from top management and key department heads even though it is costly, because the payoff is almost self-evident.

To date, skills inventories have largely been developed by engineering and research and development-oriented organizations where the high cost of recruiting and the shortage of skilled professionals made it essential to use optimally the talent already available in the company.[19] The alternative was wasteful talent stacking and failure to have adequate information on human resources.

A skills inventory must be designed so that a searcher can find specific items of information without knowing beforehand just where they are lo-

[17] *Ibid.*

[18] James T. Wolcott, "How to Develop a Skills Inventory," *Personnel,* Vol. 41, No. 3, May-June 1964, pp. 54–59.

[19] Bueschel, *op. cit.,* pp. 59–64.

cated in the file. The skills inventory is thus a register of information accompanied by a system for retrieving the information. In automating these activities, it is necessary to determine if the data in the personnel folder for each employee are accurate. Verification is usually done by interviewing each employee. The personnel records must be updated whenever any changes occur in the employee's status, skills, education, or capabilities, if the inventory is to live up to its potential in manpower planning.

A skills inventory can be a useful tool in human resource development programs since it brings into focus the present level of technical ability and the achievements to date of all employees who might be considered for participation in education and training programs. It has the particular value of being extremely factual by showing where the organization stands quantitatively and qualitatively and where it should concentrate its developmental efforts for the future.

A skills inventory gives employees a concrete demonstration that they are working for an organization where the individual does count and where his special talents are known and will be called upon. As one employee of a firm which had a skills inventory stated, "Somebody up there knows about me and knows what I can do." [20]

By offering greater internal opportunity for growth to its employees, the organization with a skills inventory may also reduce turnover among scarce professionals. The fears of job applicants who are often concerned about being lost in the labyrinthine hierarchy of large organizations can be allayed by this same tool. The employment interviewer can reassure these applicants by showing that the organization has the facts, through the skills inventory, to prevent such a loss of identity.

In many firms the training departments spend vast amounts of time on such tasks as collecting and reducing data on program attendance, typing course completion notices, filing forms, compiling statistics, and writing monthly reports on program participation. All of these jobs often have to be done manually; and, because most systems are not integrated, many systems duplicate parts of others. Files tend to be large and disorganized, and when a report has to be prepared, many hours are spent in preparing it. The clerical staff gets tied up with a mass of routine, repetitive, and costly jobs. The training department at Rocketdyne Division of North American Aviation (now the North American-Rockwell Corporation) computerized this function many years ago and has solved some of these problems.[21]

[20] Wolcott, *op. cit.*, pp. 54–59.

[21] Walter B. Wentz, "Time to Automate Your Training Records," *Personnel,* Vol. 37, No. 6, November-December 1960, pp. 74–78.

Management at North American had to decide how far the training department should be automated. By using a flow chart, the old training system was analyzed to determine if documents were being passed back and forth between the same people and if persons who had nothing to do with the training program were acting as go-betweens in the flow of paper work. Next, the company's EDP experts recommended specific machines and techniques, including proposals on both installation and operational costs.

The benefits of computerization at the Rocketdyne Division were numerous. Course titles, dates, student names, departments, attendance records, grades, and completion notices were processed by the computer. Many monthly reports were automatically printed. The training department was able to provide special data, statistics, and reports with ease and accuracy. Computerization had eliminated previously disruptive office activities required in digging out information or compiling a "crash" report for management when they were requested.

The new system resulted in a 50 percent reduction in both forms and files and a net 40 percent reduction in the number of operations performed. The new system was so flexible that tripling the work load would increase the cost $30 per month. Under the old system, a similar increased work load would have required hiring a new clerk at a cost of more than $400 per month. The training department was provided with the capability of accumulating a large supply of raw material which may be valuable in future years.[22]

Organizations should look at their training departments to see if their present information systems are routine, repetitive, and time-consuming. If the current system has these characteristics, automating the training records may offer greater opportunities for more efficient and less expensive administration of training programs as well as pertinent information about employees that could be used in the manpower skills inventory.

COMPUTERIZATION AND COMPENSATION DATA
FOR IMPROVED MANPOWER DECISIONS

In many organizations compensation information has long been available from the company's tabulating equipment. However, more extensive use of the computer is beginning to yield significant improvement in various pay programs. By use of the computer, internal pay rates can be compared with the rates prevailing in the external market. Data on distributions by salary averages, quarters of the range, and employee salary history can be reproduced quickly. The computer can be, and also is,

[22] *Ibid.*

widely used in processing data for salary surveys.[23] Most organizations believe that the savings achieved by reducing turnover and by not paying higher rates than necessary in the market are important advantages gained from computer utilization.

Another advantage of computerized wage and salary data is the speedy control given the salary administrator. He can quickly spot misclassified employees and salary irregularities. Salary budgets can be compared with projections or with the budgets of comparable departments in the organization.

'An especially valuable application of computerization is the use of the computer to simulate wages and salaries. By simulating various wage and salary trends, the company can obtain a projection of its compensation expense in the future, given the existence of specific compensation policies and rules. This device offers a ready means of testing alternative solutions to facilitate choosing the best course of solving myriad compensation problems.[24] Compensation planning data can thus be integrated with manpower planning data.

The use of electronic computers and related equipment can indisputably result in a vastly expanded capability for accomplishing clerical and administrative operations associated with manpower planning. On the other hand, these new tools are often unlikely to produce immediate savings and may even lead to increased costs. Unless properly utilized and programmed, the computer may create more problems than it solves.

One ingredient absolutely necessary to the success of any administrative innovation, including EDP, is cooperation. No system can function very well against the will of the people involved. Since today the manpower specialist is being called upon to contribute more directly to organizational goal attainment, there is little doubt that the computer can be an indispensable aid to him in this new environment. The question is: How? Answers can be found in a closer look at the composition of skills inventories and one of the prime inputs to these, namely, performance appraisal data. We turn to these topics next.

INFORMATION SYSTEMS AND SKILLS INVENTORIES: CONCEPTUAL ASPECTS

As we have seen, manpower planning involves the analysis of a wide variety of data and information. We need a better understanding of the terms "information" and "data" before we can explain the operation of a skills inventory and the manpower specialist's role in relation to it.

[23] Bueschel, *op. cit.,* pp. 59–64.
[24] *Ibid.*

In the past, information has been identified as synonymous with data, facts, news, and similar phenomena. In the new field of information technology, a distinction is made between information and data. Information is regarded as the use of selected data for the reduction of the amount or range of uncertainty. From this standpoint, simply increasing the amount of data or facts does not of itself decrease the degree of uncertainty surrounding a decision. The distinction between data and information is predicated on this distinction: data are materials to be used inferentially but have not been evaluated for their worth to a specific individual in a particular situation. Information is inferentially intended material evaluated for a particular problem, for a specified individual, at a specific time, and for the explicit purpose of achieving a definite goal. Thus, what constitutes information for one person in a specific instance may not be the same for another or even for the same individual at a different time or for a different problem. In other words, information concerns selected data; that is, data selected with respect to problem, user, time, place, and function (the reduction of uncertainty).[25] Information technology, or the state of the art in information management, has now reached the point where many of the things that we have dreamed about, wished and hoped for, are now both feasible and practical.

In the determination of manpower requirements, there are two types of informational system approaches. First, we can specify the characteristics that we want to have in each system. For example, we can pinpoint exactly how we want to develop a capabilities file or a skills inventory. Then we can write one computer program specifically for capabilities, another for skills inventories, and still additional ones for various purposes. In other words, we can develop a group of specific systems and computer programs for each application in each organization.[26]

The second approach is that of the general-purpose system. In most applications of such a system, we have a requirement to maintain a file of information, to enter new information into that file, to remove old information, to select records from files, to extract information from these records, to process this information, and to provide reports. The general-purpose system permits management to accomplish a particular application at greatly reduced time and cost for computer programming. Within the last ten years, some efforts have been made toward the development of general-purpose software to perform such applications on general-purpose computers.[27] The result of a general-purpose system is to provide manage-

---

[25] Peter P. Schoderbek, ed., *Management Systems,* Wiley, New York, 1967, pp. 43–44.

[26] John A. Postley, "The Data Processing Revolution," in *Proceedings of a Conference on Electronic Data Processing and Personnel Management, op. cit.,* p. 3.

[27] *Ibid.*

ment with information so that it is better able to manage the organization. The information contained in the memory of the computer pertains to all employees in the organization and can be quickly retrieved. The information system also combines in one location files which have traditionally been scattered among various parts of an organization.

With a general-purpose system, line and staff managers in the organization have access to the manpower file data maintained in machine-retrievable form. Thus, through teletypes into offices throughout an organization, managers can have access to part of the data base concerning all manpower in their employ. This means that they will have access to the file data through methods and equipment which at first might appear to be futuristic figments of the imagination but which are already being used today and will increasingly become operational.[28]

As a result of some of the developments in electronic data processing which we have been discussing, many leading organizations today have undertaken major revisions in their manpower record-keeping procedures. In effect, they have conducted extensive reviews of present and anticipated manpower information requirements and have devised comprehensive record-keeping systems. In these reviews of operations there has been a clear tendency toward centralizing all records dealing with the organization's manpower into a single integrated file. At the same time, sophisticated techniques for maintaining and using the file of manpower information have been devised. In general, these new procedures would not have been possible without the availability of modern data-processing equipment.[29]

Organizational Needs Met by Skills Inventories

Whether it is called a "manpower information system," a "personnel register," or a "skills inventory," the general-purpose system generally has the same objective: to consolidate information about the organization's manpower resources into a flexible format which can serve a wide variety of needs. There are at least five important organizational needs which can be met by such a system.

First, the system should make possible a continuing census of the organization's skill resources in a framework suitable for manpower planning and projections. Manpower-census figures are required for various government reports and may be useful in answering requests made by nongovernmental agencies. Skill-census data are essential for bidding on government contracts and for evaluating an organization's capabilities.

[28] E. H. Dohrmann, "How Computer Techniques Can Help in Personnel Management," in *Proceedings of a Conference on Electronic Data Processing and Personnel Management, op. cit.,* pp. 7–9.

[29] John R. Hinrichs, *High Talent Personnel,* American Management Association, New York, 1966, pp. 61–62.

Specialized census breakdowns are needed for administering employee benefit plans, for labor union contract negotiations and administration, and for public relations or college relations purposes. One integrated skills inventory can be designed to serve all of these varying needs.

Second, the inventory should be a source of information for calculating and evaluating manpower trend data over time. Turnover rates, accession rates, and rates of skill development and upgrading should be available as a base for manpower planning and projections and for other analyses and reports as well.

Third, the skills inventory should serve a manpower search and placement function. Readily accessible and detailed data about present employees' backgrounds and capabilities should lead to better selection of people to fill position vacancies as they occur. The availability of this kind of information should also assure that no potential candidates are overlooked for promotion or for optimum manpower utilization.

Fourth, the inventory should serve an important audit function and thus promote better manpower management throughout an organization. For example, it can be used to determine the extent to which performance appraisals are being carried out, the way in which salaries are being administered, the emphasis being placed on developing human resources, or the extent to which employees' skills are not being appropriately utilized.

Fifth, a properly designed skills inventory should be sufficiently flexible to serve as a source of information for manpower research purposes. It can provide a base for studies of selection, of the factors contributing to or blocking career success and mobility, and for evaluations of staffing standards and ratios.[30]

When we consider the aforementioned diverse objectives and uses of a skills inventory, it is clear that the inventory must include a broad range of information about the organization's employees. However, most of this information is already available in one form or another in many organizations, and usually can be generated by a manual or computerized system. For example, in almost every organization there is already one basic record system which is hopefully current and accurate—the payroll. Most of the input to the payroll record consists of data which are also central to a skills inventory file: position classification, organizational location, salary, educational level, marital status, and the like. Therefore, in building and maintaining a skills inventory an obvious first step is to tap the flow of information used to maintain the payroll file. Similarly, all other existing sources of manpower information should be tapped to keep the skills inventory current. These sources might include participation in training programs, the results of periodic performance appraisals, benefit plan

[30] *Ibid.*, pp. 62–63.

records, and the like. The main task is to consolidate the needed material and to put it in a form so that it can be used easily.[31]

Vital Information Items in Skills Inventories

Although the particular items that could be included in an inventory are wide-ranging, the following items contain most of the basic types of information which should be included. First, there is personal history data, such as age, sex, marital status, number of dependents, and draft and military reserve status. Second, there is basic skills information, which would include formal education, previous job experience and training, experiences and training acquired in the employing organization, hobbies, facility with foreign languages, and other areas of special competence. Third, there are the special qualifications of an individual such as foreign travel and residence, patents, publications, honors, and other types of recognition, memberships in professional or other occupationally significant organizations, and any record of special assignments completed. Fourth, there is the individual's salary and occupational progression history. This would include his present and past salary as well as a history of the positions which he has occupied and the rates of advancement in his career. Fifth, there are various items of company data which are useful. These would include benefit plan data, retirement information, seniority and service dates, and other related items. Sixth, there is the capacity of the individual. Included here would be performance appraisal information, any results from psychological test scores, and significant health information. Seventh, and last, are job and location preferences as well as any other special interests which the employee might have that could have a bearing on his employment and occupational utilization.[32]

Launching and Maintaining Skills Inventories

In addition to using and building an initial skills inventory, there are the problems of implementing and maintaining it. There are four basic stages in implementing and maintaining the inventory: planning, initiating, verifying, and maintaining it. Each of these is worth some elaboration.

Most of the pertinent considerations in planning the contents of the inventory have already been covered. It is clear that any decision about information to be included in the inventory must be based on decisions about the uses which the inventory is to serve, about the form in which the information will be recorded and stored, about the ways in which the data will be retrieved and analyzed, and about the feasibility of collecting and maintaining the information. It is impossible to list guidelines for making

[31] *Ibid.,* p. 63.
[32] *Ibid.*

such decisions which can be applied in all organizations. Each organization undertaking a skills inventory has to evaluate its own needs and its own capabilities carefully in deciding on content.[33]

In initiating the inventory, much of the information can be drawn together from existing sources such as payroll records, personnel jackets, salary records, benefit plan records, and training records. Usually gathering this information will be time-consuming and costly, especially because transcribing these existing materials into a format appropriate to a comprehensive skills inventory involves clerical and supervisory expense.[34]

Some of the desired data will not be available from records and can be obtained only through a special survey of employees. For example, it is frequently necessary to reinterpret data on previous employment experience or training in terms of the skills attained rather than the recital of job titles held or the names of training programs completed. Usually the individual employee will have to be consulted in such cases. Similarly, the only way to determine interests and job and location preferences is to query the people in question. It is usually best to keep direct surveys of employees to a minimum and to draw upon existing sources to the fullest possible extent.[35]

After the data pertaining to each employee have been assembled and transcribed into the appropriate inventory format, it is important to make sure that they are correct and that they give an accurate skill profile of the employee. The responsibility for verifying the data to be used in the inventory can logically be assigned to the employee himself. After all, it is to his best interest to see that his file in the centralized skills inventory is accurate and complete. It is particularly necessary that he verify the data obtained from existing records because frequently these will be outdated, incomplete, or subject to possible errors in transcribing. Each employee should therefore be presented with a "hard" copy—a printout from the computer, in the case of mechanized data—of his record in the manpower inventory. He should be requested to audit and update it as needed.[36]

Over the long run, a skills inventory will be only as good as the procedures set up to maintain it. In any organization, manpower resources are constantly changing and growing. Data start to become obsolete from the moment they are fed into the information system. Unless initial plans include procedures for dealing with these changes, the information will very soon become useless. In other words, without careful attention to manpower inventory maintenance, it is quite possible that many of an

[33] *Ibid.*, p. 64.
[34] *Ibid.*
[35] *Ibid.*
[36] *Ibid.*, pp. 64–65.

organization's manpower policies and programs will be based on obsolete, inaccurate manpower data. The unglamorous job of avoiding this pitfall is probably one of the most important tasks in any organization. For it is only from some form of skills inventory that an organization can hope to achieve meaningful skills planning and manpower projections. It is only from skills planning that an organization can hope to achieve effective human resources development. Finally, as we have been suggesting throughout the book, effective manpower planning and the development of human resources are clearly the major key to present and future organizational vitality.[37]

Some Specific Systems of Skills Inventories

We have been discussing the various kinds of information that are used in manpower planning. The design of the information retrieval system that provides the desired information is therefore very important.

Information retrieval, whether it be information about manpower or any other facet of organizational management, presupposes an information system. Such a system, broadly speaking, consists of a file structure to index and hold information, an input language for entering new information into the system or changing the information currently in the system, an interrogating language for couching retrieval requests, a body of programs for performing the various processing tasks, a program language for specifying new information-processing algorithms, and, finally, a language to control the operations of the system.[38] The actual retrieval of manpower information is often very slow, costly, and sometimes impossible. Computer systems can also be very costly and they can also be slow if only a small amount of information is desired and access to the computer is limited. Through time sharing it is possible to avoid some of these problems.[39]

The particular information retrieval system used for manpower planning may involve two or three subsystems in the practical situation. A computer system may be used to develop manpower inventories and to search many individual records rapidly. A manual system may be used to discover the career progression of individual persons. A third system may be devised that provides information for productivity studies and is closely related to an organization's financial information system. Regardless of the number,

---

[37] *Ibid.*

[38] Schoderbek, pp. 451–452, citing Robert A. Colilla and Burnett H. Sams, "Information Structures for Processing and Retrieving," *Communications of the ACM,* 1962, p. 11.

[39] Eric W. Vetter, *Manpower Planning for High Talent Personnel,* Bureau of Industrial Relations, University of Michigan, Ann Arbor, 1967, p. 81.

the particular combination of systems used by manpower specialists in organizations should maintain information in a form which meets the following three tests. First, is the information easily portable? In other words, can the information be easily broken out for discussion and appropriately related to the different levels in a complex organization? Second, are the data available for use on short notice? This goes back to the previously mentioned need for updating records quickly to provide management with current data. Third, once available, is the information adequate to assist in making intelligent manpower decisions? This is a double-barreled factor and involves the possibility that too much information might be generated as well as too little.[40]

The growth of manpower inventories is a relatively new phenomenon. By the early 1950s, various firms were using card sorters to help speed searches for manpower and to conduct head counts. Before that time, the United States Army had its MOS (Military Occupational Specialty) system, complete with the numerical coding of skills to five digits. By 1960 only a few companies (including, for example, Ford, International Business Machines, Standard Oil of New Jersey, and General Electric) had begun to program employee data files on computers. Perhaps several dozen have now programmed extensive data for all employees into a central computer. Basic data on manpower that can be recorded on tape in from 400 to 800 characters with each character representing a letter or number is more common than the programming of detailed information. Yet there are some skills inventories which run to 3000 or 4000 characters or more.[41]

Some of the manpower inventory programs now on-stream illustrate the size and flexibility of these inventories. IBM, a leader in this field, has unsurprisingly what is widely regarded as the country's most closely coordinated and comprehensive automated program. Several years ago when IBM launched its Personnel Data System, the latter was phased into 28 location systems, including 13 divisional units, and one headquarters file of every domestic employee, all interconnecting and using standard codes and programs. It was necessary to unify the system because most IBM locations had developed their own programs.

At IBM, the amount of information on an employee decreases at successive higher organization levels in the company. At the location where he works there are as many as 4000 characters of data on the man. In corporate-level files there are 600 to 800 characters. In effect, the manpower system keeps the bulk of the information where it is most needed. But when a division has to go outside itself for hard-to-find talent, the

---

[40] *Ibid.*, pp. 82–83. See also pp. 97–124 for an excellent example of analyzing managerial manpower requirements by means of a manpower inventory.

[41] "Describing Men to Machines," *Business Week*, No. 1918, June 4, 1966, p. 113.

headquarters file is interrogated. One such search to find a man who could consult with Apollo Moon Project engineers on induction motors uncovered 150 experts at IBM, three with Ph.D.'s.

In 1964, Kodak began to build IRIS and established a centralized computer file of 40,000 employees. In a brand new solution to the data accessibility problem, Kodak has hooked a cathode ray, similar to a television screen, to the output end of its computer, which produces a personnel record directly on microfilm. An ordinary printout of the manpower roster serves as a directory to an employee's microfilm record. The record may be reproduced on a reader-printer.

Several years ago the United States Navy had tapes on its 700,000 enlisted men as well as its 35,000 officers. The United States Employment Service with 20,000 California applicants on tape studied the feasibility of hooking the whole nation into a huge professional job applicant matching system called LINCS, which we discussed in another chapter.

Small organizations are also computerizing manpower records. For example, the State Street Bank and Trust Company of Boston with only 2000 employees has placed salary history, pension, profit-sharing, and job title data on tape and each month runs off a scalar organizational chart, a listing of employees in hierarchical order from president down to clerk.

Other companies with skills inventories include International Telephone and Telegraph, Xerox, American Machine and Foundry, McGraw-Hill, Radio Corporation of America, Honeywell, Boeing, and the General Electric Company.[42] An example of a skills inventory used by the ITT Federal Laboratories, called a capabilities index survey, is shown in Figure 2.

There is much evidence that various kinds of manpower information systems can be established in the future. For example, federal government officials have been planning the development of a storage and retrieval system for all scientific and engineering information.[43] In addition, there has been much discussion and controversy about a national roster of all American citizens which would be a type of societal manpower inventory.[44] Lastly, in one city at least, a data bank has been established for cataloging various facts about all residents.[45]

[42] *Ibid.,* pp. 113–114.

[43] "Quick Access Pool for World Data," *Business Week,* No. 1972, June 17, 1967, pp. 78–83.

[44] See, for example, Arthur R. Miller, "The National Data Center and Personal Privacy," *Atlantic Monthly,* Vol. 220, No. 5, November 1967, pp. 53–57, and letters to the editor in Vol. 221, No. 1, January 1968, p. 24; and "What the 'Data Banks' Know About You," *U.S. News & World Report,* Vol. 64, No. 15, April 8, 1968, pp. 82–85.

[45] "A City Where Computers Will Know about Everybody," *U.S. News & World Report,* Vol. 62, No. 20, May 15, 1967, pp. 78–79.

Name (Last): DOE **First:** JOHN **Initial:** W

Date: Mo 06 | Day 05 | Year 61

Personal Data

Employee Number		6 1 0 1 6
Department Number		6 4 0 1 1
Month & Year of Employment	MO 12	YR 52
Job Classification Code		2 0 7 1
Month & Year of Birth	MO 07	YR 15
Sex { 0–Male / 1–Female }		0
Highest Security Clearance		2
Citizenship		0
Degree Codes		0 8 2 / 0 8 3

Name (Last) grid: 4 | 0 | 6 | [shaded] | 0 | 0 | 0

Highest Security Clearance:
0–None
1–Confidential
2–Secret
3–Top Secret
4–Crypto.

Citizenship:
0–Native U.S.A.
1–Naturalized
2—Non-Citizen

Supervisor's Signature

Code Numbers for Degrees

Field	Associate	Bachelor	Master	Doctor
Accounting	011	012	013	014
Biology	021	022	023	024
Bus. Administration	031	032	033	034
Economics	041	042	043	044
Engineering	–	–	–	–
Aeronautical	051	052	053	054
Chemical	061	062	063	064
Civil	071	072	073	074
Electrical	081	(082)	(083)	084
Industrial	091	092	093	094
Mechanical	101	102	103	104
Other	111	112	113	114
English	121	122	123	124
Law	131	132	133	134
Physical Science	–	–	–	–
Chemistry	141	142	143	144
Mathematics	151	152	153	154
Physics	161	162	163	164
Other	171	172	173	174
Psychology	181	182	183	184
Other	191	192	193	194

BEGIN HERE →

4	0	4	9	8	0
(1)	0	1	6	0	3
(2)	0	1	6	0	4
(3)	0	1	6	0	5
(4)	0	1	6	0	8
(5)	0	1	6	1	5
(6)	0	1	6	2	5

Capabilities Codes

(14)	0	0	6	0	7
(15)	0	0	6	0	8
(16)	1	2	4	0	5
(17)	4	1	8	0	1
(18)	5	1	2	0	9
(19)	5	1	2	1	0
(20)	5	1	3	0	1

(28)					
(29)					
(30)					
(31)					
(32)					
(33)					
(34)					

The ITT Federal Laboratories, a division of the International Telephone and Telegraph Corporation, has developed a Capabilities Index that covers approximately 2,500 engineering, administrative and manufacturing employees of the company. A few of the forms associated with the index are reproduced on this and the next page. They give some indication of what this one company has done to create an effective management tool.

The capabilities codes are found in a *Capabilities Reference List*, a portion of which is reproduced at right.

Figure 2 Capabilities index survey. *Source.* Walter S. Wikstrom, "Skills Inventories—Who Can Do What?," *Conference Board Record*, Vol. 1, No. 2, February 1964, pp. 54–55.

Experience Summary

Major Fields	Activities (*See Instruction for Definitions*)						
	Applied Research	Advanced Development	Design Engineering	Systems Development	Production Engineering	Manufacturing Engineering	Service Engineering
Antennas	001	002 (4)	003 (5)	004 (1)	005	006	007
Anti-Submarine Warfare	011	012 (2)	013 (3)	014	015	016	017
Cable and Wire	021	022	023	024	025	026	027

Page one of the form is shown at the left. Page two provides space for listing additional capabilities by code number. On page three are listed any capabilities for which no code can be found in the *Reference List* and any hobbies that involve special study or learned skills. Page four (above) provides space for listing the number of years experience in various activities and fields.

The *Capabilities Reference List* (below) was developed by the company for its own use. The list provides code numbers for technical, scientific, engineering and administrative skills and knowledge. This highly specific reference list runs to forty-eight printed pages, with an eleven-page supplement.

AVIATION USE OF ELECTRONICS
01601 Air Traffic Control (ATC)
01602 Aircraft Identification
01603 Aircraft Location
01604 Airport Surface Detection Equipment (ASDE)
01605 Airport Surveillance Radar
01606 Airport Zone Equipment
01607 Altimeters
01608 Approach Zone
01609 Artificial Horizon Indicator
01610 Attitude Effect
01611 Automatic Direction Finder
01612 Autopilot
01613 Beacons
01614 Blind Approach Beacon System (BABS)
01615 Channel Separation, V-H-F
01616 Clearance Array
01617 Collision Avoidance
01618 "Common System"
01619 Compass Locator
01620 Computers, ATC

01643 Inertial Navigation
Instrument Landing Systems (ILS) See INSTRUMENT LANDING SYSTEMS)
01644 Interference, Radio
01645 Landing-Zone Equipment
01646 Long-Range Radar
01647 Loran "A"
01648 Loran "C"
01649 Magnetic-Loop Surface Detector
01650 Marker Beacons
01651 Microwave Coordinated System
01652 Military Services Applications
01653 Moving-Target Indicator (MTI)
01654 Navaglobe, Navaho
01655 Navar
01656 Omnidirectional Radio Range (VOR)
01657 Point-to-Point
01658 Post Office Position Indicator (POPI)
01659 Precipitation Static
01660 Precision Approach Radar (PAR)
01661 Radar (Pilotage Equipment)

Figure 2 (*Continued*).

In the 1970s it will be difficult for even the most conservative personnel department in organizations of any size to avoid the impact of the computer. A recent survey of electronic data processing of personnel records and reports in 333 companies reveals the extent of computer utilization. Of these, 254 organizations utilized EDP in one or more phases of their operation. Only 35 had no plans to use EDP. The remaining organizations not using it either reported definite plans for EDP or had it under serious consideration. The most widespread use of EDP was, however, for payroll purposes.[46] There is every likelihood that the use of EDP for skills retrieval will continue to spread in the 1970s. Yet the main use of EDP will probably be for payroll purposes for a considerable time in the future.

In summary, a manpower skills inventory is a carefully thought out but relatively simple tool. In concept, it is merely a list of employees and their manpower strengths and weaknesses. In actuality the skills inventory may be a deck of cards or a reel of computer tape. Yet, there is no doubt that the inventory is an extremely valuable management tool and can be truly effective when it has been properly designed.[47]

There is also little doubt that the manpower specialist will find the skills inventory not only an important tool in the conduct of his work, but also an indispensable one in the 1970s. Let us next relate the inventory to other tools concerned with manpower strengths and weaknesses, specifically performance reviews.

PERFORMANCE APPRAISALS: AN OVERALL VIEW

The appraisal of individual performance is a constant accompaniment of human society. Long before the emergence of the complex organizations which dominate so much of our lives today, each man watched other men, appraising their behavior in terms of his own goals and needs and modifying his own behavior in accordance with his interpretation of what he saw. Human relationships were initiated, strengthened, or severed on the basis of personal appraisals of others.[48]

Even though we now live in a world of large-scale organizations, each of us still makes many of these personal appraisals and subsequent choices. Eventually we work out rules of thumb to guide our choices. These rules cause us to search only for the certain restricted kinds of evidence which we believe to be significant in making judgments. We differ in our ability

[46] Elizabeth Lanham, "EDP in the Personnel Department," *Personnel,* Vol. 44, No. 2, March-April 1967, pp. 16–22.

[47] Walter S. Wikstrom, "Skills Inventories—Who Can Do What?" *Conference Board Record,* Vol. 1, No. 2, February 1964, p. 56.

[48] Thomas L. Whisler and Shirley F. Harper, eds., *Performance Appraisal, Research and Practice,* Holt, Rinehart and Winston, New York, 1962, p. 1.

as judges, probably because of differences in our rules of evidence and judgment as well as our biases.[49]

We judge one another, and we are sensitive to the fact that others are always judging us. We are aware that our acceptability to other people can be affected by our ability to sense correctly what they think of us. Most of us desire to know how others judge us; yet, at the same time, some of us may be resentful of critical evaluations. This fundamental human experience of appraisal, action, feedback, and reappraisal conditions the behavior of individuals within organizations.[50]

The problems inherent in interpersonal relations must be anticipated in organizational life as well as in other types of social experience outside complex organizations.[51]

But organizations, especially large-scale organizations, pose some additional problems. These organizations have goals apart from those of the people who comprise them. Limited types of behavior are expected of the individual organizational participant for limited periods. These limited activities are expected, in the aggregate, to contribute toward the accomplishment of organizational goals. In practice, the impersonal mechanistic model of a complex organization underlying these expectations inevitably falls short of perfection for a number of reasons, which we need not go into here but are well known to students and practitioners in complex organizations.[52]

Even when the model of a complex organization works rather well in reality, it needs policing or control, and the police are usually people. They are individuals who appraise and reprimand or reward. Furthermore, these are the same people with whom one usually has to continue to associate in a working relationship. For these reasons the problems of interpersonal relations in performance appraisal loom large. In addition, organizational objectives are sometimes compromised for personal reasons.[53]

Yet we cannot turn back the clock, because complex organizations are here to stay in our society. Despite their many dysfunctions, they have great advantages even when they work less than perfectly. If a complex organization is to function moderately well in the bureaucratic tradition, with formally defined roles and replaceable manpower, then information—adequate information—must be available about the performance and capacities of its members. Where certain participants are designated as executives and are given the power of significant decision making, infor-

[49] *Ibid.*
[50] *Ibid.*
[51] *Ibid.*
[52] *Ibid.,* pp. 1–2.
[53] *Ibid.,* p. 2.

mation on performance becomes vital to their decisions and, hence, to their own success. Therefore, appraisal is inevitable.[54]

The needs of individuals and their varying abilities (including the ability to judge), the needs of the complex organization for accurate information, and the difficult problems of judgment and the transmission of information growing out of a highly personalized appraisal process set the problem of performance appraisal in the organization.[55] It is to this subject which we turn next.

Origin and Growth of Performance Appraisals

Our approach in the next several sections of the chapter is: (1) to describe briefly the origins and development of performance review (or merit rating as it was earliest known); (2) to discuss current thinking on the subject; and (3) to argue that a refined concept of merit rating is now appropriate for and, in fact, fulfills two important functions for modern large-scale organizations.[56]

We have already mentioned that the requirement that one person, usually a superior, evaluate another, usually a subordinate, in terms of an organizational criterion or set of criteria is as old as human society. One student has noted, for example, that Sin Yu, an early Chinese philosopher, criticized a biased rater who was employed by the government during the Wei Dynasty (A.D. 221–65) and pointed out that "The Imperial Rater of Nine Grades seldom rates men according to their merits but always according to his likes and dislikes." [57] A rating scale based upon personal qualities was used by the *Dublin* (Ireland) *Evening Post* in 1684 to evaluate legislators.[58] Large-scale organizations such as churches and armies have probably always used systematic rating devices, and it has been reported that at least some branches of the United States Army used merit rating as early as 1813.[59] Perhaps the first industrial application of merit rating was made by Robert Owen at his cotton mills in New Lanark,

[54] *Ibid.*

[55] *Ibid.*

[56] An earlier version of much of the material discussed in this section appeared in Thomas H. Patten, Jr., "Merit Rating: An Outmoded Personnel Concept?," *Hospital Administration*, Vol. 8, No. 1, Winter 1963, pp. 26–38. This material is published with the permission of the American College of Hospital Administrators, 840 North Lake Shore Drive, Chicago, Illinois 60611.

[57] Harmon S. Belinsky, "Evolution of Plans and Ratings of Employee Performance," as quoted in U.S. Congress, Senate, *Hearings on S. Res. 105 and S. Res. 124, Efficiency Ratings* (80th Congress, 2nd Sess.), p. 187.

[58] J. D. Hackett, "Rating Legislators," *Personnel*, Vol. 7, No. 2, August 1928, pp. 130–131.

[59] Roger M. Bellows and M. Frances Estep, *Employment Psychology: The Interview*, Rinehart, New York, 1954, pp. 118–19.

Scotland, in the early 1800s, where wood cubes of different colors indicating different degrees of merit were hung over each employee's work station and changed, as appropriate, to reflect his deportment.[60] In the federal civil service, merit rating, which has more often been called efficiency rating, has been in operation since 1887.[61] Merit rating has a lengthy heritage.[62] In many ways it is a refinement of job evaluation applied to the job incumbent and has a history paralleling that of job evaluation.

The prime impetus to the development of merit rating in American industry can be traced to the efforts of the same industrial psychologists at Carnegie-Mellon University who conducted early work in salesman selection, described in another chapter, and who developed a man-to-man rating form based upon trait psychology, which was later used by the Army in World War I in assessing the performance of officers.[63] After the war, many of the men who had been associated with this work readily secured positions in industry because business leaders were impressed by the achievements of the Army researchers and wanted to make use of the contributions of industrial psychologists.[64] However, professional psychologists were very critical of the rating scales developed by the Army group.[65] But professional objections seem to have had little or no impact on the diffusion of merit rating schemes through industry until the 1940s, although there were numerous innovations in types of rating scales and techniques for scale-construction in the interim. The so-called graphic or trait-rating scale increased in popularity in this era and remains predominant today. Such a scale merely lists personality trait names on a sheet of paper and requires that a rater check the degree to which the person being evaluated possesses these traits.

In the defense period prior to Pearl Harbor, the Army once again assembled a group of psychologists to assist in the defense effort and im-

[60] Robert L. Heilbroner, *The Worldly Philosophers*, Simon and Schuster, New York, 1953, pp. 98–99.

[61] Frank A. Petrie, "Is There Something New in Efficiency Rating?," *Personnel Administration*, Vol. 13, No. 1, September 1950, p. 24.

[62] For a more detailed account see Thomas H. Patten, Jr., "The Development and Current Status of Industrial Merit Rating" (unpublished M.S. thesis), New York State School of Industrial and Labor Relations, Cornell University, 1955, pp. 50–148.

[63] Walter Dill Scott et al., *Personnel Management*, Third Edition, McGraw-Hill, New York, 1941, pp. 213, ff.

[64] Scott et al., *Personnel Management*, Fifth Edition, p. 248.

[65] One of the earliest and perhaps best critiques is that by Rugg. See Harold Rugg, "Is the Rating of Human Character Practicable?," *Journal of Educational Psychology*, Vol. 12, No. 11, November 1921, pp. 425–438; No. 12, December 1921, pp. 485–501; Vol. 13, No. 1, January 1922, pp. 30–42; No. 2, February 1922, pp. 81–93.

prove its rating system.[66] The principal fruits which subsequently grew out of research conducted during World War II were the development of the forced-choice technique and the critical-incidents approach to merit rating.[67] Although these innovations represented methodological and substantive improvements over the earlier man-to-man and graphic scale systems, specifically by abandoning the use of trait names and building rating systems upon observed behavior, they have not become generally adopted in industry, perhaps, in large part, because they are more expensive systems to construct. For example, in a survey reported in 1947, 106 of the merit-rating plans used by 125 companies consisted of graphic scales; in another survey in 1951, 73 graphic scales were found in a total of 93 plans; in a survey reported in 1952, 114 of 130 plans were found to be of the graphic type; and a survey reported in 1957 showed that, of 140 companies, at least 100 of them used a graphic scale or variation of it.[68] No more recent surveys of widespread organizational practice have apparently been published in the last decade, but graphic scales probably are still the most widely used. Very generally, then, because of the failure of recent rating innovations to gain widespread acceptance, it can be concluded that the persistent problems which have caused personnel managers to be dissatisfied with merit rating for the past forty years are still with us. These problems are (1) insufficient spread of score, (2) halo, (3) differences in standards among raters (as manifested in leniency, severity, and central tendency), (4) unreliability, and (5) lack of validity.[69]

In view of these problems it is not surprising to find extensive discussion in the management and personnel literature in which the function of merit

---

[66] Walter V. Bingham, "Psychological Services in the United States Army," *Journal of Consulting Psychology,* Vol. 5, No. 5, September-October 1941, pp. 222–224.

[67] Two of the basic writings describing these techniques are E. Donald Sisson, "Forced Choice—The New Army Rating," *Personnel Psychology,* Vol. 1, No. 3, Autumn 1948, pp. 365–381; and John C. Flanagan, "Critical Requirements: A New Approach to Employee Evaluation," *Personnel Psychology,* Vol. 2, No. 4, Winter 1949, pp. 419–425.

[68] Walter R. Mahler, "Some Common Errors in Employee Merit Rating Practices," *Personnel Journal,* Vol. 26, No. 2, May 1947, pp. 68–74; Lawrence G. Spicer, "A Survey of Merit Rating in Industry," *Personnel,* Vol. 27, No. 6, May 1951, p. 517; Roland Benjamin, Jr., "A Survey of 130 Merit-Rating Plans," *Personnel,* Vol. 29, No. 3, November 1952, pp. 287–294; and *Merit Rating of Rank-and-File Employees* (Survey No. 41 of BNA's Personnel Policies), Bureau of National Affairs, Washington, 1957, pp. 1–5. See also Robert Fitzpatrick and Clifford P. Hahn, "Personnel Research in Industry," *Personnel,* Vol. 31, No. 5, March 1955, p. 425.

[69] John C. Flanagan, "The Quantitative Measurement of Employee Performance," in *The Periodic Review of Employee Performance and Progress,* Industrial Relations Center, University of Chicago, Chicago, pp. C-3, C-4.

rating based on traits has been fundamentally questioned. To be sure, many of these questions have been raised because of disenchantment with the validity of trait psychology. However, some of the newly emergent interests of management (in such fields as organizational planning and manpower development) have led to new postulates relative to human behavior which conflict with the trait framework of thought. For example, since the Hawthorne studies,[70] many personnel managers have obtained a new perspective on employee behavior and view individuals not as creatures motivated by traits and innate qualities but rather as members of formal organizations and informal groups, status-incumbents behaving in ways governed by various role prescriptions. Similarly, manpower specialists have recognized that the company organizational structure can be modified through planning to tap the potential of human resources and have determined, in sum, that management is not limited to identifying and selecting individuals with immutable traits to fill slots in an inflexible organization.[71]

Lastly, the presumed "executive shortage" of recent years has directed interest to a search for means for taking an inventory of the existing executive talent in an organization, and abstractly defined traits have not been found helpful as measures of potential. However, in this field, there have been greater problems in blocking out just what development of a manager is and who should be developed and how.[72] Merit rating systems (usually called by a different name when referring to managerial, professional, and technical manpower, such as performance appraisal) have often been used in this context when selecting individuals for participation in university management education programs.

Contemporary Concepts of Performance Appraisal: Control and Development

The emergent interests of contemporary management provide a perspective for understanding contemporary concepts of rating. Basically, there has been a significant semantic and conceptual change in thinking about appraisals: use of the term "merit rating" is declining, and the focus upon "merit" has been replaced by concentration on management-by-objectives and empirical performance standards. For example, in a survey made a decade ago of 23 governmental and industrial organizations, it was

[70] See Fritz J. Roethlisberger and William J. Dickson, *Management and the Worker,* Harvard University Press, Cambridge, 1939.

[71] See James C. Worthy, "Organizational Structure and Employee Morale," *American Sociological Review,* Vol. 15, No. 2, April 1950, pp. 169–179.

[72] See, for a critique, Erwin K. Taylor, "Management Development at the Crossroads," *Personnel,* Vol. 36, No. 2, March-April 1959, pp. 8–23.

found that the term "performance appraisal" (or an equivalent) was then being commonly used to describe systems of wage and salary administration based upon periodic reviews of individual rates and pay with advances ("merit increases") recommended by organizational superiors after considering such factors as performance, time since last increase, budgetary allotments, pay range from the job or position, profit position, and seniority. In other words, the term merit rating had to a large extent been dropped, and such terms as progress review, performance evaluation, or employee appraisal were starting to be used as substitutes. Of even greater significance was the fact that in the study it was found that rating plans having titles which suggested that the program related to the employee's personal characteristics rather than his performance or that included an exact or mathematical measurement were distinctly passing out of vogue.[73] Another author has suggested that merit rating has had more euphemistic aliases than any other technique used by personnel managers.[74] Today the term merit rating seems quaint to the ears of the sophisticated manpower specialist.

There has also been increasing recognition of the concept that the value of a merit-rating system has little or nothing to do with the measurement of merit regardless of how the latter is defined. Rather, the value in merit rating is seen in the bringing together of the superior and subordinate for the purpose of discussing the latter's performance.[75] The existence of a rating system implies that such meetings will take place at regular intervals, and there are no functional equivalents of merit rating. That is, there are no other organizational devices which will assure that meetings of the kind described will take place for the same purpose. This is not to imply that all evaluative meetings are the same and that there are not significant differences in the content, duration, and interpersonal skills which differentiate performance evaluation sessions. Such differences can be acknowledged, but still the point remains: there is no generally accepted substitute for

---

[73] George E. Brown, Jr. and Allan F. Larson, "Current Trends in Appraisal and Development," *Personnel,* Vol. 24, No. 4, January-February 1958, p. 52.

[74] See Bernard J. Covner, "The Communication of Merit Ratings: A Philosophy and a Method," *Personnel,* Vol. 30, No. 2, September 1953, p. 88.

[75] This point has been made repeatedly in the recent past. See such typical discussions as E. W. Chopson, "Service Ratings Won't Serve Two Masters," *Public Personnel Review,* Vol. 15, No. 4, October 1954, pp. 171–175; Douglas McGregor, "An Uneasy Look at Performance Appraisal," *Harvard Business Review,* Vol. 35, No. 3, May-June 1957, pp. 89–94; Philip R. Kelly, "Reappraisal of Appraisals," *Harvard Business Review,* Vol. 36, No. 3, May-June 1958, pp. 59–68; Kenneth E. Richards, "A New Concept of Performance Appraisal," *Journal of Business,* Vol. 32, No. 3, July 1959, pp. 229–243; and Rensis Likert, "Motivational Approach to Management Development," *Harvard Business Review,* Vol. 37, No. 4, July-August 1959, pp. 75–82.

appraisal meetings which can fulfill equivalent control and human-resource development functions in modern large-scale organizations. The generalization applies equally for hourly, salaried, and higher managerial personnel. In view of its centrality, then, what additional reasons are there that merit rating has fallen into disfavor with management?

The Limitations of Rating Tools

Let us consider certain of the influences on post-World War II industrial relations and manpower. It can be argued today that, in merit rating for rank-and-file or hourly employees as well as for nonexempt clerical-level salaried employees (all of whom generally have no more than a high-school education), there is a strong emphasis on evaluating past performance and on providing pay increases based upon the latter. Merit rating is less emphasized for the purpose of appraising the potential of such individuals for higher-line positions (except, perhaps, in the case of hourly employees for foreman vacancies) because noncollege graduates probably will not move into staff or higher management positions in the future. In addition, for employees who are members of industrial-type unions, a merit rating is probably the least significant item influencing the amount of their pay. For example, many industrial-type unions are opposed to paying different rates for the same job (i.e., "spread" rates) and generally favor flat wage increases across-the-board. In practice, this relegates merit rating for use only in giving small increases within grades, which often cover only a narrow spread in rates. In addition, in many unionized firms a rating can be protested through the grievance procedures, which suggests that ratings applicable to unionized manpower lack today the control efficacy with which management would like to see them endowed.[76]

Another problem which organizational management has had to face up to in this context—and one which has further undermined confidence in the efficacy of ratings—is the difficulty of gauging employee contributions, particularly in manufacturing firms where it has become increasingly difficult to identify at what precise point in production there is an employee action which interferes with or improves quantity or quality. Because of this difficulty in making assessments, both managements and unions have, in many instances, agreed that merit rating can have at most only a limited role. General dissatisfaction with the mechanics and lack of validity of rating systems have undoubtedly, as a consequence, hastened the decline of merit rating for rank-and-file manpower in many firms. Nevertheless, it is still argued in some quarters that varying rates should be paid for the

[76] "Whatever Became of Merit Rating?," *Personnel,* Vol. 34, No. 4, January-February 1958, pp. 8–18.

same jobs because employees differ in motivation and how well they carry out the duties of the same job. While it is possible to describe many hourly rated and clerical jobs by pinpointing specific duties and establishing criteria, and thereby providing a basis—probably one we would often be hard put to defend—for differential pay, there seems to be little evidence or sympathy for this point of view in large-scale organizations or that such rating schemes are increasing or will increase in the near future.[77] Since the control function in firms with union contracts is partly defined by the labor-management agreement and related institutional factors and the development of unskilled and semiskilled hourly and lower-level salaried personnel is accomplished largely through on-the-job training, the future role of merit rating for such employees will probably be one of further declining importance. In other words, the control and development functions are carried out by means and arrangements other than merit rating. The wage-setting function is handled largely, if not entirely, by the union contract and the accretion of job evaluation decisions stretching back over the post-World War II period. Similarly, procedures for establishing rates on new jobs (such as those caused by automation) have become virtually institutionalized, and merit rating has been shunted aside from this procedure because it is of only peripheral concern.

With respect to higher managerial and salaried personnel, the future role of merit rating is likely to be different. For such individuals the distinction between "merit increase" and "performance review" alluded to earlier is likely to become even more accentuated. There are at least two reasons for this. First, if the contemporary perceived "executive shortage" is an accurate reflection of the availability of managerial manpower, then the practice of firms to assess their managerial work force for the purpose of identifying individuals with potential will become more widespread. This means interest will not be focused primarily upon past performance as a basis for awarding pay increases but rather upon past performance as it provides clues for future managerial potential—for development for higher-level positions. Some kind of a rating form will probably always be viewed as useful as a basis for assessing talent in the firm and discussing an employee's development in an appraisal interview—at least no functional equivalent seems to be on the horizon.

Secondly, performance reviews will probably become more widespread in the future for higher managerial and salaried personnel because such reviews provide an effective control mechanism in the installation and operation of management-by-objectives systems. Control in this sense refers to making known and understood the results an employee must

[77] *Ibid.*

accomplish in his work and assuring that he achieves these results.[78] The focus on the control function seems defensible because organization implies control, and merit rating seems to be essentially a mechanism for making duties known and assuring that they are carried out, which is merely another way of abstractly describing control. All the so-called "purposes" of rating—basis for pay increases, discovering employee "weaknesses," assigning work—seem meaningful only in the context of control.[79] Except for work situations where superiors and subordinates work together so closely that an awareness of his superior's estimate of him has been communicated informally to the subordinate through a process akin to inculcation, only formal performance reviews can in theory fulfill the vital control function. Since we cannot assume that all supervisors and managers will communicate their evaluations informally or even that all subordinates could fully understand such subtle forms of communication, we must of necessity have a formal evaluative approach. The question then becomes: what approach is consistent with the development-control concept of performance evaluation that we have been emphasizing? The answer is found in the concept of management-by-objectives, which was apparently first stated in a seminal book [80] by one of the most astute students of management, Peter F. Drucker, although the idea has now almost become common coin of the managerial realm and the concept is no longer immediately associated with Drucker. Earlier students of management, of course, had also stressed the need for objectives, such as Harrington Emerson.[81]

MBO—MANAGEMENT BY OBJECTIVES

For higher managerial and exempt salaried manpower, the procedure described by Douglas McGregor, which has received considerable attention in the past decade, seems to imply the development-control concept and provides a feasible means for carrying out the aforementioned vital

---

[78] The control concept was suggested to the author in an article by Whisler, although his definition of the concept and use of it are different. See Thomas L. Whisler, "A Realistic Rule for Merit Rating," *Journal of Business*, Vol. 28, No. 1, January 1955, pp. 29–36.

[79] For a typical but older list of "purposes" of rating see *Plans for Rating Employees* (Studies in Personnel Policy No. 8), National Industrial Conference Board, New York, 1938, p. 5.

[80] Peter F. Drucker, *The Practice of Management*, Harper, New York, 1954, pp. 121–136, where he discussed "Management By Objectives and Self Control."

[81] Ernest Dale, *Management: Theory and Practice*, McGraw-Hill, New York, 1965, pp. 168–175.

organizational functions using a management-by-objectives approach. His thinking and suggestions may be summarized in the following manner.

McGregor is, first of all, particularly critical of the judgmental nature of performance rating in which the rater is placed in the position of appraising the worth of a fellow man. The emphasis in recent years upon the manager as a leader who strives to help his subordinates achieve both their own and the company's objectives is obviously inconsistent with the role of the manager as a judge, which is, of course, demanded by most rating plans, and perhaps particularly the trait-laden graphic scales.

To get around this difficulty, McGregor recommends that the subordinate establish short-term performance goals for himself. The superior, who retains the veto power on goals, assists the ratee only after the subordinate has completed a good deal of thinking about his job, made a careful assessment of his own strengths and weaknesses, and formulated some specific plans to accomplish his goals. The superior, in effect, helps the man relate his self-appraisal, his "targets" so to speak, and his plans for the ensuing period to the realities of the organization. This entire procedure directs attention away from vague generalities and back to specifics in the organizational setting.

The first step in the process is to arrive at a clear statement of the major responsibilities of the position as they work out in practice. This is not to be a formal job description but a document drawn up by the subordinate after studying the company-approved statement of position requirements. The superior and subordinate discuss the draft jointly and modify it as may be necessary until both of them agree that it is adequate.

Working from the statement of responsibilities, the subordinate then establishes his goals or "targets" for a projected time period. These targets are specific actions which the man proposes to take and are explicitly stated and accompanied by a detailed account of the actions he proposes to take to reach them. This document is then discussed with the superior and modified until both are satisfied with it.

At the conclusion of the projected time period, the subordinate makes his own appraisal of what he has accomplished relative to the target he set earlier, substantiating the appraisal with factual data whenever possible. Then the subordinate and superior have an appraisal "interview" which is, in effect, an examination by the two of the subordinate's self-appraisal. The interview culminates in a resetting of targets for the next six months.

As a consequence of this approach, it is possible to provide the kind of guided experience necessary for manpower development while avoiding the pitfalls of judgmental rating. Furthermore, this approach makes it possible to carry out the control function of the organization, which requires that the individual do the work he is assigned, and to shift the emphasis from appraisal of supposed traits to the analysis of actions relative to goals.[82] The manifest superiority of this approach to the stereotyped coaching interview [83] can be readily seen. While different in administration from other sophisticated approaches, McGregor's approach appears to meet all the requirements of an effective rating plan, such as having clearly understood objectives, providing for obtaining "sound" performance data, and using developmental information wisely and frequently.[84]

THE FEASIBILITY OF MBO-ORIENTED SYSTEMS

Other scholars of management, such as Philip R. Kelly and Thomas L. Whisler, have commented upon McGregor's approach to MBO. Kelly has indicated agreement with McGregor but somewhat expands his concept to what he calls an "organization review." Kelly does not describe a completely articulated evaluation program but indicates he would begin much like McGregor with a "job clarification" phase which would be followed by a "job reclassification" phase involving salary administration and based upon experience obtained while the subordinate was carrying out the job and ultimately a "re-examination" phase, apparently for examining mutual problems of the superior and subordinate and for renewing efforts to improve performance.[85]

Whisler takes issue with the McGregor approach primarily on the grounds that superiors are not as a rule interested in developing subordinates, although they are interested in assuring that subordinates are adequate to their present positions. In effect, Whisler endorses the control feature of McGregor's approach but doubts its manpower developmental value. Whisler believes the lack of interest in development can be attributed to several factors: in few organizations is "payoff" related to developing subordinates; developmental efforts cannot be gauged in any event; development is regarded as paternalistic and is avoided. He believes organizational superiors under the pressure of time and effort are inclined to do only what enhances their own standing in the organization. He does not consider the fact that their own promotion may hinge upon having a qualified replacement available. Ultimately, Whisler recommends that

---

[82] McGregor, *op. cit.*, pp. 90–93.

[83] For a description of this see Spencer J. Hayden, "Getting Better Results from Post-Appraisal Interviews," *Personnel*, Vol. 31, No. 6, May 1955, pp. 541–43.

[84] Walter R. Mahler and Guyot Frazier, "Appraisal of Executive Performance," *Personnel*, Vol. 31, No. 5, March 1955, p. 434.

[85] Kelly, *op. cit.*, pp. 66–68.

evaluating current performance be separated from evaluation of future potential. The former he would have superiors do and the latter would be done by the operating and other committees in the organization as well as peer groups who could observe individual subordinates at work on temporary assignments.[86]

Whisler's proposal is interesting and refreshing but does not fully consider the dynamics of management. There is no evidence, for example, to support the view that executives will accept as accurate and meaningful the testimony of a peer group or other committee as an adequate measure of a "comer." It would be easier to defend the hypothesis that executives in large-scale organizations tend to be cautious and place greater, if not exclusive, confidence in how the "comer's" performance appears to them as a consequence of having seen some of his work or seen him in action, however unrepresentative or atypical this observation may be. If they do not "see" his work, they will probably never accept an evaluation of him under any circumstances.[87] It can also be hypothesized that committee and peer-group evaluations are no more rational or objective than those of a ratee's organizational superior. It is perhaps less adequate to evaluate a man's potential when he carries out a special assignment than it is to evaluate him when he is performing assignments in a normal organizational context and developing the skills and relationships needed to be effective in that context.[88]

In summary, the development of performance rating in the past 60 years has been marked by changes in types of rating systems, but underlying the most popular system, graphic rating scales, has been a trait psychology. Dissatisfaction with the validity of these systems and increasing recognition of the value of superior-subordinate discussions centering around performance have given rise to a new emphasis which differs from the old concept of rating traits or qualities. Merit rating of the latter type is outmoded. The new concept of performance appraisal which is used by

[86] Thomas L. Whisler, "Performance Appraisal and the Organization Man," *Journal of Business*, Vol. 31, No. 1, January 1958, pp. 19–27.

[87] For an empirical study of this and related phenomena see Thomas H. Patten, Jr., "Organizational Processes and the Development of Managers: Some Hypotheses," *Human Organization*, Vol. 26, No. 4, Winter 1967, pp. 242–255.

[88] For other elaborations of the dynamics of rating related to or elaborating upon McGregor's concept see Arch Patton, "How to Appraise Executive Performance," *Harvard Business Review*, Vol. 38, No. 1, January-February 1960, pp. 63–70; Rensis Likert, "Motivational Approach to Management," *Harvard Business Review*, Vol. 37, No. 4, July-August 1959, pp. 75–82; George S. Odiorne, *Management by Objectives*, Pitman, New York, 1965, *passim;* Marion S. Kellogg, *What to Do About Performance Appraisal*, American Management Association, New York, 1965, *passim;* and George W. Torrence, *The Motivation and Measurement of Performance*, Bureau of National Affairs, Washington, 1967, *passim.*

organizations for control and developing personnel seems practical and promising, especially for higher-level exempt technical, professional, and managerial manpower.

The personnel psychologists who boldly experimented with rating scales years ago would probably be discouraged with the direction of contemporary thinking in the field in which they pioneered. In their day, a rating scale was a sophisticated advancement because it provided a framework for ordering thoughts. Today we regard their orderly system as unsuitable for adequately measuring complex behavioral phenomena. We prefer to use simpler tools that make it possible to implement management-by-objectives or empirical performance standards. We have, in a sense, gone full swing back to where we were in rating prior to World War I, but we hopefully have learned from our efforts. It is only a rare individual who today asks, "Whatever became of merit rating?," and searches for a perfectly objective instrument.

Inasmuch as performance appraisal tends to be a well-nigh universal phenomenon in organizations, the choice is really not whether to appraise or not to appraise. The choice is either (1) lack of planning and systematization of appraisals or (2) a concerted effort to devise appraisal procedures and systems with maximum validity. From this standpoint, the process of appraisal is viewed as a vital aspect of the utilization of human resources in an organization. If the particular systems used for performance evaluation have any validity, the goals of the organization will probably be furthered. On the other hand, if they are invalid, it is quite possible that organizational mediocrity or decline may result.[89]

RESEARCH ON NEW APPROACHES TO PERFORMANCE REVIEW

In the period since World War II when management-by-objectives systems and the establishment of empirical performance review standards became popular, a great deal of interest has centered upon either altering the performance review form or some aspect of the performance review situation in order to improve the usefulness of performance review systems in organizations. The literature that has appeared in the postwar period is certainly voluminous and beyond our capability to summarize here.[90]

[89] Wendell French, *The Personnel Management Process,* Houghton Mifflin, Boston, 1964, pp. 190–191. See this text or any other leading book on personnel management for a chapter on the subject of merit rating or performance appraisal which covers considerations relating to the subject which we have only covered generally here, such as detailed descriptions of the various systems. Also see Richard S. Barrett, *Performance Reviews,* Science Research Associates, Chicago, 1966.

[90] See Whisler and Harper, *op. cit.,* for an excellent summary of the literature not only since World War II but prior to that time.

However, it is worthwhile to at least take an overview of some of the main kinds of research which have been reported and then to turn to an approach to performance review which, while not necessarily a strict logical outgrowth of some of the research cited, is one which can be utilized by manpower specialists in organizations and is consistent with the development and control concepts of performance review previously discussed in this chapter.

The General Electric Company has been one of the most active organizations in the United States in conducting research in performance appraisal. For a number of years it has retained behavioral scientists in its corporate staff and has operated an Individual Development Methods Service concerned in large part with performance appraisals.[91] In its research, General Electric has stated a number of different findings about performance reviews. For example, GE studies indicate: criticism in the appraisal situation has a negative effect on the achievement of goals; praise in a performance review has little effect one way or the other; performance improves most when specific goals are established; defensiveness resulting from a critical appraisal produces inferior performance; coaching should be a day-to-day, not a once-a-year activity; mutual goal setting, not criticism, improves performance; interviews designed primarily to improve a man's performance should not at the same time weigh his salary or promotion in the balance; and, finally, participation by the employee in the goal-setting procedure helps produce favorable results.[92] These and other studies of General Electric relate to the development of managers rather than employees at all levels and emphasize the management-by-objectives concept and the positive aspects of the appraisal interview situation. More recently, General Electric has elaborated on the management-by-objectives concept in the establishment of its own version of it called WP and R, or Work Planning and Review.[93]

The importance of the appraisal interview itself in developing manpower has long been stressed. Different approaches that can be used have been discussed at considerable length by noted industrial psychologists.[94] This

[91] For the ideas of the head of this service on performance reviews, see Kellogg, *op. cit.*

[92] Herbert H. Meyer, "Split Roles in Performance Appraisal," *Harvard Business Review,* Vol. 43, No. 1, January-February 1965, pp. 123–124. See also Emmanuel Kay, et al., "Effects of Threat in a Performance Appraisal Interview," *Journal of Applied Psychology,* Vol. 49, No. 5, October 1965, pp. 311–317.

[93] Edgar F. Huse, "Putting in a Management Development Program that Works," *California Management Review,* Vol. 9, No. 2, Winter 1966, pp. 73–80.

[94] Norman R. F. Maier, "Three Types of Appraisal Interview," *Personnel,* Vol. 34, No. 5, March-April 1958, pp. 27–40. See also his book on this subject, *The Appraisal Interview,* McGraw-Hill, New York, 1961, *passim.*

has led to the interest in training programs to improve the skills of raters.[95] It appears that all of these programs which conceive of the improvement of raters as being the key to an improved performance review really stress the mechanics of the review itself rather than the underlying concepts and the measurement problems involved in translating the concepts into an operational system.

Other companies have also stressed management-by-objectives plans in performance appraisals, such as the Kimberly-Clark Corporation. For the past several years the latter organization has been using a plan in the development of professionals and managers in one part of the organization. A great deal of interest and a high degree of participation have been engendered among the individuals participating in the plan.[96]

On the other hand, the Carborundum Company has reported some disenchantment with the use of a management-by-objectives appraisal plan. It has found that most managers were unwilling to counsel their subordinates regularly, no matter what techniques of performance appraisal were offered to them. Even when objective data were available, managers could not automatically release statistics to employees and assume that they would properly interpret them and take whatever action was necessary to improve performance. Secondly, the performance data used in results-oriented appraisals were designed to measure end-results on a short-term basis rather than the specific means to accomplish those ends. Often, this may have resulted in the sacrifice of the accomplishment of long-range goals for the purpose of achieving a shorter-range objective. Third, these types of appraisal systems did not eliminate the personal idiosyncrasies that shape each manager's dealings with his subordinates. For example, the organizational superior who fears conflict will devote the appraisal session to praising the subordinate for his successes. He may even settle for targets lower than he should rather than stretching to attain more challenging targets on the grounds that he might fall short in attaining them. Finally, it is questioned whether the understanding that is supposed to develop between the organizational superior and the subordinate as they work together defining responsibilities, goals, and measurements really comes about. Ordinarily a manager wants to feel that he is in control of the work situation. Consequently, he is more comfortable setting targets for his subordinates than in working with them to arrive at mutually agreeable objectives. Because the organizational superior knows that he, after all, is responsible for his subordinates' results, the target-setting sessions tend

[95] Joseph F. Miraglia and Robert F. Powell, "A Training Program in Appraisal-Interviewing," *Training Directors Journal*, Vol. 17, No. 2, February 1963, pp. 18–23.

[96] See David Wilkerson, "A Results-Oriented Development Plan," *Conference Board Record*, Vol. 3, No. 3, March 1966, pp. 40–45.

to become something of a charade, with the superior either trying to manipulate the subordinate into giving him back his thinking, or else dictating what he expects the man to achieve. Carborundum also doubts that the management-by-objectives approach has the value often asserted for developing subordinates, primarily because few managers relish discussing the personal characteristics and drives of the subordinates with them, or are qualified to identify other people's strengths, weaknesses, and underlying personal problems. Moreover, the goal-oriented process itself tends to relegate the whole problem of individual development to the background. Inasmuch as the development of human resources is a long-term process, it is very difficult to expect results with any degree of precision. In management by objectives the emphasis is more on attaining organizational goals than it is on developing human resources as such.[97]

Another effect of performance reviews which has been given considerable attention in the postwar period is the use of peer ratings. During World War II, in the course of extensive research on group-rating techniques, the armed forces developed a number of methods of manpower assessment based upon co-worker evaluations. These were called "buddy ratings" and were used to select such key manpower as pilots and applicants for officer candidate school. They are still used today in the armed forces in the rating procedures of service schools, as the basis for promotions, and in a variety of other decisions affecting manpower. Many of these studies have found peer nominations to be quite predictive of future performance. In fact, there is evidence that peer nominations on leadership at officer candidate school were significantly better indicators of field performance than any other single predictor from the same level.[98] Although the evidence from industrial studies is less numerous, there is some to suggest that the use of peer ratings has value in making predictions about promotions.[99]

Few organizations today advocate the use of peer ratings as a substitute for the rating of subordinates by organizational superiors. Yet this may be an approach which has greater validity for assessing potential than others that are quite widely used. Perhaps peer ratings coupled with the use of assessment centers combine to offer the best tools in identifying manpower with potential for organizational advancement. That peer ratings are superior to other types of ratings in assessing past performance is a question of a different order.

[97] Charles J. Coleman, "Avoiding the Pitfalls in Results-Oriented Appraisals," *Personnel,* Vol. 42, No. 6, November-December 1965, pp. 24–33.
[98] Gene S. Booker and Ronald W. Miller, "A Closer Look at Peer Ratings," *Personnel,* Vol. 43, No. 1, January-February 1966, pp. 42–47.
[99] Harry E. Roadman, "An Industrial Use of Peer Ratings," *Journal of Applied Psychology,* Vol. 48, No. 4, August 1964, pp. 211–214.

Finally, it should be mentioned that despite the work of General Electric and other organizations which seem to favor the stress upon positive work results and building upon the individual's strengths in developing him (rather than correcting weaknesses), some have suggested that praise as a type of fuel which motivates and stimulates people in the work setting needs to be reappraised. That is to say, praise or any statement that makes a positive evaluation of a person may result in discomfort, uneasiness, and defensiveness. There is no reason to assume that people always enjoy praise. Part of the reason is that praise carries a kind of threat in the sense that it involves something that one must defend himself against. Thus, while we are likely to feel uncomfortable when we are negatively evaluated, we may similarly feel uncomfortable about a positive evaluation, if for no other reason than a person praising us is clearly sitting in judgment of us.[100]

Although the evidence concerning the role of praise in changing one's performance is not conclusive, to raise the subject is to point to some of the extreme difficulties in performance appraisal in organizational settings.

A Performance Appraisal Method: Concepts and Format

The mainstream of developments in appraisals since World War II has been a proliferation of approaches to performance reviews on the part of pace-setting complex organizations. The results of experimentation with different concepts, methods, forms, and the like have not been fully researched, nor probably will they ever be because of the difficulties in doing this. Nevertheless, it is desirable to describe a workable system of performance review, which we do next, although we cannot defend its validity and reliability to an appreciable extent. However, it can be stated that the particular approach advocated or variants on it have been widely used in American industry, and the system suggested is generally built around the management-by-objectives or performance standards concept.

The performance review system proposed for the use of manpower specialists in developing human resources in complex organizations is based upon the assumption that managers within organizations are responsible for the development of subordinates reporting directly to them. Managers thus would be expected to take some interest in the development of their subordinates. In doing so they make their own jobs easier because their subordinates in theory gradually become more proficient in the conduct of assigned work.

It is also assumed that one of the most efficient ways for managers to

[100] Richard E. Farson, "Praise Reappraised," *Harvard Business Review*, Vol. 41, No. 5, September-October 1963, pp. 61–66.

develop subordinates is to keep them clearly informed of their responsibilities and how well they are performing in those duties. Employees whose performance is deficient in one way or another can be given training or coaching to meet the standards set by the organizational superior or agreed upon through management-by-objectives target-setting. At the same time, the organizational superior can work closely with subordinates in discussing work assignments and in planning their completion. Perhaps it is implicitly assumed that there will be an interpersonal climate in which self-development is stimulated and interpersonal communication is reasonably authentic. Within this context, a performance review can be used to control the assignment of work and to develop subordinates.

In using performance appraisals for developing human resources, it is assumed that development depends only to a minor extent on the particular form used but to a major extent upon the interpersonal relationships between the superior and the subordinate. This thought is consistent with our heuristic confidence in the universality of the apprenticeship model and the idea that individuals learn job responsibilities as they become socialized to the organization. (The apprentice model provides for occupational and other learning to take place and is described in the next chapter.)

There probably is no time period as a minimum between which performance reviews should take place. For new employees it is likely that performance reviews should be given within the first several months, simply because the newly hired person is likely to be concerned about his performance and to desire feedback and knowledge of results. Also from an organizational standpoint, it seems logical that an evaluation should be made of him and his performance before there is any commitment made to continuity of employment. Thus, in many organizations we ordinarily have probationary periods for new employees.

The outer limits to a performance review could be up to one year for experienced employees whose performance can best be measured after sufficiently lengthy periods of time in which to complete work have passed. On the other hand, there are good reasons for giving performance reviews to employees regardless of their length of service if they have changed work assignments or there have been noticeable alterations in behavior on the job which require explanation. In addition, it may be a wise manpower policy to allow managerial employees to schedule and conduct performance reviews whenever they consider them useful for a legitimate purpose at hand. This thought is not to suggest that the performance review be used to punish an employee for a short-range or incidental deviation from a typical pattern of behavior on the job. It is simply to suggest that the rigid scheduling of performance reviews to accord with the calendar need not rule out the possibility of performance reviews at unscheduled times.

Underlying the use of performance reviews in a formal setting is the day-to-day evaluation of subordinates by organizational superiors. Insofar as performance reviews are an integral part of the work situation, managers who are performing capably are likely to look upon the performance review situation as simply an occasion in which the day-to-day informal appraisals passed on to employees are merely formalized for the record. To this extent, the day in which the formal appraisal is held should contain no surprises. Unfortunately, the performance review day is often one characterized by trauma and strife when the organizational superior has failed to communicate previously his evaluation of the employee's behavior informally in the day-to-day work situation.

The type of performance review system we have in mind can best be explained by considering the performance review form, Figure 3. It can be seen from this figure that the form to be used is a very simple one covering the name of the employee and certain straightforward information describing his position and location in the organization. Information is also available indicating the date of the performance review and the period covered.

The form itself lists on the left-hand side of the page the various position responsibilities of the employee. On the right is a list of the performance incidents or trends that typify the employee's performance since the last performance review. This type of form is particularly useful because the manager giving the performance review need simply list on the left the specific position responsibilities of the employee, either by considering the management-by-objectives sessions which he and the employee participated in or by considering the official position description of the employee's work, assuming that the employee is perhaps at a lower organizational echelon and performance standards are more pertinent than broad objectives of a managerial type. Considerable freedom is given for the statement of these responsibilities, and it is possible to use as many sheets of paper as necessary to accommodate the different responsibilities. Normally the front side of an ordinary 8½ × 11 sheet of paper would be sufficient to list the responsibilities for almost all employees.

On the right side of the page, the performance incidents can be stated and lined up against the specific position responsibilities. It is important to note that the performance incidents or trends that should be listed are those that are typical (rather than those that are unusual) and adequately characterize the employee's performance since his last review. We recognize that it is possible for a manager giving the performance review to fail to cite typical incidents or trends and to use the performance review form incorrectly. Consistent with the literature which we have cited, perhaps training on how to identify incidents or trends and prepare them for inser-

Name	Soc. Sec. No.	Period from Covered	To	Date of Review
Department	Staff, Division, Branch	Organization Code No.		Classification

Position Responsibilities	Performance Incidents or Trends that Typify Employee's Performance Since Last Review

Improvements or Lack of Improvements Since Last Review

Specific Action to be Taken to Improve Performance

Are the Normal Requirements Met Regarding:
Attendance Yes ☐ No ☐   Punctuality Yes ☐ No ☐
If Not, Explain.

Describe Any Other Characteristics Which Affect the Employee's Performance and Which Require Classification.

Prepared by	Title	Reviewed by	Title

Employee's Comments (Freely Express Your Views on the Completeness of the Review, Accuracy, Etc.)

Use back of page if necessary.

Employee's Signature   Date

Figure 3 Performance review form.

tion on the form will avoid some of the pitfalls possible in not focusing upon an appropriate time-frame.

On the bottom of the page in Figure 3, there are several other categories of information. Improvements or lack of improvements since the employee's last performance review may be noted. Specific action to be taken by the organizational superior to assist in the improvement of the performance of the subordinate may also be listed. For those who wish to make observations on the employee's attendance and punctuality there is a small amount of space for describing any other characteristics which affect the employee's performance and which require clarification. As with the space provided for position responsibilities and performance incidents, additional pages can be allocated for amplification of any of the comments which the rater wishes to make relative to the items of information appearing on the bottom of the performance review form.

The last few lines of the performance review form contain additional descriptive information concerning who prepared the form and the organizational superior of the person who prepared the form. By involving two levels of organizational management in the preparation and administration of the performance review, the rater is in a stronger position in the conduct of the appraisal interview than he would be if he had not discussed the appraisal with his superior. This is a strength grounded in multiple-judgment and organizational power. Specifically, he has had his organizational superior review the form and made any adjustments which the latter considers significant. Thus the employee will normally believe that the review is just and not merely the opinion of his organizational superior.

Another feature of the form is the space allocated for the employee's comments so that he can express himself on the completeness and accuracy of the review or on other matters which he thinks were omitted or improperly stated. Obviously, employees experiencing a performance review are in a situation involving the exercise of authority. The management-by-objectives and performance standards concept used in performance reviews are intended to remove some of the authoritarian sting of the organization and inject some democratic participation in the review on the part of the employee being rated. Nevertheless, it would be naive to assume that many employees will disagree with the review and feel perfectly free to express their reaction. However, the opportunity is provided on the form for some employee feedback and it is likely to be gotten in at least some circumstances.

Lastly, the employee is asked to sign the review simply to indicate that it was given. If he refuses to sign, the rater need simply indicate that the employee refused to sign. In these situations some avenue of appeal should be available so that the dissatisfied employee can obtain either an interview with the organizational superior of the rater or perhaps discuss his own plight with the manpower specialist or the representative of the personnel department.

Administering the Appraisal: Some Mechanics

In administering a performance review using the form which we have been discussing, it is convenient to think about the preparatory aspects of the performance revision situation from the standpoint of the person making the appraisal. First, the person preparing the form should ask himself a number of different questions. How have I determined that the responsibilities and duties on the form adequately describe the job which the employee is actually doing? What have I done to assure that the employee knows what his specific position responsibilities are? What have I done to assure that the employee knows the quality and quantity of work expected in the performance of his position duties? What measures have I taken to be certain that the performance incidents or trends cover the entire period since the last review and constitute a proper representative sample? What methods and techniques were used by the employee to carry out his assignments? What have I done to evaluate the strong and the weak points and to avoid evaluating all aspects of the employee's work behavior as average? What have I done as a supervisor to help carry out plans for improving the performance of the employee which were made at the time of the last performance review interview? What preparations have I made to answer questions about salary increases should these questions come up, even though the purpose of the performance review is control of work assignments and individual development rather than an occasion to discuss the possibility of a pay increment? What circumstances exist which are beyond the employee's control and are affecting his performance? Does the employee show aptitudes and interests that suggest he may be more suitably placed in another position or line of work? What measures have I taken to make sure that this performance review represents the best unbiased judgment of the employee's typical performance in the time period covered? Why has the employee performed at the level which he has for the period covered?

The individual who has asked himself questions such as those suggested is probably as well prepared as he can be to conduct a performance review. His next task is to conduct the performance review interview itself.

The rater should begin by creating an interpersonal atmosphere that is conducive to effective two-way communication, which is, of course, much more easily said than done. Sufficient time should be allowed so that the interview will not be hasty. The specific manner in which the atmosphere is established apparently plays a very important part in the conduct and subsequent results of the performance review interview. As we have seen from the General Electric research and from other studies previously mentioned, there remains considerable debate over the proper way to create an interpersonal atmosphere which will result in a performance review that is successful from the standpoint of the organization and that of the individual. Probably more than any other aspect of the performance review, the particular manpower development policies of the organization apply with potency here.

The rater should be capable of stating his observations as clearly as possible. Obviously, individuals differ in the extent to which they are verbally articulate. It is perhaps best to emphasize the performance of work rather than the traits of the individual in order to focus the attention on specific objectives in the work situation and performance standards rather than elusive and controversial traits. Such an approach avoids adjectival "name-calling." Whether it is best to begin with positive comments rather than negative is really not known.

Whether direct questions should be more numerous than indirect questions would again depend upon many idiosyncratic elements of a particular performance review interview. However, it is probably worthwhile to close the interview with a summary to set up a plan for improvement with agreed-upon objectives and standards and target dates for the accomplishment of these.

In the course of the interview itself, it is possible that any number of topics might come up, about which it is difficult to provide general guidance. In fact, it is the wide variety of topics, personalities, reactions, and organizational settings in which performance reviews take place that complicate our discussing the actual interview in more specific terms.

In any event, after the performance interview has been completed, the rater should reflect upon what was accomplished. He may do this by asking himself a number of questions such as the following. Specifically, what was accomplished during the performance review interview? Were the planned objectives of the interview met? What new items of information were brought up in the course of the interview that had not been previously considered? What can be done to assist the employee in developing himself on the job? To what extent was the employee willing to engage in self-appraisal? In what areas were there disagreements, and what is planned to be done about these areas of disagreement? What can I do in the period between the present and the next performance review to assist the employee in attaining organizational objectives and meeting performance standards?

The type of performance review form and the surrounding circumstances for the performance review discussed above should be regarded as a workable approach that needs further research to test its value. The concepts embodied in it are consistent with some research but not necessarily with all research on performance reviews. The approach set forth is prescriptively stated but less confidently regarded than the ease with which the statements were asserted.

Certainly, the ideas advanced are consistent with the control and developmental concepts of performance review which we have been discussing in this chapter. The type of form suggested can be used for employees at all organizational levels although persons doing the rating may resist the development of a form such as that suggested for clerical employees or those doing repetitive work. It may be totally inappropriate for use with unionized hourly employees, but such persons, as we saw earlier in the chapter, are becoming less and less subject to performance appraisal of the type discussed in the chapter. Also, in a later chapter it will be suggested that an abbreviated form could be used in evaluating the performance of college co-ops. Again, the type of form to be used is probably less important than the concepts behind the approach. The form suggested here avoids the trait psychology and seems to be workable from the standpoint of management-by-objectives and performance standards.

CONCLUSIONS

In this chapter we have been discussing management information systems and the use of appraisals of human resources or performance reviews in developing manpower. We discussed the need for meaningful data on human resources in modern complex organizations and the place of real-time and conventional manpower information systems. We discussed the problems inherent in obtaining and maintaining usable information and the special problems of using subjective and objective information. The manpower inventory or "balance sheet" was viewed as the core of human resources analysis in an organization and an essential part of any manpower plan. The inputs for classifying talent and experiences were reviewed, and special attention was given to use of performance reviews in obtaining insight into the quality of an organization's manpower. Little was said which bears on the use of organizational human resources information systems upon national manpower planning and vice versa, although the reader can easily determine that we are approaching the time in our society whereby we can obtain a great deal more information about people than ever before and use this in planning.

Performance reviews were seen as an important tool in appraising human resources but as having many weaknesses. Various methods of appraisal were quickly reviewed although the details of each system that has evolved in history were considered beyond the scope of our interest. For years there has been a rather futile search for the best method of performance appraisal; but the more rating methods change, the more they seem to remain the same. Trait-name-oriented graphic check-off scales remain predominant as they have for 60 years.

Serious unresolved problems in appraisals remain. They include insufficient spread in scores or ratings ("central tendency"); halo; differences in standards, communications skills, and observation skills among appraisers (which are reflected largely in the leniency and severity of ratings); unreliability in ratings; and the lack of validity in ratings. Some attention was given to what can be done to improve the appraisal process, and a particular type of performance review form was described and its use explained.

Although psychological tests may have an important bearing upon whom is developed in the first place in an organization by "screening in" and "screening out" human resources selected or rejected for employment or training, testing per se was omitted from the discussion. Instead, we discussed the appraisal of people at diverse organizational levels and focused upon the concepts of management-by-objectives and the use of performance standards for appraising employees at all levels. Some attention was given to post-appraisal evaluations and the feedback of performance results to employees. We also discussed the integration of appraisals with the learning theory concept of knowledge of results.

Throughout, we discussed the need for control in organizations: clarifying the organizational structure, identifying and assigning tasks, setting standards of performance, accomplishing organizational objectives, and satisfying organizational members to the extent feasible. The use of performance reviews in developing employees was stressed and the possible contradiction between the authoritarian cast of performance reviews and democratic styles of management were mentioned.

The last word on performance reviews is certainly not in yet. The use of management-by-objectives as a democratic type of goal setting and type of participative management seems to be consistent with much contemporary management theorizing and a possible alternative to dysfunctional bureaucratic managerial methods. Yet there may be other types of organizational structures built upon personal autonomy, exchange, and bargaining which at a future date would probably require the thinking through of an entirely new approach to performance reviews. In any event, the transition has been made to the use of performance reviews that stress behavioral items and eschew trait names. At least in pace-setting firms the transformation has been started although probably far from completed. This transition is consistent with the growth of the behavioral sciences since the early 1960s and seems to be indicative of the direction in which performance reviews are headed in the 1970s.

CHAPTER 7

Apprentice and Technical Training

A case could probably be made that apprenticeship is the basic model underlying a multitude—if not virtually most—of manpower development activities. Apprenticeship as a model has no serious competitor or peer among development methods used in large-scale organizations today.

The idea of training through apprenticeship goes back to ancient times where the records of Egypt, Greece, Rome, and Babylon reveal evidence of plans for passing on the skills of artisans to the workers of the next generation. Weaving, shorthand writing, flute playing, hair dressing, and nail-smithing were among the earliest apprenticeable trades historically. The practice of indenturing apprentices was common throughout Europe during the Middle Ages and was brought to the United States by the early settlers. Apprenticeship has remained as the most popular means by which the craftsmen throughout the ages have passed their skills along to their successors, thereby preserving the arts and skills of one generation for the benefit of the next.[1]

In apprenticeship the competent and experienced craftsman (rather than a book or comparable source) is the repository of the skills of the craft. Without his willingness to transmit his knowledge of techniques to others, it would be practically impossible to train the next generation of skilled manpower. Fortunately, craftsmen throughout the ages have taken this responsibility seriously and have willingly passed along their skills to the young of the next generation through the process of socialization.[2] Yet this process has not been without its imperfections and blockages.

SKILL

Before proceeding to discuss apprenticeship and stating the approach used in the chapter, we must stop and examine an important initial

[1] Charles A. Hall, ed., *Apprenticeship*, Southern States Apprenticeship Conference, Houston, 1961, p. 2. For a concise history of apprenticeship see Eugene V. Schneider, *Industrial Sociology*, McGraw-Hill, New York, 1957, pp. 29–59.

[2] *Ibid.*

stumbling block: the definition of a skill. We have used the term up to this point without defining it, except to suggest it involves a knowledge of techniques or a human art. We pause here not to offer a final word on a complicated term but simply to indicate our awareness of the problems it creates and a possible way of understanding it more adequately. We then return to analyzing apprenticeship as a basic learning model underlying a multitude of programs for developing human resources, focusing upon the development of skilled craftsmen as an illustration.

There are many different views on the nature of skill. The term has been used to include numerous different human acts: tracing figures, painting, operating a lathe, speaking a language, bomb aiming, flying, shot-putting, conducting a surgical operation, electrical-wiring, and the like. Years ago psychologists tended to concentrate their attention on the response (or effector processes) and thus to stress those parts of a skill which were primarily motor. More recently, psychologists have turned their attention to the input of skills (or receptor processes) and particularly to the display of and the part played by perception. In reality, skill in patterns of movement must often be coupled with skill in perceiving when to carry out the right action at the right time if the person performing is to attain the goal in his behavior.[3] In a word, motor and perceptual skills are complementary.

Skill may thus be viewed as a continuum from those which are predominantly habitual to those which are mainly perceptual. At one end are the motor skills; at the other, the perceptual or insightful, which determine for the person when the external environment is favorable for motor skill display. Between, lie skills at various places along the continuum, depending upon the relative importance of habitual and perceptual aspects in the perfected skill.

If this conceptualization is valid, then it is important for the learner and the instructor to decide where the particular skill with which they are concerned lies on the continuum. This decision will often be difficult to make and may not be determinable in a definitive way. Changes are constantly occurring in many jobs which affect the position of particular skills on the continuum. For example, many skilled-trades jobs formerly involved much manual work and physical effort. But today power can be employed from an outside source (such as electricity), and the tradesman merely directs its application. In general, we might conclude that there is a tendency today for the accent in industrial skills to no longer be on the motor act but on the perceptual aspects of the task. Many skills in industrial jobs

[3] B. N. Knapp, "A Note on Skill," *Occupational Psychology,* Vol. 35, Nos. 1 and 2, January and April 1961, pp. 76–77.

have thus moved along the continuum toward the predominantly perceptual end.[4]

The conceptualization of skill described above brings together various psychological theories and may clarify some of the hitherto contradictory results of experimental inquiries into skills. Applied to contemporary skilled-trade apprenticeship, we might conclude that many such trades are becoming more perceptually oriented (especially, for example, machine repair, electronics, and hydraulics) and fewer are grounded on repetitive use of motor skills (such as bricklaying, metal polishing, and plastering).

Manpower specialists need to know, if they already do not, that human motor abilities are complex and that people differ in subtle ways in manipulative and dexterity skills. However, since these differences are to an extent measurable and identifiable, it is possible to use various techniques for selecting and placing people for jobs which require a large amount of motor skill. For example, learning curves can be used to measure motor skill acquisition, particularly among machine operators and hence for some aspects of apprenticeship. If normative curves for a particular skill can be developed, the progress of the trainee can be related to the norms to (1) give him learning feedback, (2) provide management with an assessment of his progress, and (3) indicate what training objectives have been stably attained. Feedback may help to avoid incorrect responses and motivate the trainee to progress. The skill can be overlearned; practice distributed to the extent feasible; and learning transfer facilitated.[5] Perceptual skills are much more difficult to measure than simpler motor skills but can be gauged to some extent by psychological tests. However, many perceptual skills in their most complex form would require measurement of higher-order thinking (such as complex problem-solving skill), and we presently lack effective tools for this purpose.

In sum, the apprenticeable trade today involves the acquisition of skill, but the legacy of the craftsman has constantly changed from generation to generation except in rare instances. Trades have waxed and waned. Skill requirements have also changed. In turn, different kinds of manpower have been needed to perform acceptably as apprentices.

The rise of the technician, which we discuss at the end of the chapter, is importantly connected with the deskilling of engineering work and the restructuring of certain perceptual and motor skills into jobs that fill the gap between the skilled trades and professions.

[4] *Ibid.*, p. 78.

[5] John R. Hinrichs, "Research on Human Motor Skills—Implications for Industry," *Journal of the American Society of Training Directors,* Vol. 16, No. 5, May 1962, pp. 39–40. For a more general treatment of skill acquisition, see W. Douglas Seymour, *Industrial Skills,* Pitman, London, 1966.

ENLARGEMENT OF THE CONCEPT OF APPRENTICESHIP

Broadly conceived, apprenticeship may be defined as a formal or informal agreement between a person lacking skill or knowledge and another who possesses these (either a person or an organization) whereby the novice is provided an opportunity to learn in exchange for his services for a stipulated time period. Usually the novice or apprentice is paid for his services at a wage rate or salary considerably below that of a fully qualified practitioner in the field to which he is apprenticed. At one time, particularly in the skilled trades, the agreement was not only expressed in formal articles of indenture but also often rather harshly administered so that the apprentice was in a semi-servile status. The broadened definition of apprenticeship which we are offering in this chapter could include such a formal agreement or merely reflect a verbal understanding between the parties.

The opportunity for learning in an apprenticeship heavily involves on-the-job work experience. Learning-by-doing is its very essence. The apprenticeship may be viewed as the student; his organizational superior(s) as the teacher(s); and the work experiences as the primary teaching tools. Sometimes it is found more convenient and economical to help apprentices learn by having them attend a school where they are grouped together and instructed in a classroom. This is basically what takes place when industrial skilled-trades apprentices are enrolled in high-school or community-college courses in "related instruction" in such subjects as shop arithmetic, blueprint reading, mechanical drawing, or principles of electricity. Classroom instruction and on-the-job training are thus complementary.

This same concept of apprenticeship applies to developing professionals, such as nurses, medical doctors, high-school teachers, and lawyers. In each of these professions there is an implicit apprenticeship model, although the term apprenticeship is not usually applied to the relationship. Others are used, such as internship. The period of related instruction extends over many years.

As we shall see in subsequent chapters, cooperative education and the training of inexperienced college graduate trainees in industry are also based upon the apprenticeship model. The same is true of some foreman training where the foreman's organizational superior (the general foreman) is expected to take the initiative in developing the line supervisor on the job. Some observers mistakenly assume that the bulk of foreman training in America consists in learning manipulative techniques and social skills (loosely, a type of perceptual skill) in the classroom setting. Not only are such assumptions unproven, they are also erroneous and naive as to the extent such knowledge exists, can be packaged, communicated, understood, and applied. We should not ignore either the role of the general foreman in teaching apprentice foremen or the formal classroom subject-matter of foreman training that transcends human relations and includes subjects such as tools, machines, and equipment; budgets and cost control; quality control; production control; and the contents of the company-union labor agreement.

Despite the universality of the apprentice model we actually know little about its developmental value in comparison with other possible models, perhaps because the latter are fewer in number and less widely used. Actually, they tend to be included in the apprentice model and consist of two polar types: training-on-the-job or exclusive classroom instruction. To be sure, there are variants in these polar types, such as guided training on the same job, rotated job assignments, and the use of the classroom as a laboratory, as in sensitivity training, and as a pure lecture hall. We look into some of these subsequently in the book, particularly in the chapter on executive development, a field which is noted in part by the stress given in it to in-residence college-level management education, which may or may not be deliberately integrated with on-the-job training.

AN OVERALL PERSPECTIVE

Apprenticeship was at one time more than the avenue of entrance to a trade and all the professions and the bridge between formal education of an exclusively classroom type and industrial or other employment. Originally, apprenticeship was preparation for life and functioned to develop character and good citizenship. Indenture and the apprentice master's role in discipline were justified on these grounds.[6] The moral overtones are much lighter today, but skilled-trades apprentices are often still subject to penalties from an overseeing joint labor-management apprentice committee if they behave contrary to the agreement upon which the apprenticeship is based. Professionals working as interns in hospitals and law offices are expected to learn the morality and ethics of their occupation as well as the techniques. Hopefully, they do.

It should be made perfectly clear, however, that the essence of apprenticeship is not democratic give-and-take in interpersonal relations but rather an authoritarian relationship. All the apprentices on-program in an organization are theoretically equal with one another in status and develop the competitive camaraderie that students tend to generate. However, the apprentice clearly possesses in theory less power, prestige, and income than his journeyman teacher. Probably in no place is this more

[6] Schneider, *op. cit.,* pp. 29–59.

obvious than among medical students and interns [7] and law clerks [8] in law "factories" whose period of service as apprentices may smack more of peonage and drudgery than professional status and intellectual excitement.

The danger inherent in such vocational education, whether it be job training or training for a professional occupation, is that unless provision is made for liberal education somewhere in the person's life cycle he may become aware only of his technological responsibilities but not of his social and moral responsibilities. He becomes in this way a specialist in means but indifferent to ends, which are considered the province of another specialist. For these reasons the kind of manpower development we have categorized as apprenticeship may be viewed as a species of vocational education that, as one leading educational philosopher has put it, "represents the greatest threat to democratic education in our time." [9] However, much of all education is ultimately vocational. The Ph.D. in one of the liberal arts who hopes to earn a living as a teacher is obtaining vocationally oriented training whether he calls it this or not.

In view of the widespread use and durability of the apprenticeship model, and despite its imperfections for providing a democratic learning environment, it would appear that manpower-planning and human resource development specialists would do well to scrutinize it carefully and use it where it is needed rather than set up exclusively classroom learning experiences of one kind or another.

We have examined apprenticeship in this chapter in its most well-established form: in the development of persons for the skilled trades. Inasmuch as we provided a detailed examination in an earlier chapter of how to conduct a study of manpower planning for apprentices in the skilled trades at the level of a business organization, no further elaboration of apprentice needs projection techniques is required in this chapter. We proceed by considering the issues involved in moving from planning to apprentice human resource development.

Our approach in the chapter is as follows: we quickly review the evolution of skilled-trades apprenticeship; discuss the role of unions in apprenticeship; outline some of the contemporary problems in administering apprenticeship programs and how they can be solved; analyze the issues involved in selection, including the selection of minority group members

---

[7] Stephen M. Creel, "Our Backward Medical Schools," *Atlantic,* Vol. 217, No. 5, May 1966, pp. 46–50; and Oliver Cope, "The Future of Medical Education," *Harper's Magazine,* Vol. 235, No. 1409, October 1967, pp. 98–103.

[8] Erwin O. Smigel, "The Impact of Recruitment on the Organization of the Large Law Firm," *American Sociological Review,* Vol. 25, No. 1, February 1960, pp. 56–66.

[9] Sidney Hook, *Education for Modern Man,* New Enlarged Edition, Knopf, New York, 1963, pp. 200–201 ff.

for entry into the skilled trades; review various developmental techniques in use for training apprentices and the role of private trade schools in the future; state some apprenticeship standards; review the skyrocketing growth of technician occupations and its impact on organizations; outline some of the European approaches to apprenticeship; and, finally, draw relevant conclusions.

HISTORICAL EVOLUTION OF APPRENTICESHIP

Apprenticeship in America never acquired the scope or prestige that it enjoyed in Europe. It was established as a means of instructing the poor in most of the colonies by the middle of the 17th century. There was a further impetus to apprenticeship in the practice of indenture of those persons who, unable to pay their passage from Britain, bound themselves out to masters in the colonies for a specified period as a way of working off the debt incurred by their voyage. The terms of indenture ranged from five to ten years, varying from colony to colony. The system was most prevalent and rigid in the South, where it remained in effect until the importation of Negro slaves in the 18th century offered a cheaper source of labor. In the northern colonies, the apprentice fared somewhat better because the increase in population and the growth of cities offered him more favorable economic prospects on completion of his indenture.[10]

On the whole, however, the economic and social development of the United States did not encourage the continuance of this form of craft training. The economic freedom that became relatively easy to obtain as the country expanded westward and the rapid spread of modern manufacturing were important causes in the gradual decline of the system. In the face of the advancing industrialization, a number of old trades tried to maintain their position in the economy by the extensive use of cheap apprentice labor. The result was that when organized labor entered the scene early in the 19th century, one of its first preoccupations was the limitation of "apprentice breeding." In an effort to halt the hiring of apprentices as substitutes for skilled adult workers the new American labor movement fought for the enforcement of the age limit and length of term in all apprenticeship agreements. After the Civil War, it sought legislation to set apprenticeship standards. Some of the states in which manufacturing was prominent actually enacted apprenticeship laws, and the unions themselves increasingly dealt with the problem by including apprenticeship clauses in their collectively bargained agreements.[11]

[10] Alfred Kahler and Ernest Hamburger, *Education for an Industrial Age,* Cornell University Press, Ithaca, 1948, pp. 18–19.
[11] *Ibid.,* p. 19.

None of these measures was nearly as decisive for the later development of apprenticeship as the swiftly changing economic conditions throughout the United States. As industrial production expanded, employers increasingly looked upon the training of apprentices as less and less worthwhile. Neither employers nor American-born workers were eager to enter agreements that would be binding on them for a period of years. Similarly, there was no pressing economic necessity for large-scale apprenticeship training as long as immigration provided an ample supply of journeymen. Moreover, the need for skilled labor apparently increased slowly. To a great extent, industry could make use of semiskilled and unskilled labor, especially since many of the goods that required precision work and high skills were being imported. In any event, labor unions cannot justly be accused of having barred American youth from learning a trade during this period because the collectively bargained agreements allowed for considerably more apprentices than were actually employed.[12]

The general decline in participants in apprentice-training programs after 1950 is shown in Table 1. Increases in the absolute number of journeymen can be noted, but the ratio of apprentices to the skilled-trades labor force shows an overall dramatic decline. The relative stability of the ratio between 1910 and 1920 can be explained by the effort made during World War I to cope with the supply of skilled labor. The economic crisis of 1929–33 and the resulting mass unemployment of the great depression reduced apprenticeship to minute proportions so that even today its recovery has been poor, comparing statistics for 1920 on the number of apprentices, the skilled-trades labor force, and the ratio between the two.

Training in all its forms was at a standstill during the 1930s when immigration with its rich supply of journeymen had virtually ceased. By 1937, although unemployment was still widespread, there was a scarcity of skilled labor in many trades. Growing public awareness of the situation finally led to passage of the National Apprenticeship Act (called the Fitzgerald Act), sponsored jointly by management and labor, in that same year. This was the first federal legislation relating to apprenticeship.[13]

In looking at the Fitzgerald Act, which expresses our national apprenticeship policy for developing skilled tradesmen only, it is interesting to note that the law both defines what apprenticeship is and what standards should be followed in conducting programs. Yet, in contrast with some European apprentice programs that call for state control, manpower policy on this topic in the United States is completely voluntary and mainly hor-

[12] *Ibid.,* pp. 19–20.
[13] *Ibid.,* p. 21. See also Edward E. Goshen, "Twenty-fifth Anniversary for Apprenticeship Program," *Jounal of the American Society of Training Directors,* Vol. 16, No. 8, August 1962, pp. 52–53.

Table 1   Apprenticeship in the United States, 1860–1969

Year	Number of Apprentices	Total Labor Force in Main Apprentice- Using Industries	Ratio
1860	55,326	1,850,034	1:33
1880	44,170	3,837,112	1:87
1890	82,057	5,091,293	1:62
1900	81,603	7,112,987	1:87
1910	118,964	11,623,605	1:98
1920	140,400	13,922,102	1:99
1930	77,452	15,094,080	1:195
1940[a]	92,360	16,374,676	1:177
1950	116,789[b]	18,189,000[c]	1:156
1960	85,282[b]	20,393,000[d]	1:239
1966	85,000[e] (estimate)	22,900,000[f]	1:270
1968 (June)[g]	225,000	n.a.	—
1969 (January)[h]	240,000	n.a.	—

[a] Figures for 1860–1940 are from Alfred Kahler and Ernest Hamburger, *Education for an Industrial Age,* Cornell University Press, Ithaca, 1948, p. 20. Their data for 1860–1910 are from Paul H. Douglas, *American Apprenticeship and Industrial Education,* Columbia University Press, New York, p. 74; for 1920 and 1930, from the *Statistical Abstract of the United States, 1937,* 58th Edition, Government Printing Office, Washington, 1937; and for 1940, from the *Statistical Abstract of the United States, 1946,* 67th Edition, Government Printing Office, Washington, 1946, p. 183. All the foregoing data are for apprentices and the total labor force in the manufacturing, construction, and mining industries only from 1860–1940. Data for other years are reported on as comparable a basis as possible except those for 1968 and 1969 which are less carefully defined and include all federally registered programs.

[b] "Experienced Civilian Labor Force, by Sex and Occupation, 1950 and 1960 and by Selected Characteristics, 1960," *Statistical Abstract of the United States, 1966,* 87th Edition, Government Printing Office, Washington, 1966, p. 233.

[c] "All Employees and Production Workers (Annual Average) in Nonagricultural Establishments by Industry: 1950, 1959, and 1960," *Statistical Abstract of the United States, 1961,* 82nd Edition, Government Printing Office, Washington, 1961, p. 208.

[d] "Nonagricultural Industries—Number of Employees, and Number, Hours and Earnings of Production Workers: 1960 and 1965" [All employees, average annual number], *Statistical Abstract of the United States, 1966,* 87th Edition, Government Printing Office, Washington, 1966, p. 222.

[e] *Negroes in Apprenticeship* (Manpower/Automation Research Monograph No. 6), Manpower Administration, U.S. Department of Labor, Washington, August 1967, p. 6.

tatory, encouraging employers and labor unions to set up apprenticeship programs.[14]

The Fitzgerald Act is administered presently by the Bureau of Apprenticeship and Training of the United States Department of Labor. The Bureau's principal functions are: to indicate the need for apprenticeship and training, not only nationally, but, with local cooperation, in particular areas; to stimulate business and industry to analyze their own special and individual skilled manpower needs currently and in the future in the expectation that they will do something about these needs; and, where necessary and within available resources, to provide technical assistance, training aids, and materials to industry.

The Bureau conducts research studies of the need for skills in the nation's economy and the extent to which management, labor, government agencies, and individuals are taking steps to develop the necessary skills. It tries to make the public aware of the need for apprenticeship and training; to publicize outstanding training systems; and to encourage employers, unions, and individuals to take appropriate action to insure a balanced number of skilled workers.

The Bureau also encourages national employers and union organizations to adopt policies and procedures that will create a favorable climate for the development of apprenticeship and skill improvement systems. It works with management, unions, and state apprenticeship and community agencies to develop the organizational machinery for training programs and apprenticeship systems. Lastly, through its technical staff, it develops training aids and other techniques to increase the effectiveness of training and serves as a clearing house for training materials.

To carry out the Fitzgerald Act's mandate of promoting apprentice welfare, the Bureau also reviews apprenticeship programs in states that have

---

[f] "Nonagricultural Industries—Number of Employees and Number, Hours and Earnings of Production Workers: 1960 and 1966 [All employees, average annual number], *Statistical Abstract of the United States, 1967,* 88th Edition, Government Printing Office, Washington, 1967, p. 226.

[g] F. Ray Marshall and Vernon M. Briggs, Jr., *Equal Apprenticeship Opportunities,* Policy Papers in Human Resources and Industrial Relations, No. 10, Institute of Labor and Industrial Relations, University of Michigan-Wayne State University, November 1968, p. 55.

[h] *U.S. News & World Report,* March 24, 1969, Vol. 66, No. 12, p. 72.

[14] Felician F. Foltman, "National and State Apprenticeship, 1960–66: Up-to-Date or Out-of-Date?," in Center for Studies in Vocational and Technical Education, University of Wisconsin, *Research in Apprenticeship Training,* Proceedings of a Conference, September 8–9, 1966, pp. 126–127.

not established their own apprenticeship agencies. If these programs meet certain minimum standards, the Bureau issues them a certificate of registration, which is sought after as a form of recognition that the apprenticeship program has some stature. The Bureau also issues certificates of completion to individuals who successfully fulfill the requirements of a registered program in states that do not have a certification program.[15]

Having been in operation for more than 30 years, an evaluation of the Fitzgerald Act is long overdue. Actually, however, very little research has been carried out on apprenticeship in the United States. And none of this has concerned itself specifically with evaluating the Fitzgerald Act. For example, the first significant evaluation of apprenticeship was made before the Fitzgerald Act was enacted.[16] The second, by Slichter, was a monumental study of industrial relations published in 1941, which in one chapter covers apprenticeship in the pre-World War II period.[17]

In the landmark study by Slichter, emphasis was placed upon control of entrance to the trade. Among the many findings was that in almost no instances were apprentice ratios in operation then based upon statistical analysis of the retirement and death rates among journeymen, the growth of the trade, or the proportion of beginning apprentices who would complete their courses. In other words, the manpower planning and timing of the training of skilled workers had by no means been solved.

The third study was published by Slichter and his colleagues in 1960 and focused on the post-World War II period. Like the 1941 study, apprenticeship was looked at as simply one field in industrial relations.[18] The study is worth a few words of elaboration.

In the post-World War II period there was a considerable growth of interest in apprenticeship among both employers and unions. The upsurge of interest was caused by the great shortage of skilled workers and the growing demand for them, to changes in technology that enhanced the need for new skills, and to the fact that the craft best able to supply skills was likely to get the work. Other causes of renewed interest were, of course, the postwar booms in construction, capital goods, and durable

---

[15] Martha F. Riche, "An Assessment of Apprenticeship—II. Public Policies and Programs," *Monthly Labor Review,* Vol. 87, No. 2, February 1964, p. 144. See also Bureau of Apprenticeship and Training, Department of Labor, *The National Apprenticeship Program,* Government Printing Office, Washington, 1953.

[16] See Paul H. Douglas, *American Apprenticeship and Industrial Education,* Columbia University Press, New York, 1921.

[17] Sumner H. Slichter, *Union Policies and Industrial Management,* Brookings Institution, Washington, 1941, pp. 9–52.

[18] Sumner H. Slichter et al., *The Impact of Collective Bargaining on Management,* Brookings Institution, Washington, 1960, pp. 59–103.

consumer goods as well as the high level of demand for many forms of military goods due to the various international conflicts since the end of World War II.

Increasingly, there has been an interest in manpower planning for apprenticeship to avoid the old-fashioned hit-or-miss methods. Nevertheless, there remains a crisis in apprenticeship, and heroic efforts of the Bureau of Apprenticeship and Training to stir up interest in apprenticeship has, overall, met with meager results.[19] In view of the persistent decline in apprentice registrations and certifications, public policy directed toward promoting the development of apprentice programs and encouraging the adoption of certain standards for apprentice projection could really stand reassessment at the present time.[20]

EVALUATING APPRENTICESHIP: SOME PRELIMINARY PERSPECTIVES

To gain a perspective on evaluating apprenticeship programs in the United States, it is important to emphasize, first, that apprenticeship programs are a product of the spread of collective bargaining. The latter includes approximately 125,000 agreements in nearly all industries, involving not only the approximately 130 international unions affiliated with the AFL-CIO, but also the unaffiliated labor organizations.[21] Thus, we can clearly see that there is an important third party in the reciprocal relationship between the employer and the apprentice, namely, the union.

Inasmuch as patterns of collective bargaining in the United States vary considerably, the type of apprentice program bargained correspondingly differs. Thus, where there is industry-wide bargaining, there may be a single national agreement covering hundreds of thousands of workers within an industry and large numbers of apprentices. In a small shop, there may be only one or two skilled tradesmen covered by an agreement. Some unions have not sought apprenticeship programs in their agreements either because they do not represent anyone in an apprenticeable trade or because they are not interested or successful in convincing an employer that a program should be established.

Apprenticeship is not mandatory and in this respect importantly unlike our public school system. Management, labor, and the government must

[19] *Ibid.*, pp. 5–103.
[20] Riche, *op. cit.*, pp. 147–148.
[21] Vernon E. Jirikowic, "Apprenticeship and the American Labor Movement," in *Research in Apprenticeship Training,* Proceedings of a Conference, September 8–9, 1966, *op. cit.*, p. 31.

decide voluntarily to cooperate in starting an apprenticeship program. The traditions and policies of the union toward apprenticeship, the attitude of the employer, employment fluctuations within an industry or corporation, the promotional efforts of the state and federal government, the supply of skilled manpower, and the presence or absence of other institutional or on-the-job forms of training are among the important variables which determine whether a bona fide apprenticeship program will be established. For example, by tradition and practice different unions in different industries have different degrees of control over labor market entry. Hence, they have a differing interest and concern with the problems of supplying and training manpower. Any industry which is dependent upon the union's supplying the necessary manpower is likely to cooperate with that union in establishing apprenticeship programs to a far greater degree than an industry which has not abdicated this responsibility and relies upon its own efforts in recruiting workers.[22]

Throughout the years, the AFL-CIO has encouraged and tried to enhance the development of apprenticeship programs, but it has not attempted to speak for and in behalf of any affiliated union. The Federation has assumed that each affiliate would handle its own apprenticeship problems in light of the circumstances of the industry or locality involved.[23]

The position of the AFL-CIO on apprenticeship has meant, in effect, that international unions have adopted a diversity of approaches and emphases.[24] As a result, discrimination against entry into the skilled trades by minority group members, particularly Negroes, has been widespread and has declined only slightly in the last few years.[25]

Discriminatory admission policies of various kinds appear to have restricted apprenticeship to the sons of union members and to have otherwise successfully blocked the entry of persons intended to be kept out. Employers have also been negligent in their responsibility for developing apprentices, and they too can be charged with discrimination. Also, their failure to initiate bona fide apprenticeship programs is tantamount to their not stepping up to their manpower development responsibilities.

At least two facts stand out when looking at apprenticeship as a man-

[22] *Ibid.*, pp. 31–32.

[23] *Ibid.*, pp. 32–33.

[24] See Slichter et al., *op. cit.*, pp. 85–101 for several examples of union programs operating as of the late 1950s. See also Jack Barbash, "Union Interests in Apprenticeship and Other Training Forms," *Journal of Human Resources*, Vol. 3, No. 1, Winter 1968, pp. 63–85.

[25] The first major exploratory research study in this area has only recently been completed: F. Ray Marshall and Vernon M. Briggs, Jr., *The Negro and Apprenticeship*, Johns Hopkins Press, Baltimore, 1967.

power problem. First, contrary to the impression given by current commentators, the apparent shortage of apprentices is not a new phenomenon. Second, statistics concerning apprenticeship are notoriously unreliable.[26]

It appears that three major trade groups account for almost 90 percent of the registered apprentices. Of these, 65 percent of all apprentices are in the building trades of the construction industry, 15 percent are in the metal trades, and 8 percent in printing. The remaining 12 percent are found in diverse occupations, with some concentration in such trades as stationary engineer, cabinetmaker, and butcher. In general, the workers in these trades have long been organized in strong craft unions which actively participate in apprenticeship training.[27]

More than one-half the 45,000 establishments in the United States operating apprenticeship programs are in the contract construction industry. But the number of apprentices employed in manufacturing exceeds those in construction. Approximately one quarter of all apprentices are employed in establishments with 500 employees or more. More than one-half the apprentices in the metal trades are found in large establishments (defined as those with more than 500 employees). Inasmuch as construction firms tend to be relatively small, it is reasonable to assume that their apprenticeship programs are generally small, thus accounting for the relatively more programs in the contract construction industry but fewer apprentices in training. The same situation applies to the printing industry.[28]

An area with considerable potential for apprenticeship and other on-the-job training is the federal civil service. For example, of the approximately two million employees of the federal government in 1960—and government employment has expanded substantially in the years since then so that today one out of six workers is employed by governments— ten percent were classified as skilled workers. But there were fewer than 3000 apprentices employed at that time by the federal government. More than one-half of these were working in ship-and boat-building industries. By the same token, there were few apprentices found in state and local government employment.[29] In summary, it appears that there are many potential training stations for apprentices but the opportunity to use them

[26] George Strauss, "Apprenticeship: An Evaluation of the Need," in Arthur M. Ross, ed., *Employment Policy and the Labor Market,* University of California Press, Berkeley, 1965, pp. 305–306.

[27] All these figures pertain to a survey completed in 1962. See Phyllis Groom, "An Assessment of Apprenticeship—III. Statistics on Apprenticeship and Their Limitations," *Monthly Labor Review,* Vol. 87, No. 4, April 1964, pp. 391–393. See Barbash, *op. cit.,* pp. 65–67 for similar findings.

[28] Groom, *op. cit.,* p. 394.

[29] *Ibid.*

for training is not utilized. Consequently, this historically well-known problem and its lack of solution require a closer analysis, which we turn to next.

APPRENTICE DYNAMICS: A CAPSULE OF PROBLEMS

Although skilled-trades apprenticeship purports to be a systematic approach to the training of skilled tradesmen, the concepts, goals, and structure are so diversely perceived as to suggest that its characteristics as a method for developing human resources are largely in the eye of the beholder. Indeed, there are wide disparities in the determination of what is an apprenticeable occupation and what the term apprenticeship training means. Clarification of concepts is essential for any evaluation of the effectiveness of apprenticeship and the derivation of plans of action to improve it.[30]

As we have seen, apprenticeship offers a training structure in which the principal tool of learning is provided by the "live" work situation of actual employment. However, all types of employment offer learning potential through work experience; or, to state it differently, learning by experience is a concomitant of all life situations, including the work situation. Therefore, if apprenticeship is to be something more distinct and unique than unguided and unplanned "work experience," it must have structural elements which maximize learning effectiveness in the place where the experience is obtained.[31]

A description of the structure of the job processes in an apprenticeable occupation is the current practice in much apprenticeship. The categories of work experience established on this basis are quite broad and loosely integrated. Studies of apprenticeship have established that, in most instances, apprentices receive random work-experience exposure. The latter often coincides poorly with the job processes and time sequences which have been established as the framework for the apprenticeable occupation. Also, very seldom have manpower specialists validated whether or not the job processes have been covered by work experiences and, even more importantly, whether or not the requisite skills have in fact been learned. Unless there is this validation, apprenticeship cannot be distinguished from other work-experience structures.[32]

Another aspect of apprenticeship that requires clarification is found in the anomalies posed by the term "apprenticeable occupations." The ter-

[30] Leon S. Tunkel, "Discussion," in *Research in Apprenticeship Training,* Proceedings of a Conference, September 8–9, 1966, *op. cit.,* p. 150.

[31] *Ibid.*

[32] *Ibid.,* pp. 150–151.

minology of "journeyman" and "apprentice" is, of course, carried traditionally from the medieval guilds in which the occupational distinction
between the two suggested that there were certain levels of complexity in
the journeyman skills of an occupation. These levels of complexity were
generally expressed by the minimum time period in which the skills could
normally be acquired, leading to the designation of journeyman. It becomes difficult, then, to reconcile the variations in time periods leading to
the same accreditation, namely, journeyman, when different periods of
preparation in the same trade are required to obtain the journeyman designation. Here again, in order for the conditions of apprenticeship to have
some articulation within a learning net, the levels of skill complexity, as
reflected in the duration of the apprenticeship, would apparently require
accreditation reflecting differences in the levels of complexity rather than
time.[33]

Yet apprenticeship today is completely built around time. For example,
the common conception of a skilled-trades apprentice is a person of
employable age who has been carefully selected and placed in a training
situation where, over a period of years, he will be trained in all the skills
of a craft. For best learning results, certain minimum standards are generally recognized as essential. First, the occupation must be a craft requiring a number of years of training. The terms of apprenticeship range from
two to six years, although the majority are four or five years. Second, the
apprentice must be employed on a full-time basis, in reasonably continuous
employment on a full-time basis, working under the supervision of experienced craftsmen and on a class of work requiring the skills of a craftsman.
Third, an apprentice must be covered by a written agreement, usually called
an indenture, outlining the terms of employment and training. Figures 1
and 2 illustrate respectively old and modern indenture forms, but both
still reflect a concept of time. The agreement includes a schedule of work
experience and a schedule of wages. The typical agreement in operation in
the United States requires that an apprentice attend courses in related
and supplemental instruction, usually away from the job, for a minimum
of 144 hours per year, for each year of the apprenticeship.[34] Apprenticeship
is thus a type of contract between two parties extending over time and involves reciprocal obligations. Apprenticeship systems also function to regu-
late entry into the skilled trades, and necessarily, as we have previously
remarked, involve a third party: the union.[35]

The role of related instruction in apprenticeship today casts still another
note of confusion and contradiction. As mentioned, for those apprentice-

[33] *Ibid.*
[34] Hall, *op. cit.,* p. 12.
[35] Kate Liepman, *Apprenticeship,* Routledge and Kegan Paul, London, 1960, p. 14.

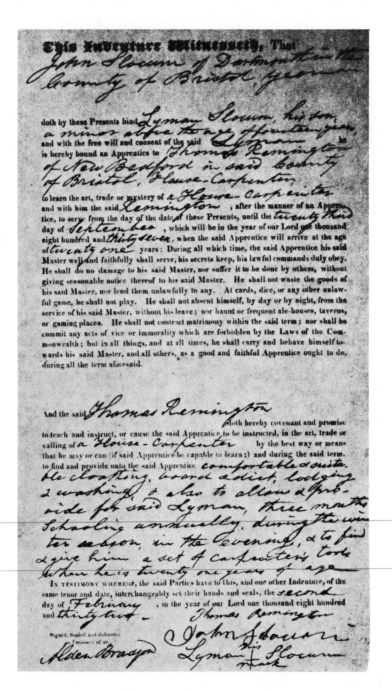

Figure 1 Apprentice indenture form of the 19th century. *Source* Ronald Perry, *Apprenticeship—Past and Present,* Government Printing Office, Washington, p. 16.

The undersigned agrees to provide employment and training in accordance with standards named herein.

R. T. Smith Construction Company
(Employer)

Newark, New Jersey
(Address)

(Employer)

APPRENTICESHIP AGREEMENT
Between Apprentice and Joint Apprenticeship Committee

THIS AGREEMENT, entered into this __2nd__ day of __February__, 19__62__

between the parties to __Newark Carpenter Joint Apprenticeship Committee__
(Name of local apprenticeship standards)

represented by the Joint Apprenticeship Committee, hereinafter referred to as the COMMITTEE, and

__Thomas M. Curtis__ born __April__ __1__ __1942__ hereinafter
(Name of apprentice)   (Month) (Day) (Year)

referred to as the APPRENTICE, and (if a minor) _____ hereinafter
                                               (Name of parent or guardian)

referred to as his GUARDIAN.

WITNESSETH THAT:

The Committee agrees to be responsible for the placement and training of said apprentice in the

trade of __Carpentry__ as work is available, and in consideration said apprentice
agrees diligently and faithfully to perform the work incidental to the said trade during the period of
apprenticeship, in accordance with the regulations of the Committee. The Apprenticeship Standards
referred to herein are hereby incorporated in and made a part of this agreement.

Credit for previous experience at trade, if any __500__ | Hours. | Apprenticeship remaining __7500__ | Hours.

Other conditions _____

In witness whereof the parties hereunto set their hands and seals:

/s/ Thomas M. Curtis [SEAL]   /s/ John P. White [SEAL]
(Apprentice)   (Representative of Joint Apprenticeship Committee)

2216 Grant Road, Newark, N.J.   Secretary
(Address)   (Title)

_____ [SEAL]   _____ [SEAL]
(Parent or guardian)   (Representative of Joint Apprenticeship Committee)

                                     (Title)

Registered by the __Bureau of Apprenticeship and Training, U. S. Department of Labor__
(Name of registration agency)

By _____ Title _____ Date __February 9__, 1962

Available through Bureau of Apprenticeship and Training,
U. S. Department of Labor, Washington, D. C.

Figure 2 Recent apprentice indenture form. *Source* Ronald Perry, *Apprenticeship—Past and Present,* Government Printing Office, Washington, p. 18.

295

ship programs which have been registered by governmental agencies, related instruction of at least 144 hours a year is a requirement of the program. The validity of this requirement is contradicted by the fact that one-half or more of the apprentices who received certificates of completion of apprenticeship do not receive or participate in any organized form of related instruction.[36] The on-the-job phase is apparently not deliberately structured to learn the trade in phases.

There is no question that occupations vary in the extent to which practical and theoretical knowledge are fundamental to craftsmanship. However, the existence of a body of theoretical knowledge is one of the key criteria in identifying an apprenticeable occupation. Apprenticeship certification in the absence of satisfactory completion of related instruction would therefore seem to be contrary to the entire concept of apprenticeship as well as denial of the fact that there is a theoretical element to the practice of a craft or occupation. Obviously, there are difficulties in providing related instruction for all apprentices, particularly in rural areas where there are travel problems involved in attending classes, although these problems could perhaps be surmounted by correspondence courses. However, the alternative of overlooking the requirement of related instruction is insupportable and when done violates the entire concept of apprenticeship as an efficient system for transmitting craftsman skills.[37]

There are two additional factors which impugn the validity of the apprenticeship concept as it is currently implemented in the United States. First, one-half or more of the currently practicing journeymen have become journeymen without participating in an apprenticeship program. Second, on-the-job training, sometimes coupled with related or other classroom instruction, has emerged since the early 1960s as a viable form of occupational training subject to various types of state and federal financial support. These on-the-job training designs are frequently indistinguishable from their apprenticeship counterpart except that they usually are of shorter duration (up to one year). Thus if one takes a critical look at apprenticeship programs which minimize or eliminate related instruction, the inescapable question then becomes: what are the differences between apprenticeship of this type and on-the-job training programs? Perhaps they are different stages of the same concept? If they are, is there not an artificial overlap, with attendant inequities because of the application of federal and state subsidy funds to on-the-job training?[38]

[36] Tunkel, "Discussion," in *Research in Apprenticeship Training,* Proceedings of a Conference, September 8–9, 1966, *op. cit.*, p. 151.

[37] *Ibid.*

[38] *Ibid.*, p. 152.

Unless apprenticeship programs live up to the standards applicable to them, on-the-job training programs may become such viable competitors that the need for attenuated apprenticeship can be seriously challenged. There are a number of reasons for this, each of which is worth mentioning. First, on-the-job training permits extension of the well-tested theory that orderly and controlled work experiences, with the supporting classroom related instruction, is a highly efficient training method. Second, on-the-job programs place the emphasis where it belongs, namely, on whether or not the skill or knowledge has been acquired rather than on arbitrary time periods, as is the case so often in apprenticeship. Third, on-the-job training permits skill development from one level to the next, consistent with the demands of the marketplace. Yet, it still offers reasonable guarantees that a person has acquired the skill and knowledge of one phase in an occupation and is therefore eligible for training in the second phase, including eligibility for the requisite wage. Fourth, to the extent that there is a beginning and ending of an on-the-job training program, these can be reliable indicators to employers that the participants they are considering hiring have probably attained the ability levels which the program is intended to develop.[39]

There are still other problems in apprenticeship which have not been mentioned. First, skilled occupations have been downgraded in status in recent years, as a result of which fewer persons are attracted to them. The traditional pay differential between skilled and unskilled workers has eroded to the point that there is no real incentive for youth to train for the skilled trades. Second, skilled-trades apprenticeship is playing a lesser part in our hierarchy of training systems because the newer skills needed today are intellectual rather than manual. This is not a mere distinction of perceptual versus motor skills. Rather, it is a difference based upon learning the higher-order perceptual skills developed through college education in which universities provide a more efficient training approach and experience than can ever be found in the restrictive on-the-job training such as is found in attenuated apprenticeship. Third, persons are being guided into growth occupations rather than the skilled trades because the number of skilled craftsmen has remained relatively static, if not actually declined, as was suggested in Table 1. Fourth, apprenticeship has not engaged in any imaginative research and has, overall, retained a rigid and inflexible posture. Fifth, apprenticeship has been reserved almost exclusively for "blue-collar" workers, thus excluding many service-sector occupations. Sixth, because apprenticeship has been largely controlled by organized labor, it has been oriented to their interests of job and wage control rather

[39] *Ibid.*

than toward training as a developmental process. Seventh, apprentice journeymen ratios are deliberately set to prevent persons from acquiring skilled-craftsman status.[40]

PLYING THE SKILLED TRADES WITHOUT APPRENTICESHIP: MUDDLING THROUGH

Desirable as apprenticeship may be, in the United States the skilled trades have learned to adjust to imperfect programs so that, in fact, most journeymen do not learn their trades through apprenticeship. As a result, the dire predictions of national catastrophe because of shortages of skilled tradesmen are less serious than they appear to be on the surface.[41]

Because managements and unions seem to be able to muddle through the alleged shortages of skilled tradesmen, one need only look closely at the work situation in organizations to determine how this muddling through works out.

To begin, the evidence suggests that the construction and metal-trades industries have room for a large number of workers who are less skilled than apprenticeship programs could in theory turn out. Many jobs do not require journeymen with complete all-round training but instead can be carried out by people who are acquainted with parts of the overall job. In this way journeymen who know the total job can act as key men, provide supervision, and perform the difficult parts of the job. The lesser-skilled men can then be employed on the routine work.[42]

Some large companies have sought to increase their supply of skilled workers by upgrading some of these helpers or especially competent specialists who acquire experience working closely with skilled craftsmen. Such individuals are sometimes known as upgraders or changeover personnel although they are often thought to be less qualified than a full-fledged apprentice program graduate. There is little doubt that helpers, upgraders, and change-over personnel often achieve journeyman status through a kind of bootlegged learning process.

If few journeymen ever serve an apprenticeship, we might ask: how do those without the training gain entry into the trade? Certainly entry and exit into a particular company or industry is not accomplished as smoothly and regularly as the ebb and flow of tides. The unions play an important part, particularly in the building trades. To obtain a clearer picture of this, it is worthwhile to examine the process by which craftsmen gain entry into

---

[40] Foltman, "National and State Apprenticeship, 1960–1966: Up-to-Date or Out-of-Date?," *op. cit.,* pp. 126–130.

[41] Strauss, "Apprenticeship: An Evaluation of the Need," *op. cit.,* p. 311.

[42] *Ibid.,* pp. 311–312.

the union and then review the means by which they obtain their training. The process is not difficult to identify. In addition to apprenticeship there are two other main channels of entry into skilled trades locals: (1) transfers from other locals and (2) direct admission of people who have obtained their training (if any) outside the union's jurisdiction.[43]

Transfers play a particularly important role in redistributing the number of skilled workers in the United States. Although skilled tradesmen are thought to be primarily in a local geographical labor market, it appears that in most trades there are a certain number of individuals who obtain rudimentary training in rural areas and admittance to rural locals and then migrate to the big cities where they are accepted for union membership on a transfer basis during the peak season when there is plenty of work for everyone. In areas where the unions are quite weak, employers often must hire nonunion men, and then the union is faced with the choice of either accepting these men as members or not being able to organize the jobs. Once accepted as union members, these employees gradually work their way into more strongly unionized parts of the country through migration.[44]

Direct admission supplies another method of entry into the trade. The process by which journeymen are directly admitted to a union varies according to the local and according to economic conditions. There are times when a local will be closed to everyone except for sons of members. There are other occasions when the labor market is tight and almost anyone can be admitted without question. In still other circumstances the union business agent determines qualifications through a brief interview. Sometimes this interview is followed up by the granting of a two-week permit and future examinations in which the applicant must demonstrate his ability with tools in the presence of a local examining board.[45]

THE JOE MCGEES AND OTHER SLEEPERS

It is believed that often there is a good deal of opposition to permitting men to enter the union without completing an apprenticeship. Entry in this fashion is called back-door entry, and those who "steal the trade" in this manner are called "Joe McGees" in the lingo of the building trades. There are short-run advantages to these direct admissions which the union appreciates. Direct admission, for example, enables the union to take on men when they are needed. Apprenticeship, on the other hand, involves a forecast with projection of future manpower needs, and many unions fear to expand their apprenticeship program too rapidly, not knowing what busi-

[43] *Ibid.,* pp. 316–317.
[44] *Ibid.,* pp. 317–318.
[45] *Ibid.,* pp. 318–319.

ness conditions will be like three to five years later when the apprentices complete their program. Also, men who are directly admitted into the union enter only during the busy season when all the regular members are working and opposition to admitting others is lowered.[46]

Many business agents recognize that from a long-run point of view direct admissions are unwise and should not be encouraged. For example, the presence of unskilled men in the union makes the business agent's life more difficult. These men are harder to place, more likely than skilled men to insist on various types of featherbedding, and more prone to generate internal schisms in the union when they insist that limited job opportunities be shared equally. Also, of course, poorly trained men threaten the craft's sense of pride and identification. All these tensions and antipathies between long- and short-term factors may explain why most craft unions have a strong formal commitment to apprenticeship as the primary means of entry but in practice obtain the bulk of their membership through other channels. Appreciating these considerations, one can thus understand what he hears when union officials talk about the need for strengthening and expanding the apprenticeship system yet under other circumstances these same men insist that their own trades have a more than adequate supply of skilled men.[47]

We have yet to explain how the Joe McGees learn their trade. There is little evidence available. Perhaps there are at least five other channels which have not been mentioned through which Joe McGees can obtain training for skilled apprenticeable occupations. These include: (1) completion of part of a formal apprenticeship; (2) informal apprenticeship; (3) learning the trade in a nonunion sector of the industry or a related industry; (4) attending a vocational school; and (5) working one's way up from an unskilled or helper classification through a step-by-step process of stealing the trade. Although these five categories overlap they do point to possible ways in which individuals attain journeyman status outside of a formal apprenticeship.[48]

There is little doubt that a large proportion of the dropouts from apprenticeship programs continue to work in the field in which they were trained and eventually attain a journeyman's classification. In fact, some trades have machinery by which apprentices become journeymen directly without completing their training. Thus it has been estimated that of every 200 men who enter apprenticeship, about 100 complete their work. Of the 100 who drop out, 39 stay in the trade, and 33 eventually obtain jobs as

[46] *Ibid.*, pp. 319–320.
[47] *Ibid.*, p. 320.
[48] *Ibid.*, pp. 320–321.

journeymen, foremen, or contractors. Of the 39 dropouts who stay in, 32 complete at least two years of apprenticeship.[49]

There are various ways in which a person can make the transition from apprentice to journeyman without finishing his formal training. For example, some unions allow a man with two years' apprenticeship to take an examination which upon passing will automatically certify him as a journeyman. By short-circuiting his training in this way, he loses his right to a "certificate of completion," but he is nevertheless a journeyman in all other respects.[50]

On the other hand, should the worker fail the examination, it may be suggested that he join an advanced apprentice training group, unless he is not qualified for apprenticeship due to age or some other reason. When the latter is the case, he may be admitted to the union as an "improver" (actually a nonapprentice trainee) until he passes the examination or becomes discouraged and seeks other opportunities. Of course, some unions do not permit improvers. Nevertheless, the improver system does admit a significant number of workers to journeyman status in certain crafts and dilutes the skill of the trade.[51]

Another approach is to allow "overage" apprentices, who start at the age of 25 years or older, to become journeymen automatically after 2 years of training, as long as they have completed their regular school work (but again they obtain no certificate of completion). Some unions offer examinations periodically which any union member can take. Those who pass can be certified as journeymen. Still other unions accept apprentices as regular union members after a few months of apprenticeship. Once a person becomes a union member, he is fairly well assured of continued employment in the trade and often at the journeyman's rate regardless of whether he completes his apprenticeship.[52]

There are additional ways in which a person dropped from an apprenticeship may use it as a short cut to becoming a journeyman and being rewarded with a pay increase. A good number of Joe McGees have apparently gone through some kind of informal unregistered apprenticeship without an indenture and with little or no related instruction in the school room. How many persons in the United States are currently undergoing such an apprenticeship is difficult to determine because there is the se-

---

[49] *Ibid.*, pp. 321–322. These data apply only to the building trades and are limited in their general applicability.

[50] *Ibid.*, pp. 322–323.

[51] A. J. Grimes, "Personnel Management in the Building Trades," *Personnel Journal,* Vol. 47, No. 1, January 1968, pp. 44–45.

[52] Strauss, "Apprenticeship: An Evaluation of the Need," *op. cit.*, pp. 322–324.

mantic problem of deciding what constitutes an apprenticeship. If we accept the definition posited earlier in this chapter, we would limit the definition of a skilled-trades apprenticeship to one that met the criteria for registration with the Bureau of Apprenticeship and Training of the United States Department of Labor. If we loosen the definition, it is very likely we would find that there is a great deal of unregistered apprenticeship and quasi-apprenticeship training, particularly in manufacturing and among nonunion firms. We would probably also find in some cases that the unregistered programs are as sound as many which are registered even though there are few external pressures to compel unregistered programs to maintain high standards. In any event, it is very possible that many craftsmen have participated in apprentice training that was informal—in many cases, very informal.[53]

Many Joe McGees were, of course, provided with experiences by which they "stole" their trade. For example, some undoubtedly picked up the trade while serving in the armed forces. The great weakness of such training is not that it is not of high quality (because it often is) but rather that it is not continued sufficiently long to give a person the proper grounding in the trade. On the other hand, apprentices may obtain credit for trade experience or training in the armed forces which reduces the period of their apprenticeship.[54] Another way of stealing the trade is to learn the rudiments of it on a farm (which is frequently the source of learning for carpenters). Production craftsmen quite often learn their jobs as maintenance men in manufacturing plants or in shipyards and subsequently "work their way up," as they put it. Still others pick up the trade by working for nonunion firms and then eventually through having their employer organized or through securing a new job in a union shop become union members.[55]

In a number of trades it is possible to work one's way up through the ranks to the journeyman's status. Thus, a person may start as a production worker on a very simple piece of equipment in a machine shop and gradually work his way up to more complicated tools, and, as he moves in a haphazard fashion from one sort of an operation to another, become what is called a "homemade" machinist. This type of employee may not have the versatility or the background which a graduate apprentice might possess, but he may be perfectly acceptable for the employer's purposes.[56]

There is little doubt that considerable skill can be picked up by observa-

---

[53] *Ibid.*, pp. 324–325. See also Howard G. Foster, "Nonapprentice Sources of Training in Construction," *Monthly Labor Review*, Vol. 93, No. 2, February 1970, pp. 21–26.

[54] Slichter et al., p. 67.

[55] Strauss, "Apprenticeship: An Evaluation of the Need," *op. cit.*, pp. 325–326.

[56] *Ibid.*, p. 326.

tion on the job. Laborers can learn a great deal about carpentry and brick-laying simply by watching (though they can probably learn much more if they are allowed to "spell" a journeyman). People working in helper classifications are in a very favorable position to learn a considerable amount, particularly when a helper is assigned to a journeyman and the two are regularly assigned to a job alone. In the past in such cases when the helper was a Negro the inherent learning resources of the job were not utilized because he was prohibited from cashing in on his knowledge.[57]

A person's chance to gain experience on more complicated equipment may depend on: (1) his ability to make friends and find a "sponsor" who will help him out; (2) his relationship to his first-level supervisor, who is in a position to assign him to jobs on which he can gain experience; and (3) fortuitous circumstances, such as an emergency or rush order during which the usual occupational barriers may be let down.[58] Still another way to obtain experience is for the person to exaggerate and embellish the amount that he has had and "bull" his way into a journeyman's job. In sum, through a variety of ways people learn to "steal" the craft bit by bit without going through any period of formal training.[59]

A few people move into a journeyman's classification directly on completion of a program in a vocational school. Whether the graduates of a trade school are adequately prepared for assumption of a journeyman's status is dubious.[60] There is considerable feeling today that the graduates of these schools are usually students who performed unsatisfactorily in a high school or were behavioral problems there and "dumped" into vocational schools as a last resort. Many then drop out of school. Quite often the predominantly vocational high school contains outmoded equipment, old facilities, demoralized teaching staffs, and a total environment which is inimical to learning.

In summing up what we have been discussing concerning the administration of apprenticeship programs, it should be noted that the skilled-trades occupations in which apprenticeship is most common—construction, metal trades, printing, and automobile mechanics and repairmen—are largely associated with strong unions, distinct crafts, small firms, high turnover of employees among firms, and, consequently, attachment of the worker to the labor market as a whole rather than a particular firm. Individual employers in these industries are often too small to provide adequate training programs by themselves. Also, they have relatively little incentive to undergo the expense of providing apprenticeship training since

[57] *Ibid.,* p. 327.
[58] *Ibid.,* p. 327.
[59] Strauss, "Apprenticeship: An Evaluation of the Need," *op. cit.,* p. 327.
[60] *Ibid.,* p. 328.

there is little point in training men who may soon leave to work for another employer. Further, the gains obtained from training are much higher from the point of view of the industry as a whole than from that of the individual firm. For these reasons, the industry-wide apprenticeship program represents an attempt to do collectively what the individual firms are unable or unwilling to do alone.[61]

A different kind of labor market structure exists in most of manufacturing. Through devices such as seniority, employees become attached strongly to the individual firm and, as a result, employers have less reason to fear that an employee, once trained, will subsequently leave. Furthermore, individual employers, particularly the larger ones, find it in their economic interest to train their own men. For this reason there is less need for external agencies to promote training. Thus apprenticeship is rarely organized on an industry-wide basis, and the programs that exist may be very informal.[62]

The function of apprenticeship in the building trades today thus seems largely to be that of training skilled key men. The proportion of job entrance provided by each trade's apprenticeship program seems to be quite closely related to the skill mix which that trade requires. This may mean that, despite the concern voiced about immediate shortages of apprentices in the future, an immediate crisis of skilled tradesmen will probably be forestalled as it has been in the past. This observation does not mean that apprenticeship programs should not be improved and enlarged, but it does suggest that Cassandra-like predictions of calamity for the nation are unwarranted.[63] The nation will muddle through.

SELECTION OF APPRENTICES

In recent years considerable attention has been given to the techniques used to select employees at all organizational levels. The attention that has been given to apprenticeship selection procedures has been a source of considerable controversy, primarily on the grounds that the kinds of psychological and other tests used to select apprentices have been unvalidated, essentially culture-bound, and patently discriminatory.

The extent such tests have been used throughout the country is not known because so little research has been done on apprenticeship. However, there probably are important differences between the use of tests in selecting apprentices who would enter the skilled trades in large manufacturing organizations. Therefore, in discussing the selection of apprentices,

[61] *Ibid.*, p. 329.
[62] *Ibid.*, pp. 329–330.
[63] *Ibid.*, pp. 330–331.

we must give attention to existing practices, administrative arrangements used (such as selection committees), and the problems of identifying qualified apprentice candidates from minority groups.

Organizations which operate apprenticeship training programs have individually established selection practices based upon factors usually known only to themselves. Knowledge of what those factors are and the relative importance assigned to each in the selection of applicants for entry into apprenticeship would be of value to other organizations thinking about installing new programs or seeking to improve selection practices in existing programs. Such information, however, is not widely available; and, when it is, it is usually reported in such general terms as to be almost valueless.

In one of the few studies of this topic reported, data were obtained in Michigan, one of the major industrial states making extensive use of skilled manpower and ranking eighteenth in the ratio of registered apprentices employed. Defining small companies as containing 1 to 100 employees and large companies as containing 101 or more employees, this study of Michigan manufacturing industry found only 3.59 percent of the small and 12.91 percent of the large companies maintained apprentice training programs. A systematic sample was drawn from a list of these manufacturing companies, and data were obtained from 86 percent of the small and 91 percent of the large companies in the sample.[64] This study provides the most useful information available in published form on apprentice selection in manufacturing, but it is obviously limited as to its scope and applicability. However, the research was conducted prior to the enactment of the Civil Rights Act of 1964, which has important implications for apprenticeship. Apparently information on selection procedures for apprentices entering skilled-trades jobs outside of manufacturing organizations has not even been reported to the extent covered in this Michigan study.

The conclusions from the Michigan study reveal that there are a number of selection practices. It was found, for example, that neither seniority in the company nor family relationship in the trade were prime requisites to ensure consideration as an applicant for apprenticeship training. On the other hand, the possession of manipulative skills needed to be immediately productive on the job was considered important, especially for applicants in small companies. Evidence of satisfactory work experience and recommendations furnished by the applicant's school were also considered basic in selection. While recommendations from previous employers

[64] Richard H. Hagemeyer, "Apprentice Selection Practices in Michigan's Manufacturing Industries," *Journal of the American Society of Training Directors,* Vol. 16, No. 2, February 1962, pp. 28–30.

were considered very desirable by both large and small companies, recommendations from friends or acquaintances were not considered important by the large manufacturing companies, although the smaller ones did attach some significance to these recommendations. High-school graduation was practically a requirement for being chosen as an apprentice, but a record showing the applicant's relative success in school, as evidenced by his grades, was considered of lesser importance. Information about hobbies which revealed the applicant's interest and aptitude in mechanical things was considered valuable in the selection of applicants. It was also thought that high-school students planning to apply for an apprenticeship should be encouraged to take courses in algebra, geometry, shop mathematics, and industrial education while in school.[65]

Seventy-five percent of the large and 32 percent of the small companies used tests in selecting apprentices. Typical tests used were those of intelligence (such as the Wonderlic Personnel Test) and those for mechanical abilities (such as the Bennett Test of Mechanical Comprehension). Companies had set a mean minimum score which an apprentice must achieve in order to warrant consideration as a program candidate. Some companies established different minimum raw scores for certain trades. Variations were made because experience had suggested that different trades would require different levels of skills and aptitudes. Some companies used selection procedures with point systems of evaluation providing for different weights among the tests and other criteria used in selection. However, most small companies selected candidates without the benefit of knowing their potential as indicated by scores on mechanical aptitude, mental ability, and specific skill tests.[66]

Eighty-six percent of the small and 93 percent of the large manufacturing firms in Michigan responding in the survey required a probationary period of employment. The length of this period varied from 500 to 2000 hours. The trial period was considered an important aspect of selection during which the apprentice's abilities and potential could be observed and evaluated. The use of a period of probation as the final phase of the selection procedure thus suggests that the entire process of choosing apprentices cannot be regarded as completed until the end of the probationary period.[67] The probationary period, of course, puts the burden of proof of performance upon the apprentice and can be a useful supplement to strengthening apprenticeship in manpower development to the extent that poor performers are weeded out during this period.

[65] *Ibid.*, pp. 31–35.
[66] *Ibid.*, pp. 32–34.
[67] *Ibid.*

The Michigan study indicated that only a small percentage of those companies engaged in manufacturing were developing apprentice-trained skilled tradesmen to replace those needed, either due to unavoidable losses or required by plant or production expansion. Yet, there are at least a few companies in Michigan that have been renowned for their apprenticeship programs. For example, the Ford Motor Company started apprenticeship in 1915 and since that time has graduated more than 11,000 apprentices, many of whom served for their entire work careers in the skilled trades while others became supervisory employees and plant and staff managers. In recent years as many as 2000 apprentices have been enrolled at one time.[68]

Turning to the selection of apprentices for the skilled trades outside of manufacturing industry, we find little information, except constant reference to the discrimination in selection against members of minority groups. To balance the picture, it should be noted that discrimination against minority group members also has occurred in selecting applicants in manufacturing industry. Yet, the prevailing view seems to be, without very much supporting published evidence, that the issue of discrimination is most severe in the selection of apprentices in nonmanufacturing industry, apparently because the overwhelming number of apprentices is found in the construction, maintenance, and metal crafts.

Criticisms have been voiced against apprenticeship in manufacturing companies on the grounds that all apprentice programs necessarily discriminate against middle-aged and older workers. The argument is made, for example, that the discrimination that takes place is caused by the premium put on high scholastic ability in selection, which may have no necessary relationship to the ability to do the job as a craftsman. Similarly, the ten-year experience requirement for employment as a journeyman which exists in some industries as a substitute for approved apprenticeship program completion is regarded as unreasonably long. Furthermore, apprenticeship is called outmoded because the concept applies to teenagers and boys but not to adults who also are family breadwinners. In essence, it is held that the only practical and proven method of acquiring skill is through upgrading, which is democratic and workable, as shown by its utilization during wartime and other periods in which there is a shortage of manpower. Thus, it is argued that discrimination not only exists but is inherent in apprenticeship in manufacturing as well as elsewhere in industry.

[68] "50 Years of Opportunity," *Ford World,* Vol. 2, No. 13, June 25, 1965, pp. 4–5. See also for an unusual history of apprenticeship, National Ford Department, UAW-AFL-CIO, *A History of Skilled Trades in UAW Ford Plants,* UAW-AFL-CIO, Detroit, 1964.

THE NEGRO AND APPRENTICESHIP PROGRAMS

In recent years efforts by Negroes to gain admission to apprenticeship programs in the building, machinist, and printing trades have received widespread attention. There have been many forms of demonstration such as picketing, construction-site entrance-blocking, sleep-ins in union halls, and violent clashes with police. Conflicts at construction projects financed by government funds are symbolically significant as well as visible to the citizenry and industry. In response both to the public furor and to the notable absence of Negro apprentices, public authorities in the United States have adopted a variety of remedial measures.[69]

Table 2   Distribution of Negro Apprentices in Skilled Trades in Selected Cities

Trade	Total Apprentices	Negro Apprentices	Percent
Electricians	960	14	1.5
Sheet-metal workers	432	12	2.8
Carpenters	3273	70	2.1
Ironworkers	301	4	1.3
Plumbers	906	14	1.5
	5872	114	1.9

Source. F. Ray Marshall and Vernon M. Briggs, Jr., "Negro Participation in Apprenticeship Programs," *Journal of Human Resources,* Vol. 2, No. 1, Winter 1967, p. 53. Data are for four states and 21 large cities outside the South. Less than 2 percent of the total apprentices are Negroes. By January 1, 1969, 9360 Negroes were enrolled on federally registered programs totaling 240,000 apprentices. *U.S. News & World Report,* Vol. 66, No. 12, March 24, 1969, p. 72.

The extent to which there has been discrimination against Negroes in apprenticeship can be clearly determined from an examination of Table 2.[70] Historically, craft unions, more than industrial unions, have been guilty of excluding Negroes from their membership. Restrictive decisions on entry into the union and the seniority system have over the years functioned to condone the exclusion of Negroes from apprentice training pro-

[69] F. Ray Marshall and Vernon M. Briggs, Jr., "Remedies for Discrimination in Apprenticeship Programs," *Industrial Relations,* Vol. 6, No. 3, May 1967, p. 303.
[70] More detailed data can be found in Marshall and Briggs, *The Negro and Apprenticeship, op. cit., passim.*

grams. Specifically, craft unions have established standards sufficiently "high" to assure closed shop conditions and thereby exercise tight wage and job control.[71]

The South has traditionally been the training ground for Negro skilled tradesmen, and the bulk of Negro journeymen in the building trades are still employed in the South. Negro slaves and freemen provided, of course, a significant source of trained artisans in the antebellum South. Yet at present we find Negro apprentices relatively scarcer than Negro journeymen in the South.[72] The evolution of the state of affairs from one where Negroes were prominent in the skilled trades in the South to one where they are virtually absent except in the smallest possible numbers today is itself an interesting aspect of the history of national manpower development.[73]

Contrary to what we might expect, the imbalance of employment in the building trades, where most apprenticeship exists, is approximately the same, North and South; and during the past 70 years the overall pattern has gotten worse, rather than better. Unless the pattern changes, Negro employment is likely to decline still further, inasmuch as the trades in which Negroes are best represented are the "trowel trades" (bricklaying, cement masonry, and plastering) and, to some extent, carpentry, in contracting, whereas those in which they are poorly represented are expanding.[74] This underrepresentation may be due in part not so much to discrimination against Negroes as it is to discrimination for relatives and friends, particularly in the building trades. In addition, the lack of motivation among younger Negroes to enter membership, lack of knowledge of how to apply, and inadequate training and education all have contributed to the present imbalance.[75]

Since the early 1960s there have been a number of sanctions exercised in the hope of getting Negroes into apprenticeship programs. Although these sanctions have perhaps had the effects of creating a climate which is conducive to change, have tended to educate various publics about apprenticeship and civil rights, have led to the formalization of apprenticeship standards and programs, and, finally, have caused some apprenticeship sponsors to raise their qualifications, there is little evidence that any of

[71] Irving Kovarsky, "Management, Racial Discrimination and Apprentice Training Programs," *Academy of Management Journal,* Vol. 7, No. 3, September 1964, pp. 199–200.

[72] George Strauss and Sidney Ingerman, "Public Policy and Discrimination in Apprenticeship," *Hastings Law Journal,* Vol. 16, No. 3, February 1965, pp. 287–289.

[73] For the details of this history see F. Ray Marshall, *The Negro and Organized Labor,* Wiley, New York, 1965, *passim.*

[74] Negroes have traditionally filled laborers' jobs, too, but these are not skilled jobs.

[75] Strauss and Ingerman, *op. cit.,* p. 329.

them has caused Negro apprenticeship enrollment to increase in large numbers.[76]

Even small gains in minority group member apprentices are considered breakthroughs by job placement experts who are familiar with the construction industry. Though, as we have seen, Negroes are well represented nationally in the unions of the trowel trades, there is still hardly any way for a laborer to become a member of the cleaner, better-paid, more highly skilled mechanical craft unions, such as the electricians, plumbers, steamfitters, ironworkers, and sheet metal workers. Only very recently in the case of the latter have some of the diehard lily-white unions in the building trades started to crack and admit Negroes.[77] An important exception would be Local 3 of the International Brotherhood of Electrical Workers in New York City, one of the largest single locals in the building trades, that has an unparalleled program to assure substantial Negro and Puerto Rican apprentice recruitment and training.[78]

In addition to legislation, two approaches which have been used to enable Negro apprentices to pass selection hurdles are (1) pre-apprenticeship programs and (2) special coaching designed to prepare the individual to pass the entrance examinations. The objective of a pre-apprenticeship program is primarily to equip disadvantaged youths with the knowledge and experience necessary to compete for apprenticeship openings. In most instances the enrollees in these programs lack high school diplomas, have graduated from substandard schools, or in other ways are manifestly poor risks for acceptance in apprenticeship programs. The effectiveness of these pre-apprenticeship programs is not known. Depending upon whom one relies for an evaluation in lieu of systematic evidence, opinions about existing pre-apprenticeship programs range from ringing endorsement to thundering disapproval.[79]

Pre-apprenticeship programs have been specifically designed in recent years to prepare the potential apprentice to pass the tests which are given to applicants. These kinds of "prep" classes avoid the Herculean job of providing general remedial education by focusing instead on how to take written and oral examinations, in which there is a review of such subjects as basic mathematics, spatial relations, and practical reasoning. It has been reported that a hard-headed approach using cram sessions designed to prepare apprentice candidates with weak backgrounds for passing selection

[76] Marshall and Briggs, "Remedies for Discrimination in Apprenticeship Programs," op. cit., pp. 318–319.

[77] Thomas R. Brooks, "A Job Program that Works," The Reporter, Vol. 37, No. 8, November 16, 1967, pp. 28–30.

[78] Marshall and Briggs, The Negro and Apprenticeship, op. cit., pp. 60–62.

[79] Ibid., pp. 218–222, 147, 260–261.

tests can be effective. The preparation used was a rather narrow but compact sharpening up of the candidates for passing specific tests, involving a kind of gamesmanship.[80]

These types of cram sessions are essentially deliberate attempts to subvert the purposes for which selection tests are, in theory, established. Assuming that these tests are designed to screen out the kinds of persons who cannot perform well in the work, rather than intended to be discriminatory in an odious sense, preparing individuals to pass the tests by intensive training in test passing would apparently defeat the purposes of the tests. If the tests, on the other hand, have not been validated on the work populations in the employing organizations which test the apprentices, then presumably this gamesmanship could be justified. If the tests were validated on skilled-trades populations, training in test passing would seem to confound the purposes behind using selection tests because the training would be geared only to the behavior sampled in the tests. Even when used, the tests may be better predictors of how well the apprentice will do in school in related instruction than on the job. Insofar as selection tests used today are seldom viewed as measures of acquired learning which needs to be supplemented by the employer to make the candidate job-effective, tests have taken on a negative cast and are regarded more as tools for rejecting applicants than for positive purposes.

In recent years the shenanigans involved in the use of selection tests across the board have attracted the attention of government officials. As a countermeasure the federal government has indicated that in the future it plans to require reports including the number of apprentices of each sex and minority group plus information on the standards and selection procedures of all apprenticeship programs.[81]

THE MANPOWER SPECIALIST AND DISCRIMINATION

The responsibility for overcoming obstacles to equal opportunity for entry into apprenticeship rests upon industrial and other employing organizations, government, civil rights groups, unions, and the educational system of the country. We turn our attention to the kind of contribution the manpower specialist in the organization can make. The activities which the other aforementioned parties might consider are not discussed here.[82]

[80] Brooks, op. cit., p. 29.

[81] "Bigger Stick to Fight Job Bias," Business Week, No. 1959, March 18, 1967, pp. 84–86.

[82] Marshall and Briggs, The Negro and Apprenticeship, op. cit., pp. 229–245, discuss these. See also Thomas S. Isaack, "Community-Apprenticeship," Training and Development Journal, Vol. 22, No. 8, August 1968, pp. 38–43.

Manpower specialists should recognize that many Negroes in the United States are disadvantaged in meeting the qualifications for entry into apprenticeship programs. Negroes do not do as well as whites on written tests, and these tests appear to be culturally biased in the sense that they are often standardized only on white population.[83] Even worse, they are not validated on industrial populations in the employing firm. The questionable use of tests is further compromised when a joint apprenticeship committee develops its own test and allows the test to be undependably administered. Overly emphasizing the weight given to oral interviews can be still another drawback, especially if Negroes are turned down because they do not present themselves or their reasoning for a job choice very effectively in the interview.

Clearly, the manpower specialist in an organization can correct some of these problems. Steps he could take would include the following: reviewing oral and written testing procedures to assure that they are realistic in terms of the requirements for the trades; communicating to the Negro community that all qualified applicants will be accepted for apprenticeship; notifying various community relations organizations, civil rights groups, and Negro leaders when apprenticeship classes are being formed; establishing channels of communication and effective working relationships with Negro community leaders (by retaining experts or consultants in race relations, if necessary) in order to clear up misunderstandings; maintaining careful records pertaining to application decisions which could be available for inspection by authorized persons or agencies; seeking out qualified Negroes for apprenticeship (rather than passively processing the applicants who appear at the employment office); and providing realistic information on the nature of apprenticeship training to civil rights groups and others interested in the subject.

He might also recruit apprentices from such programs as the Job Corps and arrange for summer work programs for youngsters who are members of minority groups. Programs for developing human resources that give minority youths an opportunity to gain first-hand experience in large-scale organizations should open new horizons for them and assist in expanding the work socialization process. Similarly, any efforts the manpower specialist makes to improve public vocational high schools and avoid their becoming dumping grounds for poorly motivated and ill-prepared minority group students would seemingly be worthwhile.[84] In essence, the role of the manpower specialist is to be a communication link between his employing organization and the outside groups which have an interest in this

[83] For background see Robert M. Guion, "Employment Tests and Discriminatory Hiring," *Industrial Relations,* Vol. 5, No. 2, February 1966, pp. 20–37.

[84] Marshall and Briggs, *The Negro and Apprenticeship, op. cit.,* pp. 229–245.

particular topic and to devise programs responsive to the problems we have been discussing.

ADMINISTERING PROGRAMS: SOME OVERALL VIEWS

An apprenticeship program may be administered in accordance with the range of conditions under which it is organized. Hence there is great variety. The Bureau of Apprenticeship and Training has offices in every state. Its administrative powers are complicated by the fact that 30 states have their own apprenticeship statutes administered by respective state apprenticeship councils. Minimum standards are set forth under both the federal and state laws. An apprenticeship program can be registered by BAT if its specific requirements comply with the federal minimum standards. As of October 1966 there were 40,437 federally registered programs in the United States, of which 31,157 were in states having state apprenticeship councils.[85]

There may be any number of situations in which apprentice training can take place effectively. These may range from a small shop employing one apprentice through a multi-plant industrial setting employing hundreds or even one thousand or more apprentices, to an area training program in the construction industry involving many general contractors, labor organizations, and crafts employing hundreds of apprentices. Thus, for example, one of the most effective recruitment and training programs for apprentices includes 650 high-school graduates taking a four-year course dividing their time between schooling at the manufacturing-trades apprentice school in Detroit and training in approximately 80 Detroit-area tool and die shops. The program as of several years ago had graduated more than 3000 apprentices and had a dropout rate of less than 5 percent. The program is 30 years old and is believed to be one of the oldest and most effective in the United States.[86]

Although the administration of apprentice programs varies with the circumstances, it usually falls within three general types. First, there are employer-administered programs. In a small shop or in a large industry where employees express through their union the wish to have management conduct the program, or, where there is no union, the management of the industry may establish an apprentice program by drawing up a set of standards, selecting the required number of apprentices, and placing them in training. The employer may establish a related instruction program within the industry or firm, or he may decide to send his apprentices to

---

[85] Marshall and Briggs, "Remedies for Discrimination in Apprenticeship Programs," *op. cit.*, pp. 304–305.

[86] *Detroit Free Press,* June 16, 1965, p. 10F.

existing apprentice training classes in the local public schools. Except in a very small shop, the employer will probably find it necessary to designate some person to supervise the training program and keep the necessary records.[87]

Second, there are craft joint apprenticeship committees, which are the type most commonly used for individual crafts. A craft JAC is normally composed of an equal number of representatives from management and the union, with a chairman and a secretary elected from the membership of the committee. JACs usually seek help and counsel from representatives of the BAT, state apprenticeship councils, and local or state educational agencies. They frequently invite representatives of these organizations to attend meetings of the committee and to act as advisors and consultants.[88]

Third, there is the area apprenticeship committee. This administrative arrangement is essential when dealing with crafts in the construction industry. During a four- or five-year training program, apprentices in the building trades may be on the payroll of many different employers. In order to learn their trades, the apprentices must be rotated through the various work processes of the trade, and they are required to attend classes in related instruction. An individual contractor cannot supervise the training of an apprentice after he has left his employment. For this reason, contractors and unions cooperate in forming area apprenticeship committees to administer and supervise the training of building-trades apprentices throughout the training period. Participating employers and unions subscribe to area standards and cooperate in carrying out the policies of the area joint committee. The latter selects apprentices from available applicants, signs and registers indentures, supervises apprentice training on the job and in the classroom, and enforces the area standards. All of this is accomplished through voluntary participation by all the parties (contractors, unions, and apprentices) who recognize the need for the training of skilled men and are willing to give the necessary cooperation to accomplish this purpose.[89]

TRAINING TECHNIQUES AND THE JOB SITE

In previous sections of the chapter we have already alluded to the various ways in which apprentices are developed and supplied to employers. Included here would be such processes as training in the armed forces, formal training in trade or vocational schools, picking up or stealing the trade, formal apprenticeship through an understudy progression method,

[87] Hall, *op. cit.,* p. 6.
[88] *Ibid.*
[89] *Ibid.,* pp. 6–7.

upgrading or changeover of personnel within a large company, improvers, and immigration (which is a device to attract skilled craftsmen from one geographical area to another).[90]

We require, however, a closer look at the specific techniques involved in the actual training of apprentices. We must give attention to the immediate supervision of apprentices in on-the-job training, often called job-site training, and the role of related instruction.

The quality of immediate supervision of apprentices undergoing training is thought to affect substantially the success of apprenticeship. It is a consideration to be weighed regardless of the type of administrative arrangement of the program, that is, whether it be employer-administered, JAC-administered or area-administered apprenticeship. The various committees themselves cannot perform this more direct supervisory function and conduct the actual learning experiences.

In most instances the employer of apprentices designates some individual to supervise apprentice training and to be responsible for the overall program including the on-the-job training and related instruction in the classroom. This person may supervise one craft, or he may supervise a number of crafts, depending upon the number of apprentices and the number of skilled trades. In his duties he will administer the work experience of apprentices on the job, arrange for and require attendance at related instruction classes, and maintain the required records of training and study. In many instances, as previously indicated, he will also have an active part in the selection of applicants.

It is important to note that the adequate supervision of apprentices during their training period is one of the most important aspects of apprenticeship. Furthermore, it is a phase of apprenticeship which distinguishes apprenticeship training from other types of training.[91] For these reasons apprenticeship activities should be placed under the wing of the manpower specialist in the organization.

Job-site training is defined as that part of the training program of an apprentice which occurs on the job, with the apprentice actually performing work on a category of work requiring the skills of a craftsman, as distinguished from that part of the training program which normally occurs in the classroom. Many regard job-site training as the essence of apprenticeship because a carefully planned and scheduled program of training at the job-site conjoined with association with competent craftsmen according to a scheduled plan is seen as the age-old key to skill acquisition. In other words, an apprentice must follow a schedule of work experiences and processes to develop the skills, judgment, habits, and

[90] Slichter et al., *op. cit.,* pp. 66–69.
[91] Hall, *op. cit.,* pp. 6–7.

attitudes necessary for successful performance in the craft. And certain study and schooling are essential. But the performance of work of the same class and under the same working conditions as that of the experienced craftsman spells the difference between apprenticeship and the great majority of other occupational training programs. Planned progress is also important because in most occupations improvement is usually made through a series of loosely related organizational positions of varying responsibility until the worker reaches the limit of his opportunities or ability; however, in apprenticeship the period of training is formal and is planned in advance.[92]

Perhaps some of the reasons that cooperative education and college graduate training programs often fail in the industrial setting are that they lack planning and the identification of the sequences of jobs that prepare a person for performance in a professional position. Apprenticeship is perhaps more carefully planned, at least, in theory; it is often violated in practice. However, we lack empirical studies which compare and contrast the advantages and disadvantages of apprenticeship training with other means of acquiring skills.[93]

At the job site the apprentice must learn the skills of the craft, how to perfect their application, and how to use them to meet varied job assignments. The particular skills must first be identified because they pertain to the performance of an operation. A craftsman, for example, performs many operations, all of which require varied degrees of skill, both in the performance of the same operation and different operations. In other words, there are different standards of performance in the application of the skill, and the difference is determined by the class of work to be done. For example, the turning of a rough axle requires a standard of performance different from the turning of a precision shaft for an electric motor. The operation is the same but the quality requirements are not.

The difficulty inherent in the skills required for various processes also helps us in identifying skills and providing progressive training for apprentices. For example, some operations in a skilled trade are simple and easy to learn whereas others require a high degree of coordination in timing and judgment. Turning a straight shaft is less difficult than cutting a thread. Milling a straight keyway is less difficult than milling the teeth on a gear. Milling a spur gear is easier than milling a helical gear.[94]

In providing for the progression of apprentices, attention should be given to selecting jobs that do not require a high standard of performance

[92] *Ibid.,* p. 18.
[93] Marshall and Briggs, "Remedies for Discrimination in Apprenticeship Programs," *op. cit.,* p. 319.
[94] Hall, *op. cit.,* pp. 19–22.

at first, then later increasing the requirements of accuracy and performance as the apprentice progresses in his training. In apprenticeship, the less difficult operations are assigned in the early part of the training program, and the more complex operations are assigned later. This approach provides the apprentice with an opportunity to develop skill and judgment on tasks within his ability at any given time and makes easier the learning of the more complex operations when he has advanced to that level.[95]

From the standpoint of learning assignments, the manpower specialist who supervises the development of apprentices must first consider the level of advancement of the apprentice and then the skill required to perform the job under consideration at the time. The job is selected because the apprentice needs additional practice, the job requires exacting performance, or the job involves the performance of a new operation which the apprentice needs to learn. The apprentice in time learns the skills of his trade by learning to perform the operations required on many different jobs. As he masters one skill after another, his assignments are broadened and he may be given any assignment which involves the operations already learned. With the broadening experiences of a variety of work situations, he is given assignments which are more complex and which require progressively more exacting standards of performance from the craft which he is learning. Thus, the apprentice learns to complete an increasing variety of jobs with constantly increasing precision.[96]

It should be recalled that skilled craftsmen are the repository of the skills of the craft. Ideally, the apprentice soon becomes aware of the fact that the experienced craftsman possesses something which he lacks. While he may not be sure what it is, the apprentice does know that he has not, as yet, acquired the standard of ease of performance of the craftsman. The apprentice finds that his problem is to learn the skills, perfect their application, learn to apply them in combination with other skills, and, finally, bring his performance up to that set by an experienced craftsman. An apprentice finds that he can accomplish this only by having practice on a great variety of jobs under the supervision of men who are already skilled. He must learn to plan his work, to determine quickly the correct sequence of operations, and to make the necessary adjustments while the work is being done.[97] Somehow he must develop a personal strategy for learning from journeymen. It is this vital interpersonal communication between the apprentice and journeyman about which we know least. How do individual differences among the dyads of journeymen and apprentices affect skill acquisition?

[95] *Ibid.*, p. 22.
[96] *Ibid.*, p. 22.
[97] *Ibid.*, pp. 22–23.

In the theory of apprenticeship we assume that the craftsman desires to and is capable of communicating with apprentices assigned to work beside him. In theory it is also assumed that no two apprentices in the same craft need necessarily follow the same sequence. Each learns the craft as a whole but follows his own order of progression and rotation among jobs at the job-site.

It is important that the apprentice not be "shuttled" from job to job without any consideration of the effects of his learning or without references to the "time element" involved in skill acquisition. A record should be kept of the "type-job" as well as the rating reports of the immediate foreman of the apprentice. However, these matters are largely mechanics rather than the guts of learning through interpersonal interaction. The importance of interaction cannot be underestimated.

Related Instruction

Turning to related instruction, it should be noted that the mastery of a craft requires more than the ability to perform the manipulative operations which constitute the job. A journeyman cannot be considered as having mastered his craft until he is able to make the necessary calculations and technical decisions which are necessary before manipulative operations can be started. The ability to make these calculations and decisions is acquired through a study of certain techniques. Thus, similar to many other occupations in an industrial society, competency as a skilled craftsman involves mastery of both the theory and practice of the occupational field of work.

Related instruction is a broad concept. It is concerned with the theory of a craft and the kinds of knowledge a skilled tradesman must have in order to apply the skills of his craft. It also includes information about a variety of matters, such as knowledge of: machines used in the trade; materials and supplies; the environment in which the trade is practiced (such as data on wages, working conditions, advancement potential, relationship to other occupations, and the like); technical topics (such as applied science, mathematics, drawing and blueprint reading, and the like); and, lastly, tools, instruments, and other devices of the trade. In other words, related instruction is organized from subject matter selected through careful analysis of the work experience schedule.[98]

There is considerable variability in the amount, quality, and style of related instruction for apprentices. Recently a study was completed in California which provided considerable information on related instruction as it occurs in the construction, printing, and machinist trades. It is worth elaboration here, despite the fact that the general application of the find-

[98] *Ibid.*, pp. 30–31.

ings is not known, because so little research has been done on the effectiveness of related instruction.

Approximately 71 percent of all apprentices were enrolled in related instruction, according to the study. Although it is standard policy that all apprenticeship programs should include a minimum of 144 hours of related instruction per year, enrollment rates seem to vary greatly from trade to trade and state to state. Most related instruction classes are held in the evening, although a few are held on Saturdays or weekdays. Substantial difficulties arise in providing related instruction in smaller communities and rural areas, mainly because the class sizes would be relatively small. The provision of it in smaller communities may require mixing apprentices in several trades together or perhaps ultimately resorting to correspondence courses. In most instances related instruction is given at local high schools, often in vocational classrooms, or possibly in a community or junior college or technical institute. Most apprentices who attend classes of related instruction go on their own time without pay.[99]

Apprentices are less happy about their related instruction than about almost any other aspect of their apprenticeship. Most attend classes against their will. They feel the classwork is impractical, irrelevant, boring, and a waste of time. Most are especially antagonistic toward studying mathematics.

Very often apprentices had specific complaints about instructional methods. These feelings of antipathy were intensified by the fact that in most cases the apprentice had to attend school after working hours, when he was tired and was not paid. Most, apparently, were intellectually able to do well at the college level but personally did not desire to return to a classroom situation and resisted anything presented to them in theoretical terms. This feeling was compounded by the fact that the apprentices studied in California typically had little sense of vocation. They had drifted from job to job finally ending in apprenticeship. With notable exceptions, they felt little intellectual challenge in their work and had little desire to learn more than was absolutely essential to do their present jobs.[100]

Given the teaching difficulty of the related instruction situation, good instructors are necessary, but they are difficult to obtain. The effective instructor in apprenticeship does more than merely impart knowledge. He acts as a "role model," demonstrating through his attitude and behavior

[99] George Strauss, "Related Instruction: Basic Problems and Issues," in *Research in Apprenticeship Training,* Proceedings of a Conference, September 8–9, 1966, *op. cit.,* pp. 57–59.
[100] *Ibid.,* p. 59.

what a skilled craftsmen should be. Coupled with several other functions—such as acting as a father-confessor—it is difficult to find the kind of person who can fulfill this kind of role, especially in trades such as ironworking and roofing. Few people who know these subjects are likely to take an interest in instruction.[101]

School districts have the formal right to appoint the instructors who teach apprenticeship courses, but they have difficulty in locating suitable instructors and rely upon the JAC to nominate suitable candidates to teach. Regardless of the outcome, there are difficulties in securing adequate instructors. The instructional situation itself with heterogeneous classes causes further problems. To the extent that instructors are not professional teachers and are untrained, students are undermotivated if not sometimes hostile, and classes are heterogeneous if not disorganized, instructional techniques become quite crucial and themselves present severe problems.[102]

The types of instructional techniques used to give related instruction vary. In some states the practice is to have each student work at his own pace in a workbook. The workbook consists of material to be read, problems to be solved, and short tests to be taken. In addition, the workbook often lists assignments to other books, which should be available in the school library.

In many respects, the workbook is like a correspondence course; and the use of workbooks often turns the class into something like a one-room schoolhouse or a supervised study hall, with each student or group of students at approximately the same level studying by themselves. Not surprisingly, many students see this approach to studying as pointless and indicate that they could learn as much at home where it is quiet and move at their own pace.

However, few instructors rely entirely on workbooks. Many spend their time presenting lectures or demonstrations which are of general interest to the class, bringing in outside speakers or movies, conducting class discussions of actual work experiences, or providing manipulative training. In any event, it is quite obvious that the instructional techniques used for developing apprentices are rather mediocre.[103]

Job Site Versus Related Instruction

The relative merits of job-site or on-the-job training as opposed to related instruction have frequently been debated. Most apprenticeship originally took place on the job, and it was not until the 1920s that related instruction became widely accepted.

[101] *Ibid.*, pp. 59–60.
[102] *Ibid.*, pp. 61–62.
[103] *Ibid.*, pp. 62–63.

Many argue that vocational schools should do the entire job today. They believe, first, that since the firms that hire apprentices are becoming increasingly specialized, on-the-job training inevitably is also becoming specialized, despite JAC efforts to police it. If this is the case, only a minority of apprentices receive a well-rounded education, which also is needed. Second, apprenticeship is a much better organized form of training than merely picking up the job in a haphazard way by means of work experience. Thus, there are advantages in planning and directing the development of an apprentice through formal instruction, which cannot be matched by haphazard experience. Third, learning in school may be faster and more effective than learning on-the-job if for no other reason than learning in school is full-time whereas learning on-the-job is largely secondary to the employer's insistence that the apprentice put in a full day's work. Fourth, on-the-job an apprentice can frequently learn sloppy ways of doing things whereas in the classroom situation he has the time to be taught the proper way. (It is of course assumed that the instructor knows the right way himself.) Fifth, many of the old skills which required high degrees of manual dexterity and knack are becoming obsolete while the perceptual skills involved in such new trades as electronics demand greater intellectual ability, which are better learned in school than on the job.[104]

The arguments against vocational schools' providing apprenticeship training are well known. First, on-the-job training is considered cheaper than school training because the apprentice may earn while he learns, thereby relieving the taxpayer of a substantial burden. Second, learning on the job is more realistic than learning in a classroom. Trainees are more motivated when they do a real job than when they perform a classroom exercise. Third, classroom training tends to become antiquated and artificial. This is caused by the fact that it is too expensive for schools to be constantly buying new equipment as it comes out and to keep the training of apprentices abreast of the current state of technology. Training on obsolete machines and equipment can be worse than useless. Fourth, traditional on-the-job training has worked fairly well, with the graduates of such programs holding very good positions and enjoying high pay.[105]

In reality it is not so much a matter of "either or" as a matter of "both and." In other words, apprentices can have the advantages of both training on the job and in school. The real question is the extent to which there should be a combining of one or the other. The inherent rigidity in requiring that every trade should have 144 hours of related instruction annually does not recognize that some trades are more intellectually demanding than others and are deserving of greater treatment in the class-

[104] *Ibid.,* p. 64.
[105] *Ibid.,* p. 65.

room. Despite the many disadvantages of classroom instruction, it is more likely that apprentices will receive a thorough, well-rounded training there than they will on the job itself, particularly if one is thinking about the hit-or-miss training on the job received by many apprentices in the building trades.[106]

An important aspect of the controversy regarding on-the-job versus related training is the strong feeling in some circles that schools should not engage in skill practice or manipulative training. Three arguments are made against manipulative training. First, some unions believe that when the schools start providing manipulative training, they will be in a position to bypass the apprenticeship system altogether and will have, in effect, prepared people to work as scabs. Second, some people believe that modern technology is so complicated that 144 hours per year for related instruction provides far too little time to study the underlying theory of a skilled trade. As a consequence, none of this valuable time should be diverted to mere handwork. Third, it is argued that manipulative training is more expensive than lecture and self-study because it requires supplies, modern equipment, and considerable space. Where school budgets are tight, school administrators may be unenthusiastic about buying expensive equipment.[107] The problem is accentuated today because of rapid cycles of technological obsolescence.

Nevertheless, there is a real need for manipulative training, especially where the apprentice does not have an opportunity to rotate from job to job. Also, manipulative training is justified where the skill is practiced on the job but only in a slipshod manner. In some cases, practice of the skill in the safe environment of the classroom is required before the apprentice can ever begin to perform any aspect of a trade on the job. Lastly, certain trades have very little theoretical content and involve primarily hand skills, such as metal polishing, cement masonry, and plastering.[108]

Despite the various pros and cons there is little doubt that related instruction can be made more effective. In general, related instruction classes should be homogeneous rather than heterogeneous. Within the schools, more can be done to break down artificial lines between trades and establish common classes for apprentices at the same stage of understanding where it actually exists. For example, classes in mathematics, welding, safety procedures, or estimating could be taught to several groups of students at once, provided that the students are at the same stage of training. Common courses can also be arranged for groups of trades with related technologies. In addition, more can be done to motivate students

[106] *Ibid.,* pp. 64–65.
[107] *Ibid.,* pp. 66–67.
[108] *Ibid.,* p. 68.

and to correct absenteeism as well as to reduce the period of related instruction for students who do unusually well in school. Perhaps the requirement for completion of an apprenticeship should follow the practice of many European countries where, before a person is admitted as a journeyman, he is required to pass a comprehensive written and practical test—even one taking several days.[109]

PRIVATE TRADE SCHOOLS

There is little doubt that apprenticeship training is primarily the responsibility of industry and unions, but a great deal of help can be obtained from experienced vocational teachers and administrators, particularly in the organization and preparation of teaching materials and the development of teaching methods.[110] Schools of various kinds have a role to play.

In contrast to the types of training techniques which we have been discussing above, there remain a number of private vocational or trade schools in the United States, some of which are known as "racket" schools. Such schools were established to attract the gullible person with promises of quick vocational or trade education which would allegedly lead to instant jobs upon graduation. The basis for the appeal is the stated demand for skilled employees as well as the unsatisfied demand of fast-developing and booming industries. These despicable consumer racket schools have flourished in the past as when after World War II thousands of veterans desired training for jobs. These schools have programs which prepare individuals to become qualified mechanics and technicians in the aviation industry; practical nurses; operators of heavy equipment, such as bulldozers, graders, scrapers, tractors, and steamshovels; carpetlayers; airline hostesses; and electronic data-processing technicians. Some of the schools offering this training undoubtedly provide sufficient background for certain semiskilled occupations. Yet many are, in essence, operating rackets which do not prepare their graduates for employment and certainly are inadequate in developing skilled tradesmen.[111]

Yet, over the years a number of private trade and business schools have been established in the United States which are perfectly legitimate and meet the training needs of the population. In many instances these schools probably duplicate the offerings of public vocational schools. Nevertheless,

[109] *Ibid.*, pp. 68–69.
[110] Hall, *op. cit.*, pp. 32–39.
[111] Robert E. Mackin and Charles W. Stickle, "Phony Schools," *Parade,* June 13, 1965, pp. 12–13. See also "How Good Are Computer Schools?," *Business Week,* No. 1988, October 7, 1967, pp. 97–105.

the well-known two-year private business schools typically found in the downtown sections of American cities throughout the country are a valuable educational adjunct to the public school system, providing a marketable education for those persons who are willing to pay tuition to obtain vocational preparation quite similar to that offered publicly in many areas.[112]

APPRENTICESHIP STANDARDS

Apprenticeship standards are a means of converting the fundamentals of apprenticeship into a functioning and workable activity. The purpose of standards is to establish uniformity and continuity in a program of training, including selection, administration, work schedules, and other conditions of employment. Guidance in the development of standards is provided by the JAC both on a statewide and national basis and by the BAT.[113]

Apprenticeship standards contain a number of important items. First, they include the definition of a skilled-trades apprentice, which would normally be approximately that stated earlier in the chapter. Second, the standards indicate the qualifications for apprenticeship. These would include the age limits, which are normally between 18 and 25, although the upper limit may be waived for individuals with military service. Also included would be an educational requirement, such as high school or equivalent and standard physical health qualifications. As was previously discussed in reviewing the Michigan study of apprentice selection techniques, companies often use character references as a qualification for apprenticeship. Third, included in standards is the apprenticeship agreement on indenture, which gives direction and purpose to the program of training and insures that the person trained will, in theory, at least have completed the apprenticeship. The usual agreement form provides space for a brief statement of the conditions of employment and training, including wages, hours, probationary period, and an outline of work processes and related instruction.

Fourth is the term of apprenticeship, which is normally stated in both total hours and years. Most apprenticeships require a term of 8000 hours or four years although some are longer and a few are shorter. Decisions are made for the appraisal of an allowance of credit for previous experi-

[112] Jay W. Miller and William J. Hamilton, *The Independent Business School in American Education,* McGraw-Hill, New York, 1964. See also A. Harvey Belitsky, *Private Vocational Schools and Their Students,* Schenkman, Cambridge, 1969.

[113] Hall, *op. cit.,* p. 15.

ence of value. Many programs provide a method of transferring an apprentice from one registered program to another for apprentices in the same craft, thereby strengthening the program in the community.

Fifth is the probationary period, which ranges from three to six months. As we previously indicated, the probationary period extends the period of selection beyond immediate employment selection. During the probationary period the agreement may be terminated by either the apprentice or the employer upon request. After this period, the agreement is cancelled only after some formality as specified by the standards.

Sixth is apprentice wages. In establishing an apprenticeship wage schedule, the administrators of the program consider a number of matters. They try to establish a starting wage which is sufficient to attract high-quality applicants. They structure the schedule so that there is advancement at regular levels and a scheduled increase of wages of the apprentice such that toward the end of his apprenticeship his wages ultimately reach those of a journeyman.

Seventh is the subject of hours. Normally, apprentices work the same schedule as journeymen. However, as previously stated in most instances, an apprentice works under the immediate supervision of a journeyman during the first three years of a four-year apprenticeship.

Eighth is the ratio of apprentices to journeymen. In many instances, local standards provide for one apprentice for the craft plus one additional apprentice for each predetermined number of journeymen. The number of apprentices is expressed as a ratio of apprentices to journeymen, the objective being to provide a sufficient number of craftsmen to meet future needs. In determining the specific ratio for a trade or collection of trades, the local administrators of the program must recognize the economic conditions affecting the employer, the specific experience a particular organization or employer association has acquired relative to apprentice turnover, and the steps that can be taken to provide reasonably continuous employment for apprentices.

Ninth is the schedule of work experiences. This schedule is needed to prepare a plan in which training for the development of job skills will take place. The schedule is prepared after an analysis of the craft has been made and time assigned to learning the various phases of the craft.

Tenth, and last, is related instruction, which we have discussed above. The hours spent in the classroom are not counted as hours worked and wages are not paid for class attendance unless this instruction is given during working hours. Apprentices are normally advised of conditions under which they are paid and not paid during the period of their service.[114]

[114] *Ibid.,* pp. 12–14.

THE GROWTH OF TECHNICIANS

Apprenticeship is a type of education that prepares people for working careers and must over and over again be adapted to a democratic society in which the techniques of production are constantly changing. Changes in manpower requirements should cause educational programs to be modified so that they will be viable.

We have seen the evolution in the 20th century of what has been termed "vocational-technical" education. The latter is a type of education which is vocational in objective and technical in content. It is often designed to prepare persons for, or upgrade them in, technical occupations which do not require graduation from a college of engineering. These occupations include engineering aides, technical specialists, technical production and maintenance supervisors, and specially combined occupations such as technical salesmen. Positions in these fields are usually filled by persons who get there through varied and often devious routes of education and training. Persons in these occupations are frequently referred to as technicians.[115] Yet the term technician should not be limited to engineering support manpower.

The educational institutions which offer curricula for vocational-technical education are of many types. They include technical high schools, technical institutes, junior colleges, vocational or trade schools at the secondary level, university extension services, and training programs in industry. The programs are varied and the cut-off point between vocational-technical training and trade training is not altogether clear. In fact, the training differences may be of degree rather than kind. For example, the mechanical technology program offered at grade levels thirteen and fourteen appears most definitely vocational-technical whereas bricklaying is essentially a skilled trade. Technical institutes are particularly intended to provide a form of vocational education primarily concerned with the training of persons who may be described as technicians. Yet, the term technician does not fit all persons for whom technical institute education is of value. Technicians may be defined as those workers who are classified in the occupational structure between engineers who have graduated from college and the skilled craftsmen. In general, technicians are persons who perform tasks which require a less extensive training in technology and the basic sciences than is given to the engineer and yet require more technological training and less training in manipulative skills than is the case of

[115] Lynn A. Emerson, *Industrial Education in a Changing Democratic Society* (Bulletin 33, October 1955), New York State School of Industrial and Labor Relations, Cornell University, Ithaca, 1955, p. 52.

the skilled craftsman.[116] They occupy a rather ambiguous organizational status and apparently suffer from the marginality which such situations generate.[117]

In contrast with the branches of engineering and the skilled trades, technician occupations do not fall into a limited number of clearly defined and obvious classifications. They are characterized by diversity. The training needed for technician jobs is equally diverse. Certain of these jobs permit persons with proper technological training to attain competency with a relatively short period of breaking in. These people can enter such jobs immediately on completion of their formal training, as in drafting. Some require previous experience in a skilled trade, such as perhaps a tool engineer.[118] Further complicating the situation is the fact that the technician may work under a wide variety of payroll titles, most of which do not include the word technician.

To avoid compounding the existing confusion as to who is a technician, it has been suggested that technicians be subdivided into two types, the engineering technician and the industrial technician. The distinction between the two would be that the engineering technicians have jobs of relatively wide scope calling for a wide level of mathematical, scientific, and applied technical ability. They are usually oriented toward one of the major fields or branches in engineering. It is thought that they need a broad post-high-school education, with emphasis on applied technology, to prepare them to assist engineers and scientists. They may generally be described as being "field oriented." On the other hand, industrial technicians operate within a narrower range of activities and are usually considered "job oriented." Their work is said to center on specific jobs such as quality control, inspection, production-line trouble-shooting, and the like. Perhaps they need less knowledge of mathematics and science than the engineering technician and can get by with a more limited background in technology. On the other hand, they may need more training in the development of manipulative skills.[119]

We are witnessing in the United States today a number of persistent problems in apprenticeship and changes in job requirements which not only are causing the establishment of such new programs as pre-apprenticeship for minority group applicants and desires to shorten apprenticeship in the

---

[116] *Ibid.*, pp. 52–53, 19.

[117] William M. Evan, "On the Margin—The Engineering Technician," in Peter L. Berger, ed., *The Human Shape of Work*, Macmillan, New York, 1964, pp. 83–112.

[118] Emerson, *op. cit.*, pp. 52–53, 20–21.

[119] Carl J. Schaefer and Robert E. McCord, "Needed: A Definition of the Technician," *Technical Education News*, Vol. 22, No. 5, June 1963, p. 23. See also A. C. Bodeau, "What Abilities Do Technicians in Industry Need?," *Technical Education News*, Vol. 24, No. 1, September 1964, pp. 1–3.

traditional skilled trades where the emphasis is essentially upon manipulative skills but also some changes on the opposite end of the spectrum, where skilled-trades occupations shade into technician work. Modern journeymen, for example, require repeated refresher training and retraining in response to automation. Journeymen employed in large manufacturing firms especially need a continuing type of technical training to keep abreast of changes in the work environment. Over time, the buildup of technical knowledge given these journeymen through repeated and diversified retraining places them in an occupational category beyond that of the traditional craftsman. Or perhaps the modern craftsman in many trades should be viewed as a new kind of technical expert or technician.

In recent years there have been several interesting applications of training programs designed to prepare people for this zone of occupational competency between skilled tradesmen and technicians. One such program was conducted for 30 young high school graduates who had relatively no knowledge of machine tools but were being put through a training program of several months' duration after which they would not only be operating the machines and knowledgeable as to their interrelationships but also supervising others in a precision ball-bearing manufacturing operation. Some would ultimately become foremen. In the program the men were exposed to training on the job whereby they learned how to set up and run off the products the machines could make. In the classroom they learned basic principles of measurement, shop mathematics, mechanics, blueprint reading, machining theory, and shop practice.[120] The result was of course a combination of abbreviated apprenticeship and abbreviated technician training.

A different tack was taken by the Seafarers International Union and the Marine Engineers' Beneficial Association in which a program was devised to enable unlicensed seamen to undertake training to become marine engineers. Although seamen are clearly not skilled tradesmen in any sense, the program is interesting because it represents two unions' attempt to remove financial and other obstacles in order to develop technical manpower. More specifically, the program provided that the Seafarers would pay $110.00 weekly from their union to persons who attended classes for 30 to 90 days while studying for marine engineers' licenses at a school in Brooklyn. Those who passed their Coast Guard licensing examinations were given waivers of the $1,000.00 initiation fee in the Marine Engineers' Union. To qualify for the program, a seaman had to be 19 years old with three years of watch-standing experience in an engine department job.

[120] "Getting Their Bearings," *Business Week,* No. 1737, December 15, 1962, pp. 146–148.

They attended classes 6 hours a day in such subjects as mathematics, electricity, and marine regulations. The program was needed for a number of reasons, an important one being that the handful of commercial schools that provide purely vocational training in the maritime field cannot fill the gap for marine engineers. A rise in need caused by substantial numbers of marine engineers nearing retirement and the shipping requirements for the conflict in Viet Nam gave impetus to the program.[121]

Perhaps even more to the point than these two illustrations is the program started at the Douglas Aircraft Company a number of years ago which was specifically intended to convert skilled workers into super-skilled, aerospace electronics technicians. There were important correlative changes in manpower requirements as the company switched from aircraft to missile and space-system production which generated the need for the program. For example, in 1951 the ratio of hourly production workers and technicians to engineers and scientists was 10.5 to 1. In 1963 it was down to 1.6 to 1. In the missiles and space-systems division of Douglas the ratio of hourly production workers to engineers and scientists was 3 to 4. However, in the aircraft division, production workers were still on top by a ratio of 3.5 to 1. The hourly production worker was thus less numerous, and, where he survived, he was both more skilled and more versatile. The rigid tolerances and quality control requirements of spacecraft demanded skill whereas its custom-made nature required employee versatility.

Inasmuch as long assembly lines with single jobs to be performed were on the way out, Douglas had found that it was prudent and wise to employ people with a number of skills who could carry out varied assignments as they were moved around the plant. By the same token, the union encouraged its members to take advantage of special training programs in electronics, computing techniques, and other specialties in order to adapt to the new materials, new processes, and new tools.[122]

Several years later, a unique on-the-job apprenticeship program designed to convert skilled workers into the kinds of technicians needed was started. The program was a joint project of Douglas and the International Association of Machinists and represented a sharp manpower policy change for the company. Until that time Douglas had conducted training courses for thousands of executives and tens of thousands of production workers but shied away from the kind of complicated, long-term program required to train the types of technicians in the industry. A complex of factors, in-

[121] "What a Union Does to Fill a Shortage," *Business Week,* No. 1909, April 2, 1966, pp. 105–106.
[122] "Why Aero-Space Needs Flexible Men," *Business Week,* No. 1764, June 22, 1963, pp. 44–48.

cluding commitments made in collective bargaining, advanced the concept that the new apprenticeship program could eliminate all need to fill higher job classifications at Douglas from outside the company.[123]

The Douglas-IAM program is intended to produce all-round electronics technicians, firmly grounded in the theory and practice of many fields: production techniques, component testing, circuit adjustments, maintenance, research and development projects, and advanced electronics systems. The enrollees must absorb 8000 hours of paid training and 700 hours of related evening classes in four years. The classes are offered nights at cooperating junior colleges, and the academic requirements for the program can be fulfilled in nine months each year. The courses emphasize higher mathematics (including analytical geometry and calculus), electronics, and such electrical-engineering specialties as DC theory, materials engineering, electronics circuits analysis, instrumentation, and radar principles. The fourth year of study will include the sciences of the future, such as atomic energy, computer sciences, plasmas, lasers, and masers. Apprentices can qualify for an associate of arts certificate (the standard junior college "degree") by taking social science courses during the summer, for which Douglas will pay. Each apprentice will also specialize somewhat and receive a journeyman rank in one of five specialties: research and development, manufacturing, missile production, test or ground support equipment, and test electronics. It is quite clear that this is a challenging and difficult program. Workers who survive it and show additional ability will be considered by Douglas as prime candidates for supervisory positions. Selection criteria are equally stringent because applicants must not only meet the usual age and educational requirements for apprentices nowadays but also earn passing grades in an electronics aptitude test given by the California State Employment Service and a difficult mathematics test given by the cooperating junior colleges. Lastly, Douglas and the union are also discussing the possibility of modifying apprenticeship programs to train machinists and welders in skills that are today becoming almost as complex as electronics.[124]

Another striking example of the upgrading of apprenticeship training is reflected in the establishment of area vocational schools and extended programs of industrial education in the states of the South. Formerly a part of the country oriented towards agriculture and the textile industry, the South has made a reassessment of its economic future and by means of tax lures and the provision of impressive systems of vocational-technical schools tried to induce employers to locate new plants in the various

[123] "Douglas Upgrades the Apprentice," *Business Week*, No. 1897, January 8, 1966, p. 80.
[124] *Ibid.*

southern states. There is little doubt that these efforts have been successful in such states as Virginia, North Carolina, South Carolina, Georgia, and perhaps other states of the old Confederacy as well. The development of these vocational-technical schools is a prime example of the interpenetration and cooperation of local and state government, school systems, and private industry.[125]

Still another case in point, bridging the technical and skilled fields at a higher level perhaps, is the field of industrial design, which has blossomed into a profession in the last 35 years. In 1936 there were only six graduate industrial designers in the United States and they were all from the Carnegie-Mellon University, which pioneered a program starting in 1932. Today there are more than 8000 designers working in corporate design departments or the offices of independent design consultants. They have become a powerful force in shaping the design of all sorts of goods from packages to presses. Yet, there are only 1400 students of industrial design in colleges throughout the United States and only about 250 graduates per year, at least in recent years.[126]

The status of industrial designers—called "stylists" in the automobile industry—is still ambiguous despite the acknowledged value of their work in stimulating sales. Actually, the field is very broad, and designers find it difficult to agree on an exact definition of their work, which is, of course, part of the cause of their problem of ambiguous status.

In general, designers are not licensed by the state, and there is little agreement on exactly what their function is. There is disagreement on what stage they should get involved in the design of a product and how much weight their opinions should be given.

What is meant by the term itself presents problems because it has a vague connotation. In fact, it is clearer what design is not rather than what design is. For example, the term design does not mean engineering design nor making things attractive by applying beauty. The goal is to shun extraneous decoration and to study structural elements in nature that are most economical of materials and energy. There is little doubt that industrial design has become the basis for an important new occupation.[127] It is the source of styled obsolescence and a cause for concern among consumers, managers, and manpower specialists for different reasons.

[125] Twentieth Century Fund, *Manpower Planning in the South,* Twentieth Century Fund, New York, 1967, *passim.*

[126] "Students Show Designs to the Men Who Know," *Business Week,* No. 1703, April 21, 1962, p. 161.

[127] "Putting Design on the Track," *Business Week,* No. 1959, February 25, 1967, pp. 94–98. See also Ralph Caplan, "What Executives Should Know about Industrial Designers," *Think,* Vol. 34, No. 1, January–February 1968, pp. 13–16.

There are also some signs that computers may not only take a load of detail from the designers but also perhaps at some future date take over the entire designing and tooling of automobiles.[128] Whether computers will be able to replace the truly creative individual who designs or whether they will be more apt to replace only draftsmen, detailers, and persons called designers who are something less than stylists (such as certain workers who are concerned with a translational aspect of overall design) is a moot question.

Probably the greatest application of computers in automotive design will be in using them for the numerical control of machines that will produce templates, wood models, and many types of dies. It has been suggested that numerical control could have its greatest impact upon the replacement of skilled tradesmen, perhaps transforming them into technicians with an enlarged or somewhat redefined job.[129]

In sum, the requirements of our expanding technologically oriented economy have resulted in a growing emphasis on the demand for technicians. Projections made several years ago indicate that the total new technician manpower needs for the nation between 1963 and 1975 range from about 877,000 to nearly 1,300,000.[130]

The shortage of technicians has been felt for some time and has been a source of innovative ideas in developing technicians. For example, the shortage of cooks has led the Culinary Institute of America to establish cooking as a skilled, respected "profession" attractive to young Americans. It has publicized the need for cooks and provided trained cooks to act as teachers offering vocational courses in cooking through a university.[131]

The shortage of competent technical instructors remains a problem in not only training technicians but higher-level technical personnel as well.[132]

The training of technicians is a massive undertaking in the armed forces

[128] "Computers Speed the Design Cycle," *Business Week*, No. 1836, November 7, 1964, pp. 91–93.

[129] See "Ford Lifts Lid on Secret," *Business Week*, No. 1898, January 15, 1966, pp. 140–142. This article suggests the extent to which numerical control may replace conventional methods, particularly for dies requiring a long lead time or critical dies. There is perhaps no technical reason why all dies could not be made by numerical control.

[130] Bureau of Labor Statistics, *U.S. Department of Labor, Technician Manpower: Requirements, Resources, and Training Needs* (Bulletin No. 1512), Govenment Printing Office, Washington, 1966, p. 3.

[131] "Turning Cooks into Teachers," *Business Week*, No. 1660, June 3, 1961, pp. 104–105.

[132] See Gene L. Jackson, "Technical Instructors," *Training and Development Journal*, Vol. 20, No. 7, August 1966, pp. 54–56; and for a discussion of the problem in Britain, Alfred B. Sloan, Jr., "The British Approach to Recruiting Technical Faculty," *Technical Education News*, Vol. 26, No. 2, December 1966, pp. 12–14.

and particularly the United States Air Force, which not only has the problem of retraining technical personnel to keep them up to date but also the initial training of technicians who are constantly leaving the Air Force as their discharges take effect.[133] A similar problem in private industry arises in trying to induce technicians to serve at remote outposts at missile tracking stations and the like. RCA has responded to this problem by attempting to train Eskimos, Alaskan Indians, and others to be technicians.[134]

The last example is provided in the experience many state governments have had in attempting to attract and retain engineers, particularly civil servants. In Massachusetts, for example, the problem was recognized and responded to in a program having two phases. First, a large group of employees were trained as technicians. Second, those technicians who had demonstrated a high degree of aptitude and ability were given the chance to be trained as civil engineers. Classes were offered at various locations throughout the state, and a technical institute contracted to organize and conduct the first phase of the program. Somewhat similar to the approach used at the Douglas Aircraft Company, the Massachusetts program made use of the associate certificate as a form of recognition of educational achievement. Participants attended classes three evenings each week for 30 weeks a year and were rotated on various jobs. The state paid the tuition for these trainees.[135]

Education and training programs for technicians will undoubtedly be on the center of the stage in educational planning in the United States in the years ahead.

THE ROLE OF PUBLIC VOCATIONAL SCHOOLS

In several places in the chapter, reference was made to the place of public vocational high schools, particularly in offering related instruction to apprentices. Comments were also made on the contemporary problems facing vocational education at the secondary level in the United States. By and large, these institutions are not looked to by manpower specialists as the source for skilled craftsmen or technicians. Even though some use is made of them in providing related instruction, it is thought that after an apprentice has completed his secondary education in a vocational high school he should still attend related instruction, perhaps in the same school with the same teachers after graduation once he becomes an apprentice!

[133] "Where Job Retraining Works," *Business Week*, No. 1712, June 23, 1962, pp. 49–52.

[134] "Going Native the Electronics Way," *Business Week*, No. 1800, February 29, 1964, p. 52.

[135] Donald F. Reilly, "Upgrading Employee Skills in Massachusetts," *Public Personnel Review*, Vol. 28, No. 3, July 1967, pp. 182–183.

In some instances the related instruction would be waived on the grounds that it would simply duplicate what the apprentice has already learned. Yet the reputation of these schools is rather poor at the present time and the future direction which these schools should take as a part of overall national educational planning is a subject of considerable controversy.

Perhaps a look backwards would suggest the guidelines which could be considered in the future for vocational schools. It was not until the middle of the 18th century, when Benjamin Franklin and Thomas Jefferson offered the first challenge to the established pedagogical order, that education in the United States departed from that which existed in Britain at that time, essentially built around grammar schools and the Oxbridge tradition. Both Franklin and Jefferson were aware of the burgeoning in Europe of new educational theories that stressed the unity of school and everyday living, the value of learning through doing, and the importance of developing manual skills. As products of The Enlightenment, both exposed ecclesiastical authority, sectarianism in education, and the tyranny of tradition. Both were keenly conscious of the implications of the increased knowledge of natural science for the individual and society. Their thinking on the usefulness of education and practical achievements provided an ideological backdrop in which vocational education in America was started.[136]

During the 19th century vocational education in Europe advanced rapidly. At first called "useful," "practical," "utilitarian," "scientific," or "technical" rather than vocational, these educational programs were begun early in the century in Germany, partly to overcome the commercial lead of the British. These early efforts recognized the value of the social and economic efficiency in vocational training and specifically the desirability of bringing the best training to the largest number of people in the shortest possible time. The result would be, of course, to increase the national resources of skilled manpower. Then, as now, the leading thinkers realized that the country that organized its human resources into the greatest reservoir of skills would assume an industrial and commercial advantage. Such a reservoir has always been of extreme importance to nations with limited natural resources, and the Germans were quick to sense this key to British and Dutch success. Thus, by the end of the 19th century, the German *technikum* and the continuation school were models for vocational educators around the world.[137]

In the United States, throughout the 19th century, public opinion was overwhelmingly concerned with the great issues of general education: free

[136] Kahler and Hamburger, *op. cit.*, pp. 8–9.
[137] Grant Venn, *Man, Education and Work*, American Council on Education, Washington, 1964, p. 40.

schools, democratization of the class-torn school system in order to bring equal opportunity to all children, and the training of competent teachers at a time when teachers were ignorant and ill-prepared for their occupation. Early in the century there were some short-lived movements in support of manual labor schools and mechanics' institutes, which foreshadowed later trends in the direction of vocational schools as we have come to understand them.

The British, Austrians, Swedes, Italians, French, and Russians gradually adopted vocational education along the lines of the German model. But in the United States the growth in vocational education occurred primarily after the Civil War. The population was growing as immigration soared. New inventions, modern machinery, improved means of communication, the evolution of urban areas, and the growth of material wealth all facilitated the improvement and spread of education. Subsequently, there were urgent demands for the abolition of child labor and for the enforcement of compulsory school attendance. Thus, by the turn of the century the average term of schooling was gradually extended to an eight-year elementary and subsequent high-school course. In time, the public schools became adequate agencies of education. The schools mirrored in their social composition the entire population of an increasingly industrialized and urbanized nation. In the light of this situation, educators recognized manual training and vocational subjects as necessary components of the school curriculum and reached a general agreement in their devotion to democratic ideals and the principal of learning by doing. As a consequence, they recognized both the need for vocational education and the reforming power inherent in education itself. However, then as now there were strong differences of opinion on the precise roles to be accorded vocational and manual training by the schools.[138]

John Dewey, in a remarkable synthesis of conflicting ideas, assigned to vocational education its place in his system of continuous reconstruction of experience for educational purposes. He urged the integration of basic occupational activities with cultural education and with progressive methods in the classroom in order to produce a higher type of worker and thus prepare for the democratization of industry itself.[139] Another group of educators favored the establishment of separate public vocational high schools, considering this development as indispensable for industrial workmanship in a democratic society, for a national industrial efficiency, and for the responsible interest on the part of the worker in the social problems of the day. Controversy arose as to whether there should be separate schools or whether the vocational subjects should be taught within com-

[138] Kahler and Hamburger, *op. cit.*, pp. 12–14.
[139] *Ibid.*, p. 14.

prehensive high schools. Debate began on this subject about 75 years ago and continues to this day. As a consequence of this debate, we have seen the emergence in the United States of the predominantly vocational high school (located today to a large extent in the inner-ring areas of the older and eastern cities); a variety of technical, classical, and science high schools; and the comprehensive high school which offers college preparatory, commercial, general, and vocational educational within the same institution.[140]

Junior colleges, community colleges, and technical institutes have also gotten heavily involved in vocational education. Their existence may herald the end of comparable vocational training at the secondary level. Another such challenge to the status quo is found in area vocational schools which crosscut both the secondary and junior college levels.[141]

SOME EUROPEAN TRENDS

In Europe, vocational training and apprenticeship have taken a different tack and flourished. The achievements of the Soviet Union are largely attributable to the careful nurturing and development of technical education.[142]

Similar to the United States, the employment of youth today in Europe is becoming more of a problem as greater numbers of young people enter the labor force each year. All the countries have recently increased their emphasis on basic education, some having added one year of compulsory schooling. The traditional age for labor force entrance has been affected by the rise in the legal school-leaving age and by the increase from 8 to 9 years in the amount of required schooling for everyone. But most young people in Europe still leave school before completing their secondary education.[143]

Apprenticeship training in Europe is now given in almost all countries within the hours of a normal work week. The details of the apprenticeship standards are spelled out in the written contract; and the contracts, in turn, are regulated by public authorities, employers, and unions, as they have

[140] *Ibid.,* pp. 14–18, 53–66.

[141] Michael Russo, "Area Vocational Schools," *American Education,* Vol. 2, No. 6, June 1966, pp. 13–19. See also Samuel M. Burt, *Industry and Vocational-Technical Education,* McGraw-Hill, New York, 1967.

[142] For a review of vocational education and apprenticeship in Europe as it evolved over the 19th century and up to the World War II period, see Kahler and Hamburger, *op. cit.,* pp. 244–311.

[143] "Trends in European Apprenticeship," *Monthly Labor Review,* Vol. 89, No. 4, April 1966, p. 396.

been for many years. In many occupations apprenticeship has changed relatively little over the years in spite of technical and social change.[144]

Because there has been a shortage of young people in all countries until recently, European employers have been willing to train apprentices in spite of the costs. Few students in Europe are willing to go directly from school into employment without some form of recognized apprenticeable training. As a consequence, industrial and commercial apprentices are numerous in European firms. For example 75 percent of all German boys and girls leave school at 14, but nearly all the boys and one-half the girls become apprentices. Apprenticeships are offered in 124 trades, ranging from hog raising to organ building and typically take three years to complete.[145]

Yet in Europe only a small proportion of those who complete apprenticeships remain as skilled craftsmen. Some fill in time until they can obtain adult jobs whereas others become unskilled workers in industry. A few go on for higher technical training or take advanced training to become supervisors. Similar to the United States, one of the major problems is whether a sufficient number of apprentices can be recruited who will go on to become master craftsmen or do supervisory work.[146]

In Europe, the tradition of apprenticeship as the principal means of providing vocational and technical education remains virtually unbroken. It is almost impossible to move into technicians' jobs and supervisory positions without first becoming an apprentice. However, the rapidly increasing demand for technicians has forced educational authorities to modify the requirements of full craftsman training for entry to technician-training institutions. Similar to the United States, the educational authorities are reexamining the content of related instruction, the teaching methodology used, and the timing of instruction in relation to actual skill training. Recently, European vocational schools have played a role in improving related instruction and have tried to find and train teachers for apprentices. Concentrated courses in large, centrally located, well-equipped schools are also being developed. Employers and unions are working to improve the training which apprentices receive on the job.[147]

In summary, the trend in Europe is toward greater concentration of the supervision of apprenticeship programs in national, regional, state, or

---

[144] *Ibid.*

[145] *Time,* Vol. 81, No. 18, May 3, 1963, p. 105.

[146] "Trends in European Apprenticeship," *op. cit.,* pp. 396–397. For lengthier discussions of apprenticeship in Europe which are relatively up to date, see *European Apprenticeship,* International Labour Organization, Geneva, 1966.

[147] "Trends in European Apprenticeship," *op. cit.,* p. 397.

local authorities. Apprenticeship is becoming less a matter of policing and more a matter of consulting and persuasion. With the rising costs of apprenticeship, employers are tending to train only those in a few highly skilled trades where shortages exist. In many countries there is fear that the government may eventually have to take on all training of apprentices.[148] Yet, there is no question that apprenticeship is flourishing in many countries.

Although a closeup view would probably highlight the differences, the overview which we have described above suggests that many of the problems of apprenticeship in the United States find expression in Europe. However, the long-established apprenticeship tradition in Europe has made apprenticeship a more viable method for producing skilled craftsmen and for a very large number of other subprofessional positions.

CONCLUSIONS

Certainly one of the reflections of the manpower revolution in the United States is our failure to develop a sufficient number of skilled tradesmen in line with projected needs. To some extent our deficiencies in producing craftsmen is a disputable and, at times, devious numbers game.[149] But we have seen that the manner in which individuals acquire skilled-trades positions suggests that the methods employed do not maximize the supposed inherent advantages of apprenticeship. However, little if any research has been conducted which proves that the learning model of apprenticeship is superior to any other.

On the face of it, the planned use of job resources, the systematic tapping of the repository of knowledge possessed by the skilled craftsmen, and the careful use of related instruction to supplement practice with theory seem to provide a potent learning combination. By extension, the fundamental concepts of apprenticeship appear to be applicable to a wide variety of interpersonal, occupational, and organizational settings. The model itself seems to be explicit in such learning situations as law, medicine, teaching, and the professions generally. Indeed apprenticeship was *the* method of learning before aspects of the subject matter to be learned were identified, isolated, and packaged as related instruction to be taught in group situations in a classroom.

Among the actions that are warranted for extending the use of apprenticeship for developing skilled tradesmen are the following. If employers are to hire sufficient apprentices to meet their long-range manpower needs,

---

[148] *Ibid.*

[149] Lawrence F. Doyle, "An Evaluation of Apprenticeship: Growth or Stagnation?," *Training and Development Journal*, Vol. 21, No. 10, October 1967, pp. 2–12.

consideration should be given to making it financially attractive for them to hire apprentices. For example, after World War II, veterans constituted approximately 90 percent of the total apprentice enrollment. Subsidies provided by the G.I. Bill accounted for this enrollment. Employers assisted in the training because they were socially responsible but even more because it reduced the cost of obtaining skilled workers.[150] Perhaps it would be worthwhile to institute subsidies on a more durable basis. An alternative might be for organizations to assume the cost of training apprentices as a social responsibility and to make internal budgetary adjustments for decentralized divisions and plants so that they are encouraged to hire and train apprentices over the long-run rather than be searching the labor market in the short-run for upgraders, changeovers, and improvers on the assumption they are preferable manpower or at least good enough for getting by. Overcoming excessive profit consciousness might be a better solution than subsidy.

The voluntary nature of our national apprenticeship legislation should be reexamined. Consideration should be given to requiring employers engaged in defense contracting to train specific numbers of skilled workers. Hopefully, such an arrangment would assure an increment to the national skilled manpower pool.[151]

Apprenticeship training should be extended to the service industries and a number of white-collar jobs, such as in sales. As we have seen, such apprenticeships have been in successful operation in Europe for many years. In the United States, there have been signs that apprenticeship can be structured to prepare individuals for essentially technician occupations. There are ample grounds for changing apprenticeship from concentration on blue-collar occupations to include the growing number of white-collar jobs.[152]

There is a pressing need for all persons associated with apprentice training to communicate more effectively with one another and to conduct research on apprenticeship. Except for a rather large amount of descriptive information on procedures for establishing apprenticeship programs and the outlines of specific programs, one finds little meaningful information in published sources concerning apprenticeship. More discouraging, there exists relatively little controversy in the existing literature on changing various provisions in apprenticeship to determine what the appropriate length of a skilled-trades apprenticeship should be, in what fields appren-

[150] Felician F. Foltman, "An Assessment of Apprenticeship—I. Apprenticeship and Skill Training—A Trial Balance," *Monthly Labor Review,* Vol. 87, No. 1, January 1964, p. 34.

[151] *Ibid.*

[152] *Ibid.*

ticeship has the most applicability, the value of pre-apprenticeship, and the best patterns for learning specific skills. A more creative and innovative approach would be desirable not only on the part of BAT, but also on the part of employers, unions, and educators.[153]

For example, it would be highly desirable to carry out a task analysis of all the apprenticeable trades and determine as rationally as possible what they require in basic shop training and knowledge of machines, tools, and other devices. Optimal plans for rotational learning would also be identified. This task analysis would be followed by an analysis of the needed related instruction and the elimination of frills. Rather than continuing to use workbooks and lectures, attention should be given to using programmed instructional devices and other modern tools of instructional technology in training apprentices. The results of such a study of learning specific skills might be to reduce the time needed to acquire trade skills, provide better trained journeymen, and accommodate the entry of new apprentices at various stages of learning. Unions, of course, would need to be persuaded to support such fundamental reconsiderations.

Public policy on child labor and public education should be reexamined with a view to permitting apprentice training to begin at an age earlier than 18. The average skilled-trades apprentice in the United States in recent years has been approximately 26 years of age. The fact that he is in his 20s, often with a family, implies that he will be dissatisfied with a wage that is a fraction of the journeyman's wage. It would be desirable to have younger persons in apprenticeship, especially if these younger persons were comprised of the currently jobless youth who cannot or perhaps should not go to college and who cannot find a job because they are untrained and have little to offer employers.[154]

The opportunity to enroll in apprenticeship training programs should be open to all qualified persons regardless of race, color, or creed.[155] Enrollments in apprenticeship will be little more than a drop in the bucket in solving some of the minority group employment problems in the United States because the number of skilled-trades positions is limited; nevertheless, in a democratic society the possibility for enrollment should be open to all. Advanced placement should be considered for well-prepared or partly trained apprentice candidates. In this connection, serious consideration should be given to validating the tests used in apprenticeship selection and ceasing the preparation of apprentices to pass tests. Industrial management should, in turn, establish the proper basis in validity so that it can look upon the tests as valid predictors of success in apprenticeship. If in-

---

[153] *Ibid.*
[154] *Ibid.*, pp. 34–35.
[155] *Ibid.*, p. 35.

dustrial management takes the position that the tests are to be used as measures of the deficiencies of the applicant that could be corrected by later education and training (which after all was the purpose that Alfred Binet had in mind when tests were first established many years ago), then tests would serve an entirely different function than they now serve. A sound decision is necessary on this matter if gamesmanship is to be avoided in the selection process.

We need to have more accurate data on the number of apprentices in training, both in formal and informal programs. We also need better data regarding future occupational needs. Complete and more accurate data will help policy makers as well as practitioners to form more precise judgments about the nature of the gap, if any, between the supply and demand of skilled workers. More important, better data will permit better manpower planning and human resources development programming.[156]

Many of the proposals on improving apprenticeship prepared almost 50 years ago in the authoritative study by Douglas[157] have come to pass. New proposals are warranted in our era of manpower revolution. The manpower specialist in organizations as a part of his job should think through the proposals which are in the interest of his employing organization as well as the nation and the apprentice. Much hard thinking remains to be done.

At the same time, the manpower specialist should keep in mind the extent to which the apprentice model can be applied in the development of all types of manpower in the organization. He should also be alert to the democratic and authoritarian elements inherent in apprenticeship and the implications of these for creating the kind of climate in an organization which is most conducive to the development of people. It may be that apprenticeship is the most effective model for developing the skills of individuals but because of its very nature creates authoritarian interpersonal relationships in organizations and reduces the possibilities for injecting more democracy into work settings.

[156] *Ibid.*

[157] Douglas, *American Apprenticeship and Industrial Education, op. cit., passim.*

CHAPTER *8*

Foreman Training and Predicaments of a Changed Status

According to almost all accounts, one of the most piteous characters on the contemporary industrial scene in America is the industrial production foreman. He is the harried, confused, hard-working, underpaid, undertrained errand boy of modern manufacturing management.

The foreman is truly the forgotten man of industry in America today, particularly in the largest of manufacturing organizations.[1] For almost three decades observers have been commenting upon the erosion of his position, and his epitaph has been written many times. Interest in his plight has tended to be cyclical rather than sustained, and many manpower scholars today have crossed him off their lists of potentially interesting subjects.[2]

Industrial managers, too, may have lost interest in the foreman per se, although in recent years there has been a surging feeling of uneasiness in some quarters that organizations are thin in talent for positions in manufacturing management. Capable candidates for production manager and plant manager positions do not seem to be coming along in the management pipeline in many firms, probably because the personnel input into

[1] For a detailed up-to-date treatment of this subject upon which the present chapter is largely based, see Thomas H. Patten, Jr., *The Foreman: Forgotten Man of Management,* American Management Association, New York, 1968. Acknowledgment is given the American Management Association for use of these materials.

[2] Writing in 1956, Walker, Guest, and Turner stated: "The foreman, the forgotten man of a few years ago, has become almost the most talked about in the industrial world." See Charles R. Walker et al., *The Foreman on the Assembly Line,* Harvard University Press, Cambridge, 1956, p. 1. By 1963, Hutchinson concluded once again that "the foreman is the forgotten man in industry." See John G. Hutchinson, *Managing a Fair Day's Work* (Report 15), Bureau of Industrial Relations, University of Michigan, Ann Arbor, 1963, p. 105. This view was generally confirmed in a front page *Wall Street Journal* story by Herbert G. Lawson, "The Foreman's Life," on March 23, 1966.

first-level supervisory positions is thought to lack the requisites for greater responsibility. This awareness has caused some attention—perhaps not more than a ripple—to be redirected to the foreman, but this is an interest generated less by concern for the present foreman than for the development of the future higher manufacturing manager. Meanwhile, the foreman goes about his tasks as before and either adjusts to his incessant frustrations or leaves the job to seek a more placid existence in another line of work.

MANPOWER PLANNING AND THE FOREMAN

The specific techniques which can be used in projecting the needs for foremen are the same as those discussed previously in the book and were illustrated in an earlier chapter. As a result, there is no reason to repeat an explanation of them here. Yet, the need for determining the number, types, and time-phasing of foreman candidates for training cannot be over-stressed. Indeed, the lack of consideration which managements have displayed in recruiting, training, developing, and retraining foremen has been deplorable. Although basic to the resolution of some of these manpower problems affecting the foreman is adequate quantitative and qualitative needs projection, the field requiring the most attention is restoration of managerial status to the foreman and hence the reason for its being the focal point of the chapter.

The predicaments of the changed status of the foreman deserve greater attention than they have been given in recent years. Of greater moment are resolutions to some of these predicaments, which require manpower planning, too. Throughout this chapter we dwell less on the dreary devolution of the foreman's status than upon positive actions which the manpower specialist should consider in a program of restoration and revitalization of the role of the industrial foreman.

DEFINITION OF A FOREMAN

In the chapter, we concentrate upon what is commonly known as the "industrial production foreman," that is, the first-level supervisor who is employed in the large companies in such mass-production industries as automobiles, electrical products, rubber, and steel. We also pay some attention to supervisors of maintenance employees in mass-production industry and supervisors of quality control or inspection. We recognize, of course, that the term "foreman" includes a multitude of different jobs, some of which in the smaller firm are almost like manufacturing vice-presidents.

Inasmuch as foremen are employed in a wide variety of plants and in-dustries, it may be an impertinence to assume that a chapter could be written about foremen in general. Technological change in the chemical and petroleum industries has probably eliminated the position of produc-tion foreman in many instances. Production workers have been replaced by dial-watchers who spend their work day observing instrument panels and console operators who are supervised by graduate engineers quite unlike the production foreman as traditionally understood. We have tried to be as realistic as possible in discussing the foreman, and the context in which we have placed him is probably the most general. By focusing on the industrial production foreman, and still discussing foremen in other contexts, occasionally, we hope, thereby, to provide a discussion which should interest readers in a variety of different industries and organizations.

We should probably start by defining more specifically what a foreman is and differentiating between his organizational status and that of other persons found in the industrial environment called working leaders, straw bosses, or gang bosses. Our concern is not with the informal group leader but rather with the bona fide foreman. Commonly, he is known as the first-line supervisor. Actually, he is the first level of management in an organization and is carrying out line supervisory work, that is, he is ultimately responsible for securing adequate production. Although we could define the foreman in terms of other specific job responsibilities which he carries out, there are some differences in responsibilities from firm to firm and industry to industry, and securing adequate production is a common denominator from an organizational standpoint.

We further define the foreman as a managerial employee who supervises the work of nonmanagerial employees.[3] In the typical case, the foreman is paid a salary and supervises the work of hourly employees. The extent to which the foreman is responsible for planning, organizing, staffing, con-trolling, directing, budgeting, reporting, and carrying out similar classical-traditional managerial functions varies considerably from firm to firm.

If we examine the word "foreman" itself, the exercise is quite revealing. If we separate the word into two parts, we get "fore-man." Actually the origin of the supervisory job is a hybrid. One forebear was the "master" recognized in common law who was a real boss. As recently as 1880, there were plants in New England where the foreman was a genuine entrepreneur bidding on the job of production, hiring his own men, orga-nizing them for work as he saw fit and making his living out of the difference between his bid and his actual costs. But the foreman's job also grew out of the old lead man of ditch diggers or tow-rope pullers who was

---

[3] For the legal definition see Walter L. Daykin, "Legal Meaning of 'Supervisor' Under Taft-Hartley," *Labor Law Journal,* Vol. 13, No. 2, February 1962, pp. 132–138.

the "fore-man" because he had the forward position in the gang and whose authority consisted mainly in chanting the "one, two, three, up" that set the speed for the group. The German word *Vorarbeiter* or the British word *charge-hand* connote this meaning better than our "foreman." [4] Still another source of the word is found in the ancient position of foreman of a jury in trials at law.

The foreman today may be looked upon as the forward man in relationship to the hourly work force. In this sense, he is not a mere "charge-hand," that is, someone in charge of the hired hands. He is less than this and more than this. Interestingly enough, in Great Britain to this day the structure of the manufacturing work force often has at its lowest level a person called a charge-hand, who is a type of hourly paid foreman. Immediately above the charge-hand organizationally is a person called a foreman; however, in the United States, the foreman is, in theory, not merely another of the hired hands but a member of management.

The Supervisory Connotation

The title "supervisor" covers more than 400 different names in the United States census classification of occupational titles, including such varying position designations as traffic supervisor, mine pit boss, buck swamper, corral man, boom-master, gang leader, and route supervisor.[5] There are more than one million foremen in the United States today.[6] Persons who have filled the position of foreman have felt the brunt of both mass-production technological advances and organizational changes emerging in large-scale bureaucratic organizations.

To millions of workers, their foreman is the immediate boss—the one who really counts in assigning work and in creating the social climate of their work group. To an earlier generation who saw him as a feared but respected figure, the foreman was the colorful "bull-of-the-woods." To the social scientist, the foreman and his changing status are perceived of interest for various purposes in studying human organization.[7] To management, the foreman is the forgotten man in production.

Very few foremen who are employed today in plants in mass-production industries can adopt the posture of the "bull-of-the-woods." These produc-

[4] Peter F. Drucker, *The Practice of Management,* Harper, New York, 1954, p. 320.

[5] Delbert C. Miller, "Supervisors: Evolution of an Organizational Role," in Robert Dubin, ed., *Leadership and Productivity,* Chandler, San Francisco, 1965, p. 104, citing Bureau of the Census, *1960 Classified Index of Occupations and Industries,* pp. 39–45, 73–75.

[6] Miller, *op. cit.,* p. 105, citing Bureau of the Census, *Current Population Reports,* Labor Force, Series P-57, No. 200, March 1959, p. 16.

[7] Miller, *op. cit.,* p. 105.

tion foremen simply do not have the broad scope and freedom of action in production of their supervisory forbears. Relatively few production foremen now supervise the making of an entire product. They make a part which is intended to be joined with other parts at some point in assembly. As products have become more complex, and as product lines have become larger and more varied, the individual foreman no longer has the information needed to schedule production, even for his own department or smaller unit. Either his line superiors or, more commonly, a staff department has taken over the job of determining production schedules. The foreman thus follows a production plan drawn up by someone else.[8]

Inasmuch as the work group of the foreman typically makes only a part of the total product, they and the foreman may not be able to determine how slight changes in that part may affect the whole. Therefore, responsibility for making design changes must rest elsewhere in the organization. Because the variety of materials available today make it a complicated matter to make changes in production methods, the production or manufacturing engineering department sets the rules in this area. Correspondingly, with the foreman's subordinates restricted to making standard parts in standard ways, it has seemed logical to establish a group of inspectors or quality control personnel (reporting elsewhere) to decide whether the foreman's subordinates have done so.[9] Underlying all these matters is the serious business of cost control, which too is directed by staff people. It could, therefore, be expected that the foreman would have little say in this area but should make certain that the performance of his department minimizes variances in cost control reports and is as efficient as possible.

In theory, the foreman still supervises his people. But what does "supervision" mean in practice? In many companies he usually has the final word on who is hired for his department, but his selection is probably limited to those employees or applicants who get past a personnel department screening. The foreman may recommend that someone be fired but the recommendation will probably be reviewed by his organizational superiors as well as the industrial relations department before being carried into effect. He may administer discipline but an agreement with a labor union will specify the nature of the disciplinary action and the offences which are subject to this action. With the proliferation of National Labor Relations Board rulings and arbitrators' decisions, the very words which the foreman can say to a worker may be circumscribed. Even in the absence of a union,

[8] Walter S. Wikstrom, "Can the Foreman Be a Manager?," *Conference Board Record,* Vol. 2, No. 7, July 1965, p. 11.
    [9] *Ibid.*

the foreman may find his freedom to decide limited to actions that are in accord with binding personnel policies, long-standing practices, and established procedures of his employing organization.[10]

The Slide Down in Status

One-hundred and fifty years ago, the economy of the United States was undergoing the early stages of industrialization. The first large-scale industries to emerge were textiles, railroads, and steel. We really have no way of knowing whether the status of the foreman in all those industries was identical years ago. The organizational structures of firms varied; and, the industries were significantly different in, among other factors, technology, geographical location and concentration, and ethnic composition of the work force. However, according to scattered impressionistic accounts, there is little doubt that the foreman was an important figure in management.[11]

It is usually assumed that the conditions which gave rise to the current predicaments of the foreman, particularly in the large, mass-production industries, are traceable to the growth in size of firms, minute subdivision of work, unionization of hourly workers in the 1930s, and proliferation of staff specialists in firms in those industries.[12]

Up to 1900 the foreman was virtually the sole authority in the domain of production; his power extended under some circumstances to demanding bribes and constant payola in exchange for employment.[13] About the time of World War I, when Frederick W. Taylor's disciples were introducing the industrial engineering tools of scientific management, significant incursions into the foreman's authority were made, causing the removal of some of his responsibilities. Various staff specialists asserted an interest in such areas as quality control, production control, cost control, work standards, and personnel administration, and split these areas from the foreman's jurisdiction.

[10] *Ibid.*, pp. 11–12.

[11] Cyril Curtis Ling, *The Management of Personnel Relations,* Irwin, Homewood, Illinois, 1965, pp. 37–38.

[12] J. Carl Cabe, *Foremen's Unions: A New Development in Industrial Relations,* University of Illinois Press, Urbana, Illinois, 1947, pp. 7–28. See also Charles P. Larrowe, "A Meteor on the Industrial Relations Horizon: The Foreman's Association of America," *Labor History,* Vol. 2, No. 3, Fall 1961, pp. 388–390; Herbert Northrup, "Unionization of Foremen," *Harvard Business Review,* Vol. 21, No. 4, Summer 1943, pp. 496–504; and Herbert R. Northrup, "The Foreman's Association of America," *Harvard Business Review,* Vol. 23, No. 2, Winter 1944, pp. 187–202.

[13] John A. Fitch, *The Steel Workers,* Russell Sage Foundation, New York, 1911, pp. 143–144, citing in part *National Labor Tribune,* April 19, 1884.

The period of the Great Depression and unionization drives of the 1930s hastened the decline, which accelerated even more after the outbreak of World War II. By the latter time, status problems and unfavorable wage relationships drove thousands of foremen into a union of their own, the Foreman's Association of America (although there were many other supervisory unions of minor importance prior to this period). After 1947, when the Taft-Hartley Act was passed, foreman unionization in mass-production industry subsided because employers were no longer required to recognize or bargain with unions of supervisory employees.[14] From time to time scholars have questioned the desirability of restoring the union status of foremen to the pre-Taft-Hartley conditions, and one occasionally reads about congressmen urging this same change in the position of the foremen.[15] However, it seems unlikely that changes of this sort will come about in the near future. For all practical purposes, if the status of the foreman is to be changed, it will have to be brought about through managerial action in organizations.

Concepts of the Foreman Based on Research

Social scientists who have studied the plight of the foreman over the years have come to virtually identical conclusions in the majority of research analyses. Writing in the 1940s when the foreman's problems were perceived as most acute, some behavioral scientists characterized the status of the foreman as being a "man in the middle" and as the "master and victim of double-talk." [16] Others described the foreman as being a "marginal man," [17] while still others noted that the foreman was a"member of two organizational families." [18] These are overlapping concepts and simply indicate variously the alienation of the foreman from management. A small number of dissident studies exist denying the appropriateness of these characterizations of the foreman's position and offering alternative

[14] Cabe, *op. cit.*, pp. 29–68.
[15] For example, Thaddeus J. Dulski, "Plight of the Foremen in American Industry," *Congressional Record—House,* March 30, 1962, pp. 4231–4232.
[16] Fritz J. Roethlisberger, "The Foreman: Master and Victim of Double-Talk," *Harvard Business Review,* Vol. 23, No. 3, Spring 1945, pp. 285–294. For a similar article see Burleigh B. Gardner and William F. Whyte, "The Man in the Middle: Position and Problem of the Foreman," *Applied Anthropology,* Vol. 4, No. 1, Spring 1945, pp. 1–28.
[17] Donald E. Wray, "Marginal Men of Industry: The Foremen," *American Journal of Sociology,* Vol. 54, No. 2, January 1949, pp. 298–301.
[18] Floyd C. Mann and James K. Dent, "The Supervisor, Member of Two Organizational Families," *Harvard Business Review,* Vol. 32, No. 2, November-December 1954, pp. 103–112.

formulations.[19] Meanwhile, research on the current status of the foreman continues by a variety of individuals.[20]

Some of the most recent studies have confirmed that the position of the industrial foreman has not changed greatly since World War II. Broadly, the foreman remains the link between management and the hourly employee and comprises the point at which the employee experiences management and management relates to the employee. Foremen have a difficult time in identifying with management and function largely as day-to-day problem solvers. They are subject to a variety of control systems in such areas as costs, quality, meeting the schedule, and the like. More important, they are required to satisfy the administrators of what are often conflicting control systems. They are harassed more than helped. They are expected to obtain results in production while acting as shock absorbers of organizational pressures brought to bear by higher management in an effort to induce hourly employees to obtain stipulated levels of production consistent with quality, cost, personnel, engineering, and work standards. It is therefore easy to understand why it is often asserted that the foreman never receives praise but only criticism because he cannot always satisfy the conflicting demands of the administrators of the control systems. He can always do better and is never perfect. Similarly, because he works in a difficult, fast-paced environment—and one that is often hot, dirty, and noisy as well—we can readily understand why the position is a drain on the foreman's energy, as well as one which provides little more than borderline job satisfaction.

In some of the companies concerned in recent years with doing something about the foreman's predicaments, intensive studies have been made of specifically how the foreman spends his time; and adjustments have been made in the nature of the foreman's position responsibilities in order to transform him into a true manager.[21] In fact, in some companies the

---

[19] Brian R. Kay, "The Foreman's Role: Theme with Variations," *Personnel,* Vol. 40, No. 3, November-December 1963, pp. 32–37; and Wilmar F. Bernthal, "Foremanship: Business's Achilles' Heel?," *Business Horizons,* Vol. 1, No. 2, Spring 1958, pp. 111–119.

[20] Three different types may be found in the following: George Strauss, "The Changing Role of the Working Supervisor," *Journal of Business,* Vol. 30, No. 2, July 1957, pp. 202–211; Richard L. Halpern, "Employee Unionization and Foremen's Attitude," *Administrative Science Quarterly,* Vol. 7, No. 1, June 1961, pp. 73–88; and Dubin et al., pp. 1–132, *passim.*

[21] William W. Mussmann, *Management Development, A Ten-Year Case Study,* (Studies in Personnel Policy, No. 140), National Industrial Conference Board, New York, 1953; Chester E. Evans, *Supervisory Responsibility and Authority* (Research Report No. 30), American Management Association, New York, 1957; Harry E. O'Neill and Albert J. Kubany, "Observational Methodology and Supervisory Be-

Table 1   College Education Completed by Foremen

Education	Percentage of Foremen Aged				
	25–34	35–44	45–54	55–64	25–64
4 years college or more	9.1	5.0	3.3	1.1	4.8
1 to 3 years college	12.2	10.3	8.1	6.7	9.4
Total with college exposure	21.3	15.3	11.4	7.8	14.2

Source. Kenneth Hopper, "The Growing Use of College Graduates as Foremen," *Management of Personnel Quarterly,* Vol. 6, No. 2, Summer 1967, p. 7, based on *U.S. Census of Population,* 1960.

foreman's position has been significantly modified so that he is genuinely the manager of his own area and not merely a coordinator of staff services or a production troubleshooter. As yet we do not have a great deal of information indicating the success of these efforts, but it is of interest that organizations are taking action of a fundamental type.

In still other organizations, considerable attention has been given to piecemeal efforts to resolve at least a few of the problems, such as analyzing the social background and characteristics of foremen in a firm in order to make manpower projections. These studies are helpful to management if they reveal the number of foremen needed in the future as well as the characteristics they should possess. Their value would increase correspondingly if they resulted in stability of salaried employment for the foreman and became the basis for planned human resources development.

EDUCATIONAL ATTAINMENT OF FOREMEN

In the past, foremen throughout the United States have come from the hourly ranks and have possessed a high-school education (or less) plus extensive work experience in production.[22] This observation is supported by the data in Table 1, which indicate that older foremen tend to have

havior," *Personnel Psychology,* Vol. 12, No. 1, Spring 1959, pp. 85–95; Chester E. Evans, "Contrasting Views of the Foreman's Responsibility," *Personnel,* Vol. 34, No. 1, July-August 1957, pp. 32–33; and Quentin D. Ponder, "The Effective Manufacturing Foreman," *Proceedings of the 10th Annual Meeting of the Industrial Relations Research Association,* 1957, ed., by Edwin Young, Industrial Relations Research Association, Madison, pp. 41–54.

[22] Kenneth Hopper, "The Growing Use of College Graduates as Foremen," *Management of Personnel Quarterly,* Vol. 6, No. 2, Summer 1967, pp. 2–12.

Table 2 College Education of United States Foremen

Industry	Number of Foremen	Percent 1 to 3 Years College	Percent 4 or more Years College
Construction	101,634	7	1.1
All manufacturing	694,041	10	6
Metal industries	126,238	10	6
Machinery except electrical	65,781	9	4
Electrical machinery and supplies	61,165	14	9
Transportation equipment	81,765	13	6
Motor vehicles	39,565	11	6
Other transportation equipment	42,200	14	6
Other durable goods	96,170	8	4
Textiles, textile products, and apparel	53,871	6	4
Other nondurable goods	209,051	10	7
Railroads and railway express service	35,413	5	0.6
Transportation *except* railroad	26,927	9	1.9
Communication, utilities, and sanitary services	57,617	10	4
Other industries not reported	200,944	9	5
All foremen	1,116,576	9.4	4.8

Source. Kenneth Hopper, "The Growing Use of College Graduates as Foremen," *Management of Personnel Quarterly,* Vol. 6, No. 2, Summer 1967, p. 7, based on *U.S. Census of Population,* 1960.

lesser education than younger foremen. Throughout industry there appear to be relatively few foremen who are college graduates and in no case greater than 9 percent, as can be determined from Table 2.

Despite their limitations in formal education, foremen have over the years moved into higher-level positions in production management, such as general foremen, superintendents, production managers, and even plant managers, staff manufacturing managers and, occasionally, general managers of divisions, and heads of corporations. Today, however, some managers believe that employees who work their way up the organizational hierarchy through production along the lines indicated are less desirable as manufacturing executives than college graduates who, although they lack the years of production experience, have a broader base of education to draw upon in carrying out management work. As a consequence, many large companies have in the past decade attempted to recruit college graduates off the campus for placement in production.[23]

[23] *Ibid.* and Stephen Habbe, *College Graduates Assess Their Training* (Studies in Personnel Policy No. 188), National Industrial Conference Board, New York, 1963, 80 pp.

The results of placing college graduates in the production foreman position are not clear; many firms have experienced high rates of turnover in these placements. For management, this instability created another new predicament regarding foreman manpower. It would like to attract college graduates into production and hopefully secure 15 or 20 years later an individual who is not only well steeped in production but also has a sufficiently broad academic background so that he will be an effective production executive at high organizational levels. But few college graduates appear to have the staying power required to become well grounded in production before they are moved upward.

The diversity in experiences among organizations that have tried to attract and retain college graduates as foremen can be illustrated by some anecdotes. The author has been told of circumstances whereby one college graduate placed in a production foreman's job at the beginning of the day shift had become so disenchanted that he had quit before lunch. Another gave up his job because he was dissatisfied with the intellectual wavelength of his hourly rated subordinates. As he put it, the most intelligent conversation he had with his workers in six months as a foreman was an argument over whether Venezuela was located in South America!

It is difficult to know what conditions in general make for retention and turnover of college graduate trainees in the foreman slot. It may be surmised that many individuals attend college with the main purpose in mind being avoidance of work in a factory. These persons do not want to be employed as hourly employees and also have no interest in becoming foremen. To some extent their motivation in attending college has nothing to do with an interest in learning but rather an interest in avoiding the hardships, noise, dirt, abuse, long hours, and hard work associated with factory employment. They desire white-collar employment in a staff capacity and often study subjects in college which supposedly qualify them for work in such subject-matter fields as accounting, marketing, advertising, public relations, quality control, production control, personnel, and industrial engineering.

A number of firms have successfully utilized college cooperative students or college graduates in production over the years. For example, General Motors plants have been using students enrolled in the General Motors Institute as foremen before they received their bachelor's degree from GMI. A number of universities in America which have operated cooperative education programs have placed their undergraduate students in industrial settings where they have worked as foremen. But the novelty in the situation is apparently many firms that have never done it before are now giving some thought to placing college graduates and college co-ops in foremen positions. For example, the Ford Motor Company since 1960 has placed a number of college graduates and co-ops in foreman positions with as yet long-run indeterminate results.

Studies of the circumstances governing the successes and failures of recruiting, selecting, placing, training, and retaining college graduates and co-ops as production foremen are the new frontier in research on the foreman. Industrial firms appear to be extremely concerned with this area. There may be opportunities here for studying the foreman's job from both the classical-traditional authority-responsibility-accountability, and behavioral science standpoints. Presumably with a higher caliber person in the foreman's position, production management can be restructured to take advantage of the alleged superiority of new-style college-graduate foremen, but this has yet to be demonstrated.

HUMAN RELATIONS AND FOREMAN SELECTION

At the end of a session in a company's "charm school" (the pejorative name given to the on-going supervisory training program), a foreman was heard to remark, "Why do they (management) waste all this time and money trying to make us a bunch of human relations suckers who go around trying to adjust people when what they really want and ask about all the time is the number of units that were shipped out the back door at the end of the last shift." This type of cynical dismay is not at all unusual and has probably been vented by many foremen in many different organizations over the years. The comment highlights the inconsistencies between what the foreman perceives as a drive to get out production and management's stated interest in whatever constitutes the prevailing concept of the day in "good human relations."

Human relations in industry is a subject which extends back to the research conducted at the Hawthorne plant of Western Electric and is intimately connected with foreman development in the 1920s and 1930s. Prior to this time, of course, many industrialists and social scientists were concerned with the problem of worker motivation and productivity in the factory setting. Yet, we customarily equate the genesis of human relations with the Hawthorne studies.

Production has always had an inherent authoritarian cast to it. This orientation of production is presumably based upon the concept that someone (or some accountable group) must decide on the objectives of an industrial organization in terms of what is going to be produced and sold and then plan and implement a course of action for manufacturing. Subordinates in the work situation are expected to bend to meet the demands of the production schedule. The role of democracy in production management has, in practice, been given short shrift although many academic writers on management and motivation have stressed the desirability of the injection of more democracy in industrial problem solving and decision making. The practicing manager is likely to reject this suggestion on the grounds that it is unworkable. As a matter of fact, he probably has never seriously considered any experimentation with democratic participation in the conduct of production management. The academician is likely to retort: "How do you know democracy does not work if you have not tried it?"

In American industry, traditionally, persons have apparently been selected to be foremen for one of two reasons: either because they have been on the job for a long period of time, or because they are expert workers. An impressive physique and authoritarian mien were not considered disqualifying. In firms in which the work required the foreman to supervise employees who had special or highly trained skills, the man who was chosen to be a foreman probably had shown himself to be a proficient skilled-trades worker. On the other hand, where foremen were chosen to head up production or assembly line workers, the supervisor's need for special background or experience in the skilled trades was minimal. As a result, we would typically have found a foreman in a machine shop with a background as an expert machinist, but the foreman on the assembly line was probably a former hourly employee with considerable service, a good labor relations record, and a reputation for being previously effective on the job. Undoubtedly he would also have had the approval of his own foreman and endorsement from local management.[24]

One of the considerations in the selection of foremen over the years has been the extent to which psychological tests could be used in making these choices. A great deal of work has been carried out by industrial firms and by industrial psychologists consulting with firms to validate batteries of tests for selecting foremen.[25] It would be inappropriate here to review the literature on selection test validation studies of foremen. The literature, especially the periodical literature of industrial, applied, and personnel psychology, is constantly making available the results of various studies. It should be consulted for up-to-date information. Suffice it to say here only that tests for the selection of foremen should probably be validated on specific company populations and in no way simply adopted by a firm uncritically in the hopes that a selection battery used in one organization is *pari passu* applicable in another.

[24] Alfred R. Lateiner, *The Techniques of Supervision,* National Foreman's Institute, New London, 1954, p. xiii.

[25] For a fairly recent review of much of this literature, see Thomas W. Harrell, *Managers' Performance and Personality,* Southwestern, Cincinnati, 1961, especially pp. 109–126.

Other than the subject of psychological testing, there are additional considerations that should be given weight in selecting new production foremen. Today not only for reasons of morality but also for reasons of compliance with prevailing federal and state legislation, it is important that all employees be given equal opportunity to be considered for a foreman's position. This does not mean that all employees should be viewed as equally qualified by reason of education, experience, or personal characteristics. It simply means that all hourly rated employees in a plant should feel free to apply for a foreman's position and know the procedures for making such application. The existence of an equal opportunity policy should be underpinned by procedures which are disseminated through plant bulletin boards, the plant newspaper, and other media that are available and constitute a pipeline to the hourly work force. It is hypothesized that the establishment of such a climate within a plant will encourage many individuals to apply for the production supervisory position who otherwise would not. In this way management is enabled to attain the best candidates and employees are likely to feel that the environment is free of discrimination as well as positively characterized by a merit employment policy.

Certainly it can be agreed that an equal opportunity policy is preferable to selection based upon favoritism or "who-you-know." To implement further an equal opportunity policy, it is important that the candidate for a production foreman's position be evaluated by a selection board rather than a single individual. In order to make the greatest use of the knowledge of job requirements and the abilities of persons in the plant, it is preferable to have a plant foreman selection committee composed of several members of higher production management (such as superintendents and general foremen), possibly the plant manager and production manager, in addition to such plant staff service department heads as the industrial relations manager, production control manager, quality control manager, and perhaps the plant controller or traffic manager. They can through consensual validation and multiple judgment presumably choose the best-qualified candidates.

It is helpful to have a rational screening procedure in operation so that the selection committee is not required to consider a number of individuals who are obviously not suited for the foreman position. Therefore, pace-setting companies normally establish certain basic selection criteria for foreman candidates. Although these vary considerably from company to company, it is worthwhile for an organization to identify the education, experience, employment record, physical condition, and the character requirements of the candidate for the foreman position.

In respect to formal education, companies normally consider whether the foreman is the graduate of an apprentice program or high school or has the equivalent in educational background. In experience, companies might look for at least two to five years of shop or factory employment. Any individual who has spent this amount of time in a work situation probably has a fundamental understanding of what it takes to be a successful production employee and some appreciation of the problems which production employees have in satisfying the foreman.

The employment record of the candidate for the foreman position should in general indicate that he has satisfactory labor relations, attendance, and conduct records. This does not mean that management should look for sheeplike individuals for the foreman's position; but, by the same token, it should try to avoid apparently recalcitrant, undependable, and hot-headed individuals who may have trouble in adjusting to the complicated requirements of work as a production foreman.

Insofar as the position requires movement about the plant and the ability to function in a noisy, fast-moving, technological environment, it is obvious that the plant physician or another medical doctor retained by the company should examine the physical condition of foreman candidates.

Lastly, the character of the foremen candidate should be reviewed by obtaining statements of recommendation from the candidate's former organizational superior(s). For example, the foreman candidate who is endorsed by his own foremen or supervisors whom he has worked under in the past may be a better candidate than one who cannot secure these recommendations. Obviously, such letters may be more subjective than objective, and the selection committee must be circumspect in evaluating the content of these recommendations. Nevertheless, it would be unwise not to use this potential source of additional information about the foreman. It should not be regarded, however, as an infallible index of his character.[26]

The selection committee in its deliberations regarding candidates and in its personal interview of candidates who appear before it can ask additional questions which may reveal the character of the foreman candidate. Throughout the entire process of selecting production foremen, the plant industrial relations department usually acts as the coordinator in announcing the availability of openings (preferably, of course, after having completed a manpower planning projection), screening candidates, providing application materials, and following up procedurally on the paper work necessary to complete the applicant's candidacy in preparation for the selection committee.

[26] For parallel ideas, see Gordon S. Watts, "Selection of Candidates for Foremanship Training," *Journal of the American Society of Training Directors,* Vol. 16, No. 2, February 1962.

TRAINING NEW FOREMEN

Following the ultimate selection of new production foremen is the vital training phase. Foremen who are selected may, as soon as vacancies open, either be (1) placed in the foreman's position directly (perhaps only in cases where the person has had some prior supervisory experience), (2) enrolled in a preforemanship training program and then placed in the foreman's position, or (3) perhaps appointed a trainee foreman, undergoing foremanship training while carrying out the position requirements under the direction of the general foreman. These are the various patterns for training arrangements, although there may be others as well. Candidates passed over in the selection procedure because other candidates appeared to have stronger credentials may have their names placed upon a roster of persons qualified for the position and reconsidered at a future date should vacancies open for additional new foremen.

The employee is selected from the pool of applicants. Whether he is appointed a preforeman, trainee foreman, or full-fledged foreman, he must in some way be told about his work. As a minimum, he must understand the labor-management agreement. In the post-World War II period most foremen have also been given strong doses of training in human relations in industry. A number of writers have recently suggested that these two emphases in supervisory training have overlooked the importance of the contribution of the foreman to the profitability of the firm, which should be a key area of training.[27] It is not surprising to find individuals bringing up once again the question of training for profit, inasmuch as the managerial environment of the plant is geared to cost control (and contribution to the profitability of a divisional profit center in a decentralized corporation). Perhaps the strong stress upon human relations training has the same fundamental objective, based upon the theory that the production foreman with superior human relations skills can extract the highest degree of productive contribution from the members of his hourly work force and meet cost standards. At least this charge has been leveled at those associated with the human relations in industry movement: management is concerned with human relations only because this interest will pay off in production and profits. This charge may or may not be true depending

[27] See, for example, Harold Koontz, "Training Managers for Profit," *Training Directors Journal,* Vol. 18, No. 8, August 1964, pp. 10–17; and George S. Odiorne, "The Need for an Economic Approach for Training," *Training Directors Journal,* Vol. 18, No. 3, March 1964, pp. 3–12; and George S. Odiorne, "Training for Profit," *Journal of the American Society of Training Directors,* Vol. 15, No. 8, July 1961, pp. 7–18.

upon the organization under consideration. Certainly, the cause-and-effect relationship is more easily stated than implemented.

The issues involved in training production foremen are numerous and can be given only generalized treatment here. First, there is the question of the extent to which the foreman should be given training in a classroom setting or training on-the-job under the conduct of his immediate organizational superior. Obviously, these are not necessarily mutually exclusive approaches to training because the foreman can be appointed to the position and tutored on-the-job by his general foreman while he attends supervisory training conferences either during or after working hours with other newly appointed foremen. In this way the new foreman learns about his specific work and job environment by carrying out the position requirements and by being coached and counseled by his general foreman. If the latter is incompetent as a developer of subordinates, it is quite likely that the foreman will have difficulty in learning his job. On the other hand, if the general foreman is a capable developer of men, then training on-the-job can be successfully used to develop foremen.

Whenever there are a number of newly appointed foremen, it is sometimes economical to group them together in formal classes and to provide instruction using conferences. In these situations the experts from the plant staff service department can lead conferences or act as resource persons in conferences led and coordinated by instructors from the plant industrial relations department. The general foreman may not be in as favorable a position as the plant staff service department experts to acquaint the foreman with many of the control systems in operation in the plant. By using conferences, this deficiency can be overcome.

A second distinction that should be made in discussing the development of foremen is the extent to which this training should consist of "education" or "training." The purposes in training foremen have been very diverse over the years,[28] but in many firms these objectives are still common:

1. Assist in controlling costs while obtaining quality production in sufficient quantity.

2. Help the foreman understand his own job, the plant as a whole, and his place in it.

3. Provide knowledge of human relations, leadership, and techniques for developing subordinates.

4. Prepare the foreman for positions of greater responsibility.

5. Provide information about the management-union agreement, programs and policies of the firm, economics, and other matters which management wishes to communicate.

[28] For example, Vernon G. Shaefer and Willis Wissler, *Industrial Supervision*, McGraw-Hill, New York, 1941, p. 26.

There have thus been elements of both education and training in the development of foremen.

Foreman Training Off-the-Job

In discussing supervisory training, it is worthwhile to consider approaches to the development of foremen beyond the factory walls, which are still exceedingly popular in the United States today. As far back as 60 years ago, it was not uncommon to find forums and conferences taking place among factory foremen for the purpose of discussing technical problems. Some of these discussion groups ultimately become "foremen's clubs." By the early 1920s the existence of a number of these foremen's clubs led to the creation of federations of foremen's clubs. In 1924, a convention was sponsored by one of these federations which drew representatives of industry from 40 cities throughout the United States. Shortly thereafter, the National Association of Foremen was established as an educational effort designed to help develop foremen as intelligent industrial managers.[29] The National Association of Foremen subsequently played a unique role in the development of the foreman. It took organizations, such as the National Association of Foremen and later the American Management Association, to acquaint top management with changing ideas of interpersonal relations and to pave the way for the effective maturation of the personnel function in industry. Only as top management accepted and supported new concepts in organizational behavior and took on the responsibility of training and retraining foremen could the personnel function assume its ever-growing obligations and tasks. In the process of educating foremen in the newer ideas and methods as well as in the relationship between foremen and staff service experts, the National Association of Foremen made a significant contribution to the development of personnel administration in industry, which has continued to the present time in the National Management Association, which is the new name for the old NAF.[30]

But, perhaps the greatest contribution to the development of the foremen outside of the factory walls has been made by the American Management Association and other educational institutions, such as the Bureau of Industrial Relations at the University of Michigan, and the extension programs of other universities such as Purdue, Wisconsin, and Michigan State which have continued to have an interest in the development of foremen and have offered special educational and training programs for foremen.[31]

[29] Ling, op. cit., p. 371, quoting from Thomas Spates, Human Values Where People Work, Harper, New York, 1960, pp. 76–77.

[30] Ling, op. cit., pp. 371–372.

[31] For example, see Harry S. Belman and Thomas F. Hull, "Industrial Supervision Training at Purdue University," Training Directors Journal, Vol. 22, No. 10, October 1958, pp. 37–41.

There are still other organizations which have offered foreman training. In the 1930s and the 1940s, the YMCA took a strong interest in the development of better foremanship in America. One of their main vehicles in trying to improve foremanship was the aforementioned foremen's clubs. Sometimes these clubs were composed of all the foremen in an individual plant, but more often they were composed of the foremen of all industries in a particular community.

These clubs had a multitude of purposes ranging from the improvement of management through providing educational opportunities to helping foremen make a better contribution to the communities in which they lived.[32]

No studies evaluating the effectiveness of these foremen's clubs have come to the attention of the author. It has been suggested by some writers that, as economic conditions for the industrial production foreman worsened in the 1940s, these clubs became the nucleus around which locals of foremen's unions were established. Whether this was generally the case or not would be difficult to determine, although it seems quite plausible. The YMCA is still continuing such foremen's clubs, but their apparent effectiveness at the present time is not known. Anyone who has looked into the current status of the foreman will find few references to YMCA clubs today, but they are, nevertheless, a force on the scene in developing foremen.

Content of Foreman Training

During World War II when it was necessary to make maximum use of manpower, the War Manpower Commission was established and the Training Within Industry (TWI) programs were launched. These were very practical "how to do it" training programs in which maximum use was made of the foreman in training the hordes of workers (many of whom had been out of the labor force for years) who flooded the munitions plants, shipyards, and factories engaged in war production.[33] There is no need here to review the details of the TWI programs except to indicate that they, perhaps more than any other innovation, reinforced the idea that not only could workers be adequately trained on-the-job but that foremen too could be trained on-the-job to learn the responsibilities of their positions.

Using the definition of education mentioned above, it should be noted that perhaps the most popular area for educating foremen over the years

---

[32] Glenn Gardiner, *Better Foremanship*, McGraw-Hill, New York, 1936, pp. 298–301.

[33] See Alvin E. Dodd, *How to Train Workers for War Industries,* Second Edition, Harper, New York, 1942; and William K. Opdyke, "Training Within Industry," *Harvard Business Review,* Vol. 20, No. 3, Spring 1942, pp. 348–357.

has been in the field of basic economics. In fact, in some companies foremen were being given economics education (as well as education on costs, materials, human relations, and the like) prior to 1920.[34] In the 1940s and 1950s there was an upsurge of interest in educating foremen in economics to show them their place in management under the free enterprise system. This was, of course, an era when there was considerable fear of Communism in the United States, and prevailing beliefs among some influential managements were that the economic literacy of the population was low. Some companies believed that it was essential that foremen be given explanations of how the American business system operated so that they would be better defenders of free enterprise and not susceptible to the reasoning of left-wing economic thinkers and the blandishments of unions that were supercritical of managerial profits. The variety of programs ranged from the blatantly propagandistic to the reasonably sophisticated.[35]

With their concern over the Employment Act of 1946 and the increasing popularity of Keynes' economic theories, companies have continued to offer economic programs to show that a free enterprise system operates best if left to itself with little or no government intervention. More recently, it has been suggested that companies have become somewhat disenchanted with their economics education courses and have tried to get their ideas on economics and business across through the annual meetings, newsletters, employee publications, and other communications media.[36] The exact status of economic education for foremen today is not entirely clear, although undoubtedly many programs are still in existence.

Many influential groups in the country continue to feel that the American citizenry in general is poorly informed in economics and that more programs, new approaches, and better ideas for teaching economics are needed in order to correct misconceptions and to provide basic information.[37] This need would apply equally to foremen.

Another important area in education for foremen has been, as mentioned, that of human relations in industry. Courses on this topic range between education and training and often have a heavy emphasis upon the

[34] Ordway Tead and Henry C. Metcalf, *Personnel Administration,* McGraw-Hill, New York, 1920, pp. 145–160.

[35] For a review of some of the programs in operation at this time at Eastman Kodak, Johnson and Johnson, Standard Oil Company (New Jersey), Pennsylvania Bell Telephone, and one division of the General Motors Corporation, see Lynn A. Emerson, ed., *Developing Understanding of Basic Industrial Economics,* New York State School of Industrial and Labor Relations, Cornell University, Ithaca, 1948, *passim.*

[36] George V. Moser, "Changing Fashions in Economic Education," *Management Record,* Vol. 22, No. 10, October 1960, pp. 18–21.

[37] *Economic Literacy for Americans,* Committee for Economic Development, New York, 1962, *passim.*

362 Foreman Training and Predicaments

latter. A vast amount of the training provided foremen in industry is on this topic.[38] In fact, the early research in the relay-assembly test-room experiment at the Hawthorne Plant of Western Electric was intended to supply case material for supervisory training courses. Such courses had already been standard at Hawthorne before the human relations research was launched and existed mainly to teach the company's rules and policies to new supervisors. Apparently even in the 1920s many supervisors already had "a new conception of leadership" at least at the verbal level and had all the paraphernalia of "saying a cheery word" to their subordinates and in other ways trying to appear to be oriented toward workers.[39]

Over the years there have been many changes in the approaches to training supervisors in human relations, which we need not dwell upon here. Although there have been frequent allegations made that this training somehow was successful in teaching supervisors how they could manipulate their subordinates, there is little evidence to prove that these efforts have been successful. By and large, persons who make this assertion have a naive view of the difficulties involved in changing human behavior and assume that there is some type of "charm" that supervisors can learn quickly and apply unsuspectingly to the detriment of their oafish, credible subordinates. This view is not only a naive misconception but a sinister insult to the intelligence of most hourly employees. Yet, there is little doubt that companies continue to cast about for new approaches to supervisory training in the hope that they will come up with a nostrum that can be surreptitiously gotten across. Some programs have reportedly stressed that discipline should give way to "leadership" and persuasion and authority should yield to "an understanding of human behavior." [40] Such sugar coating and label changing has been typical of the search for the Holy Grail in human relations in industry.

The most recent trend in human relations is to apply directly social science ideas in the training of supervisors. This field is often called "sensitivity training" and has given rise to considerable controversy among training specialists and academicians.[41] As we discovered in an earlier chapter this field possesses great potential.

[38] E. W. Mumma, "Approaches to Training Supervisors in Human Relations," *Journal of the American Society of Training Directors,* Vol. 16, No. 3, March 1962, pp. 24–26.

[39] Henry Landsberger, *Hawthorne Revisited,* New York State School of Industrial and Labor Relations, Cornell University, Ithaca, 1958, pp. 16–21.

[40] Loren Baritz, *The Servants of Power,* Wesleyan University Press, Middletown, 1960, pp. 130–134.

[41] See, for example, Chris Argyris, "A Brief Description of Laboratory Education," *Training Directors Journal,* Vol. 17, No. 10, October 1963, pp. 4–8; Chris Argyris, "In Defense of Laboratory Education," *Training Directors Journal,* Vol. 17, No. 10,

A final word, however, should be said about the *range* of education and training activities in industry for foremen. Although it is very true that training in labor relations and human relations is most common, there are many instances in which foremen are given training that goes far beyond these two subject-matter areas. For example, in the automobile industry, in one company, newly appointed foremen were for more than a decade given 100 or more hours of classroom instruction in a wide range of supervisory responsibilities. Approximately 30 hours were given to such subjects as handling new employees, training hourly employees, maintaining discipline, and other activities concerned with manning the operation. About nine or ten hours were devoted to developing and maintaining quality. Twenty-one hours were given to cost planning and control. About six hours were devoted to production schedules and learning how to schedule work and manpower. Three hours were given to the use of staff services, which essentially were sessions acquainting the foreman with the nature of these services. Eighteen hours were devoted to tools, machines, equipment, and materials. About 13 hours were devoted to acquainting the foreman with the inherent possibilities of constructive thinking, involving such varied problems as work simplification, company policies, procedures, and practices. Ten hours were given to an examination of the effect of economic forces on the automobile industry. These sessions were scheduled in two-hour blocks twice per week outside of the foreman's regular working hours. This particular program was probably one of the most comprehensive and elaborate used in mass-production industry. However, in scaled-down fashion probably many aspects of it were utilized by other companies in their efforts to train newly appointed foremen.

Many firms have established and operate an on-going series of supervisory training sessions for new and experienced foremen, which are used to communicate with them and provide information, improve their skills, and in some instances (hopefully) change their attitudes. More recently, there have been a number of developments in supervisory training in which sophisticated simulations are used to develop the foreman's skill in problem solving and decision making. An example of this would be the "Genco Program" made available by the Kepner-Tregoe organization to pace-setting firms throughout America.[42] Many other new programs and con-

October 1963, pp. 21–30; Chris Argyris, "A Comment on George Odiorne's Paper," *Training Directors Journal*, Vol. 17, No. 10, October 1963, pp. 31–32, 37; George S. Odiorne, "The Trouble with Sensitivity Training," *Training Directors Journal*, Vol. 17, No. 10, October 1963, pp. 9–20.

[42] The rationale for the Genco Program can be seen in the Kepner-Tregoe organization's Apex program described in Charles H. Kepner and Benjamin B. Tregoe, *The Rational Manager*, McGraw-Hill, New York, 1965.

cepts are coming into use and can be identified by examining the literature of personnel administration and training.[43]

Once supervisors are selected, trained, and placed on the job, their organizational superiors carry out their managerial role by observing their work and making decisions concerning their performance and future progress in the organization. When managers manage, they, by the very act, train subordinates (for good or ill depending on the proficiency of the manager).

SUPERVISORY STYLE AND LEADERSHIP

Insofar as managers and supervisors are said to be responsible in organizations for the development of subordinates, a term has come into popularity which refers to this phenomenon and reflects generally how supervisors carry out this duty. Supervisory style may be defined simply as the way in which a supervisor (such as a foreman) conducts himself in relationships with subordinates. The concept is normally tied up with authoritarian and democratic styles of supervision, production orientations and people orientations, and the interpersonal environment in the work organization.

Our view of this subject may be regarded as somewhat iconoclastic, but it is in line with the reaction that has recently set in against the uncritical acceptance of many of the ideas of Douglas McGregor,[44] Rensis Likert,[45] as well as less well-known behavioral scientists. This is not to suggest that the ideas of McGregor and Likert are in any way to be criticized because industrial managers have naively accepted them and perhaps in some cases applied them in simplified ways in which they were never intended to be utilized. The point is simply that Theory X and Theory Y as stated by McGregor were essentially hypotheses, not proven theories based upon extensive substantial research. Given the tendency for industrial management to be continually jumping on the latest human relations bandwagon and then becoming disenchanted at the end of a short ride, it is not surprising that a reaction has set in (or, at least, started to set in) against the participative management fad, although in reality the stature and underpinning of this concept should by no means be dismissed flippantly as simply another fad. The basis for the popularity of the concept deserves

[43] Bradford B. Boyd and Burt K. Scanlan, "Developing Tomorrow's Foreman," *Training Directors Journal,* Vol. 19, No. 5, May 1965, pp. 44–52.

[44] His main ideas are stated in *The Human Side of Enterprise,* McGraw-Hill, New York, 1967.

[45] His leading ideas are stated in *New Patterns of Management,* McGraw-Hill, New York, 1961; and *The Human Organization,* McGraw-Hill, New York, 1967.

serious attention, and we provide it. We then expand the participative concept beyond the foreman-subordinate relationship to include the foreman in the multiplicity of his role sets and job responsibilities.

The subject of supervisory style could perhaps best be reviewed by considering all of the literature by modern management experts. They do not necessarily agree on the appropriate style of supervision, either from the standpoint of obtaining productivity or from that of building satisfactory interpersonal relations in the workgroup. For example, on the very same campus two opposing schools of thought flourished. One need only compare the views of Rensis Likert and those of George S. Odiorne [46] during the 1960s to obtain a dramatic contrast in point of view by two leading figures both looking over about the same data or phenomena from different perspectives. Yet, it is worthwhile to examine some of the concepts of style discussed today.

The social-psychological subtleties involved in supervisory style, although extensively studied, require still more analysis in future years. There is increasingly coming into existence a literature which explains why supervisory training programs fail.[47] The earlier studies of failures in supervisory training at International Harvester were also notable as harbingers.[48] The predispositions of workers toward foremen and the possible potential conflict involved in this relationship require greater study if we are to fully appreciate the effects of supervisory training.[49]

Closely associated with supervisory style is the frequent reference made to the foreman's leadership responsibilities. It is not often clear as to what is meant by leadership; therefore, the term often has an empty ring to it. Nevertheless, the term continues to be used and is a veritable watchword in the study of line supervision. As a consequence, it is worthwhile to consider the concept of leadership in style at some length.

[46] See George S. Odiorne, *How Managers Make Things Happen,* Prentice-Hall, Englewood Cliffs, 1961; and his "Reality in Management," *Michigan Business Review,* Vol. 19, No. 5, November 1967, pp. 18–23.

[47] For a recent example, see A. J. M. Sykes, "The Effect of a Supervisory Training Course in Changing Supervisor's Perceptions and Expectations of the Role of Management," *Human Relations,* Vol. 15, No. 3, August 1962, pp. 227–243.

[48] Edwin A. Fleishman, "Leadership Climate, Human Relations Training, and Supervisory Behavior," *Personnel Psychology,* Vol. 6, No. 2, Summer 1953, pp. 205–222; and Edwin F. Harris and Edwin A. Fleishman, "Human Relations Training and the Stability of Leadership Patterns," *Journal of Applied Psychology,* Vol. 39, No. 1, February 1955, pp. 20–25. For further background see Charles L. Walker, Jr., "Education and Training at International Harvester," *Harvard Business Review,* Vol. 27, No. 5, September 1949, pp. 542–558.

[49] For an interesting study in this vein, see A. J. M. Sykes, "A Study in Changing the Attitudes and Stereotypes of Industrial Workers," *Human Relations,* Vol. 17, No. 2, May 1964, pp. 143–154.

Out of this discussion of leadership in the literature of personnel management and the behavioral sciences at least two different useful concepts pertaining to style have emerged. One of the most important of these is Philip Selznick's idea of institutional leadership, which is not very applicable to supervisors such as foremen one level above nonsupervisory employees, but clearly delineates the distinction between executive leadership duties and those of managerial personnel having lesser responsibility in the organizations.[50] Such duties as determining the business in which a corporation should be engaged, defending the integrity of the organization from outside onslaughts, building a sense of mission, and motivating managers to collaborate are so different in degree from the foreman's leadership responsibilities that there is what amounts to a difference in kind. The second is the concept of interpersonal influence, which has been developed by many writers and applied effectively to foremen, salesmen, and many other statuses in organizations. It may be said that contemporary foremen are not expected to be institutional leaders in Selznick's sense but are required to be interpersonal influencers, effective in convincing their subordinates to meet management's expectations on production, costs, quality, and the like.

In a definition which still has relevance in the context we have been discussing, Tead, an early applied psychologist, stated: "Leadership is the name for that combination of qualities by the possession of which one is able to get something done by others chiefly because through his influence they become willing to do it."[51] Tead then departs from much contemporary thinking by stressing the "combination of qualities," such as enthusiasm, intelligence, imagination, affection for people, and technical knowledge, rather than the influence process itself. Tead was, of course, writing at a time when psychologists were interested in the trait theory of individual personality whereas today behaviorally oriented theory is in vogue. Yet, Pelz writing a quarter of a century later in a widely cited article takes off on the same idea as Tead (without stressing trait names).[52]

Many human relations or leadership style training programs aim at teaching the foreman how to get results from his people with the limited resources left to him either of compulsion or reward. The gist of these programs is that he has to learn to lead by influence and persuasion. Leading by influence alone, without the equivalent of either the carrot or

[50] Philip Selznick, *Leadership in Administration,* Harper and Row, New York, 1957, *passim.*

[51] Ordway Tead, *Human Nature and Management,* McGraw-Hill, New York, 1929, p. 149.

[52] See Donald C. Pelz, "Influence: A Key to Effective Leadership in the First-line Supervisor," *Personnel,* Vol. 29, No. 3, November 1952, pp. 209–217.

the stick tends to become quite an art. Leadership by persuasion consists, first, in creating a work situation today's generation of employees regards as at least satisfactory, and then showing the worker his part in it and how to benefit from it. One might say that the entire enterprise becomes in this way one great big carrot. The stick is the threat of banishment from the feast, not by anyone's arbitrary decree, but by failing to measure up, to meet the group's standards, to get along with people, in a word, self-banishment.[53]

Rough-and-Ready Style Formulas

Clearly, then, at the foreman level leadership style and human relations are considered vital. Practical rough-and-ready formulas are often sought by management to simplify what it is believed foremen should know, such as the four F's (be firm, be fair, be friendly, and be factual) or some other homily. For example, foremen may be told that all the human relations wisdom of all time was stated by Socrates, Plato, and Christ and can be broken down into three phrases, which foremen should apply every day in the work situation: know thyself; be thyself; love thy neighbor.

There is nothing inherently wrong with the four F's or other homilies, but do they comprise the sum total of all behavior that is needed for a person to be an effective foreman? This we do not know, but the sophisticated person sees them, of course, as really only broad statements of values, not specific guides to action in the complexity of the manufacturing world. There are many such generalized formulas floating around, and they probably have some validity—at least, they appear to contain common sense in our culture. It would be of interest to identify those which are appropriate at different levels of the organization and to determine what can be done to make them more operational and valid.

Higher Management's Perceptions of Foreman Style

People in higher management—line and staff—live in a different world from that of the foreman and affect different supervisory styles. They, too, have the problem of motivating subordinates, but the results which they are after, as for example in staff work, may be less tangible than the results expected of the foreman. The performance of staff personnel cannot be measured so easily or readily as that of the foreman. The foreman is subject to evaluation by all the plant staff service departments as well as by his own boss (the general foreman), and has, of course, a daily efficiency report which indicates whether his costs are out of line.

[53] Edwin F. Beal and Edward D. Wickersham, *The Practice of Collective Bargaining,* Revised Edition, Irwin, Homewood, Illinois, 1963, pp. 129–130.

The performance of supervisors in staff functions is often tempered by organizational politics. Thus managements are likely to be more tolerant—knowingly or unknowingly—of the performance of staff people. Also, staff supervisors are likely to have subordinates who are not union members. The existence of organizational politics and the lack of unionized subordinates are two important factors which make for a different world in comparing the line and staff supervisor and in considering supervisory style.

Also, people in higher management typically have more education and come from a different social background in comparison with foremen. Possibly, people in higher management are more sophisticated in human relations, and the people problems that arise in staff areas are of a different order. For example, we are told that managers "wear masks" [54] and that they are very much aware of the political environment. They fail to build "authentic relationships" and their predominant human relations problem, it would seem, is breaking down barriers to authentic relationships and penetrating these masks. Those who advocate sensitivity training are, of course, very much inclined to view management in the terms just described.[55] Foremen may wear masks too, but their style is to be more earthy and action-oriented—with perhaps more easily penetrated masks!

One of the complexities in discussing supervisory style today is that higher managers, when they speak about the foreman, either unconsciously or deceitfully, talk of the foreman as a manager in the textbook sense. When confronted with the fact that the foreman may be only a trouble-shooter or a coordinator, or someone who simply pours over a list of telephone numbers to obtain plant staff services that bear upon resolving emergency production problems, higher managers are inclined to accept this interpretation, but at the same time suggest that he ought to be different. Yet, over the years it is management which has consented to the devolution of the foreman to what he is. When inconsistencies of this type are brought to the attention of managers, they will then typically acknowledge the fact that the foreman is a forgotten man and occasionally state that it is a pity. They will also usually agree that the problems of the foreman have been swept under the organizational rug and forgotten. Thus, they will shrug their shoulders and change the subject to something more interesting and of central concern to management.

Foremen cannot be told universal principles of how to do their jobs by higher managers because there are no such principles of supervisory style. Much of the job of supervision, in the final analysis, is dealing with people

[54] Alfred J. Marrow, *Behind the Executive Mask*, American Management Association, New York, 1964, *passim*.

[55] See as an illustration, Chris Argyris, *Integrating the Individual and the Organization*, Wiley, New York, 1964.

on a face-to-face basis and trying to influence or persuade them to do something. This is usually what is loosely meant by the terms "motivation" or "leadership" when they are applied to the foreman's job and supervisory style.

Since there is today no generally accepted theory of human behavior, there cannot be a general theory of motivation, much less a theory of motivating the foreman's subordinates. To take the argument one step further, there obviously is no general theory of motivating production employees across the board. There may be such theories in the future, but their development depends upon the concomitant growth of valid and reliable knowledge in the behavioral sciences.

In lieu of the lack of bona fide principles, foremen who are attending training sessions are often given checklists of behavior, against which they are asked to review their own conduct on the job. Perhaps they can learn empirically this way because the information they receive is a starting point upon which they can build a body of knowledge and insights. In time, the accumulated fund of such experiences may provide the foreman with a *modus operandi* (which may turn out to be effective or ineffective). He will be conditioned by his boss and the organization as well as his own values and the fund of information which he builds up based upon experience. The formal and informal rules of the organization in which he works provide the cues to which much of his behavior is attuned. The rules of organizations are variable from company to company, although it could be expected that, because there are some similarities in law, the norms, and environment, similarities in supervisory behavior will appear and are required by the job. This hit-or-miss use of unproven precepts and guided or unguided work experience amounts to throwing the foreman to the dogs in developing supervisory style, but is probably the most common method used in many firms.

Participative Management Concepts and Style

Persons such as McGregor and Likert developed their thoughts on participative management from much of the research on the involvement of groups in decision making and a number of parallel developments in the behavioral sciences.[56] At the same time, individuals such as Maslow were working on the theory of the prepotency of needs.[57] The confluence of these seminal ideas is without question the mainstream of most pace-

[56] They, for example, were influenced by such studies as Lester Coch and John R. P. French, Jr., "Overcoming Resistance to Change," *Human Relations,* Vol. 1, No. 4, August 1948, pp. 512–532.

[57] See Abraham H. Maslow, *Motivation and Personality,* Harper and Row, New York, 1954, *passim.*

setting managerial thinking about human relations and supervisory styles today. These ideas tend to minimize the active supervisory role of the foreman other than as an organizational linking pin and enthrone the work group as problem solver, if not decision maker as well.

For many years individuals have been raising questions about the generality of participative management and have indicated replication studies were warranted, particularly to examine the place of intervening group processes in these studies.[58] More recently there have been several in a similar vein; for example, a provocative review of the literature on the small primary work group published in 1966 raises a number of fundamental questions, suggesting that modern management is too complex for workers to share in it, although they may engage in limited forms of self-government at the work level.[59] Another makes a number of basic criticisms of the use of survey research data in the study of supervisory style and human relations upon which much of the theory of participative management is based.[60] Even in the popular literature of management, questions are now being raised to the effect that participative and group approaches do not work well with all people and in all situations.[61]

However, perhaps the most basic criticism and most detailed analysis of the validity of the participative supervisory style was made by Robert Dubin. In 1965 he published a provocative analysis of much of the literature of supervisory style and reviewed some British studies of supervision which are not well known in the United States.[62] In essence, he concluded that there is no one sure-fire effective style of supervision.

The practicing manager is not likely to arch his eyebrows at Dubin's conclusion because he probably feels intuitively that this observation is true. Academic scholars are also likely to find the conclusion unsurprising. As previously mentioned, two well-respected scholars on the same campus, Likert and Odiorne, held vastly different conceptions of supervisory styles. Likert, a psychologist and sociologist who has been heavily involved in survey research for many years, and an impressive following of his distinguished colleagues and former students advocate participative management in human relations. Odiorne, an economist and former practicing manager, who is now a very prominent management educator, stresses the importance in supervisory style of making things happen and getting re-

---

[58] One such study is by Philip M. Marcus, "Supervision and Group Process," *Human Organization,* Vol. 20, No. 1, Spring 1961, pp. 15–19.

[59] Maxine Bucklow, "A New Role for the Work Group," *Administrative Science Quarterly,* Vol. 11, No. 1, June 1966, pp. 59–78.

[60] Stephen Sales, "Supervisory Style and Productivity: Review and Theory," *Personnel Psychology,* Vol. 19, No. 3, Autumn 1966, pp. 276–286.

[61] Robert C. Albrook, "Participative Management: Time for a Second Look," *Fortune,* Vol. 75, No. 5, May 1967, pp. 166–170, 197–200.

[62] Dubin, ed., *op. cit.*

sults. This is more than a difference in stress between means and ends. These fundamentally divergent conceptions of supervision should have tipped off others that supervisory style needs a great deal more study and curtailed some of the contemporary genuflecting toward various apostles of style.

Style as a Situational Variable

Several generalizations should be made to sum up what we have been suggesting about supervisory style. The behavior of the foreman affects the productivity of the employees by being appropriate to the work setting. Differing technologies seem to call for differing supervisory styles. Culture makes a difference in supervisory practices. The more a production process resembles a unit- or batch-technology, the greater is the probability that employee autonomy and its supervisory counterpart (general rather than close supervision) will be appropriate. The more a technology resembles a continuous-production system, the more appropriate is close supervision. As a consequence, there is no "one best" method of supervision. Variety in supervisory behaviors may no longer be considered a matter of simply choosing the one best for all settings, but rather a challenge to understand where each does or does not work. As far as is presently known through careful research, the influence of supervisory behavior on productivity is indeed small. The impact of supervision on work behavior is probably curvilinear. That is, a unit change in a particular supervisory behavior does not necessarily produce a corresponding change in worker response through the range of supervisory action. Much of this behavior has a threshold above which the behavior is responded to by others but below which the behavior produces little or no effect. Evidence supports the view that if a small amount of a particular type of supervisory behavior may be good, a great deal may be very bad indeed. This optimization notion is often overlooked in the theory and practice of human relations in industry.

An important technological trend is making for a fundamental shift in industry away from the management of people to the management of things. This means that supervisory work is changing its character and that executives must, therefore, constantly face the difficult problem of organizational design and the choice of operating goals for foremen and all other supervisors. In the future, supervisors will be largely concerned with controlling quality and the operating emergencies that influence the performance of the production process.

Lastly, all the studies of human relations tell us little about how much productivity is affected by individual supervisory practices. There remains the task for more future study involving the analysis of variance of simultaneous factors affecting individual output.[63]

[63] *Ibid.*, pp. 46–50.

An Approach to Supervisory Style in General

Where does this critique of supervisory style leave us? Are we advocating a form of managerial nihilism? We are not. We suggest another point of departure which we believe is pragmatic and may bridge the gap between Dubin's shrewd analysis, managerial nihilism, and simplistic thinking. The point of departure would consist of a basic assumption and an *ad hoc* list of hypothetical supervisory skills which could be practiced, keeping this assumption in mind. These skills are formulated on the basis of reading the literature on supervisory style, personal experience, and perhaps the most undependable criterion of all: what appears to be common sense. The latter is, of course, merely one man's judgment and should be regarded more as a thought-starter than thought-concluder.

Following one observer we would start with the following assumption:

"The central hypothesis offered here is that regardless of organizational level or type of work, *men will work hardest, gain most personal satisfaction, and contribute most to the organization as a whole if they regard contributing to the work objectives of the component as the best available means to fulfilling their own work values now and in the foreseeable future. In this frame of mind people are more likely to be motivated toward high productivity, creativity, and self-discipline by forces from within themselves, instead of just meeting the minimum required by 'external' pressure.*" [64]

The average foreman—if there is such a person—is a pragmatic, action-oriented person who probably cares little for "theory." He is not looking for concepts, but rather for concrete suggestions on how to do the job better. He becomes rather difficult to train because he has his own theories, even though he does not realize it. For example, when a foreman states, "Religion and politics do not mix, so I don't talk politics on the job," or "Let's face it, we all work for money," or "Women are tougher to supervise because they are more emotional than men," or any other similar aphorism, he is in effect stating a theory. Inasmuch as many foremen have not attended college and perhaps developed the critical facility higher education might provide, these aphorisms are accepted as valid beliefs, and they become a basis for behavior. If through training an attempt is made to challenge these beliefs or substitute more sophisticated concepts for them, the trainer is likely to run into difficulty. The foreman may cling to his folksy beliefs even though the more scientific theories have greater validity. He needs a framework that makes sense of his offhand observations.

[64] David A. Emery, "Managerial Leadership Through Motivation by Objectives," *Personnel Psychology,* Vol. 12, No. 1, Spring 1959, p. 67, italics in original.

Also, the foreman like any other person has his total life experiences which he brings to the job. He is likely to see self-interest as the wellspring of motivation and use this as a starting point for many of his assumptions about how people behave in the work setting, if indeed not everywhere in social life. He necessarily draws on his life experiences in carrying out his work—what else could he be expected to do? If he is taught subject matter in a training session on supervisory style which is inconsistent with these beliefs, he is more likely to reject the materials in the training session than he is to deny his life experiences. Despite this barrier and many others, it is possible, of course, to communicate with foremen through training sessions.

We are suggesting that communications in these sessions be devoid of dogmatism about the inherent evil in Theory X and the universal advocacy of Theory Y of participative management. We propose that the supervisory styles advocated in training sessions be broadened to include other concepts and give greater cognizance to the technological imperatives of the industry in which the production foreman is employed. In other words, the field of organizational behavior should be opened up more widely so that we can obtain better insight into it rather than assume that the Holy Grail of supervisory style has been found once and for all time. Also, we would recommend as part of a broadened concept of supervisory style that some reference be made to the style the foreman should maintain in his relations with peers, superiors, and staff service department representatives, as well as subordinates. The venerable usage of the concept of style as it relates to subordinates is incomplete; to view the remainder of the supervisor's job as being an organizational linking pin is to fail to ask questions about the relevant style in other role sets, which may eventually be shown to be more important than relations with subordinates.

Turning to the *ad hoc* list of hypothetical supervisory skills, we suggest that there are certain techniques, attitudes, and skills which the line supervisor must develop, specifically those that enable him to establish and maintain working relationships with his employees, his fellow supervisors, organizational superiors, plant staff personnel, and, to a lesser degree, the general public. He may learn many of these skills as an outgrowth of his day-to-day work experience. However, in formal training conferences, and particularly in conferences involving case analyses, he will be given an opportunity to test his supervisory skills without being held accountable for any adverse results. At the same time, he will see how other supervisors approach the same problems and how their concepts and approaches differ from his. He can learn a great deal about supervisory skills and interpersonal relationships in such sessions.

Since the line supervisor gets his job done through the efforts of individuals, the acquisition of interpersonal human relations skills is important to him if he is to become effective in carrying out the requirements of his position. Although it is difficult to define these skills and provide examples of concrete steps to be taken to assure successful supervisory work performance once they are learned, it is possible to indicate the kinds of organizational behavior in which these skills have relevance. The following items are listed as a guide to the production foreman in reviewing the area of establishing and maintaining relationships.

1. Establishing effective working relationships with employees.
    (a) Providing "two-way" communication with employees; keeping them up to date on important and necessary department information.
    (b) Developing an on-the-job relationship with employees so that they will want to come to the supervisor to discuss problems.
    (c) Understanding that each employee is different with respect to job performance and individual behavior and generally must be handled in a manner which gives appropriate recognition to these individual differences.
    (d) Observing employees on the job, both in individual and group situations, in order to help them with job performance and job relationships.
    (e) Discussing, periodically, with employees their job performance and how they can improve their job skills, attitudes, and knowledge.
    (f) Inducing employees to feel they are actively participating in the organization rather than merely doing a job.
    (g) Instilling in employees the feeling that their jobs are important.
    (h) Understanding that problems in human relations stem, in large part, from differences in perception—two or more people viewing the same situation in different ways—remembering, however, that the factual work situation (rather than someone's view of it) may need to be changed to resolve human relations problems.
    (i) Having a competent technological knowledge of the jobs employees are performing; understanding how much time is needed to do each job; and developing the facility to overcome difficulties that grow out of work situations and conflicts of interest.
    (j) Permitting employees to work independently when they know their jobs, but maintaining control over them so that the supervisor achieves the desired results.

(k)   Avoiding the display of authority and the use of continuous and unnecessary pressure when supervising employees, including not passing on the pressure the foreman may be under in emergencies to employees.

(l)   Avoiding the adoption of a "know-it-all" attitude; being especially careful when handling older and experienced employees to take steps which make use of their years of know-how.

(m)   Avoiding the display of authority and unnecessary stress on the status differences between line supervision and employees; winning the respect of employees by being competent, playing fair, and taking an interest in their problems and how these govern their job performance.

(n)   Listening to employees when they discuss job difficulties or new job situations; asking employees for their ideas as to how the job might be done and using their ideas insofar as possible.

(o)   Not passing the buck when the supervisor makes a mistake; being aware that employees generally know when the fault is not theirs.

(p)   Giving credit where due; when criticism of an employee is required, doing this in private.

(q)   Avoiding personal prejudices in dealing with people and situations.

(r)   Making job assignments, wherever possible, in accordance with some scheme of advancement and avoiding favoritism in making these assignments.

(s)   Supervising employees in such a manner that they will look upon the supervisor as enthusiastic and resourceful.

(t)   Developing a reputation for liking one's work as a foreman and knowing how to handle problems.

(u)   Following plant rules personally and enforcing plant rules.

2. Establishing an effective working relationship with fellow foremen.

(a)   Providing technical and nontechnical information upon request.

(b)   Interpreting, where required, plant or organizational policies and practices to associates, particularly newly appointed foremen.

(c)   Treating fellow supervisors equitably; that is, not providing assistance for some supervisors and then refusing the same assistance to others.

(d)   Providing acceptable parts, components, assemblies, products, or materials to other departments so as to avoid additional or unnecessary work on the part of receiving-department personnel.

(e) Handling work or other requests within reasonable time limits.

(f) Discussing plant problems concerning other line supervisors directly with the supervisor involved insofar as possible, rather than with his superiors (to the extent that such a practice does not violate established organizational relationships).

(g) Following the chain of command when dealing with other foremen.

(h) Understanding that other line supervisors in the department may manage their operations differently; developing an acquaintanceship with their methods of handling their employees and production operations so that coordination of departmental activities can be accomplished.

(i) Knowing the principal problems people face in other areas of the plant and doing what can be done to minimize rather than contribute to those problems.

(j) Lining up work at the end of the shift for the incoming work group; preparing written communications advising the incoming line supervisor of any production or maintenance problem that he may encounter; making certain the work area is clean and orderly for the next shift.

3. Establishing an effective working relationship with organizational superiors.

(a) Implementing effectively and promptly policy statements received from organizational superiors; making suggestions as to how they can be most effectively implemented.

(b) Following the established supervisory channels when requesting information or services.

(c) Handling directions or orders quickly and efficiently.

(d) Discussing problems in which difficulty is anticipated with higher management before taking action.

(e) Reporting to management on actions taken, if required.

(f) Reporting to management concerning existing problems that the supervisor does not have the authority to handle.

(g) Keeping management informed of problems in the foreman's area and the steps taken to correct them. (This involves not overcommunicating by providing details on problems the line supervisor is expected to handle, but, on the other hand, not undercommunicating. A decision as to what should be communicated depends upon the development and exercise of sound judgment, and this skill can only be learned by experience—and by occasionally making bad decisions and learning from them.)

(h) Participating in the suggestion plan.

(i) Handling position responsibilities in accordance with corporate, division, and plant policies.

4. Establishing an effective relationship with plant staff service department representatives.

    (a) Understanding the principal functions of the plant staff; giving counsel and technical assistance in the areas of their specialized knowledge and experience, and operating planning and control systems.

    (b) Understanding that the staff may be authorized in certain areas to act for and in the name of line management, that is, that there is staff as well as line authority.

    (c) Following organizational channels when dealing with plant staff service department representatives.

    (d) Sharing the responsibility with staff service department representatives for the improvement of organizational relationships.

    (e) Consulting staff service department representatives on problems relating to their area of special interest; contacting them before the problem becomes serious.

    (f) Cooperating with staff service department representatives when working out production problems or other work-area problems.

    (g) Knowing that staff services may not be provided automatically and that plant staff service personnel should be contacted for needed services and advice.

    (h) Providing effective communication with employees and with organizational superiors when staff service representatives assist in solving problems relative to departmental activities.

5. Establishing an effective relationship with the general public.

    (a) Acquainting friends and others (when asked) with corporate activities (which are not confidential) that provide a favorable view of the corporate employer.

    (b) Speaking well of the corporation or employing organization and recommending its products or services.

    (c) Acquainting others with the corporation's interest in civic and governmental affairs and in being a good corporate citizen.

    (d) Acquainting others with the corporation's research facilities and programs (which are not confidential); providing information concerning the corporation's interest in quality.

    (e) Actively participating in and supporting civic and community activities.

6. Keeping himself up to date on at least job-related skills and knowledge.

(a) Taking the initiative for self-development through reading, attending meetings, asking questions and conversing with others.
(b) Cooperating in organizational efforts made to prevent manpower obsolescence.

Obviously, there is nothing about this list that makes it any more credible in making a normative prescription about supervisory style than a simplistic statement about democratic and participative management. The interpersonal skills identified can be practiced by foremen who motivate themselves and by others to fulfill organizational goals while also meeting their own interests. Massive research remains to be done in organizational behavior to determine if this formulation is valid, reliable, and practicable.

There is also obviously little that distinguishes this list from innumerable laundry lists of desirable supervisory behavior that have existed in the personnel literature for decades. Yet it does have value in pointing to the fuller dimensions of the supervisory job.

A PROGRAM OF REVITALIZATION

In this section of the chapter we examine a set of interrelated actions which manpower specialists should consider in resolving some of the problems and predicaments of the foreman which we have been reviewing. The actions can be grouped into three broad areas: (1) locating and interesting candidates for the position of foreman; (2) according prestige and recognition to line supervisors; and (3) retaining and promoting competent foremen into the ranks of higher production supervision.[65]

Locating Foreman Candidates

In general, the principal source of candidates for line supervisory positions in American industry has been and remains the hourly work force of the particular company. In general, also, employees selected for the foreman position are probably among the "better" (defined variously as highest producing, best behaved, most effective in social skills, etc.) hourly employees in the organization, many having probably been versatile utility workers who by relieving others learned a variety of jobs and thereby increased their worth as employees. Similarly, it is likely that the general foremen were selected from the best foremen; and presumably the higher levels of production supervisors were, in turn, selected from the better employees in the lower levels (although there probably has been a great

---

[65] Some of these ideas in less developed form also appear in Thomas H. Patten, Jr., "Revitalizing the Role of the Foreman," *Management of Personnel Quarterly,* Vol. 5, No. 2, Summer 1966, pp. 34–43.

deal of chicanery and sponsorship where rational selection procedures were not in operation).[66]

In many organizations, employees who have completed a skilled-trades apprenticeship have been preferred as supervisors and therefore selected as foremen because they possessed not only work experience but also vocational or technical training which was thought helpful for carrying out the responsibilities of a foreman. Often the most technically competent man was by virtue of this skill considered the best foreman candidate, although many times such persons were later found to be unable to supervise others. Over the years, organizations which promoted from within to secure foremen and members of higher-level production management found that their supply of qualified candidates was gradually depleted. This was caused by continuing selection from a rather constant pool in companies where additions were worked over and screened several times for selection.

The repeated selection from a constant pool created a shortage of above-average talent, with serious consequences. Because the hourly work force could no longer be regarded as a sufficiently large pool for supervisory talent in the future, companies started to look outside their organizations for candidates. In the process, they sought criteria for locating and interesting persons in applying for the position.

Criteria for Choosing Among Interested Candidates

In considering hourly employees who apply for foreman positions, a company has certain information contained in its records regarding each candidate which it always lacks when it must choose among applicants from the local labor market. For example, it can review the employee's work history, labor relations record, and various supervisors' opinions as to the employee's potential for work as a foreman. When considering walk-in and write-in candidates for foreman positions, it is more difficult to obtain meaningful information for making a selection decision, usually because reference and employment checks often yield innocuous information in a firm or industry related to the one in which he is applying for employment. The following criteria, based upon some impressions and the limited data available, are suggested as being possibly useful in choosing foreman can-

---

[66] Sponsorship is a somewhat ignored topic in the literature of management, but references to it occur in sociology. See Orvis Collins, "Ethic Behavior in Industry: Sponsorship and Rejection in a New England Factory," *American Journal of Sociology,* Vol. 5, No. 7, 1946, pp. 293–298; and Melville Dalton, "Informal Factors in Career Achievement," *American Journal of Sociology,* Vol. 56, No. 5, March 1951, pp. 407–415. One of the most sophisticated discussions of the subject can, however, be found in Norman H. Martin and Anselm L. Strauss, "Patterns of Mobility Within Industrial Organizations," *Journal of Business,* Vol. 29, No. 2, April 1956, pp. 101–110.

didates, particularly those who walk-in or write-in and have some college or a college degree, assuming we are thinking about a firm which wants to gradually upgrade the educational calibre of its line supervisory work force.

Educational background. Probably a technical background would be desirable, although an engineering degree would not be required. Persons who switched from an engineering to a business curriculum would be acceptable. Programs in production supervision or related fields would be desirable.

Academic grade-point average. In general, any passing grade-point average would be acceptable. It is likely that the students (especially graduate students) with the highest grade-point averages would have a multitude of employment opportunities and would not be likely to consider production supervision, except as a last resort or because of a special interest.

Personal characteristics. Age: Applicants who are older than the average college graduate, that is, between the ages of 25 and 30, would be preferable. The most important factors are apparent maturity and emotional stability.

Appearance: Individuals who by their stature and bearing suggest they can secure results from others without appearing to be "bulls-of-the-woods" may be most desirable. They should be more than 5'10" and 170 pounds.

Marital status: Married students with family obligations are preferred because they may give production supervision a longer trial than would a person with greater mobility. Residence at the time of employment of the application should be within a 200-mile radius of the employing location because such persons may have a geographical commitment to the area, which could further strengthen the likelihood of their giving foremanship a substantial trial.

Initiative: There should be some evidence of motivation toward hard work and a willingness to accept responsibility. Applicants who were employed during their college years in part-time or full-time work would be given special attention.

Family background: Candidates who have been exposed to production operations through the experience of their fathers, relatives, or close friends would be desired. Individuals from those segments of society in which there has been no close connection with production operations may be less desirable.

Experience. Special attention should be given to applicants who have worked as machine operators or assemblers or as general factory employees at some point in their lives.

Extracurricular activities. Candidates who were active in outside activities and held positions in campus organizations should be preferred on the theory that they may have developed rudimentary social skills and the ability to lead through interpersonal influence.

These criteria have not been tested by experience, nor should they be regarded as amounting to stereotypes. They provide a first approximation based upon the grounds that college-educated candidates who have these attributes will probably be preferable to individuals with entirely different backgrounds and orientations. Perhaps the ideal foreman in mass production would be someone who has the practical supervisory experience combined with a technical college education, but we really do not know. It is not being suggested that foreman candidates should be academic failures or solely students with low grades. It is possible, however, that the average or below-average student may make a better adjustment to work as a foreman because his opportunities for employment in other capacities by large companies are normally poorer than those of other students.

Only research can verify whether the proposed criteria are meaningful. And certain demographic processes may even rule out the need to consider them. Undergraduate enrollments skyrocketed between 1960 and 1970. This means that there will be many college graduates available in the labor market during 1970 through 1980, many of whom may be willing to work for relatively less than current graduates require. Also, they may be eager for any kind of industrial employment, including positions as production supervisors. The situation would be somewhat similar to the 1930s when there was a surplus of engineers willing to work for available wages. The educational upgrading process currently in operation in American society may serve to cheapen the value of a college degree so that in the next decade college graduate status may have as much significance as high-school graduate status has today and the expectations of the college graduate will be scaled down accordingly.

Applying Manpower Policies

Let us now return to some thoughts on new manpower policies which may have value in taking another look at the firm's existing work force and some supplementary ideas on college recruiting and training programs to secure foremen.

It was previously mentioned that persons who have completed an apprenticeship not only possess a desirable background but also have a work experience and a work orientation that should help them adapt themselves successfully to the foreman position. In a manufacturing company the desirability of having skilled-trades specialists in positions requiring knowledge of a mechanical nature as well as of supervision seems particularly logical. However, in the past, many journeymen have not been attracted to production foreman positions because their compensation would suffer. Others, of course, probably ruled themselves out as temperamentally unsuited to supervision.

It may be desirable for organizations to require as a matter of policy that a skilled-trades employee have experience as a production foreman before he can become a skilled-trades foreman. Companies could initiate inventories of their own skilled-trades work force so that they would have an adequate idea of the corpus out of which they can draw production foremen. Then a specific approach could be devised for interviewing and explaining the advantages of production supervision to skilled-trades employees, and the position could be used as a building block in the career development of manufacturing executives. The participant would gain by obtaining the experience of supervision, and the organization would derive the benefit of having technically competent craftsmen as production supervisors for portions of their careers.

In addition to the encouragement of skilled-trades personnel, a firm should as a matter of policy continue to encourage other hourly employees to apply for positions as foremen. Even though the pool of candidates may be drying up or well picked over, it is important that hourly employees know that this avenue of mobility is available to them and that equal opportunity to express interest in and apply for supervisory jobs is a manpower policy carried out in practice.

It is essential that a firm have a specific selection policy and workable procedures for not only screening but also training new foremen. Psychological tests validated upon company populations should be used in selection wherever possible. A curriculum of supervisory development conferences built upon specific training needs, supplemented by orientation and on-the-job experiences, should be devised. It may also be desirable to recruit and train qualified production foremen candidates in advance of actual needs, although such preforemanship training may have a negative effect on the man if there is a long time interval between completion of training and assumption of the foreman position.[67] Preparatory to establishing a preforemanship program, special arrangements on budget and head-count relief should be worked out so that manpower from the hourly

---

[67] Crosby S. Grindle, "Pre-Supervisory Training—Yes or No?," *Training Directors Journal,* Vol. 19, No. 1, January 1963, pp. 12–13; and Dorothy Pertuiset, "Pre-Supervisory Training—Yes or No?," *Personnel Journal,* Vol. 43, No. 11, December 1964, pp. 617–621.

ranks can be trained and retained on the roles to fill future vacanies when they occur.

Lastly, there are several actions that can be taken to attract and encourage inexperienced college graduates to work in production. It may be desirable to establish an accelerated advanced "racetrack" type of program for a small number of unusually well-qualified college graduates who would be recruited for placement as production foremen (using perhaps the selection criteria previously described). These individuals would be given a special opportunity to move up the production supervisory ranks in a relatively short period of time, such as three years. The opportunity for rapid movement and increased responsibility at an early age should induce some of these individuals to make an adjustment to the difficulties of line supervisory work and seriously consider spending a major portion of their industrial careers in production. To achieve this objective, an organization must carry out careful manpower planning and be prepared to honor promotional commitments to successful candidates in the time period indicated.

Another source of college-trained personnel is utilization of college cooperative trainees, as previously indicated in the chapter. Some persons may doubt that young men between the ages of 19 and 21 can succeed as foremen, but there is evidence that co-ops have been successful in this difficult role in a number of companies. Several colleges have developed production-supervision curricula and have enrolled students who profess a strong interest in production. Some of these co-ops who work in industry have been able to obtain the sympathetic attention of experienced foremen, who tend to adopt a fatherly attitude and look upon them as ambitious "sons" who are making their way in the world by alternating college attendance and work-experience periods. On the other hand, some of these same foremen often openly oppose assisting college graduate trainees because they perceive them not so much as "sons" but as permanent, on-the-scene, competitive threats to their own jobs. Also, foremen may resent the movement of college graduates into soft, relatively well-paying staff service department jobs early in their careers simply because they possess a degree. They take out their resentment at being buffeted by the control systems run by the college "punks" by displacing their hostility on college trainees recruited to be foremen. In many respects all the possible bases for interpersonal clashes among different age and educational groups are inchoate in these situations and are well known to readers with factory experience.

Still another source of college graduates is the planned employment of college students during summer vacations. Most large companies hire college students as "walk-ins" for hourly jobs during summer vacations. It would be preferable for a firm to hire a number of carefully screened college students for summer employment for the purpose of acquainting them with line supervisory work and interesting at least some of them in becoming production supervisors after graduation. It is possible that there are college students who because of their lack of knowledge of production have ruled out working in this area after they receive their degrees.[68] Those who obtain experience in production during the summer months may find the area to their liking, particularly if they are properly indoctrinated to the job and firm and are shown that it can lead up the line on a career basis because of the alleged scarcity of college-educated manufacturing executives in may firms. Adequate indoctrination can be carried out if students who are selected are inducted into employment through the salaried personnel employment office as well as through hourly employment and treated as potential salaried employees after graduation. Steps could be taken to counsel the students on career opportunities in the organization after graduation, and occasional meetings should be held after working hours during the summer with higher levels of production management in which the problems and dynamics of manufacturing are discussed with them. Although the students would be placed in hourly jobs for the duration of the summer, it would be recognized that the company has a special interest in them; and strong follow-up with them regarding placement possibilities as line supervisors after college graduation would be initiated. For example, the company college recruiters should look up these students while they made their regular campus rounds during the academic year and thereby express the firm's interest in their educational progress and possible future employment.

In general, most companies would prefer to recruit from the immediate geographical area in which the plants are located. This policy has the advantage of minimizing recruitment expense as well as attracting persons who may have a geographical preference for the area in which they reside and in which the plant is located. Although there is wisdom in this policy, experience has shown that in recruiting candidates for vacancies as foremen, such as through newspaper advertisements, individuals with especially strong backgrounds in production supervision residing in locations remote from a firm also express interest in considering employment in a new geographical area. Often companies do not invite these candidates to their locations for interviews because it has been felt that payment of travel and moving expenses for candidates for employment at the foreman level is

[68] Paul Donnelly, "College Students as Vacation Replacements," *Personnel Journal,* Vol. 43, No. 3, March 1964, pp. 147–148; and Henry L. Tosi and Robert Starr, "Does a Summer Intern Program Result in Better Selection?", *Personnel Administration,* Vol. 30, No. 2, March-April 1967, pp. 44–48.

difficult to justify. In a relatively tight labor market, this point of view is shortsighted. But, regardless of the labor market, if a company is serious about locating and interesting well-qualified candidates for the foreman position, it is important that a flexible policy for payment of travel and moving expenses be established. In a decentralized company with profit centers, such a policy can be devised by dividing the expense for travel and moving between the division and the plant (or corporate headquarters and the plant) so that it is economically attractive to the plant to hire the best foreman candidates available regardless of their location.

All the actions indicated above, when fitted together as part of a concerted effort to locate and interest candidates for the foreman position, should have value in improving the input to the supervisory work force. These actions would all be pointed to the resolution of one cluster of problems but would not comprise the total solution. Let us next turn our attention to actions required to accord status and recognition to members of the existing supervisory work force, a second major cluster of problems.

According Status and Recognition to Line Supervisors

One of the real burrs in this thicket of problems is that of convincing line supervisors that they are members of management. In all likelihood, in most firms the vast majority of foremen and general foremen started employment on the hourly roll and moved into salaried status only after considerable hourly service. As a result of this background and their being subjected to a wide range of control systems operated by plant staff service personnel, many line supervisors feel themselves continually harassed, quite vulnerable to reports of less-than-perfect performance, and extremely unsure of their continuing ability to remain in a managerial status. Many of the studies mentioned in this chapter have concluded that line supervisors perceive themselves as already in the marginal position of being neither workers nor managers of their work areas, and any additional doubts caused by management's lack of concern simply compound their frustration. In consequence, they cannot identify with either the hourly employees they supervise or with management; and they thereby comprise an insecure marginal status group.

Supervisory training conferences can be of some value in helping line supervisors identify with management, but they cannot be relied upon as a final solution because, as is well known, much of the success of the transfer value of training depends upon the total managerial and organizational environment set and controlled by higher levels of management.[69] If management provides meaningful training sessions and communicates its

[69] Harris and Fleishman, "Human Relations Training and the Stability of Leadership Patterns," *op. cit.*

policies and plans to line supervision in advance of their public announcement, a basis may be laid for the start of fostering identification. If these sessions are offered during working hours, many line supervisors will resent leaving their work to attend them unless there is definite value in their being present. Much depends upon the quality of the materials, the competency of the conference leader, and the extent to which the training has demonstrable value.[70] The scope and content of this training should, in our judgment, coincide with the description of the production foreman's job presented earlier in the chapter. Beyond that type of training would be efforts to improve, as needed, the reading, writing, and speaking skills of foremen.

There is a wide range of actions that should be taken to assist the foreman in identifying with management. Higher levels of supervision should not bypass him in dealings with hourly employees. Management should communicate more thoroughly with the foreman so that instances do not arise, for example, whereby the union committeeman learns of the results of a grievance settlement before the foreman and communicates the findings to the affected hourly employee before the foreman knows of the outcome.

The plant newspaper can also be used to focus attention on the contribution of line supervisors. Efforts should be made in it to single out the accomplishments of individual foremen by news and feature stories and by securing personal recognition from higher levels of management in instances where line supervisors have performed unusually well. But such recognition in itself can achieve little unless it is accompanied by a host of other actions.

In addition to overt attempts made to convince line supervisors that they are members of management, it is important to clarify the activities of foremen and plant staff service departments, as we suggested earlier in this chapter. A common complaint of many foremen is that they do not know what their responsibilities are, particularly in regard to the hiring and disciplining of hourly employees and the levels of authority they have been assigned to carry out these responsibilities.[71] This dilemma causes them to have serious interpersonal clashes with plant-level staff service specialists. These specialists in operating their competing control systems tend to compound the problem by burdening the foremen with paper work. In

[70] Many of the elements which should be built into training programs, including supervisory programs, have been well stated in a recent sophisticated presentation on industrial training: David King, *Training Within the Organization,* Educational Methods, Chicago, 1964.

[71] See Amitai Etzioni, "Human Relations and the Foreman," *Pacific Sociological Review,* Vol. 1, No. 1, Spring 1948, pp. 33–38.

general, line supervisors are, of course, more oriented toward direct action than they are toward preparing reports and similar duties involving written communications. They have a natural aversion to the verbal, whereas this is the forte of the staff specialist. Not surprisingly, they collide. In principle, paper work should be reduced to the absolute minimum for the foreman.

Span of Control and Organizational Relationships

Another problem which confronts the line supervisor and can be re-solved by management action is lengthy span of control. The span of control of the foreman should give cognizance to not only the number of hourly employees reporting to him but also to the special area in the plant covered, the kinds of operations supervised, and the complexity of the machinery, if any, being operated under his direction. It would be a simple matter to analyze the ratios of foremen to hourly employees and to make adjustments so that it would become possible to minimize the physical and mental strain on foremen who have too many subordinates, too much area to cover, or to many machine operations to be supervised properly. It is dangerous to establish these ratios by apparently reasonable rules-of-thumb as devised by masterminds in the staff who are divorced from the realistic dimensions of the problem and see it only in terms of numbers.[72] It is preferable that ratios, if used, be determined by analyzing specific plant situations and tailor making plans based upon the examination of the current shop situation. Such an analysis need not increase the number of foremen in a plant but can indicate areas in which there should be a more equitable distribution of the work load. There may, nevertheless, be situa-tions where foremen should be added. Or perhaps in some instances fore-men can be eliminated if an organization decides to make the foreman the manager of his area—a true manager.

In recent years, there has been considerable attention given to the spe-cific contribution and role of the general foreman. There again manage-ment can take action to resolve an obvious problem. Odiorne suggests that the main duty of the general foreman today should be to train foremen. In essence, the general foreman's job is to "check and correct" the work of subordinate foremen. Depending upon a specific statement as to the activi-ties involved in "checking and correcting," it may be that Odiorne is suggesting that the general foreman has as his responsibility managing foremen, that is, he should be a manager rather than a roving trouble-shooter or "utility" foreman, which is apparently his present role in many organizations. In any event, the specific functions of the general foreman today are not entirely clear, and it appears that there may be some indus-

---

[72] For a pertinent discussion see Robert M. Guion, "The Employee Load of First Line Supervisors," *Personnel Psychology*, Vol. 6, No. 2, Summer 1953, pp. 223–244.

trial situations where the organization's objectives and the effectiveness of the foreman could be mutually achieved by eliminating the general fore- man position. There would be some apparent economies in doing this, although there may be dangerous circumstances generated if the organiza- tional superior of the foreman has, as a result, a span of control which is too long. But there is some evidence from studies made at Sears, Roebuck —obviously a retailing rather than a production organization—which sug- gests that fairly long spans of control improve morale and efficiency.[73] It would be worthwhile for organizations to consider eliminating the general foreman position on an experimental basis in some activities and to take "before" and "after" measures to determine the resulting economies and efficiencies. Experimentation should provide some insight into a tolerable span of control. If it is found that the main role of a general foreman is a relief or utility foreman and that this is a necessary function, the firm which experiments will obtain verification of this fact and can take the action desired to reconstruct the line supervisory work force.

Status Protection and Perquisites

Consistent with the thought of according differential status and recogni- tion by position level is the concomitant thought of giving special privileges to those who deserve them simply by virtue of that status. In other words, if line supervisors are members of management, they should be treated as members of management and given all the perquisites which that status implies. Thus, in an organization, line supervisors should be given choice parking spots and desirable eating areas in the plant. They should either be assigned a certain part of the cafeteria or provided with a separate dining room. Depending upon the circumstances, barber shop and shirt laundry facilities could be made available to foremen. Even though paper work should be kept to a minimum, foremen will continue to have many reports to complete, and they should be given office facilities, including a desk in a reasonably quiet location, and whatever clerical assistance would help them to reduce the time required for filling out reports. The typical "stand-up" desk given foremen may be a space-saver on the shop floor, but it hardly provides the conveniences needed for concentration and accuracy in completing reports or for offering occasional relaxation from the com- motion of production.

Another important contribution to according status and recognition to foremen would be giving them "permanent" salaried employee status. In

[73] William F. Whyte, "Small Group and Large Organizations," in John H. Rohrer and Muzafer Sherif, eds., *Social Psychology at the Crossroads,* Harper, New York, 1951, pp. 141–419; and James C. Worthy, "Organizational Structure and Employee Morale," *American Sociological Review,* Vol. 15, No. 2, April 1950, pp. 169–179.

many firms one of the most serious barriers to attracting and retaining foremen is the considerable movement of foremen between the salaried and hourly personnel rolls. If an individual has moved between these rolls several times, it can safely be assumed that he eventually will lose interest in becoming a foreman and has good reason to believe management is not sincere when it asserts the foreman is a member of management. He is treated like a hired hand, dispensed with when not needed. It also becomes exceedingly difficult for such a person to identify permanently with management. Similarly, other hourly personnel who might be attracted to the foreman position decline to apply for it because of this movement and the instability of supervisory tenure.

There is already some evidence that union stewards in a few firms have shown greater leadership ability than foremen.[74] There may be many instances where stewards are better trained than foremen.[75] If the lower echelons of the management hierarchy are thus made unattractive, talented, aggressive individuals may seek mobility through the union hierarchy. This mobility should be encouraged, too; but where shortages of management talent exist, companies would do well to assure that their best employees are enabled to move, if they wish, into lower management. Even more desirable would be the career planning of positions so that the path to middle and higher management is integrated with movement into lower production management.

It is vital, therefore, that action be taken to protect the status of foremen who have performed satisfactorily in the position for a given time period—for example, 24 months. We propose that all foremen who have satisfactorily carried out the responsibilities of the position for a two-year period be maintained in salaried status regardless of fluctuations in the hourly work force. If careful manpower planning is carried out, it should be possible to assure foremen that they will at least have their status protected to the same extent that all other salaried employees have this assurance. Obviously, the line supervisor should not be granted much more than other salaried employees, but why should he be given less and accept treatment as a second-class citizen? In periods when they are not supervising hourly employees because of a reduction in force, the affected foremen could be given special assignments in the plant staff service departments or elsewhere, pending their reassignment as foremen. It is possible that many foremen placed on these special assignments may ultimately remain in plant staff service activities once their talents become known or

---

[74] Harold F. Rothe, "Who's the Better Leader—the Foreman or Union Steward?," *Factory Management and Maintenance,* Vol. 108, No. 8, August 1950, pp. 240 ff.

[75] Harold R. Nissley, "Supervisory Training: Ten Years Behind or Ten Years Ahead?," *Personnel,* Vol. 28, No. 6, May 1952, pp. 491–495.

as they develop additional skills. Importantly, they would not revert to the hourly rolls and be gradually demoralized in the game of manpower ping-pong that prevails in many mass-production firms.

Every firm should, through salary surveys or other means, assure that its foremen are paid competitively. In addition, differentiation should be made in the salary grade levels of foremen based upon the complexity of the work for which they are held accountable and the other considerations enumerated above that make foremen's jobs inherently unequal. Unequal pay for unequal work in proportion to the inequality is a useful principle throughout the organization, and there is no reason why it cannot be applied to foremen.[76] This differentiation will require the application of job evaluation, probably using one of the available systems and the multiple judgment of plant managerial personnel in ranking the relative difficulty of different production foreman positions. They may also be good reason to allocate merit increase funds specifically for line supervisors to reward strong performers (assuming the organization is sufficiently large to employ a good number) and to administer their salaries as a separate cluster in the structure in order to assure that foremen are equitably treated in compensation vis-à-vis plant staff service specialists.

Another task which pace-setting managements now ask foremen to undertake in the effort as. firms implement federal manpower programs designed to place, train, and upgrade poorly educated and poorly skilled minority group members is implementing the policy of including workers hitherto screened out of jobs. Foremen will be supervising and guiding the integration of these individuals. Perhaps this added task should be evaluated as a compensable pay factor to determine if it causes foremen to be deserving of extra compensation. Supervisors will need to have some understanding of the dynamics of social processes and the environmental forces at work which affect the excluded.[77] The difficulties inherent in this task are reminiscent of a similar one in World War II when foremen made the extra effort needed to develop older workers, women, minority group members, and other people out of the mainstream and previously excluded from jobs. Foremen today could legitimately ask themselves why they remain excluded in practice from management and from coverage under the prevailing labor relations legislation in the light of what they are being asked to do to implement national manpower policy. Yet, they probably will accept their status and dependably turn to their jobs as they have in the past. Undoubtedly a case could probably be made that their jobs should be evaluated in higher pay grades because of their responsibility for carrying out the company's poverty-war responsibilities.

[76] Beal and Wickersham, op. cit., p. 45.

[77] Daniel H. Kruger, "Job Economics in the Responsible Society," Employment Service Review, Vol. 4, No. 7, July 1967, p. 27.

One last action which should be helpful is to streamline the position title of line supervisors. In order to break with the past, consideration should be given to changing the position title of the foreman and general foreman to something which more accurately reflects the work of a foreman as the manager of his area. It is suggested that the foreman be called "production supervisor" and general foreman be called "department manager." These position titles are equivalent to those used in many staff activities in many large organizations, and the carry-over into the line may give new prestige to the foreman and general foreman. We cannot be naive and assume that the changing of a title is, in itself, going to have great impact, but coupled with the other proposals for according status and recognition, changing the position title may be the capstone for all the remainder: it would signify that management was serious about changing the foreman's status in every respect from the greatest to the least important.

Retaining and Promoting Line Supervisors

There is ample evidence that many individuals regard the production foreman and general foreman positions as "dead-end" positions and refuse to apply for them.[78] The difficult environment in which the work of production supervision is carried out, the hypothesized disesteem in which supervisors are apparently held in many organizations, the unsteadiness of the position because of periodic cutbacks and reversion to hourly status, and the inadequate prestige in relation to that of plant staff service department specialists all combine to discourage individuals from becoming line supervisors. Therefore, the retention and promotion of above-average talent in the line supervisory work force depends not only on the caliber of the person initially selected for these positions but also on according some recognition and status to the person who becomes a foreman so that he wishes to remain a line supervisor. All of these actions are closely interrelated. The following are proposed as specific means which may assist the manpower specialist in retaining and promoting line supervisors who have been attracted to the field of production and feel they are securing some recognition.

To begin with, much obviously can be done to assist in the development of line supervisors by making certain that the initial manpower input to the supervisory work force has potential. Talented output cannot be developed out of mediocre input. Inasmuch as we have already elaborated upon this point in this chapter, it need only be mentioned here.

The development of human potential can, however, be fostered by the kinds of actions taken by general foremen and superintendents in carrying

[78] See, for some evidence, Ely Chinoy, "The Tradition of Opportunity and the Aspirations of Automobile Workers," *American Journal of Sociology,* Vol. 57, No. 5, March 1952, p. 455.

out their work. To a large extent individuals in industry learn by on-the-job experience. The inherent learning resources of the job can be used to develop a subordinate by giving him work assignments that are progressively more difficult and more varied in order to use the job for development. The higher levels of line supervision must be instructed on how to develop subordinates by skillful use of assigned work. They can be provided with specific information on developmental techniques but, of course, whether they will act as developers of men will depend upon many factors. Some training should also be directed toward changing the attitudes of line supervisors who are not oriented toward developing subordinates. It is suggested that recognition and extra remuneration be given to those general foremen and superintendents who display ability in developing subordinates; this may encourage at least some to become "man-builders" as management spends its money consistent with stated intentions.

One of the unsolved problems in the development of the foreman is determining where he might move after several years of capable performance as a foreman. Earlier in the chapter, we noted some evidence which showed that years ago foremen were looked upon as the logical candidates for plant superintendent positions and could reasonably aspire to these positions. Obviously, if there are general foreman or superintendent positions available to him because the organization is sufficiently large to require three levels of line supervision, the foreman who desires movement can hope for eventual promotion to these positions (unless there is the stultifying policy of promoting college graduates only). If there are very few in-line positions to which he can aspire, the question becomes where else in the organization he would fit.

Ambiguity in the Status of the Foreman's Bosses

General foremen and superintendents are supervisors of supervisors. In order to qualify for these positions, the foreman would need to demonstrate the kinds of abilities, skills, and attitudes required for this work. Unfortunately, the position requirements of general foremen and superintendents have never been clearly identified and are considered a "mess." [79] In some organizations, as we indicated, the general foreman is used as a utility foreman filling in for absent, newly appointed, or weak-performing foremen. In these instances the main purpose in having general foremen is to develop or prop up foremen. On the other hand, sometimes the general

[79] Views on this topic diverge but are symptomatic of the unclarity that exists. See Clark C. Caskey, "Is There a Mess in Middle Management?," *Management of Personnel Quarterly*, Vol. 3, No. 3, Fall 1964, pp. 27–32, and Curtis J. Potter, "The Care and Feeding of Middle Managers," *Management of Personnel Quarterly*, Vol. 4, No. 1, Spring 1965, pp. 16–19.

foreman may have considerable responsibility, possibly approaching that of a plant manager if the general foreman is actually the highest-ranking supervisor at work in the plant as, for example, might be the case on the night shift in a large plant. Often the superintendent has considerable managerial responsibility (day-, afternoon-, or night-shift) and is rarely, if ever, conceived of as being a relief or utility general foreman. Superintendents customarily have significant responsibility in production, maintenance, or some other sphere of manufacturing operations.

In view of the unclarity surrounding the position requirements for being a general foreman or superintendent, it becomes difficult to indicate what it may take to help the foreman qualify for these positions. This is clearly a case where careful organizational planning must be carried out before manpower planning and career path planning can be implemented. As a potential supervisor of production supervisors should the foreman be given more or less orthodox management training in the POSDCORB functions: planning, organizing, staffing, directing, controlling, reporting, and budgeting? Possibly he should also be given training in human relations, creativity, problem analysis and decision making, and education in basic economics, cost control, and related topics, if he has not had these previously.

As a potential manager outside of production, we might want to consider these and/or alternative courses of action. There are ways of rounding the rough edges on diamonds. Possibly the foreman should be enrolled after working hours or even on a cooperative basis in a community college or technical institute or even a degree-granting college where he can acquire knowledge in depth in a business- or engineering-related field.[80] Clearly, experimentation along these and other lines is warranted and constitutes yet another new frontier in foreman development.

We lack answers as to the type of environment and conditions under which college graduates and other young people learn most effectively. A considerable amount of research is required in the area of learning before we can feel sure that we are on firm ground in specifying a detailed approach beyond the apprentice model concept we have expounded. Companies and universities could mutually benefit by exploratory research in this crucial area of adult learning methodology and theory.

Short intensive seminars sponsored by universities and occasionally the longer management education program of universities can be used in help-

---

[80] Possible programs along these lines could be patterned after some of those described in the literature. See Jess E. Burkett, "Unspecialized Men for Special Responsibilities in Business and Industry," *Training Directors Journal,* Vol. 17, No. 12, December 1963, pp. 40–46; and Thomas W. Gill, "Continuing Education at NOL," *Training Directors Journal,* Vol. 19, No. 2, February 1965, pp. 8–13.

ing line supervisors who have shown potential by work performance to realize their full capacity. It is highly desirable that any organization establish procedures whereby above-average talent can be given the opportunity to develop further, either through outside organizations, such as universities, the American Management Association, or similar institutions. An educational leave-of-absence policy of the proper type which allows employees to remedy educational deficiencies would also have value. In this way, able employees who are not college graduates can acquire additional education and compete better with college graduates for promotion to higher management positions.

However, the wise firm of the future with a commitment to the development of human resources will stress less the possession of a college degree than the competency of the man. In fact, there is accumulating evidence that it may be far preferable to assist experienced employees in production to become higher-level managers in production and manufacturing and related activities than college graduates who lack this commitment or have but a hazy conception of what they are getting into.

In any event, no organization should shut the door of opportunity to people with less than a college degree. To do so is to introduce an undesirable "meritocracy" into the work situation and to fail in optimum manpower utilization. A system based on meritocracy implies a type of competition in which individuals move ahead and are given further opportunities on the basis of their very early achievement, with position in later life increasingly and irreversibly determined by schooling in youth. The "late bloomer," the early rebel, the person from an educationally indifferent home—all of them, in a full-scale meritocracy become victims of a senseless irreversibility of decision.[81] There are signs that large-scale bureaucracies are becoming internal meritocracies as far as foremen and hourly employees are concerned. The accompanying blockages to mobility could become industrial social dynamite.

CONCLUSIONS

The ideas expressed in this chapter may appear to the reader to be an ambitious attempt to improve the status of production foremen in one fell swoop. We have encompassed a multitude of activities which undoubtedly would result in considerable expense for a firm. Many manufacturing organizations simply could not afford to take all of the elements of this program and translate them into action at one time because of the cost

[81] Jerome S. Bruner, *The Process of Education,* Vintage Books, New York, 1960, p. 77.

implications and the lack of certainty as to their effectiveness.[82] However, each of these elements is related to the other, and it is likely that all of them must be carried out sooner or later if the predicaments of the foreman are to be resolved. At the moment, firms are attempting to resolve the problems on a piecemeal basis and somewhat uncritically endorse the latest managerial nostrum. Of course, fads shift over the years. Money spent in this manner on fads is probably money wasted because it cannot have the effect of a well-financed concerted effort on many fronts simultaneously.

Although we lack all of the research bases we would like to have to be certain of the wisdom of the approach suggested, we believe that it would be highly worthwhile for a firm to start on a program emphasizing as many of these elements as possible. Any firm can decide with which elements it wishes to start by analyzing its present programs and then setting priorities as to those elements it lacks and believes it needs most. In many instances reported to date, the best that American management has been able to do is to improve the foreman's economic position without restoring his status.[83]

In lieu of action, management must face up to the fact that it really does not want the foreman to be member of management and that he is to remain simply, as in Britain, a "charge-hand" acting as a straw boss over the hired hands (of which he is one even though he may not be paid by the hour) or a human shock absorber between higher production supervision and the union of hourly employees. As we noted earlier, one well-known study has suggested that if the production process could be smoothly engineered and administered, there would be no need for the contemporary production foreman because he has value now only to the extent the process is fallible.[84] With better planning and more elaborate automation, a human problem-solving coordinator or "production assistant"[85] may not be necessary, and thus the foreman is tolerated tempo-

---

[82] IBM made many such changes in the early 1950s. See Drucker, op. cit., pp. 325–328. See also Wikstrom, "Can the Foreman Be a Manager?," op. cit., pp. 12–15; and his later detailed report, Managing at the Foreman Level (Studies in Personnel Policy, No. 205), National Industrial Conference Board, New York, 1967.

[83] Solomon Barkin, "A Trade Unionist Appraises Management Personnel Philosophy," Harvard Business Review, Vol. 38, No. 5, September-October 1960, pp. 59–64.

[84] Charles R. Walker, The Foreman on the Assembly Line, Harvard University Press, Cambridge, 1966, pp. 9–33, 129–149.

[85] Some companies have taken this approach by dividing the lowest level of the line supervisory work force into foremen (who function as true managers) and production assistants (who are troubleshooters directing their efforts at solving problems coincident with production stoppages and breakdowns). See for example: "Upgrading Foremen with an Ax," Business Week, No. 1641, February 11, 1961, pp. 110–112.

rarily, but looked upon as eventually expendable. This may in time prove to be the most realistic view of solving the manpower problems of the foreman; but, whatever the position taken by management, everything indicates some meaningful manpower policy should be formulated rather than leaving the line supervisor in the chaos he typically finds himself in many large organizations today. For those firms oriented toward a positive program, it is recommended that the actions described in this chapter be given serious consideration.

The industrial production foreman is a classical case of multiple responsibilities, limited authority, and high accountability—and very obvious visibility when he fails to meet the standards set for each responsibility. Management can act to clarify the formal organization to help him and should start to think broadly about job redesign and technological change as it has forced the diminution of the foreman's role. It should also take action to enhance the foreman's "image," that is, his status and his self-perception as a member of management by tackling some of the aforementioned problems. The behavioral scientist can help by retreating from dogmatism and considering the validity of varying supervisory styles appropriate to the factory technology. The democratic-participative style advocated in the management literature has become a pat answer that is clearly a simplistic solution to a complex problem. There is surely more to solving the foreman's problem than the suggestion he should get his subordinates to participate more democratically in problem solving and decision making and that he (the foreman) should, in turn, be brought into management on the same basis. His are problems that involve manpower planning of several types and basic organizational and personnel actions if foremen are to be properly developed.

CHAPTER 9

Executive Development Programs

In this chapter we examine the growth of executive development programs, their objectives, evaluations made of them, and their place in an industrial society. This endeavor will necessarily involve us in an exploration of mystique, technique, and critique. In many respects we will be chasing an elusive phantom whose capture would be most welcome by experts on manpower and organization.

The mystique of managing and management has led students of management to search for what makes managers successful. We still do not know the answer to that problem. In many respects we may not have advanced much beyond the crude insights of the Prussian military general staff.

It has been stated that the latter placed each officer in the Prussian armed forces into one of four categories. These categories were: brilliant-lazy, brilliant-ambitious, stupid-lazy, and stupid-ambitious. Then the officers were assigned as follows: The brilliant-lazy were assigned duty as field commanders, for they would make quick, accurate decisions based upon the detailed research and information presented by staff officers and subordinate line officers. The brilliant-ambitious were assigned duties as members of the commander's staff, for they would accurately and reliably gather the detailed information needed by him in order to make decisions. The stupid-lazy officers were assigned duties of a routine nature where they could be constantly supervised and were given little or no responsibility. The stupid-ambitious officers were eliminated from the service because their ambition coupled with their stupidity would get everyone into trouble.

Obviously, this example is somewhat facetious and oversimplified but the terms used are relative and refer to observed performance, personality, and general makeup of the individual rather than to academic grades or scores on tests. Much of what is done today in executive development, at least among naive organizations, seems to be on the same plane as the old simplistic grading approach allegedly used by the Prussian general staff.

In this chapter we approach the subject of executive development by first discussing the mystique from a more serious standpoint than we have to this point. Second, we examine the specific techniques used in executive development. This will involve us in examining systems and procedures as well as some of the model corporate schools and their evolution. Third, we turn our attention to a critique of executive development systems as well as the various management education programs conducted by colleges, universities, and other organizations. We examine certain model programs such as those of the University of California (Los Angeles) designed to prevent educational obsolescence among engineering managers, the program offered by the University of California (Berkeley) with its forward-looking curriculum which focuses upon current social issues, the Sloan Fellowship Program at the Massachusetts Institute of Technology, which culminates in a Master's Degree, and the Harvard Advanced Management Program.

We also give some attention to other new special programs that have been devised for developing executives, such as those designed to develop managerial manpower in government, to make experienced American executive talent available overseas through the Executive Service Corps, and to use business sabbaticals for development purposes.

Executive development has become of increasing interest in European countries in recent years. Before we conclude the chapter we pay some heed to these developments in Europe and their implications. Then we bring the chapter to a conclusion.

CONCEPTS OF EXECUTIVE DEVELOPMENT AND EXECUTIVE MANPOWER PLANNING

Executive development is a multifaceted concept that is not altogether clear because different organizations define the concept differently. For some the concept means simply appraising the performance and potential of managerial employees at a certain organizational level. For others executive development refers to projecting needs for supervisors, managers, and higher-level executives. To still others the concept refers to total replacement planning, including the organizational intake of college graduate trainees, college cooperative students, and new managerial employees as well as all types of in-service training, in-house management education, university-level in-residence and nonresidence programs, and the offerings of developmental programs by management associations and consultants. Sometimes compensation and organizational planning are regarded as integral parts of the executive development concept. If looked upon from this multifaceted point of view, executive development becomes rather amorphous and subsumes many specific plans and programs that can perhaps best be understood if looked at individually and then interrelated.

The basic ideas behind executive development, at least in its modern versions, seem to go back to the early thinking of such manpower tools as the "promotional chart," "the qualification chart," and "the personnel control chart." [1] These tools were developed by manpower specialists of an earlier era to introduce rational manpower planning in organizations so that the replacement process would be made visible and controllable. In the last 30 or 40 years it seems that the replacement of manpower has become the central concept in executive development from which all others stem.

For the purposes of this chapter, we shall not offer a definition of executive development but simply use the term to refer to the multitude of processes already discussed. We shall sharpen our terminology as we go along so that the concept is broken down into parts which can be discussed with some precision. In order to do this it is necessary to discuss, on the one hand, manpower projection techniques and, on the other, human resource development opportunities. It is helpful as a first step to discuss manpower planning and the development of human resources by considering executive employees at various organizational levels.

For most large manufacturing organizations today, manpower needs can be determined by projections made for college graduates, cooperative students, apprentices, and, to a lesser extent, executives, managers and staff supervisors. The latter three categories are not too numerous in smaller organizations, and executive manpower needs probably can be easily identified by inspecting an organizational chart in preparation for an annual management development review of whom would replace whom in case of death, retirement, quits, and the like.

For other categories, particularly foremen, we normally would project manpower needs and adjust to meet the particular instructional needs for development. Apprentice needs may be projected if the organization is large. Apprentices, if they are on a federally registered program, are taking a prescribed sequence of courses. Similarly, co-ops are enrolled in universities and follow a curriculum prescribed by the institution, which in theory is integrated with on-the-job experiences to combine in providing an optimum learning opportunity.

College graduates, staff supervisors, and managers typically do not have courses planned for them unless they enroll in a college course after work-

[1] Walter Dill Scott, *Personnel Management,* Second Edition, McGraw-Hill, New York, 1931, pp. 141–150, 162–163, and 282–294.

ing hours or attend an in-residence management education program. These kinds of employees typically learn through an apprenticeship of sorts in which the organizational superior controls most of the learning resources.

IMPORTANCE OF STAFF SUPERVISORS AS A BUILDING BLOCK

Executive development planning should begin at least with first-level staff supervisors, if not with planning for the development of nonsupervisory technical and professional employees. However, one of the most neglected subjects in manpower planning and sound human resource development is that of the first-level staff supervisor (in any functional field of business organization). We are told by Dale and others that the initial breakthrough of the college graduate into a supervisory position, based upon his recognized high level of performance and some minimum length of service, is probably the most important step in his career.[2] Here he distinguishes himself from his peers and for the first time is no longer a doer but a supervisor of the work of others. Many young people are unprepared for this change in their responsibilities and have difficulty in making the transition.

We know very little how firms project needs for first-level staff supervisors, how candidates are selected, and how new supervisors are trained. We perhaps know a great deal more about planning for, selecting, and developing foremen. The new staff supervisor remains a mystery. Because of the lack of information on this topic, our knowledge consists largely of impressions and ideas that should be viewed as hypothetical. Apparently people "slip" into these positions and their development ensues as they carry out work and are exposed to organizational processes.

What is meant by the term "staff" supervisor, and what kinds of persons occupy these positions? In order to answer these questions, it is important to consider first-level staff supervision in plants and decentralized sales offices, at the division level, and at the corporate staff level in large-scale business organizations. At each level we are likely to see entirely different types of persons from the standpoint of demographic characteristics.

In plants, staff supervisors are likely to be doing work which is so closely integrated with production that their contribution to the successful outcome of the production process is as indistinguishable in its importance as that of line supervision and the efforts of hourly rated employees. For this reason plant staff departments are often called "service departments." The staff supervisor in a plant is correspondingly called a supervisor in a plant staff service department. This work is vastly different in various respects

[2] Ernest Dale, *Management: Theory and Practice,* McGraw-Hill, New York, 1965, p. 57.

from supervisory work in the staff of a division or a corporate staff in a large-scale organization. Yet, some students of management would insist that there are universal aspects of supervisory or managerial work and the similarities outweigh the differences.

In any event, and although the process has never been thoroughly re-searched, individuals become staff supervisors. By virtue of the fact that they supervise the work of other people they are managers by definition and potentially high-level executives. When a person becomes a supervisor for the first time, it may be said that he has then developed to the point of becoming a manager and has experienced some aspects of the man-agement development process itself.

It seems that most management development programs are built on the assumption that the manager to be developed has already progressed to the point at which his further development depends upon either manage-ment education, a planned job rotation move, or some similar arrangement to assist in his growth. The gap between the time a person enters the em-ploy of an organization and is appointed a supervisor and subsequently viewed as a candidate for formal executive development activity highlights the gap in manpower planning for the development of managers. We shall say no more about this problem here but subsequently in the chapter turn back to some specific techniques which can be utilized for improving the executive manpower-planning process itself. An analysis of why there is such a gap brings us to consider the many unknowns in management skills and the development of managers.

THE MYSTIQUE OF MANAGEMENT

The importance of managerial skill and knowledge and the investment in human capital have become widely recognized as a necessary prerequisite to nonhuman capital investment.[3] The key role of managers in particular has recently come to the fore once again, which is a kind of contemporary perspective on modern entrepreneurship as it operates in an era of complex organizations. Thus, two manpower experts remind us that managerial resources, similar to capital, must be accumulated and effectively em-ployed or invested in productive activity. In important ways, the problem of the generation and accumulation of managerial resources is similar to that of capital formation. A nation's economic development may be limited by a relative shortage of this critical factor or may be accelerated signifi-

---

[3] This section of the chapter draws heavily upon the excellent survey of the litera-ture by Kenneth McLennan, *Managerial Skill and Knowledge*, Industrial Relations Research Institute, University of Wisconsin, Madison, 1967, pp. 1–18.

cantly by a high capacity to accumulate it.[4] Correspondingly, an organization's ability to attain its objectives and develop in planned ways is dependent upon its managerial resources.

The managerial shortage in the United States during World War II provided a dramatic example of the importance of managerial employees during an emergency situation. This experience pointed to the importance to the nation of information about managers and their jobs and led to the spate of books and articles from about 1945–60 on the perceived executive shortage and the need for executive development programs. The need for more and higher quality information about managers and their work, it has long been recognized, can be of assistance to the individual firm in allocating its own managerial resources so that the organization may achieve its goals. The problem of the duties to be performed by management and the skills necessary to perform them has been a subject of inquiry for management writers since the turn of the century and remains in hot controversy today. We still do not possess the information we ought to have if we are to understand more adequately some of the skills and knowledge necessary to perform various types of managerial jobs and how managers acquire their skill and knowledge. More specifically, we cannot answer the following fundamental questions thoroughly; therefore, we tend to drift widely in executive manpower planning and development.

Do the skill and knowledge requirements for managerial jobs vary with organization level, size of organization, the functional area of job, and other variables? If they do, what is the nature of these variations? Some writers believe there is a world of difference between executives (the top ten percent of managers in an organization) and lower managers and would reserve the term "executive" only for the former.

What are the patterns, if any, in the acquisition of skill and knowledge for managerial jobs? What methods of training do managers consider most useful? What methods have they used most frequently during their own careers? What is the nature of the most valuable training or developmental experience which various groups of managers have had during their careers? How important is the person's present organizational experience in acquiring job knowledge?

A useful backdrop against which to discuss the empirical research pertaining to these two questions can be provided by a brief review of some of the more theoretical management writings relating to the two major questions stated above, beginning with the question of the skill and knowledge requirements of managerial jobs.

[4] Frederick H. Harbison and Charles A. Myers, *Management in the Industrial World,* McGraw-Hill, New York, 1959, p. 19.

From the earliest management theorists to the writers of modern classical-traditional management textbooks, the emphasis has been more on the duties to be performed by managers than on the skills and knowledge required to perform them. Henri Fayol (1841–1925), the French pioneer theorist, classified the various activities of an industrial enterprise into six groups: technical, commercial, financial, security, accounting, and managerial. He then identified five main functions within managerial activities: planning, organization, command, coordination, and control.[5] Many modern writers of the classical-traditional schools have retained Fayol's list with only minor changes. For example, some five decades later Koontz and O'Donnell[6] described the functions of the manager's job as planning, organizing, staffing, directing, and controlling. Most of the functions seem to be simply another way of describing rational thought processes and are deductively derived.

It is apparent that these writers use the term "function" to mean the general activities which managers must perform in some concrete way to accomplish the overall goals of the organization. Most classical-traditional management theorists have generally held that the functions performed by the manager are the same regardless of his place in the organizational structure or the type of enterprise. Using this premise, management writers have then developed a series of prescriptive principles for each function. The resulting "principles" or rules-of-thumb then become very general in nature and are, in most cases, arrived at by deductive reasoning (though in some cases the deduction may be based on a few subjective observations).[7]

It is important to note that some classical-traditional management theorists make a distinction between managerial and nonmanagerial skills.[8] Functions are things that managers characteristically do or are responsible for while techniques (managerial skills) refer to the way these functions are carried out. Nonmanagerial skills are technical and professional skills usually exercised by staff specialists, such as lawyers, accountants, salesmen, and engineers. When a manager uses one of these skills directly, he is no longer acting purely as a manager. From this essentially deductive reasoning management writers then arrive at two conclusions which are of interest in the study of management jobs and thinking about executive development:

---

[5] Henri Fayol, *General and Industrial Administration,* Pitman, London, 1949, p. 3.

[6] Harold Koontz and Cyril O'Donnell, *Principles of Management,* Third Edition, McGraw-Hill, New York, 1964, pp. 39–40.

[7] See Thomas H. Patten, Jr., "Organization Processes and the Development of Managers: Some Hypotheses," *Human Organization,* Vol. 26, No. 4, Winter 1967, pp. 249–250.

[8] Koontz and O'Donnell, *op. cit.,* p. 45.

404   Executive Development Programs

1. Technical skills are not an important part of a manager's job, though at times a manager may be forced to use or fall back on technical skills in his job by performing technical tasks. Normally, he should do the managing rather than do the doing.

2. Managerial skills (to be used in performing the functions of planning, directing, organizing, and controlling) can usually be expressed in terms of qualities important to success in the managerial job. Qualities and personality traits frequently mentioned in management textbooks include intelligence, leadership ability, communication skills, cultural interests, moral virtues, good judgment, and initiative.[9]

The list varies from author to author and has contributed to the mystique of what it takes to manage and manage "effectively."

The classical-traditional management school of thought has undoubtedly made an important contribution toward an understanding of the process of management. But it has not been very successful in identifying the types of skills and knowledge required by the participants engaged in the process of managing. The influence of the school has nevertheless been great: it has initiated a large volume of literature on subjects such as "what is needed to be a successful manager" and has sparked off a great controversy with the behavioral scientists. Unfortunately, there is a great deal of variability in the quality of the traditional literature: much of it tends to be of an anecdotal nature.[10] This does not mean that this body of literature is of no value; on the contrary, many of the writers brightly illuminate the nature of managerial jobs. However, their lack of empiricism has brought severe criticism from modern researchers, such as the aforementioned behavioral scientists.[11]

Organizational Behavior Theorists

An early reaction to the classical-traditional management approach developed during the 1930s. This reaction was crystallized in the work of

[9] Roger Bellows et al., *Executive Skills,* Prentice-Hall, Englewood Cliffs, 1962, pp. 3–13. See also Koontz and O'Donnell, *Principles of Management,* McGraw-Hill, New York, 1959, p. 313; however, in their 1964 edition previously cited, Koontz and O'Donnell are less specific about the qualities necessary for successful management.

[10] For recent examples of the "anecdotal" type of writing see David D. Ewing, *The Managerial Mind,* The Free Press of Glencoe, New York, 1964; P. J. Brouwer, "The Power to See Ourselves," *Harvard Business Review,* Vol. 42, No. 6, November-December 1964, p. 156; Walter Guzzardi, Jr., *The Young Executives,* New American Library, New York, 1964; and Perrin Stryker, *The Character of the Executive,* Harper, New York, 1961. Both the Guzzardi and Stryker books originally were articles in *Fortune.*

[11] See for one of the strong opening salvos, James G. March and Herbert A. Simon, *Organizations,* Wiley, New York, 1959, p. 32. Since then the *Academy of Management Journal* has been peppered with pro and con articles on the best way to conceptualize management. No end to the controversy is in sight.

Elton Mayo and other writers of what used to be called the human relations in industry school in industrial sociology and is now called organizational behavior. Emphasis shifted from the formal approach of Taylorite scientific management and formal deductive management theory which had flourished since the writings of Fayol to greater concern for the informal aspects of management and inductive theorizing.

Initially, human relations theories were considered most useful in explaining the motivation of nonsupervisory employees, but gradually they became accepted for interpreting the behavior of persons at higher levels of the organization. As a result, ideas about the supervisory practices of managers above the first level of management were affected. Because of the lack of emphasis on the techniques of management found in the classical-traditional approach to management, human relations concepts were accommodated and introduced into modern management textbooks where management was frequently defined as getting work done through people. The main component of managerial jobs was now seen as the supervisory role and consequently the major skill requirement was skill in human relations, interpersonal relations, leadership, persuasion, and the like.[12]

Although the emphasis on this approach to the study of managerial jobs has diminished during the past decade, human relations skills are still considered an important part of all managerial jobs.[13] Sensitivity training is in current vogue and comprises a variation of some earlier ideas about group dynamics. However, it appears that the older form of training in human relations is still probably the most important single subject-matter area in short-term foreman management developing programs, whether conducted on an in-plant basis or as part of a university extension program, despite the fact that little evidence has been presented to show the real benefits to the business firms participating in such training programs.[14]

Another landmark reaction to the early classical-traditional managerial

[12] Thomas H. Patten, Jr., *The Foreman: Forgotten Man of Management,* American Management Association, New York, 1968, pp. 123–147.

[13] For a modern development of the human relations aspect of managerial jobs see Robert Tannenbaum et al., *Leadership and Organization,* McGraw-Hill, New York, 1961. For example on p. 79 he asserts: "(T)he successful leader is one who is keenly aware of those forces which are most relevant to his behavior at any time. He accurately understands himself, the individuals and group he is dealing with, and the broader social environment in which he operates.

"But this sensitivity or understanding is not enough. . . . The successful leader is the one who is able to behave appropriately in the light of these perceptions. If direction is in order, he is able to direct. If considerable participative freedom is called for, he is able to provide such freedom."

[14] For an example of a modified sensitivity program of the human relations type where an attempt is made to measure the cost savings to the organization, see Robert R. Blake et al., "Breakthrough in Organization Development," *Harvard Business Review,* Vol. 42, No. 6, November-December 1964, pp. 133–155.

writings, in addition to that of Elton Mayo's, was contained in Chester Barnard's book, *The Functions of the Executive.*[15] Barnard, an experienced telephone company executive, conceived the organization not simply as a group of persons, nor as a hierarchical structure of formal relationships, but as an action system in which both the formal structure and the individuals within the system were equally important. The action aspect stressed the importance of interpersonal cooperation and communication within the system. This notion of the organization was much different from the one held by the early classical-traditional writers who were concerned almost exclusively with deductive abstractions pertaining to the formal structure.

Barnard and Mayo proved to be the forerunners of a new wave of social researchers who, though varying in their disciplinary orientation, all emphasized the need for empirical data as a basis for generalizations concerning the problems of management. The impact of this trend also became evident in the study of management jobs, and several empirical studies provided greater substance to our understanding of the so-called functions of management.

Research Studies on Managing, Work Sampling, and Traits

Following the human relations approach to the study of managerial jobs, investigators at the University of Michigan conducted a number of empirical studies on how leadership practices related to productivity and morale. One of the results of these studies reported by Kahn and Katz [16] stressed the importance of supervision in relation to productivity. The authors identified several variables (closeness of supervision, the extent of employee-centered supervision, the supervisor's ability to play a differentiated role, and group cohesiveness) which were related to the productivity of an organizational group. A similar approach was taken in a group of studies at the Ohio State University. Here the researchers identified two factors which were related to supervisory behavior: "consideration" (mutual trust and rapport between the leader and his group and more participation in decisions by the group) and "initiating structure" (assigning tasks, defining production goals, etc.)[17] A supervisor may be high in both these factors; and there is a suggestion that this combination in a leader-

[15] Chester Barnard, *The Functions of the Executive,* Harvard University Press, Cambridge, 1938.

[16] Robert L. Kahn and Daniel Katz, "Leadership Practices in Relation to Productivity and Morale," in Dorwin Cartwright and Alvin Zander, eds., *Group Dynamics, Research and Theory,* Harper and Row, New York, 1961, pp. 554–570.

[17] See Edwin A. Fleishman et al., *Leadership and Supervision in Industry,* Bureau of Educational Research, Ohio State University, Columbus, 1955.

ship style may be the optimum one as far as effectiveness in supervision is concerned. The research at Ohio State also pointed out the importance of the environment in which the supervisor operates; this environment in many cases determines the leadership style that is allowed. As in the research conducted at the University of Michigan, the results showed that there was no positive relationship between morale and productivity.

These two groups of studies were mainly concerned with first-level supervisors; there were few implications suggested for middle- and top-management jobs. From the point of view of answering the questions mentioned earlier in this section of the chapter, the emphasis of these previous leadership studies on first-level supervisors is too restricted. Other deficiencies in these studies from our standpoint are that the leadership styles are expressed in very general terms, and the specific skill and knowledge requirements of higher-level managerial jobs are not identified.

Another approach to the study of managerial jobs has been to attempt to describe through work-sampling techniques what the manager actually does during his working day. This behavioral approach as applied to top-level managerial jobs was presumably initiated by Carlson in Sweden, and a number of studies have followed in the United States using the same general methodology.[18] These studies tend to show the amount of time spent interacting with other managers at various levels in the organization, as well as the amount of time spent at meetings and performing other activities. However, apart from stressing the importance of communications skills in executive work, the results of these studies are of limited value in identifying any other skill and knowledge requirements of managerial jobs.

As has already been pointed out, the classical-traditional approach to the nature of the manager's job in many cases led writers to emphasize the importance of a list of rather vaguely defined traits and qualities which the manager should possess. The literature of management—especially the popular—is liberally sprinkled with examples of such traits. These traits are, in a general way, usually related to the manager's personality, and the implicit assumption seems to be that if a manager has the "right" personality he will be a success in the managerial job. The trait approach has been repeatedly challenged by recent empirical studies, particularly those included in the Ohio Leadership Studies. These studies were based on the premise that the pattern of leadership behavior within the organization was based on the demands of each position along with structural factors (such

---

[18] See Sune Carlson, *Executive Behavior,* Strombergs, Stockholm, 1951. For a summary of the application of the behavioral approach to the study of management jobs see Robert Dubin, "Business Behavior Behaviorally Viewed," in George B. Strother, ed., *Social Science Approaches to Business Behavior,* Irwin, Homewood, Illinois, 1962.

as the responsibility-authority structure and the structure of interactions).[19] Yet it should not be implied that the trait approach is no longer considered important. On the contrary, with changes in the development of personnel practices, there has been a continuing effort to develop and improve selection and testing techniques for employees at all levels in the organization oriented toward trait and quality measurement. Much research has also been conducted on identifying leadership traits, but as yet no completely satisfactory relationships have emerged.[20] The study of executive positions by Hemphill[21] is an illustration of the rejection of the trait approach oriented toward the personality of the manager. In place of the trait approach Hemphill concentrated on the job demands of the managerial position. He administered a special questionnaire on managerial jobs to 93 top- and middle-level executives. The questionnaire contained a checklist of some 200 specific items describing the activities, responsibilities, authority, and other requirements of managerial jobs. The respondent estimated the extent to which these items were present in his own job. By the statistical technique of factor analysis, it was possible for Hemphill to determine that the relative importance of these items to the various executives could be explained by a limited number of underlying factors. He found that there were ten underlying factors which explained most of the variations in responses to the items on the checklist. In other words, he found that there were ten factors or dimensions which were common to almost all executive positions, although the importance of each factor or dimension was likely to vary from one type of executive position to another. These dimensions were as follows: staff service, business control, human affairs, exercising broad powers, personal demands, supervision of work, technical (products and markets) planning, business reputation, and preservation of assets.

The dimensions tell us something about the activities involved in management jobs. However, they are not really very informative from the standpoint of planning for the development of executives, and their usefulness is restricted because of the general terms in which they are stated. A more serious weakness is that these dimensions provide little insight into the types of skill and knowledge required for various managerial jobs. To

---

[19] Most of the basic premises on which the Ohio State Leadership Studies were based can be found in Ralph M. Stogdill and Carroll L. Shartle, *Methods in the Study of Administrative Leadership* (Business Research Monograph, No. 80), Bureau of Business Research, Ohio State University, Columbus, 1960.

[20] Much of this research has been reviewed in Thomas W. Harrell, *Manager's Performance and Personality,* Southwestern, Cincinnati, 1961. He makes a plea for more research in this area.

[21] John K. Hemphill, *Dimensions of Executive Positions* (Business Research Monograph No. 98), Bureau of Business Research, Ohio State University, Columbus, 1960.

this extent the dimensions are not really much more revealing than the renowned statement of the classical-traditional managerial functions.

Another study important to the quest for information on managerial jobs was conducted at the University of Minnesota by Mahoney.[22] This study identified eight job dimensions which were similar to the functions of management jobs described by some of the classical-traditional theorists. These dimensions were called planning, investigating, coordinating, evaluating, supervising, staffing, negotiating, and representing. Six other job dimensions, which were related to specialized job knowledge, were identified. These dimensions were called employees, money and finance, materials and goods, purchases and sales, methods and procedures, and facilities and equipment. The job performance pattern of 450 managers was described according to the proportion of total work time spent on each of these job dimensions. An attempt was then made to classify the respondents as "planners," "investigators," "coordinators," and the like.

These relatively recent studies by Hemphill and Mahoney are perhaps an improvement on the previous work in describing managerial work qua work. However, both of them have the same weakness in that they have been unsuccessful in isolating the skill and knowledge requirements of various managerial jobs. Previous studies in classical-traditional theory have placed as much emphasis on the general activities performed by managers. From the standpoint of executive development, it is as important to know the skill and knowledge necessary to perform these activities because this information would become the focal point of all training, education, development, and allocation decisions for managerial manpower.

Managerial Skill Acquisition

Turning to the second set of questions we raised earlier in this section, let us next review some leading studies of what is known about the skill and knowledge acquisition patterns for managerial jobs.

There have been a number of studies already conducted in the general area of the background and training of managers. In Britain, a well-known study was conducted to determine the career patterns of managers and how managers had been produced in the past.[23] This study suggested that there were a series of ideal types in managerial career patterns in Britain. However, this study is sociological and not focused narrowly on skill

[22] Thomas A. Mahoney et al., *Development of Managerial Performance,* Southwestern, Cincinnati, 1963.

[23] R. V. Clements, *Managers: A Study of Their Careers in Industry,* Allen & Unwin, London, 1958.

acquisition. Another British study of the Acton Society Trust [24] surveyed the educational background of some 3000 managers and the selection and training policies of some 50 large organizations. Still others in this vein could be mentioned,[25] but none tells us what we would like to know in specific detail about managerial skill and knowledge acquisition.

In the United States recent interest has been shown in the need for more information about employees in the managerial, professional, and technical segments of the labor force. Bass conducted a study [26] of the educational background of some 6000 employees (professional, technical, and managerial) drawn from a very large number of firms. Another study has also been made of the contemporary scientific revolution in terms of the composition of its managerial leadership.[27] The report indicates that increasingly more managers today have a scientific and engineering background than in the past. A few of the other recent studies of managers and their backgrounds [28] contain a considerable amount of relevant information on various selected groups of managerial employees (usually top-level executives). This information reveals a great deal about social mobility patterns and the role of education in fostering mobility, but again it does not point to much more than the broad skills and knowledge that managers presumably acquired in formal educational institutions and in a lifetime of work experience.

[24] *Management Succession,* The Action Society Trust, London, 1956.

[25] Roy Lewis and Rosemary Stewart, *The Managers: A New Examination of the English, German, and American Executive,* New American Library, New York, 1961, pp. 58–110; and Frederic Hooper, *Management Survey,* Penguin Books, Baltimore, 1960, pp. 149–207.

[26] Henry L. Bass, *The Education of Management in American Manufacturing,* mimeograph, Graduate School of Public Administration, Harvard University, no date, probably 1964, cited in McLennan, *op. cit.,* p. 16.

[27] Jay M. Gould, *The Technical Elite,* Kelley, New York, 1966.

[28] See, most recently, Robert C. Allbrook, "How to Spot Executives Early," *Fortune,* Vol. 78, No. 1, July 1968, pp. 106–111; and the earlier *Fortune* study of 900 executives in Herrymon Maurer, *Great Enterprise,* Macmillan, New York, 1955, pp. 95–101; Mabel Newcomer, *The Big Business Executive: The Factors that Made Him, 1900–1950,* Columbia University Press, New York, 1955. This study has recently been updated in *The Big Business Executive, 1964.* See also Myles L. Mace, *The Growth and Development of Executives,* Graduate School of Business Administration, Harvard University, Boston, 1950; William H. Whyte, Jr., *The Organization Man,* Doubleday, Garden City, 1956, has some pertinent information. The classic study by W. Lloyd Warner and James Abegglen, *Big Business Leaders in America,* Harper, New York, 1955, is still relevant for the career patterns of top business leaders. A more recent discussion of Warner's work is contained in W. Lloyd Warner, "The Careers of American Business and Government Executives: A Comparative Analysis," in G. B. Strother, ed., *Social Science Approaches to Business Behavior, op. cit.* See also Stanley C. Vance, "Higher Education for the Executive Elite," *California Management Review,* Vol. 8, No. 4, Summer 1966, pp. 21–30.

In the literature of management, personnel, and training and development, there is a vast amount of published material, though some of it is of the how-to-develop-the-successful-executive type; [29] and there seems to be a lack of empirical research using large samples of respondents. Some of it is quite perceptive and has much face validity, being based upon the reflective introspection of individually successful managers.[30] Some of it points up the very confusing nature and mixture of the components of the broad skills (and to confound the picture more, shifts from managerial skills to the "true" nature of organizations in which the skills are used). More explicitly, some observers have pointed out that we have been moving in two different conceptual directions in discussions of the development of managerial skills and techniques.

On the one hand is the view that administration can be made into a science or technology. An organization is studied in terms of its mission and structured in a particular way. Information is generated, processed, analyzed and a formal decision-making technique is used to arrive at a policy. On the other hand is the view that administration is a political process in which the implementation of a decision is at least as important as its content. This means securing the active, willing cooperation of employees functioning less as subordinates and more as colleagues. The concept of administration as a technical skill versus the concept of administration as a social or political process is epitomized by the image that the press has created of Robert McNamara as the administrative technocrat while someone like Sargent Shriver is pictured as the model of the administrative politician. Regardless of the truth or falsity of these particular images, the dichotomy they represent is real. The problem of combining these skills in one person or of organizing their cooperation in the same institution is a major challenge.[31]

Other segments of the managerial skills literature range from the light, almost tongue-in-cheek [32] to the heavy and seriously quantitative [33] which might be unrecognizable as management to all but a few mathematically

---

[29] A detailed example worth examining is George C. Houston, *Manager Development,* Irwin, Homewood, Illinois, 1961.

[30] For an excellent example see Theodore O. Yntema, "The Transferrable Skills of a Manager," *Journal of the Academy of Management,* Vol. 3, No. 2, August 1960, pp. 79–86.

[31] Joseph W. Garbarino, "The Industrial Relations System," cited in Luvern L. Cunningham, "Implication of Collective Negotiations for the Role of the Principal," in Stanley M. Elam et al., eds., *Readings on Collective Negotiations in Public Education,* Rand McNally, Chicago, 1967, p. 309.

[32] Antony Jay, *Management and Machiavelli,* Harcourt, Brace and World, New York, 1968.

[33] Leonard Hein, *The Quantitative Approach to Managerial Decisions,* Prentice-Hall, Englewood Cliffs, 1967.

skilled managers. However, despite the existence of a number of studies on managers and managing, it does not appear that agreed-upon ideas about specific managerial skill and knowledge acquisition patterns have crystallized.

As a consequence, it may be that we have only scratched the surface in the field of executive development and really have little to go on. The best way out of our present morass may be the careful evaluation of studies that do exist, giving punctilious attention to the findings and their meaning together with ideas for replication studies and other research intended to deepen our understanding of the multiple facets of executive development and management.[34] Meanwhile, organizations will need to be aware of the nature of managerial jobs and the changing nature of the skill and knowledge components required to perform these jobs. In this way they will perhaps be in a better position to allocate managerial resources to meet their own needs, but they still need all the help they can get to crack the mystique of management and to thereby learn the foundation of what it takes to make executive development planning and programming work.

TECHNIQUES OF EXECUTIVE DEVELOPMENT

If the mystique of executive development presents barriers to the conduct of effective executive manpower planning and programming, the techniques also have strong deficiencies. In other words, if it is difficult to set objectives in developing executives because we are unsure of the requirements for effective performance in managerial work, it follows that the development of techniques and tools are correspondingly weakened.

Perhaps one of the reasons that there has been such a strong emphasis upon tools, techniques, and gimmicks in the literature of executive development may be attributed to the fact that manpower specialists in organizations have in the past fallen back upon the use of paper programs and tools in order to impress their organizational superiors with their efforts. As a result, many organizations have had attractive paper programs, forms, and the like but have accomplished very little by way of executive development. To this day, there is a continuing search for new forms and techniques, the implicit assumption perhaps being that once these are found the problems of manpower planning and developing of executives will somehow go away. Nothing could of course be further from the truth.

The fundamental consideration in executive development programs should be providing for management succession. In many companies this

---

[34] Such an approach is well illustrated in the symposium reported in Frederic R. Wickert and Dalton E. McFarland, eds., *Measuring Executive Effectiveness*, Appleton-Century-Crofts, New York, 1967.

is done intuitively without the use of any formal tools. Although the use of tools will not necessarily forestall the operation of bias and the intrusion of political factors in managerial succession, the use of tools when followed up by a critical questioning of their use by persons at higher levels in an organization will tend to minimize these dysfunctional consequences. Certainly, in a large organization it is not practicable to rely upon the intuitive approach, and it is in such organizations that the use of formal tools started and has spread.

In addition to the specific tools themselves are the various corporate schools and institutes which have been established to conduct the human resource development aspect of executive development programs. These schools may be looked upon as a kind of tool. Among the schools which are most prominent are the General Electric Management Development and Research Institute at Crotonville, New York, and the IBM Institute at Sand's Point, also in New York State.

A third approach that might also be considered a tool of executive development is the use of management education programs which have now been established in almost 50 universities throughout the United States. There is considerable variability in these programs according to content, duration, purpose, and similar considerations. An important type of program, which we discuss subsequently, is the kind designed to prevent the educational obsolescence of engineering and technical managers.

In the next section of the chapter we consider the first of these techniques, namely, the formal replacement planning and evaluation systems used internally by organizations for the purpose of executive development. These systems are discussed from the standpoint of how they can be strategically operated by the manpower specialist. In the next two sections of the chapter we turn respectively, to the corporate management development institutes and university-level management education.

Formal Replacement Planning

Manpower planning for executive resources rests upon the forecast of future needs of the organization, which is required to determine the size and nature of the manpower-planning task as well as to give it purpose and direction.[35] Once these needs have been determined they must be translated into both the quantity and quality of executive manpower needed as well as related to dates on which the needs will have to be met.

[35] Two excellent sources concerned with projections and forecasts in planning for the executive manpower development task are: John R. Hinrichs, *High Talent Personnel,* American Management Association, New York, 1966, pp. 9–65; and Eric W. Vetter, *Manpower Planning for High Talent Personnel,* Bureau of Industrial Relations, University of Michigan, Ann Arbor, 1967, *passim.*

		Placement Required					
Position	Present Incumbent	1971	1972	1973	1974	1975	Reason
President	J. Brown				x		Retirement
Vice-president, Finance	S. Green			x			Possible promotion
Controller	B. Black			x			Possible promotion
Director, Management Planning	—	x					New position
Vice-president and General Manager, "x" Division	—		x				New product division to be formed
General Sales Manager, "x" Division	—		x				New division
Manufacturing Manager, "x" Division	—		x				New division
General Sales Manager, Paint Division	S. Williams	x					Inadequate performance
Manufacturing Manager, Paint Division	G. Gray					x	Retirement
Division Controller, Paint Division	L. Blue		x				Possible early retirement—health
Corporate totals		6	24	13	8	4	

Figure 1   Executive needs summary. *Source.* Based upon Willys H. Monroe, "Strategy in the Management of Executives," *Business Horizons,* Vol. 6, No. 1, Spring 1963, p. 38.

The entire process of executive development planning begins with an audit of key positions in existence at a given point in time. Next, future positions needed to carry out organizational plans for growth, diversification, reorganization, new products, or changed operations are identified and translated into executive manpower requirements.[36]

Figure 1 contains an example of an executive needs summary. It shows the specific positions to be filled, required staffing action by time intervals, and reasons for the needed action. It should be noted that the positions illustrated are direct reflections of the needs of the organization both in the near future and longer term. This appraisal of needs, both of the organiza-

[36] Willys H. Monroe, "Strategy in the Management of Executives," *Business Horizons,* Vol. 6, No. 1, Spring 1963, p. 37. Much of the discussion which follows is based upon this excellent presentation by Monroe.

tion and of specific executive needs, forms the foundation for constructing executive manpower plans.

Once the nature of executive needs is established, an inventory of the existing executive human resources must be taken. This inventory is developed from an objective appraisal of each executive to determine his principal strengths, shortcomings, present performance, and future potential. The appraisal of executive manpower thus involves an examination of each executive's personal history as well as a specific personnel appraisal. Figures 2 and 3, respectively, illustrate a possible personal history form and a personnel appraisal form containing data on a hypothetical Mr. William R. Ryan who is appraised as of January 1, 1970, simply for illustrative purposes.

Since the personal history and personnel appraisal are the basis for the executive manpower inventory, the accuracy of the data is of paramount importance. The individual appraisal is the source document for strategic executive manpower planning; for assessing the suitability of the individual to his present position; for determining his readiness for greater responsibilities; for planning his career and individual development program; and, with the appraisals of other executives, for matching available executive talent with the needs of the organization.

Although neither Figure 2 nor Figure 3 should be considered the final word in the proper manner in which to record personal history and executive appraisals, they do provide a format that should be useful. More specifically, the personal history includes information such as name, birth date, date of service with the present organization, education, other pertinent information, *ad seriatim* experience with other employers, and *ad*

Name:	William R. Ryan		
Birth date:	March 3, 1925		
Service date:	June 22, 1959		
Education:	9/42–6/43	Mech. Eng.	Michigan State University
	9/45–6/48	Mech. Eng. (BSME)	Michigan State University
	9/51–6/53	Business Ad. (MBA)	Harvard Business School
Other data:	6/43–8/45	Combat Engineer	U.S. Marine Corps.
	6/65–present	Board Member	Ind. Mgt. Club of Los Angeles
	Proficient in reading, writing, and speaking German.		
Experience with other employers:			
	6/53–6/56	Design Eng.	Capital Tool Co., New York
	6/56–6/59	Asst. Chief Eng.	Logotype Tool & Die Corp., New York
Experience with present employer:			
	6/59–3/61	Mgr., Ind. Eng.	New York Plant
	3/61–4/65	Prod. Mgr.	Chicago Plant
	4/65–present	Gen. Mgr.	Los Angeles Division

Figure 2 Personal history form.

Mr. William R. Ryan

General Manager,
Los Angeles Division

Time on position: 4.8 Years
Age: 44.9 Years

Evaluation of Performance

Mr. Ryan's product recommendations have had a significant bearing upon his division's long-range plans. His analysis of product potential and its exacting presentation to top management prompted the decision in 1966 to enter the high-priced widget market. In 1968 penetration was at 15% and in 1969 at 24%, with further growth expected for 1970. He has followed-up on all aspects of the new product campaign and has kept warranty expenses low. He deals effectively with the union and has eliminated the historically old trend toward wildcat strikes in the Division. He is analytical in his approach to work and has a reputation for developing subordinates who qualify for and are moved into promotional positions.

Evaluation of Promotability

Q (Qualified now)   Director of Product Planning—Corporate Level
                            Vice-President—European Manufacturing Operations
WE (With experience)   Vice-President—Engineering—Corporation Staff
                            Vice-President—Manufacturing—Corporation Staff
                            President—Large Overseas Subsidiary

Evaluation of Potential

Possessing an unusual combination of engineering-business education, unusual analytical ability, a flair for production problem solving, and product-planning skills, Mr. Ryan is clearly capable of moving still higher in the corporation. Although he could remain in Los Angeles one to three more years, he should be given consideration for the positions to which he is evaluated Q when they are likely to be open.

Replacements

Q	Ralph J. Dustin (41)	Asst. Gen. Mgr.	New York Division
WE	Alfred A. Burlough (40)	Mfg. Mgr.	Corporation Staff
WE	Seymour S. Davis (38)	Product Plng. Mgr.	Corporation Staff

Figure 3   Personnel appraisal.

seriatim experience with the present employer. Dates and a minimum amount of descriptive information about work experience and prior employers are provided to enlarge upon the person's background but without going into too much detail.

Value of Appraisals in Executive Development

Similarly, the personnel appraisal is prepared to tell some facts about the performance of the individual in his present position as well as some subjective reactions to his performance and potential. Positions for which he would be qualified immediately or within two years are also noted. In addition, the names, ages, position titles, and locations of possible internal replacements are listed.

These rather simple forms, which probably had their genesis with the Standard Oil of New Jersey management development system years ago, comprise a useful beginning point for an inventory.[37] Job incumbents' names are used, and the performance write-ups are completed in a manner which stresses concrete achievements as subjectively perceived by the individual's organizational superior, documented insofar as possible by objective illustrations. Such a system does not lend itself well to comparing individuals within an organization based upon a graphic rating scale or on the basis of trait names, yet it does provide a tool of useful potential in executive development, especially in large organizations. Figure 4 provides a possible list of the standards that should be considered in developing and using executive appraisals.

When the appraisals of the executive group are assembled into an executive inventory, it becomes possible to assess the quality of the group in terms of strengths in specialized fields, weak spots, and the total capacity to meet the possible challenges of the future. This initial evaluation of the executive inventory should provide the basis for determining the size and urgency of the executive manpower planning task. The inventory of accurate individual appraisals is the framework for constructing appropriate executive manpower-planning strategies. It may be hypothesized that the accuracy of these appraisals depends very much upon the extent to which the highest levels of management adopt a questioning attitude towards the thoroughness and thought that went into the appraisals by the persons who did the rating. The degree of accuracy achieved is of course less than a scientific measurement than it is a device for forcing lower levels of management to prepare appraisals which they are willing to defend and constitute their true opinion of the performance of the person who is rated.

The strategic management of executive manpower resources in executive development as a device for organizational goal attainment begins with a systematic matching of appraised executives with the present and future requirements of the particular organization. This could include replacing persons, shifting responsibilities among executives, going outside the organization for specific talents, acquiring talent through corporate acquisi-

[37] For more detailed up-to-date discussions see Leon Megginson, *Personnel: A Behavioral Approach to Administration,* Irwin, Homewood, Illinois, 1967, pp. 251–306; and Robert B. Burr, "Management Development," in Robert L. Craig and Lester R. Bittel, eds., *Training and Development Handbook,* McGraw-Hill, New York, 1967, pp. 363–395.

Appraisal methods should be tailored to key in with the organization's needs.

Several diverse appraisal methods, focused on securing evidence of performance, should be used.

The system should be integrated in such a way that evidence from one part of the program can be cross-checked with findings from other parts.

A direct evaluation should be made of the executive's performance using yardsticks of performance and appraisal of specific accomplishments.

The executive should be evaluated in terms of other jobs and other executives.

An appraisal program should be repeated periodically to measure the development of those who have potential for promotion.

A careful written appraisal should be made to document findings and conclusions and to serve as a reference point for measuring development progress.

A program should be flexible enough to be applied to all management levels, for constant movement occurs in management echelons as promotions, replacements, and transfers are made.

Management appraisal should be applied to all executive personnel because everyone in a management position is part of the reservoir of future talent.

The program should be readily understood by the executive group to assure their active participation in its conduct and to allay any fears that they might otherwise possess.

The program should be easily administered to encourage management confidence in the plan and to assure its continuing success.

Records should be kept confidential to protect the individuals involved and to prevent a carry-over of previous findings.

Figure 4   Some standards for executive appraisal. *Source.* Willys H. Monroe, "Strategy in the Management of Executives," *Business Horizons,* Vol. 6, No. 1, Spring 1963, p. 39.

tions, or risk taking in the selection of the relatively untried executives for key spots. The specific action taken depends upon the particular requirements of an organization and their urgency. Four common problems can be cited to illustrate how executive manpower actions come to real focus in a business organization: improving executive strength, planning for management succession, staffing realigned organizations, and planning acquisitions and mergers. Each of these problems is discussed below primarily from the standpoint of executive manpower planning strategy. It should be noted that the manpower element is only a part of the total problem in which the organization's objectives, plans, and policies are also pivotal considerations.[38]

Despite their drawbacks, the strength of an organization can be reasonably assessed from the results of appraising incumbent executives. Essential managerial positions, in which outstanding performance is deemed

[38] Monroe, *op. cit.,* p. 39.

vital to success, can be specially evaluated to guide strategic decision making. Figure 5 is a simplified illustration of an appraisal of organizational strength in a part of a hypothetical complex organization. The figure reveals questions that must be answered in any attempt to improve the executive strength of the particular organization. Should this organizational arrangement and the present staffing be retained, modified, or radically altered in view of both current and anticipated needs? Should any specific executive changes (such as promotions, demotions, terminations, the introduction of an outsider) be made because of these needs? What might be the consequences of not changing the present management group? What might they be of making substantial changes? Can the poor performers be motivated to improve sufficiently to warrant their retention? Could they be better utilized in another part of the organization? [39]

The manpower-planning strategy selected to improve the organization will depend in large measure on the responses made in answer to the questions which were just stated. Any knowledge of available talent obtained from the review of personal histories and personnel appraisals in the executive manpower inventory, both of an individual and group nature, would provide key inputs for these decisions and for the selection of appropriate strategic moves.

Planning and Implementing Executive Succession

When there is an inventory of appraised executive talent, an orderly plan of succession to key executive positions can be designed, including the moves to be made and the optimum timing. Qualified replacements for key executives can be identified, as we did in Figure 3, their readiness for various positions can be determined, and the general supply of available candidates within the organization against probable need can be inventoried. Using raw material such as that displayed in Figure 2, the management succession planning chart shown in Figure 6 can be developed. The latter chart shows the management backup condition of the organization and points to possible weak spots in succession planning. Where weak spots or shortages of qualified candidates are identified, "emergency" replacements can be designated as stopgap or caretaker position incumbents until a more qualified man is ready or recruited outside the organization.[40]

The analysis of situations in parts of a total organization where replacements are scarce can pinpoint executive manpower shortages and suggest appropriate strategic planning for their resolution. Once again, critical decisions must be made before selecting the most suitable executive manpower-planning strategy. Answers should be given to such questions as the

[39] *Ibid.*
[40] *Ibid.*, p. 40.

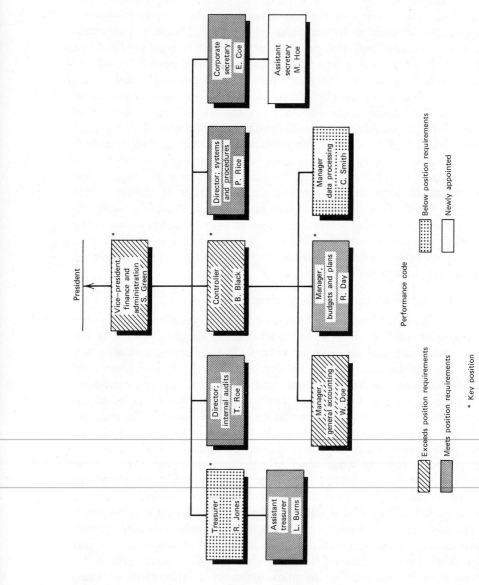

Figure 5 Organizational strength analysis. *Source.* Willys H. Monroe, "Strategy in the Management of Executives," *Business Horizons*, Vol. 6, No. 1, Spring 1963, p. 40.

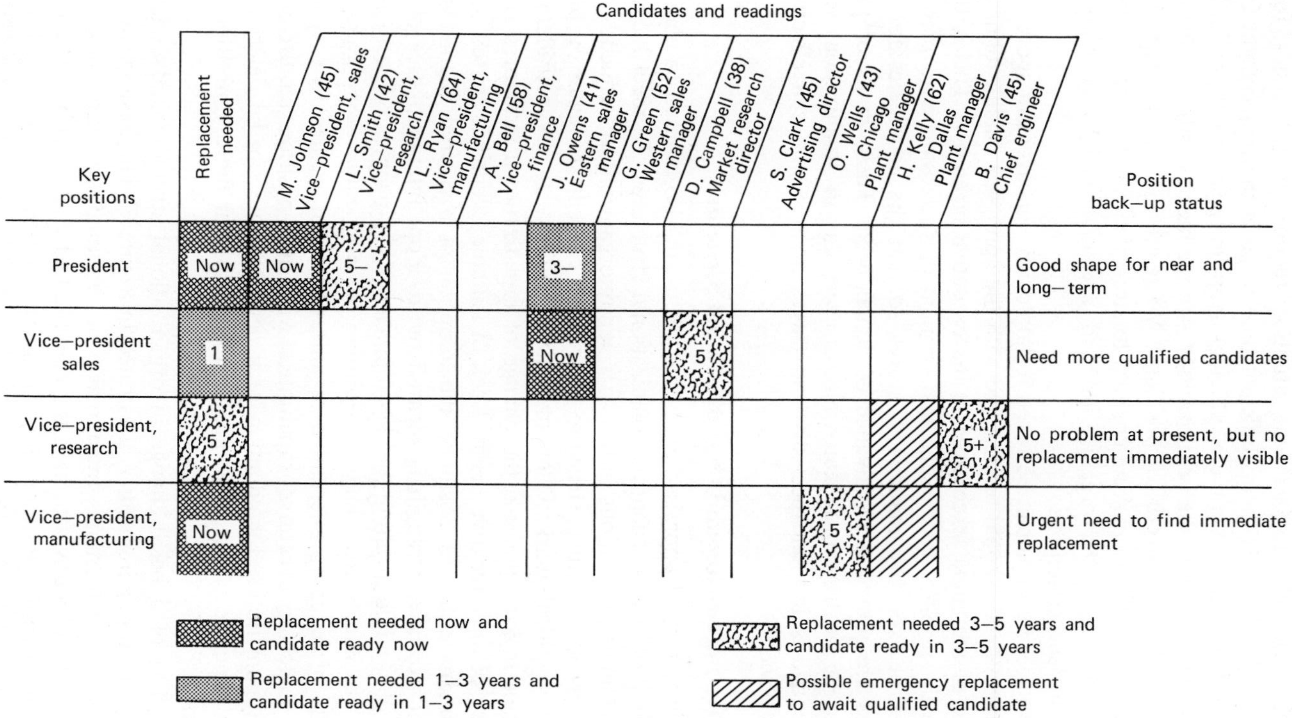

Candidates and readings

Key positions	Replacement needed	M. Johnson (45) Vice-president, sales	L. Smith (42) Vice-president, research	L. Ryan (64) Vice-president, manufacturing	A. Bell (58) Vice-president, finance	J. Owens (41) Eastern sales manager	G. Green (52) Western sales manager	D. Campbell (38) Market research director	S. Clark (45) Advertising director	O. Wells (43) Chicago plant manager	H. Kelly (62) Dallas plant manager	B. Davis (45) Chief engineer	Position back-up status
President	Now	Now	5—			3—							Good shape for near and long-term
Vice-president sales	1					Now		5					Need more qualified candidates
Vice-president research	5									5		5+	No problem at present, but no replacement immediately visible
Vice-president manufacturing	Now								5				Urgent need to find immediate replacement

Legend

- Replacement needed now and candidate ready now
- Replacement needed 1–3 years and candidate ready in 1–3 years
- Replacement needed 3–5 years and candidate ready in 3–5 years
- Possible emergency replacement to await qualified candidate

Figure 6 Executive succession planning chart. *Source.* Willys H. Monroe, "Strategy in the Management of Executives," *Business Horizons*, Vol. 6, No. 1, Spring 1963, p. 40.

following. Does the replacement situation require going outside for a suitable backstop, or is there sufficient time to grow the replacement from within the organization? Is there sufficient depth in replacement possibilities for the key positions in the organization? Are the best executives scheduled to move into the most critical positions? What are the various degrees of risk in standing pat, in making changes to strengthen the backup situation, and in rearranging the organization and executive manpower plans to prepare for succession? [41]

Before specific steps can be taken to implement management succession, replacement needs should be matched with the appraised qualifications and potential of individual executives in the executive inventory. This is done because the primary task in the management of succession is to plan the sequence of executive manpower moves so that the candidates for key positions are prepared in advance of actual need. These kinds of plans will prevent the tragedy repeated almost every day in organizations when an executive is lost unexpectedly and leaves no one who can effectively take his place.[42]

Executive Succession and Organizational Structure

The inventory of appraised executive talent can also be used to plan for the staffing of new or changed organizational structures. To meet the constantly changing conditions in business, many organizations frequently find it necessary to alter their structure in order to concentrate better on products, geographical markets, or specialized abilities. A key consideration limiting or making possible the change of organizational structures is the adequacy of top executive talent. Lack of suitable talent has caused many organizations either to postpone the adoption of a desired change until sufficient executive strength is secured or to adopt interim phases of the desired plan while awaiting the development of key people. When there is knowledge of executive human resources, it is possible to appraise the feasibility of manning alternative organizational arrangements by systematically matching executive capabilities with new position requirements. The optimum timing for adoption of a new structure can be determined, and the sequence of executive moves needed to staff the organization can be planned.[43]

The effect of a basic change in organizational structure and concepts upon executive requirements is illustrated in Figure 7. The basic change is, obviously, a switch from a functional to a divisional structure using some of the existing executives to man the new product-line structure. The number of key executive positions is substantially increased, of course, by this

[41] *Ibid.*
[42] *Ibid.,* p. 41.
[43] *Ibid.*

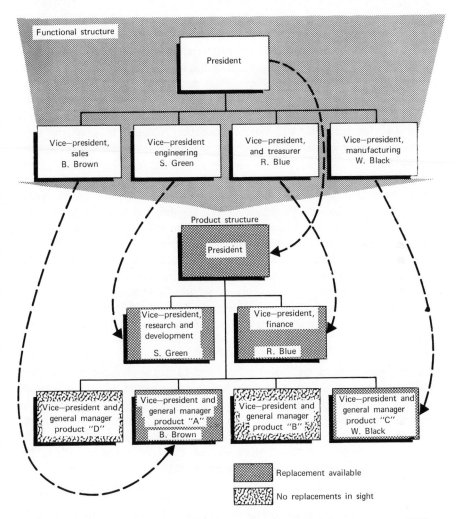

Figure 7   Staffing a proposed organization with executive manpower. *Source.* Willys H. Monroe, "Strategy in the Management of Executives," *Business Horizons,* Vol. 6, No. 1, Spring 1963, p. 42.

basic change from a functionalized to an essentially divisionalized structure; and a new key position, Division General Manager, emerges. This type of an organizational change points to a number of manpower decisions that must be faced before the new organizational concept is adopted. The following questions must be answered. Is there a sufficient number of qualified executives to staff the revised organization now? Should intermediate phases of organization be designed to provide the time and opportunity for developing executives to meet the changed requirements of the new proposed structure? What is the degree of risk involved in placing executives who are considered not fully qualified at present in the new positions? How urgent is the adoption of the new organization? In addition to these general organizational questions there are a number of specific questions concerning the strengths, potential, and possible placement of individual executives. Source information for resolving these individual issues and for planning the executive moves required to man the new structure is secured from the executive inventory, personal histories, and appraisals.[44]

Plans for the expansion or diversification of a corporation can be more clearly evaluated when a knowledge of available executive talent exists. Armed with this knowledge, key decisions regarding the need for management in specific opportunities for acquisition can be more realistically made. Questions such as the following can be answered at least in part. How important a factor is the caliber of management in the organization to be acquired? Should specific functional strengths be sought to supplement the executive capabilities in the acquiring firm? What is the best way to integrate the merging organizations and executive manpower to secure the best balance of talent among the human resources involved? [45]

Timing and Sensitivity to Learning Situations

These examples of executive manpower planning illustrate the importance of careful management of executive resources as a part of overall strategic organizational management. The timing of executive moves is directly related to the urgency of both the needs and the plans of organizations. The individual handling of specific executives in terms of career planning depends upon the nature of the business situation. Plans for organizational growth, diversification, perpetuation, and improvement and the appropriate executive manpower strategy to meet them are patently built upon the quality of the executive inventory.[46]

The real key to all strategies in the management of executive resources is the development of the individual executive. Human resource development programs aimed at meeting the appraised needs of both the individual and the organization should be directly related to each segment of the manpower plan.[47] There is now sound evidence of the practicality of a comprehensive simulation model of careers in management that can give coherence and relevance to the various pieces of the selection, training,

---

[44] *Ibid.*, pp. 41–42.
[45] *Ibid.*, pp. 42–43.
[46] *Ibid.*, p. 43.
[47] *Ibid.*, p. 43.

motivational, and promotional process in organizations. Such a model or system will also provide a matrix for examining the merits of different research and operating possibilities, and a perspective for planning and testing the means to improve important elements in the costly and relatively primitive process of executive development that is common in organizations today.[48]

Clearly, an important starting point for building tailored development programs is a realistic assessment of the organizational environment as it pertains to executive growth. Such environmental factors as compensation levels, executive attitudes, promotional opportunities, performance requirements, and working relationships among executives have a strong and direct influence upon the individual's motivation for self-improvement. A systematic evaluation of the organizational environment against a background of both executive and organizational needs should point to specific changes that ought to be made to assure an effective environment for executive development.[49]

Computerization of Records and Simulation Models

Through the use of computers, it is now possible to build a simulation model of the entire growth process for managers which gives due attention to all identifiable environmental considerations.

Using the quantitative and qualitative information available from the executive development inventory, an executive manpower information system can be established that will help manpower specialists and managers make promotional decisions which are compatible with the optimal long-term benefits both to the individual and the organization. The proposed system is schematically shown in Figure 8. The facilities would be used for the necessary coding, storage, retrieval, analysis, and study of data which could be used for manpower planning. As the model is now envisioned, the manager would make his selections for executive positions in a perfectly normal and independent fashion. Any properly qualified manager would have access to the appropriate bank of manpower information in the central data storage and processing system as shown in Figure 8. From his desk he could ask for and receive complete information about all persons in the storage bank who meet the specifications he designates. The manager could change the specifications, ask for special analysis, and, in general, obtain (to the extent that prior inputs have been adequate) answers to any question that he wishes to ask the computer. He must be

---

[48] Lawrence L. Ferguson, "Better Management of Managers' Careers," *Harvard Business Review*, Vol. 44, No. 2, March-April 1966, p. 152.

[49] Monroe, *op. cit.*, p. 43. See also Gordon McBeath, *Organization and Manpower Planning*, Second Edition, Business Books, London, 1969, pp. 27–216.

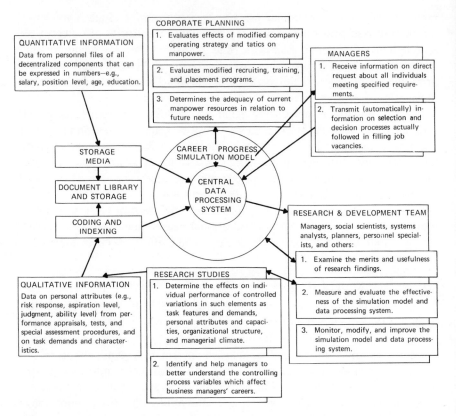

Figure 8   A simplified managerial manpower selection and career-planning model. *Source.* Lawrence L. Ferguson, "Better Management of Managers' Careers," *Harvard Business Review,* Vol. 44, No. 2, March-April 1966, pp. 139–152.

able to interrogate the computer in terms of the attributes, characteristics, and limitations he wants to impose. He could, at his command, obtain whatever information is available that might help him reach a decision on a manpower move. From a listing of qualified candidates he would finally make a choice and a promotion would be accomplished.[50]

After a sequence of actions concerning the selection of an executive have been completed by the use of the central data-processing system in the career progress simulation model, there would be available for analysis a complete history of the process of selection the manager actually went through. When a sufficient number of these selection histories have been recorded, there would then be available for examination and study the evidence of the real selection process managers use in filling executive

[50] Ferguson, *op. cit.,* pp. 149–150.

positions. Thus the system would allow the individual seeking promotion to receive a confidential "handicapping" of his chances for success in different possible career routes. A person's career history would reveal a series of objectives whose successive attainment provided a basis for more refined estimates as to the likelihood of his achieving more demanding goals. Specifically, he can inquire as to the odds that he will reach a certain type of position or level in the organization at a particular age. If he finds that the odds are unfavorable, he can ask the computer to assess—in the light of his present work experience, educational history, special training, personal attributes, age, performance record, and the like—what he must do to have a 50–50 chance of reaching his goal within a specific time. Individuals could make effective use of such manpower information to alter their own personal-planning timetables so as to match their qualifications and experience with various opportunities in a much more realistic, self-determining, and democratic fashion than is possible under current conditions of limited and inexact information.[51]

Furthermore, the information about current conditions on various career paths could be periodically summarized and used for a number of other purposes beyond feeding back information to aspiring managerial candidates. Research studies could also be conducted to determine the effectiveness of the organization's compensation structure in attracting, retaining, and motivating individuals. Factors affecting the optimal timing of job changes could be studied as could the extent and nature of changes induced by special educational and training programs. Studies could be made of how an individual's career is influenced by climate, aspirational level, managerial style, supervisory values, and many other considerations. Means for more nearly optimizing the utilization of human resources employed and predicting the specified nature, costs, and advantages of possible changes in them may become apparent and could be subjected to objective testing and evaluation.[52]

From a long-range standpoint, the complete system could provide essential manpower data in a central source that reflects the inputs from and status of manpower in hundreds of decentralized organizational components in a complex enterprise. This advantage makes it possible for the manpower specialist to examine the composite effects of individual manpower decisions made by hundreds or thousands of managers at any point in time. Consequently, the system can simulate the effects of different strategies, tactics, and criteria for manpower decision making. In addition, manpower specialists and corporate planners can examine changes in policies and practices that will optimize the use of available resources and maintain

[51] *Ibid.,* pp. 150–151.
[52] *Ibid.,* p. 151.

control over the human resource developmental processes for the proper distribution of talents. Planners can determine new objectives, monitor their effectiveness, and be prepared to introduce corrective measures quickly, if needed. Appropriate reserves or balanced inventories of talents can be maintained to enable the organization to cope with foreseen demands as well as with changing economic, competitive, and international conditions. It goes without saying, perhaps, that the competitive advantages in availability and use of the needed individual talents will be directly translatable for a business into leadership in design, new products, costs, volume, and profits.[53]

Eventually, reliable predictive patterns of career progress in organizations will begin to emerge. Eventually, also, a kind of calculus for the management of human resources will be developed that will provide for differentially weighting personal skills and attributes in relation to corresponding job demands and developmental opportunities. Intelligently used computers can handle these data-processing and analysis problems while still leaving to the personal judgment of those executives involved the choice between individuals with different characteristics. Perhaps most important of all, the career-planning process will become a more truly participative one. Managers will be in a much more secure position as far as making sound manpower decisions are concerned. Subordinate managers will be in a position to do more intelligent planning for their own development based upon full information about procedures, values, opportunities, and requirements. At this ultimate juncture, career planning in organizations will become a two-way process with all the parties fully aware of the critical considerations that affect them.[54]

Philosophical Underpinnings

To this point we have been discussing the various mechanical and computerized techniques for implementing individual executive development programs. Equally important to a successful executive development program is the basic philosophy that underlies the conduct of development plans and programs. A practical philosophy of executive development, which can help to implement manpower planning, includes orienting individual development efforts towards improved position performance. If an organization adopts this philosophy, concentrated attention must be given to on-the-job development techniques that are focused on performance. Therefore, performance appraisals are essential as a tool in the kit for executive development. Moreover, planned individual development programs must be tailored specifically to the appraised needs of each execu-

[53] *Ibid.*
[54] *Ibid.*, p. 152.

tive and aimed at meeting clear-cut organizational objectives and needs as translated into executive manpower planning.[55]

Looked at another way, individual executive development may be perceived as the action aspect of executive manpower planning. The implementation of strategy in the management of executive resources is largely conducted through a continuing follow-up developmental effort. In order to coordinate this individual development programming and executive manpower-planning strategy there are some rules-of-thumb and manpower policies that are worth mentioning here. First, the aim of executive development should be the strengthening of the organization through improved executive performance. Second, tailored individual development programs should be designed to meet the objectively appraised needs of both the individual and the employing organization. Third, individual development programs should be sufficiently flexible to permit changes in emphasis and rate to meet the changed conditions in an organization. Fourth, development should be made available to all executives. This kind of policy will strengthen the executive inventory and provide the maximum talent for strategic management of executive manpower. Fifth, techniques for development which are job related should be emphasized. Emphasis should be placed on the incumbent's present job rather than some position in prospect. The techniques used should include the establishment of demanding performance goals, selective job assignments, well-chosen task force and project team assignments, counseling and coaching, planned job rotation, and the use of formal management education where appropriate. Sixth, progress in individual development and in meeting the objectives of the organization should be measured periodically through reappraisal of the executive group.[56]

In addition to the above rules-of-thumb and policies, are some others which were developed as a consequence of experience simulated by General Electric in conducting its Management Research and Development Institute and were stated some years ago by the former director of that institute. Added to the above, the seventh rule of thumb would be: development is not something which you would *do* to a man but is something which he attains through job performance and employment in an organization. Eighth, there is no ideal cluster or mixture of personality traits which can be used as a guide in executive development. Ninth, executive development involves moral and spiritual values. Therefore, it should not only be available to all members of the managerial group, but, in addition, decisions made in respect to it should be carefully considered and premised upon equal opportunity. Lastly, although management is increasingly taking

[55] Monroe, *op. cit.*, p. 43.
[56] Monroe, *op. cit.*, pp. 43–44.

on professional-like aspects, more needs to be known about it, and experimentation in executive development is warranted.[57]

CORPORATE INSTITUTES FOR EXECUTIVE DEVELOPMENT

Assuming that executive manpower is both the most valuable and most perishable of the key resources of an organization, many businesses and other organizations have given greater care and attention to its preservation and improvement than was the case 30 or 40 years ago. In addition to adapting and installing some of the techniques for executive development which we discussed above, some firms established corporate institutes quite similar to colleges which offer short courses for their executive groups in order to assist them in developing what are perceived as managerial skills and knowledge. In some instances these institutes were developed because firms changed their organizational structure and philosophy and desired to acquaint their managers with the new structures and policies stemming from decentralization or centralization as the case might be. In other cases organizations either were not able to enroll a sufficient number of their managers in university-type management education programs or believed that these were too general and not specifically geared to help the individual organization. Still other firms probably established their institutes either to imitate pace-setting firms that had established them or because they had a conviction that something had to be done to respond to the deficiencies of their existing executives and the perceived numerical shortage of executive manpower in the years ahead. Certainly the post-World War II business expansion and the low birth rate of the depression induced many firms to take action in executive development. Thus, for reasons of one kind or another executive development institutes have been established by such companies as General Electric, IBM, American Telephone and Telegraph, Chrysler (in a special Institute of Engineering since 1933, off and on), International Harvester, Johnson & Johnson, Westinghouse Electric, and numerous other organizations both public and private. None of these institutes is a carbon copy of the other. Therefore it is difficult to talk about them in any generalized manner. For the purposes of illustration we take a close look at the General Electric Management Research and Development Institute that was established in 1955 after which the IBM Institute established in 1959 is designed.

[57] Moorehead Wright, "Individual Growth: The Basic Principles," *Personnel*, Vol. 37, No. 5, September-October 1960, pp. 8–17. Similar thoughts can be found in Charles D. Flory, ed., *Managers for Tomorrow*, New American Library, New York, 1965, pp. 172–185.

General Electric's Innovations

General Electric Company's Management Research and Development Institute at Crotonville, New York, was established in 1955 and quartered at the estate of the late well-known management consultant Harry Hopf, who lived in a 32-acre estate 35 miles north of New York City, the home of General Electric's headquarters. When the $2.25 million staff college was established it looked like as significant a step for GE as the establishment of its research laboratory in 1900 looked.[58]

Between 1956 and 1961, when the nine-week Advanced Management Course operated, approximately 1500 GE managers graduated from the course. The institute shut down until early 1964 after which it reopened with a modified AMC and other courses. During the 1956 through 1961 period a GE divisional general manager who sent a subordinate to Crotonville paid $2,650.00 of his division's funds for tuition, room, and board. In addition, the trainee's salary for the period and his transportation was also paid while he attended sessions at Crotonville.[59]

The AMC course at GE was launched as a sort of crash program to upgrade the higher echelons of GE's newly decentralized management. The program was intended to have a definite termination point. The nine five and one-half day weeks of intensive lectures, discussion sessions, and project work on GE's world-wide business environment and ways of dealing with it were aimed specifically at the 1700 executives in the company's four top levels of management. It included immediate subordinates of the general managers of the various decentralized profit centers (or departments, in the GE organizational terminology). It was thought that about five years would be needed for all these levels of executives to complete the AMC. By early 1961 about 80 percent of the departmental general managers, all but one of the higher-ranking divisional general managers, and five members of the executive office had attended the AMC.

It was intended that the GE institute would provide management training of a multifunctional type to men who had already reached a level that would be equivalent to a vice-presidency in a smaller company. This was to be training in the classical-traditional functions of management. It was not intended that the AMC course would cover such specific business operational functions as finance, marketing, engineering, and personnel, subjects which were to be left to more specialized courses. AMC was in-

---

[58] "GE Institute Nears End of Run—Now What?," *Business Week,* No. 1644, March 4, 1961, p. 50.

[59] *Ibid.*; and "GE's 'College' Is Back in Session," *Business Week,* No. 1797, February 8, 1964, p. 78.

tended to concentrate on management theory and economic, social, and political issues, a more abstract approach to overall business policies and general management. It was thought that this type of subject matter would be most appropriate to help the managers in decentralized locations to define the new roles required as a result of the change from the former higher centralized type of management.[60]

The AMC course drew upon both company and outside lecturers. Divergency in points of view was deliberately built into the program. There was considerable required and recommended reading and a strong emphasis upon 12-man discussion groups. In addition each participant was required to work out a "strategy project" suggesting future policies for GE and a "carry back action plan" for himself.

At the end of the programs, it was generally found that the participants were vague about how they could apply the experience and what they specifically gained from it. Participants could point to specific things that they learned about GE, of course. Managers from widespread parts of the corporation became acquainted with one another. Yet they found it difficult to explain how their new awareness of world problems and corporate philosophy helped them to do their jobs better. Observers from outside GE criticized AMC as being too long, too expensive, and too theoretical.[61]

After being shut down for about three years, GE reopened the AMC, as we have seen, and extended its duration to thirteen weeks rather than the prior nine weeks. The old nine-week course was streamlined and squeezed into a six weeks' seminar composing the midsection of the new thirteen week program. As before, the older AMC portion was concerned with perspective and environment, led by outside experts in the social, political, and economic trends that affect the decisions of GE management.

However, some new ingredients were added in the first and last layers in the new educational sandwich that GE put together. The course opened with a three-week section developed and almost exclusively presented by GE's own top management. This was a kind of cram course of selected key information helpful in managing a product department or the equivalent in General Electric. In the third and final phase of the curriculum, intensive analysis of cases was utilized as is typical of curricula in pace-setting graduate schools of business administration. The GE managers analyzed about 50 cases, discussion of which was led by experienced professors of business administration from leading universities. The new AMC course

---

[60] "GE Institute Nears End of Run—Now What?," *op. cit.*, pp. 50–51.
[61] *Ibid.*, pp. 50–55.

was also to be offered on a much more limited basis and to be carefully observed for a considerable period of time into the future.[62]

The General Electric Management Research and Development Institute is clearly a quantum addition to executive development that cannot be matched by many other organizations which lack GE's financial and other resources. Therefore, it could be expected that other organizations which have attempted to establish their own institutes have usually curtailed their ambitions and vastly scaled down their institutes in comparison with General Electric.

Public Sector Executive Development

In addition to institutes established in the private sector, government has also been recently interested in executive development institutes. In 1957 there were virtually no courses for the training of nonmilitary governmental employees. Beginning in 1958 the Government Employees' Training Act placed responsibility for executive development with the Federal Civil Service Commission. The latter legislation was in marked contrast to the attitudes toward training executives that prevailed up to that time. Previously, powerful committee heads in Congress had voiced hostility toward any ventures in executive development for many years. In fact, in 1938, the Controller General had ruled that the Department of Agriculture could not expend funds for training purposes. That ruling significantly affected the subsequent history of executive development in the federal government.[63]

In the period between 1957 and 1959 the Brookings Institution inaugurated a series of conferences for federal executives in the upper levels of the career service. These conferences were held at Williamsburg, Virginia, and were broadly oriented towards mind-stretching rather than emphasizing managerial techniques or tactics which federal career executives could use more directly on their jobs in government. In many respects the concepts underlying the program were like those used at General Electric, only properly scaled for executive work in government.[64] Several years later the powerful Committee for Economic Development composed of leading American businessmen suggested that the federal government should give greater attention to executive and professional development, concen-

---

[62] "GE's 'College' Is Back in Session," op. cit., pp. 78–79.

[63] Douglass Cater, Developing Leadership in Government, Brookings Institution, Washington, 1960, p. 8.

[64] Ibid., passim. See Marver H. Bernstein, The Job of the Federal Executive, Brookings Institution, Washington, 1958, for a pertinent study of the work of appointed political executives at the policy level.

trating on the government's career (civil service) managers.[65] Brookings has continued to make programs available in the past decade whereby government executives learned more about private industry and executives from the latter were provided an opportunity through seminars to become acquainted with the executive job in government.[66]

In 1968 the Civil Service Commission conducted the first Federal Executive Institute. This Institute was planned to be the capstone of the federal employee's training programs that have been functioning since 1958. About a dozen eight-week classes were conducted for about 30 executives in the higher levels of the Civil Service. The purpose was to provide a deeper understanding of overall federal goals and programs and to give the executives a sense of common purpose in how their work related to state and local governments. The faculty was divided between a resident career staff, appointed for not more than five years and a resident consultant staff, engaged for three months to one year. The latter was comprised of corporate professionals as well as people from the nation's universities, research institutes, and other organizations.

For the future, a permanent campus will be established complete with modern classrooms and dormitories within 50 miles of Washington, D.C. The design for this institute springs from several years of experimentation with executive manpower development and training methods under the direction of the Brookings Institution and the Civil Service Commission.[67]

Other branches of government have long been interested in executive development programs. The Industrial College of the Armed Forces is an example of one such type of program.

A British Innovation

In Britain there has been a strong interest in the education of businessmen and public officials since the establishment in the late 1940s of the Administrative Staff College at Henley-on-Thames. The Henley program, supported principally by the employers of those attending it, is residential, housed on an attractive estate maintained for the purpose, and extends for three months. The composition of the membership of each program was originally intended to be about equally divided between executives in business and from the public services. The candidates are iden-

---

[65] Committee for Economic Development, *Improving Executive Management in the Federal Government,* Committee for Economic Development, New York, 1964, pp. 35–42.

[66] "Learning How Government Ticks," *Business Week,* No. 1699, March 24, 1962, pp. 136–140; and "Bureaucrats Meet Company Brass," *Business Week,* No. 1864, May 22, 1965, pp. 176–178.

[67] "The Bureaucrats Get Their Own B-School," *Business Week,* No. 1971, June 10, 1967, pp. 69–72.

tified by their employers as being considered for broader responsibilities. There are special discussion groups at Henley (called syndicates) and a small faculty of Henley staff in addition to some outside lecturers. The Henley experience has been emulated in the United States and inspired the establishment of administrative staff colleges for government officials.[68]

It is difficult to determine present trends concerning the future corporate and other management and executive development institutes. There is a growing awareness of the need to prevent executive obsolescence.[69] It might therefore be predicted that we shall see more of these institutes in the future rather than fewer.

MANAGEMENT EDUCATION

We now turn to the last of the three techniques for executive development, namely management education. By this term we mean in-residence types of programs in which executives at various organizational levels gather together on a college campus for a period of time ranging from a few days to a few months for the purposes of education. (Although the usual locale is a college campus, it is quite possible to use some other setting such as a residential estate or other facility removed from the place of work of the program participants.) In order to grasp the significance of management education, it is necessary to turn briefly to relevant background which explains the evolution of this very important type of device for executive development in an industrial society.

Scope and Origins

Data are provided in Figure 9 which indicate the extent of university level management education programs in the United States at the present time. There are at least 40 institutions offering these kinds of programs although some universities have several different programs of different duration. In addition, in past years there have been other programs functioning which for one reason or another have been discontinued. Similar to cooperative education, management education is largely an American innovation.

In the United States, undergraduate education for business began with the establishment of Wharton School of Finance and Commerce at the

---

[68] Ward Stewart and John C. Honey, *University-Sponsored Executive Development in the Public Service,* Government Printing Office, Washington, 1966, pp. 5–7. This source contains a great deal of information on the subject of executive development in government including a review of a number of existing programs in various universities.

[69] See Harry Levinson, "Is There an Obsolete Executive in Your Company—Or in Your Chair?," *Think,* Vol. 34, No. 1, February 1968, pp. 26–30.

University	Date Started	University	Date Started
California (Berkeley)	1959	Northeastern	1960
California (Los Angeles)	1954[a]	Northwestern	1951[a]
Carnegie-Mellon	1954	Ohio State	1955
Chicago	1957	Oklahoma	1957
Cincinnati	1960	Oklahoma State	1954
Columbia	1952[a]	Pomona	1957
Cornell	1953	Pennsylvania State	1956
Emory	1951[a]	Pittsburgh	1949
Florida	1960	Richmond	1955
Georgia	1953	South Carolina	1959
Harvard	1945[a]	Southern Methodist	1953
Hawaii	1954	Stanford	1950[c]
Houston	1953	Syracuse	1953
Indiana	1951[a]	Texas	1955
Iowa	1941	Texas A & M	1953
Kansas	1955	Utah	1957
Louisiana State	1960	Virginia	1958
M.I.T.	1932[b]	Wabash	1955
Michigan	1954	Washington (of St. Louis, Mo.)	1955
North Carolina	1954	Western Ontario	1949[d]
		Williams	1956

Figure 9   University-level management-education programs in the United States. [a] Several programs; the earliest is shown. [b] Sloan Fellowship Program dates back to 1932; MIT also has other programs. [c] Sloan Program dates back to 1950; Stanford has other programs in addition. [d] This is a Canadian program, of which there are others less well known and less frequented by American executives, such as Banff, Queen's, and Atlantic.

University of Pennsylvania in 1881. Subsequently, other undergraduate schools were founded at the University of Chicago and the University of California prior to 1900. After 1900 such schools proliferated so that by the mid-1960s there were probably about 600 business administration programs either in undergraduate or graduate schools or in separate divisions or departments of colleges or universities. However, the university-level management education program for older men in executive positions was not really foreshadowed in this rapid growth of business education.[70] In part these programs were needed because business curricula did not produce a sufficient number of trained potential managers.

To be sure, in the years when business administration education was

[70] Kenneth R. Andrews, *The Effectiveness of University Management Development Programs,* Graduate School of Business Administration, Harvard University, Boston, 1966, pp. 16–17.

growing in the colleges and universities, the old War and Navy Departments sent career officers to some MBA programs. Also, men who had spent some time in business occasionally returned to full-time schooling at their own expense. But management education programs came much later.

Roots are to be found in three developments of the late 1920s and 1930s. First, the Graduate School of Business Administration at Harvard University, usually called the "Harvard Business School," offered special sessions for business executives in the summers of 1928 and 1929. These were attended by almost 400 men, about one-half of whom were college graduates. About one-quarter of them had their expenses paid by their employers. The course was of six weeks' duration. The program comprised five different courses, and the participants enrolled in only one of the five. In 1930, after the crash of the stock market, the courses were shortened to one month; and then there was a suspension of them until 1936 when they were resumed for only one year. They then expired permanently in 1937.[71]

Second, the Sloan Fellowship Program began in 1931 at the Massachusetts Institute of Technology. This program was one year's duration and is in a sense the oldest continuing management education program in existence which was especially designed for men actually occupying management positions.

Between 1931 and 1942, 78 men accepted Sloan Fellowships. The program was suspended from 1942 to 1949 and was renewed after that time and expanded so that today there are approximately 45 Sloan Fellows enrolled in the program at any one time. Participants attend the program for a 12-month period; and, if they successfully complete the work, they are granted a Master's Degree from MIT.[72]

The third development in the 1930s which foreshadowed the rise of management education as we have described it was a business executive discussion group that evolved in 1935 at the Harvard Business School. Discussions in this group tended to transcend far beyond the specific and detailed problems facing management into the larger issues of business and society. The existence of this group established a close relationship between the Harvard Business School and a number of seasoned businessmen.[73]

The groundwork having been laid, it was perhaps inevitable that, with the advent of World War II, universities would be looked to as a national educational resource for preparing men displaced from less essential occu-

[71] *Ibid.*, pp. 17–18.
[72] *Ibid.*, pp. 18–19.
[73] *Ibid.*, pp. 19–28.

pations for jobs in war production. In 1942, the armed forces established 90-day courses in which civilians could be transformed into officers (the so-called "90-day wonders"). At this same time, Harvard and Stanford Universities were asked to design a short course for businessmen to help them make the transition to the management of war production. By early 1943 the first war production training course was introduced, and seven such sessions were ultimately completed before the end of the war.

These courses of 15-weeks' duration comprised the logical lineal predecessor of modern management education and established many of the features which have become characteristic of such education. The participants in the program ("retreads," as they called themselves) took several courses and had their tuition paid for by the federal government. About one-third of the men were sent by their companies, and two-thirds paid their own additional expenses. They left their families to live on campus. They attended regular classes for which substantial study was required.

Some of those sponsored by their companies were sent not only to learn skills relevant to war production but also to prepare for promotion to greater responsibility. In each successive course, the proportion of men sent to be prepared for promotion rose until finally it was approximately four-fifths of the enrollees. Also, in time the curriculum changed so that there was gradually a greater emphasis on human and administrative problems.[74]

Enlargement of Programs Since World War II

Both Harvard and MIT were urged by the participating companies to continue offering their courses after the war not so much to retrain executives but to prepare men for increased responsibility. Stanford decided to discontinue its program, but it resumed it later in 1952. On the other hand, at Harvard in September 1945, the Advanced Management Program (AMP) was initiated for men sent by their companies. The course length was 13 weeks. The executives attending were required to live in dormitories, and except for two weekend breaks, were not expected to see their families or return to work in their organizations. This program became at once and has remained the largest and longest of the university management education programs for senior executives. The needs that produced it and the impact of its own contribution were within ten years to carry this type of extension of university education throughout the world.[75]

As we saw in Figure 9, within ten years after the end of World War II, a large number of universities had installed management education pro-

[74] *Ibid.*, pp. 28–29.
[75] *Ibid.*, p. 30.

grams. 1953–1955 were the peak years of program establishment. The growth of these continued until about 1960, after which the starting of new programs tapered off. In the interim a number of programs that were started were subsequently abandoned. Yet, there is no doubt that there was phenomenal growth in management education programs between 1945 and 1960, to the point that a new dimension was added to the mosaic of American educational institutions.

An Educational Patchwork Quilt in Perspective

The diversity among the management education programs makes it extremely difficult to discuss them in any coherent manner. Moreover, a good many of the programs seem to change in minor ways almost annually. Nevertheless, it is desirable to discuss some of the broad features of the programs. Subsequently, we discuss in more detail a few of the programs of different types. However, for the purposes of a more general analysis, it is worthwhile to consider the management education programs in existence according to the following broad categories. First, is the program residential or nonresidential (and therefore was it full- or part-time)? Second, is its subject matter drawn essentially from the liberal arts or business? Third, is its subject matter essentially a broad inquiry into the administrative processes of general management and offered to executives from a cross section of organizations, or is it specialized in either subject matter or clientele? Fourth, is the program of long or short duration?

Turning back to whether the programs are residential or nonresidential, we will probably find that better than 90 percent are of two-weeks' duration or longer and have as clientele persons in general management. For all practical purposes, management education programs are residential and full-time. The longest programs are those for junior executives at MIT, Stanford, and Harvard. Harvard is currently offering the advanced management program which lasts for 13 weeks and the program for management development which is given twice a year and lasts 16 weeks. The other programs range generally from two to six to nine weeks.[76] The outer limits of the range would be from two weeks to one year (the latter being the MIT Sloan Fellowship program).

During the decade from 1949 to 1958 when management education programs were at the height of their popularity, more than 10,000 individuals sponsored by their companies attended this form of education. Prior to 1949, 1100 individuals had attended the Harvard AMP program alone.[77] Since 1958 it is likely that attendance at executive development programs in the United States has averaged about 2500 persons per year, although

[76] *Ibid.,* pp. 30–31.
[77] *Ibid.*

this figure is essentially a guess based upon somewhat impressionistic evidence reported in the mid-1960s.[78] If this figure is meaningful, it would suggest that within the last decade approximately 25,000 persons have participated in management education programs. Perhaps 23,000 of these attended the residential programs lasting two weeks or longer and aimed essentially at general management.

About ten percent of management education programs are essentially concerned with broad coverage courses in business administration and last a year or longer, designed for managers already at work. The best known of these types of programs is the Executive Program of the University of Chicago which has long had a reputation of being a rigorous two-year part-time course for men working in the Chicago area who desire to obtain an MBA degree after having earned undergraduate degrees.[79] It should be mentioned that in addition to the relatively long nonresidential courses which we have discussed there are a number of short nonresidential courses offered throughout the country. These are extremely heterogeneous and resist classification.[80]

Turning to subject matter, it should be noted that probably no more than a handful of management development programs have centered on the liberal arts. Among the most prominent of these have been the courses offered to executive manpower of the American Telephone and Telegraph Company at the University of Pennsylvania, Dartmouth, Williams, and Swarthmore Colleges. (The Pennsylvania and Swarthmore courses have been discontinued in recent years.) Among other liberal arts programs that are well known we should include the Wabash College program and the Aspen executive program (which is not university sponsored but appeals to executive clientele to some extent).[81]

Subject matter in executive development programs varies considerably. The kinds of programs that are of most interest in developing general management manpower focus upon administrative processes and general management and apply to a cross section of industry. Yet, numerically there are more courses that appeal to more localized clientele and stress a diversity of subjects such as banking, public utilities, hospital administration, financial controls, engineering management, and credit management.[82]

[78] Edmund K. Faltermayer, "Some Firms Question Value of Management Development Seminars," *Wall Street Journal*, February 21, 1962, p. 1. No central source maintains statistics on annual management education enrollments.

[79] *Ibid.*, pp. 19–32. See also Reed M. Powell, "Two Approaches to University Management Education," *California Management Review*, Vol. 5, No. 3, Spring 1963, pp. 87–104.

[80] Andrews, *op. cit.*, pp. 31–32.

[81] *Ibid.*, pp. 32–33.

[82] *Ibid.*, pp. 33–35.

In addition to all the foregoing categories of management education, there is an uncountable miscellany of hundreds of institutes, seminars, workshops, conferences, and short intensive courses which range anywhere from less than a day up to a week or more. Some universities through their extension and continuing education activities in the period of a year offer literally hundreds of such short intensive programs. It is dubious if any of them would qualify as management education in the sense that the term is being used in this chapter. Yet they are used to educate managers.

Undoubtedly the quality and impact of these brief programs vary widely. Their principal significance is what they symbolize: a desire for knowledge, assistance, and the exchange of experience by managers; and the willingness on the part of business schools to attempt an educational or training offering within brief periods of time in which managers can satisfy their wants and needs. The growth of the idea of continuing education for management and the coming together of people in organizations and the faculties of universities for such courses are important developments which have led to important changes both in education and in organizational management. In any event, the executive who sets out for a three-day institute, no matter how hastily it is put together, is in at least approximately a learning frame of mind. He neither thinks that he knows it all nor insists that his own experience is the best teacher.[83]

The Andrews Evaluation Study—Summary of a Landmark

In the years since longer-duration management education programs have established themselves in the American educational scene, a number of attempts have been made to evaluate one or more specific programs.[84] The most monumental of these evaluations is that by Kenneth R. Andrews of the Harvard Business School, which deserves some attention and is considered in the paragraphs that follow.

The Andrews study was intended to answer the question: How do we appraise the effectiveness of management education programs and justify rationally the expenditure of executive time and organizational money? This question was considered of immediate concern to companies and of at least secondary importance to universities. It was important to the latter because, if the resources of the nation's business schools are already meager in the light of growing enrollments, the diversion of faculty from traditional programs to executive courses should be explained.[85]

[83] *Ibid.*, pp. 34–36.
[84] These attempts would include Andrews, *op. cit.;* Powell, *op. cit.;* and R. Winston Oberg, "Top Management Assesses University Executive Programs," *Business Topics,* Vol. 11, No. 2, Spring 1963, pp. 7–27.
[85] Andrews, *op. cit.*, p. 1.

In order to evaluate the programs, Andrews constructed a rather sophisticated questionnaire that was sent to 10,000 participants in the 39 leading management education programs. The rationale was that managers' reports on executive development programs in universities were the most meaningful which could be obtained on the subject. The assumption was simply that the executives were responsible adults whose judgments should carry the most weight regarding program evaluation simply because they knew most about the experiences which they had, even though their perceptions might be subjective and biased.[86]

Ultimately, questionnaires were obtained from approximately 60 percent of the total population included in the study. Andrews focused on the evaluation of the 39 leading programs, many of which are included in Figure 9. Missing would be three Canadian Schools (Atlantic, Banff, and McGill), State University of New York at Buffalo, Case-Western Reserve, Colorado, Illinois, Ohio University, University of Oregon, Michigan State, University of Pennsylvania, University of Southern California, and University of Washington. Of these schools at least Buffalo, McGill, Michigan State, Oregon, Pennsylvania, and Ohio University have discontinued their executive programs since 1958. In any event, the programs that Andrews focused upon were the leading programs and the ones that carried prestige, were oldest in time, and the most influential in organizational effect.

Program Similarities

The 39 were remarkably alike in stated purpose, for most indicated that they were intended to help executives function more effectively in their present positions and to help them prepare for promotions. An increased tolerance and understanding of the various functions in organizations, recognition of the importance of human relationships in organizations, and expanded awareness and broader understanding of the economic, political, and social environment of business were other common purposes of all the major programs. The striking similarity in the objectives of these management education programs can be attributed to the influence of the colleges upon each other, to the conventional style of stating purposes, and to a common perception of a clearly defined need felt in the top levels of management.[87] Thus, all the programs examined by Andrews aimed to "broaden," that is, to expose the participants to new horizons and to enlarge their outlook toward the events taking place around them.

The intention to modify one's point of view rather than to inculcate procedures, teach information, or recommend specific values and attitudes is much different from the emphasis found in typical undergraduate or

[86] *Ibid.,* pp. 2–3.
[87] *Ibid.,* pp. 36–38, 277.

graduate education in business administration. In contrast to the usual college course, the management education programs presupposed experience and emphasized (instead of knowledge) change, increased awareness, and reexamination of previous experience.

This difference in educational goals had important consequences. First of all, the laudable purpose of broadening one's perspective carries with it the virtual impossibility of quantifying results. This is because the extent of breadth desired is not finite. Every person begins at a different starting point. The second consequence was the creation of a different curriculum and teaching process. The subject matter studied by executives was necessarily not organized by company, industry, or technology. Instead the many courses taught fell into the following eight categories: the human problems of administration in organizations; labor relations; policy formulation, general management, and the tasks of top management; the social, economic, and political environment of business; marketing management; financial management; control, accounting, and other uses of quantitative data; and certain personal improvement courses, such as public speaking, rapid reading, conference leading, executive health, and the like.[88]

Unique Educational Process

Perhaps the educational process itself even more dramatically distinguished the management education program from the conventional academic undergraduate or graduate course of instruction. For example, the role of the faculty differed quite sharply from that usually assumed in courses offered graduates and undergraduates. Likely to be of about the same age as the executives, the professor appeared more as an equal than as a superior and served often as a moderator, discussion leader, or chairman rather than a teacher. Also, he did not give grades, mark examinations, or presume to pass judgments in any formal way on the individual work performed. Very little written work was required in most management education programs because executives often appear lost without their secretaries, and they are already hard-pressed to revive their reading capacities. Not supported by typical forms of academic coercion, the professor depended upon the intrinsic interest of the material and the issues he presented for study and upon the responsiveness of the executives in his course. The professor was helped either by the innate conscientiousness of the executives in his sessions or by their wish to do well before one another as peers. By the same token, the faculty was generally judged for their ability to stimulate useful experience for the participants rather than by their standing as scholars or their rank in the profession, which, of course, was often unknown by the participating managers.

[88] *Ibid.*, pp. 39–40.

Though lectures were used in many management education programs, discussion was the central and most essential educational activity in all programs. Both in small study groups and in larger class sections, discussion and interaction among the executives comprised the natural medium for exchange of experience. This exchange was challenged, stimulated, and questioned by the professor; but the conversation was seldom an exchange between student and teacher. The need to make so much discussion meaningful placed a heavy demand upon the faculty, and it by no means followed that a professor who was successful in a conventional classroom setting was equally successful in the management education program.[89]

The Typical Management Education Student

Although it is difficult to generalize on the basis of conglomerate data, Andrews found it possible to put together a summary which indicates the broad dimensions of his findings. The representative executive leaving his home and office for a period of two to thirteen weeks to return to a campus life is very different from what he was as a youth. He is a well-adjusted American male, a college graduate, married with children, and in his early or mid-forties. Typically, he had worked successfully for his employer for 17 years. In view of the regard for him by his superiors and his own success, he was not contemplating working for another employer after completing the management education or indeed at any future point. In four out of five cases, he was to be at the departmental management level shortly after completing the management education program. He had last been promoted three years before his enrollment in management education. He did not typically request that he be sent to a program, but when the idea was suggested to him he welcomed it. He perceived in the suggestion his employer's regard for him. He expected as a result of that regard—not his attendance—to find himself promoted sometime after the program had ended.

He approached the renewal of formal education with a disposition to learn something and an acknowledgment that he had something to learn but with no specific expectations of what it would be. He looked forward to a stimulating interchange of ideas and information with managers on the same organizational level as he from many different industries. He would ultimately find that this was what he obtained.

Middle-of-the-road or conservative in politics, undoctrinaire in argument, ready to consider the point of view of others, optimistic and emotionally stable, the typical participant seemed to his colleagues and to most of the faculty who worked with him to be an extraordinarily straightforward person of conspicuous good will. Easily bored by statistics, theory,

[89] *Ibid.,* pp. 43–44.

and lectures about almost anything, easily offended if he was treated like an undergraduate, he was still intensively interested in problems, in new ideas about dealing with them, and concepts about the relationship of business to society. Whatever were the limitations of his experience, it seemed not to have twisted him or to have disqualified him for possible personal growth in the future.[90]

Essential Findings of Andrews

The Andrews study, like all of its predecessors, seems to have concluded that four out of five participants are markedly favorable toward the management education program which they attended. To be sure, favorability varies by program and class in response to hundreds of variations. Favorability also seems to be related to the participant's previous education; his knowledge of the purposes, content and activities of his program; and to the reservations with which he approached the experience. Typically, his enthusiasm dropped sharply after he plunged into campus life, rose toward the end of the program, and held steady over time thereafter or perhaps increased. He attributed the value of the program to classroom activities and to study for class rather than to recreation or to association with other participants. Rather than rejecting the professors as impractical, he usually praised their confidence and the methods they employed. He did the work which they assigned. His opinion of the management education program remained unaffected by subsequent promotion or the lack of it and was sufficiently durable not to fade out in time. His evaluation was based on the conviction that his attendance in the course was worth his time, effort, and separation from his family and job and his employer's money.[91]

In respect to the impact of the management education experience upon the participant's managerial skill and knowledge, "broadening" is mentioned often—and many evaluations made do not go far beyond citing this vague term. Broadening is, of course, essentially the purpose of all the programs which are considered pace-setting, such as the bulk of those in Figure 9. Broadening redresses in one way or another the narrowing effects of unvaried experience in a functionally restricted aspect of an organization. To the extent that broadening is so extensively cited, it can reasonably be deduced that the programs have probably had this effect.[92]

Andrews concludes that there are many implications for university and company action that grow out of his study.[93] From the standpoint of the manpower specialist in organizations, certainly one of these implications

[90] *Ibid.*, pp. 68–70.
[91] *Ibid.*, pp. 123–124.
[92] *Ibid.*, pp. 154–155.
[93] For an excellent discussion of the details of these see *ibid.*, pp. 184–255.

that should be mentioned is the following. The mission of the management education program should be to teach the integrative and policy skills of general management and advanced work in one or more functional fields. Inasmuch as decentralization is characteristic of many organizations today, the study of the aforementioned topics is as legitimate for managers in middle as in senior positions. Emphasis on future developments, on the relationship of the organization to its environment and of business to society, on the formulation of viable programs and objectives, and on the nature of a business organization as a human institution is especially appropriate for the university-type program. Moreover, the time is now at hand not only for the particularization of mission and clientele among the various university programs but also for a classification of the separate developmental functions of company and university-level programs. The two different kinds of executive development should be complimentary in purpose and effect.[94] It is in the area of policy formulation and the behavior of people in organizations that management education programs in universities relate most closely to the developmental processes operating within an organization and can be most effective. Whether or not the university program makes a contribution in developing executives with these skills depends in large part upon the quality of the organization's strategy in manpower planning and the nature of its climate for growth of human resources.[95] Effective management education can be cancelled by poor manpower planning and a hostile organizational environment.

The learning consequences of democratic give-and-take in the management education seminars but also during evening hours after classes have ended have been repeatedly cited as the main values attributed by managers to college-level in-residence management education programs. This finding underscores once again the importance of interpersonal relations in learning. Indeed, it has often been suggested that the value of management education depends almost exclusively on the personalities and experience-mix of participants who happen to be present at the same time during a particular course offering. The study by Andrews would suggest that much more than the quality of interpersonal relations are involved in the perceived value of management education, but his study also tends to suggest the importance of this topic. Let us next turn to several illustrative management education programs.

Harvard Advanced Management Program

As we have seen, the Harvard 13-week Advanced Management Program is the oldest and best known of the management education programs. The

[94] *Ibid.,* p. 238.
[95] *Ibid.,* p. 249.

program is presented twice annually in the spring and fall and typically has a class size of 150. It enjoys wide national and international geographical distribution and industry representation. The average age of executives attending is 43.8 years and most have had an average of 17.2 years of service in their sponsoring organization. The program caters to high middle and top management.[96]

The intention of the program is to prepare individuals for top-management responsibilities through the study of broad problems of the firm as a whole and the relation of the firm and its environment. Emphasis is placed upon greater awareness of the human aspects of organization and of the responsibilities—other than economic—of business leadership. Specific courses include administrative practices, problems in labor relations, business and American society, business policy, marketing administration, and cost and financial administration, none of which is excessively technical. The program faculty is drawn exclusively from the Harvard Business School and is given a full-time assignment without other teaching responsibilities at any time in the academic year. The teaching methods have differed depending upon the individual instructors but, by and large, have stressed the use of the case method in all courses. The classes usually meet in two large sections but are also organized into small study groups which meet daily.[97]

In the last ten years a few changes have been made in the Advanced Management Program. These include the production of an extensive case collection for a climactic cross-course examination of the top management problems of an important company in great detail with reports presented to its top management. Also, such changes as the following have been made: the introduction of lectures and seminars on developments in the behavioral sciences which affect the future of business administration; more attention to international business; experimentation with a complex business game; an introduction to statistical decision theory; and an attempt to intensify the intellectual challenge of the course materials.[98]

Whereas AMP is intended for experienced executives who are, or are already selected to be, in top management positions, the Harvard Program for Management Development is designed to meet the requirements of younger men currently filling responsible positions at the operating level who have demonstrated by their performances that they are potential top-echelon managers. The PMT is a 16-week operationally oriented course, intended to equip young managers to handle their day-to-day assignments better and to prepare them to assume increasing responsibility in the years

[96] *Ibid.*, p. 280.
[97] *Ibid.*, pp. 280–281.
[98] *Ibid.*

ahead.[99] Altogether, since the Harvard Business School launched its executive training programs in 1943, more than 6000 people from nearly 1000 organizations have attended its AMP or PMD programs. Harvard is now attempting to raise $6,000,000 in order to expand its Management Education facilities.[100]

MIT Sloan Fellowship Program

The Sloan Fellowship Program at MIT dates back to 1931 but was suspended for a number of years during and following World War II. In many respects it is radically different in concept from the AMP or the PMD programs at Harvard. It is a 12-month program leading to the degree of Master of Science in Management and is designed to broaden and develop outstanding but typically specialized young executives for more general and senior management responsibilities in the future.

Forty-five Sloan Fellows are selected each year from both industrial and nonindustrial organizations. They are between 32 and 38 years of age and typically have 10 to 15 years of successful experience behind them. Thus, they can anticipate 30 to 35 years of significant contributions to their organizations ahead of them. They come from both the United States and abroad and are nominated by their employers. They are selected by MIT and designated Alfred P. Sloan Fellows and awarded $1000 fellowships and other funds provided by the Alfred P. Sloan Foundation.[101]

The Sloan Fellowship Program is not a vocational program. There are no techniques or tools offered in it which a man can apply directly back on the job as soon as he has completed his residency at MIT. The goal is to develop the individual intellectually, to create an awareness of significant new concepts and forthcoming critical issues. In fact, as a Sloan Fellow the individual may go through an unlearning process, leaving behind stereotypes and subjective judgments which fail the test of objective analysis. It is expected that he will finish the rigorous and demanding year at MIT with a strong motivation and confidence to go on learning and growing long after he has left the campus.[102]

Whenever possible, the Sloan Fellows work in groups of 15 or 22, which are rotated during the year. Working in small groups facilitates a close informal relationship with the faculty at MIT. The Fellows are encouraged to draw on the total resources of MIT and during the year may also take

[99] *Management Programs at the Harvard Business School,* Graduate School of Business Administration, Harvard University, Boston, 1967, pp. 6–7.

[100] "Corporate 'Old Grads' Help Finance Expansion of Harvard's Executive Education Facilities," *Business Week,* No. 1974, July 1, 1967, p. 58.

[101] *The MIT Alfred P. Sloan Fellowship Program* 1967–1968, Alfred P. Sloan School of Management, Massachusetts Institute of Technology, Cambridge, 1967, p. 3.

[102] *Ibid.,* p. 7.

courses from Harvard University, which is located not far away in the same city (Cambridge, Massachusetts). Whatever success the program enjoys—and it is substantial—derives primarily from the contributions of the faculty of the Sloan School of Management and the associated Departments of Economics and Political Science at MIT. Sloan Fellows enjoy the rich cross-fertilization of ideas made possible by a close association with one another and with industry and government leaders. But it is thought by the Sloan staff that no meaningful and lasting learning experience can take place without a full-time, competent, and devoted faculty.[103]

The year at MIT is considered to be a full and demanding year, calling for extensive reading, critical analysis, and active participation in classes, discussions, and field trips. Participation involves what is tantamount to a 55- or 65-hour work week. Part of the requirement for completion of the program, which has the effect of making it a serious challenge, is the writing of a Master's thesis. The remainder of the program includes course work in such subjects as: economics and finance; management information and control; quantitative methods; law; operations management; industrial dynamics; labor relations and public policy; organizational behavior, including participation in a one-week laboratory in sensitivity training; and a variety of seminars and related courses.[104]

The Sloan Fellowship Program has also followed the belief that the businessman-turned-student can learn as much from contact with top men in government and industry as he can from classroom work. Thus, the Sloan Fellows methodically work their way through the offices of a bevy of federal executives in Washington as part of their participation in the Sloan Program. In addition, they visit industrial executive suites and travel to Western European capitals, visiting industrialists and governmental leaders.[105]

From the original six annual participants, the Sloan Program grew to 15, then to 30; and today each class numbers 45 men, representing a wide variety of industries and activities. Similar to Harvard and other schools, MIT has also branched beyond the initial exploration in management education. It now has a program for senior executives, which consists of nine weeks of seminar discussions, substantial reading assignments, and a client-consultant relationship with the Sloan School of Management faculty. In many respects this program, appealing to a different executive audience, has many of the features of the Sloan Fellowship program only scaled down to an abbreviated time period.[106] In addition, as previously indicated in the chapter, it should be noted that a version of the Sloan Fellowship

[103] *Ibid.*, pp. 13–15.
[104] *Ibid.*, pp. 16–17.
[105] "Executive Training by Meeting the Best," *Business Week,* No. 1753, April 6, 1963, pp. 46–47.
[106] For more details see Andrews, *op. cit.*, p. 293.

Program has also been established at the Graduate School of Business Administration, Stanford University.

The Executive Program at the University of California at Berkeley

It can be seen from Figure 9 that the University of California at Berkeley has been involved in management education going back to at least 1959. Since that time it has evolved several versions of a management education program. The one being offered in the late 1960s was unique among all such programs in the United States.

The present offering is called the Executive Program and is a departure from traditional executive development programs by being specifically geared to the social and economic problems of the 1960s and the 1970s. The program is of four weeks' duration and is of the in-residence type. The participants read 130 books and monographs and attend 110 hours of classes exclusive of after-dinner seminars and evening meetings with graduate students from the Graduate School of Business Administration at Berkeley. The program essentially plunges executives into an intensive study of those external events that, although not directly related to business, exert a subtle impact upon it, such as the War on Poverty, Civil Rights demonstrations, conflicts in urban areas, international politics, open-heart surgery, the economics of medical costs, crime, business statistics, the balance of payments, and similar topics. This emphasis clearly differentiates the Berkeley program from all others available today because it focuses upon the world around the businessman. In past sessions as many as 50 professors from the resourceful Berkeley faculty have been drawn upon to create a curriculum so broad that the participants could sample what is going on in almost every area of national interest.[107]

In addition to the Berkeley faculty, field trips and guest speakers are utilized to round out the program. Moreover, the diversity among the participants itself brings change into the learning situation. For example, the 200 alumni run the gamut of large- and medium-sized companies, domestic and foreign corporations, the armed forces, federal agencies, state and local governments, different cultural and minority groups, and both sexes. Since the program's inception in 1959, 75 corporations have sent more than one manager; and since the mid-1960s new companies have been enrolling in the program at a 30 percent annual rate.[108]

As an entirely new departure in management education, the Berkeley program, when it matures, may take either of two directions. First, it could become a place for distinguished scholars and public figures to meet with an elite management student body. In this way it would have one of the

[107] "B-School Throws Away the Book," *Business Week,* No. 1964, April 22, 1967, pp. 104–106.
[108] *Ibid.,* p. 106.

same features of the Sloan Fellowship program. Secondly, the program could incorporate more of the "continuing education" philosophy. In other words, the faculty could fly to regional seminars, meet with alumni, and bring them up to date. This would be a new departure in adult education. Whatever the ultimate direction, the program is intended to do more than educate the participant concerning contemporary changes. It is also intended that they should be able to forecast changes and to initiate them within and outside their employing organizations.[109]

Modern Engineering Program of the University of California at Los Angeles

In addition to management education programs, there are others which are intended to improve the technical competency and prevent the educational obsolescence of engineering and technical personnel. Others are intended to prepare engineers for management positions. For example, the MIT Sloan Fellowship Program was initially started in 1931 to assist engineers who had risen above the strictly technical level to learn executive skills.[110]

The Sloan Program may be regarded as focused upon one end of the spectrum of problems in developing competent engineering manpower. At the other end is the fluctuating level of undergraduate engineering enrollments, which has been a preoccupation of manpower experts since 1951, if not before.

It should be noted that in 1951 the various engineering professional societies formed the Engineers' Joint Council which concerned itself with engineering manpower and in particular the need to awaken young people's interest in engineering. In any event, manpower experts believe there has been a poor job of the engineering profession's selling itself to young people as a creative field of endeavor. Engineering also has obtained a black-eye from the stockpiling of engineers by large companies. Malutilization of engineering talent resulted in the assignment of college graduate engineers to tedious routine work which used only a limited part of their professional background. The toughness of the academic program in engineering also drove off enrollees. These problems when coupled with the high attrition rate in college and the grind of the curriculum itself have combined to reduce the number of undergraduate engineers.[111]

Still another problem in developing engineers in recent years has been the need to change the undergraduate engineering curriculum so that it will be consistent with the requirements of the Space Age. The fast pace of

---

[109] *Ibid.,* p. 108.

[110] "Executive Training by Meeting the Best," *op. cit.,* p. 46.

[111] Edmund K. Faltermayer, "Engineering Enigma," *Wall Street Journal,* July 27, 1962, p. 1 ff.

today's technology makes knowledge stale very quickly. In engineering this rapid obsolescence often means that the graduate finds that in five years one-half of what he has learned is no longer valid or useful. As a result, many engineering schools have moved toward offering generalized rather than specialized curricula, leaving up to industry the task of providing specialized training for young engineers.

The basic educational problem that has stemmed from these other problems is whether the engineering curriculum should emphasize the basic sciences of design and similar engineering fundamentals. Undergraduate engineering education in the future is likely to split off into two groups, one emphasizing the scientific orientation and the other stressing design. Inasmuch as only one to two percent of engineering graduates go on for a doctorate, the job of specialized training will largely be handed over to the graduate schools and to industry. More broadly, it is quite possible that engineering schools in the future will assume one of three basic roles. Some will take on the job of filling the present needs of industry. A smaller number will train people who will staff presently undreamed-of industries based upon undreamed-of technology. And, third, a tiny handful will turn out graduates who will set the new engineering standards.[112]

Inasmuch as MIT has long been the cornerstone of the nation's engineering education, the changes made in its curriculum over the last nine years are probably a harbinger of what is ahead for the best of American engineering schools. If this is the case, the stress at MIT on eliminating barriers between engineers and scientists, between theories and their application, and in training students so that their fundamental approach and their knowledge will be valid ten to twenty years hence will probably be most influential in modifying curricula at other schools.[113]

Figure 10 depicts the phenomenon which we have been discussing and is especially appropriate when considering engineering obsolescence. The diagram shows the work-life of an engineer as a beam cantilevered on his basic engineering education. As he moves out on the beam, it will deflect in proportion to the distance from his basic education. If we consider the value of a professional engineer to society as directly related to his technical competency, as the beam deflects, his competency decreases and his value to society diminishes. For a time, some support to the engineer's technical competence is given through job-related experience. But this decreases rather rapidly and contributes to his support for only ten years or less. Assuming that our total fund of engineering and scientific knowledge

[112] "The Fine New Art of Educating Engineers," *Business Week*, No. 1804, March 28, 1964, pp. 142–148.

[113] "MIT's New Breed of Engineers," *Business Week*, No. 1794, January 18, 1964, pp. 54–58.

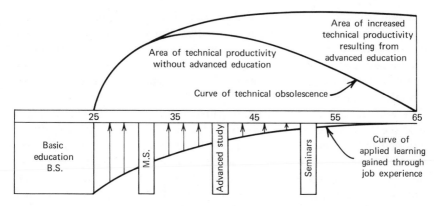

Figure 10 Engineering obsolescence cantilever. *Source. Northeastern University Graduate Cooperative Programs in Engineering and Mathematics* (brochure), p. 3.

doubles approximately every eight years, one's working life must therefore become a continuing educative process, with the first step being toward advanced fundamental training in one's specific occupational or professional field.

Let us elaborate further on the engineering obsolescence cantilever in Figure 10. One's education beyond the basic bachelor's degree may be obtained through an educational program leading to a master's degree in one specialty. Through this program, a person will learn to use the advanced tools of his occupation or profession and to begin specialization in an area of professional interest. Armed next with the master's degree, the individual may then specialize further in a doctoral program or continue his education on a part-time basis while practicing his occupation or profession. Throughout his career he will need, then, to update his education continuously through advanced study, formal courses, selective reading, attending the meetings of professional societies, seminars, and other forms of part-time education. It, therefore, becomes obvious that technical competency is a function of education, and today's professional engineer cannot afford to fall behind.[114]

The problem of coping with the onrush of science and technology is likely to be largest, ironically, for the best engineers and particularly for the man who has not stuck with some narrow specialty over the years but has risen into management and been given responsibility for a diverse engineering group or a development laboratory. His problem is basically that he finds it increasingly difficult to understand what the young men

[114] *Northeastern University Graduate Cooperative Program in Engineering and Mathematics* (Brochure), pp. 2–3.

under him are talking about. He will wonder how he can manage men with whom he can hardly communicate. He is likely to feel inadequate in judging the capabilities of which of these men should be hired and advanced or in evaluating a proposed development program when his own education is hopelessly out of date. The solution has been found in programs such as the Modern Engineering Program at UCLA.[115]

Many of the existing management education programs are not of much use to the engineering manager because he needs a special kind of educational help. He probably lacks the scientific background he would need to take individual courses in quantum mechanics, plasma physics, cryogenics, magnetohydrodynamics, solid-state electronics, inertial guidance, nuclear engineering, and matrix algebra. He also lacks the time it takes to reeducate himself from the bottom up and needs something in between. What he requires has not existed in the framework of conventional education, but it does exist under the sponsorship of institutions concerned with management education.

The idea for a course that would meet these interstitial needs was identified in 1959 at a meeting of the American Society for Engineering Education.[116] Since 1961, UCLA has been offering an intensive six-week course entitled Modern Engineering for 30 to 35 engineering and scientific managers consistent with the need.

Most of the instruction in Modern Engineering has been provided by UCLA professors, but some outstanding scientists and engineers from local industry and other universities have also been used. The reasoning basic to the program is that the engineering executive must be able to analyze, evaluate, and perform syntheses from all available information relevant to the job. This requires that he be acquainted with recent developments in engineering and with the new tools and techniques for future application. The program is designed to teach principles rather than specifics, to orient participants in modern technical concepts, and to explore the nature of probable future trends. The program is keyed to the needs of senior personnel from the armed forces who are involved in research or must evaluate sophisticated proposals from industry as well as for industrial managers.[117]

The UCLA Modern Engineering Course has had an interesting and

[115] George A. W. Boehm, "Bringing Engineers Up to Date," *Fortune,* Vol. 67, No. 5, May 1963, p. 120.

[116] *Ibid.*

[117] *Modern Engineering for Engineering Executives,* Department of Engineering, University Extension, University of California, Los Angeles, 1964, p. 3; and "Tough Cram Course for the Brass," *Business Week,* No. 1713, June 30, 1962, pp. 90–94.

significant offshoot. Two engineering executives from General Electric attended the first program and returned with considerable enthusiasm for it. As a consequence, General Electric built a modern engineering program of its own with some of the ideas developed at UCLA. G.E.'s version of modern engineering was offered at a hotel in Saratoga Springs, New York, and consisted of some 100 lectures spread over six weeks.[118]

The UCLA program remains the model for strengthening a manager's knowledge of science and engineering as opposed to the traditional management education course which is intended to teach engineers managerial skill and knowledge. Considering the importance of engineering manpower for the future of the United States and for industrial organizations, it is quite likely that such engineering courses are going to increase in the future if the tendency to cope with educational obsolescence is sustained.

The Liberal Arts Programs

Of all the programs that have been designed to broaden managers and to make them aware of their environment, there is little doubt that the liberal arts programs are conceptually closest to these ideals. The earliest and most well known of the management education programs in the liberal arts was the Institute of Humanistic Studies for executives initiated and supported completely by the Bell Telephone System and operated at the University of Pennsylvania. Managers with high potential, selected from the third and higher levels of supervision, were released from their jobs to spend a full academic year at the university. Courses were grouped into four major fields, namely, science, philosophy, history, and the arts. The program started with a course in practical logic and a short transitional course in business history. The latter was followed by a history of economic thought, world art, history, the esthetics of music, analytical reading, world literature, social science, philosophy of ethics, and the history and meaning of science. As these specialized courses neared completion, the various areas of knowledge were integrated and related to the present-day world in courses presented during the final weeks. The program culminated in a detailed study of James Joyce's *Ulysses,* a course in modern architecture and city planning, one on American civilization, and, finally, one in political science and international relations.[119]

The teaching methods used included lectures, discussions, seminars, and field trips. The latter included visits to the United Nations Secretariat;

[118] Boehm, *op. cit.,* pp. 121, 179–180.

[119] Morris S. Viteles, " 'Human Relations and the 'Humanities' in the Education of Business Leaders: Evaluation of a Program of Humanistic Studies for Executives," *Personnel Psychology,* Vol. 12, No. 1, Spring 1959, pp. 1–28.

attendance at Philadelphia Orchestra concerts; trips to New York, Washington, and Philadelphia museums; and attendance at lectures, exhibitions, and other cultural activities to be found in and around Philadelphia. The Institute faculty included professors from the University of Pennsylvania and nearby colleges. In addition, there were more than 100 guest lecturers who were also outstanding in their respective fields. The reading of many books was a strong and central feature of the program. These were supplied to the student and represented the nucleus of a substantial library to which he could add subsequently in his life. The presentation of books was viewed as a significant step in achieving one objective of the program, namely, to motivate participants to accept the concept of intellectual activity as a never-ending process to be continued throughout life.[120]

The Institute of Humanistic Studies for Executives ran for about seven years, and about 130 executives completed the course. Bell Telephone indicated that the program was worthwhile, but it was experimental. After the Institute was started in 1953, the Bell System created four other shorter programs somewhat similar in type. For example, in 1956 Bell established one eight-week session a year at Williams and Dartmouth Colleges. In 1957 they established three eight-week sessions a year at Northwestern University. A series of 14-week sessions that began at Swarthmore College in 1956 was abandoned in 1958.[121]

In its later years the Bell program at the University of Pennsylvania had difficulty in securing enrollments both within the Bell System (and from outsiders when it was offered to other corporations). One reason the Institute was difficult to sell to other organizations was that it was no quick, easy introduction to the arts and no simple course of practical management skills with a garnish of humanities. Rather, it was a long, serious, intensive program of lectures, readings, and discussions of esoteric subjects, as previously indicated. Most of the participants worked very hard and they considered that the program brought about an important change in their lives. For example, some former participants reported that they were buying fine art for their homes as a consequence of having learned to appreciate it and had begun to stock up on books and classical records. They stated that the courses made them more aware of changes in the world around them and helped them relate change to other times and other societies. Students from the earlier years in the program testified that the wider outlook which they had learned stayed with them. Some reported that they took a much broader view and were making much more critical analyses of

[120] *Ibid.*
[121] "No More Humanities for Brass," *Business Week,* No. 1607, June 18, 1960, pp. 123–124. For more details see Peter E. Siegle, *New Directions for Liberal Education for Executives,* Center for the Study of Liberal Education for Adults, Chicago, 1958.

both on- and off-the-job problems. They also reported that decisions did not come as spontaneously as previously and more of the opposite point of view is automatically understood.[122]

Evaluation of the Bell Program

The only published systematic evaluation of the Bell Program extant was carried out by Viteles, a famous industrial psychologist. He found that the participants had acquired guides for distinguishing what is significant from what is commonplace and of transient value, especially in recognizing the origin, nature, and importance of literary and artistic trends. Participants acquired a better understanding of the forces within the individual and his society which affected the development and operation of a civilization and its institutions. They acquired an increased understanding of the nature and history of social, economic, and political institutions and of the problems arising in them. In this respect they will probably become better prepared to deal with these kinds of problems in contemporary society. In addition, exposure to the humanities led program participants to attach greater importance to ordinarily neglected values which have or can contribute to enriched intellectual and emotional perspectives. Along this dimension, they saw movement toward the realization of a major objective of the Institute program.[123]

After the demise of the Institute of Humanistic Studies for Executives at the University of Pennsylvania, it was not long before the counterpart programs at Williams, Dartmouth, and Northwestern were also phased out. Yet there were other independent experiences in the use of liberal arts for executives. For example, there were programs at Clark University, Wabash College (which is still continuing), Pomona, Denver, Akron, and Vassar (which had an institute for women in business).[124] And by the middle of 1965 managerial liberal arts education had been somewhat revitalized as IBM installed a program of its own operating out of Colgate University. IBM had for a while been a participant in an AT&T program. It decided to start an eight-week cram course in the arts, philosophy, economics, psychology, and communications for the purpose of managerial "enlargement" or broadening. Each course in the program was specifically

[122] "No More Humanities for Brass," *op. cit.,* p. 124.
[123] *Ibid.* For other evaluations see E. Digby Baltzell, "Bell Telephone's Experiment in Education"; Wilfred D. Gillen, "Why Should a Company Spend Money in This Way?"; and Charles A. Nelson, "The Liberal Arts and Management," all in Robert A. Goldwin and Charles A. Nelson, eds., *Toward the Liberally Educated Executive,* New American Library, New York, 1960, pp. 15–22, 23–24, and 105–119, respectively.
[124] For the details of these programs, see Siegle, *op. cit.,* pp. 29–66.

intended to contribute to the broadening of communication capability among participants.[125]

By the mid-1960s the telephone company was back again in liberal arts education for executives. By this time 700 to 800 upper- and middle-management men had taken an AT&T humanities program. Building upon a so-called leadership course that was begun at Dartmouth in 1959, a parallel program was started at Carleton College in Northfield, Minnesota, in 1963. The idea behind the revived program was to study certain novels, biographies, histories, and essays for insight into the anatomy of leadership and persuasion. Only three courses were included in the curriculum, but all were based upon heavy reading assignments in the liberal arts.

Though the programs at IBM and AT&T were different in focus and curriculum, they had several things in common. For example, both were experimental. This means that although both companies had extensive experience in educating employees, neither had been able to prove that management competent in the liberal arts was more competitive in the marketplace. The programs were small compared to other training the companies have undertaken over the years. The students selected were top performers.[126]

The Aspen Program

Perhaps the most durable of all the liberal arts programs for executives is the one conducted by the Aspen Institute for Humanistic Studies in Aspen, Colorado. This program was started by the late Walter P. Paepcke of the Container Corporation of America in an effort to help executives understand the society in which their businesses exist, and it continues to add blue-chip business executives to its roster of participants.

Originally, the Aspen program was designed to expand the executive's understanding of his role in society and the responsibilities that go with leadership. The developmental approach is to provide a unique environment for the whole man in which cultural immersion and recreation are mixed in a kind of regenerative process.

The program is not merely another college or intracompany summer management education program. Instead, at Aspen there are a number of two-week sessions each summer called the Aspen Executive Program. The participants are stimulated to develop their own convictions. This is approached through exposure to selected reading of the world's greatest philosophers, scholars, economists, historians, and political leaders; daily meetings with a bold and stimulating group for informal discussion of the ideas found in the readings, with special emphasis on the application of

[125] "Specialists Try a Wider Track," *Business Week,* No. 1874, July 24, 1965, p. 56.
[126] *Ibid.,* p. 57.

these ideas to current problems; and lectures and panel discussions by authorities on international affairs two evenings a week, each followed the next morning by informal discussions with the leaders. The Aspen Musical Festival and the Aspen Music Year run concurrently with the executive program, thereby providing an intimate association between the participants and the world's most eminent musicians and musicologists. Also, a health center is integrated into the life of the executive program.[127]

Actually, the Aspen Institute for Humanistic Studies pioneered in seminars for executives in order to expose them to rather lofty examination of such enduring ideas in the evolution of Western thought as freedom, equality, justice, power, and the destiny of man. Approximately 1200 persons had partaken of this intellectual broth by the mid-1960s, guided by moderators from the fields of education, the arts, science, labor, theology, and government.[128]

Executive development using liberal arts programs has had a checkered history. The vicissitudes of the telephone company program and the consistent popularity of the Aspen program suggest contradictory patterns. We might conclude that there is only a mild interest in the use of liberal arts programs for management education today. Yet we cannot say that they are on the way out. It is quite clear that they have had problems in recruitment, at least as far as the AT&T programs are concerned. Despite the unclarity of the role that they are intended to serve in management education (beyond "broadening"), it is quite clear that evaluating liberal arts programs for executives is equally as difficult as evaluating liberal arts education for anyone. Therefore, we shall not attempt to do so here.

Using Management Education Programs: Some Guidelines

It was recently estimated that American business firms in an effort to fight the increasing problem of executive obsolescence put about 500,000 executives through on-the-job training courses, management seminars, and formal academic programs during 1966 alone, which was nearly twice the number put through such programs in 1961.[129] The management education programs of the type we have been discussing in this chapter are obviously a very tiny part of the sum total of executive development programs in operation in the United States today. Yet, because they are concerned with the highest-potential manpower, they are worthy of the detailed considera-

---

[127] Siegle, *op. cit.*, pp. 49–52. See also the various annual reports of the Aspen Institute for Humanistic Studies for the details of specific offerings.

[128] *Denver Post*, August 8, 1965, p. 291.

[129] Robert J. House, *Management Development: Design, Evaluation, and Implementation,* Bureau of Industrial Relations, University of Michigan, Ann Arbor, 1967, p. 9, citing T. Bray, "Obsolete Executives," *Wall Street Journal,* January 24, 1966, p. 1.

tion we have given them. It therefore becomes very important, from the manpower specialist's standpoint, to consider the factors and guidelines pertinent for executive participation in management education.

Participants who seem to have benefited the most from management education programs share several characteristics, such as better-than-average ability, capacity to embrace new ideas and solve novel problems, strong interests, and a favorable attitude toward the developmental experience provided them. The last characteristic is especially important because of the difficult personal adjustments these programs impose.

As we have seen, typically the management education program participant is in his 30s or 40s and long removed from coping with the amount of reading and studying the regimen of management education will entail. The reading load is heavy, and the unfamiliarity of the program activities often combine to make the experience trying and frustrating. Genuine interest and effort are required to surmount these difficulties. In general, it is a disservice to the man, his organization, and the university to send an unqualified candidate to such programs.[130]

Selection Considerations

To avoid waste, organizations should know the man they intend to send to a program and the characteristics of specific management education programs. In this sense, the organization must be like a physician diagnosing a case or situation.

Organizations vary in the methods used to select men for participation. In some instances the organizational superior simply nominates an individual for the program. In other organizations where there is more sophisticated manpower planning, some consideration is given to performance appraisals and organizational planning requirements in deciding upon whom should be sent to management education programs. Whatever the method used, most candidates are selected because they have demonstrated potential that warranted accelerated development. However, sometimes candidates are chosen for other reasons. For example, sometimes a man is sent because it would appear that he had been discriminated against were he not selected. Sometimes selections are based on the hope that problem managers who have not responded to other approaches might be improved by attending a university program. Lastly, the programs are sometimes used as a means of rewarding older men, even though it is recognized they are unlikely to progress further.[131]

Finding the right program for a manager is largely the responsibility of

---

[130] John H. Gorsuch, "Making Better Use of University Programs," *Business Horizons,* Vol. 6, No. 1, Spring 1963, p. 58.
[131] *Ibid.*

the employing organization. An organization that fails in this is subject to serious indictment. Yet many fail to diagnose effectively the individual needs of an executive. It seems that the managers who benefit the least from participating in programs come from organizations that lack any sound performance appraisal method.[132]

From the standpoint of the manpower specialist, management education programs have quality probably only in terms of their ability to meet the defined needs of the individual executive. Some managers will study and learn best in a city atmosphere. Others of equal maturity and potential must find a program far removed from the tempo and confusion of a city. Those who tend toward introversion should go to one type of program whereas those who are more extroverted should go to another. Executives sometimes dislike programs because of the eating arrangements whereas others dislike programs because their privacy is invaded. The point is that each program is effective and the best for certain types of executives. None is categorically best for all managers.

It is the responsibility of the manpower specialist in the employing organization to determine the subject matter, surrounding circumstances, and the learning process that each executive requires. In respect to the learning process, this is a function of individual differences. Some people learn best by ear and, therefore, enjoy lectures; some people learn best by reading and dislike lectures. Some management education programs include little reading, whereas others include heavy reading assignments. As for case analyses, bull sessions, and business games, some managers like these and some do not. Some managers are very intolerant of others' opinions and perhaps should go to longer programs where there will be a greater opportunity to break down an individual's intolerance. There are also differences of a cultural nature reflecting perhaps the varying values and attitudes of different parts of the United States. Considerations should be given to these in choosing a program for each executive.[133]

The task of matching the manager with the program is not the exclusive responsibility of the employing organization, however. It must be shared by the university. Yet, very few universities offering management education programs have real selection processes.[134]

In preparing a candidate to attend a management education program, it is important that the executive be consulted and involved in this decision concerning his development. Thus, an organization should cooperate with an executive who is about to leave for a university program by aiding him

---

[132] Allison V. MacCullough, "University Courses for Executives," *Management Record,* Vol. 19, No. 5, May 1957, p. 3.

[133] *Ibid.*

[134] *Ibid.*

in numerous ways to cover his position while he is absent. He may not be able to put aside his responsibilities during the period of his attendance. His job responsibilities must be completely delegated to others while he is gone. This is sometimes a stumbling block because organizations hesitate releasing a key man for management education. Yet no one is indispensable in a large organization because we find that jobs are covered when individuals are on vacation or when they die unexpectedly. Therefore, with adequate planning people can be freed from their responsibilities and sent to management education programs. Skillful executive counseling can assist in preparing the man for attendance.[135]

Preparing for the Manager's Return

The peers, superiors, and subordinates of the manager attending a management education program must be prepared for the manager's return after program participation. Sometimes the manager's various organizational associates feel that some kind of change should take place when the manager returns. In addition, the participant also often wants to make changes based upon what he has learned while on the program. An organization must have well-developed plans for the participant's reassimilation upon his return.

An organization has two obligations to the man and to itself upon his return. First, it should provide him with time to take an inventory of his recent experience, to reevaluate his philosophy, to assess and calibrate new views and attitudes, and to plan his new course of action and mode of conduct. The second obligation is the creation of a new climate which permits experimentation and the right to try and to fail in making innovation.[136]

Measuring Specific Value of Participation

The specific value to an organization of participation in management education programs is difficult to assess. In a sense, all the programs are good and all are bad and all are different, depending upon the participant. There are some rules of thumb which are pertinent. First, no program should be judged solely by one man's participation and subjective impressions. Variety in the types of programs and the learning processes prevent the views of any one person being definitive. The devotion of the faculty to the management education job is an important variable because there are few professors who are mature, intimately acquainted with big business, and, at the same time, scholars and experts in subject matter. Programs which have "visiting firemen" may not be better than those with residential

[135] *Ibid.*, pp. 3–4.
[136] *Ibid.*, p. 4.

professors because the integration of their contributions to the program is extremely difficult.

Second, the organization's objectives in sending a manager must be predetermined. These objectives then constitute the basis for measuring changes in the participant.

Third, changes in the graduate of a program should not be looked for prematurely, perhaps not for one year or more.

Fourth, changes that are likely to count heavily are to be found in the managerial climate of the organization only after a significant proportion of all its executives have become program graduates.

Fifth, the total growth of an individual should be evaluated, not the numerous segments of growth, of which the management education program participation was only one!

Finally, it should be realized that an objective appraisal of management education programs is extremely difficult because the required factors for a controlled educational experiment are largely impossible to manipulate.[137] Therefore, most evaluations have (as in the case of Andrews) resorted to subjective or testimonial approaches. Perhaps the ultimate test of the management education program is whether it extends the mind to comprehend the world rather than shrinks the world to fit the mind of a specialist.

Removing the Pomp and Stressing Results in Performance

Some organizations have dropped the pomp and ceremony which was characteristic of their executive development programs in the early 1950s and have replaced these with sophisticated approaches for individual learning. These organizations distinguish sharply between the formal programs and the organized, individually managed approaches designed to stimulate and help their managers build competence. Stress has been placed upon changes of job responsibilities or lateral transfers in manager development. Appraisals have been sharpened to insist upon the use of fact-oriented judgments rather than highly structured approaches or the off-the-cuff personal opinions of managers. Greater emphasis has been placed upon involving top executives in making executive development decisions. There has even been a return to the "crown prince" syndrome on the theory that the process of planned development is inherently selective; therefore, it is desirable to concentrate executive development efforts on promising individuals rather than carry out unfocused efforts. Leading organizations tie discussions and decisions on manpower with business-planning and organizational-planning decisions. Individuals considered for executive development are "tested under fire" and given challenging assignments to determine if their performance is adequate. Lastly, when management education

[137] *Ibid.*

programs have been used to supplement opportunities for learning and development within the organization, emphasis has been placed upon using the shorter rather than the longer management education programs. Greater stress has been placed upon shorter and special-purpose programs which probe a single facet of management in considerable depth for a one- or two-week period. These are courses designed and run by outside professionals for presentation on an in-company basis in such topics as problem solving and decision making, sensitivity training, and the fundamentals of finance. Finally, most educational programs, particularly the special-purpose courses, have been increasingly offered in an atmosphere of tension, pressure, and competition in which the individual becomes very active in the learning process. This is sometimes coupled with testing and an evaluation of the participant's performance in the educational and training program. Some of this new emphasis amounts to making executive development much more concrete than it was a decade or more ago.[138]

Stress on Building Men through Organizational Resources

In other words, in organizations where executive development is most successful today, line executives have assumed responsibility for developing their immediate subordinates and overseeing that these subordinates, in turn, recognize their responsibility to develop their men. Under this approach, each individual's development plan is unique and based upon a study of his own needs by his organizational superiors. The overall effort is thoughtful and well organized. Performance appraisal is still central in executive development but appraisal becomes a continuous, cumulative process. As promising younger managers are tested in increasingly difficult job assignments, management constantly adds to its knowledge of individual capabilities and of the organization's total manpower resources. Management has much more realistic expectations in regard to what can be anticipated from university-level in-residence management education programs. There is also increasing use made of executive manpower development specialists who spend the major part of their time on planning human resource development programs for executive manpower.[139]

We are perhaps on the brink of the closest possible cooperation between business and other organizations and universities for educational purposes. The rapid obsolescence of education obtained in college has become a matter of great concern to our universities as well as to the industries that attract our most intelligent graduates. Continuing programs of formal instruction are needed so that executives and other persons may return repeatedly to the classroom throughout their productive lives, supplement-

[138] Robert K. Stolz, "Executive Development—New Perspective," *Harvard Business Review*, Vol. 44, No. 3, May-June 1966, pp. 133–141.
[139] *Ibid.*, pp. 142–143.

ing their own experience with the new knowledge spawned from many other minds. Conversely, many changes are taking place in industry and in technology about which university professors and academicians are not fully aware. Manpower can be attracted from industry and utilized on a part-time or evening basis to instruct in colleges and universities in their area of specialism. In this way the ties between organizations and the educational community can be strengthened. Also, educational plans could be established and sabbaticals might be given to individuals who desire to return to the academic environment for study. In many respects the bonds between industry and education can be strengthened for the benefit of both.[140] Undoubtedly they will in the years ahead, but there are many signs at present that there will be an uneasy equilibrium in relationships for the foreseeable future.

OTHER APPROACHES TO EXECUTIVE DEVELOPMENT

The chief methods of executive development have already been discussed above in the chapter. There remain innumerable other techniques which are used. It will not be possible to cover all of them; however, for illustrative purposes three other techniques will be mentioned. The first of these is an example of a popular program presenting the principles of management by a leading American consultant. This program is not necessarily typical of the full range of programs of its type, but it is a pertinent example of how instruction in managerial skills and knowledge is being handled. Second are executive manpower policies that provide for sabbatical leaves and for the provision of teachers to organizations on a leave-of-absence basis. In a way these are complementary policies. Third is the relatively new concept of using retired executives in a service corps for the purpose of developing organizations or locations where they are in short supply. Let us examine first the aforementioned training program on managerial skills and knowledge.

Programs Stressing Classical-Traditional Principles

Some firms have utilized programs based on the classical-traditional principles of management in training not only staff supervisors but also higher managers and even foremen. One of the most well known of these courses was developed by Louis A. Allen Associates for Armco Steel Company and later filmed.[141] This course has some human relations con-

---

[140] Neil W. Chamberlain, "The Corporation as a College," *Atlantic Monthly,* Vol. 215, No. 6, June 1966, pp. 102–104.

[141] "Film Textbook Builds Talent Pool at Armco," *Business Week,* No. 1584, January 9, 1960, pp. 54–60. Five thousand employees at Armco from vice-presidents to foremen participated in this program.

tent but consists largely of identifying and describing such traditional management functions as planning (which, according to Allen, involves forecasting, establishing objectives, programming, scheduling, budgeting, establishing procedures, and developing policies); organizing (which includes developing organizational structure, delegating, and establishing relationships); leading (involving decision making, communicating, motivating, selecting people, and developing people); and, lastly, controlling (which includes such activities as establishing performance standards and then measuring, evaluating, and correcting performance).[142] Although many of the ideas in his course are similar to those appearing in the literature of management stated by such pioneers as Henri Fayol or James D. Mooney, Allen has structured his materials somewhat differently and carefully integrated them. Between 1954 and 1964 Allen made studies in 385 business, governmental, and institutional enterprises throughout the world. Each concept, principle, and definition set forth by Allen has been critically reviewed by 12,500 managers throughout the world. He regards the results of this critical appraisal as having "the hard muscle of practical fact and will apply with validity to the manifold problems of management wherever they may be found and in whatever language they may be voiced." And also:

"The theoretical framework we have developed to accommodate the realities of management practice is based upon the assumption that management is a specialized kind of work which represents a maturation of leadership. A manager is a particularly competent, knowing, and, hopefully, most effective kind of leader. His purpose is to enable the people he leads to work most effectively together with him. To accomplish this, he devotes most of his time and energy to performing certain kinds of specialized work which only he is organizationally capable of performing with maximum efficiency. The four functions and nineteen activities of management are identified and defined, their logic is established, and the major requirements of successful practice are developed . . . [in Allen's course and the book]."[143]

Among other results the program provides participants with a common vocabulary for managerial phenomena. If an organization does not use a face-validated system such as that suggested by Allen, it is important that it develop its own common language of management and that it be used across the board. Much time is lost and effort wasted in contemporary organizations because members of management do not speak the same

[142] Louis A. Allen, *The Management Profession*, McGraw-Hill, New York, 1964, p. 68.
[143] Allen, *op. cit.*, pp. vii–ix.

language or think in comparable terms, which if corrected could improve performance. Organizations with access to programs such as that offered by Allen may teach the classical-traditional principles of management to managers and thus can avoid the need for establishing a corporate school or using an in-residence management education program in a university.

Sabbatical Leaves

Sabbaticals for managers of complex organizations are closely akin to liberal arts management education programs. As we have seen, big business attracts many bright young college graduates. But after employment industry places these young men in a long, narrowing career tunnel which will steadily stifle the excitement of their youth. Time spent on the job, on homework for the job, in travel, in business entertaining, in mulling over the problems of the next day and the conflicts of the past one combine to deprive managers in large organizations of the time needed to explore their intellectual curiosity in fields beyond those directly related to their employment. Sabbatical leaves would provide the opportunity for mind stretching in much the same way that is inherent in the programs offered by the Aspen Institute and formerly through the Institute for Humanistic Studies operated by the AT&T.[144]

The idea of a sabbatical leave for managers in complex organizations is taken from the venerable concept as it applies to institutions of higher learning. Harvard University was the first to have a sabbatical leave policy, beginning in 1880. The purposes of sabbatical leaves are to provide teachers with an opportunity for self-improvement through a leave of absence with full or partial compensation following a designated number of years of consecutive service, quite often after six years. Sabbatical leave involves three essential elements: purpose, compensation, and a definite period of prior consecutive service in the institution.[145] Sabbatical leave also usually implies a definite obligation for the recipient to return to his institution for further service for at least one year and in some cases a longer period of time.

The idea of sabbaticals for managers seems radical at first blush. Yet, it should be recalled that members of the United Steel Workers Union who satisfy certain eligibility requirements may obtain three months' vacations. Similarly, electrical workers who are members of the International Brother-

---

[144] Richard B. McAdoo, "Sabbaticals for Businessmen," *Harper's Magazine,* Vol. 224, No. 1344, May 1962, pp. 39–40.

[145] Walter Crosby Eells and Ernest V. Hollis, *Sabbatical Leave in American Higher Education* (Bulletin No. 17), Government Printing Office, Washington, 1962, pp. 1–3, citing Carter V. Good, ed., *Dictionary of Education,* McGraw-Hill, New York, 1959, p. 424.

hood of Electrical Workers in the New York City area obtained the five-hour day several years ago through collective bargaining and have put the New York City electrical contracting industry on a 25-hour week, although electricians typically work a longer week at overtime rates. It has frequently been suggested that hourly employees be given a paid sabbatical similar to that enjoyed by teachers. To some extent all of these union negotiated or proposed reductions of the work year or work week are radical. They are straws in the wind, however, and there is good reason for managements to consider reduced working time for managers. There remains the question of how the time not worked can be optimally used. Educational program participation and sabbatical leaves are a possible answer.

One version of the sabbatical program for executives would grant the leave every eleventh year rather than the seventh year as in academic life. This arrangement would give the average young man entering industry in his early 20s approximately four years off during his life cycle of employment, assuming he works for the same organization throughout his career. Such amounts of leave would not necessarily be as costly as might appear. For example, for the organization paying a 52 percent tax in profits, each of these dollars costs only 48 cents. The organization that paid a manager two-thirds of his regular salary while on sabbatical would be spending proportionately less than the university that provides only one-half pay to the teacher on leave. Perhaps the intellectual refreshment and opportunity to obtain new perspective would justify the expense. The granting of sabbaticals could be arranged so that the organization does not lose the services of a key man at a critical juncture in its operations. There seems to be no existing functional equivalent in management of the sabbatical for giving executives the chance to refresh themselves. Such a new perspective could hardly be gained by a vacation of four weeks, which is probably the closest thing to a functional equivalent.[146]

Sabbatical leaves could also be tied in with the assignment of managers to institutions of higher learning for the purposes of teaching. Interactions between complex organizations and institutions of higher learning are likely to intensify in the future, as we have previously noted. In order to help offset the increasing shortage of capable teachers and at the same time facilitate the development of managerial manpower, organizations might consider granting a year's leave of absence to a small number of qualified employees for the purposes of teaching at the collegiate level. These individuals could receive their regular salary and expenses while on leave serving as teachers. On completion of their assignments they would then return to their original or equivalent positions in the employing organization. Such an executive manpower policy would not only help institutions

---

[146] McAdoo, *op. cit.*, pp. 41–42.

of higher learning but also provide a chance for an executive to relocate himself in an entirely different environment and give some thought to his own development. If he were to teach courses connected with his specialty, the very fact that he had to prepare himself for classes would be a worthwhile professional developmental experience. Tulane and Southern Illinois Universities have already made starts in this direction with their executive-in-residence programs.[147] Organizations presently offering various types of sabbatical leave, often called fellowship programs, tend to be technologically oriented and include Eastman Kodak, RCA, IBM, GM, North American Rockwell, Dow Chemical.[148]

A variant on the sabbatical year is the concept of farmout. The latter is a technique for extending the on-the-job training of an executive beyond the confines of his own organization by literally farming him out to a consulting firm or another organization that agrees to employ him for a stated period in a capacity offering the particular kind of experience he needs. It may be viewed as external job rotation. By its very nature farm-out is applicable principally to the younger manager who exhibits exceptional potential. Similar to sabbatical leaves, farm-out periods would be approximately one year in duration. As in the case of job rotation, the farmed-out manager must be given a productive work assignment. It may be easier to negotiate farm-out arrangements with management consulting firms than with other organizations, for they are more apt to find ready use for such men. However, once the potential of the farm-out device is fully appreciated, it may be possible to work out reciprocal agreements between two or more organizations. In terms of salary, the employing organization pays the farm-out manager what his services are actually worth to it, with his own employing organization making up the difference between that amount and his current salary, if any.[149] The same compensation payment is worked out for sabbaticals and executives placed on leave for collegiate teaching.

Use of an Executive Peace Corps

In addition to the use of sabbaticals, another developmental technique is expressed in the form of the International Executive Service Corps (IESC), also known as the "Executive Peace Corps." During the 1950s activities carried out by the predecessor to the federal Agency for Inter-

[147] "Resident Executive to Help University Bridge Gap Between Curriculum, Business," *Business Week*, No. 1964, April 22, 1967, p. 103.

[148] J. Roger O'Meara, *Combating Knowledge Obsolescence*, Studies in Personnel Policy No. 209, National Industrial Conference Board, New York, 1968, *passim*.

[149] Willard E. Bennett, *Manager Selection, Education and Training*, McGraw-Hill, New York, 1959, pp. 99–100, 44–46.

national Development (AID) enabled about 7000 managers to share their managerial experience, skills, and know-how with businessmen in the underdeveloped countries of the world. During that same decade the number of foreign managers trained in the United States amounted to more than 6000. The activity was one of the largest cooperative ventures of United States government and United States management.[150]

Several prominent Americans pressed the idea of an Executive Peace Corps in the late 1950s and early 1960s. Their interest was echoed by David Rockefeller when he addressed the 13th International Management Congress (CIOS) in 1963. He proposed that a managerial task force of free enterprise sponsored, directed, and staffed by the private sector of the developed countries be established. Finally, a synthesis of ideas produced the IESC in 1964, and the first volunteer executive was sent overseas early in 1965. Since that time it has been involved in hundreds of projects.[151]

IESC is today a private, nonprofit, nongovernment agency staffed and directed by industrial organizations. A grant from the Agency for International Development (AID) provided the initial financial support for the Executive Peace Corps. In return, the IESC planned to obtain increasing support from industry. AID's interest in the venture was occasioned by its own objective of raising the economic level of underdeveloped countries. IESC was seen as a vehicle for making financial aid more meaningful by giving the private sector the opportunity to supply expert managerial manpower in underdeveloped countries.[152]

More than 80 percent of the members of the Executive Peace Corps are successful businessmen who have retired from their regular career jobs. They are retained on short-term contracts to provide assistance to client organizations in underdeveloped countries. Most of the volunteers are in their mid-60s or late 50s, but there are some in their 40s. The latter are "mid-career" managers on loan from their employing organizations. The Corps would like to expand their roster of these mid-career executives because sometimes a need arises for expertise in an area that cannot be filled by available retirees.

Bids for manpower to serve overseas have been welcomed by some United States companies who see the IESC assignment as a means of giving their people some useful developmental exposure to overseas operations. For several organizations that are either contemplating or have already begun small-scale expansion overseas, the IESC tour has become a training

[150] "ICA 'Hires' Top Brass to Teach Abroad," *Business Week*, No. 1635, December 31, 1960, pp. 46–49.

[151] Harold M. F. Rush, " 'Executive Peace Corps Aids Free Enterprise Abroad," *Conference Board Record*, Vol. 3, No. 9, Summer 1966, p. 42.

[152] *Ibid.*, pp. 42–43.

vehicle. Other organizations have used the IESC assignment to give their managerial manpower an opportunity to accept increased responsibility away from the supervision of their employer.[153]

The few reports on the effectiveness of the IESC indicate that the retired managers who volunteered their services have left a store of know-how behind in return for a deep sense of satisfaction as a consequence of their participation.[154] Thus, in addition to the Job Corps, Teachers Corps, VISTA (Volunteers in service to America), we have the International Executive Service Corps or a new type of social and economic service which has important developmental aspects to it.

In addition to IESC there is also an organization known as SCORE, which stands for Service Corps of Retired Executives. This organization consists of about 3000 volunteer ex-managers who advise small businesses in the United States. The federal Small Business Administration was credited with establishing SCORE. Organizations such as SCORE and IESC are valuable because they make full use of retired executive manpower resources for the benefit of both the retiree and the total society and economy. Additional purposes are served when retired executives combine to offer services through a management-consulting organization.[155]

The full utilization of executive manpower is also reflected in the existing National Defense Executive Reserve Program (NDER). The reserve consists of about 3500 business executives who have agreed to serve with emergency mobilization agencies of the government. NDER would provide the nucleus of executive manpower to staff emergency governmental agencies. Executives who participate in it are required to undertake some training, but very little of it takes place in Washington.[156] As with all the other techniques for executive development which we have discussed above, the Reserve provides yet another relevant source.

EXECUTIVE DEVELOPMENT IN SELECTED
EUROPEAN COUNTRIES

In concert with changes in management education in the United States, executive development programs have been growing in Western Europe. On the other hand, the Soviet Union has not made any appreciable use of

[153] *Ibid.,* p. 44. See also "Moving Into Action," *Business Week,* No. 1839, November 28, 1964, pp. 58–60.

[154] "Executive Peace Corps: It Works," *Business Week,* No. 1884, October 9, 1965, pp. 84–86; and Robert Sheehan, "Those 'Retired' Management Missionaries," *Fortune,* Vol. 76, No. 3, September 1, 1967, pp. 106–108, 146–148.

[155] "Learning from Experience, Inc.," *Business Week,* No. 1969, May 27, 1967, pp. 106–108.

[156] "Businessmen's Reserve," *Business Week,* No. 1899, January 22, 1966, pp. 4–5.

management education programs, as we have defined the term in this chapter, although governmental managers in that country have long since been aware of education and training in developing human resources and have paid heed to the changing problems of factory management in the economy.

Management education in Europe has largely developed since the end of World War II. In many countries before the war there were schools of commerce and technology which offered people training in commercial and industrial practice. Through them passed a substantial percentage of the owners and managers of small- and medium-sized firms.

About 60 years ago one or two universities in Britain offered courses in the principles of management. About this same time studies in business economics were established in Germany. But such offerings were few and isolated. It was the new thinking of the postwar reconstruction period which led to the explicit recognition of a need for management education. Much of the new thinking was clearly influenced by experience in the United States.[157]

Three factors were chiefly responsible for the growth of management education in Europe. These were the search for efficiency as the key to renewed and expanding production; the realization that managerial ability was a main element in achieving efficiency; and a new emphasis on education as a process throughout life in response to new knowledge and changing conditions.

It was perhaps natural for Europe faced with the immense problems after the war to turn to American doctrine and practice for solutions to these problems. From the late 1940s to the present, there developed through numerous channels, notably through the European Productivity Agency, a two-way flow of academic and business leaders, teachers, and students, propounding or studying American business practice and new ideas on management education. Thus by 1960 some 25 institutions at the university level in 16 European countries were offering a full-time one-year management course for college graduates. An equal number offered shorter or part-time courses. There were more than 100 courses of one kind or another for practicing executives. Innumerable programs for students at all levels were developed by technical colleges, business associations, and private enterprise.[158]

By the early 1960s doubts were increasingly voiced as to the appropriateness of American doctrine and teaching methods when transplanted to Europe. As products of the American way of life, they were themselves

[157] Organization for Economic Cooperation and Development, *Issues in Management Education,* Organization for Economic Cooperation and Development, Paris, 1963, p. 55.

[158] *Ibid.,* pp. 55–56.

in a state of continuous development. Much of what was being imported was already becoming out of date in the United States by the time it had been established in Europe. More importantly, there were fundamental differences in the structure of education in Europe, and the pattern of business enterprise there made it difficult for the American institutions to take hold and function.

In Europe a secondary education of the classical type still retains pride of place over vocational studies as a preparation for life and for higher education at the university level. The older universities adhere firmly to their traditional pursuit of knowledge for its own sake and grudgingly admit vocational studies into their curricula. Where they do, it is by broadening the range of such established faculties as those in economics, social sciences, and the natural sciences rather than by the creation of altogether new or interdisciplinary departments. European educational traditions tend to preclude short, intensive, specialized first degree programs. The time spent in graduating is seldom less than four or five years and sometimes extends to eight years.[159]

Another consideration is that the young European begins his business career later than his American counterpart and generally with a broader-based education. He must move fast in his chosen career if he is to reach responsibility in his thirties, and he has less time or inclination to step aside from his job for additional course work in management education. Also, he will find himself in a business climate varying greatly between countries and firms and generally one very different from the American scene. This is particularly true because European enterprise is characterized by the small family firm. In fact, many large organizations are still family owned and managed. Although the counterpart to the American managerial revolution may be spreading in some European countries, management is still not regarded as a distinctive function in its own right.[160]

Still another consideration is the difference in attitudes toward authority in Europe. Relationships between employers and employees conform neither to the American patterns of collective bargaining and employer-employee relations nor to one another. Paternalism is not universally rejected (nor, of course, is it in the United States). In some countries the direct exercise of authority from the top is accepted and rather common. Typically, the number of higher executives is substantially smaller than in America, and the autonomy of Boards of Directors is greater.[161]

In management (as in much else) Europe presents a scene of diversity to the point where the question has been asked whether there is a Euro-

[159] *Ibid.*, p. 56.
[160] *Ibid.*
[161] *Ibid.*, pp. 56–57.

pean pattern that can be set alongside the pattern of American management education which we have previously discussed in the chapter. Perhaps the only defensible generalization would be that the path of management education indicates that each country has adapted and developed it in conformity with its own particular culture, educational pattern, and needs.[162] As a consequence, we shall simply point out some illustrative cases involving Britain, France, and the Soviet Union, without trying to expatiate upon the influence of American-style management education in Europe.

The United States still surpasses Europe in managerial manpower strength. This leadership may be attributed to the facts that most European countries have insufficient national educational goals and weak management and that the United States spends much more money than Europe on research and development, thereby enjoying a growing technological advantage. Europeans are learning that it is innovation not invention that creates jobs, or, to put it another way, that it takes good management to make something out of brilliant technology.[163]

Britain

Turning first to Britain, it is of interest to note that as of 1960 no university in Britain offered a master's degree or a Ph.D. in Business Administration. There were generally a few courses which might be regarded as equivalent to a bachelor's degree in business administration, for example, the BCom. There was relatively little postgraduate work in management, despite the fact that many of the larger British business companies have had excellent internal management training programs for many years.[164]

In the later 1960s a number of changes were then made in management education in Britain. For example, 40 technical colleges and colleges of advanced technology are now providing courses for the new diploma in management, which is sponsored jointly by the Ministry of Education and the British Institute of Management. If these courses are taken on a full-time or "sandwich" (cooperative) basis, they can be completed in six months of study with some period of residence. In addition, since early 1965 Britain has had two business schools in operation (at London and

---

[162] *Ibid.,* p. 57. See also Lewis and Stewart, *op. cit.,* pp. 11–56; and Rosemary Stewart, "The Socio-cultural Setting of Management in the United Kingdom," *International Labour Review,* Vol. 94, No. 2, August 1966, pp. 108–131; and "The New Fire in British Business," *Business Week,* No. 2036, September 7, 1968, pp. 88–92.

[163] Robert E. Farrell, "Europe's Lag in Business Skills," *The Reporter,* Vol. 38, No. 2, January 25, 1968, pp. 22–24.

[164] Tom Lupton, "Management Education: Who, What, and Why?," *The Manager,* Vol. 31, No. 5, May 1963, p. 35.

Manchester) which are patterned after the Harvard Business School and the MIT Sloan School of Management.[165] One-year courses in management at the postgraduate level are also now being given at such universities as Cambridge, Birmingham, Edinburgh, Glasgow, Leeds, and Sheffield. Sandwich courses for practicing managers are conducted at Churchill College (Cambridge) and at Bristol and Sheffield Universities. Summer schools of three to four weeks' duration aimed at middle management are organized at Cambridge, Edinburgh, Dundee, and Oxford. In addition, the Administrative Staff College at Henley-on-Thames, previously mentioned in the chapter, still runs its 12-week course at the middle or senior management level for an average of 60 managers. In addition, there are many internal management training programs in industry, and a considerable expenditure is now being made on these courses. For example, ICI alone trains 700 to 1000 managers a year at its staff training center at Kingston-on-Thames. Shell Mex and BP run an internal career development program at Codicote. The various nationalized industries operate staff colleges or residential training centers. Lastly, there are programs run by a number of management consulting firms, of which the Sundridge Park Management Center, the Urwick Management Center, and the Bilton House Center are examples.[166]

Dozens of the British management education programs are conducted in mansions located in rural parts of England, as is the case for some American management education programs. Training given in these mansions varies widely. Some of the sponsoring companies concentrate almost exclusively on their own specific policies and techniques. At Chelwood Vachery, for example, the British-American Tobacco Company has an educational plant somewhat comparable to the General Electric Management Research and Development Center at Crotonville, New York.

Other British management education courses cover the entire spectrum of management. Still other programs restrict their courses to junior managers whereas others offer courses to everyone from the youngest management trainee to the oldest board member.[167]

Similar to American management education programs, the British approach combines a certain amount of recreation with the educational program. However, managers in training in Britain state that what they like best about management education is the chance to learn about man-

---

[165] "Mentors for Britain's Flagging Management," *Business Week,* No. 1937, October 15, 1966, pp. 190–198.

[166] John Cockcroft, "Education for Management," *The Manager,* Vol. 31, No. 1, January 1963, 25–26.

[167] "Stately Homes are B-Schools for the British," *Business Week,* No. 1872, July 17, 1965, pp. 52–56.

agement in their own company and about other people's jobs and problems. Use is also made in Britain of visiting lecturers from universities and technical colleges, but probably greater use is made of the faculty of company officials. The emphasis on actual business experience and management know-how characterizes most of the company and consultant education centers in Britain. This orientation may guarantee their survival despite the parallel growth of industry-sponsored "staff colleges" such as Henley-on-Thames and the government-sponsored school at Cranfield, as well as the more recent buildup in the management education offerings of universities and technical colleges. But the awakening in academic circles to the study of management will have to be even more thorough before it can satisfy more than the estimated 1000 British companies that now support management education. Nevertheless, there is no doubt that management education is presently booming in Britain.[168]

France

For social, cultural, and other reasons management education in France differs significantly from that in Britain. A few words on the French background are needed to grasp the evolution of management education in that country.

In the mid-1950s Georges Doriot, a well-known professor of industrial management at the Harvard Business School, persuaded the Paris Chamber of Commerce that its traditionally contemptuous view concerning formal business training had to be abandoned if the growing need for trained industrial managers in France was to be met. The Chamber set up an advisory committee of businessmen to start a project along these lines, and European and American corporations contributed funds. Finally the school commonly known as INSEAD (from its French name, *Institut Européen d'Administration des Affaires*), the European Institute of Business Administration, opened its doors in Fontainebleau to its first class in 1959. INSEAD also had IMEDE as a prototype to follow, which was a management education institute founded in 1957 at Lausanne, Switzerland, by the Nestle Foundation, heavily influenced by the Harvard Business School case study method.

Perhaps the best business school on the continent today, INSEAD has built a reputation as a sort of Harvard Business School of Europe by carefully selecting its applicants and training them so rigorously that they are eagerly recruited by the large international companies. The curriculum emphasizes an international approach to business problems and the impact

[168] *Ibid.*, p. 58. For more detail on Britain, see T. M. Mosson, *Management Education in Five European Countries,* Business Publications, London, 1965; and Lewis and Stewart, *op. cit.,* pp. 151–163.

of the Common Market on industry. The school limits enrollment from a single country to a maximum of one-third of the total class. Approximately one-quarter of the student body is French. Entering students are required to have a university degree equivalent to the bachelor of arts in the United States. This requirement is occasionally waived for outstanding young businessmen with a minimum of five years of experience. To be eligible for admission an applicant must speak at least two of the school's three official languages (French, German, and English) and be capable of carrying out reading assignments in the third. Proficiency in three languages is considered a minimum for an executive to function efficiently at the international level in the new European environment where national boundaries have less and less meaning.

The program is of nine months' duration, and the student carries a heavy academic load. Classes meet for six days a week except for one Saturday off each month. There is a heavy emphasis on the use of cases, as at the Harvard Business School. There is an annual field trip, as in the Sloan Fellowship Program. The permanent faculty is small, but guest lecturers from various European countries help in instructing the students.

INSEAD lifts its students out of long-fixed European business propensities by stressing practical problems, discouraging narrow specialization, and insisting that they take a global view of every business opportunity. More than 80 percent of its graduates are now employed outside their homelands. About 86 percent of the graduates work in the European offices of international firms.[169]

INSEAD caters to 120 students from dozens of countries both European and non-European; hence, it is not entirely aimed at the Frenchman who desires management education. France's business elite consists of graduates of the famed *École Polytechnique,* the most prestigious among France's half dozen *grandes ecoles* or postgraduate schools. Known by its graduates as the *"X,"* alumni of the *École Polytechnique* inevitably wind up running most of France's biggest private and state-owned companies. For example, of France's 50 largest companies today, 32 have X graduates in one or both of their two top executive positions.[170]

After finishing their schooling, graduates of the X are obliged to work for the government for ten years or serve in the armed forces. About 20 percent usually choose a military career (which before the war was around 50 percent). Graduates can avoid their ten years of government service by repaying the government $7000.00 for their two years' education. Some

[169] "Europe: A Trilingual Business Education," *Fortune,* Vol. 69, No. 2, February 1964, pp. 51–56; and *Time,* Vol. 85, No. 15, April 9, 1965, p. 100.

[170] "The School That Breeds France's Business Elite," *Business Week,* No. 1968, May 20, 1967, pp. 184–186.

private French companies will recruit a talented X graduate by agreeing to pay the $7000.00 to the government.

Inasmuch as most *Polytechniciens* spend their first ten years in government, that fact is what gives France's business establishment its unique quality: the link between business and government. When graduates of the X complete their governmental service and, as many do, switch over to private business, the old school tie remains. The thick annual directory of the X is used for making contacts in business or government. The directory lists more than 10,000 graduates four times, by class, residence, job, and alphabetically. With many decision makers in business and government in France bound by a common tie to the nation's most distinguished school, it is understandable that the distinction between business and government itself becomes blurred.[171]

The curriculum at the X has only one purpose: to teach the 300 students enrolled how to reason, analyze, and resolve problems. The courses revolve around the sciences and higher mathematics. Problems are dealt with strictly in abstract terms and nothing even faintly resembling a business course is taught. There are no electives. The two-year curriculum is in all respects most demanding. All students admitted to the X must pass their baccalaureate examination with honors. They must then pass a two-year intensive cramming program to enter the X. No matter what career a *Polytechnicien* may have in mind, going through the X will help him get there.[172]

At the end of both the first and second years at the X, the *Polytechnicien* must take written and oral examinations in mathematical analysis, algebra, geometry, thermodynamics, physics, political economy, history, literature, languages, and drawing. If he passes his final examinations, he receives an engineering diploma.[173]

Most *Polytechniciens* realize that their broad, mind-building courses at the X have left them with no particular career field. Therefore, they go on to a "school of application" where for another two years they study and specialize. They may go, for example, to the School of Mines, the National School for Administration (which develops civil servants), the School of Natural Resources, or the government civil engineering school. About ten percent enter industry directly.[174]

Ironically, the best business school in France does not come near the X in prestige, even though it is among the six *grandes ecoles*. Paris's *École des Hautes Commerciales* (or HEC) has been turning out 300 graduates a year since the latter part of the 19th century, but few of its graduates are

[171] *Ibid.*, p. 186.
[172] *Ibid.*
[173] *Ibid.*
[174] *Ibid.*

in the top ranks of business or government. By contrast, graduates of the *X* are expected to be capable of administering any business or governmental agency, even if they lack practical experience. In fact, very few business executives have worked their way up through the marketing or sales functions, as is the case in the United States. More than one-half of France's 100 largest companies are managed by men with engineering backgrounds, and the rest are largely run by lawyers.[175]

Criticism of the *X*'s enormous influence, particularly in linking business and government, is not likely to change anything. The French government is, however, planning to establish its first graduate school of business administration. Pending the necessary approvals, a school using the case method fostered by the Harvard Business School will be established by 1972 as part of the HEC. In the past, HEC graduates have been limited to mainly second-string management positions in sales, marketing, and finance, while the top management spots have gone to graduates of the *X*. With the new school, young business-minded Frenchmen would then have available for the first time a complete management training program within France's government-operated educational system. The new school would differ from INSEAD in its government connection. (As previously mentioned, INSEAD is sponsored by Harvard and the Paris Chamber of Commerce.) It is quite likely that the continuing economic development of France requires a management education *force de frappe,* which means much more than one graduate school of business administration! [176] There is already at least one clarion call to Frenchmen that they must act now.[177] The mid-1968 general strike in France is also symptomatic of the *malaise* in French higher education.

Despite its national vicissitudes in the post-World War II period, France is a strong industrial nation in the process of an important transformation. To this end, the connection between education and economic development is slowly being recognized.

Thus, a number of provincial cities that have long languished in the backwaters have had time to develop high-technology enterprises that point to the future for France's economy. For example, in Grenoble which is one of the fastest-growing areas in France, the business community has capitalized on a great scientific school, the 628-year-old University of Grenoble, and a government-sponsored nuclear center.[178]

---

[175] *Ibid.,* p. 188.

[176] "France Readies Plans to Establish Harvard-like Graduate Business School," *Business Week,* No. 2008, February 24, 1968, p. 154.

[177] Jean-Jacques Servan-Schreiber, *The American Challenge,* Atheneum, New York, 1968, 291 pp.

[178] John Davenport, "A Fast-Growing Provincial Town Points France's Future in High-Technology Industries," *Fortune,* Vol. 65, No. 3, March 1967, p. 69.

IBM Center in Holland

Turning briefly to a third European country, it is of interest to examine some of the early experience of the IBM World Trade Corporation's European Educational Center in the Dutch town of Blaricum, for it displays some of the problems caused in the undiluted export of American-style management education. A few months after IBM established the Center patterned after American models, it found that the care and feeding of executives is not the same the world over. For example, many European executives guarded their weekends at home much more jealously than did Americans. They resisted the idea of showing up at Blaricum on Sunday night to be ready for training sessions early Monday morning. As a result, IBM changed the arrival time to Monday morning.

A second problem was the ban on alcoholic beverages at Blaricum. It was found that most visiting Europeans were accustomed to having wine at their meals and resented their not being able to obtain it.

A third problem arose when the aversion of the average European businessman to rooming with anyone was ignored. They considered that they had been gravely insulted when they were placed two persons to a room.

A fourth problem was the failure of IBM to foresee the difficulty of keeping groups together for the informal evening bull sessions that are considered by some an important feature of management education in the United States. At Blaricum the men tended to flock together by nationality groups in order to relax without any language barriers. And since Blaricum was only 16 miles from Amsterdam the visitors tended to leave the premises at night and seek the attractions of the city.

These four examples illustrate how difficult it is to transplant an accepted institution to alien soil.[179]

Soviet Management Education

Lastly, let us turn to the USSR. If one were to examine Soviet educational institutions, he would find that they do not contribute substantially to the development of managerial skills or knowledge. This assertion is particularly true in engineering educational programs, although more courses in economics and business administration have been added to the curricula of many engineering institutes recently. Yet, almost all Russian managers have engineering degrees; few have business degrees; almost none possess a liberal arts background. "Broadening" plays no role in the philosophy of Russian higher education.[180]

It is rather surprising that so little time has been devoted to business,

[179] "IBM's Dutch Eden Has Its Thorn," *Business Week,* No. 1591, February 27, 1960, pp. 105–106.

[180] David Granick, *The Red Executive,* Doubleday, Garden City, 1961, p. 48.

economics, and management education at engineering schools inasmuch as the great majority of managerial manpower in Soviet industry consists of persons trained as engineers. Yet, in some programs the Soviet student does acquire an insight into the formal procedures and regulations pertaining to the planning and organization functions of management. He may even acquire some insight into the management functions of direction, staffing, and control. However, the emphasis is likely to be on descriptive, static, and nonoperational aspects rather than the dynamic aspects of management.

The key elements of the managerial job are not even defined or clearly spelled out in formal instructional programs in the Soviet Union. The student receives almost no instruction in principles, criteria, concepts, or other guidelines to be used in performing managerial activities. Little if any attention is given to problem solving and decision making and the analysis of alternatives, human motivation, individual behavior, leadership, and various other traditional topics covered in American management and business administration courses. Actually, the Soviets have condemned "bourgeois sociology" and western advances in the study of human relations, organizational behavior, and motivation in industry.[181]

The Soviet system of formal education for management apparently operates on the assumption that some managers are born good managers, others develop through the process of living and managing, but managers cannot be produced in the classroom. In essence, the Soviet position appears to be that the art of management can only be learned and perfected through managing, without recourse to science, principles, theory, or education.

The Soviet institutions do not use such devices as case problems, role playing, problem solving, independent projects, and sensitivity training to simulate the real life management world and serve as a means for applying the theory and concepts learned. Yet, it is important to point out that the Soviet educational system does employ a number of devices for simulating the managerial world and for management development.

One simulative device is the creation of a tight organizational world of their own for the students while in school. Specifically, the extracurricular life of the Soviet student is highly organized, filled with meetings, committees, and various other activities, such as a comprehensive system of student self-government. A system of mass indoctrination through education, mass media, and the party channels also operates at the same time. Students must plan, organize, staff, and control their activities, delegate authority and exact responsibility, and gain the cooperation of the student

[181] Barry M. Richman, *Management Development and Education in the Soviet Union,* Graduate School of Business Administration, Michigan State University, East Lansing, 1967, pp. 188–189. See also pp. 127–188, for the detailed background.

membership through effective direction, leadership, and motivation in extracurricular activities. These organizational activities are taken seriously by the Soviet student body, and outstanding service is a significant factor in the evaluation of students for employment upon graduation. Through this process of natural selection many students are labeled as potential managerial material for industry.[182]

The combining of formal study with practical work experience in Soviet education programs may also have some favorable effects on management development. There is the widespread assignment of students to work as laborers during alternating periods in their formal education in a work-study type of arrangement. As a consequence, this experience probably instills in students some appreciation of labor and human relations problems at the grass-roots level. It also means that if the student moves up the managerial hierarchy in his later career, he will have had firsthand exposure to the procedures at the bottom rungs of the organization where tangible operating results are achieved. He will be familiar with the problems, behavior, and needs of the work force; and this experience may well enhance his effectiveness as a manager and leader.

It should be noted that relatively few contemporary American managers have worked as laborers at any time in their careers, as compared with Soviet managers. Fewer still have gone through an educational program that bridged formal study with the real world through related employment, except cooperative students. However, it is generally believed that formal education for management development is far more advanced in the United States than in the Soviet Union. The Soviets perhaps have much to learn from us, and it appears that their educational system will converge somewhat in the direction of ours in the future.[183] But it cannot be denied that the desirability of enabling young people to relate the theory and practice of subject matter which they are studying through work experience has been far less fully exploited in the United States than is the case in the Soviet Union.

International Business

Because of the growth in international business in the post-World War II period, questions as to the exportability not only of the management concept but also of management education have arisen on many occasions. The parallel growth of international business curricula in undergraduate and graduate schools of business has also been a notable development.[184]

---

[182] *Ibid.*, pp. 189–190. Granick, *op. cit.*, pp. 46–73 makes these same essential points.
[183] Richman, *op. cit.*, pp. 190–191.
[184] "How Business Schools Welcome the World," *Business Week*, No. 1997, December 9, 1967, pp. 118–124.

Recently, attention has been given to means for making American business management know-how available in crash and cram programs to industrialists and educators from underdeveloped countries.[185] This type of program is one possible answer to the question of how to train leaders to run multinational companies. INSEAD is, of course, a response to this problem, especially in the European Common Market.

The boning-up of American managers planning to be sent overseas in Berlitz language cram courses is almost legendary and another manifestation of a solution to the problem. The affiliation of the American Institute for Foreign Trade with the American Management Association in early 1963 was a form of positive recognition by the AMA of the strategic importance of specialized management training in the field of foreign commerce. Since that time the AMA has been actively involved in preparing executives for overseas assignments.

Indeed, we have probably just started to scratch the surface of international business and its implications for executive development, not only in the United States but elsewhere in the world. The next significant shift in American-style executive development may very well be in thinking through plans and programs for executive and other manpower in internationally oriented business and other organizations.

CONCLUSIONS

In this chapter we have scrutinized the multiple facets of executive development and tried to explore the mystique, technique, and critique of the subject. We found that our gaps in knowledge about managerial work and skills and knowledge required for executive success pose almost insurmountable problems for management education because we lack a reasonably clear direction toward which educational goals can be set. Moreover, the serious problems caused by gaps in our knowledge of management skills and perceived shortages of managers since the 1950s resulted in the establishment of a number of corporate schools as well as in-residence university-level management education programs.

We found that the management education programs differ according to their specific objectives, content, the learning process, faculty, physical facilities, and the number of participants. Such model types as the MIT Sloan Fellowship Program, Harvard Advanced Management Program, two programs offered at the University of California, and several liberal arts programs were discussed.

In general, most persons who have participated in management educa-

[185] "Spreading the Business Gospel," *Business Week,* No. 1775, September 7, 1963, pp. 99–100.

tion programs indicate that they liked them and that the experience was broadening.

Although it is difficult to generalize, it does appear that the management education concept developed in the United States was translated and introduced into Europe, and adjusted to accord with the requirements of the environment in different countries. Management education in the United States and selected European countries has been necessary not only for business managers but also for executives in a variety of organizations, including government.

Manpower planning for executive development has a different character than the type carried out for persons at lower organizational levels. For example, in most organizations fewer individuals are involved, and systematic replacement and developmental planning on almost a personal basis is possible.

Performance appraisals and individually tailored rotational plans together with individually tailored developmental plans are coming into increasing use in executive development. In the last five years more selective use has been made of management education programs than hitherto, and organizations have started to determine what types of internal learning experiences can be most effectively utilized for developing executives. The excessive stress on the use of forms and pretty manuals in executive development, which characterized the early 1950s, seems to have now given way to more sophisticated thinking.

Pace-setting complex organizations have found that education is a lifetime process and that the minds of executives must be periodically retooled. Management education is viewed as a kind of school of advanced study for managers in which this retooling can take place.

A rising number of short intensive management education courses offered by consultants, noncollegiate institutions, and professional associations have become popular in recent years.

The liberal arts programs occasionally used in management education have tended to decline, although some, such as the one offered at Aspen, have continued to be successful.

Increasing attention has been given in recent years to preventing technical educational obsolescence among engineering and scientific specialists and managers.

The executive shortage which has been experienced around the world will probably be with us in the next decade or more. The rise of the international business orientation prevalent among firms in leading countries throughout the world indicates there will be an increased need for a new type of executive development, namely, that of the manager competent to function in the multinational corporation and organization. Inasmuch as we have done so poorly in learning what it takes to be successful as a manager in more limited types of organizations, the difficulties which we face in developing managers for international businesses and other organizations constitute real and disturbing manpower problems for the future. In other words, we might conclude by stating that we need more research so that we can obtain better knowledge of not only how adults develop but also of how high-talent adults in key positions in complex organizations develop, and particularly in organizations oriented toward world enterprise.

CHAPTER *10*

College Cooperative Education Plans

There is a story, perhaps aprocryphal in which it is told that the dean of a college could determine in what year a returned alumnus graduated by the suggestions the alumnus made for revising the curriculum. In broad terms the dean's system was this: men one to five years out of college would ask: why didn't you teach me how to make a living? For those in the age group from 30 through middle age, the comment would be: why didn't you teach me the fundamentals? And, the 60 to 65 year age group would demand: why didn't you teach me how to live? There is a moral in this story for both industry and manpower planners. What a man needs to make a living, what a man learns to perceive over time as the fundamentals of his profession or occupation, and, to a considerable extent, the creative part of his working life, which goes into the synthesis of what he calls "living," are conditioned by industry. Cooperative education can be used as a tool to break down the barriers between formal educational systems such as schools and universities and industry.[1]

In this chapter we explain the creation and expansion of work-study plans of education as a unique form of cultural transmission in industrial society and as a variant on apprenticeship. Our approach is to first define cooperative education; second, explain, its purpose and values; third, relate this form of education to manpower planning; fourth, discuss its history; fifth, outline model programs of cooperative education in operation; and, sixth, review various techniques and tools for administering cooperative education in industry.

Our attention in the chapter is directed toward college cooperative education plans rather than toward cooperative education at the high-school or secondary level. Manpower specialists in industry are likely to have some interest in the possibilities of utilizing cooperative students who are enrolled

---

[1] Clarence H. Linder, "Breaking Down the Barriers Between Industry and Education," in *Highlights of the Conference on Cooperative Education and the Impending Educational Crisis,* Dayton, Thomas Alva Edison Foundation, 1957, p. 23.

486

in business, distributive, trade, and industrial education curricula at the high-school level.[2] Likewise, they may be interested in work-study programs for needy college students financed under the Economic Opportunity Act. The administration of these programs from the standpoint of the manpower specialist in industry is somewhat different from that for other college students.[3]

In the latter part of 1967 some industrial companies announced that they were planning to "adopt" high schools in which the student body was composed largely of minority group members. The purposes were many, but one was to teach business skills and provide a general work orientation to youngsters, particularly potential high-school dropouts.[4] These programs add a new dimension to work-study plans. They may also be viewed as a part of business' initial involvement in the war on poverty.[5] However, the high-school and poverty-war foci are not those of this chapter. Our stress is upon cooperative education for graduate and undergraduate students in various college curricula.

DEFINITION OF COOPERATIVE EDUCATION

Cooperative education may be defined in different ways. Perhaps the most widely adhered to definition at the present time is one which was stated in 1961 when the most significant research report on college cooperative education was completed. This definition was as follows: "The cooperative plan of education is defined as that educational plan which integrates classroom experiences and practical work experience in industrial, business, government, or service-type work situations. The work experience constitutes a regular and essential element in the educative process and some minimum amount of work experience (at least two different periods of work, totaling at least 16 weeks) and minimum standards of perfor-

[2] See, for example, "How Retailers Woo Bright Young Talent," *Business Week,* No. 1988, October 7, 1967, pp. 116–118.

[3] For an excellent up-to-date review of cooperative education at the secondary-school level, see Ralph E. Mason and Peter G. Haines, *Cooperative Occupational Education,* Interstate Printers and Publishers, Danville, 1965, *passim,* and pp. 378–386 for junior-college programs. The work-study program of the Economic Opportunity Act of 1964 has allowed more than 100,000 needy students to continue their education, although this program is different from traditional cooperative education. See Margaret Nolte, "Work-Study Programs in Colleges and Universities," *Personnel Journal,* Vol. 46, No. 10, November 1967, pp. 740–744.

[4] For example, see *Detroit Free Press,* October 25, 1967, p. 3A, and November 1, 1967, p. 3A for the programs of Michigan Bell Telephone Company and the J. L. Hudson Company.

[5] See "Business Takes New Role: Training 'Unemployables,'" *U.S. News & World Report,* Vol. 63, No. 20, November 13, 1967, pp. 97–98.

mance are included in the requirements of the institution for a degree. In addition, there must be liaison between the administration of the institution and the employing firm. The essential criteria . . . are that the work experience be considered an integral part of the educational process, and that the institution take a definite responsibility for this integration." [6]

This definition of cooperative education is more inclusive than those used previously by students of the subject. For example, this definition does not require that the student alternate between periods of classroom attendance and periods of on-the-job work; it does not require that the student be paid for his employment; it does not require that the work experience be definitely related to the student's field of study; and it does not require that the student's work become progressively more difficult.[7] Yet, in many cooperative education programs operating today it would be found that students do alternate periods of instruction in school with periods of work, that the work experience is related to the student's major field, and that the successive cooperative work assignments of the student become progressively more difficult as he advances educationally. Also, in most instances it would be found that students enrolled in cooperative education are normally paid wages for the period in which they are employed.

Inasmuch as the word *cooperative* does not always convey the final idea to the person who hears or reads it, the term *work-study* has been devised as a synonym. To the uninitiated the word cooperative might suggest simply that the student is easy to get along with and cooperative in that sense. Actually, the word means that the student is enrolled in a work-study plan that integrates the theoretical knowledge available in a university with the practical work experiences available in a work situation. The cooperation or collaboration between universities and employers enables the student to obtain a college education and to acquire practical on-the-job experience along with it in the same time frame.

PURPOSE AND VALUES

The cooperative or work-study plan of education is based upon two fundamental considerations regarding how people learn in a complex society. First, every profession or occupation for which students are preparing contains certain knowledge elements that cannot be taught in the classroom. These elements can be learned only by direct on-the-job experience, work-

[6] James W. Wilson and Edward H. Lyons, *Work-Study College Programs,* Harper, New York, 1961, p. 19.

[7] These specific criteria were stated in Henry H. Armsby, *Cooperative Education in the United States,* [Bulletin 1954, No. 11], Department of Health, Education and Welfare, Office of Education, Washington, 1954, p. 1.

ing with people who are already in the particular occupational field. In some professions, this requirement for learning is met by the principle of internship. In other occupations, it is met by apprenticeship (of which internship is, of course, conceptually similar). Second, most of the students in America must find employment on a part-time basis while they are in school and during their vacation periods in order to earn money to offset part of the cost of their education. In many cases, the jobs obtained have no relation to ultimate career aims and, therefore, do not contribute substantially to the occupation or professional development of the student.[8] Obviously, these jobs contribute to the socialization of students in an industrial society, but they often provide experience in fields of work totally unrelated to fields in which the student would like to acquire experience.

On the other hand, cooperative education often satisfies the dual desire of providing income-producing jobs that at the same time extend and amplify learning. Under a cooperative education program, the educational institution designs an academic calendar which allows the insertion of work periods at various intervals in the academic curriculum. The institution assumes the responsibility for finding positions which are related to the students' professional and occupational objectives and which thus provide work experience that enhances knowledge associated with educational aims. These jobs are wage-paying positions in organizations and as a rule produce income by which students can finance their education.[9] Cooperative education does not appeal to all students nor should it be blanketly proposed as a better plan than conventional schemes.

Role of the "Co-op Coordinator" and "Pairing"

Undoubtedly the key factor in making cooperative education operate as intended is the faculty cooperative education coordinator (hereinafter simply called the "coordinator"). His responsibility is to find employers in the student's fields of interest and to bring these employers into a cooperative relationship with the institution. Very often, this responsibility means that the cooperating employer must be willing to provide work to be shared by two students, one of whom works on the job while the other attends college. At the end of a specified period of time (such as a quarter, semester, or trimester) the two students change places, which keeps the job continuously filled, while each of the students assigned to it is enabled to spend one-half of his time in college. This arrangement is called *pairing*. The length of the period of alternation between work and study varies among different educational institutions, as does the total amount of work expe-

---

[8] Roy L. Wooldridge, *Cooperative Education and the Community Colleges in New Jersey,* National Commission for Cooperative Education, New York, 1966, p. 2.
[9] *Ibid.*

rience required and the point in the student's curriculum at which work experience starts.[10]

The two-man team principle is generally followed in cooperative education programs. However, it is not universally followed, nor is it considered a fundamental principle of the cooperative system. Some institutions have arranged their cooperative programs so that all their students go to work at the same time, with all returning to the college at one time. Even those institutions that use the two-man team arrangement have found it desirable in certain instances to provide only one cooperative student for a given job, provided it can be handled in such a way as to permit him to return to college for the regular class period. The essential feature, then, of cooperative education is not the pairing of students but rather alternation between periods of employment in organizations, regulated by the university, and periods of classroom instruction at the university.[11]

Diverse Values of Cooperative Education: The Student

The values of cooperative education may be viewed from several different perspectives. There are a number that pertain to the development of people for industrial occupations and professions; some which accrue to educational institutions; still others which pertain to employers of cooperative students; and additional ones that apply to the graduates of cooperative programs as well as to the community at large, which would include the total population of a society as well as the community of all employers.

From the standpoint of the individual, there are a number of values inherent in cooperative education and we should perhaps consider these first. Not all of these advantages to the individual have been proven by empirical research, but they are frequently cited as holding true. First, by coordinating work experience with the on-campus educational instruction, theory and practice are more closely related, with the result that students find greater meaning in their studies. Second, the coordination of work and study increases student motivation. As students see connections between what they are learning on-the-job and on-campus, greater interest in academic work develops. Third, in the case of many students, work experience contributes to a greater sense of responsibility for their own efforts, greater dependence upon their own judgment, and the corresponding accentuated development of personal maturity. Fourth, the work experience phase enables the cooperative student (henceforth called a "co-op") to develop a greater understanding of people and greater skill in getting along with others. This advantage might be summed up as the development of greater skills in human relations. Because they are forced to make inter-

[10] *Ibid.*
[11] *Ibid.,* p. 3.

personal contacts with adults in a variety of work situations and often to meet people from various socioeconomic backgrounds, the work experience phase of cooperative education tends to break down the segregation of college students into wholly adolescent communities which prevail for them on college campuses. Instead of becoming socialized to an adolescent youth culture the co-op, as opposed to the non-co-op, must also make an adjustment to an industrial culture in which adults predominate. Fifth, cooperative education helps co-ops to become oriented to the world of work. Most college students are very concerned about their future lifework and want to know more about the range of occupations available to them. They also want to know more about the potential and limitations of these fields as well as the qualifications demanded and their own fitness for them. Cooperative education furnishes students with opportunities for exploring their own abilities in connection with real jobs. While working, they find a direct means for gaining vocational information and vocational guidance not only in the occupations in which they are employed but also in a number of related fields. In the process, co-ops have a chance to test their own aptitudes more fully than is normally possible on-campus. Furthermore, co-ops are enabled to understand and appreciate more fully the meaning of work to the individual and the function of occupations in providing the wide range of goods and services characteristic of the American economy. Sixth, cooperative education plans make higher education possible and attractive to many people in America who would not otherwise go to college. The earnings of co-ops while on the job have enabled many to attend college who could not finance their education without it. The assurance of having a job while in college makes co-operative education seem practical and attainable to many youths and their families who have had no previous connections with colleges and are skeptical not only of college itself but also their own potential to be successful in college-level educational programs. The benefits of making college entry available to people who might not otherwise attend also redound to the nation, which has increasing needs for well-educated people in science, engineering, business, and the professions. Seventh, cooperative education may give the student contacts which are useful in later occupational placement once he has received his college degree. Lastly, it may also give many students a head start in salary and position level after they graduate from college and enter the world of work on a full-time basis.[12]

Values to the Educational Institution

Among the specific benefits to educational institutions are the following. First, cooperative education makes possible a more economical use of the

[12] Wooldridge, *op. cit.*, pp. 6–7.

college plant and facilities. This is caused by the split of the student body into two equal groups, about one-half attending classes on campus while the other group is off-campus at work (assuming that we are thinking of the type of cooperative plan that operates in this manner, as most do). Consequently, only one-half the student body is in school at one time. This arrangement means that an institution that converts from a conventional educational pattern to the cooperative plan can nearly double its enrollment using the same physical facilities. It also means that tuition income for the institution may be doubled because two students alternate in occupying each seat in class, and each pays a full tuition charge. It also means that more students can be graduated to meet the manpower needs of employers and the nation. Second, cooperative plans may enable the faculty to keep in better touch with industry, government, the professions, and employing institutions of all kinds. The improved contact may result in more effective teaching because faculty members are kept up-to-date on the latest developments in practice.[13] One professor of economics explained his reaction to exposure to cooperative students as follows:

"My first experience in teaching under the cooperative program gave me a shock. A student with considerable ability had been doing rather indifferent work in the beginning course in economics. Upon returning from his cooperative job with the Department of Labor in Washington, he said to me, *I learned more economics from my job in Washington than I did in your course.* This was not a tactful remark for a student to make and the boy's statement upset me at the time.

Were a student returning from a job to make a similar statement now, I would dismiss it by retorting, *Of course you learned more on the job than you did in my course. Look at all the facilities in Washington, including the large number of economists to instruct you in the practical application of the subject.* More to the point I would try to make the boy see that his cooperative job and his campus experiences were on two different levels. His off-campus experience should prove stimulating, give him facts and raise fundamental questions about our economic system. In the classroom we are trying to develop theoretical analysis, to engage in sustained reasoning and to see economics as an integrated whole. The two experiences should complement each other and contribute to a more fundamental understanding of the subject . . . ."[14]

One might deduce from this statement that cooperative education has the effect of keeping faculty members on their toes. This may be a humbling

---

[13] Wooldridge, *op. cit.,* p. 7, citing Tyler, *op. cit., idem.*

[14] Comment by Valdemar Carlson, *Cooperative Education and the Impending Educational Crisis, op. cit.,* p. 34.

experience for a smug, self-satisfied individual who feels he has all the answers and repeats year-in and year-out the same lecture with unchanging material, tired old concepts, and dated illustrations.

Third, the cooperative program is likely to generate active support for the educational institution from industrial and other employers. The relationships which are established through the placement of students foster a greater recognition of the services that the institution renders to employers and thus may furnish a basis for moral and financial support of the institution.[15] Obviously, the services of a university extend beyond the provision of manpower competent to fill positions in the occupational structure. It is nevertheless true that universities that can fulfill at least this manpower-production function are probably in a better position to obtain the support they require to function in all their areas of interest.

Values to Industry

From the standpoint of industry, there are a number of values in college cooperative programs. First, co-ops constitute an excellent source of manpower for semiskilled and subprofessional work. In many industries there are dozens if not hundreds of jobs that fall within these categories. Sometimes these jobs are filled by high-school graduates and other times they are filled by graduates of junior colleges or four-year institutions. These positions are important from the employer's point of view because he wants them adequately filled while avoiding the cost and inconvenience of excessive turnover. The utilization of cooperative students for these positions often provides a practical solution. Co-ops placed in such jobs are likely to bring them enthusiasm, interest, and a higher than normal level of ability (unless these jobs are being filled by college graduates, which may lead to high turnover caused by malutilization). Student motivation and the supervisory participation of the college cooperative coordinator practically assure the continuity in these positions sought by the employer.[16] Co-ops used in this manner become a source of competent manpower filling positions productively in the short run while constituting a long-run pool for promotions after graduation into the technical and professional ranks. Jobs designated as co-op positions can then clearly become important training stations used by the manpower specialist in career planning and for providing technicians.

Second, cooperative programs have value for employers by contributing to the recruitment and retention of gifted employees, as well as retaining such people in their own communities. Employers generally find that their cooperative programs help maintain a flow of partially trained manpower and manpower in training into their organizations. The mere existence of

[15] Wooldridge, *op. cit.,* p. 8.
[16] *Ibid.,* p. 9.

a program itself attracts promising young people into diverse occupational areas and thereby enriches the manpower pool of the employer. Also, employers may use the cooperative program as an actual testing ground to identify and select persons with needed abilities and talents. Specifically, during the co-op's work periods the employer can study the aptitudes of the co-op within the actual environment of his own organization, using his own supervisory personnel to observe and assess the co-op's performance. These observations and evaluations can be used as an initial basis for sound judgment about the student's long-range potential as a permanent employee. Experience indicates that approximately 50 percent of the co-ops exposed to this process will remain with their employers after graduation.[17] Of course, during the process co-ops will normally be paid wages which are less than those that would be required for career-type employees performing the same kind of work (that is, at lower quarters of the salary grade or perhaps under an *ad hoc* co-op salary schedule). Although research results are scant, it appears that savings in payroll costs are possible. On the other hand, if the developmental opportunities afforded the co-op by the employer are considered by the co-op as inadequate, he may reject a position offer of employment after graduation and choose to work elsewhere. In these instances, employers may retain a great deal less than 50 percent of the co-ops who work for them and conclude that co-oping is economically unjustified. Clearly, the economic advantages of co-oping must be viewed by each organization in the light of co-op performance and retention, alternative sources of employees in the labor market(s), and its long-range manpower plans and policies.

The third advantage in cooperative education for employers is improving the level of maximization in talent utilization. The use of co-ops to handle duties performed by higher-paid employees releases the latter from performing work beneath their skill level and frees them for higher-level positions. This does not necessarily mean that these workers are replaced by co-ops but rather that they are relocated to positions that may be more challenging and better paying than those assumed by the co-ops. The positions that are liberated by this upgrading can become the aforementioned permanent training stations for co-ops. Such an arrangement is mutually beneficial to the co-op, the employer, and workers with aspirations for higher-level positions. The co-op gains experience; the employer optimizes the use of manpower at different organizational levels and with differing degrees of personal competency; and the full-time regular employee finds himself properly engaged in tasks commensurate with his capabilities.[18]

Fourth, inasmuch as work-study programs are proven to be a major

[17] *Ibid.*
[18] *Ibid.*, pp. 9–10.

factor in creating the opportunity to attend college for many young people who otherwise would not be able to do so, industry gains by obtaining manpower of which it would normally be deprived if there were no cooperative programs (or alternative human resource development programs). This advantage is the same as the one we previously discussed, except here we are looking at it from a different standpoint. In certain segments of society parental approval and emotional and some financial support might be denied youngsters who aspire to attend conventional colleges. Yet, these types of support are more readily granted if the college is a cooperative institution.

Looked at another way, from the standpoint of industry and the community, the cooperative institution produces significant returns on a number of levels. It begins to introduce cultural changes in the poorly informed and culturally deprived segments of the population. It upgrades the training and skills of adults who would otherwise have limited capacities as employees and wage earners. It probably also lessens the sense of isolation of culturally deprived families from the mainstream of community life and integrates them into the broader society. The effects are to introduce a number of social and economic values into the communities and industries in which cooperative education plays a part.[19]

In the popular mind cooperative education is often thought to be a program which enables students to work their way through college financed by benevolent industrial managements who receive inexpensive labor as an exchange for taking on the co-ops. The cooperative education program is thus viewed as industry's contribution to the improvement of human resources by subsidizing the education of needy students. Actually, this conception of cooperative education is outmoded despite its popularity in some quarters. Cooperative education should be looked upon essentially as a method of work-study in which practical experience is integrated with academic learning. When the theory and practice complement one another, supposedly a better education results.

COOPERATIVE EDUCATION AND MANPOWER PLANNING

In a previous chapter we discussed the projection of manpower needs in various kinds of organizations and indicated that in identifying those needs one possible device for developing technical and professional employees in response to them was the use of college cooperative education plans. These plans and training programs for inexperienced college graduates may be viewed as serving the same basic purpose, namely, to bring into an organization qualified young persons who can carry out technical and

[19] *Ibid.*, pp. 8–9.

professional work. Furthermore, it is possible to utilize both cooperative trainees and college graduate trainees as supervisory personnel despite their relative youth. A number of American industrial organizations have in recent years been using both co-ops and college graduates as foremen and staff supervisors.

One of the fastest-growing groups of employees in modern large-scale organizations comprises technical and professional nonsupervisory employees carrying out the work of staff and service specialists. The group would include people working as accountants, industrial engineers, outside salesmen, quality-control analysts, personnel representatives, buyers, and the like, literally hundreds of different jobs. Manpower planners are concerned with the most effective means of assuring that their employers attract and retain an adequate and dependable supply of such qualified technical and professional manpower at a minimum cost.

The technical and professional segment of the labor force of the United States has been the fastest-growing segment since about 1950. Modern large-scale organizations generally require that persons who fill technical and professional positions possess at least a bachelor's degree and increasingly a master's degree, although the "requirement" is quite arbitrary and imposed in many instances simply because college graduates are available and being increasingly produced by educational institutions. Despite the high levels of unemployment in the early 1960s, there were very few college graduates with technical and professional skills who were seeking work. In fact, organizations were attempting to hire more college graduates than were generally available.

Considering the manpower needs generated by replacement and expansion in many organizations today, there is every reason for manpower specialists to consider the recruiting, selecting, developing, and retaining of co-ops as one part of the approach toward human resources development in order to meet organizational manpower requirements. There is also ample reason for organizations sustaining co-op programs to consider the expanded use of co-op programs to provide master's degrees for employees who are considered in need of further education either to remain proficient in their present jobs or to qualify for promotional or higher-level technical positions in the future. Organizations can thus use co-op programs offered by undergraduate colleges as well as those available in graduate schools. In many instances, both levels of education could be made available to full-time employees during the work day or evenings or weekends. In this way co-oping for adults would be worked out, with the initiative for enrollment coming from industry or other organizations.

In sum, the manpower projection techniques discussed in earlier chapters apply with equal force to co-ops, subject to the limitations discussed as applicable to all levels of employees in large-scale organizations. In other words, there is no more difference in projecting the needs for technical and professional employees than there is in doing the same for apprentices, foremen, or other types of positions. However, there are important differences in the programs for developing human resources—specific people, who can qualify as foremen, apprentices, technicians, or professionals. There is, of course, some interchangeability between these classifications, for foremen positions can be filled by college-graduate trainees as well as by co-ops. However, the important consideration for the manpower planner is that once he has made his manpower projection he can then decide upon plans of action for fulfilling the manpower needs through utilization of pertinent training programs. Cooperative educational plans should certainly be included among the alternative methods of developing human resources.

HISTORICAL BACKGROUND

Cooperative education was founded in the United States at the University of Cincinnati in the School of Engineering in 1906 by Dean Herman Schneider. He developed his idea of the cooperative plan while he was a professor at Lehigh University. While there, he found that nearly all of those graduate engineers who made outstanding contributions soon after graduation had had practical experience before graduation, either through part-time work, vacation work, or staying out of school to work and save money. This led Dean Schneider directly to the idea that perhaps the optimum educational experience was one which combined industrial work experience with the classroom. In this way a man would not have to wait until he graduated to start his industrial experience. When Dean Schneider moved to Cincinnati, he succeeded in selling his idea to a group of manufacturers and finally convinced the rather skeptical faculty of the university that his plan had possibilities.[20]

Twenty-seven students enrolled in the cooperative engineering curriculum at the University of Cincinnati in 1906. By 1919 the engineering co-op enrollment had risen to 780, and it was working with 135 different firms. In that same year the co-op curriculum was extended to business administration students, and one year later all the engineering courses were put on a co-op basis. Since its early founding at Cincinnati, college cooperative education has spread to many other institutions and to many other curricula.[21]

[20] Henry H. Armsby, "What Is a Co-op Program?," in *Cooperative Education and the Impending Educational Crisis, op. cit.,* pp. 6–7.
[21] *Ibid.,* p. 7.

The first period of growth in college cooperative education was from 1906 to 1942 in which a moderate but steady increase in the spread of plans took place. Eight out of ten institutions that began cooperative education continued its operation, and by 1942 there were 30 successful programs in the United States. Even the severe depression of the 1930s, when jobs were difficult to find, failed to halt the growth of college cooperative plans.[22]

The second period of expansion began in 1946, after the close of World War II. During the war, most cooperative plans had been discontinued in favor of the emergency acceleration of academic programs. With the postwar reconversion, cooperative education resumed its growth; and in the period from 1946 to the present the number of participating cooperative institutions had increased vastly. Nine out of ten institutions that initiated cooperative education during this period are continuing it at present.[23]

By early 1967, there were 110 colleges and universities offering undergraduate and postgraduate cooperative programs with an enrollment of 56,000 students in such programs. During their work periods co-ops earned in excess of $95,000,000 per year. At that time there were more than 3000 American industrial firms and other organizations employing students on work-study plans.[24]

Of the approximately 110 colleges utilizing cooperative plans in 1970, there are a number of model programs, which we discuss in more detail later in the chapter and briefly here. For example, the cooperative plan of education was adopted at Northeastern University in 1909 and has been in continuous operation ever since. In recent years, more than 9000 undergraduate students have been enrolled in five-year cooperative curricula, leading to bachelor's degrees in engineering, liberal arts, business administration, education, pharmacy, nursing, physical therapy, and physical education and recreation. Approximately 6000 upper-class students, and more than 200 graduate students, alternate quarters of full-time academic work with quarters of full-time employment in more than 1300 industrial and other organizations throughout the United States and Canada. Northeastern has become the largest institution of higher education in the United States wholly committed to the work-study plan of education. The College of Engineering at the University of Detroit has had a cooperative program since 1911. Since its inception the plan has been expanded to include students in architecture, accounting, and at the graduate level in the various fields of business administration. An interesting facet of the cooperative

[22] Wooldridge, *op. cit.,* p. 3.

[23] *Ibid.*

[24] News release of the National Commission for Cooperative Education, Monday, April 24, 1967.

program at the University of Detroit is the availability of the engineering program to students transferring from other collegiate institutions. Working agreements are in effect with more than 30 affiliated colleges and universities whose preengineering curricula are designed to facilitate the transfer of students into the cooperative program at the University of Detroit.

Another well-known cooperative education program is that conducted by Antioch College. Antioch has used the cooperative plan since 1921 and requires all students to participate in it. In fact, co-op credits are required for graduation. The college enrolls approximately 1800 students and maintains 900 on campus at any one time, the others being on work assignments. The students have freedom of choice in selecting their co-op jobs.

Antioch is very concerned with the impact of the total off-campus experience on its students. It deliberately uses the word "extramural" to indicate such experience beyond the walls in its co-op program, which is staffed by the "extramural department." Because the co-op experience is regarded as educational, the employers of co-op students are regarded as "field faculty." [25]

Recent Growth

The reasons for the accelerated growth of cooperative education plans in recent years are numerous. First, many educators previously committed to orthodox curricula have begun to accept the work-study principle as worthwhile in higher education. They have seen cooperative education meet the tests of time and performance over a long enough period to win approval as being academically sound. Second, many educators have accepted, if not welcomed, the role of industry as a valuable active force in the educative process. This change of attitude has probably been brought about in part by increased interrelationships of faculties and industry in consulting and research undertakings. Also, colleges, particularly private institutions, have been financially forced to rely upon contributions from industry in order to survive. This reliance has fostered a more sympathetic understanding of the mutual problems of education and industry. Third, the reciprocity between higher education and industry is fundamentally rooted in the requirements of our complex technology. Industrial management has become increasingly aware that universities are the primary source of future managers. Therefore, they have become concerned with the quality of higher education and academic standards.[26] In turn, universities have become aware of the need to utilize the learning resources

[25] "The Cooperative Plan," *Antioch College Bulletin,* Vol. 62, No. 1, October 1965, pp. 1–2.
[26] Wooldridge, *op. cit.,* p. 4.

available inside industry rather than to attempt duplicating them. Duplication would, in many instances, be prohibitively expensive and financially undesirable because universities simply would not have sufficient funds to continually purchase the tools, machines, laboratory and other equipment required to provide up-to-date instruction.

In addition to the numerical increase of universities with cooperative educational plans, there has also occurred a spread of the work-study idea over a broader spectrum of curricula. It is true that cooperative education is thought of by some people as exclusively identified with engineering, but this misconception stems from the fact that it began in an engineering school and has enjoyed its greatest growth in technical education. Since 1946, however, there has been a marked proliferation of cooperative education into other areas such as business administration, education, and the liberal arts. It has also expanded slightly into junior colleges, community colleges, and technical institutes, but, by and large, it is overwhelmingly identified with the four- or five-year programs leading to the bachelor's degree.

Graduates of cooperative programs in recent years have generally been offered starting pay five to ten percent higher than that offered to classmates without experience who get their college degrees in four years. Universities with such work-study plans report that graduates are in heavy demand and that they could find jobs for two to five times as many as are graduated.[27]

Much of the expansion of cooperative education plans can be attributed to the efforts made by the National Commission for Cooperative Education since the early 1960s. The commission, which is an outgrowth of research efforts and conferences supported by the Thomas Alva Edison Foundation in the late 1950s, carried on a very effective campaign to disseminate knowledge about the advantages of cooperative education and to encourage educational institutions to adopt cooperative plans.

Another impetus for expansion is a newly established organization. Representatives of universities and employing organizations have since early 1964 developed a Cooperative Education Association, which is designed to provide a more broadly based professional association for persons interested in cooperative education than previously existed. For decades until the early 1960s, the American Society of Engineering Education had maintained a Cooperative Education Division. Perhaps the ASEE was the logical place to professionally quarter cooperative education when it was largely confined to engineering curricula and co-ops, but as cooperative education expanded its perimeters specialists in it thought that the stature and the philosophy of cooperative education demanded a professional

[27] *U.S. News & World Report,* Vol. 62, No. 5, January 30, 1967, p. 89.

association of its own. The National Commission for Cooperative Education endorsed the idea of a Cooperative Education Association and the Cooperative Education Division of the ASEE also gave it its support. As a consequence, the CEA was started and has grown to more than 400 members.[28]

Research on Cooperative Education

Until the early 1960s there were very few objective investigations of the educational effectiveness of cooperative programs. Perhaps the first study was made in 1927 and was designed to find out whether engineering graduates of cooperative programs were as competent as graduates of regular programs, in spite of the fact that cooperative students generally spent about 20 percent less time on the college campus than did regular students. The data were supplied by graduates of two institutions which were alike as to environment, number of students enrolled, size and general quality of the faculty, and quantitative requirements for graduation. They differed only in that one institution had a cooperative program and the other, an all-residence curriculum. The findings of the study were largely inconclusive, although revealing in some important respects. It showed no marked differences between the two groups of students in the number of positions occupied by graduates in a given period after graduation; the relationship of fields of work of graduates to courses pursued in college; levels of positions occupied; and the earnings and rates of advancement of the graduates. Also, inasmuch as the period that had elapsed since the establishment of cooperative courses was not great (less than 20 years) it was quite possible that sufficient time had not passed so that the graduates of the two curricula could be studied.[29]

Another of the rare studies made of cooperative education was reported in 1944. This study was a report on cooperative education programs at the Rochester Institute of Technology. In the study it was found that more than 90 percent of the students enrolled in the co-op program had been placed in jobs allied to their major fields of study. About four-fifths of the students reported that their work became more meaningful as a result of their work experience. Seventy-five percent stated that they were motivated

[28] Donald C. Hunt, "And It Happened This Way," *Journal of Cooperative Education,* Vol. 1, No. 1, November 1964, pp. 3–4. For the background on other organizations concerned with cooperative education, see: Clement J. Freund, "The Cooperative System—A Manifesto," *Journal of Engineering Education,* Vol. 37, No. 2, October 1946, p. 6; and Henry H. Armsby, *Cooperative Education in the United States* [Bulletin 1954, No. 11], *op. cit.;* as well as scattered articles over the years in the *Journal of Engineering Education.*

[29] Ralph W. Tyler, "Educational Values of Cooperative Education," in *Cooperative Education and the Impending Educational Crisis, op. cit.,* p. 35.

in their schoolwork as a result of their work experience. More than 80 percent of the graduates indicated that their cooperative work had been of considerable value to them, and an equal number stated that they would again elect a cooperative education plan if they were to repeat their education.[30]

Except for scattered research conducted by graduate students for dissertations and other materials which are fugitive, up until 1961 there existed little beyond individual testimony concerning the objectively and subjectively perceived values of cooperative education. Recognizing needs for both the expansion and extension of cooperative education and the fact that higher education faced many challenges within the following decade, Charles F. Kettering suggested and arranged for the Thomas Alva Edison Foundation to sponsor a conference on cooperative education in 1957. This was the first national conference on cooperative education to be attended by representatives of more than 80 colleges and universities and by representatives of nearly 100 firms employing cooperative students at that time. The purpose of the conference was to examine the existing working models of cooperative education because they offered active demonstrations of what might be one way of serving effectively some of the enlarging student population seeking advanced education.

Most Recent Research Study

This conference in 1957 revealed that cooperative education had been adapted to a variety of forms of higher education: public and private institutions, residential and nonresidential colleges, and liberal arts and professional curricula. It was found that there were many kinds of businesses and professions using cooperative education and that those experienced with cooperative education were enthusiastic about its educational and social merits. However, the conference also revealed the need for an objective scientific comparison of cooperative education with conventional education because no real evaluation of the philosophical purposes and broad values and no comprehensive documentation of the methods and results of cooperative education had ever been carried out.[31]

As a result of the conference and subsequent work, the Study of Cooperative Education was formally inaugurated during 1958. The final results were published in 1961 and constitute a monumental evaluation of cooperative education which has not been equalled since then. Because of its importance and the richness of its evaluative findings, it is worth giving some attention to this study so that manpower specialists can comprehend its significance.

[30] *Ibid.,* pp. 35–36.
[31] Ralph W. Tyler, "Conclusions and Recommendations," in Wilson and Lyons, *op. cit.,* p. 3.

The plan of the study was: (1) to select a representative sample from the population of cooperative institutions and a sample of noncooperative institutions which, insofar as possible, would be comparable to those cooperative institutions included; (2) to collect data from a sample of students, graduates, faculty, and administrators which would be germane to the purposes of the investigations; and (3) to collect relevant information from a sample of firms which employed cooperative students. The total of institutions participating consisted of 22 cooperative programs and 16 noncooperative programs. From each of the cooperative programs, selected faculty members were asked to complete a brief questionnaire regarding their views on several pertinent questions about cooperative education. One hundred sixty-three of these questionnaires were completed. Data were collected from questionnaires and interviews with the coordinators of cooperative programs of the 17 institutions in the sample operating cooperative programs. Data relevant to the purposes of the study were also collected by means of interviews and questionnaires from 30 industrial concerns employing cooperative students. Each participating institution was asked to administer to a random sample of freshmen and senior students in the selected programs certain specially prepared questionnaires. The institutions further participated by making available the names and addresses of graduates from these programs of the classes of 1958, 1955, 1953, 1950, and 1939, samples of whom were sent questionnaires. Of 4012 questionnaires 2476 were returned, a 61.7 percent rate of return. All interviews were planned and conducted by the National Opinion Research Center of the University of Chicago.[32] Although there were some important methodological problems limiting the generalization of the findings of this research, it remains the best available to the present time.

Based upon questionnaires returned by the students, it was found that there is greater contrast in perceived environmental characteristics among liberal arts, engineering, and business curricula than there is between cooperative and noncooperative programs within each curricula. There appeared to be no single or characteristic environmental setting common to all programs of cooperative education. Instead, cooperative education was found within a variety of settings.[33]

Looking at social class characteristics, it was found that a larger proportion of noncooperative students, including freshmen, seniors, and graduates, had origins in upper and upper-middle social classes.[34] At the same time, the data revealed that a larger proportion of cooperative students and

[32] Wilson and Lyons, *op. cit.*, pp. 19–25.

[33] *Ibid.*, p. 40.

[34] These classes were defined using W. Lloyd Warner's Index of Status Characteristics, as described in W. Lloyd Warner et al., *Social Class in America*, American Book-Stratford Press, New York, 1949.

graduates came from the upper-lower and lower-lower classes. The data also showed that a larger proportion of liberal arts students and graduates —whether cooperative or noncooperative—came from the higher social strata than did students and graduates of engineering and business programs. Conversely, more engineering and business students and graduates had origins in the lower social strata than did liberal arts students and graduates. These data on social class give clear support to the contention that cooperative education provides educational opportunities for a greater number of young people from the lower social strata than does noncooperative education. Cooperative education thus is a means of making higher education financially possible to a large group of young people. Except for social class, cooperative students in almost all other respects are like their noncooperative counterparts. As a corollary, there is no specific cluster of characteristics which clearly sets the cooperative student apart from the noncooperative student.[35]

Employers reported rather enthusiastically about the hiring of cooperative students because employment provided them with a flow of talent into the organization. Co-ops, at the time of graduation, had a breadth of knowledge about the organization and its operations which could not be obtained without employment. The employers reported that the cooperative education plan furnished them with the opportunity to train students in the ways of the organization and furnished them with the opportunity to observe the students over a period of time and select the most able for permanent employment. As a consequence, co-oping tended to cut down the cost of industrial recruitment and make it more efficient. Employers also reported that cooperative education provided the organization with capable persons performing in semiprofessional jobs. The professional staff could then be released for other duties commensurate with their talents. Employers mentioned, finally, that they believed they were making contributions to education and giving service to the community when they participated in cooperative education plants.[36]

Turning from industry to the university itself, the results of the research showed that faculty members believed co-op work experience helped give a sense of reality to the learning of the students. The addition of this dimension provided a great incentive to the student for his academic work. Faculty members believed that co-oping contributed substantially to the student's ability to apply theory to concrete situations. Cooperative work experience thus assisted the student in the development of mature judgment. Yet the practical aspects of cooperative education were not so emphasized that the student's ability to think creatively was stifled. Lastly,

[35] Wilson and Lyons, *op. cit.*, pp. 41–43, 64.
[36] *Ibid.*, p. 70.

faculty members believed that there was little, if any, academic loss for cooperative students because of a need for review on return to the campus after a cooperative work period.[37]

Looking at the cooperative student himself, the research discovered that the academic behavior of cooperative and noncooperative students within each of the three curricula (engineering, business, and liberal arts) was quite similar. This similarity was also noted in the measurement of the intellectual needs among the different students. Cooperative students stated that they planned to continue, and as many cooperative students actually had continued their education beyond the undergraduate level as was true for noncooperative students. All these data may be interpreted to mean that the cooperative education plan does not tend to curtail student interest and motivation for academic striving, including aspirations for graduate education.[38] However, cooperative students and graduates believed that their programs of education provided them with greater opportunity for practicing the application of concepts and principles to concrete situations than did noncooperative students and graduates.[39]

Differences were found between cooperative and noncooperative graduates in their specification of the ways in which their college programs prepared them for their present employment and the ways in which they felt they might have been better prepared. That their institutions provided them with a sound general education was stated by more noncooperative than cooperative graduates. Opportunities to learn about the world of work were cited more often by cooperative than noncooperative graduates. The desire for more exposure to the world of work was advanced by a substantially larger proportion of noncooperative graduates than former co-ops.[40]

As should be expected, the study showed clearly that cooperative students earned a considerably larger proportion of their college expenses than did noncooperative students. The study revealed that a considerably larger proportion of cooperative students and graduates felt that college attendance would have been doubtful or impossible had they not been able to earn some portion of their expenses.[41]

Reflecting on the value of the cooperative educational experience, students and graduates are satisfied and endorse cooperative education. The vast majority of these did not feel unduly delayed in starting their careers because of the fact that cooperative programs are usually five years in

[37] *Ibid.*, p. 86.
[38] *Ibid.*, pp. 96–97.
[39] *Ibid.*, p. 101.
[40] *Ibid.*, p. 115.
[41] *Ibid.*, pp. 122–128.

length. Interruptions in classwork caused by periods of employment did not make their academic work more difficult. They were not confused in trying to practice the concepts and principles learned. Interruptions in classwork did not cause forgetting of material covered in class prior to episodes of employment. The work experience did not discourage the student's interests in theoretical aspects of their major field of study. In summary, the data clearly indicate that the vast majority of cooperative students and graduates felt that their original hopes and expectations for selecting cooperative education were realized.[42] Retrospective reflections perhaps generally tend to be favorable, but the fact remains that virtually no negative second thoughts cropped up among co-ops and former co-ops.

Overall, the Study of Cooperative Education showed quite clearly that the academic potential of cooperative students is equal to that of non-cooperative students. It showed that the cooperative experience provided meaningful opportunities for the student and afforded him opportunities to practice application of what he was learning in the classroom. Enthusiasm for cooperative education was shown by all the parties concerned: students, industry, and universities having cooperative plans. Cooperative students were able and did enter into the life of the college as effectively as non-cooperative students. The five years of college required by most cooperative programs was not regarded as a handicap in getting started in a career. Co-oping was socially desirable in the sense that the financial remuneration received by students for cooperative work made higher education feasible for many talented youths who might otherwise find college financially prohibitive. Co-oping made possible the more effective utilization of college facilities and fulfilled the hopes and expectations of those who selected this particular type of educational plan.[43]

MODEL COOPERATIVE PLANS

Reference was made earlier in this chapter to the diversity of cooperative educational plans. In this section of the chapter we sketch five different cooperative plans to indicate the diversity of approaches being used by educational institutions. Four of the five plans are undergraduate, and one is graduate.

In the next section of the chapter we then examine the manner in which manpower specialists in organizations can carry out their responsibilities for administering cooperative educational plans regardless of the model type.

Cooperative education plans, which are perhaps America's most distinctive contribution to higher education, when viewed from a closeup perspective vary greatly in details. There are differences between schools

[42] *Ibid.*, pp. 129–137.
[43] *Ibid.*, pp. 155–158.

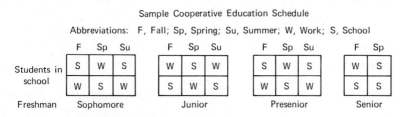

Figure 1   Sample cooperative education schedule.

because of the nature of schools as well as differences between specific fields of study and undergraduate and graduate work.

Figure 1 displays a sample cooperative education schedule, assuming that the particular school under consideration operates on fall and spring semesters with a summer session and that cooperative students spend their entire freshman year on campus studying. It further assumes that the co-oping work-study periods begin in the sophomore year and extend through the senior year. As can be seen from this schedule, the completion of a normal four-year college program takes five years under the cooperative plan.

Furthermore, Figure 1 indicates the "pairing" concept previously mentioned in the chapter. For example, beginning in the sophomore year one group of students (indicated by S) are at school whereas an equal number of students (indicated by W) are at work. This pairing and division of the student body making alternate use of the college plant and the work training stations continues for the last four years of college. Finally, at the senior year both groups have completed an equal number of work and study periods and are eligible to receive their baccalaureate degrees provided they have satisfied all the academic standards of the cooperating educational institution. (It should be noted that the cooperative plan is often accompanied by a new academic class level called the "presenior," reflected in Figure 1.)

The model suggested in Figure 1 would require adjustment to accord with universities operating on the trimester, quarter, or some other less common method of dividing the academic year. These adjustments simply reflect changes in the structure of the schedule rather than any fundamental conceptual changes in the basic ideas indicated.

Northeastern University

Turning to the first specific model cooperative program, let us consider Northeastern University, located in Boston, Massachusetts. In 1909, when it was known as the Cooperative School of Engineering of the Boston

YMCA, Northeastern became the second institution in the United States to adopt the cooperative education plan, beginning with eight students in engineering. Similar to the early plan at Cincinnati, the academic calendar in the early years called for one week of school and one week of work as the alternating pattern. As the years went by and the program grew, Northeastern experimented with various one-week, two-week, five-week, and ten-week periods of alternation. Finally, it developed the quarter system and extended the co-op program from an initial four years to five years in order to meet the academic requirements of the various university accrediting bodies. As the university grew, co-oping was extended beyond engineering into business administration, liberal arts, education, pharmacy, nursing, and physical education. At times, optional full-time four-year programs have been offered to students at Northeastern; however, the basic educational pattern has always been the work-study alternation of cooperative education. In recent years, only students in liberal arts have been allowed to elect a four-year noncooperative or conventional program. In 1965, Northeastern introduced cooperative education into the graduate level and currently operates two-year cooperative programs leading to the Master of Science Degree in Engineering, Mathematics, Pharmaceutical Sciences, Sociology, Actuarial Science, and Professional Accounting.[44]

At Northeastern, freshmen spend the entire year in full-time study. The four upper-class years are those involving alternate periods of work and study. About 1300 employers, two-thirds of whom are located within commuting distance of Boston, provide work experience for the co-ops. The remaining employees are located elsewhere in New England, along the Atlantic Seaboard, and throughout the remaining parts of the United States. Occasionally, students have worked in foreign countries as co-ops. Satisfactory performance in these work assignments is as essential for graduation as satisfactory performance in the student's academic studies.[45]

Northeastern has a rather large department of cooperative education in which there are a number of coordinators. These are the aforementioned specialists in placing students on assignments related to their major field of study. They locate full-time jobs for the students. Freshmen, since they have no previous cooperative work record to be used as grounds for selecting their first job assignment, are placed in work based upon their scholastic record in high school and academic achievements at Northeastern. When they have completed three twelve-week periods as freshmen, they then are separated into Division A and Division B while sophomores. Those in Division A start the college year with a term of classroom instruction, while those designated as Division B commence their first cooperative

[44] Northeastern University, *1966–1967 Cooperative Education Handbook*, p. 4.
[45] Northeastern University, *Co-opportunities at Northeastern University*, p. 6.

work assignment. At the end of the first academic term those in Division A and Division B simply change places with their alternates and continue on this plan for the duration of their upperclass years.[46] The patterning of A and B in work-study would follow the S and W legend shown in Figure 1.

The coordinator is the key specialist who places students on assignments related to their major field of study and locates full-time jobs. The coordinators discuss the career objectives of the co-op and answer any questions that they may have. Insofar as possible they attempt to match the abilities and desires of student with available work opportunities. Coordinators also arrange for interviews between the co-op and the potential employer. If the employer is located in close geographical proximity to the school, usually he will interview the co-op at the place of employment. However, it is possible for an employer to interview the student on campus, and this is done. If the decision is made to hire the student, he reports for work and remains on the co-op program unless there is a desire for change on his part or his performance is not regarded as appropriate by the employer. Depending upon economic conditions, the co-op training stations may be closed by the employer and the co-op will be out of a job. When these co-op layoffs do occur, normally the co-op does not receive unemployment compensation, and it becomes the job of the college cooperative coordinator to locate another position for the co-op.

The coordinator also makes regular visits to the employer to determine how well the co-op is performang and to determine if the co-op has any unsettled grievances or dissatisfactions which he wishes to voice to the coordinator.

In sum, the coordinator discusses the co-op's progress with his supervisor and confers with the co-op at the conclusion of each cooperative work assignment throughout his career at the university. In addition to a record of all academic grades, the co-op coordinator also has before him the official employer's evaluation form, which is a type of performance review report. Since 1962 a number of cooperative universities and employers have adopted a simplified performance review form recommended by the Cooperative Education Division of the ASEE and now by the Cooperative Education Association. This form is shown in Figure 2.

The typical performance review form is an abbreviated type of graphic scale in which the employer describes and evaluates on the front side how the co-op performed during the work period. The other side can be used by the co-op to provide the same information regarding his perception of the work assignments he was given. With the performance review tool the co-op coordinator is able to obtain a measure of the co-op's progress on

[46] *Ibid.*

(Name of School)

Employer's Evaluation of Cooperative Student

Name_____   Class_____   Course_____

Work Period_____   Assignment_____

Employer_____

INSTRUCTIONS: The immediate supervisor will evaluate the student objectively, comparing him with other students of comparable academic level, with other personnel assigned the same or similarly classified jobs, or with individual standards.

RELATIONS WITH OTHERS

- ☐ Exceptionally well accepted
- ☐ Works well with others
- ☐ Gets along satisfactorily
- ☐ Has some difficulty working with others
- ☐ Works very poorly with others

ATTITUDE — APPLICATION TO WORK

- ☐ Outstanding in enthusiasm
- ☐ Very interested and industrious
- ☐ Average in diligence and interest
- ☐ Somewhat indifferent
- ☐ Definitely not interested

JUDGMENT

- ☐ Exceptionally mature
- ☐ Above average in making decisions
- ☐ Usually makes the right decision
- ☐ Often uses poor judgment
- ☐ Consistently uses bad judgment

DEPENDABILITY

- ☐ Completely dependable
- ☐ Above average in dependability
- ☐ Usually dependable
- ☐ Sometimes neglectful or careless
- ☐ Unreliable

ABILITY TO LEARN

- ☐ Learns very quickly
- ☐ Learns readily
- ☐ Average in learning
- ☐ Rather slow to learn
- ☐ Very slow to learn

QUALITY OF WORK

- ☐ Excellent
- ☐ Very good
- ☐ Average
- ☐ Below average
- ☐ Very poor

ATTENDANCE: ☐ Regular ☐ Irregular   **PUNCTUALITY:** ☐ Regular ☐ Irregular

OVER-ALL PERFORMANCE: Outstanding | Very Good | + Average − | Marginal | Unsatisfactory

What traits may help or hinder the student's advancement?

Additional Remarks (over if necessary):

This report has been discussed with student   ☐ Yes   ☐ No

(Signed)_____   Date_____
               (Immediate Supervisor)

This form is recommended by the Cooperative Education Division, ASEE

Figure 2   Performance review form.

the job as well as his scholastic attainment. The coordinator can then judge at least grossly whether the co-op has successfully combined the theory of the classroom with the practical experience of the work-a-day world.

Schools such as Northeastern also require that the co-op periodically complete more lengthy reports on their cooperative work experience. These reports together with the others discussed above provide the coordinator with additional information to make certain that the co-op is advancing in line with his ability. In general, the better jobs are held by the better-performing co-ops. The employer is usually interested in retaining the more proficient performers at the end of the co-op's formal education at the university. The co-op coordinator thus plays a strategic role in the development of the co-op and is the important bridge to the community of employers.[47]

The growth of Northeastern University and the prominence it has gained in cooperative education resulted in the reorganization of the Department of Cooperative Education at the school and the formation of a Division of Cooperative Education in 1964. The division consists of three departments: the Center for Cooperative Education, the Department of Graduate Placement Services, and the Department of Cooperative Education. The Center conducts research in the expansion, development, and improvement of cooperative curricula. It also makes available consulting services to schools and colleges that are considering adopting cooperative education. About 21 faculty coordinators work in the Department of Cooperative Education and seek to maintain approximately 3500 jobs for the 7000 upper classmen co-ops at Northeastern.[48]

Graduate Co-op Programs

In 1956 the first graduate program in cooperative education was started at Northeastern with 15 students in electrical engineering, a field in which the greatest technological expansion has taken place in the last two decades. Ten years after starting graduate cooperative education, Northeastern grad co-op registrations were in the vicinity of 300, with approximately one-half in engineering and the remainder in such fields as mathematics, pharmacy, actuarial science, and professional accounting. This 10 years of operation at the graduate level has largely proven that the basic ideas of cooperative education can be applied as successfully to graduate education as they have historically been applied to undergraduate education.[49]

The basic concepts in graduate cooperative education and the definition of it are very similar to those of undergraduate cooperative education. Yet there are a few important distinctions. When a student enters graduate

[47] *Ibid.*, pp. 8–10. See also Mason and Haines, *op. cit.*, pp. 124–128.

[48] Northeastern University, *1966–1967 Cooperative Education Handbook, op. cit.*, pp. 4–13. See also Roy L. Wooldridge, *Analysis of Student Employment in a Cooperative Education Program,* Center for Cooperative Education, Northeastern Massachusetts, Boston, 1966.

[49] Alvah K. Borman, "Graduate Study: A New Approach Through Cooperative Education," *Journal of Cooperative Education,* Vol. 3, No. 1, November 1966, pp. 10–11.

cooperative education, he is a professional by virtue of having obtained his first degree in his field. In addition, he has demonstrated his theoretical competence by being accepted for graduate work. As a rule, he is in the top one-quarter of his undergraduate class and usually an above-average person in other respects. There are other important distinctions and they hinge upon the fact that the graduate co-op requires a different kind of effort on the part of the co-op coordinator if he is to be adequately placed.[50]

Placement on the job is carried out in three ways. First, approximately one-half the graduate co-ops at Northeastern are students who were formerly on undergraduate co-op programs. Many of these students were highly regarded by their employers and they wished to remain with them while studying for graduate degrees. In effect, the situations solved the customary undergraduate co-op placement problem because the training stations already existed. However, with grad co-ops the co-op coordinator must ascertain that the job is a professional job and that all the requirements of the philosophy of cooperative education can be met.

Secondly, in other situations the prospective co-op is working in his field of interest and wishes to remain associated with a specific employer, but the latter is not acquainted with cooperative educational plans. In this case, the co-op coordinator will have to do some missionary work to indoctrinate the employer in collaborating with the school. At Northeastern a number of organizations have been won over and incorporated graduate cooperative education into their overall training opportunities. In some instances, these firms encourage new or current employees to take advantage of the opportunity for graduate cooperative education.

Thirdly, in still other situations the co-op coordinator discusses the various employment opportunities that exist with the student and determines which of these is best suited to the student's career goals. The student is referred to prospective employers for interviews. The coordinator must then satisfy himself that the employer will meet the requirements of the program. All of this means that the placement of graduate students is more flexible than that of undergraduates. The graduate student is more likely to be mature, his interests are likely to have developed, and he is more sure of his goals. Perhaps most important of all, he is a professional working in a professional field.[51]

Graduate co-ops are normally paid higher salaries than undergraduate co-ops. Of course, some are already on the payroll of an employer, and the co-op program amounts to arranging for tuition refund or possibly time-off during working hours to attend classes (assuming all the require-

[50] *Ibid.,* p. 13.
[51] *Ibid.,* pp. 17–18.

ments of the school program can be met in this manner). A unique situation possible under graduate co-oping is the writing of a thesis. In some cases a student is allowed to do his thesis work on a problem or project with his cooperating organization. If this situation is allowed, coordination must be maintained between the student's faculty advisor and the industrial or organizational supervisor for whom the student is working. Usually, it is the responsibility of the co-op coordinator to set up the necessary liaison channels to affect the coordination.[52]

University of Detroit

Turning to another cooperative education program, let us consider those in operation at the University of Detroit. Begun in 1877 by a nucleus of four Jesuits and 87 students, the University of Detroit has since expanded to more than 11,000 students. When the College of Engineering was established in 1911, a cooperative training program followed. In recent years the program has been expanded to students in the School of Architecture, the Accounting Department in the College of Commerce and Finance, and the Master of Business Administration program in the Graduate School. A unique feature of the Detroit program is, as previously mentioned, that the College of Engineering also makes its cooperative program available to students transferring from other collegiate institutions. Working agreements are in effect with about 30 affiliated colleges whose preengineering curricula are specifically designed to facilitate transfer of students into the cooperative program at the University of Detroit.

Students enter the cooperative phase of their educational program when they are certified as eligible by their respective deans. This certification is based upon successful completion of all prerequisites within their programs. The number of years usually required to obtain certification for entry into the cooperative phase is as follows: Accounting, 2 years; Engineering, 2 years; Architecture, 3 years; Master of Business Administration, 4 years, assuming recipiency of a baccalaureate degree. The cooperative education schedule varies for each of these programs although the basic principle of work-study is implemented consistent with the philosophy of cooperative education. For example, determination of whether one's cooperative education begins with an academic or the training period for MBA candidates is dependent upon the requirements of the cooperating firm and the course requirements of the student. Performance reviews, periodic training re-

---

[52] *Ibid.*, p. 18. Other schools having graduate cooperative programs of one kind or another include the University of Cincinnati, University of Detroit, and Virginia Polytechnic Institute.

ports on cooperative experience, a certain standard of accomplishment in course work, and satisfactory completion of the work periods are indispensable to completing the requirements for a degree under the cooperative education plan.[53]

Antioch College

Turning to the fourth model cooperative program, let us consider Antioch College, which is located in Yellow Springs, Ohio. Antioch has a reputation for being forward-looking and liberal in outlook. Antioch's aim as an educational institution is to equip its students to live effectively in a complex world. In order to do this, Antioch believes that broad experience as well as knowledge are required.[54]

Antioch has been using a cooperative plan since 1921 in order to enable students to live in communities that differ from the college campus and to broaden their understanding of the world in which they live. Thus the purpose of the plan is educational. It is not designed primarily for students to work their way through college.[55]

Antioch regards successful extramural experience as so important that it is a major degree requirement for all students, men and women, in all fields of study. Because the experience obtained in co-oping is educational the employers become, in effect, field faculty.[56]

Antioch has identified three work periods over an academic year's time. The students' first jobs are usually elementary ones so that they can learn basic skills, try out different kinds of work, or determine where they fit in or perform best. In the process, students learn how to get a job done, work with others, carry personal responsibility, and observe how an organization operates. Depending upon the nature of the job, the employer's expectations, and the student's interest, students may return to the same employer for two or more work periods, either to do the same work or perhaps progress to an assignment that requires more experience and background. Employers have used Antioch students for jobs that they could expect bright but untrained teenagers to hold, and for responsible, preprofessional positions that able, trained, and experienced young men and women could fulfill.[57]

---

[53] University of Detroit, *Cooperative Education Program,* pp. 8–25.

[54] "The Cooperative Plan," *Antioch College Bulletin,* Vol. 62, No. 1, October 1965, p. 1.

[55] *Ibid.*

[56] *Ibid.*

[57] *Ibid.,* pp. 1–2. For a recent evaluation of the Antioch program see D. Keith Lupton and Joan Schwartz, "The Other Half of Cooperative Education," *Journal of Cooperative Education,* Vol. 3, No. 1, November 1966, pp. 22–28.

Other liberal arts colleges operating widely variant versions of the basic cooperative educational plan include Goddard in Vermont, Bard in New York, and Wilmington in Ohio.

In addition to the aforementioned colleges there are many others which offer cooperative education, but their programs contain still other distinctive features which cannot be easily summarized. For example, the cooperative program at Cornell University is largely a prestige honors program although it is clearly in the work-study pattern.

General Motors Institute

The last type of cooperative plan which we discuss is that offered by the General Motors Institute in Flint, Michigan. Founded in 1919 and sponsored by the General Motors Corporation since 1926, GMI is the only accredited undergraduate college maintained by an industrial corporation in the United States. Over the years, approximately two-thirds of the more than 7000 graduates of GMI have remained at General Motors in engineering and management positions. GMI graduates are represented in the ranks of management holding such positions as Executive Vice-President, Group Executive, General Manager, Chief Engineer, Plant Manager, Project Engineer, and many other similar and lower positions of managerial responsibility. The school is fully accredited as a bachelor's degree-granting institution and is supported entirely by General Motors, either directly by grants or indirectly through wages paid to cooperative students, who in turn pay tuition, and also through special charges to GM plants for specialized programs in management development and the various technical fields.[58]

Fundamentally, GMI is an engineering college granting degrees with specialization in mechanical, electrical, and industrial engineering. To gain admission to GMI an applicant must secure both the approval of the GMI admission committee and the sponsorship of a GM operating unit, such as a plant. The successful applicant then embarks upon a five-year program divided into alternating six-week periods between academic study at the Institute and full-time work at one of the more than 140 participating plants throughout the United States and Canada. The student pays all his own expenses and $724.00 tuition annually out of the salary received from the participating unit, a salary usually about $2300.00 net per year. During the fifth year, the GMI student works full time at his participating unit and the preparation of a thesis required for graduation. Superior students can apply for a special arrangement during this fifth year to earn a master's

[58] "Engineers Tailor-Made for General Motors," *Business Week*, No. 1161, July 1, 1961, pp. 48–49; and General Motors Institute, *1967–68 Engineering Program Catalogue*, pp. 5–6.

degree in science or engineering at another institution, which is called the "bachelor-master's" program. In recent years General Motors Institute enrollment has been about 2600 with, of course, less than one-half that number on campus at any one time. There are slightly more than 200 full-time faculty members.[59] Very few faculty members possess Ph.D. degrees. Probably more of the faculty than found in other colleges have extensive managerial and engineering experience in industry.

Students at GMI have no commitment to complete the five years, nor does the Institute or the sponsoring unit have an obligation to continue the arrangement. Attrition over the five years is about one-third, which probably reflects the careful screening of students. About one-half of the students entering GMI are in the upper 10 percent of their high-school classes. Because General Motors is one of the highest-paying organizations in the world, the co-op who graduates from GMI probably earns a great deal more money as a consequence of participating in work-study at General Motors than in many other companies.

Although GMI has been very productive from the standpoint of providing managerial personnel for General Motors, it has some drawbacks. First, it is extremely expensive. For example, in 1966, GM's aid to education amounted to $11.4 million but about $4.4 million or about 39 percent of the total went for support of GMI.[60] Few companies could support such an educational endeavor. Second, extreme corporate inbreeding is another criticism frequently made of GMI. Although 65 to 70 percent of its graduates remain with GM, the GMI graduates are only a tiny corps among the thousands of GM management employees. In fact, at the present time GMI is producing only about 15 percent (or less) of General Motors annual requirements for college graduates. This statistic would suggest that although GMI does tend towards some present inbreeding, it by no means shuts out the graduates of other universities from employment at GM. The inbreeding charge may be more viable for top management because prior to the 1950s college recruitment was lower and the relative number of GMI graduates inputted and retained would have loomed larger.

Third, it has been asserted that the program produces narrow-minded and shortsighted individuals who may have been exposed to little beyond the General Motors way of managing and carrying out professional and technical work. Although this criticism may have some merit, it is quite clear that GMI provides education not available elsewhere with the emphasis on the kinds of knowledge, skills, and attitudes that General Motors needs. With the establishment of the bachelor-master's plan, individuals

[59] "Spawning Ground for Industrial Leaders," *Training in Business and Industry,* Vol. 3, No. 1, January 1966, p. 24. Tuition and salaries are changed from time to time.
[60] General Motors Corporation, *Annual Report,* 1966, p. 15.

can be exposed to opportunities beyond GMI and GM plants and thereby avoid the possible parochialism inherent in work-study situations limited to GM and GMI. It is also possible that the GMI program is equal to the best in engineering and no more parochial in the overall than any other technically specialized curriculum.

In summary, we have been discussing some model-type cooperative education plans. The first two were at Northeastern which offers graduate and undergraduate cooperative education for almost the entire student body. The third was the University of Detroit which offers cooperative education on a selective basis and has integrated its offerings with the pre-engineering curricula of a number of other institutions. Fourth, we discussed Antioch College, which requires that its students participate in cooperative education and contains a student body which studies only the liberal arts. In discussing these model programs we made reference to other schools which have comparable programs. Lastly, we examined the co-operative engineering program at the General Motors Institute, which is a unique program and one much admired.

Although cooperative education plans in the United States have historically been tied closely to engineering education, in recent years their application has been extended beyond this field. There is every likelihood that in the future their expansion will continue into still other fields of education.

ADMINISTERING COOPERATIVE PLANS IN ORGANIZATIONS

The manpower specialist in organizations plays a role in cooperative education which is analagous to that of the co-op coordinator in the university. The manpower specialist is responsible for assuring the success of cooperative education plans in the employing organization. To that extent he may be looked upon as the analogue of the co-op coordinator, except he is in the employer's setting. In many organizations the person responsible for administering cooperative education plans would be the training director, personnel manager, or some other representative of the industrial relations department.

We previously discussed the manpower-planning implications of cooperative education plans and suggested that cooperative plans be used to assure the organization of an adequate supply of eventual college graduates who have demonstrated technical and/or managerial aptitudes. This same purpose can, of course, be attained by the direct employment of college graduates after they have received their bachelor's degrees. The important administrative problems for the manpower specialist in conducting cooperative education plans is to identify training stations that can be used for co-ops and to establish the necessary controls for assuring that development takes place. The problem of manpower projections involving co-ops is of lesser importance and can be handled in making an overall manpower projection for a plant, division, or total organization.

Developing human resources by means of cooperative plans requires that considerable thought be given to the recruitment, selection, placement, training, and retention of the co-op trainee. Cooperative plans can meet organizational manpower needs by offering a source of new personnel with professional, technical, or managerial training and aptitudes or specialized skills where normal employment and on-the-job developmental activities cannot be expected to provide an adequate supply.

Selection of Co-ops

Inasmuch as co-ops are college students and must meet at least minimum academic standards in order to remain in college and participate as co-ops, these standards in themselves act as a selection device. The organization hiring co-ops can often choose from among those with the better grades or other qualifications desired.

Normally the employing organization retains the right to reject or accept students, and those accepted must meet the employment and work performance standards of the employer. At the same time, no commitment is made by the employer (or the co-op, for that matter) regarding continued or permanent employment.

Normally, co-ops are considered regular employees and are given leaves of absence from employment when they are attending school. Usually they are given performance reviews utilizing a form similar to that identified in Figure 2 earlier in this chapter. These performance reviews are normally given at the end of each work period by the supervisor under whom the co-op was employed. Although the performance reviews have many purposes, they essentially provide information as to the co-op's abilities, capacities, and interests, which is essential for their placement and continuation in the program. Secondly, they can be used to determine areas where additional experience might be desirable.

Forestalling the Layoff of Co-ops

One of the most serious problems in administering a cooperative program from the standpoint of the manpower specialist in industry is to continue the program at least at a minimum level through adverse as well as prosperous business years. Whether cooperative education in the United States would survive a depression such as that which we experienced in the 1930s is a moot question. Certainly during 1958, which was the last year in which there was a serious economic setback affecting cooperative education plans, cooperative programs were able to survive.

To give co-op programs viability the manpower specialist should install a policy which recognizes the development of human resources as a legitimate business expense and a necessary investment to insure the manpower strength of the employing organization in the future. His responsibility in carrying out this policy involves the following. He must work with line-and-staff managers to determine the planned utilization of selected work assignments having training value in which trainees can do productive work. He must determine that the number of co-ops employed be maintained continuously at a level adequate to meet the organization's long-range manpower needs. He must assure that each trainee, as a requirement for continuance in the co-op program, demonstrate his ability to perform at a high level. He must make certain that the supervisor of a co-op evaluates his performance and determines if the co-op is showing potential that can be developed. When it is demonstrated that co-op trainees are meeting these requirements, the organization should normally give them an opportunity to complete their work phase of the work-study program without interruption.

Establishing Controls for Co-op Retention

In carrying out some of these program administrative responsibilities, the manpower specialist may be assisted by the co-op coordinator from the university who periodically will visit co-ops on the job and determine if they are benefiting and contributing. Any problems that are identified in respect to the work experience phase of the cooperative plan can be mutually worked out by the co-op, supervisor, coordinator, and manpower specialist.

Effective manpower planning requires that provision be made for retaining in the organization's employ all co-ops who satisfactorily complete the work-study program. Under cooperative education plans, the problem of retention is complicated by the fact that the co-op often returns to college following his last work experience and is interviewed on the campus by recruiters from other organizations prior to his graduation. (Figure 1 indicates how this peculiar situation develops at the end of the senior year.) The employing organization's chances of retaining graduating co-ops in full-time positions are strengthened if co-ops receive a specific job offer during their last work period and prior to returning to school. Therefore, one of the tasks of the manpower specialist is to set up an advanced-warning signal system by which he can determine if a position offer is going to be made to a co-op, to have a specific offer made to him, indicating salary, description of the work he will be performing, a suggested date for reporting to work, and the like, so that the co-op knows what he can expect from the employer. If the co-op wishes to remain with the employer but in a different part of the organization, the manpower specialist should make arrangements whereby the co-op can be given consideration for employment elsewhere. Similarly, if the employing organization does not plan to extend a job offer, the co-op should be notified so that he can make his plans for job searching. Of course, if the employing organization has no interest in retaining co-ops and is conducting or participating in a cooperative educational plan out of a socially responsible desire to improve the development of human resources in the total community rather than selfishly for its own organizational improvement, then the suggested steps can be ignored.

Use of Meaningful On-the-Job Training Resources

Proper use of the job for the development of the person is essential in cooperative education. The manpower specialist has an important role to play in making the job all that it should be in this respect. The abilities of co-ops can best be determined by observing them on jobs in which they do productive work commensurate with their maturity, education, and experience. As the co-op proves himself through performance, he should continue to be challenged by placement on work of steadily increasing complexity. The manpower specialist should be alert to the co-op's performance and be planning the arrangements to assure the co-op's movement and placement in due time.

Careful selection and identification of the kinds of work which have developmental value and control of job assignments are necessary. If responsibility for the identification and use of work assignments is retained by the manpower specialist, it is most likely that the work phase of the work-study plan can be structured to have developmental value.

Once a determination has been made as to the kinds of work experience best suited for the co-op's development, the co-op should then be assigned to that kind of work under a supervisor. Similar to any other employee, the co-op should be answerable only to his supervisor. The supervisor should, in turn, be responsible for evaluating the performance of the co-op as a basis for determining whether or not he will be continued on the program. The manpower specialist oversees this process and works with supervisors to make sure that they carry out their developmental responsibilities.

Budget and Headcount Allocation Controls

There is one powerful tool which can be given to the manpower specialist and used by him to make the cooperative education plan effective. If the budget and headcount allocation for co-ops is taken away from the plant or department budget in an organization and centralized under the manpower specialist, it is relatively easy administratively for him to stabilize the number of trainees and permit each part of the organization to utilize the best training stations available for human resource development with a minimum of difficulty.

Installation of such an administrative plan requires reallocation of existing allowable headcounts so that line-and-staff managers in effect lose budget and headcount allocations but are given in return the services of employees that are required to carry out the work. For example, if a department has twelve employees and X dollars for salaries, two employees and a certain amount of money to cover their salaries may be taken from the department manager's budget and headcount. The same is done in a number of other departments. The result is to generate throughout an organization, let us say, 30 positions and a rather large amount of money for salaries. The manpower specialist is held responsible for this budget and the assignment of co-ops to these 30 positions. However, he "gives back" to each department manager the services of persons (now co-ops) who were moved from the department and all the line authority needed for effective supervision. Inasmuch as the co-ops are budgetarily under the authority of the manpower specialist, they can be withdrawn by him from their assignments in the department manager's area of work and assigned elsewhere if it is determined that the department manager is not providing developmental experience in what are now truly training stations. In this way, the manpower specialist has considerable leeway to exert pressure in removing individuals from positions when they are not being provided developmental opportunity. (Likewise, he must be responsive to department managers who report inadequate performance by co-ops.) On the other hand, if the manpower specialist does not have the authority to remove co-ops (which would be the case if for headcount and budget purposes they were assigned to the line or staff department manager), then the manpower specialist would be relatively powerless to make certain that co-ops are given the kind of work experience best suited for their development. The administrative centralization of cooperative education under the manpower specialist has many more virtues to it from the standpoint of conducting an effective program than any other form of administrative arrangement.

Compensation of Co-ops

Other aspects of pay and costs affecting cooperative education should be briefly mentioned. The pay of co-ops should be geared to the level of education which they possess at the beginning of a particular work period. This means that a higher salary would be paid for a senior or presenior than a student entering his first or second work period. By the same token graduate co-ops are paid more money than undergraduate co-ops. Organizations which are employing co-ops from a variety of schools on semester and quarter plans find it convenient to have a single salary schedule which relates the academic progress of the student to the level of pay. In addition, the specific level of pay set is based upon the pay for this same type of work carried out by regular employees. A competitive salary is established, and the co-op is by no means viewed as "cheap help."

Integrating College Graduate and Co-op Plans

Ordinarily the cost of recruiting a co-op into the employ of an organization is a great deal less than the cost of recruiting a college graduate. The reasons for this are several. First, campus interviewing costs for recruiters' travel expenses, not including salaries, are much higher for recruiting college graduates. Second, co-op program graduates are normally not paid travel and relocation expenses, whereas college graduate trainees often are. Third, the advertising expenses for college graduate trainees will likely be substantial. Fourth, the expenses for running a full-blown college recruiting department with all the associated expenses, including the building and cementing of college relations, have become very high since the early 1960s when many leading corporations got involved in the intensive recruitment of college graduates. The result is that the average cost per hire for co-ops is probably only 20 or 25 percent that of hiring college graduates. However, detailed meaningful statistics on this important topic have never been published, and the above is largely surmise.

Organizations that utilize cooperative education plans are often confronted with the question of deciding how the co-op plan should be integrated with the college graduate development plan. For example, if an individual has co-oped with an employer for four years, should he after graduation then be placed upon a college graduate program in the employer's organization? Of course, the answer depends very much upon the extent to which the college graduate program would provide complementary, different, or still more complex training experiences.

If it is possible to provide college graduate programs that build upon the prior cooperative experience, then there is no reason for not allowing co-ops to participate in college graduate training. On the other hand, if there can be no meaningful sequence of developmental experiences devised, then there is no reason to place the co-op on a college graduate program.

We have already seen that it is possible for undergraduate co-ops to continue co-oping on the graduate level. In addition, there is no reason why any professional employee who is qualified and admitted to graduate schools having cooperative education plans cannot participate in these plans although he may not have been an undergraduate student on a cooperative plan. There are thus many ways in which cooperative plans and college graduate plans can be meaningfully integrated to develop the person and at the same time to serve the organization.

MANPOWER PROBLEMS IN COOPERATIVE EDUCATION

There is little doubt that the cooperative education plan is a sound plan of higher education and has a number of distinct contributions to make. Manpower specialists should be well-acquainted with cooperative education and give greater thought to solving some of the problems associated with it so that it can expand and make a greater contribution than it has in the past toward the development of human resources.

There are a number of basic problems associated with the future of cooperative education which we quickly review next, and there are a number of actions currently being undertaken to expand cooperative education in the United States. The problems may be viewed from the standpoint of manpower specialists, college coordinators, employers, and cooperative students.

The first basic problem is that too often cooperative programs of employment are geared to economic conditions. Often, both the number of jobs available and the quality of those jobs from the standpoint of their educational value are seriously curtailed during periods of economic recession.[61] Organizations which have committed themselves to cooperative education plans must realistically reduce some of their training stations during a recession. However, the radical extirpation of training stations and their equally radical reestablishment after a recession has ended cannot be condoned as educationally or economically wise.

Second, co-ops are not always used or given employment in ways that best draw upon their capabilities and that provide them with the most suitable educational experiences. Obviously, the types of assignments given to co-ops would vary depending upon their educational level and maturity. For example, an assignment in the mailroom or as a messenger could be perfectly appropriate for a co-op during his first work experience period. In the process, he could learn about the organization, meet individuals at various levels, and develop some of the basic attitudes necessary to become an employee in an organization. Yet, continued work experiences at such a humble level are inconsistent with the idea in cooperative education of challenging the student, giving him the opportunity to use effectively the knowledge and skills that he has acquired on-campus. This single issue

[61] Wilson and Lyons, *op. cit.*, p. 149.

seems to be largely the basis of any strained relationships that have arisen between cooperative educational institutions and cooperating firms.[62]

Third, employers generally dislike the practice of having cooperative students employed by several different organizations in the various work periods during their college careers. They would prefer that the co-ops have all their experience with one company. There are two reasons for this preference. First, there is a disruption in the work because of the training involved; and, second, there is a loss of contact with co-ops and a lessened claim on them for subsequent full-time employment after graduation. Most cooperative institutions understand this point of view but a few believe that the limitation of students to one organization may not be in the best interest educationally for the students.[63] Yet, it should be noted that unless there is dissatisfaction with the co-op on the part of the employer or dissatisfaction with the employer of a serious nature on the part of the co-op that the co-op is likely to remain with one employer. In cooperative institutions such as Antioch where the extent to which the co-op is retained by the employer after graduation is of little or no concern, there is probably a great desire that the co-op have exposures in more than one organization. In other cooperative plans where the employer's main interest in cooperative education is to retain the co-op after graduation then the problem of remaining with one firm is a serious one.

Fourth, though not a universal problem, in certain industrial and governmental agencies the task of employing co-ops is difficult because they either create problems in union shops or do not conform very well to civil service regulations. These are not insurmountable problems but they require working out.[64]

Fifth, a most frequently cited problem by employers is retaining co-ops (especially the best ones) full-time as employees after graduation. Retention rates vary considerably, perhaps from a low of 15 to 25 percent in some companies and industries where the cooperative work experience is poorly regarded by the co-op to the high of 65 to 70 percent retention experienced by General Motors, which in a certain sense administers a "captive school," GMI. In general, it appears that engineering graduates return to their cooperative companies most frequently, with business school graduates second, and liberal arts graduates third.[65] Consistent with post-World War II trends, an increasing number of young people are going to graduate school, and this certainly includes the best co-ops. Manpower specialists should set up administrative arrangements to keep in touch with

[62] *Ibid.*
[63] *Ibid.*, pp. 149–150.
[64] *Ibid.*, p. 150.
[65] *Ibid.*

these ex-co-ops and try to lure them back to the employing organization after recipiency of the graduate degree, much as they do when dealing with co-ops who are drafted.

Six, the variation of academic calendars among schools presents problems. It is perhaps too much to expect that all schools will in the future go on an identical educational schedule. Employers often try to solve the problem of placing co-ops on different schedules by keeping a pool of jobs open for cooperative students. Others try to solve it by hiring pairs of students from a single institution and assigning them to a specific division, department, or job, keeping them there on an alternating basis throughout their period of employment.[66] Such arrangements do not provide as much flexibility as employers would desire, but they can be tolerated.

Seventh, many students overemphasize the financial rewards of cooperative employment. Coordinators have noted that the primary manifestation of this problem is that students are reluctant to take or actively resist taking cooperative jobs which are relatively low paying despite the fact that these jobs might offer great educational value. Closely related to this problem is another, namely, the problem of orienting students to view their cooperative employment as an integral part of their total education. Coordinators note that often students view their employment solely as a means of securing financial aid for their education or that they become so involved in the details of their job that they are unable to relate it effectively to their total education.[67] The resolution of these problems rests in communicating more thoroughly with students to acquaint them with the objectives of cooperative education. It is perhaps ironic that students would have a mercenary attitude toward co-oping rather than one consistent with the educational philosophy of cooperative plans. Yet this can perhaps be explained by the fact that many co-ops are from lower socioeconomic levels and take an instrumental view of cooperative education. Co-op alumni seem to have a more balanced perspective, although they may have forgotten an earlier mercenary orientation.

Eighth, some faculty members either resent the interruptions in their courses brought about by cooperative employment or almost completely ignore the fact that students have work experience within the context of their educational programs.[68] Ironically, this attitude too is inconsistent with balancing the theory of the classroom with the practice learned in the work situation. However, it does not seem to be a serious or widespread problem.

The future of cooperative education looks bright provided that the phi-

[66] *Ibid.*
[67] *Ibid.*, p. 151.
[68] *Ibid.*, pp. 151–152.

losophy, purposes, and nature of cooperative education are more carefully and thoroughly presented to parents, the public, and manpower specialists in organizations. It is particularly important for industrial and other organizations to consider themselves partners with the school engaged in the joint effort to develop human resources. Closer liaison and more continuous communication could contribute to this end.[69] It would be simplistic to think that a panacea, however.

Educational institutions could improve the image of cooperative education by selecting only highly qualified students for cooperative education and establishing rigorous standards of proficiency for remaining in the cooperative program. Educators should also give more attention to devising new techniques so that the students' time while on work periods can be more effectively used in carrying out assignments of the university. Cooperative institutions could also improve their contribution by seeing that co-ops are counseled more regarding their own career objectives and their potential. By the same token, industry could improve cooperative education by counseling students too.[70]

The National Commission for Cooperative Education proposed in 1962 that cooperative education expand within the following five to ten years consistent with a number of goals. First, the Commission proposed doubling the number of colleges and universities offering cooperative education programs from 60 to 120. Second, it suggested increasing the number of students enrolled in cooperative education programs from the estimated 30,000 in 1962 to 75,000 in 1972. Third, it recommended strengthening some of the existing colleges and universities, perhaps especially liberal arts colleges, by helping them adopt the economic and educational benefits of cooperative education. As opportunities arose it would also aid new colleges to adopt cooperative education plans.

The Commission indicated that these goals could be reached by five sets of action. First, it would provide consultation services by experienced cooperative administrators to colleges working on the transition to cooperative education. Second, it would make available teams of persons who could work intensively with individual colleges to assist in the transition to cooperative education programs that would become self-supporting. Third, it would provide for the in-service training of persons who could fill coordinators' positions at colleges adopting cooperative education. Fourth, it would make available a public information program to create a better understanding of cooperative education by educators, parents, students, industry, and the press. Fifth, it would publish special case materials

[69] *Ibid.,* p. 152.
[70] *Ibid.,* pp. 153–154.

needed by the administration, faculty, and staffs of individual colleges and by employers showing how to move into and solve the various problems of cooperative education.

The desirability of obtaining these goals can easily be seen and defended by manpower specialists who have analyzed how cooperative education can assist them in developing human resources for their organizations. The specific recommendations proposed by the National Commission for Co-operative Education should clearly make sense to manpower specialists who give thought to the ways in which the goals can reasonably be implemented.

CONCLUSIONS

In this chapter we have explained the creation and expansion of work-study plans of education. Beginning more than 60 years ago, college cooperative education in the United States has expanded and has become perhaps the unique American contribution to higher education. The idea has been picked up abroad and the counterpart of co-oping is well-known in Britain but referred to as "sandwich courses." [71]

These plans involve work and study and can be looked upon as a variant on the apprenticeship model.

Cooperative students and graduates tend to be overrepresented in the lower socioeconomic levels in American society. Various research studies have shown that co-ops are not intellectually inferior to non-co-op students.

Co-op programs can be used by manpower specialists to acquire qualified talent for their organizations and to at the same time allow the processes of social mobility to operate.

Co-operative education is educationally sound to the extent that when it is properly administered it allows the theory of the classroom to be complemented by practical experience.

Although cooperative education has in the public mind often suggested the subjective image of "earn while you learn," it has objectively enlarged equal opportunity and upward mobility for many individuals. It should not be understood or defined entirely as a device for allowing the full play

[71] P. F. R. Venables, *Sandwich Courses,* Parish, London, 1959. For more recent work see G. P. Thorley Lawson, "Sandwich Degree Courses: Industrial Training and Its Assessment," *Technical Education,* Vol. 8, No. 4, October 1966, pp. 450–453; H. L. Houghton, "The Training Aspect of Sandwich Courses," *Technical Education,* Vol. 8, No. 2, April 1966, pp. 167–171; and D. Spurgeon, "Industrial Training for a Sandwich Degree in Production Engineering," *Technical Education,* Vol. 8, No. 4, October 1966, pp. 448–453.

of democratic values because it also has potential economic advantages for the hard-nosed businessmen and rational manpower specialist.

Cooperative educational plans are particularly appropriate today because the current "state of the art" in engineering and business cannot be learned solely in the classroom. Cooperative education can potentially motivate students to learn by orienting them to the world of work and providing an opportunity to tie theory and practice together.

There are a variety of different cooperative educational plans in operation in the United States. In the past decade graduate cooperative education has been started. Yet cooperative education remains popular at the high school level, particularly in the distributive field.

The success of cooperative education plans hinges partly on the activity of the coordinator in the university and partly upon the manpower specialist in industry. The success of co-oping also depends upon certain mechanics in administration, such as the utilization of organizational work plans and the progressively increasing complexity of work assignments for the co-op as he shows his capability to perform previously less-demanding jobs. There are a number of administrative refinements that will be necessary in the future for making cooperative education plans workable.

Co-op programs in organizations increase in their learning value to the extent co-ops are developed by receiving planned successively more difficult assignments, given knowledge of results in performance reviews, and supervised by managers interested in human resources.

Manpower projections made in organizations should provide for absorption and retention of co-op graduates as a part of the master manpower plan. Co-oping can then be effectively used to provide organizations with a flow of trained human resources and as a testing ground for selection after graduation. Co-op programs can be integrated in various ways with college graduate training programs.

Co-oping may disrupt organizations as paired co-ops alternate periods of work and study. Yet, the training costs of co-oping are mitigated by the lower salaries paid co-ops in comparison with full-time professional and technical employees and the reduction of recruitment expense in comparison with college graduate trainees.

Historically, co-op programs have been vulnerable to being eliminated by organizations in times of economic adversity. This problem is circumvented when there is a permanent allocation of co-op job stations under a firm manpower plan. It is important that top management plan, endorse, and protect co-oping if this form of education and training is to develop people as intended.

The nub of the cooperative education problem is whether co-oping human resources are developed for industrial society broadly conceived or for the employing organization. The particular manner in which an organization will structure its cooperative education plan depends upon how it perceives the goal of cooperative education.

There is every likelihood that in the future cooperative education will expand and play an ever-larger role in the development of human resources.

CHAPTER 11

Development of College Graduate Trainees

In this chapter we analyze the aspirations, expectations, and mobility of college graduate trainees in large-scale organizations and indicate the dimensions of the problems they present for their employing organizations in recruitment, selection, placement, development, and retention. The cluster of problems surrounding the college graduate trainee presents management of organizations with some of the most difficult problems in manpower planning and the development of human resources. These problems are especially critical today because inexperienced college graduates are increasingly regarded by top administrators in business, governmental, military, and other types of organizations as the sole managerial hope of the future.

ORGANIZATIONAL DISENCHANTMENT: THE BASIC PROBLEM

Complicating any analysis of the development of college graduate trainees are two problems which might be characterized as: "the great young man hunt" and "the business-is-for-the-birds syndrome." These problems are referred to in the literature by other terms such as: "the crown prince complex," manpower "restlessness," and the need for controlling the youthful yeast that leavens the mountain of dough involved in manpower turnover. Although these are somewhat facetious characterizations, they point to the well-known high rates of turnover and disenchantment which young people are experiencing in large-scale organizations and undoubtedly constitute a prime personnel problem for the manpower planner.

Despite a rapidly rising curve of enrollments in colleges, the recruitment rush at the exit door of these same institutions of learning for college graduate trainees, particularly holders of the MBA (Master of Business

Administration) degree, is even greater in some respects. Surely, one of the most bizarre and absurd fads ever to sweep American industry is this contemporary clamor to collect college graduate degree holders for every white-collar position. The intensive college recruitment movement shows no sign of abatement. Yet, at the same time there is apparently very little careful manpower planning to identify which organizational positions require college degrees and which do not.[1] Often this determination is made by fiat. The recruitment movement has even resulted in the development of a guide which provides all pertinent information to college graduate trainees about leading American corporations.[2]

Although this love affair between the college graduate and the American corporation—and, in fact, large-scale organizations of all kinds—continues, very little research has been conducted exploring the happiness and fruitfulness of this marriage. The largest research study reported to date was an analysis of 26 different training programs conducted by 14 companies in which 1074 graduates of the company training courses provided information. The major finding of this study was the high enthusiasm of young college-trained men for their companies and for most of the things that happened to them after they entered industry. Yet, the level of enthusiasm varied by program and by company, although in no instances was it low.[3] Other studies which cover a great deal of ground tend to be reported in anecdotal terms; and, although they provide interesting insights, they hardly give enough evidence to more than whet the appetite of the curious.[4] Storm signals in the marriage are nevertheless becoming clearer.

Our approach to discussing systematically the problem of the development of college graduate trainees in this chapter is to examine the subject from several different standpoints (which constitute subtitles in the chapter). First, we discuss the manpower planning implications. Second, we examine in detail the "business-is-for-the-birds" syndrome, which has actually been given a great deal of attention and, while sounding facetious, is definitely a serious underlying problem, whose full impact is still being debated as we enter the 1970s. Third we look at the various considerations involved in college graduate recruitment and some of the resolutions to

[1] George S. Odiorne and Edwin L. Miller, "Selection by Objectives: A New Approach to Managerial Selection," *Management of Personnel Quarterly,* Vol. 5, No. 3, Fall 1966, p. 3.

[2] Ernest A. McKay, *The Macmillan Job Guide to American Corporations for College Graduates, College Students, and Junior Executives,* Macmillan, New York, 1967.

[3] Stephen Habbe, *College Graduates Assess Their Company Training* (Personnel Policy Study No. 188), National Industrial Conference Board, New York, 1963, pp. 3–6.

[4] See John S. Morgan, *Managing the Young Adults,* American Management Association, New York, 1967.

these problems which seem to have been worked out. Fourth, we give special attention to the recruitment, development, and training of Negro college graduates, and the results of these efforts. Fifth, we provide an overall look at the many training problems that are connected with the development of college graduate trainees and try to point to possible solutions.

MANPOWER PLANNING

For many managers who entered the labor market during the depression days of the 1930s, the entire phenomenon of companies' sending representatives to the colleges to seek employees has an unreal air. When these men first started industrial employment, it was not uncommon for an employer to use the criterion of a college diploma merely as an arbitrary screening device for winnowing out the many applicants for each position. Those employed were generally not hired for managerial and staff positions but rather were likely to start as laborers, clerks, or in other low-level positions.[5]

Today college recruiting has grown to the point where more than 75 percent of all American college students obtain their first jobs through the university placement office. The amounts of money spent on college recruitment, the time and ingenuity applied to it, and the systematic coverage of almost every college in the search for able young men have continued almost unabated, in good times and in recession, since the end of World War II. Although there was some college recruiting prior to the war— George Westinghouse is alleged to have begun surrounding himself with young engineering graduates many years ago—the major emphasis upon college recruiting has come during the period since World War II. Whether this trend will continue is a matter of some concern, but realistically it appears that there will be increasingly more rather than less college recruiting in the years ahead.[6]

Within ten years after the war various companies had become aware that college recruiting was extremely competitive and that they were running into resistance in recruiting college graduates. For example, Sears Roebuck reported more than a decade ago that they had become increasingly concerned about the much publicized apathy of college students toward retailing as a career. It found in its discussions with placement

[5] George S. Odiorne and Arthur S. Hahn, *Effective College Recruiting* (Report 13), Bureau of Industrial Relations, University of Michigan, Ann Arbor, 1961, p. 1.

[6] *Ibid.,* pp. v and 1, citing Richard S. Uhrbrock, *Recruiting the College Graduate,* American Management Association, New York, 1953.

directors in colleges throughout the country that similar comments were made by students about the attractiveness of other industries.[7]

Also, during the early 1950s much of the interest in management development that had developed in the postwar period was stressing that the effectiveness of these developmental efforts depended largely upon the kinds of persons who initially entered management. In order to produce competent executives, it was necessary to have qualified college graduates as professional and technical employees who would ultimately qualify for management. These kinds of individuals, sometimes called "crown princes," were looked upon as the ultimate salvation to the executive manpower problem, not only in industry but also in large-scale organizations of all kinds.[8] Despite this awareness of the need for high-caliber manpower input in order to achieve a subsequent executive output years later, organizations apparently talked more about the problem than devised rational solutions to it.

As far as can be determined from the literature, modern organizations have advanced very little in projecting their needs for college graduate manpower in such a way that the projection points to the number of college graduates with given educational backgrounds that should be recruited in an academic year.[9] As we saw in an earlier chapter it is possible to identify position vacancies at all organizational levels and to plan upon filling at least some of them with college graduate trainees or cooperative education trainees. Similarly, it is possible to fill anticipated vacancies by promotions from within using manpower that possesses less than a college degree. Yet, it seems that most organizations conduct their college recruiting on a hit-or-miss basis; and, while they may have a particular numerical goal in mind for an academic year, this number is based upon short-run guesswork rather than carefully conducted manpower planning.

We need not repeat here the techniques which apply in projecting college graduate needs. However, it is well to mention again that projections are possible and should be made as a part of the total manpower planning in an organization. Neglect of manpower planning for this important group by organizations is difficult to understand because few would argue that the caliber of college graduates entering an organization and retained by it

---

[7] R. E. Barmeier and R. J. Kellar, "How College Graduates Evaluate Job Factors," *Personnel,* Vol. 33, No. 5, March 1957, pp. 490–491.

[8] Max Ways, "The Crown Princes of Business," *Fortune,* Vol. 48, No. 4, October 1953, pp. 150–153, 258–268.

[9] An important exception would be IBM. For an outstanding analysis of some of the thinking in that firm, see John R. Hinrichs, *High-Talent Personnel,* American Management Association, New York, 1966, pp. 9–133.

will have a significant imprint upon the future of the organization and its capabilities in attaining its objectives.

THE BUSINESS-IS-FOR-THE-BIRDS SYNDROME

Perhaps the importance of manpower planning for college graduate trainees has not resulted in concrete planning because for at least the past decade the frenzied recruitment of trainees has been a preoccupation of personnel departments in organizations. Recruitment has been a significant problem for a variety of reasons. The number of trainees has not equaled the demand, the quality of trainees available to industry in particular has declined because many people have decided to enter graduate school, the armed forces have drained much manpower from the civilian labor force, young people have taken a greater interest in social service occupations (such as the Peace Corps or, to much lesser extent, VISTA) than in the past, and, perhaps most important of all, an antipathy has presumably developed between young people and industrial employment. Although the dimensions of this antipathy are debatable, there is little doubt that it exists and that it has caused considerable worry both among manpower planners and line and staff managers.

In the United States industrial top management has historically had more education than the general population.[10] Since World War II, the college degree has become virtually the passport to salaried professional and managerial employment, with ramifying effects upon college curricula, the enrollment crush, financing education, building facilities, and the like. The essential problem is that while college graduates are in the greatest demand, they now appear to be in the least supply.

Students of all types of ability, but particularly those with high grades, are ardently wooed. Yet, the extent to which academic performance predicts executive success and effectiveness is nevertheless controversial. For example, the American Telephone and Telegraph Company, which several years ago annually recruited 2500 to 3000 trainees on the nation's campuses, has found that academic grades are the best indicator of how a candidate achieves later in his career in the organization, whereas extracurricular activities are the least reliable. As a consequence AT&T picks only men from the top one-half of the college graduating classes.[11] In a study made in a leading Ivy League university, it was found that there is

[10] Stanley Vance, "The Education of Industrial Executives," *California Management Review,* Vol. 8, No. 4, Summer 1966, pp. 21–30.

[11] "The Bell Is Ringing," *Time,* Vol. 83, No. 22, May 29, 1964, p. 76. For more detail see Roy W. Walters, Jr., and Douglas W. Bray, "Today's Search for Tomorrow's Leaders," *Journal of College Placement,* Vol. 24, No. 1, October 1963, pp. 22–23, 104–116.

a direct correlation between high grades and high salaries.[12] On the other hand, some studies suggest that grades do not predict future earnings.[13]

Psychological tests are also widely being used in order to make early predictions of management potential among college graduate trainees. Some organizations assert that they are having considerable success in predicting who will move into top management based upon test scores. In turn, these test scores may ultimately prove useful when transformed into use for selecting college graduate trainees either on campus or after they have appeared on company premises for screening interviews.[14]

Turnover and Anti-Business Sentiment

If the "business-is-for-the-birds" syndrome is the main public "image" problem of American industry in recruiting college graduate trainees today, turnover of these young people is probably the prime managerial manpower problem.[15] Indeed, the perpetuation of proficient management is dependent upon the organizational intake of capable young people. Detailed statistics on their turnover based upon published studies are difficult to obtain. One of the few such studies of trainees reports turnover of 39 percent for the duration of a three-year program for recruits with bachelor's or master's degrees in science and engineering.[16] Another study reports 80 percent turnover of college men within three and one-half years of placement in saleswork.[17] Still another reports *retention* of 67 percent of its trainees over

[12] "Brown University Finds a Correlation between School Grades and Salaries," *Business Week*, No. 1972, June 17, 1967, p. 104.

[13] Rollin H. Simonds, "College Majors, Grades vs. Business Success," *Business Topics*, Vol. 14, No. 3, Summer 1966, pp. 7–12. See also "Good Scholars Not Always Best," *Business Week*, No. 1695, February 24, 1962, pp. 77–78.

[14] "How Do You Pick an Executive Winner?," *Business Week*, No. 1905, March 5, 1966, pp. 108–110.

[15] This phrase, already used several times in the chapter, was used by Roger M. Blough of U.S. Steel in his, "Business *Can* Satisfy the Young Intellectual," *Harvard Business Review*, Vol. 44, No. 1, January-February 1966, p. 49. The related idea of "Business Isn't Where the Action Is" was the theme of Duncan Norton-Taylor's, "The Private World of the Class of 1966," *Fortune*, Vol. 73, No. 2, February 1966, pp. 128–132 ff. The controversy seems to have been sparked off by a front-page business story by Roger Rocklefs' "Scorning Business," *Wall Street Journal*, November 10, 1964, pp. 1 ff. The controversy is by no means ended. For a very recent reaction see "Top Students Sell Business Short," *Business Week*, No. 1984, September 9, 1967, pp. 134–140, and the deluge of letters to the editor on the subject in subsequent issues of *Business Week* and *Fortune*.

[16] William M. Evan, "Peer-Group Interaction and Organizational Socialization: A Study of Employee Turnover," *American Sociological Review*, Vol. 28, No. 3, June 1963, pp. 436–440.

[17] Andrall E. Pearson, "Sales Power Through Planned Careers," *Harvard Business Review*, Vol. 44, No. 1, January-February 1966, p. 105.

the history of its program.[18] (However, this group of trainees is from the General Motors Institute, a degree-granting institution serving GM and "captive" in the sense that its graduates are lesser exposed to outside opportunities than those of schools subjected to intensive recruitment through the college placement office.) Turnover of 50 percent after several years' employment seems to be the norm.[19] Differences between organizations, occupational fields, and industries could be very wide (with perhaps high turnover among banks and retailing and relatively low turnover in pacesetting manufacturing firms), although this observation needs further verification.

The alleged anti-business sentiment is apparently strongest in the schools that have the highest academic standards and where American industry in the past has carried out its most ardent solicitation of recruits. In fact, it is held that the lower a man's academic standing, the more likely he is to choose business as a career. There is a growing feeling that a person with a bachelor's degree is considered by some to be virtually a dropout and that he should get at least a master's. Undoubtedly, efforts to avoid the draft have also been a factor encouraging students to continue their education in recent years.[20] Yet, the tendency to go on educationally remains strong and is growing, whatever its inspiration.

Young college graduates today also in many instances possess a formidable self-confidence, never having faced a serious depression and having been too young to have a meaningful understanding of the World War II holocaust. In addition, the idea of making a significant contribution to human welfare appears to be especially strong among younger people today. They seem to be more aware than their parents of social problems in the world and consider tackling these as a challenge. Business, on the other hand, is in bad repute because it has not been tackling these problems to any extent (although some activity has followed in the wake of the civil rights riots since 1965) and can consequently be viewed as "not where the action is." Of those college graduates who have worked in industry during summer vacations, many have gained the impression that business is unexciting and uninteresting. Some have felt that they were subjected to pressures toward conformity, and the jobs available do not supply much responsibility. Liberal arts students, particularly, have little

---

[18] "Engineers Tailor-Made for GM," *Business Week,* No. 1161, July 1, 1961, p. 49.

[19] Edgar H. Schein, "How to Break in the College Graduate," *Harvard Business Review,* Vol. 42, No. 6, November-December 1964, p. 68; and Thomas H. Patten, Jr., "Peer Groups in Industry," *American Sociological Review,* Vol. 29, No. 1, February 1964, pp. 100–101. See also "Over Half of College Graduates Leave First Jobs in Three Years," *Training and Development Journal,* Vol. 24, No. 9, September 1970, p. 43.

[20] Norton-Taylor, *op. cit.,* pp. 128–131.

vocationally to offer business in the short run and are often low priority men in college recruitment. Coupled with jokes against business made by professors, the rejection of interviews on campus at leading colleges by the better students and protests against recruiters from companies making war materials, developments that have taken place since the mid-1960s have suggested to industrial and other recruiters that they need not stop on certain campuses of prestigious universities any more in their search for manpower.[21] In short, it might be said that the business world does not hire the liberal arts graduate, and he returns the compliment by accusing the business world of crassness, conformity, extreme cautiousness, and, on occasion, outright stupidity.

To some extent, the current campus disdain of business results from something that in itself is laudable: the insistense of very many students that they want to make a "contribution to society." It is not always clear what young people mean by that concept, but the desire speaks well for them and for the society that produces and sustains them. What is disturbing, though, is that many of these students appear to think that business does not contribute to society. There is a significant irony here. The students' attitudes, their freedom from economic pressures and concerns, and their security reflect the national affluence that business has contributed to so abundantly. Moreover, the social ideals and values that many students feel cannot be served in, or by, private industry can be realized only through economic growth, which in the United States has historically meant the expansion of private industry. It appears then that many college students arrive at graduation with a strong desire to improve their society but possess only a hazy understanding of how their society works. In other words, if college students were to be shown the reality behind both theories, they could see that in the economy of the United States growth largely depends upon the efforts and decisions of private industry. This means that young people could learn that business offers them opportunities to "contribute." [22] In fact, perhaps one of the main tasks of the manpower specialist in establishing educational and training programs for college graduate trainees is to take it upon himself to provide material which would give these trainees a better explanation of how industry contributes to the American economy and society. Such a program could make a start in eliminating some of the basic problems behind the syndrome.

Although estimates of student hostility toward business may be exaggerated—it is alleged that they will become more tolerant when they are faced with the necessity for earning incomes to support families—it is

---

[21] *Ibid.*, pp. 131–132, 166–172.

[22] "The Recruiter Doesn't Stop Here Anymore," *Fortune,* Vol. 73, No. 2, February 1966, pp. 102–104.

quite possible that the purported atrophy of American business is due to a kind of irrelevancy, that is, the pursuit of profit and a feigned interest in social responsibility but opposition to the war on poverty and other activist social programs of our era.

In any event, many informed observers are pointing out that young people in American colleges and graduate schools today are far less attracted to a career in business than were their predecessors 10 or 15 years ago. This opposition is not necessarily the same as hostility toward business as some observers point out but more simply a lack of interest in business. The real reasons behind the disenchantment with a business career are numerous. Business has lost a good deal of its advantage as an employer both in respect to pay and opportunities. Business has failed to live up to its intellectual promises. The basic values supported by business have been looked at by young people and have been appraised as sadly wanting.[23] Each of these is worthy of consideration because of its connection with organizational manpower policy.

Need for Managerial Talent

Up to about 1960 no alternative employer could match the salary which the young college graduate was offered by business, and especially by the large corporation. Pay scales in other fields of employment, especially in government and higher education, were just beginning to rise from their depression lows. Also at this time, the opportunities in business greatly outnumbered those in other fields of work. It was during these postwar years that American business largely made the great transformation from "manual" to "knowledge" work and built up large new staff activities in all areas, each demanding the employment of educated people in substantial numbers. Finally, a job in industry offered young people the best opportunities for advancement. Government and higher education had attracted large numbers of young people in the 1930s and early 1940s, if only because business had fewer openings in those years. As a result, in the years after World War II, government and higher education were amply staffed with the graduates of 20 years before who were still young and in mid-career.[24]

Industrial management, by contrast, in the early postwar years was overage. Many managers had gone to work well before the Great Depression of the 1930s, and an ambitious young man starting to work for a corporation in the late 1940s and 1950s could reasonably expect rapid advancement. However, today, the switch to "knowledge" work in industry

[23] Peter Drucker, "Is Business Letting Young People Down?," *Harvard Business Review,* Vol. 43, No. 6, November-December 1965, p. 49.

[24] *Ibid.,* pp. 49–50.

has been substantially accomplished. Precisely because business hired so many of the able young men of the 1940s and 1950s, opportunities for advancement today are more limited than they were prior to 1960. In other words, the managerial people in organizational positions to which newcomers could aspire are themselves young and have many more years of eligible service before they reach retirement. In contrast, it is hypothesized that government and higher education today are growing hollow in their age structures as the New Deal and World War II generations are aging. Thus, while entrance pay in government and higher education is still lower than it is in business, the gap is constantly narrowing. All of this means that the competitive position of business as a career attractor will continue to deteriorate further in the next few years as young people seek opportunities elsewhere.[25] These demographic facts of organizational age groupings are thus of considerable importance to the manpower specialist who has been caught up in the postwar college recruitment scene.

Yet it cannot be said that the brightest and ablest young men are being lost to business because they take jobs elsewhere. Actually, they go on to graduate school in increasing numbers, and many industrial firms neglect to recruit at the graduate schools (particularly the graduate schools of arts and sciences rather than the graduate schools of business and engineering). This means that the great bulk of graduate students are often not considered prospects by the college recruiter.[26] Of course, sophisticated manpower specialists have recognized this fact and started to recruit some graduate students from the liberal arts fields.

Passive, Unchallenging Training Programs for Activists

Perhaps business' worst mistake in dealing with young people is the establishment of college graduate training programs that tend to make the jobs of young educated people as unimportant as possible, as undemanding as possible, and as boring as possible. Many college graduate trainees look for and accept work with organizations which offer training programs. However, the program as it operates is often inappropriate both culturally and psychologically. In fact, in many instances the college graduate training program only disguises the fact that the company does not know what to do with the new employee. In most instances, there is no need today to continue a young man's schooling within a company. If he lacks knowledge, he is probably better off if he takes an evening course in a local university after working hours rather than attempt to fill the knowledge gap by working as a trainee without a real job, without real responsibility, and without a real challenge. Moreover, the trainee ap-

[25] *Ibid.*, p. 50.
[26] *Ibid.*, pp. 50–51.

proach is psychologically inappropriate today because the college graduate has already had 16 years of formal education and is more interested in work than additional study. If he were still interested in studying, he could do it in a school rather than on a job. Most young people are far more interested in being challenged to show what they have learned than to spend more time as passive learners in an industrial classroom setting.[27]

Organizations which stress on-the-job training rather than formal classroom training tend to make the bottom jobs in management as small and undemanding as possible. They compound the problems of motivating and retaining young people by attempting to attract young men with ambition and initiative in large numbers to these kinds of positions. The reaction of young people is predictably one of disenchantment when they find out how small, cribbed, and confined their jobs are. Moreover, when they enter business they usually expect industrial management to be reasonably rational, organized, and purposeful. In practice, they often find management is largely hit-or-miss, hunch, prejudice, opinion, and a question of "who is right" rather "what is right." In addition, they are told not to "make waves." This disenchantment of the men entering management with the malaises of bureaucracy gradually filters back to their juniors who are still in college and graduate school. The subsequent communication based upon the negative learning experiences is undoubtedly one of the reasons why today's younger generation is much less interested in a career in industrial management than its predecessors were only a few years ago.[28]

The Clash of Values and Bases for Resolution

A last area—basic values—may well be the most important one leading to the disenchantment of the younger generation of college graduates with business as a career. In essence, young people have very definitely come to expect leadership from management in respect to social and moral values. They have typically been told a great deal regarding the social responsibilities of business, both by college professors and by businessmen themselves. They are quite confirmed in their beliefs that management should give leadership, should be committed, and should act according to what it believes is right. When they find values applied to business affairs which may be less enlightened than those prevailing in the total society or a willingness to do the least to get by rather than to do the right thing, they may be profoundly shocked and conclude that business is immoral. In other words, their standards for managerial behavior are severe, not because they are hostile to business, but, on the contrary, because they have come to expect very much from it. If American business wants to be

[27] *Ibid.*, pp. 51–52.
[28] *Ibid.*, pp. 52–53.

considered a preferred career opportunity by the younger generation, it will have to satisfy the expectations of the young in respect to the values and commitments of business to society fully as much as their expectations regarding salaries and promotions.[29]

Others have argued that business can satisfy young college graduate trainees and that the "business-is-for-the-birds" syndrome is an unsupported conclusion built upon inadequate data. They argue that the most intense competition which business faces for college graduates today comes from the colleges and universities that recruit candidates for their graduate schools. Many of these individuals ultimately receive their graduate degrees and seek employment in industry. Citing fragmentary evidence from a variety of sources, these defenders of careers in business point to two conclusions. First, college graduates are entering the market place in satisfactory numbers to meet the current manpower requirements of industry. Second, of those bypassing the market place now, a growing proportion of them are seeking advanced degrees in business administration and other disciplines designed to equip them for eventual leadership and top management roles in industry.[30]

The foes of the syndrome deny that business is dull and routine, a place where conformity rules, a jungle where acceptable standards are readily compromised by corner cutting in the drive to meet competitive pressures, and a place where the freedom of comment, criticism, and dissent are stifled. Rather, business is held to be honorable because service to the material needs of man is clearly a prerequisite to the satisfaction of his intellectual and spiritual needs. Also, there are in industry as many dedicated men as can be found in other fields of work who find their greatest personal reward in the knowledge that they have performed a worthy economic service to society. Intelligent college graduates are needed so that industry can attain and surpass the objectives it has set. Only people with inventive minds, original ideas, and unrutted patterns of thought can meet the challenge of change in the industrial organization of today and the greatly multiplied challenges of change that are on the horizon.[31]

A third and last point of view regarding the "business-is-for-the-birds" syndrome is found among those who argue that the controversy centers around differences in value judgments. These values are essentially separable into two orientations, the pragmatic and intellectual. People with pragmatic value orientations are likely to be interested in careers in industrial management and to be capable of making the adjustments required to this kind of a life. These people often solve problems intuitively or judgmentally

[29] *Ibid.,* pp. 54–55.
[30] Blough, *op. cit.,* pp. 49–52.
[31] *Ibid.,* pp. 53–57.

and can easily accept a hierarchy of power. On the other hand, persons with an intellectual value orientation tend to accept a hierarchy of intellect or talent and tend to think analytically and conceptually. They are least able to make a continuing adjustment to employment in industry. Perhaps the very superior sort of person who is able to understand, to tolerate, even to appreciate, the inherent strengths and weaknesses in both value orientations to the realities of life in our society is likely to be the type of manager most eagerly sought by industrial management.[32]

To some extent the distinction between the pragmatic and intellectual value orientation is almost the same as that between the theoretical and the practical. Perhaps the kind of young person who is likely to be able to understand, tolerate, and appreciate the theoretical and practical value orientations is one who has participated in a cooperative education program as opposed to a college graduate trainee whose main experiences in respect to business are limited to summer vacations or part-time employment. In fact, we might hypothesize that the co-op most closely approximates the "right young man for business."

In order to improve its image among young people, business and large-scale organizations of all kinds might consider offering better career opportunities to the brighter young people. Organizations must remove the shackles of seniority and inane management training courses where they exist. Next, business organizations particularly should present to young people a more honest picture of the American economic system and of the practice of management. By means of information and education, business should take whatever action is required to demolish the image of muscular anti-intellectualism which it possesses and which repels the better-educated young people.[33]

Colleges and universities also can make a contribution to eliminating the "business-is-for-the-birds" syndrome. They can do this by combining the intellectual discipline of the liberal arts with the action goals of business in the educational curriculum. This job would be a challenge to education and involve not only devising a list of appropriate subjects but also building in the curriculum a certain type of pedagogic emphasis. It means giving the students a real challenge so that they feel that there is something worthwhile and exciting about learning, not for its own sake or for personal satisfaction, but for practical use in a life of action involving other people. Businesses can help colleges and universities by making clear what kind of education it is that they want and why they want it. Any suggestions made cannot be too "first job" oriented or too vocational—in a word—too prag-

[32] John S. Fielden, "The Right Young People for Business," *Harvard Business Review*, Vol. 44, No. 2, March-April 1966, pp. 76–77.
[33] *Ibid.*, pp. 80–81.

matic. Most business subject matter eventually bursts into a number of the underlying social and behavioral sciences and mathematics, such as economics, sociology, psychology, and statistics. These are, of course, fundamentally liberal arts subjects. Young people who master these and who are enabled to perceive their relationship to employment in industry as managerial, professional, and technical employees are likely to find that there is exciting and significant scope for intelligence and even intellectuality in the world of practical action. Colleges and universities that are trying to do this kind of job are increasing in number and caliber. It remains for industrial management to recognize this fact and provide the needed interest, advice, and encouragement so that brighter young people will be attracted to the study and practice of industrial management.[34]

Improving the Recruitment of College Graduate Trainees

The rush toward college recruitment has surprised many observers who have not kept fully abreast of the changing needs for human resources in our urban-industrial society. Some of the most significant changes that have taken place in the American labor force suggest why college recruitment has vastly expanded. First, there has been a drastic rise in the number of professional, technical, managerial, and staff specialists in industry. It shows no signs of abatement. Second, there has been a leveling off and in some instances a decline in the number of unskilled workers needed by firms. Third, there has been a demand for more skilled-trades workers. Fourth, there has been an increase in the number of service, clerical, and sales workers and a further drastic falling off of the ranks of farmers and farm workers.[35] Momentary reflection upon these changes leads one to wonder where the needed manpower for the rising number of professional, technical, and managerial positions will come from. The answer has been: college recruitment.

The entire subject of college recruiting is fraught with decisions which have historical significance for our society, even when the two immediate parties, the recruiter and the college graduate trainee, are not always aware that such decisions have any further meaning than their individual desires.[36] The college recruiting movement has had a far-reaching impact upon the public employment service, promotion from within policies in large-scale organizations, the influx of students into college, the establishment of many kinds of training programs, and thinking in the field of personnel administration concerning the optimum utilization of educated manpower. As a rough rule of thumb, college recruitment has meant that organizations

[34] *Ibid.,* pp. 81–83.
[35] Odiorne and Hann, *op. cit.,* pp. 2–3.
[36] *Ibid.,* p. 17.

interview approximately ten college students on campus per employee gained. This means that one recruiter should be able to find one student per day of campus interviewing on the average, if he is able to interview ten students properly in one day on campus.[37] It has also meant that organizations seem to be guided by the reputation of the school and the reputation of the graduates in choosing places where they wish to recruit.[38] As we previously noted, however, in some of the Ivy League colleges and other prestige schools such as the "Big Ten" state universities, MIT, Stanford, Cal. Tech, and the University of California, where large numbers of undergraduates go on to graduate school, recruiters have found slim pickings in recent years. The lack of students interested in industrial employment has caused them to add smaller schools as well as those with lesser reputations to their list of places at which they should recruit.

Recruiting is, of course, an investment in human capital with the significant payoff some five to ten years ahead. Manpower planning, when it is properly carried out and based upon real needs in an organization, should result in hiring the right number of college graduates and having working jobs ready for every one of them. This desirable state of affairs results if there are long-range projections of needs in the organization and a predictable rate of growth and stability in the business or service provided by the organization.[39] The essential problem in recruiting college graduates is that manpower planning often blows hot and cold so that in many organizations college recruiting is almost a guessing game.[40] These problems eventually lead to college recruiting being a manhunt in which the college recruiters themselves are essentially order takers for manpower determined perfunctorily to be needed by the employing organization. Frequently, the indications of manpower needed in these circumstances are changed on whim so that college recruiting becomes a very erratic game in which the recruiter, the college graduate trainee, the placement office in the university, and the employing organization seem to be operating without regard to a rational manpower plan.[41]

This state of affairs had lead some to suggest that college recruiting is a "madhouse and it's getting madder."[42] Thus, in early 1967, more than 3000 employers including the federal government were visiting 1000 cam-

[37] *Ibid.,* pp. 96–97.

[38] *Ibid.,* p. 102.

[39] Hinrichs, *op. cit.,* pp. 27–65.

[40] George S. Odiorne, "How to Get Men You Want," *Nation's Business,* Vol. 52, No. 1, January 1964, pp. 70–72, 74.

[41] For suggestions as to how the affected parties should work together, see Edgar H. Schein, "The Wall of Misunderstanding," *Journal of College Placement,* Vol. 27, No. 3, February-March 1967, p. 54.

[42] "The Great Young Man Hunt," Vol. 99, No. 5, *Forbes,* March 1, 1967, pp. 46–47.

puses to try to hire about 90,000 graduating college men and women. The federal government alone was trying to recruit 35,000 graduates this year, almost equal to all the private companies combined. Some organizations had come to the conclusion that within ten years it would be physically impossible for them to recruit and interview all the young men and women they will need because they cannot relieve company or organizational personnel from their work to carry out the recruiting task. In addition, the mounting costs of recruitment have caused many organizations to reconsider the excessive expense involved in adding one college graduate trainee to the payroll.[43] A few years ago it was estimated for example, that in one leading American corporation for each new college graduate hired, $15,000 was spent for recruiting the man and his initial training to get him into a productive job.[44] It is thus not surprising that the turnover of graduates has been of some concern.

The problems involved in college recruitment have resulted in the proliferation of writing about how to overcome some of the leading difficulties. Many of these articles focus on changing the specific techniques used in college recruitment. Still other articles concentrate upon coping with the "business-is-for-the-birds" syndrome.

In suggesting that there be changes in specific recruiting techniques, advice ranges widely. College recruiters are advised to be careful about the amount of talk which they engage in during the campus interview.[45] It has also been proposed that rather than interview students one at a time, that multiple interviewing-observation is perhaps preferable.[46]

Some suggest comprehensive programs to improve the recruitment of college graduate trainees, rather than the mere improvement of one or two techniques. The changes recommended are: more cooperation between colleges and industry; improvement of the placement service; changes in college curricula; better follow-up; improved vocational counseling; encouragement of college graduates to be more realistic about job openings; and even that colleges should consider changing their forms and policies to enable the recruitment process to run more smoothly.[47]

Overselling the potential employer has been specifically identified as a

---

[43] *Ibid.*

[44] Harry Seligson, "The Trend to Mobility," *Journal of College Placement,* Vol. 23, No. 1, October-November 1965, p. 63. An earlier study of recruitment costs per hire estimated a high of $4700 per trainee. See E. C. Kubicek, "Salary Alone Is Not Enough," *Journal of College Placement,* Vol. 21, No. 3, February 1961, p. 38.

[45] Edward M. Krech, Jr., "What Students Think of Campus Recruiters," *Personnel,* Vol. 35, No. 2, September-October 1962, pp. 72–76.

[46] Jules Z. Willing, "The Round Table Interview—A Method of Selecting Trainees," *Personnel,* Vol. 39, No. 2, March-April 1962, pp. 26–32.

[47] Roye R. Bryant, "Placement of College Graduates: Eight Point Improvement Program," *Personnel Journal,* Vol. 38, No. 2, June 1959, pp. 58–61.

major problem for the recruiter to overcome.[48] Yet, there is evidence that young college graduates view the start of a career with considerably more wariness, even cynicism, than recruiters are aware. In fact, the siren songs of recruiters are heard by anything but naive ears! [49]

Organizations have been warned repeatedly that it is wasteful to recruit the more outstanding college graduate. It is urged that they should recruit average boys who can fill job openings at least passably well but perhaps not superlatively well.[50]

Still another closely allied approach is to eschew the far-flung nationwide recruitment of college graduates and to concentrate instead on trying to interest students attending universities in the immediate geographical area of the employing organization to apply for work as college graduate trainees.[51] All these and many other techniques have been proposed as devices to combat some of the problems in college recruitment.

Improving College Relations and Understanding

In addition to changes in technique, a number of other suggestions have been proposed to counteract the aforementioned "business-is-for-the-birds" syndrome. Among other things, more organizations are taking an altruistic tack in promotional material aimed at collegians and skeptical professors to convince them that industrial firms want to help humanity as well as earn a profit. Some have made a vigorous effort to move their brightest young men up the corporate ladder faster to indicate that seniority and career velocity delays due to "lock stepping" do not exist in their firms. A few have been giving students a pregraduation preview of corporate life through a variety of special programs, including the opportunity to work in the firm during the summer vacation period. The latter type of program has not been eminently successful, as we previously indicated, although it may have dispelled some of the negative aspects of industry for a few students.[52]

Another approach has been to engage in public correspondence with students who are negative in their opinion of business. In this approach outstanding students have been asked to write letters, which would be pub-

[48] E. L. Zwerski, "The Oversell: A Major Pitfall in College Recruitment," *Personnel Journal*, Vol. 45, No. 3, March 1966, pp. 167–168.

[49] Anthony G. Athos, "Job Turnover: The Lorelei Theory," *Journal of College Placement*, Vol. 25, No. 3, February 1965, pp. 49–53.

[50] Harry R. Knudson, "The All-American Boy," *Personnel Journal*, Vol. 39, No. 2, June 1960, pp. 56–57, 67.

[51] Glenn H. Varney and Joseph P. Flemming, " 'Native Son' Days for College Recruitment," *Personnel*, Vol. 43, No. 6, November-December 1966, pp. 61–64.

[52] Albert R. Hunt, "Campus Skeptics," *Wall Street Journal*, October 23, 1967, pp. 1, 21.

lished in student newspapers circulating on various campuses throughout the country, to discuss their perceptions of business. These in turn would be analyzed and rejoinders composed by the executive of a leading corporation.[53] Closely related to this is the campaign being waged through advertisements in popular business magazines, such as *Fortune,* to come to grips with the negative image of business.[54]

A second approach is to use a seminar sponsored by a particular employer in which representatives of the firm's marketing department, for example, try to acquaint technically oriented professors with the marketing policies, plans, and procedures of the organization. The rationale behind this approach is that the best way to recruit technically trained college men for marketing jobs is through influencing their teachers. Because many faculties are comprised of men without business experience, it is thought that the seminars serve to improve communication between business and education which ultimately will result in improving the employer's acceptability to professors, who in turn will steer their graduates to the employer.[55]

A third approach is to engage graduating business students in a business game that requires them to manage a fictional company. In this computerized business exercise, recruiters from various companies observe them in solving problems and making decisions. With organizational representatives available to not only help the students but also observe them in the exercise, a rare opportunity is provided for a relaxed alert exchange of ideas between businessmen, educators, and students.[56]

Still another (and perhaps a far-out) approach in the fierce corporate fight to capture college graduates is abstract painting! For example, one firm announced it would send its controversial collections of modern art on the college circuit in order to build the corporate image among students as a forward-looking employer. The plan was to send the collection of 44 paintings to 11 universities during a 15-month period.[57]

In essence, we have been suggesting that the recruitment of college graduate trainees has become virtually a frenzied search for almost any warm body. Although starting salaries have steadily climbed in recent years in order to attract trainees, placement officials say that the location of a job,

[53] Stephen Habbe, "Business and the College Student," *Conference Board Record,* Vol. 4, No. 9, September 1967, pp. 18–26.

[54] For example, see the Olin advertisement in *Fortune,* Vol. 76, No. 7, December 1967, p. 189.

[55] "Business Lectures Professors," *Business Week,* No. 1871, July 10, 1965, pp. 65–66.

[56] "Profits Set Score at B-School Tournament," *Business Week,* No. 1959, March 18, 1967, pp. 157–158.

[57] "The Company Will Try Abstract Art Collection as Touring Bait to Recruit Collegians," *Business Week,* No. 1959, February 25, 1967, p. 112.

the type of work, and the chances for promotion seem to have greater influence than salary on the decisions of graduates to accept offers in specific organizations.[58] In one word, the trend in college recruiting has been "up." The number of recruiting companies has gone up, the number of college trainees sought has increased, and the starting salaries have continued to head in an upward direction.[59]

COLLEGE RECRUITING AND THE PUBLIC EMPLOYMENT SERVICE

The rapid growth of college recruiting came 15 or 20 years after the establishment of the federal-state employment service under the Wagner-Peyser Act in 1933. Since 1950, the college placement office has evolved into a kind of non-fee-charging private employment service functioning on college campuses throughout the country. Its services have been oriented toward the placement of graduate and undergraduate students and, to a much lesser extent, the alumni of colleges.

It was perhaps inevitable that there should be a clash between the functions of the college placement office and those of the public employment service. Manpower specialists in industry, and particularly those who engaged in college recruiting, were placed in the middle of this controversy because to a large extent they provided the business which led to the establishment of campus college placement offices.

In 1962, the United States Employment Service indicated its interest in college placement by stating its plans to establish a system of USES "Campus Placement" installations. The purpose of this plan was to improve the service given professional and managerial manpower and to try to break the image the USES has had of being essentially a manpower exchange for blue-collar workers. The College Placement Council, the professional association which is composed of college placement officers, considered the plan of the USES a veiled threat to college placement officers throughout the country. The essential objection was that the expansion of the USES in setting up campus placement installations duplicated the efforts of college placement officers and infringed upon a domain which had been legitimately carved out by them. It was also suggested that the duplication would needlessly increase federal spending and federal control across the board. Furthermore, the efforts to supplant the college placement office would probably be doomed to failure because the USES campus placement officer would in all probability not be allowed to participate on university

[58] *U.S. News & World Report*, Vol. 60, No. 23, June 6, 1966, p. 94.
[59] Stephen Habbe, "College Recruitment in 1967," *Conference Board Record*, Vol. 4, No. 2, February 1967, pp. 16–20.

committee assignments covering such areas as scholarship awards, admissions planning, student career and curriculum advising, freshmen orientation, student activities, and other aspects of student personnel administration.[60]

A survey completed by the College Placement Council in 1962 indicated that the overwhelming majority of business members of the college placement associations opposed government intervention in campus placement.[61] In addition, it was argued that government does not fit into the program of college placement because the only role of government is to fill needs where the individual organization or society cannot fulfill them. Government could legitimately provide educational materials on opportunities and careers which may not be available through other sources. It could conduct coordinated research through the cooperation of industrial, governmental, and educational organizations, and it could support communication of the research findings.

Governmental agencies could provide additional career information and assistance as requested by college placement officers or by professional placement associations. It could furnish speakers, organize conferences, and provide financial support where needed. It is even possible that the government could furnish guidance to some individuals who have peculiar problems regarding their careers. These would probably be persons who are experienced college alumni and are changing geographical areas of employment or who have developed special qualifications which some college placement offices may not be fully prepared to serve. However, even here it was assumed that as the professional placement offices of the colleges grow in statute they could in time even take over the placement of alumni. But except where government is recruiting college graduates for employment in government, it was thought that college placement activities should remain an integral part of the work of the college placement office and that government should, by and large, stay out of college placement.[62]

In the last few years the struggle between the College Placement Council and the USES has been settled to the point that the former is now acting to supplement the latter. For many years, the USES and state employment

[60] Arthur R. Eckberg, "United States Employment Service, Current Threat to College Placement," *Personnel Journal,* Vol. 42, No. 9, October 1963, pp. 461–463.

[61] *Ibid.,* p. 462.

[62] Chester E. Peters, "The Government's Role in Placement," *Journal of College Placement,* Vol. 23, No. 3, February 1963, pp. 14–15. See also, John M. Brooks, "Reaffirmation of a Philosophy," *Journal of College Placement,* Vol. 25, No. 1, October 1964, pp. 49–55. An example of an apparently successful college–employment service working relationship can be found in Virginia. See B. D. Fowler, Jr., "The Virginia College Placement Program," *Employment Service Review,* Vol. 3, No. 7, July 1966, pp. 34–36.

agencies have wanted to improve their services to managerial, technical, and professional employees and thereby break the blue-collar-serving image which they have had. Also, it is, of course, vital that the USES become more involved in the placement problems of the fastest growing segment of the United States labor force if it is to keep abreast of, if not lead, the trends.

Today, the USES and the state agencies are serving college graduates by maintaining professional placement offices in a number of large cities. Inexperienced college graduates who have been unsuccessful in obtaining employment through the college placement offices often register at state employment agencies and attempt to secure employment through referrals. Also, experienced college alumni who choose not to use the college placement office to secure employment (which rarely has the resources to provide much service) often register at the professional placement centers of the state agencies in seeking employment.

At the moment the accord reached by the USES and the CPC leaves the USES providing assistance to colleges in a number of different ways. The USES: helps students who apply at local employment offices; conducts on-campus placement services either full- or part-time (when the need exists, where the resources of the employment service permit, and when requested by appropriate college authorities); assists students in the aforementioned two ways to obtain summer or part-time employment; provides employment and labor-market assistance to college dropouts; exchanges career opportunity information for college students by furnishing college placement offices with employer job orders; and provides colleges and students with labor market information on labor supply and demand, the employment outlook by occupation, and changing hiring specifications, including salaries.[63] The upshot of this working relationship seems to mean that the CPC is now an important force in the field of high-talent manpower placement.

The GRAD System

In early 1966 the College Placement Council made a significant contribution to providing a national placement service for alumni which should further strengthen its hand in the field of manpower. It established a system called GRAD (an acronym for Graduate Resume Accumulation and Distribution) which stores the names and backgrounds of job seekers, who have worked for at least one year, in a random access computer. College

[63] Letter of Robert C. Goodwin, Administrator of the Bureau of Employment Security, in "The Approach to an Understanding," *Journal of College Placement,* Vol. 24, No. 2, December 1963, p. 33. See also John M. Brooks, "And Now . . . A Fair Trial," *op. cit.,* pp. 6–7.

graduates pay a $10.00 registration fee and have their name and background recorded as data in the computer. An employer can use the GRAD service as often as he likes by informing the computer of the kind of person he desires. The computer will produce the name and code number of each graduate who meets the qualifications submitted by the employer, and the College Placement Council will obtain the resume on the applicant from its microfilm files. The service costs the employer 50 cents for each minute of computer time and $2.00 per resume. Once he obtains the list of applicants, the employer makes his own arrangements for interviewing job candidates.[64]

In operation, the GRAD system is uncomplicated and makes sound use of electronic data-processing equipment in placement and recruiting. The alumnus to be served must have at least a bachelor's degree from an accredited college or university whose placement office is a member of a regional placement association. The alumnus simply makes known to his placement office that he is interested in being served through the GRAD system. He completes a GRAD resume from which 21 key factors are extracted and entered by teletype into an electronic file at a computer center. The facility is utilized on a time-sharing basis, and the candidate's original resume is reduced to microfilm by the college placement council for retrieval at a later time.

With the key selector factors for each candidate electronically recorded, employers are in a position to call upon the GRAD system in their search for talent. They have at their disposal the thesaurus of GRAD employment categories which enables them to cut through rapidly to the best description of the position open. They may also call upon one or all of the 21 selectors in their search. The employer may approach the GRAD system either by the installation of teletype equipment or simply by direct mail. Employers who use the GRAD system are screened to make sure that they are of the right caliber as determined by the College Placement Council. The system cannot be used by any organization that is not authorized and can only be used by an organization when hiring for its own purposes. Employers using a teletype unit to query the GRAD system have almost immediate access to the electronic file, can phrase their own questions, and will be provided a prompt response in English.[65]

In a typical case, an employing organization may inquire for applicants on the basis of 6 or 8 selectors. When this question is completed on the teletype, he may be given dozens of names of alumni whose qualifications

[64] "Computer Will Dish-up Lists of Talent for Companies Seeking College Grads," *Business Week,* No. 1906, March 12, 1966, p. 50.

[65] "Graduate Resume Accumulation and Distribution," leaflet of the College Placement Council, Inc., n.d.

are in the system and meet his specifications. If he desires, the inquiry can be restated with more closely defined requirements, and the number of qualifying applicants reduced to a more manageable number, such as 10. If too few candidates are found, the selectors may be modified to increase the roster of individuals qualifying. When he is satisfied with the number of applicants, the employer types instructions for the actual resume to be sent to him from the College Placement Council.

Then another sequence of events takes place with remarkable speed. The employer's order is relayed to a data center where resumes correspond to the chosen code numbers are retrieved, duplicated, and sent to the employer. From this point on, negotiations are carried out in the orthodox manner, in which the employer interviews the employee and decides on whether a position offer will be extended. The special feature of the GRAD system is that it makes it possible for employers to keep a job search continually in effect if desired. Thus, if the selectors chosen by the employer for the search fail to yield sufficient candidates, the file can be researched at a later time period. In addition, special provisions have been programmed into the GRAD system whereby the applicant's current employer is blocked electronically from receiving resumes. A similar precautionary measure exists for employers. They may make their electronic search of selector factors in terms of state residence but not city. Employers are in this way protected from having a competitor concentrate his employment searches on cities where they have major installations.[66] In essence, the GRAD project thus not only places opportunities of unparalleled scope at the disposal of the college graduate but also hastens the distribution of the findings to placement directors so that their offices may become the source of vital manpower information. For example, if the alumnus is placed through the use of the system, the campus placement director is informed of the employment. If no employment results in the first six months, the applicant is removed from the file and the placement director is informed of the number of times his resume has been referred to employers. The placement director then has the option of granting an additional six months to the applicant without further charge.[67] These alternatives obviously move the college placement director to the center of the manpower stage—at least in seeing that the paper work is referred or held back.

Between recruitment on campus and the existence of GRAD, the college graduate should have excellent resources in seeking employment, particularly as GRAD becomes more widely known and utilized.

[66] *Ibid.*

[67] "A New CPC Service—GRAD," *Journal of College Placement,* Vol. 26, No. 2, December 1965-January 1966, p. 40.

PICS and LINCS

A similar service is available through Western Union in their PICS (an acronymn for Professional Information Communication Service) and through another organization entitled Careerways System, both of which operate for a profit.

The United States Employment Service in collaboration with the California State Employment Service has been experimenting for several years with a service called LINCS (Labor Inventory Communications System) to place professional employees. The service has since been expanded nationally, although a certain amount of debugging and perfecting still remains before the interstate clearance of applicants lives up to its potential.[68]

The thrust of these several devices is to provide the college graduate with unparalleled manpower placement services. Coupled with other actions currently being tried in American society, these new concepts of college manpower recruitment and computerized placement have potential for solving some aspects of our most prominent social problems, to which we turn next.

Recruitment and Development of Negro College Graduates

In the United States the Negro population is approximately 20,000,000; and approximately 250,000 Negroes are enrolled in colleges and universities. Beginning in the early 1960s, industrial organizations started to give attention to the recruitment of Negro college graduates. By 1964, opportunities for Negroes who were college graduates started to open and recruitment efforts were intensified. The reasons were numerous. There was governmental pressure to open new jobs in industry through the Plans for Progress and Civil Rights Act of 1964, widespread protest activities by Negro groups attracted attention, nondiscrimination clauses in defense contracts became more numerous, and there was discrimination in reverse. Negro preferential employment started to show up in employers' desires to show good faith by overcompliance. Except for Negro women, the supply did not equal the demand.[69]

Since 1965 efforts have been stepped up even more to recruit Negro college graduates. Increasingly, companies have been visiting a greater

[68] See Herb Folkman, "LINCS—Progress Report, The Teletype Network," *Employment Service Review,* Vol. 1, No. 11, November 1964, pp. 30, 34–35; and Karl Bybee, "LINCS—Progress Report, Mechanical File Search," *Employment Service Review,* Vol. 1, No. 11, November 1964, pp. 31–34.

[69] "Industry Rushes for Negro Grads," *Business Week,* No. 1808, April 25, 1964, pp. 78–82.

number of Negro colleges, and Negroes in "white" colleges have been assiduously sought. Special efforts have been made to train visitation teams that would recruit at predominantly Negro colleges as well as improve the quality of placement services there. An important part of the problem in these schools was found to be the need to communicate convincing information to Negro youngsters, parents, and instructors about the bona fide opening of new career opportunities.[70]

In addition to the expanded recruitment, from time to time industrial organizations have pooled their efforts to obtain Negro college graduates by operating *ad hoc* "opportunity centers" wherein a group of companies would for a two- or three-day period encourage Negroes to appear in a central location and take job interviews. The organizations participating in the opportunity center would share the costs of collecting, screening, and distributing the resumes obtained. These opportunity centers often tapped Negro college graduates who were reluctant to apply for placement interviews on the college campus on the grounds that they did not believe that the companies recruiting there were sincere in their interest in talking with Negroes.[71]

It has been estimated that only five Negro college graduates are available for every 100 management-level jobs open to them. In addition, very few Negroes have in the past chosen business for a career because they have traditionally opted for such fields as teaching, government, the ministry, and social work where discrimination has been relatively mild. However, in recent years, such fields as banking and brokerage have opened their gates more widely to accept Negro college graduates. Also, Negro recruits are increasingly welcome at airlines, retail stores, and food, petroleum, aerospace, steel, automotive, and electrical manufacturing companies.[72]

Techniques for the recruitment of Negro college graduates vary somewhat from those used to recruit white college graduates. However, these differences are less a matter of specific interviewing, the reviewing of records, and information-providing techniques than they are differences concerning schools to visit, ways to encourage Negroes to give consideration to business opportunities, and means to indicate that a potential employer is sincerely interested in hiring minority group members.[73] Also, considerable attention has been given to testing, selection criteria, training required, and related matters in selecting Negroes for positions in manage-

[70] Andre G. Beaumont, "A Fruitful Year for CPS," *Journal of College Placement,* Vol. 27, No. 1, October-November 1966, pp. 50–52, 55–56.

[71] "Industry Plugs Positive Negro Job Message," *Business Week,* No. 1869, June 26, 1965, p. 34.

[72] *Time,* Vol. 83, No. 25, June 19, 1964, pp. 84–86.

[73] Robert Calvert, Jr., *How to Recruit Minority College Graduates,* Swarthmore, *Personnel Journal,* 1963.

ment. Again, there are many similarities in the use of techniques for recruiting Negroes and whites, but there are differences which hinge upon the modifications required when using the same criteria and tools for non-whites as for whites.[74]

A number of efforts have been made in recent years to have Negroes claim a larger part in the nation's economy, particularly by enabling them to participate more in small business and become salaried, managerial, professional, and technical employees in large-scale organizations. One of the most interesting of these is the program to increase the number of students that are enrolled in graduate schools of business. For example, in 1966, of 13,000 graduate business students in the country, fewer than 50 were Negro. The Ford Foundation recently made a grant which would enable the enrollment of 50 and later at least 100 Negroes in the nation's graduate schools of business.[75] These and other efforts are symptomatic of attempts presently being made to assist Negro college graduates to enter industry in appropriate positions and get started on careers in management. Much remains to be done, and there is little doubt that manpower specialists will be given the assignment to plan the development and integration of minority group members in their employing organizations.

TRAINING OF COLLEGE GRADUATE TRAINEES

Earlier in the chapter we referred to the study of 26 different training programs in 14 companies in which more than 1000 young men who had graduated from these programs responded to a detailed questionnaire covering all aspects of their training experience. We noted that the major finding of this study was the high enthusiasm of the ex-trainees for their companies and for their experiences since they joined their employing organizations. The level of enthusiasm varied by program and by company but in no instance was it recorded as low.[76]

Although a majority of the answers in the survey were favorable, close to one-third of the participants were critical of certain practices carried out by organizations. For example, 25 percent of the graduates said that they would have liked it better if their progress had been checked more so that

[74] Educational Testing Service, *Selecting and Training Negroes for Management Positions,* Educational Testing Service, Princeton, 1966.

[75] "Ford Foundation Grant for Negroes in Business," *Training and Development Journal,* Vol. 21, No. 6, June 1967, pp. 48–49. For example, a small organization has already been established which plans to use a computer to match graduates of Negro colleges with jobs at companies that cannot afford to recruit on campus. See "Two Wharton Graduates Set Up Service To Match Negro Graduates to Jobs," *Business Week,* No. 2026, June 29, 1968, p. 76.

[76] Habbe, *College Graduates Assess Their Company Training, op. cit., passim.*

they would have known if they were performing as expected or not. Thirty percent described the training course as "slow moving"; 36 percent thought the training should have been "tougher—more exacting." With respect to training objectives, the college graduate trainees asked for more facts about the business, more experience in analyzing business problems, more opportunity to show their qualifications for different company jobs, and more preparation for advancement. These negative findings point to areas in which corrective action could be taken by the manpower specialist to improve these kinds of programs.[77] Performance appraisals and postappraisal counseling could quite clearly be of use in allaying some of the problems vocalized.

It was found that the standing of a company's training program in the eyes of its graduates could be predicted with considerable accuracy by the way the trainees answered the question, "Since you joined your company, to what extent has it made use of your knowledge, skills, and abilities?" An analysis of the findings indicated that, if management was able to assign college graduates to jobs for which they felt qualified and which called for their best effort, it would have accomplished the single most crucial matter in building their morale and job satisfaction.[78]

In this particular study, 15 of the training programs were classified as on-the-job, and the remaining 11 were classified as formal. The former were relatively short courses with emphasis placed upon the development of specific skills. The latter offered longer training with rotated assignments to the different departments of the organization. When the results of the study were analyzed, it was found that only 2 of the formal courses ranked among the top 13 (the upper half) of the most favorably regarded programs. In other words, on-the-job training was favored by the graduates by a wide margin.[79]

The five most important reasons that college graduate trainees gave for accepting an organization's offer of employment were, in order: (1) the organization's reputation and future; (2) advancement possibilities; (3) the existence of a training program; (4) the opportunity to do desired work; and (5) salary.

When asked the main values of the training programs in which they participated, the graduates replied by referring to the opportunity to learn about the organization and its products; learning about the work which they would be doing after the training had ended; the influence of instructors and supervisors; and the association with other trainees. Repeatedly two considerations were mentioned in response to the question, "Of all the

---

[77] *Ibid.*
[78] *Ibid.*
[79] *Ibid.*

things that have happened to you since you joined your present company, what contributed most to your development?" Most frequently mentioned was the help and guidance that someone in the organization gave the graduate when he needed it. Second to this was the experience of being given a job and being held accountable for results.[80] Several available accounts of specific organizations corroborate these quantitative findings.

Some Programs in Brief

At the present time it appears that the Peace Corps, which rejects four out of five applicants, is the nation's largest single employer of inexperienced college graduates. Despite the rugged assignments which these trainees obtain and the demanding preparatory training, such as learning recondite languages, it appears that the challenge, idealism, and opportunity to serve continue to attract and satisfy young people.[81]

Similarly, organizations which have recruited college graduates over the years and provided meaningful and challenging training have reaped the rewards later. For example, the Bethlehem Steel Company established a management training program in 1922 (now known as the Loop Course) which was one of the earliest management recruiting and training programs in American industry. It begins in early July each year and consists of three phases: orientation to the company at the headquarters office; specialized training in the activity or field for which the "looper" was selected; and on-the-job training which prepares him for more important responsibilities.

It has given the company a home-grown, top-level executive group that marshalled Bethlehem's resources so that it became the world's second largest steelmaker. It recently provided the person who became the chairman and chief executive officer.[82]

Another example would be the college recruiting and training program of a leading accounting firm. It strives not only to recruit for its own needs but also to provide a pool of trained talent for its clients. At any one time it will have 300 college graduate trainees as employees who, after they learn the practical aspects of accounting, will be given a chance to move on to client corporations over the subsequent two or three years that they are employed by the accounting firm.

In this particular organization a partner is in charge of recruiting and attempts to obtain about 750 top college or business school graduates per year. In a recent year 90 percent of the graduates signed up were in the top 15 percent of their accounting classes whereas 30 percent had graduate

---

[80] *Ibid.*
[81] *Time,* Vol. 90, No. 17, October 27, 1967, p. 32.
[82] "Bessie Gets a New Boss," *Business Week,* No. 1797, February 8, 1964, p. 82.

degrees. Youngsters recruited are told that within 10 to 12 years if their performance is sufficiently high, they should be partners and have incomes of approximately $25,000 per year. As an alternative, if they do not reach this level in the accounting firm, they will be offered to client companies, probably at comparable incomes.[83]

Finally, to take a last example, a revitalized company in the timber and wood products industry, has conscientiously recruited men in their twenties, fresh from business school, and moved them rapidly into important managerial positions. In fact, the president carried on a fervent courtship with the nation's top business schools and tried to recruit the top four or five graduates from each school. His view is that business is changing so rapidly these days that as likely as not experience can be a liability in the conduct of managerial work. He believes that young people when motivated to out-perform themselves and given a chance to learn about the political in-fighting and salesmanship inherent in much managerial work provide the best manpower solution to organizational success.[84]

These anecdotal accounts of college graduate recruitment and training programs indicate that some firms are trying (to a greater or lesser extent) to overcome some of the problems reported by persons who have completed the college graduate training programs. When this has been the case, organizations have obtained valuable managerial manpower. In the process, they have also undoubtedly experienced high turnover and the cost associated with it.

It is clear that there are various types of college graduate training programs. Those that involve a considerable amount of classroom training could perhaps be identified as one type. Having identified this dimension, however, the alternatives for durations of the program, content, and approaches to instruction are diverse.

On-the-job programs are a second type and stress rotated work assignments and periodic performance reviews designed to let the trainee know how well his assignments were completed in the judgment of his supervisor. Again, there is diversity in the number and kinds of assignments provided trainees and in the extent on-the-job training is integrated with formal classroom training.

[83] T. A. Wise, "The Very Private World of Peat, Marwick, Mitchell," *Fortune,* Vol. 74, No. 1, July 1, 1966, p. 129. It is of interest to note that some of the earliest significant work in manpower development evolved from the controllership function in diverse organizations. See T. F. Bradshaw, *Developing Men for Controllership,* Graduate School of Business, Harvard University, Boston, 1950, pp. 21–162, 218–223, for a classical explanation of the process consistent with that developed in this book.

[84] Tom Alexander, "It's Grow or Die at Boise Cascade," *Fortune,* Vol. 72, No. 6, December 1965, pp. 180–183.

In addition, many organizations today sustain tuition-refund plans whereby a person in a college graduate training program is also given the opportunity to enroll in university-level courses after working hours (or perhaps even on released time from work during the day if the course is not offered at night) and is reimbursed for his tuition expenses, perhaps with the proviso that he receive a passing grade, or a B grade, or meet some other arbitrary criterion. It is also possible for a person to be a college graduate trainee, enrolled in several courses after-hours on a tuition-refund plan, and while working be rotated to a job such as foreman, where he may also undergo preforemanship or trainee foreman program participation. Thus a person could easily be receiving multiple developmental experiences simultaneously.

Perhaps the newest of the training programs for college graduates is the Management Internship Program of the American Management Association. This is an eight-month training program which is an extension of the AMA's world-famous program of management education. It is directed to the specific needs of college graduates who want to prepare themselves for a successful career in management. Some interns are sponsored by business firms or other organizations, but the remainder are composed of people who have spent a year or two teaching on an assignment with VISTA or the Peace Corps or who have been serving in the armed forces. College students must not have worked for their sponsors beyond summer employment. The management center at Saranac Lake is used for the program.

Unlike a business training curriculum, the AMA management internship program is not restricted to specialized areas of management. Instead, it takes the broader view, teaching skills and techniques that supposedly have universal application. Its objectives are to present a type of education, training, and concentrated drill that will prepare young men in the philosophies, principles, skills, and actual tools of management. It hopes to make them highly desirable candidates for employment in any kind of organization they wish to enter. Also, it hopes to help the college graduate to attain an intellectual maturity, emotional stability, and leadership capability much more quickly than could be attained at any other source. In the AMA tradition, the management internship program is education by management, which means that the faculty is composed of more than 150 successful practicing managers who regularly present courses and seminars for the AMA.[85] It is hoped that this program or an equivalent will be perpetrated in the 1970s.

[85] American Management Association, *AMA's Management Internship Program,* American Management Association, New York, 1967.

THE SOCIALIZATION OF COLLEGE GRADUATE TRAINEES

In view of the many problems involved in attracting, recruiting, retaining, and developing college graduate trainees, it is rather surprising that a limited amount of research has been reported on some of the underlying social and organizational phenomena (as opposed to the attitudes of college graduate trainees themselves) that seem to be at the root of the "business-is-for-the-birds" syndrome and the turnover of young people. The basic phenomena are the socialization process, situational adjustment, occupational choice, and career commitment. Each of these is worthy of some detailed treatment because they are particularly useful in analyzing the plight of the college graduate trainee.

Broadly viewed, the socialization of the college graduate trainee to the industrial setting should be integrated with his expectations of industrial employment as they were established during his lifetime, but particularly during his early adulthood as a college student. Undoubtedly, there are differences and expectations among undergraduate and graduate liberal arts, engineering, and business administration students as they perceive employment in organizations. It would seem that business students would have the greatest ease in making the transition to industry because of anticipatory socialization, that is, they undergo a certain amount of vocational training in undergraduate business schools and probably have propensities toward business which motivated them to enroll as a business major in the first place. Thus, if we begin our analysis by considering the transition of the business student to work in industry, we can approach the analysis of work socialization from the point of view of the person who presumably is best equipped to make a smooth transition. Many engineers, of course, are probably equally well prepared because they have studied engineering with a vocational goal in mind in the industrial setting. Liberal arts graduates probably have the least crystalized career objectives if they are planning to terminate their formal education at the undergraduate level and not pursue graduate studies in the arts or sciences.

Discontinuities in Learning

We might begin by comparing the experience of the undergraduate business student prior to receiving his degree with his initial experience at work. There are numerous discontinuities in the cultural learning involved. For example, a major difficulty for the recent college graduate trainee making the transition is his unrecognized but important assumption about time. For most of his life, his activities have been arranged so that there is a beginning point and ending point and relatively short time spans between.

Based upon his experience in primary school, secondary school, and college, he probably found that the amount of time devoted to a unit of work gradually decreased. For example, in grammar school each course was studied for one academic year; in high school some courses were only one half of one year; and in college, almost all of the courses taken were no more than one semester in duration.

The repetition of this pattern probably influences undergraduates to expect a continuing shortening of time span so that by the time they have entered industry they expect each job to be completed within a relatively short period of time, to be followed by movement into a different job. It is difficult for them to get used to the idea that some work is never "finished" and that they are not necessarily going to be promoted each year as they were hitherto. Changes in positional rank within industry or other organizations are hardly arranged so that promotions occur yearly simply because minimum standards have been met.

In essence, we are suggesting that there are four somewhat different dimensions of time affecting college graduate trainees: (1) from regular change to irregular change; (2) from five-month time spans for work to longer time spans; (3) from frequent completion to occasional completion of units of work; (4) from annual promotion to unscheduled promotion.[86]

Temporal Aspects of Socialization in a Changing Situation

Time influences the behavior of college graduate trainees in other ways. Inasmuch as he is a young man he has great difficulty seeing much beyond the next year and has particular difficulty in projecting where he will be five or more years from the present. Similarly, when he is told that he needs a few more years of seasoning, he cannot grasp the significance of this projected time in any meaningful way; and, consequently, it is regarded as unreasonably long. At the same time, if he is experiencing any disappointment on the job, he not only feels his past and present deprivation but extrapolates it into the future and becomes anxious about what is for him an unknown.

Anxiety is a common human reaction, but the recent college graduate may well express it in ways that more experienced men might consider immature impatience, restlessness, or naiveté. The young person may be counseled to become patient. Yet attempting to inculcate patience by talking to young men about their prospects for a lifetime career with an organization seems futile, for they can hardly conceive of the time dimensions of their first job. Perhaps most important, they do not recognize that they are more likely to behave inappropriately because they do not clearly

[86] Anthony G. Athos, "From Campus . . . To Company . . . To Company," *Journal of College Placement*, Vol. 24, No. 2, December 1963, pp. 22–23.

see themselves, their assumptions, and their limitations. Likewise, their immediate superiors may also lack an awareness of the meaning of time to the college graduate trainee. This mutual unawareness is a basic problem in the socialization of the college graduate trainee.[87]

The young man entering an organization also is unfamiliar with the concept of having a single boss. While he was a student he simultaneously had four or five different courses and perhaps as many as ten during a year. He perhaps avoided taking courses from instructors whom he disliked for apparent or perceived reasons. As a result, the trainee has grown used to the idea that he selects his superiors and that no one of them has sufficient power to govern fully his behavior. The difference between this situation and employment is quite obvious, for in the latter situation the graduate finds that his supervisor is one man, unavoidable.

In addition, as a student, the trainee encountered very different instructors who asked him to perform in very different ways during the same semester. Perhaps this is why students tend to attribute to the professor everything that they think is wrong or right with a class. The point is that students tend to focus their feelings about a course on the professor and possibly transfer this practice when they think about their supervisors in their employing organizations. However, whereas students who dislike their instructors in school, if the course is not required, could drop it and in that way the instructor, the industrial supervisor can hardly be "dropped." Thus, instead of dropping the supervisor, the disgruntled trainee may in a certain sense drop the organization by quitting.[88]

In summary, the student who becomes a college graduate trainee experiences a different situation in the employing organization than he had in the school: (1) from having many superiors to only one boss; (2) from the choice of superiors to the assignment of superiors to whom he is fully accountable; (3) from an easy "out" to few escapes; and (4) from multiple, independent evaluations by instructors to a single evaluation by a supervisor. The latter is particularly important because supervisors evaluate employees not in terms of one overall alphabetical letter, such as A, B, C, or D, but in a more subjective way, perhaps in most organizational settings without a clear common denominator between supervisors. The difference again is quite great comparing school to employment: (1) from frequent to infrequent evaluations; (2) from explicit to deduced or implicit evaluations; and (3) from understood single symbols to subtle signals. This difference is all the more important when it is recalled that college graduate trainees are conditioned to attach great importance to "grades" from their superiors. Moreover, while they look forward to being more on their own

[87] *Ibid.*, p. 112.
[88] *Ibid.*

after graduation they still need some feedback on their performance in work settings in order to reduce their anxieties about living with the freedom they have not experienced previously.[89]

Status and Cultural Changes

Still another socialization problem stems from the fact that the recently exalted position of the college senior as a big man on campus may not be followed on the job by a similar regard from peers in the work group. This lack of esteem by others, combined with a search for evaluation from a boss who is not much inclined to give "grades," produces a feeling of being "nobody." In one sense, this is merely the adjustment required from the world of youth to the beginning of the world of adults. In another sense, it is the transition to being more alone, more on their own, more in open competition with peers, and yet ultimately more dependent on one boss. These differences are unfortunately frequently overlooked in analyzing the industrial socialization of college graduate trainees.[90]

Another factor, perhaps more often recognized than those we have been discussing, is that the cultural milieu and purpose of academic life are very different from those in organizations. The real purpose of a college is the growth of its students. The college senior has been at the center of his institution's activities for four years. Professors generally worry about what their students are learning, and administrators worry about how they are living. In this way, the work to be done, or the task of the educational institution, centers on the individual development of the student. A business or other organization seldom can afford the luxury of concentrating solely on individual growth. There are many objectives to be attained, and the growth and development of recent college graduates is merely one of these.[91] Yet there appear to be a number of college graduate trainees whose goal in life appears to be to continue being trained and to learn rather than to transform this training and learning into the accomplishment of organizational objectives.[92] Trainees whose goals are those of the perpetual student obviously are going to collide with those of organizations which consider that at some point formal training must cease and stress must be placed upon the performance and contribution of the employee.

Perhaps the greatest collision of all is the difference in culture between the university and the employer's organizational setting. In preparing for work, the recent graduate studies courses which generally emphasize the

[89] *Ibid.*, pp. 112–114.
[90] *Ibid.*, p. 114.
[91] *Ibid.*
[92] Gerald G. Fisch, *Organization for Profit*, McGraw-Hill, New York, 1965, pp. 163–164.

analytical, generalized, and conceptual. His first job in an organization is usually detailed, specific, concrete, and of limited scope. Also, in college, problems have a curious way of being solved, neatly and completely. Most of them are designed so that they permit a solution, particularly in subjects such as mathematics. The problems in organizations are often not so much for immediate solving as for living with (and piecemeal solution based upon the exploitation of opportunity). This is a qualitative difference in the nature of the work and the nature of the problems it is important to discern. For all these reasons, the recent graduate needs to understand what is happening to him in the socialization process so that he can work out a personal adjustment for himself.

Forestalling Self-Defeating Behavior

Obviously, there is no quick and easy solution to smoothening the transition. Certainly, discussions with the supervisor or opportunities for groups of graduates to meet with a discussion leader to discuss the topics of mutual interest would have some value.[93] But there are other basic problems of adjustment that cannot be easily solved through discussion.

Another way of looking at the problem of the organizational socialization of the college graduate trainee is to analyze it as a problem of solving the young person's identity and his relationships to authority, typically in the setting of a large-scale bureaucratic organization. In such an organization the college graduate trainee is likely to be viewed as overambitious and unrealistic in his expectations regarding the responsibilities of advancement and in getting acceptance of his ideas. The trainee is perhaps regarded as too theoretical, idealistic, naive, immature, and inexperienced to be given very important initial assignments or to be able to cope with the realities of the job situation. He is likely to be viewed as unwilling to recognize the difference between having a good idea and the process of selling the implementation of that new idea to affected managers and nonsupervisory employees. Yet, he is also likely to be seen as potentially a highly useful resource for new ideas, new approaches, and better management, although he must be "broken in" before this resource becomes available to the organization. The organization also expects that the trainee become able to accept organizational "realities" such as power politics, seemingly unethical decisions, and apparently irrational behavior on the part of managers. It expects the trainee has the ability to generate and sell ideas. In this process, he must come to terms with his supervisor, develop an appropriate self-image, integrate himself into relevant groups within the organization, and learn the norms that apply in interpersonal relations. A certain sense of loyalty and commitment would also be expected. Yet, the trainee

[93] *Ibid.,* pp. 114–116.

has had an education which probably overemphasizes the rational, technical solution to problems and does not prepare him for the social and psychological dynamics involved in selling and implementing ideas and adjusting to irrational behavior. He will also want enough reliable feedback so that he can evaluate himself. All of this means that the expectations, aspirations, and needs of the college graduate trainee and the expectations and needs of the organization are sufficiently out of line with each other so that a considerable danger exists for both parties landing in the trap of a self-defeating induction and training program. The employing organization has to take the initiative to prevent a self-defeating pattern from emerging.[94] The manpower planner in the organization is the logical one to establish a strategy for forestalling such a pattern.

Whether the strategy is implemented through a training program for supervisors of college graduates or whether some other approach is undertaken is less important than recognizing the basic manpower problem and accepting the need for a solution. Blaming the universities categorically for giving the wrong kind of education and the college graduates for being immature are equally fruitless solutions. The manpower challenge is to recognize the great potential of the college graduate trainee and to create organizational circumstances for him that will utilize rather than defeat the very qualities which will make him valuable—his education and his youthful enthusiasm and idealism.[95] Careful selection and training of supervisors under whom new college graduates will be assigned should go a long way toward alleviating the problems discussed in this chapter. Yet, the development of supervisors who are capable of using the interpersonal relationship for effective developmental purposes, for becoming man-builders, is more easily stated than accomplished.

Upward Mobility of Trainees

If very little is known about the socialization of college trainees based upon research in the behavioral sciences perhaps even less is known about how trainees achieve upward mobility in organizations.[96] Perhaps the most meaningful study in this vein is one which has followed the development of 30 graduates of the Graduate School of Industrial Administration at the Carnegie-Mellon University.[97] All of these men completed their under-

[94] Schein, "How to Break in the College Graduate," *op. cit.*, pp. 68–76.

[95] *Ibid.*, p. 76.

[96] Robert D. Garton, "Assimilating the College Graduate: A Challenge to Industry," *Personnel Administration,* Vol. 24, No. 1, January-February 1961, pp. 10–17.

[97] See William R. Dill et al., "How Aspiring Managers Promote Their Own Careers," *California Management Review,* Vol. 2, No. 4, Summer 1960, pp. 9–15; and "Strategies for Self-Education," *Harvard Business Review,* Vol. 43, No. 6, November-December 1965, pp. 119–130. For a depth study of three of these young managers, see *The New Managers,* Prentice Hall, Englewood Cliffs, 1962, by Dill *et al.*

graduate work in engineering or science and hence are not typical of many managers in organizations. As a group, they had a high level of intellectual ability and represent the cream of the crop.

The most important single finding from the standpoint of socialization to industry is that the career progress of these men reportedly depended greatly on the strategies of heuristics that an individual employed in "his game" with the organizational environment that he encountered at work. In other words, upward mobility depended most upon the specific environment in which the person worked and the heuristics which he brought to bear in dealing with the constraints and opportunities in that specific environment. Those who were upwardly mobile perceived that they were in large organizations in which there was relative indifference to their advancement as individuals. Those who moved ahead rapidly were men who had a compelling wish to be a manager as a specific personal goal. Their behavior was governed by the desire to do managerial work or to achieve managerial income and status. They wanted to attain positions where they could act independently and be judged by results. Men who progressed slowly seemed to be less capable as agents of their own progress, less desirous for the specific benefits that a managerial position conferred, less tolerant of the perceived costs of being a manager, and more committed to and identified with their present jobs and present working conditions.[98]

Interest in becoming a manager, however, was rarely a sufficient basis for mobility. Men who wanted to advance rapidly had to pay particular attention to the expectations and standards of the men who governed their organizational fate and chances for promotion. This was not a simple matter of willingness to conform to the supervisor's desires. Inasmuch as the interpersonal and work environment changed continuously each time a man took on a new assignment or began to work with new people, he became subject to different kinds of constraints and had to search for new heuristics or rules of thumb which were likely to promote but in no sense guaranteed his success.

Often, a man's aspirations and orientation tended to be "local," directed toward finding a satisfactory resolution of problems faced in his immediate job situation. Thus, the men who made rapid progress tended to see themselves, their surroundings, and their jobs in the same way that their superiors did, even though they did not always act as the superiors would. On the other hand, the less successful men did not seem to order their heuristics for action so directly in terms of the immediate problem situation. In some cases, they seemed less aware of what was expected of them. In other cases, they preferred to follow strategies which were familiar

[98] Dill et al., "How Aspiring Managers Promote Their Own Careers," *op. cit.,* pp. 9–12.

or which they personally preferred in place of the strategies which the situation might seem to call for. Some of these tended to have a "cosmopolitan" orientation. Finally, the most mobile tended to profit by being aggressive and by taking the initiative in defining and elaborating their roles in the organization, provided they were careful to observe local norms about what young college graduates may and may not do.[99]

The process of self-education in management required in order both to qualify for advancement and to stay ahead of still younger men who have the advantage of more recent training confronts the ex-college graduate trainee after he has been employed in organizations for a few years. A great deal of what today's young managers want to learn is the same as what their predecessors wanted as they moved up through the organizational ranks. First, as they become increasingly organizationally socialized, young managers want to become more broadly oriented to the company and their co-workers. Then, after a few years, they want to develop skills as a supervisor, become expert in some phase of the organization, and learn how to make decisions and persuade others to accept them. Still later, they want to gain an increasingly broad perspective, the ability to see problems and opportunities for the organization as a whole, a concern for long-term goals and plans as well as for today's operations, and a skill for negotiating with many kinds of groups inside the organization and out. To some extent executive development programs play a role in developing human resources at this organizational level.

Yet, many managers realize that the reward structure of organizations seldom emphasizes learning. If he views his career as a game which he plays against the men who grant promotions, the payoff for the manager lies in doing the things which have an immediate rather than a long-run return. Organizations must provide the circumstances whereby the burden of learning is shifted to the individual and opportunity is provided so that the person can develop through self-education.[100]

Several generalizations can be made regarding successful strategies for self-development. First, the effort, whether it involves reading or reflecting on experience, should be selective and focused, guided by an agenda or goals for learning. The effort should be organized so that it can be sustained for a long enough period to show meaningful results. Second, the learner must be willing to admit that education consists not only of acquiring new knowledge, skills, and attitudes, but also in giving up convictions and approaches to problems that may be inaccurate and outmoded. Third, although some learning may indeed be implicit, unplanned, and unconscious, the process of education can be facilitated by seeking oppor-

[99] *Ibid.*, pp. 13–15.
[100] Dill et al., "Strategies for Self-Education," *op. cit.*, pp. 119–130.

tunities to talk or write about what is being learned, to use it, and to test whether it works. Fourth, new knowledge, skills, and attitudes are secure only when they have been integrated with those acquired earlier. Men apparently need to translate what they read or hear into familiar terms and to seek illustrations from their own experience for the ideas and concepts involved.[101]

Although these observations have some face validity, they cannot be given greater credence until they have been examined in more organizational settings. Nevertheless, the point is well made that in our rapidly changing world college-educated individuals must assume some of the burden for self-development if they are to remain effective performers in organizations over their life spans.

COLLEGE GRADUATES AND CAREER COMMITMENT

The concepts of situational adjustment and commitment are useful in understanding the reactions of the college graduate trainee to his employing organization. The person, as he moves into and out of social situations and acquires experience, should learn the requirements of continuing in each situation and of success in it. Yet, he will exhibit some consistency as he moves from situation to situation. This consistency can be explained by the concept of commitment, a term describing a variety of social psychological mechanisms. Essentially, a person is considered committed when he is observed pursuing a consistent line of activity in a sequence of varied situations over a period of time.[102]

We also know that the meaning and basic functions of work in modern urban industrial society influence situational adjustment and commitment. Work is a source of subsistence, a regulator of activities, a provider of patterns of association, a producer of identity, a supplier of meaningful life experience, and a determiner of social status.[103] Thus, work itself is freighted with the greatest of social significance, of which career commitment is only one part.

Perhaps when college graduate trainees enter work situations, those who are able to make situational adjustments in particular organizations are the very ones who can accommodate their commitment to employment in that organization. If they cannot, they make some kind of a deferment of their commitment pending a further consideration of employment opportunities.

[101] *Ibid.*, p. 127.
[102] Howard S. Becker, "Personal Change in Adult Life," *Sociometry*, Vol. 27, No. 1, March 1964, pp. 44–50.
[103] Walter L. Slocum, *Occupational Careers*, Aldine, Chicago, 1966, pp. 19–21.

Those who turn over in particular organizations may be the same individuals whose commitments cannot be satisfied there and who believe that alternative employment provides a greater opportunity for achievement of objectives to which they are committed.

In any event, it appears that the stability of a choice of an occupation after additional information about the work role becomes available varies directly with the psychological commitment to the occupation on the part of the person choosing it.[104] According to this hypothesis, we can envisage the college graduate trainee as an unstable employee because he is acquiring additional information about the work role. As he acquires this, his commitment may solidify or be changed in some respect. The restlessness, dissatisfaction, and high turnover of college graduate trainees, of course, can be expected because the young graduate is undergoing socialization from education to industry and is, by and large, casting about to find an identity for himself and a career line of work, if not responding to his emerging sense of commitment.

CONCLUSIONS

In this chapter we have analyzed the aspirations, expectations, and mobility of college graduate trainees in large-scale organizations and discussed some of the dimensions of the problems they present in recruitment, selection, placement, development, and retention for their employing organizations. A prime problem that has developed in the recent past is the "business-is-for-the-birds" syndrome, the validity of which is far from settled. The latter has developed at a time when there has been an increasing expressed need for college graduates.

The attraction of young people to the Peace Corps and other forms of employment which focus upon human service, such as VISTA, seems to be greater than that of industry. Perhaps many of these young college graduates will ultimately need to turn to careers in industry in later life because the preponderance of jobs is still there, even though governmental employment—federal, state, and local—is growing apace.

Increasingly, organizations have become more receptive to recruiting Negroes and women college graduates. This trend is in line with recent manpower legislation and the stress on equal opportunity in civil rights legislation.

Stress on recruiting and training college graduate trainees has in turn created the problem of providing acceptable careers for this highly edu-

[104] Buford Stefflre, "Vocational Development, Ten Propositions in Search of a Theory," *Personnel and Guidance Journal,* Vol. 44, No. 6, February 1966, pp. 6–13.

cated manpower. Many of the positions into which these individuals are placed appear to be unchallenging and unacceptable to them, resulting in high turnover. Turnover has implications for job and organizational redesign as well as for the social order, because it raises questions about the proper utilization of high-talent manpower and controls necessary in the educational upgrading process. Specifically, the proliferation of college graduate trainees in large-scale organizations and the demand for increasingly more may mean that the doors for upward mobility are being shut for individuals with less than a college education. Sealing off mobility in this manner may have dangerous repercussions in a democratic society.

The great college recruiting manhunt which has been accelerating since 1960 has led to some excesses in policies, programs, and procedures inaugurated by organizations in order to corral their needed manpower. Conflict has developed between the college placement offices and the United States Employment Service, which has at least temporarily been resolved. In many respects the solution has been to push the USES back into its traditional role of placing blue-collar and marginal workers and prevent it from getting more involved with white-collar manpower. Whether this delimitation of its role is in the best interests of the college graduate, employers, and the nation is debatable.

It appears that the college placement function will be the predominant manpower institution for recruiting technical, professional, and managerial personnel in the United States for many years to come. The development of computerized personnel systems such as GRAD indicates that alumni of colleges may also benefit from still another new manpower institution, which in turn may also benefit industrial and other employers if it is not restricted to college alumni.

The future of college graduate training programs is unclear. The two basic types involving on-the-job training and formal classroom training continue to exist and are often combined. The great variety in types, content, and approaches leaves unclear which is preferable from a manpower development standpoint. Perhaps those which are best are ones which test and challenge the trainees so that they obtain information on how they are performing in terms of organizational standards and perceive themselves as increasingly learning in a way which is personally satisfying.

The development of college graduate trainees in large-scale organizations remains one of the most significant manpower problems in the United States today. In this chapter we have looked at it from many different angles. It is a hydra-headed problem that is difficult to solve by programs. In the future, manpower specialists in organizations will be required to strengthen college graduate manpower programs in all respects in order to benefit the trainees, the employing organizations, and the total society.

At the present time it is not clear as to what types of actions should be undertaken or if the existing hypothesized solutions are worth testing. Indeed, the controversy is far from settled [105] that the "business-is-for-the-birds" syndrome is as potent a cause as the normal discontinuities young people can expect in being socialized to a world of large-scale organizations.

[105] "Students Still Choose Business," *U.S. News & World Report,* Vol. 64, No. 8, February 19, 1968, pp. 98–100. See also *Wall Street Journal,* April 23, 1968, p. 12 for a story on how Sears, Roebuck is now accentuating the negative a bit in college recruiting.

CHAPTER 12

Sales Manpower and Sales Training

It may seem strange that sales training is singled out for special attention in a book on manpower planning and the development of human resources. Why not separate chapters on developing personnel for purchasing, industrial relations, accounting, hospital administration, military management, or myriad other functional fields of management or in other organizational settings?

The answer can only be pragmatic. In a previous chapter we, in fact, focused upon the lower echelons of manufacturing management when we discussed the foreman and foremanship. His is a generalized job covering more than one million workers in the United States. Similarly, selling is a generalized job employing millions more workers in salesmanship. Obviously, there are important differences between selling diamonds at Tiffany's and peddling brushes door-to-door. Similarly, there are differences between being a production foreman at General Motors and a carpenter foreman at a building site. Despite these differences, there is sufficient homogeneity in each of these occupations so that we can at least examine them from the standpoint of organizational requirements and manpower development.

Foremen and salesmen are considered in some occupational classification schemes as neither managerial, technical, and professional employees nor as skilled, semiskilled, or unskilled laborers. They occupy jobs that are distinctive in the structures of organizations and are perceived as in the twilight zone of marginal status. Certainly, this characterization is true for many foremen, and there appear to be mounting evidence and similarity in conviction that the salesman is a mere leg up from the bottom of the heap and not yet accepted as a professional in any meaningful sense. Part of the problem is that "selling" is an ambiguous term.

THE UNIVERSALITY OF SELLING

In reality, there is no job which does not involve selling in the broad sense of persuasion and communicating ideas. Trainers, for example, should be salesmen of a very high order.[1] As John Dewey put it:

"Teaching may be compared to selling commodities. No one can sell unless someone buys. We should ridicule a merchant who said that he had sold a great many goods although no one had bought any. But perhaps there are teachers who think that they have done a good day's teaching irrespective of what pupils have learned. There is the same exact equation between teaching and learning that there is between selling and buying. The only way to increase the learning of pupils is to augment the quantity and quality of real teaching. Since learning is something that the pupil has to do himself and for himself, the initiative lies with the learner. The teacher is a guide and director; he steers the boat, but the energy that propels it must come from those who are learning. The more a teacher is aware of the past experiences of students, of their hopes, desires, chief interests, the better will he understand the forces at work that need to be directed and utilized for the formation of reflective habits." [2]

The field sales manager taking the trainee salesman on his rounds is certainly in part playing as much a teaching role as is anyone in a supervisory position, line or staff.

The salesman, similar to the foreman, must have interpersonal skills to be able to persuade or influence others to change their behavior in a way desired by the persuader. He must, in a certain sense, teach. To induce the other person to buy is one basic goal in selling. This common meeting-ground of the interacting situation is also the focal point of much managerial behavior. But whereas the foreman manages interpersonal situations to get work done in production, the salesman manages interpersonal situations to get work done in the form of sales. Beyond this similarity in managerial behavior, there are wide departures which need not be pursued here. Suffice it to point out that these two industrial statuses are important in many industrial organizations and should be given special attention from the human resources standpoint because of their preponderance and diffusion in an industrial occupational structure.

In addition, selling and producing are the line activities in many large-scale organizations in an industrial society such as ours. By and large,

[1] Wallace G. Southern, "The Trainer Is a Salesman," *Journal of the American Society of Training Directors,* Vol. 16, No. 9, September 1962, pp. 34–58.

[2] Joseph Ratner, ed., *Intelligence in the Modern World,* Modern Library, New York, 1939, pp. 614–615, citing John Dewey, *How We Think,* Revised Edition, pp. 35–57.

most of the other activities carried out in bureaucratic organizations are designed to assist the line functions in their basic mission of selling and producing goods and services. Selling itself may in fact be viewed as production, and we often hear of a given salesman's "production" in the selling field.

Selling and producing goods and services are not necessarily unique, of course, to industrial culture and a society such as ours. People in preliterate societies are also obviously concerned with production, and the exchange of goods and services can become the focal point for group life. The important distinction in considering an urban industrial society such as our own, in contrast with a rural agricultural society, is the scope of production, the level of technological sophistication, and the elaborate institutional structures developed for producing and selling.

In this chapter we have made a distinction between sales and marketing and dwelled on the former. Even more specifically, we are mainly concerned with personal selling, which is merely one aspect of promotion or communication with customers.[3] Personal or direct selling is defined as face-to-face confrontation between a potential customer and a salesman. Selling is thus an action-oriented interpersonal activity. Marketing, on the other hand, is defined broadly as the sum total of planning and staff work required in order to support effective sales activities in organizations. We subsequently in the chapter discuss further refinements in our conceptualization of selling and marketing, but these should serve our purposes until then.

SCOPE OF THE CHAPTER

Our basic objective in the chapter is to examine the manpower problems involved in planning for and developing an effective and competitive sales organization. Attainment of this goal is not easy because, as one expert has put it, ". . . selling as an art and science has made little or no progress since the early days of the Industrial Revolution."[4] We will necessarily analyze the changing status of the salesman and salesmanship and examine behavioral science views on these two topics inasmuch as these perspectives more than any other available today carry the potential of moving selling out of the intellectual dark ages.

Our approach in the chapter is to begin by considering manpower-planning techniques in projecting needs for salesmen. We provide a less detailed

[3] E. Jerome McCarthy, *Basic Marketing, a Managerial Approach*, Irwin, Homewood, Illinois, 1964, p. 667.

[4] Robert N. McMurry, "The Mystique of Super-Salesmanship," *Harvard Business Review*, Vol. 39, No. 2, March-April 1961, p. 113.

treatment of the use of these techniques than we did in earlier chapters on projection techniques in order to avoid repetition. Instead, we stress the alterations in basic techniques required simply because we focus on a different breed of cat, the salesman.

We proceed next to set salesmanship in historical perspective so that we can clearly grasp the mystique of the breed. This discussion will also involve us in the thicket of problems in selecting salesmen who can be developed into individual contributors and managers. The decline in the reputation of selling is a part of these problems. Then we take a closeup view of personal selling situations and the use and validity of sales formulas in developing salesmen. These topics provide all the background we then need to review the training of salesmen of various kinds, techniques of sales training, training dealers and service personnel, and the field of sales and marketing management education. We complete the chapter by pulling together a conceptual framework and series of steps that comprise a body of ideas on manpower planning and the development of the total sales and marketing work force.

INSIDE AND OUTSIDE SALESMEN

Broadly, one overriding consideration has always been obvious in thinking about sales personnel and remains basic today: the distinctions between "inside" and "outside" salesmen. Since the passage of the Fair Labor Standards Act in 1938, which has gradually covered more and more inside salesmen for wage and hour purposes, the retail salesclerk has become viewed as a distinct type of employee for pay and manpower policies purposes. Historically, the inside salesman has been viewed as a sales agent of the proprietor or ownership. Although notoriously lowly paid in the main, this type of salesman usually went unheroically about his business and was, by and large, content with his salary (or some combination of salary and commission). If he were dissatisfied, he could join the Retail Clerks International Association (AFL-CIO) or other sales unions that have been on the scene over the years, such as the Automobile Salesmen's Association, which has been organizing salesmen in dealerships in Detroit in the past few years. He probably aspired to become a buyer or department manager and was unlikely to become either, serving out his career in direct retail selling. For pay purposes he either received union-negotiated rates or, if there was no union, was paid according to the existing managerially established systems of job evaluation and compensation administration. These observations are not to suggest all inside salesmen have been carbon copies of one another or that all have been low paid. Salesmen of *objets d'art*, Oriental rugs, or big-ticket white goods may have been quite handsomely paid, depending upon the compensable factors in the job evaluation plan and commission arrangement.

On the other hand, pay and manpower policies for outside salesmen generally, such as manufacturers' representatives, sales engineers, insurance salesmen, detailers, account executives, goodwill men, and the high-powered order takers has been of a different species. People in these classifications were not covered for wage and hour purposes by the Fair Labor Standards Act and have seldom had their jobs systematically evaluated with the gamut of other jobs in their employing organizations. Rarely, if ever, have they joined unions. In terms of work content and personality, such salesmen have ranged from hapless drummers like Willy Loman [5] to such veritable entrepreneurs as Cash McCall.[6]

Our primary concern is with outside salesmen and personal selling. Much of what follows would, of course, apply equally in concept to inside salesmen and their salesmanship techniques, but we have in mind primarily outside salesmen and their planned development.

MANPOWER PLANNING FOR SALESMEN: TWO EXAMPLES

Sales forecasts, budgets, and plant and equipment expansion are among the many profit tools considered by organizations in corporate planning. One leading American firm, Minnesota Mining and Manufacturing Company, which has been planning sales manpower needs for more than a decade, uses sales dollars as the basis for all forecasts and budgets. When the firm first considered manpower planning, it speculated that if a relationship could be established between manpower and sales dollars, then it would be possible to forecast manpower for as many years in the future as sales forecasts were available.[7] Such a prognosis differs from forecasting the internal needs of a division based upon units of production, as we described the technique in an earlier chapter. We shall discuss here how corporate sales and divisional sales can be used in manpower projections and thereby augment our earlier discussion of possible techniques of manpower projections.

Assuming that there might be a relationship between manpower and sales dollars at the corporate level, 3M tried to correlate the number of managers at the end of the year to parent company sales for the year. It found a high correlation and decided not to explore possible correlations

[5] Arthur Miller, "Death of a Salesman," in *Arthur Miller's Collected Plays,* Viking, New York, 1963, pp. 130–222.

[6] Cameron Hawley, *Cash McCall,* Houghton Mifflin, Boston, 1955.

[7] Wendel W. Burton, "Forecasting Manpower Needs—A Tested Formula," in David W. Ewing, ed., *Long-Range Planning for Management,* Revised Edition, Harper and Row, New York, 1964, pp. 532–533.

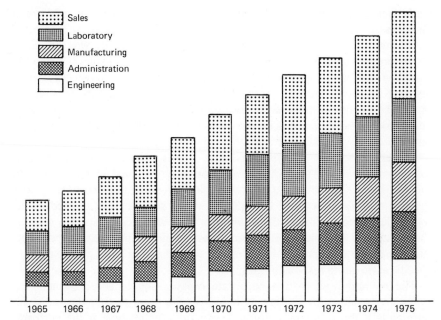

Figure 1 Corporate managerial manpower projection by functional field and year. *Source.* Wendel W. Burton, "Forecasting Manpower Needs—A Tested Formula," in David W. Ewing, ed., *Long-Range Planning for Management,* Revised Edition, Harper and Row, New York, 1964, p. 534, years changed from original.

in other areas such as units produced or sold and plant worth. At the same time, a five-year study of the management payroll was completed. The management group was divided into five key functional fields: sales, laboratory, engineering, administrative, and production. A tabulation was made of the number in each group at the start of the year, turnover during the year, and the total at the end of the year. Figure 1 depicts how these data would appear, assuming the study covered the years indicated. The figure is based upon the determination of turnover percentages including retirements within years listed.[8]

Having found that the average sales per manager is quite consistent among the annual varying numbers of sales managers and having also obtained a five-year sales forecast from the organization's economist, it became possible to make a meaningful manpower projection. The total parent company sales forecast for each year was divided by the average sales per manager, and the result was the projected total of managers for each year of the next five years. By multiplying the total number of man-

[8] *Ibid.,* pp. 533–535.

agers each year by the turnover ratios and adding the number of additional managers to be secured that year, the organization was able to determine the number necessary to develop. For example, if the study were made in 1970 looking back five years, the statistics shown in Table 1 could be compiled with the projection for 1970 as shown (no sales managers needed because turnover balances need). This same approach can be used to project below the sales manager level and, in fact, an entire corporate sales and marketing division. Let us turn to such a situation for illustrative purposes.

For another firm, the divisional sales management classifications, the total productive and total direct sales force for the past seven years, and the projections for the next five years in our illustrative corporate sales division are shown in Table 2. The total direct sales force is defined as the total sales force excluding the indirect or support sales personnel, such as those engaged in sales promotion, sales training, and technical support functions. The total productive sales force is defined as sales personnel with specific sales quota responsibilities.

The method used by the corporate organization to forecast incoming order levels and sales revenue is based on the premise that the main determinant of the company's ability to expand sales revenue is the performance of sales manpower. Accordingly, the sales forecast is developed from a projection of the organization's total productive sales force and an estimate of the productivity level. Insofar as the markets for the organization's products have been shown by long-range marketing studies to have been growing 8 to 20 percent per year depending upon the product line, the company believes its market penetration has not yet reached the optimum level and that its rationale for sales manpower projections makes sense. Yet, manpower projecting is often described in reverse to that outlined. Commencing with the sales forecast, future productivity levels are projected; and from these two factors sales manpower requirements are derived.

The projections in Table 3 comprise a five-year forecast made in 1970 for the ensuing years, based upon data available for the past ten years and two other factors. The growth in the productive sales force is established consistent with planned corporate organizational objectives. The growth in the sales management sector is based upon a projection of past ratios and takes into consideration new product development.

The historical ratios and growth rates are shown in Table 3 for the past few years, and projected levels in the next five years. For the purposes of the sales management manpower plan, it is not necessary to forecast the incoming order level, but it could be determined from the average productive sales manpower in each year and the projected productivity level.

Table 1 Historical Data on Corporate Sales Managerial Work Force

Year	Sales Managers End of Year (whole number)	Sales Managers Average during Year (whole number)	Sales per Manager Column 2 (thousands of dollars)	Percent of Turnover	1970 Sales Forecast (thousands of dollars)	Loss through Turnover (whole number)	Sales Manager Manpower Forecast for 1970
1965	72	70	211	7			
1966	77	74.5	220	5	1387		
1967	87	82	219	11			
1968	93	90	234	8			
1969	92	92.5	210	6	Average		
Average:				7	212	7	None

Source. Adapted from Wendel W. Burton, "Forecasting Manpower Needs—A Tested Formula," in David W. Ewing, ed., Long-Range Planning for Management, Revised Edition, Harper and Row, New York, 1964, p. 535.

Table 2 Five-Year Direct Sales Manpower Projection

As of December 31	Sales Management					Total Productive Sales			Total Direct Sales Force
	General Managers	Branch Managers	Zone Managers	Account Managers	Total	Basic Product	Advanced Product	Dealer Sales Representatives	
1961	8	9	16		33				178
1962	8	16	19		43				196
1963	8	17	19		44				217
1964	8	20	21		49	193		3	245
1965	8	21	25		54	207		9	272
1966	8	25	27		60	231		7	315
1967	8	25	22	10	65	231	10	9	299
1968	8	28	26	8	70	245	8	9	325
1969	9	28	25	7	69	255	7	9	339
1970	9	32	26	13	80	236	13	10	349
Projected									
1971	8	36	33	22	99	292	22	11	404
1972	8	42	34	25	109	327	25	12	455
1973	8	48	36	29	121	366	29	13	510
1974	8	55	38	33	134	410	33	14	571
1975	8	63	42	38	151	459	38	15	640

Table 3 Growth Rates and Management Ratios (1961–1970 actual; 1971–1975 projected)

As of December 31	Percentage Increase		Percentage of Productive in Total Direct	Branch Size in Total Direct[a]	Number of Direct Supervised per Manager	
	In Total Direct	In Total Productive			In Total Sales	In Basic Products
1961	10.1			10.5	4.4	
1962	10.7			8.2	3.6	
1963	10.7			8.7	4.0	
1964	12.9		80.0	8.8	4.0	
1965	11.0	10.2	79.4	9.4	4.0	
1966	15.8	10.2	75.6	9.5	4.3	
1967	−5.1	5.0	83.6	9.1	3.6	4.1
1968	8.7	4.8	80.6	9.0	3.6	4.0
1969	4.3	3.4	80.0	9.2	3.9	4.2
1970	2.9	−4.4	74.2	8.5	3.4	3.8
Projected						
1971	15.8	25.5	80.4	9.2	3.1	3.7
1972	12.1	12.0	80.0	9.0	3.3	3.8
1973	12.1	12.0	80.0	9.0	3.3	3.9
1974	12.1	12.0	80.0	9.0	3.3	4.0
1975	12.1	12.0	80.0	9.0	3.3	4.0

[a] The ratio projected for the years 1972 through 1975 is used to estimate the number of branch managers required in each of these years. The actual number of branches opened is determined from the long-range marketing study conducted in each country.

Table 4   New Manager Requirements

	1971	1972	1973	1974	1975
Total management personnel required as of December 31	99	109	121	134	151
Net additions required	19	10	12	13	17
Estimated losses					
Resignations	6	7	7	9	10
Retirements and deaths	1		1		1
Promotions and demotions	5	6	6	6	7
Total	12	13	14	15	18
Number of new management appointments required	31	23	26	28	35

Table 4 shows the number of new managers required each of the five years in order to satisfy the division's total manpower objectives.

The number of nonsupervisory personnel to be promoted to their first management assignment takes into consideration the losses from present management ranks due to resignations, deaths, retirements (both normal and early), promotions (to positions outside the direct productive force), and demotions. The projected loss rates have taken into consideration turnover experience during the past seven years and the increasing complexities of the company's product lines.

An analysis of the distribution by management classification could indicate a very young management group with, for example, one retirement due in 1971 and not another due for 12 years. The average age of the four classifications could be as follows: (1) general managers, 43; (2) branch managers, 31; (3) zone sales managers, 30; (4) account managers, 28.

An analysis could also be made of performance appraisals and available objective data, such as sales and the percentage of quota achieved, to determine the number of personnel in nonmanagement positions who are considered promotable within the next two years to zone, account, or branch managers. Because of the technical knowledge required in these positions that may be peculiar to the firm, it may decide that it is not possible to consider employment from outside the company directly into these positions. Therefore, the only manpower source would be the present sales force.

This analysis could show the following:

Number rated immediately promotable	21	1971 Requirement	31
Number rated promotable within 2 years	19	1972 Requirement	23

The number of salesmen needed in the direct and productive sales forces can be determined by the ratios included in Table 3, which is a reflection of the planning completed to attain corporate objectives. The latter were previously set by predicted order levels and sales revenues in markets estimated to be growing at research-determined levels.

These two illustrations of sales manpower planning suggest ways in which organizations can calculate the numbers of salesmen and sales and marketing managers needed. However, this kind of information is only of a limited value. The lead time needed for developing sales manpower must be put to proper use. One study showed that it took six to nine months for a new salesman to start pulling his own weight; and, as a result, unless salesmen were added to the work force well in advance of the actual need, they could not be developed sufficiently to contribute to the job. In other words, to meet the sales goal for any year it was necessary to have X salesmen on the payroll at the start of the year for every million dollars of sales forecast.[9] Failure to make proper use of lead time has placed the sales organizations of many companies today—in both industrial and consumer industries—in a pincer. They are caught between (1) an urgent need for an upgraded, expanded sales force, and (2) inadequate, ineffective techniques for the development of this manpower.[10] Coupled with these manpower and development problems are others that run more deeply and raise profound questions about whether we really know very much about selling. Until we have a better understanding of what people are being developed for in selling, it is difficult to know what should be done. This brings us to the core of the mystique in selling, which is at the heart of manpower development problems in sales.

SALESMANSHIP IN HISTORICAL PERSPECTIVE

The haggling in Oriental and Turkish bazaars and sales transactions conducted in the Medieval towns antedate contemporary salesmanship. In the past century there grew in America two new institutions that ushered in our era of mass consumption. The first of these was the retailing revolution with its two novel agents, the department store for city dwellers and the mail-order house for farmers and rural folk. The second was the growth of nationwide chains of poor man's stores, 5-and-10-cent stores selling thousands of standardized small items. Advertising blossomed and reached

[9] *Ibid.*, p. 537.

[10] Andrall E. Pearson, "Sales Power through Planned Careers," *Harvard Business Review*, Vol. 44, No. 1, January-February 1966, p. 106. See also Cecil V. Hynes, "Sales Personnel: Future Demand and Supply," *Personnel Journal*, Vol. 47, No. 8, August 1968, pp. 540–546.

out into city, town, and country over the mass media.[11] Markets became national and international and the nature of selling changed. To be sure, door-to-door salesmen, drummers, sales engineers, and their kin still exist, but salesmanship has taken on important new dimensions and the division between inside and outside salesmen has been set with the advent of the Distribution Revolution. The nature of selling has become even more confused than ever.

In the early years of the 20th century, psychologists and economists were about the only social scientists interested in selling as a social phenomenon and the salesman as an economic contributor in modern society. From 1900 to 1925 the psychologist's interest in salesmanship was focused primarily upon three problems: (1) the selection of men who would succeed as salesmen; (2) the psychological nature of selling as a form of human behavior; and (3) the training and supervision of the salesman.[12]

Sell the Individual, but Advertise to the Group

During the first two or three decades of the 20th century advertising, sales promotion, and an incipient form of market research were thought of primarily as supporting mechanisms for the payoff work of the face-to-face salesman. But nothing could be more misleading today than to describe advertising as "salesmanship in words." There is no doubt that advertising aims to sell. But salesmanship is aimed at the individual customer whereas advertising is presumably aimed at groups of consumers. Since the 19th century the new mass media have concentrated on consumer groups.[13] Thus, advertising as a spinoff from salesmanship has had the effect of fragmenting the selling job in much the same way that the proliferation of plant staff service departments and the development of production-specialized expertise have fragmented foremanship.[14]

In 1907 Dr. Walter Dill Scott published the first detailed analysis of the problems of advertising and selling from a psychological standpoint. From that time until the present, the number of books and articles written on advertising and selling has been great. Unfortunately, much of this litera-

---

[11] Daniel J. Boorstin, "Welcome to the Consumption Community," *Fortune,* Vol. 76, No. 3, September 1, 1967, pp. 120, 131.

[12] Samuel N. Stevens, "The Application of Social Science Findings to Marketing," in *Aspects of Modern Marketing* (AMA Management Report, No. 15), American Management Association, New York, 1958, p. 86.

[13] Boorstin, *op. cit.,* p. 131.

[14] One company having a product that is difficult to get across to customers (a water softener) has tried to sell them the salesman rather than the product in the raucous "Hey Culligan Man!" campaign. This approach presells the salesman and substitutes him for the service. "How to Get Salesmen through the Doorway," *Business Week,* No. 1918, June 4, 1966, pp. 84–89.

ture has been superficial, trite, and sterile; but this need not cause us to overlook the important facts and phenomena toward which the psychologists and economists of those years turned their attention.

One of the implications of this early research by Dr. Scott was to relate the field of selling rather closely to consumer research and advertising. One of the basic objectives in consumer research is to determine the wants and needs of the potential buyer. The salesman who is fortified with this knowledge is aided in achieving his objective of closing a sale. This intimate tie-in has also, of course, confused the theoretical differentiation between advertising and selling. Most advertising is indirect selling, but some of it is rather direct, judging by many of the virtual commands to buy which are barked out over the television. The main purpose of advertising is to sell the customer the product, service, or institution, or at least "soften him up" for the sale and the pitch of the salesman.[15] However, selling by means of advertising is a different order of thing from face-to-face selling involving interpersonal relations on a face-to-face basis.

Selling and Interpersonal Clashes

Experimental psychological and social science investigations in the sales field have lagged considerably behind similar work in the field of advertising. The methodology of selling has not been inspected and studied as systematically as the procedural developments in consumer research. For these reasons, psychology has not up to the present time particularly contributed to the subject of salesmanship, although there have been some very recent contributions, the principal ones being in the selection of salesmen and the introduction of psychological and behavioral science concepts into marketing. Studies of the latter type are becoming more numerous, and we comment upon some of them later in the chapter.

The relationship between psychology and salesmanship has often been misunderstood in the popular mind. In everyday life we hear much of the "psychology of selling," for a good salesman is thought to be a good psychologist, whatever this is supposed to mean. If a psychology of selling is to have any meaning, the meaning that it does take on will be one that should reflect the several facets of salesmanship. For example, salesmanship may perform a useful service in our society, but it may also cause considerable conflict and interpersonal clashes. Salesmanship not only provides an income for some people but also enables the consumer to satisfy both his material and his psychological needs more readily.

Selling implicitly introduces a clash between the salesman and the consumer because the consumer must decide on how best to allocate his in-

---

[15] Milton L. Blum, *Industrial Psychology and Its Social Foundations,* Revised Edition, Harper, New York, 1956, p. 549.

come among his various needs whereas the salesman must persuade or influence the customer to purchase his product to the possible exclusion of other products. Consumers frequently have difficulty in making up their minds as to which of their needs they need to satisfy first; and then, when the needs are identified, they may have further difficulties in deciding upon which particular product in the same line will best meet their needs. Each competing salesman will put pressure on the consumer to buy his product, not the product of the other salesman. Similarly, salesmen who sell competing brands of the same product try to exclude one another from obtaining the consumer's business. As a result, the consumer often finds the potentially useful service function in selling has become minimal because the salesman's behavior is patterned according to his own needs and interests, rather than those of the consumers'. Obviously, this can result in interpersonal clashes in the selling situation.[16]

Selecting Salesmen

The first important research concerning salesmen in America was carried out under Dr. Scott for the American Tobacco Company. Scott was searching for important differences in the psychological makeup of successful and unsuccessful salesmen and nonsalesmen. His is generally regarded as the pioneering effort, although there were a number of scholars in Europe (such as Hugo Munsterberg) who were also interested in selection testing at this time. The fact that no significant or durable results were achieved in Dr. Scott's research should surprise no one acquainted with the development of the social sciences. At the time he was active in the American Tobacco Company, instruments capable of the precise measurement of individual differences in respect to salesmanship did not exist. Since that time, the persistent quest for psychological understanding regarding salesmanship has met with more success, although it should not be assumed that definitive answers have been arrived at even as yet.[17] Salesmanship, like management and managing, has proven to be a most elusive mystique.

The earliest psychologists, such as Scott, worked by themselves in tackling selection problems. As time went on, Scott, Walter Van Dyke Bingham, and a number of other persons concentrated their energies on the improvement of tests. By the time of World War I, psychological tests had been developed which were widely used in the Army for selecting recruits. For example, the famous army Alpha and Beta tests of intelligence go back to this time period. Eventually, of course, testing came increasingly

[16] *Ibid.*, pp. 549–550.
[17] Stevens, *op. cit.*, p. 86.

to the attention of businessmen; and, after the war, the checkered career of personnel testing began when psychologists who had worked with the army during the war returned to civilian life and began to ply their craft in the industrial setting. However, these developments transcend the purposes of this chapter and need not concern us further here, other than to serve as one anchor point in the search to understand the nature of selling.

Bureau of Salesmanship Research and Turnover Studies

The formal study of salesmanship and salesmen in the United States on a broader scale goes back more than 50 years. In fact, the first major project in salesmanship can be traced to 1916. A Bureau of Salesmanship Research was founded by Bingham at the Carnegie-Mellon University in Pittsburgh. The Bureau was essentially an agency for research in selecting, training, and supervising salesmen. The Bureau was supported by a group of 30 industrial and business companies that were compelled to employ 30,000 new salesmen annually to keep intact a total work force of 48,000 salesmen. The research staff of the Bureau was comprised of ten psychologists, and the employees of sales departments for the 30 firms were made available to these psychologists for the purposes of study.[18]

Studies of testing and training salesmen have continued to the present period. Psychologists have sustained some interest in selling behavior, although much more attention has been given by them to the selection of salesmen by means of tests and weighted application blanks, marketing and advertising research, and, more recently, consumer behavior.

At the time the Bureau of Salesmanship Research was established, turnover in American industry was considered a serious problem, particularly among factory or hourly personnel. One hundred percent annual turnover was not unusual and in certain large firms exceeded 300 percent.[19] There were a considerable number of men ready to give up one job in the hope of getting a better one. For example, it has been reported that more than two-thirds of the pre-World War I separations from employment were resignations. Throughout the 1920s personnel administration endeavored to promote the idea of continuous service and thereby reduce turnover.[20]

Turnover of sales personnel remains a significant problem in industry, although it is perhaps of lesser magnitude today than overall turnover was

[18] Walter Dill Scott et al., *Personnel Management,* Fourth Edition, McGraw-Hill, New York, 1949, pp. 233–234.

[19] Walter Dill Scott et al., *Personnel Management,* Third Edition, McGraw-Hill, New York, 1941, p. 213.

[20] Sumner H. Slichter, *Union Policies and Industrial Management,* Brookings Institution, Washington, 1941, p. 100.

in America 50 years ago. Similarly, selection and training of salesmen remain as problems. In certain industries and among certain types of salesmen, turnover, selection, and training are more serious than among other industries and sales types. For example, all of these are serious problems for the managers of automobile dealerships and are among the important reasons the "Big Three" in the industry established sales and marketing training institutes for their dealers and dealership manpower.

It has been repeatedly stressed in the literature that solutions to the problems involved in developing the sales work force, including the reduction of turnover, begin with improved initial selection. Thus we are told that the failure of industry to select competent salesmen stems from such errors as: the belief that interest equals aptitude; the fakability of aptitude tests; the emphasis on conformity rather than creativity; and the subdivision of the man into piecemeal traits, rather than understanding him as a whole person. Prior sales experience is said to be less important for retail automobile salesmen and people selling insurance and mutual funds than the man's possession of "empathy" and "ego drive," the two characteristics which he must have to permit him to sell successfully. Sales training can only succeed when the raw material is present.[21]

It has been stated that with the possible exception of the president and the night watchman, the salesman's is the most independent role in the organization. No general test battery presently exists for measuring the intellectual, emotional, and interactional characteristics of applicants for salesman positions.[22] Yet, many organizations have reported success with *ad hoc* or commercially available tests locally validated.[23] The search for selection tools continues, even to the extent of reexamining the possible use of formerly discredited approaches, such as analyzing the variations in handwriting among sales applicants.[24]

[21] David G. Mayer and Herbert M. Greenberg, "What Makes a Good Salesman?", *Harvard Business Review,* Vol. 42, No. 4, July-August 1964, p. 125.

[22] James A. Belasco, "Broadening the Approach to Salesman Selection," *Personnel,* Vol. 43, No. 1, January-February 1966, pp. 71–72.

[23] John E. Wilson, "Evaluating a Four Year Sales Selection Program," *Personnel Psychology,* Vol. 12, No. 1, Spring 1959, pp. 97–104; Wayne K. Kirchner, "Predicting Ratings of Sales Success with Objective Performance Information," *Journal of Applied Psychology,* Vol. 44, No. 6, December 1960, pp. 398–403; and Wayne K. Kirchner and Marvin D. Dunnette, "Identifying the Critical Factors in Successful Salesmanship," *Personnel,* Vol. 34, No. 5, September-October 1957, pp. 54–59. Also promising is the assessment center concept. See Douglas W. Bray and Richard J. Campbell, "Selection of Salesmen by Means of an Assessment Center," *Journal of Applied Psychology,* Vol. 52, No. 1, Part 1, February 1968, pp. 36–41.

[24] S. M. Zdep and H. B. Weaver, "The Graphoanalytic Approach to Selecting Life Insurance Salesmen," *Journal of Applied Psychology,* Vol. 51, No. 3, June 1967, pp. 295–299.

EMPIRICAL RESEARCH ON THE SALES PERSONALITY

Others state that not more than one person in a thousand is so constituted that he will be successful and find challenge and security in direct sales, especially because he will not be able to accept the persistent rejection he will face. For example, a salesman of accident and health insurance is expected to make about 36 prospect contacts by cold-spearing each week. He is doing well if he can sell four of these. This means that he must steel himself to an average of 32 rejections 50 weeks in the year. Probably no one without a strong capacity to take punishment—and often a real need for constant self-punishment—can tolerate such activity. For these reasons selling is widely deprecated and the work reportedly attracts a large share of neurotics.[25]

Inasmuch as most Americans seem to need security, certainty, and a predictable future, the demands of salesmanship generally, and of specialty selling particularly, are intolerable to many people. But it is probably the high rejection rate that accounts for the phenomenally high amounts of turnover in many direct selling organizations. Much of the time a 400 percent turnover seems acceptable to sales managers—and sometimes even turnover up to 750 percent. Most firms engaged in direct selling have a hard core of 10 or 20 percent who are career-committed veterans, but the remainder of the sales work force come and go with lightning-like rapidity.[26]

Those who can make a success of selling are said to be habitual "wooers," people who have a compulsive need to win and hold the affection of others. They are not best identified as bundles of the right techniques and concepts but rather "procurers" who use the merchandise to "seduce" the prospect so that the latter "falls in love" with it and wants to buy it. Along with the desire to woo, the successful salesman has: a high level of energy; abounding self-confidence; a chronic hunger for money; a well-established habit of industry; and a state of mind which regards each objection, resistance, or obstacle as a challenge. If a salesman is not a natural wooer and has not demonstrated that he has the foregoing five qualities, he is reported a poor risk for selection. Furthermore, no training program or system of supervision can inculcate them in him once selected.[27]

Occupational Prestige

To this point, we have been suggesting very strongly that salesmen possess distinctive character and personality types, although the evidence

[25] McMurry, *op. cit.,* p. 115.
[26] *Ibid.*
[27] *Ibid.,* pp. 116–118.

for this is really more the shrill recital of impression and folklore than demonstrated fact. In addition to this basic selection problem of what to look for in prospective salesmen, there are others which bear upon the present reputation of selling as a career and the rejection of selling by college graduates and others in the post-World War II years. It seems that, ever since the play *Death of a Salesman* was widely seen, the image of Willy Loman has been around and negatively influenced people who might have considered selling as a career. To some people, all selling is reduced to the life of Willy Loman with its endless travel, superficial thinking, shallow interpersonal relationships, psychological taxations, and, perhaps more than anything else, futility and meaninglessness. In fact, in the play the salesman is depicted as one who is detached from the reality of the business world. He is shown to know little about anything and depends solely on his smile and jovial manner to ingratiate himself with his buyers.[28]

Perhaps in the popular mind the service nature of selling is glossed over, and sales work is regarded as something to be avoided, if possible. Occasionally, some recognition is given to the opportunities for high salaries and commissions inherent in some selling positions, but persons who have a socially oriented outlook are likely to avoid selling as a career. Although much has been made of the revolution in personal selling and claims advanced that the Willy Loman types are vanishing, they still seem to be around; and there appears to be little evidence that the image of the salesman has improved.[29] Not only are many young college graduates today reported as disenchanted with business as a career, but also retailing and personal selling probably are at the bottom of the list of business occupations. For example, in one recent study, researchers polled almost 1000 college men from 123 universities and found only 6 percent who were willing to give selling a try.[30]

Empirical research on sales occupations reinforces the negative stereotype.[31] Though considered a white-collar worker, the salesman is occupationally marginal to the blue-collar employee, which represents only a minor status improvement. For the lower-status manual worker, high-school dropout or graduate, or minority group member, selling constitutes the most accessible channel for occupational advancement because it requires comparatively little in terms of educational attainment, training, capital, and experience. Although the variance in income in selling is probably the

[28] Richard M. Baker, Jr., and Gregg Phifer, *Salesmanship: Communication, Persuasion, Perception,* Allyn and Bacon, Boston, 1966, p. 11.

[29] E. B. Weiss, *The Vanishing Salesman,* McGraw-Hill, New York, 1962, pp. 213–221.

[30] Baker and Phifer, *op. cit.,* p. 11.

[31] For example, Pearson, *op. cit.,* p. 105.

largest of all occupations, it is problematic as to whether the salesman's pay should be attributed to his employer or his customers. This ambiguity gives the salesman a certain occupational freedom but at the same time gives him two masters, each having a claim on his compliance and loyalty, with the two claims often competing with one another. As salesmen increase their earnings the marginal utility of their income decreases, and they seek status improvement either by moving out of sales, staying in sales but in higher prestige companies or with higher prestige products, or going into business for themselves.[32]

In a study of 66 essentially outside salesmen, based on interviews, the pastiche of comments gleaned indicated two contradictory themes: selling is (1) going up in prestige because it is becoming more professionalized; and (2) going down in prestige because increasing numbers of people are called salesmen who have no legitimate claim to the title (such as sales-clerks in department stores). The salesman's ideological strategy was to seek to garner the best from both worlds: the aura of the professional man without the encumbrances; the aura of the drummer without the loss of respect. The salesman is not very interested in questions of integrity, nor does he care to prove that his function and conduct serve community values, primarily because his inordinate stress on expedience rules out ethical considerations. He is not so much unethical as nonethical; he avoids being self-used but winds up self-using, thereby trading one form of alienation for another.[33]

The causes of the problem of low occupational prestige of salesmen are usually thought to be: (1) people do not seem able to differentiate between salesmen and retail clerks (outside and inside salesmen), and (2) historically salesmen have been unscrupulous—which we might call the "Yankee peddler syndrome." An alternative explanation might be that difference in interests between buyers and sellers is connected with the salesman's low status. This difference of interests causes distrust in situations involving interaction (or outright clashes as we previously indicated). The buyer's distrust of the seller results in a low level of prestige for selling and for salesmen as an occupational group. Yet, since we lack a generally accepted theory of occupational prestige, we cannot clearly identify the de-

[32] Gerhard W. Ditz, "Status Problems of the Salesman," *Business Topics,* Vol. 15, No. 1, Winter 1967, pp. 68–80.

[33] F. William Howton and Bernard Rosenberg, "The Salesman: Ideology and Self-Imagery in a Prototypic Occupation," *Social Research,* Vol. 32, No. 3, Autumn 1965, pp. 277–298. This is one of the very few empirical studies of salesmen. Many of its findings contradict those discussed earlier in the chapter and are based upon less systematic evidence. Some fresh insights into the role of salesmen can be found in Abraham H. Maslow, *Eupsychian Management: A Journal,* Irwin, Homewood, Illinois, 1965, pp. 220–235.

terminants of prestige level or bring about the necessary changes that would improve the status of the salesman.[34]

Although improvement in manpower input to sales jobs and revamping of the salesmanship image should be helpful in resolving some of the problems of sales manpower, there are still other persistent problems of salesmanship in America today that have important implications for manpower planning and the development of human resources in this line of work. In taking them up, it is necessary first to take a closer look at the nature of the direct selling job and consider some of the subtleties and complexities involved in it.

A CLOSEUP OF PERSONAL SELLING

It has been estimated that at least ten percent of the nation's labor force is engaged in personal selling activities. The range in sales jobs is, as we have already seen, extremely wide, although to this point we have over-simplified the differentiation to inside and outside selling. Momentary reflection on the variety of selling jobs should convince the reader of the range of these positions. For example, in industries where manufacturer-dealer relations are important, the selling jobs may be very diverse. In the automobile industry there is the omnipresent retail salesman, well known (if not notorious) to anyone who has ever purchased a vehicle off the showroom floor or the back lot in a dealership.[35] Less well-known is the field sales representative from the automobile manufacturing company who has responsibility for the sales of dealers in the zone or district in which he works (a wholesale salesman). His duties are not merely seeing that sales are sustained at acceptable levels but also to act as a kind of management consultant to the dealer advising him on service, parts, personnel, accounting, and a wide range of matters related to management of the business.[36]

A different type of environment and selling prevails in the insurance industry, and even within segments of that industry itself, considering, for example, salesmen who specialize in group insurance, fire insurance, auto-mobile insurance, or individual life policies. In recent years we have seen the rise of the sales engineer, a person who is usually concerned with selling

---

[34] John L. Mason, "The Salesman's Prestige: A Re-Examination," *Business Topics,* Vol. 10, No. 4, Fall 1962, pp. 73–77, citing in part Theodore Levitt, *Innovation in Marketing,* McGraw-Hill, New York, 1962, p. 5.

[35] For a perceptive analysis see Meg Greenfield, "Nightfight with the Nicest Guy in Town," *The Reporter,* Vol. 35, No. 1, July 14, 1966, pp. 35–37.

[36] For an analysis of the complexity of these relations in general, see Valentine F. Ridgway, "Administration of Manufacturer-Dealer Relations," *Administrative Science Quarterly,* Vol. 1, No. 4, March 1957, pp. 464–483.

technologically complicated machines or equipment, which requires engineering knowledge in order to make effective technical presentations. There are many other types of salesmen ranging from the individual manufacturer's representative to the account executive working in a stock brokerage house.

Order Getting

It has been said that every salesman's job is a little different from every other and that the tasks handled by any given salesman are continually changing. The American economy is dynamic, and the changes that take place within it affect the tasks of the salesman. These tasks may vary with company objectives, market conditions, and the changing preferences of each individual customer. Despite these differences, there are three basic sales tasks which might be found in any sales job. In some situations in industry one salesman may be required to carry out all three tasks, whereas in other situations he may carry out only one.[37]

The three sales tasks are: (1) order getting, (2) order taking, and (3) supporting the order-oriented salesman. Salesmen who are order getters and order takers are obviously order oriented in the sense that they are specifically interested in obtaining orders for their employing company. On the other hand, supporting salesmen are not directly interested in taking orders. Through a variety of devices, they function to assist the order-oriented salesman. Manufacturing firms of all kinds, and especially those who make industrial goods, constantly seek out prospective buyers and, as a result, have a great need for order-getting salesmen. Wholesalers also employ order-getting salesmen, although recently such salesmen have developed more into counselors and advisors, as in the use of the aforementioned automobile field sales managers, rather than acting merely as order takers. Similarly, retail firms employ order-getting salesmen to sell unsought goods and for making the initial contacts in selling certain delivered convenience goods. Examples of these types of salesmen would be, respectively, those who sell aluminum storm windows and those who deliver milk to the home.[38]

Order Takers

Order takers (which incidentally is not a derogatory term) complete the bulk of all sales transactions in America. A very large part of personal selling is order taking, that is, the routine completion of sales that are made regularly to the same or similar customers. The repetitive nature of this sort of business makes it extremely important and profitable for many

[37] McCarthy, *op. cit.*, p. 675.
[38] *Ibid.*, pp. 675–682.

firms. At the present time, and probably more so in the future, the order-taking function will be reduced to taking money mechanically and delivering the product, as we now see in the case of vending machines for cigarettes, soft goods, and other convenience goods. Computer reordering is already with us and promises to become increasingly diffused in the future.[39]

Order takers may be classified according to whether they are employed by manufacturers or wholesalers or retailers. The manufacturer's order taker usually has a regular route and calls upon his customers at fixed times. In selling some products to manufacturers, the order taker may find it necessary to train the company's employees in the use of the machines or products. If he sells to dealers, the order taker may be required also to train the wholesaler's or retailer's salesmen. Usually his job requires him to move about geographically and to complete a large number of calls on his customers. Typically the manufacturer's order-taking salesman handles relatively few items, or even a single item. On the other hand, the wholesaler's order takers may handle thousands of items. Because of the variety of items handled, the order takers may be reduced to mere pencil wielders who fill out forms, thereby accepting orders in the narrow derogatory sense of the term "order taker." In reality, the term order taker often applies specifically to the wholesaler's salesmen who are handling a multitude of items which virtually sell themselves. However, order taking in its most mechanical sense is commonly found at the retail level. The retail clerks encountered in stores selling convenience and specialty goods are often low-level order takers. The goods which they handle have already been thoroughly presold through advertising campaigns, and the retail clerk is required to do little beyond filling the customer's order, packaging it, and making change.[40] He does little selling.

Missionary Salesmen

Two types of salesmen have been identified who support and assist the order-oriented salesman. Their activities are directed toward obtaining sales in the long run, but in the short run they function as ambassadors of goodwill who provide specialized services. These persons may be termed "missionary salesmen" and "technical specialists." Most supporting salesmen work for manufacturers. Typically these manufacturers bear the responsibility of initiating training and promotional programs for all levels in the channels of distribution.[41]

Very briefly, a missionary salesman is employed by a manufacturer to work with his distributors and the customers of his distributors. His usual purposes are to develop goodwill and stimulate demand, help or induce

[39] *Ibid.*, pp. 682–683.
[40] *Ibid.*, pp. 683–685.
[41] *Ibid.*, pp. 685–686.

customers to promote sales of his employer's goods, assist the customers in training their own salesmen, and take orders for delivery by the distributors. In all these senses the supporting salesman is a kind of missionary for the manufacturer. Sometimes these persons are called "merchandising salesmen" because in another perspective their primary function may be regarded as to serve as an effective medium of communication between the manufacturers, his distributors, and his customers.

Lastly, a special kind of merchandising salesman or missionary salesman is the so-called "detail man." He is especially well known in the drug industry as the person who calls on doctors, dentists, pharmacists, nurses, and drug wholesalers and retailers. Quite often these salesmen have had some science training, perhaps in pharmacy, and are able to talk to the professional people both knowledgeably and convincingly. They are usually selling the reputation of the company for its products rather than any particular product.

Technical Specialists

Turning to the other type of supporting salesman, there is one commonly known as the "technical specialist" or "sales engineer." Actually these technical specialists are usually persons with backgrounds in engineering or science and may have relatively little interest in sales in the traditional drummer sense. They function as communicators insofar as they have the technical competence and ability to explain the advantages of the company's product. Inasmuch as they normally talk to the customers' technical employees, they are not required to have a high level of traditional salesmanship ability. In these types of selling cases an order getter has probably stimulated interest in the product, and the sales engineer has arrived on the scene simply to provide the details. The order getter has the task of getting past the purchasing agent or other company personnel who serve as a screen for the company. In this way the order getter locates a problem that the company is having and suggests that his employer's technical specialists can help solve it.

By way of summary, in considering salesmanship, three sales tasks have been isolated, order getting, order taking, and supporting sales. Based upon these differentiations, it should be obvious that selling is not a simple homogeneous activity. There are variations not only in types of salesmen but types of sales, products, markets, and industries. It therefore seems rather ludicrous that so much attention has been given in the literature to formula selling techniques, rules of thumb, and other simplistic approaches which seem to be based upon the assumption that selling is one identical universal process.[42] Since there is such diversity in selling tasks, the types

---

[42] *Ibid.,* pp. 686–687.

of training required for developing salesmen could be expected to be differentiated accordingly. Such is the case, as we shall see.

Let us next consider these rules of thumb and simplistic approaches to salesmanship in the sense of one's ability to handle a selling situation and the improvements to this line of thinking contributed by the behavioral sciences before turning to the specific training of salesmen itself.

SALES FORMULAS IN SELLING

Some psychologists and social scientists and many sales managers have proposed formulas for successful selling, despite the fact that they are apparently aware of the many intangibles connected with the selling process. As suggested above, many of the advocates of these systems feature sales formulas based upon a layman's interpretation of social science concepts.

It has been suggested that knowing how to handle individual customers could be made easier if the salesman understood the appropriate findings of psychology and sociology. At the present time, the behavioral sciences have not been developed to the point where it can be determined with finality which specific combination of stimuli will be made effective in dealing with customers. It is known that different individuals react differently to different stimuli in different environments. Some persons are impressed by visual stimuli, whereas others react to such senses as hearing, smelling, tasting, or touching. Reference groups, personal influence, values, attitudes, and a multitude of other considerations undoubtedly play a part.[43]

Salesmen tend to be pragmatic in their approach to selling. They start by sizing up the customer and make certain general appeals to him, gradually adapting their appeals during the sales presentation based upon their own experience with different kinds of people. In essence, the astute salesman attempts to key his sales presentation to the individual. Not knowing what may appeal to a given customer, the salesman may attempt a wide range of appeals seeking an emotional or an economic reaction. He may, of course, vary the blend of appeals for particular prospects.[44]

In the literature on salesmanship, frequent reference is made to one of the most widely known formulas for selling, which has existed since before the turn of the century, and is known as AIDA. Although the explanations of the meaning of this formula vary, the basic idea is that when a buyer is considering a purchase he has a kind of mental stream. A sale meets with less resistance when the talk of the salesman follows this mental stream. The four letters AIDA stand for attention, interest, desire, and action. Based upon the formula, the salesman is expected to begin by

[43] *Ibid.,* pp. 670–671.
[44] *Ibid.*

gaining the attention (A) of the customer. After he has done this, he is supposed to arouse in the customer a state of interest (I) and to build it up in order to create the desire (D) to buy. In theory when the desire to buy is sufficiently strong, action (A) follows when the customer actually buys the product.[45] Some people would add an "S" to the AIDA formula to stand for satisfaction, a frame of mind which is supposed to follow the act of purchasing and predispose the customer to begin the AIDA sequence once again.[46]

Sophisticated psychologists have written that assuming that such a mental stream exists in the mind of the potential purchaser is ridiculous. Moreover, it is a gross oversimplification. The chances are very slight that the mental processes of the successful salesman and the overwhelmed buyer are anywhere near as simple as the AIDA stream conceptualization implies.

Not to dwell on the point too much, but for the sake of illustration, let us consider another equally sterile selling formula: want-solution-action-satisfaction. According to this formula, the salesman has as his principal task determining the existence of, or creating, a want in his potential customer. As soon as this uneasy state of mind has made the buyer sufficiently miserable, the salesman suggests a solution to meeting needs which oddly happens to be just the product he has on hand. In order for the customer to regain his equilibrium, he must take action by purchasing the product. This satisfies him, but apparently only until another want is created at another time.[47]

A formula has even been suggested for summing up what we think we know about human learning so that it can be used by the sales trainer. The formula is a mnemonic device in which the first letter of each item on the list is learned; the formula is PESOS. We prepare the trainee; explain the job; show him how to do it; observe him do it; and then supervise him or follow up on the training. When these items are put together they spell PESOS, which felicitously means money in the sales trainee's pocket. Such mnemonic devices can probably be very useful if not used mechanically. Unfortunately, too many trainers believe that they can implement PESOS as quickly as they recite the word and do not adequately follow up in helping the sales trainee learn.[48]

This discussion of formulas is not intended to cast doubt upon the well-established theory of needs in the human personality as stated by leading

[45] Blum, op. cit., p. 550. See also the exposition by McCarthy, op. cit., on AIDA, pp. 670–672.

[46] Blum, op. cit., p. 550.

[47] Ibid., p. 551.

[48] William McGehee and Paul W. Thayer, Training in Business and Industry, Wiley, New York, 1961, p. 180.

contemporary psychologists. Actually there are various ways to conceptualize needs, and Abraham Maslow has indicated that needs are arranged in a hierarchical order according to various degrees of prepotency.[49] It is dubious, however, that the salesman must concern himself pragmatically with complex conceptualizations of this sort. For his purposes a product or service is for sale, and the consumer may buy it. The consumer may or may not need in an objective or subjective sense the product which is for sale. There is no requirement that the salesman psychologize or use pseudopsychology to comprehend these kinds of situations. Much of salesmanship is not applying psychological principles of selling. Both the salesman and the customer are complex individuals with complex motivations. Under these circumstances, a selling formula is a gross oversimplification, and sales formulas are highly artificial. In the final analysis, a salesman would probably be more effective if he were to disregard such formulations.[50]

Most sales managers and knowledgeable marketing men in industry probably today do not emphasize or naively and uncritically accept the validity of sales formulas. (Or perhaps they do; little research has been conducted on this subject.) Yet, in order to train salesmen, there must be some content and subject matter about which they can be told. Even though there are recognized variations in sales techniques, quite commonly sales and marketing managers assert the belief that there is a common core of activity that runs through all sales work. For example, in most selling situations, there are allegedly such activities as: (1) greeting the prospect; (2) sizing up or qualifying the customer's ability to buy; (3) presenting arguments to buy now; (4) overcoming objections; (5) narrowing the field down to one item to be bought; and (6) closing the sale. All of these items are concerned with salesmanship, and they can be considered social psychological only when they are thought of as the content and product of the interaction between two people. The validity of this common core of activities as a systematic delineation of all the key components of successful selling behavior has not to the knowledge of this writer been established.[51]

BEHAVIORAL SCIENCE AND SALESMEN

At several points above in the chapter, we discussed the movement from folklore and rule of thumb to the identification of salesmanship principles through the scientific study of selling. In the future we may find that gen-

[49] Abraham H. Maslow, *Motivation and Personality*, Harper and Row, New York, 1954.
[50] Blum, *op. cit.*, p. 551.
[51] *Ibid.*, pp. 551–555.

eralizations about human behavior in selling situations based upon empirical evidence collected in an impersonal and objective manner will become available.

Eliot Chapple has for many years been interested in the utilization of the interaction chronograph in measuring salesmanship ability and conducted some of the earliest empirical research on selling behavior. In some of his research in measuring salesmanship among retail salesmen [52] Chapple found that the chronograph was useful in identifying effective and ineffective salesmen based upon observed selling behavior. This innovation could assist in selection and may have implications for the training and development of sales personnel. More recently, Woodward studied selling behavior in four British department stores.[53] There is a tendency among behavioral scientists to challenge traditional ideas in salesmanship and to investigate the field, although a great deal more research is needed.

More specifically, the concepts of psychology, social psychology, and sociology have started to be applied to sales and marketing activities. In a recent ground-breaking book, formula selling was almost completely departed from and selling was discussed in behavioral and educational terms. Here the emphasis was placed upon individual cognitive and perceptual processes; the effect of groups, group membership values, and attitudes upon behavior—that of the customer as well as the salesman; and role behavior and empathy. Salesmanship was conceptualized as situation management, and behavioral science concepts were identified which would assist the salesman in managing the situation.[54]

Yet, it was recognized that there is no one way to sell. There is only an acceptable framework of ideas and concepts in the behavioral sciences that the salesman may employ to develop his own way of selling. Out of ignorance, many salesmen may never employ these concepts. Of all the social sciences probably educational psychology has the most relevance for selling behavior because, as we saw earlier, selling essentially involves educating. The main problem from the standpoint of application is that psychology, like marketing, when speaking of aggregates of persons can provide ideas that are useful in general but not necessarily applicable to specific times, places, and people.[55]

Others suggest that the salesman should also develop insight into the process of human perception if he is to manipulate successfully the attitudes,

[52] Eliot D. Chapple and Gordon Donald, Jr., "An Evaluation of Department Store Salespeople by the Interaction Chronograph," *Journal of Marketing*, Vol. 12, No. 2, October 1947, pp. 173–185.

[53] Joan Woodward, *The Saleswoman*, Pitman, London, 1960.

[54] Joseph W. Thompson, *Selling: A Behavioral Science Approach*, McGraw-Hill, New York, 1966, pp. 57–106.

[55] *Ibid.*, pp. 67–68, 107, 231.

thinking, emotional responses, and the behavior of others. Hence, a salesman must develop persuasive communication based upon his insight into
client perceptions and alter them to win a favorable response. Thus, we
are told that the persuasive sales message must be replete with communications symbols (language) that shoot the message home quickly and surely.[56]
Effective listening and rational thinking necessary to qualify customers,
overcome objections, and close the sale are also to be given due weight.

The behavioral sciences (which are, of course, themselves still evolving)
may very well hold the greatest promise for removing personal selling from
the dark corner of the sales-marketing field because they strike at the
rational foundation of personal selling and the "why" of activities associated with it. Art and science can then be blended so that our knowledge
of selling will transcend formulas and be placed on a more solid foundation.
Probably the major problem in making use of the knowledge relevant to
personal selling issuing from the behavioral sciences is the sheer volume
of material which has been developed. In the final analysis, the question of
which are the most relevant concepts in a particular dyadic salesman-
prospect relationship must be decided by the salesmen. No matter how
many formulas he consults or cookbook sources he turns to he must select
and combine eclectically from the existing tools the ones which can be
useful in performing his job.[57]

All of this means, of course, that the training content of courses for
salesmen must be flexible because we cannot communicate definitive ideas
on valid techniques in selling anymore than we can set forth the basic
principles of human behavior. We can perhaps omit reference to sham
information, but it is doubtful that final answers can be provided salesmen
on how-to-do-it. It is perhaps most useful to view salesmanship as the sum
total of knowledge, skills, and attitudes required by a salesman to serve as
the two-way communications link between his employing organization and
the customer. The salesman's goal is to insure the salability of products
and services through his behavior. Anything the behavioral sciences can
provide to improve our understanding of salesmanship in this context
would undoubtedly be an assist to the manpower planner.

THE TRAINING OF SALESMEN

The origins of sales training can be traced back many years, particularly
to retailing. We have previously discussed the work carried out at the

[56] Baker and Phifer, *op. cit.,* pp. v–vi and *passim.*
[57] James H. Bearden, ed., *Personal Selling,* Wiley, New York, 1967, pp. vii–xii,
81–82.

Bureau of Salesmanship Research at the Carnegie-Mellon University. It is quite clear that a lively interest in sales training has continued since that time.

One of the earliest corporate schools stressing sales training for outside salesmen was that of the National Cash Register Company, founded in 1894 by John Henry Patterson. This school focused upon providing salesmen of NCR products with information in a primer about the merchandise as well as sales techniques. Patterson was a strong advocate of education and saw the industrial environment as permeated with opportunities for teaching. As he put it:

"Business is only a form of teaching. You teach people to desire your product; that is selling. You teach workmen how to make the right product; that is manufacturing. You teach others to cooperate with you; that is organization." [58]

Yet, most of the earliest training of salesmen took place in retail stores throughout the country where there was a continuing need to inform the sales force of products and techniques for dealing with customers, even though this type of selling was and remains the least prestigious, poorest paying, and least demanding from a salesmanship standpoint. In a store, sales training included programs on: induction, sales systems and procedures, salesmanship and store sales policies, merchandise, supervisory development, as well as any retraining needed.[59] Many stores have successfully used programmed instruction in recent years rather than training-on-the-job in instructing sales personnel in such topics as use of the cash register, store policies on charge accounts, handling checks, making change, and closing out at the end of the day.[60] The main advantages of programmed instruction have been saving of training time and improved learning of selected aspects of work content.

The training of outside salesmen began to receive increasing attention in the 1940s. Because of ease of selling during World War II, many sales managers believed that salesmen already hired would have to be retrained

[58] "How Personnel Relations Was Born," *Business Week*, No. 1864, June 26, 1965, pp. 92–94.

[59] Maurine O. Staack, "Training in Retailing," *Journal of the American Society of Training Directors*, Vol. 11, No. 4, July-August 1957, pp. 26–27, 31.

[60] For example, see Barbara Rimbach, "A Department Store's Experience with Programmed Instruction," *Training Directors Journal*, Vol. 18, No. 4, April 1964, pp. 34–38; Joan Taylor and R. L. Reid, "Programmed Training in a London Store," *Occupational Psychology*, Vol. 39, No. 1, January 1965, pp. 57–58; and "The Quiet Revolution in Retail Sales Training," *Training in Business and Industry*, Vol. 4, No. 5, May 1967, pp. 31–35.

in order to sell successfully in the postwar buyers' market. It was also expected that large numbers of new salesmen would have to be hired to build sales forces and keep up with expected business. In a similar vein, it was anticipated that men returning to civilian life after military service and work in war industries would have been out of touch with selling for several years and would have required training if not complete retraining.[61]

The need for training salesmen arises, of course, from the fact that a newly hired salesman usually does not know the products which he is to sell, the customers, or how to sell or present products to the customers. The extent of training required depends upon such considerations as: the difficulty and complexity of the selling task, the salesman's prior education and training, the salesman's previous selling experience, and the type of buyer whom the salesman is to approach. The most difficult task in the training of salesmen is teaching salesmanship per se, which can be defined as teaching a salesman to use his knowledge of the product, market, and customer to accomplish the purposes for which he was hired.[62]

Techniques Useful in Sales Training

Frequently, salesmen are given very little and very inadequate training. Some firms encourage the salesman to study his product and trust to experimentation and experience for suggestions on methods of presentation to specific customers. Sometimes a company furnishes a sales manual or suggests using methods that have been used successfully in the past, including standardized sales presentations. Some firms have organized courses or schools for salesmen. An increasing number of companies have provided for practice selling under the tutelage of another salesman, manager, or instructor.[63] This training-on-the-job approach is essentially a sales version of the apprenticeship model we have discussed previously in the book. Increasingly, outside salesmen, like inside salesmen, are also being trained by programmed instruction. Time-saving and educationally effective programs have been developed for use in salesmanship fundamentals [64] as well as for use as one part of a broader salesman development program, integrating programmed learning with schooling in the home office, plant tours,

---

[61] Harry R. Tosdal, *Introduction to Sales Management,* Fourth Edition, McGraw-Hill, New York, 1957, p. 585.

[62] *Ibid.,* p. 585.

[63] *Ibid.,* pp. 584–585.

[64] J. S. Schiff, "Programmed Instruction to Train Men to Sell," *Training Directors Journal,* Vol. 18, No. 8, August 1964, pp. 18–20; and Raymond Hedberg et al., "Insurance Fundamentals—A Programmed Text Versus a Conventional Text," *Personnel Psychology,* Vol. 18, No. 2, Summer 1965, pp. 165–172.

and the like.[65] Programmed learning has even been successfully used to train franchised saleswomen selling cosmetics to housewives at home.[66]

The use of programmed tapes and playback machines,[67] home-study booklets and films,[68] audio tapes detailing new products or other information of value to sales personnel,[69] and video-tape television systems are other means used today to develop salesmen. Many organizations are, in essence, simply making use of all available modern communications and educational techniques to keep their sales people up to date on products and qualified to perform their work.

Sales Job Goals

It is generally agreed that it is not possible to have a successful sales training program unless the salesmen are told what is expected of them and shown how to accomplish these goals. A job description is helpful in informing the salesman what is expected of him, but not in showing him how to accomplish his duties. Much sales training breaks down because it is not designed to cope with the different backgrounds, skills, and levels of intelligence of salesmen, all of which must be considered if training is to be successful.[70]

One of the first considerations that must be properly weighed in preparing for the training of salesmen is to identify the needs of the particular sales work force. New salesmen may be divided into a number of different categories: (1) the salesman who is new to sales work as well as the company's products; (2) the salesman who has had previous selling experience but has no knowledge of the company or its products; (3) the salesman with knowledge of the company's products but no previous selling experience; and (4) the salesman with previous selling experience with the company's type of product but who has been employed as a salesman elsewhere. The type of sales training which would be required for each of these groups varies, and the sales training program which should be used for each should accordingly differ. This is not the place to discuss the

[65] Henry J. Lindsay, "Systematized Sales Training," *Training Directors Journal,* Vol. 18, No. 2, February 1964, pp. 42–47.

[66] Carol Cook, "Programmed Instruction in Direct Selling," *Training and Development Journal,* Vol. 21, No. 7, July 1967, pp. 34–40.

[67] "New Approach Pays Off in Immediate Sales Increase," *Training in Business and Industry,* Vol. 4, No. 2, February 1967, pp. 25–29.

[68] "Rexall's New Sales Training Program," *Training in Business and Industry,* Vol. 4, No. 5, May 1967, pp. 38–40.

[69] "Spreading the Message with Tape," *Business Week,* No. 1923, July 9, 1966, p. 87.

[70] McCarthy, *op. cit.,* p. 688.

specific materials which should be added or deleted for each group, but it is obvious that certain aspects of the training can be eliminated for the men who have the prior experience or background needed for the job.[71]

Content of Sales Training

The sales training program established by an industrial firm should give some coverage to the following fundamental areas of concern regardless of the preparation of the salesman: (1) company policies and practices, (2) product knowledge, and (3) techniques of selling. We shall discuss each of these and then consider other associated administrative aspects of sales training.

In respect to company policies and practices, it is important that the salesmen be provided sufficient knowledge concerning these so that he can deal effectively with the customer. A manufacturer's order-getting salesman, for example, should be thoroughly familiar with the company's policies in respect to credit, size of orders, dating of invoices, delivery, transportation costs, return goods privileges, and pricing. Salesmen should also be completely familiar with the procedures concerning reports they are expected to complete, expenses and their control, attendance at sales meetings, and other similar matters. The salesman should also thoroughly understand the administrative practices in the company as they bear upon expediting orders, securing adjustments, and generally making it easier for the customers to deal with the company. Obviously, it is extremely difficult to draw a line as to exactly how much knowledge and information a particular salesmen should have about these matters. Some companies may consider that their salesmen need training on subjects that transcend those just discussed. For example, they may believe that their salesmen should have training in company personnel policies, policies regarding possible conflict of interest, and even the company's attitudes toward economic and political questions. These kinds of training are not job related, but they have a bearing upon the salesman's employment with the firm, and may be required by the employing organization to round out the employee's fund of knowledge.

Product Knowledge

Turning to product information, the salesman must have sufficient knowledge so that he can deal effectively with customers. Again, it is difficult to draw a line and be precise in any sense that would apply across the board to a multitude of sales employment situations. The amount of product knowledge a salesman would require depends largely on the type of job he will fill and the diversity and technical complexity of the product mix.

[71] *Ibid.*, p. 689.

For example, automobile salesmen are likely to encounter a wide range of persons entering the showrooms from automobile buffs who are concerned with all of the details and minutiae of engine performance and gear ratios to those who care little about the car other than price or styling. Only empirical research could confirm precisely what items of information such a salesman ought to have in order to acquit himself well on the dealer's showroom floor. About the only general criterion that could be mentioned is that the salesman should have enough information so that he can answer the questions of the majority of customers and satisfy their inquiries, leading ultimately to a sale.

In respect to selling techniques, we have already pointed out that salesmen cannot rely solely upon formulas. There are many ways in which training in selling techniques can be carried out. It is not safe to assume that some people are born salesmen and therefore they need no training. Knowledge of salesmanship skills and psychological selection tests have not arrived at the state of development so that we can have full confidence in assuming that those whom we select will necessarily be good salesmen. As we have seen, increased research is necessary in order to validate what makes for success as a salesman.

There are many ways of training salesmen, varying from our basic apprentice model through attendance at company schools to attendance at educational institutions outside of the employing firm. Many companies find that salesmanship can be taught effectively by apprenticeship systems in which newly hired salesmen observe senior salesmen. This may involve the newcomers tagging along with the senior salesman as he makes his rounds, after which the newcomer is allowed to make trial demonstrations and sales presentations. These are followed by critiques from the senior salesman. Through a process of trial and error and experience the new salesman gradually becomes more effective in selling or is found to be deficient and a poor learner, at which time the organization may suggest that he give up selling and try some other line of work. In some firms the apprenticeship model is extensively used, whereas in others this on-the-job training follows instruction that has previously been inaugurated in the classroom.[72]

Length of Training

The length of the initial training period for salesmen varies greatly. In some selling situations it could be as brief as a part of one day, whereas in other circumstances it could last for as long as several years. Similar to all kinds of development in industry, sales training should go on indefinitely, and certainly at least as long as required to attain acceptable performance.

[72] *Ibid.,* p. 690.

In fact, sales training usually does continue indefinitely because we find that many companies use weekly sales meetings or work sessions, annual or semiannual conventions or conferences, and weekly or biweekly newsletters along with normal sales supervision as devices for perpetuating sales training and providing refresher training for even the most experienced salesmen. New products are introduced by firms. New policies are formulated. And, occasionally, clearly identified selling techniques that apply only in specific situations are made known. Because there are these dynamic elements in the work situation, it becomes necessary for sales and marketing managers to make certain that sales training continue throughout the duration of the salesman's employment.[73]

SALES AND MARKETING MANAGEMENT EDUCATION

References were made above in the chapter to different techniques of sales training and in particular to the apprenticeship model. In addition to apprenticeship, much sales training takes place, as suggested, in the classroom. Also, there are numerous management development programs that have been established in various parts of the country for sales and marketing managers. In this section we discuss some of these sales training techniques for higher-level sales and marketing personnel.

Many large firms have established corporate sales and marketing schools. One of the most popular kinds of schools is that which caters to the training of dealers. Obviously, dealers within their own organizations conduct training activities for their own employees, sometimes maintaining their own schools or using these combined with on-the-job facilities. The training of interest here is that which is provided by a manufacturer for its dealers. This type of training may range from training managers in dealerships in how to be better managers to the actual training of retail salesmen who work in the dealership. For example, in the automobile industry in the past decade, the "Big 3" have established sales and marketing centers which train dealers, managers of departments in dealerships, retail salesmen, the wholesale salesmen or field managers who are employed by the manufacturer but call on dealers, and a number of other types of automobile sales and marketing personnel.[74] In addition, there has been a continuing interest in providing service training for dealers. In this way, dealers become acquainted with the latest equipment and techniques for improving

---

[73] *Ibid.*

[74] "Detroit Adds Power to Its Dealer Training," *Business Week*, No. 1878, August 28, 1965, pp. 54–56; "Dealer Staff Training," *Training in Business and Industry*, Vol. 1, No. 1, September-October 1964, pp. 30–32; and "How to Train 58,461 Prime Customers," *Training in Business and Industry*, Vol. 3, No. 1, January 1966, pp. 32–33.

the maintenance and upkeep of vehicles and the profit opportunities involved in service.[75]

Dealer Training

Inasmuch as the dealer is the primary link between the manufacturer and the ultimate customer, it is easy to understand why manufacturers train their dealers to be more effective sales agents both through management training and through salesmanship training.[76]

In a study done in the postwar period which included such companies as Esso Standard Oil, Goodyear Tire and Rubber, Mack Truck, Carrier Corporation, Carborundum Company, and others, it was found that manufacturers believed that such training programs used for dealers increased sales, improved dealer relationships, expedited order processing, reduced customer complaints, and lowered distribution costs. Similarly, dealers reported that training helped them increase sales, improve customer relations, and obtain greater familiarity with company products. At the time the study was conducted, the methods of training used included direct mail (use of letters, postcards, bulletins, magazines, and brochures mailed to the dealer), on-the-spot training (use of company salesmen or special personnel to train dealers at their place of business), and the use of training centers (i.e., of specially equipped classrooms, model stores, or practice shops, located either at the company's home office, at district offices, or elsewhere in the field).[77]

In the study described above, it was found that each of the three basic training methods used presented problems. For example, (1) some dealers are reluctant to be trained; (2) training costs are often high; (3) company salesmen fail to cooperate in training and in following up after the training is completed; (4) qualified instructors are difficult to find. Dealers were usually quite satisfied with these company training programs, although they sometimes said that the courses are not sufficiently instructive and were too sales promotional in orientation. Despite these considerations, dealership training is quite widespread in America and probably will continue to expand in the future.

One of the reasons that dealership training is emphasized among certain American manufacturers is that relatively small retail firms are often ones

[75] "Tender Loving Care—Just for Autos," *Business Week,* No. 1933, September 17, 1966, pp. 140–144.

[76] See "New Growth Rings for U.S. Plywood," *Business Week,* No. 1873, July 24, 1965, pp. 72–75; and "Aiming at a High Score in Bowling," *Business Week,* No. 1891, November 27, 1965, pp. 124–130.

[77] National Industrial Conference Board, *Training Dealers* (Studies in Business Policy, No. 48), National Industrial Conference Board, New York, 1950, p. 1.

in which a family dominates the management. As a result, so-called "dealers' sons" programs are fairly popular. They are intended to perpetuate entrepreneurship and effective management. Inasmuch as these firms are family owned and the likelihood is very strong that the son will succeed the father in the management of the business, the manufacturer will often make provision for training the son in effective management techniques. This is to the advantage of the manufacturer and, of course, is endorsed by the dealer insofar as it is usually of interest to him that his son succeed him in the business and carry on profitably.[78]

Service Training

Brief mention was made of service training above, and we shall now return to it for additional comments inasmuch as the apparent reemphasis on service training in recent years has an important bearing for the development of human resources.

The provision of service training has important implications because service personnel are skilled or semiskilled craftsmen and mechanics. There has been a shortage of such individuals for many years in the United States. Service occupations comprise a field in which the unemployed have been retrained in recent years in order to qualify for employment, such as automobile mechanics.

The modern service center which provides for the analysis of mechanical, electrical, and other failures of vehicles (or the service centers of other industries, which are equally complex in terms of tools, machines, and equipment) require a fairly capable individual with mechanical aptitude and ability to learn. These service centers are important because they are the complement to salesmanship. If salesmanship is designed to sell products or services at a profit which are needed in the community and serve a worthwhile purpose, it seems important that manufacturers make available adequate service facilities so that once the sale is completed the buyer is assured of getting value through continued acceptable performance from the product or service purchased. Where the customer is not treated in this manner, he may become alienated from the company, lose his so-called "customer loyalty," and no longer be a prospect for purchasing products of the firm in the future. For these reasons sales and service training appear to be coming together now and probably will become increasingly harnessed in tandem in the future. Signs of this merger are already present. The integration of these two related fields carries great potential for setting forth new concepts of salesmanship and sales training which adequately bridge

[78] Cf. "When Your Real Job Is 'Son,'" *Business Week,* No. 1937, October 15, 1966, pp. 98–99; and "Whirlpool Takes Dealers' Sons in Hand to Give Them a Feel for the Business," *Business Week,* No. 1824, August 15, 1964, p. 66.

the gap between service and profit, two aspects of selling which we previously described in the chapter as being potentially in conflict with one another.

PLANNING CAREER PATHS FOR DEVELOPING SALES MANPOWER

Looking upward organizationally to developing sales and marketing executives in the corporate home office or headquarters, we would find that the desired input in the manpower development pipeline is typically not someone from a service background, a dealer's son, dealer, or often even a retail salesman. The preferred entrant to corporate sales and marketing today is, according to a recent survey of 200 leading companies, a college graduate with a strange and somewhat contradictory blend of economics and selling, psychology and product management. Ideally, he would have a liberal arts degree and a master's degree in business administration, hopefully with a major in marketing.[79] In retailing, the college graduate recruited may be given job rotation on the selling floor and assignments in such supporting departments as credit and advertising, as well as some classroom training.[80] The general picture seems to be that after selection and training to learn an entry-level job and several others which it may lead to, the employee is further developed by supervisory training, after-hours courses, evening college tuition-refund plans, in-residence campus management education programs, attendance at a corporate management school (if there is one), guided on-the-job training, job rotation, or special assignments.[81] Eventually, the sales and marketing executive with potential for movement to the top positions in these fields or to general management is identified and treated the same as managers with different functional backgrounds: his further development depends on the organization's total manpower planning system.

In view of this multitude of sticky problems surrounding sales manpower recruitment, selection, training, development, and retention, many large organizations have started major undertakings to improve their methods of attracting and systematically developing salesmen. A recent study of sales manpower development in 30 large leading companies in consumer fields has demonstrated how overhauls of traditional developmental processes

[79] "Getting More Out of the Graduate," *Business Week,* No. 1919, June 18, 1966, pp. 61–64.

[80] "How Top Retailers Build Executives," *Business Week,* No. 1865, June 5, 1965, pp. 88–95.

[81] For a pertinent discussion see LeRoy Johnson, "The Sales Job and Preparation for Management," *Management of Personnel Quarterly,* Vol. 5, No. 4, Winter 1967, pp. 33–37.

can be shaped to reduce turnover and build depth in the sales work force. These efforts amount to two basic approaches: (1) strengthening individual parts of the organization's personnel management *programs,* and (2) mounting a broad-based attack on the entire *process* of developing sales manpower in the particular organization.[82] Each of these approaches is worth more detailed examination.

Following the first approach some leading companies improved specific aspects of their manpower development programs. For example, several organizations which experienced high turnover discovered after research into the problem that sales employees hired in field locations were below the standard of those hired at headquarters. The reasons for this discrepancy were field executives often hired the first available candidate simply to fill a territory and get on with the job or hired in their own image. When hiring was centralized, a higher standard was set, turnover declined, and the sales work force improved. Other organizations had problems in the level of compensation for salesmen or blocked advancement, which were identified and rectified.[83]

Spot changes made to resolve manpower problems often have repercussions affecting other areas. For example, if hiring standards are raised, top management sooner or later finds it must upgrade the sales training program, compensation levels, and the quality and type of first-level sales supervision. Perception of the causal interconnections leads to recognition that an entire range of activities is linked and that the proper way to take action is to attack them by an integrated approach addressed to the *process* of development as a whole. This mobilization may be called the "career path concept."[84]

Career Path Concept in Sales and Marketing Management

In order to get better control of the developmental process, organizations normally begin with the demographic inventory of the sales work force and then formulate and state a specific set of policies that are designed to solve manpower problems and are supported by top management. The inventory is analyzed in the light of problems discovered in the organization. For example, firms believing their market penetration is growing too slowly might find answers in blockades in key jobs held down by men who are older, unwilling to accept change, and difficult to motivate. Or, firms might find that promotions come too slowly and reflect the phenomenon of "lock stepping," that is, the slow movement of employees by age groups and/or specific periods of service through the organization without any real regard

[82] Pearson, *op. cit.,* p. 106.
[83] *Ibid.,* pp. 106–107.
[84] *Ibid.,* p. 107.

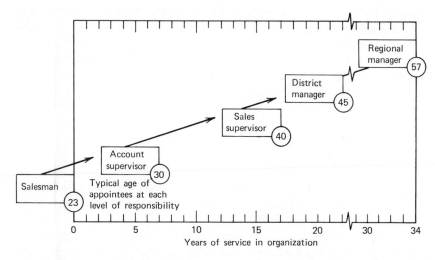

Figure 2   Example of an unattractive career path. *Source.* Andrall E. Pearson, "Sales Power Through Planned Careers," *Harvard Business Review,* Vol. 44, No. 1, January-February 1966, p. 109.

of individual performance. Ambitious, high-potential men soon realize they are up against unheroic careers and little chance for real responsibility or substantial earnings while they are still young.[85] The young college graduate trainee is particularly apt to become restless in these circumstances and subsequently may quit.

An example of such an unattractive sales career path is shown in Figure 2. This simply shows typical ages at which employees are appointed to each level of responsibility and the number of years it takes to move up the ladder in the organization. Analysis of career paths may reveal a great deal about other problems which changes in manpower development processes can solve, such as retention of poor performers, educational deficiencies among salesmen, and undesirable age gaps.

After defining their manpower problems, organizations are normally ready to lay down policies as a foundation for manpower building. These policies are guides for action toward objectives to which top management is committed. Once this commitment is established, policy decisions are made on such vital elements in the developmental process as the kind of men needed, the developmental stages through which they should and will pass, how men will be paced as they move through the developmental stages, the systems of performance evaluation and compensation that will

[85] *Ibid.*, pp. 108–109.

be used, and the role of training and educational programs. Inasmuch as there are two basic functions in any sales organization—selling and sales management (including staff marketing positions)—the career path proceeds along two corresponding lines. Some people will remain as individual contributors selling whereas others will go into a variety of line sales management and staff marketing positions, functioning in a supervisory capacity or at least outside of personal selling.[86] Both of these career paths can be pinpointed; let us consider the sales manager's career path initially.

Stages in the Career Path

The management candidate's path may be conceived of as having six hypothetical stages. For illustrative purposes, the model path starts at the beginning and follows a straight line to the end. In practice, an organization would need to compromise the model to accord with its existing manpower situation and could not effect a revolution overnight. Nevertheless, the model can be adapted to realistic work organizations.

In the first stage of his development, the I & T or Introductory and Trial stage as depicted in Figure 3, the newly hired salesman begins his work with a productive sales assignment after a prescribed orientation period (i.e., six months in the illustration, which could be extended). During the orientation stage, each assignment is intended to be productive, both in the sense of carrying with it meaningful responsibility for results and of providing an opportunity for evaluation of how well a man does. How long a man stays in this stage is determined by performance. In Figure 3, within six months the candidate can be promoted to the sales development stage (i.e., when he has been employed one year). Thus a "race track" is opened for the men who show they can perform whereas others may stay in this stage up to their third anniversary of employment. However, at this point, somewhat similar to the system of promotions for officers in the armed forces, career path planning dictates an "up-or-out" decision. In brief, the first assignment does not provide a continuing job but leads to promotion or termination. This first decision prevents the ultimate growth of an aging, mediocre sales work force and simultaneously gives an early indication to the promising performer that his strengths are recognized and his prospects good.[87]

A move to the SD or Sales Development stage represents a vote of confidence in the man. An outstanding performer could have gotten here in one year; but, importantly, everyone in SD made it by on-the-job behavior not by managerial drift or inaction. Persons at this stage may remain for

[86] *Ibid.,* pp. 110–111.
[87] *Ibid.,* pp. 111–113.

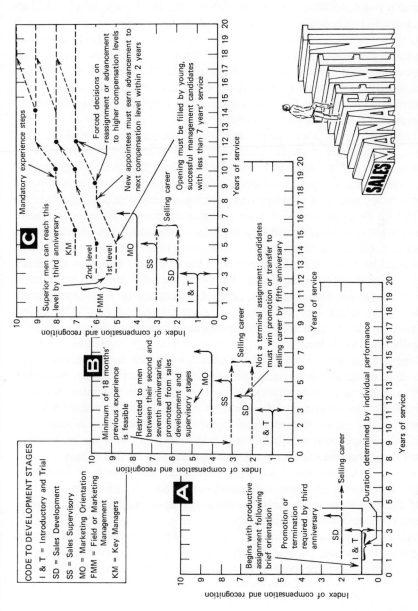

Figure 3 Sample blueprint for developing sales management. *Source.* Andrall E. Pearson, "Salespower Through Planned Careers," *Harvard Business Review*, Vol. 44, No. 1, January-February 1966, p. 112.

four years. But a man's career in the sales development stage again has a terminal point. Men who do not qualify for the third stage as management candidates automatically move into the career path for salesmen (to which we return below). The point is that a formal early decision is made on who the most promising candidates are and "late bloomers" are virtually by-passed, which may be a small price to pay for the early identification of real talent that can then be intensively groomed, encouraged, and retained. It should be noted that the sales management stage also has a "racetrack" counterpart for exceptional performers.[88]

The career path idea stresses fast tracks, formal early decisions, time limits, and an overall grand design. It recognizes moving men through the organization rapidly to keep them challenged. At the same time, the concept takes into account individual differences, pacing men according to their ability, and thus avoiding lockstepping or tenure promotions.[89]

The SS or Sales Supervisory stage comes next and represents the man's first assumption of responsibility for supervising the work of others. He reaches a critical juncture in his career here, as shown by B in Figure 3. It should be noted that the racetrack is kept open so that men can reach this third stage with a minimum of only 18 months' previous experience. Likewise, the third stage is not a terminal assignment for managerial candidates. They either are promoted within the prescribed time (five years) or they are transferred to a career salesman position as supervisory positions became available.[90]

These manpower policies for the sales work force recognize that many salesmen do falter when made managers and must, as a result, be moved out in order to provide supervisory openings and to prevent blockading. Obviously, the movement of ineffective managerial candidates back into career selling implies the double risk that once back in the sales force they still will not perform adequately and may eventually have to be removed from it. In accepting this risk, top management demonstrates that one promotion does not constitute a lifelong commitment to a man or even guarantee him tenure at lower organizational levels. It further demonstrates that the employee must meet his challenge at each level if the developmental process is to work effectively.[91]

As proven performers emerge, the need for a broadening assignment becomes important. At the fourth stage people who have demonstrated their ability to handle both selling and sales management responsibilities

[88] *Ibid.*, p. 113.
[89] *Ibid.*
[90] *Ibid.*
[91] *Ibid.*

are moved to the corporate headquarters staff for marketing orientation. Only employees promoted through three levels qualify to participate in this stage. The marketing orientation assignment is restricted to sales personnel with two to seven years of service. The assignment is confined to productive work with specific objectives and organized evaluations and is intended to provide the necessary experience leading up to a sales or marketing management position.[92]

The fourth stage brings the essentially field sales employee to headquarters for the purpose of sizing him up. It should be used to penetrate beyond the external behavior of the man and to obtain an estimate of how well he can solve problems and make decisions on the more complex issues.[93] The assignments given the employee at this stage would not be those normally in the bailiwick of career specialists in such fields as marketing research, advertising, or product planning. Rather, they would be assignments designed to expose the man to the overall strategy supporting field sales (roughly what we would designate as marketing) and to require that he complete one or more projects in these areas such as perhaps in sales promotion, sales training, market representation, and dealer development.

Employees who pass through the marketing orientation screen then move to the fifth stage of field sales management or marketing management, another critical career juncture shown as C in Figure 3. High performers could have reached stage five in three years, which is rapid movement by anyone's standard.[94] The same policies requiring demonstrated performance to remain in the position applicable at lower organizational levels apply to this one.

Finally, the career path moves some people into the top of the corporate sales-marketing activity. Even at this lofty level, career planning requires that a man's development not be left to managerial drift. Manpower development efforts are carried out by forced decisions on advancement to higher compensation levels or larger sales districts, both of which would involve performance considerations. Tendencies toward managerial inaction are thereby forestalled. However, at the top of the organization no time limit is placed upon the candidate's eligibility for promotion to higher jobs. He is at the apex of the pyramid with few places to go (other than general multifunctional management) and is probably receiving all the personal satisfactions and compensations available from work. These should make him less restive.[95]

[92] *Ibid.*
[93] *Ibid.*
[94] *Ibid.*, p. 114.
[95] *Ibid.*

The Development and Retention of Career Salesman

The foregoing has described the career path to sales management but skipped over the fate of the individual career salesman. The study of 30 large companies mentioned above in this section of the chapter found that many organizations have now started to conceive of direct selling as a much shorter career than a working lifetime and to plan their sales manpower accordingly. These companies have observed that even their best salesmen level off in performance by the time they reach age 50 or 55. As a result, these firms have moved toward policies of earlier retirement ages for salesmen while providing maximum compensation and recognition opportunities for successful salesmen as early in their careers as possible.[96] The career path shown in Figure 4 indicates how these policies can be used in developing salesmen.

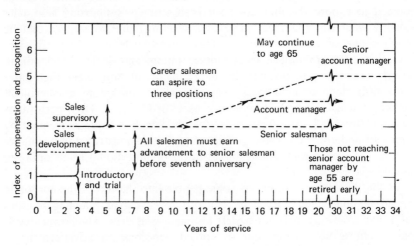

Figure 4   Sample blueprint for developing field sales organization. *Source.* Andrall E. Pearson, "Salespower Through Planned Careers," *Harvard Business Review*, Vol. 44, No. 1, January-February 1966, p. 115.

The physical demands of most selling jobs and the inevitable problems of motivation make it unlikely that most salesmen past their early fifties will be strong performers. Moreover, the possibility exists that even the most adequate salesman may level off at any age. As a result, the forced checkpoints and decisions come into play to shape the career path of the sales management candidate and to maintain high standards for career salesmen. As can be seen in Figure 4, the flow of salesmen comes from

[96] *Ibid.,* pp. 114–115.

two manpower sources: those reaching the sales development stage who remain career salesmen; and sales supervisors who are found to be more suited to direct selling. Men at the sales development stage must earn advancement to the next higher stage (senior salesmen) before their seventh anniversary with the company or again a forced up-or-out decision is made. This policy assures the early identification and weeding out of men who are not likely to be productive over their working lives. Successful career salesmen can then aspire to three recognized promotions in sales work: senior salesman, account manager, and senior account manager. Beyond these promotions senior salesmen and account managers cannot go; they retire early, leaving the selling job to younger men. Senior account managers may remain employees till 65 in recognition of their role as pivotal men in the sales organization.[97]

Early retirement is a sound remedy and consistent with policies affecting commercial airline pilots and members of the armed forces. With expanding social security benefits and liberalized industrial pension plans the basis for early retirement is already in motion in America. By using early retirement together with a grand design for sales manpower planning and human resource development, organizations are provided with tools for inventorying the human assets, controlling the developmental process, minimizing manager drift on manpower decisions, and building and retaining a competent work force.[98] When the grand design is used as an essentially qualitative complement to the quantitative sales manpower projection techniques discussed at the beginning of the chapter, the sales manpower planner has placed in his hands rational and practical tools for developing and perpetuating competent human resources. Indeed, the concepts set forth may be applied with minor alterations to diverse functions and organizations totally unconnected with sales. In any event, the tools hold great promise for manpower planners concerned with sales and marketing manpower.

CONCLUSIONS

In this chapter we have analyzed sales manpower and sales training from a number of standpoints. We have considered the origins of sales training and the mystique of salesmanship. We have shown that the behavioral sciences have provided some insight into salesmanship, mainly by suggesting that selected psychological and social psychological concepts can be applied to salesman–customer interaction. These insights are more intellectually respectable than the trite selling formulas (such as AIDA and

[97] *Ibid.*
[98] *Ibid.*, pp. 115–116.

PESOS) but need to be shored up, made more explicit, and increasingly operationalized if they are to be of practical assistance to the salesman and of theoretical value to the student of behavioral science in selling.

Manpower-planning techniques should be closely integrated with the prevailing conceptions of how salesmen, sales managers, and higher-level sales-marketing executives are to be developed. It is possible to pinpoint career paths in sales and marketing and to construct a grand design that reflects the integrity of sales manpower planning and the development of sales and marketing personnel.

Education and training programs for these types of employees are well known and extensively used in America. Although these programs vary greatly in content, scope, profundity, methodology, and the like, they share with other programs many common features. The use of selling formulas, training of dealers, stress on service and selling, and recent interest in communicating marketing concepts and orientation typify contemporary sales training efforts in industrial organization.

There is a growing tendency to centralize the sales manpower development function, guiding and controlling it with concrete, fact-founded policies, and making it a direct concern of top management. Only the strength of the American economy in recent years has spared many companies the worst consequences of outdated and haphazard methods of developing their sales manpower.[99] Steps need to be taken to get a better understanding of why the salesmen's image is poor in America and what can be done to correct the circumstances that cause it. Barring this, the spectre of Willy Loman may continue to drive off potential salesmen and thereby perpetuate the prevalence of recruitment and selection problems that hamper sales manpower development.

In many organizations the old-time salesman—the story-telling, hard-living, back-slapping hawker—has faded away. He has been replaced by the sales representative who is the market manager of his territory, who knows how to sell competitively and serve his customers as a kind of educator. He is a problem solver aware of the needs of the customer and skilled in persuasion and interpersonal communication. This changing character of the salesman's role came to light in the early fifties, gathered momentum in the late fifties, and by the late sixties became well accepted.[100] The task of the manpower planner who works with sales personnel is to assist the employing organization in developing people for the new world of selling.

[99] *Ibid.*, p. 116.
[100] Thompson, *op. cit.*, p. 21.

CHAPTER *13*

Public Policy on Manpower, Training, and Vocational Education

There is little doubt that technology has created a new relationship between man, his education, and his work, in which education is placed squarely between man and his work. Although this relationship has traditionally held for some men and some work, modern technology has advanced to the point where the relationship may now be said to exist for all men and for all work.[1] Thus all the arguments that have been mustered about industrial education are, in an essential way, arguments about the kind of role industry and large-scale organizations should play in American life. This long-debated question has left a series of contradictory assumptions in its wake, and industrial educators, like other Americans, have fashioned their own special views of the country partly out of such materials.[2]

In this chapter we review the growth of the principal federal legislation enacted to conserve and develop human resources. We point out the key features of selected laws as they have a bearing upon industry. Emphasis is about equally placed between older legislation dealing with education and human resources and the more recent manpower-planning and retraining legislation.

Table 1 summarizes the main legislation and its date of enactment. It should be a useful guide to the reader through the welter of laws. The plethora of legislation since 1961 provides ample support to labelling the decade of the 1960s as the manpower revolution decade.

The reason we discuss public policy in the context of manpower planning and the development of human resources is to show how it has evolved

[1] Grant Venn, *Man, Education, and Work,* American Council on Education, Washington, 1964, p. 1.
[2] Berenice M. Fisher, *Industrial Education,* University of Wisconsin Press, Madison, 1967, p. 3.

Table 1 A List of American Legislation on Manpower, Training, and Vocational Education

Legislative Act	Year of Enactment
Morrill	1862
Hatch	1887
Second Morrill	1890
Smith-Lever	1914
Smith-Hughes	1917
George-Reed	1929
George-Ellzey	1934
Bankhead-Jones	1935
George-Dean	1936
Fitzgerald (National Apprenticeship)	1937
G.I. Bill of Rights (Servicemen's Readjustment)	1944
George-Barden	1946
Employment	1946
National Defense Education	1958
Area Redevelopment	1961
Manpower Development and Training	1962
Vocational Education	1963
Higher Education Facilities	1963
Economic Opportunity	1964
Nurse Training	1964
Elementary and Secondary	1965
Higher Education	1965
Health Professions Educational Assistance	1965
Allied Health Professions Personnel Training	1966
Education Professions Development	1967
Higher Education Amendments	1968
Health Manpower	1968
Vocational Education Amendments	1968

over the agricultural, mechanical, and human resources eras into what we might now consider the post-New Frontier–Great Society Era. In fact, the latter era is perhaps behind us already and we are now entering a new period of the 1970s for which an appropriate term has yet to be devised. The 1970s may be the years of the fruition of the manpower revolution.

Yet, there is little doubt that a facade of affluence and abundance hides the spreading blight of social crisis in America, a set of problems compounded by insufficient economic growth, an identifiable hard-core unemployed, increasing racial tensions, student rebellions, discontent over American foreign policy, swelling public welfare rolls, chronically depressed areas, an expanding ratio of youth to the total population, and a growing disparity of educational opportunity. At the center of this crisis is a system of education that has failed in many respects to prepare all individuals for a new world of work in an advanced technological society.[3]

The social problem concept provides a particularly meaningful framework for this chapter because problems in manpower planning and human resource development have become increasingly under scrutiny since 1960. There is no question that these are key problem areas. The ameliorative values that are thought to be involved are expressed in a train of legislation involving education and training that was enacted during the Kennedy and Johnson administrations.

Although all the legislation enacted by the states and the federal government in the 19th century could be cited as prolegomena to the chapter, it is most fruitful for our purposes to review only the leading federal laws enacted prior to the 1960s and to concentrate upon those enacted more recently rather than those of isolated historical interest, except where a review of precedents assists in understanding problems and issues of the present. Specialists in manpower planning and human resource development in industry are most directly concerned with the more recent laws because this legislation must be understood as it applies to organizations today. In turn, the well-versed manpower specialist will probably want to formulate a position for himself or his organization in respect to present and proposed public policy changes so that possible legislation of the future can be influenced. The myriad of state and local laws should be examined by manpower specialists in their particularity to determine more specifically the legal norms that apply to any given geographical location in which he finds himself.

BACKGROUND ON VOCATIONAL EDUCATION

The concept of "vocation" in the manpower field is not new. People have always had to make certain career choices and have tended to dignify that choice by referring to it as a calling or vocation. But it should be noted that until fairly recent times a person's occupation was largely determined by birth. Whether the person became a minister, a craftsman, or a farmer, he recognized his vocation as something permanent or for life. Since the life's work of the son was usually the same as his father's, the son learned the rudiments of that work from his father and from other men in the community, generally by "pickup" or on-the-job methods, involving observation, imitation, and personal initiative. In the larger commercial

[3] Venn, *op. cit.,* p. 157.

centers a few skills were transmitted in a more organized manner, as through formal apprenticeship.[4]

The state of vocational affairs was well suited to a society whose institutions were based on permanency. But beginning in the 16th Century and accelerating in the next 200 years, reaching full tilt perhaps during 19th and 20th centuries, a countertrend developed, a trend suggested by the word "change." Change rather than permanency became the mark of any institution that was to survive, and the Industrial Revolution brought great changes between man and his work. The father-son "pickup" method of vocational preparation was soon swept away. In a factory and office system geared to change and marked by specialization of function, the son was not necessarily going to do the same work his father had done. Nor with the spread of mechanical and technological innovation could there be any guarantee that the father knew and could pass on to his son sufficient skills so that the latter could ply his trade through a life of changing work. In essence, the son needed new training, and he needed to obtain it by means of a new setting. These needs gave rise to a new form of education which was vocational in orientation. Spreading rapidly throughout Europe in the early 19th century, "vocational education" came to the United States at the same time but it remained for the passage of the Morrill Act in 1862 to stimulate any real start in its diffusion.[5]

As we noted earlier in the book, European society found relatively early that its limited natural resources demanded that greater attention be paid to the development and utilization of its human resources. America, on the other hand, had great natural resources. This country's commercial life centered on the rich and seemingly inexhaustible resources of the forest, mine, field, and sea. As a supplier of raw materials rather than as a processer, the United States could presumably afford to neglect the development of human skills and still remain prosperous. At the same time, many of the needed skills in the crafts and trades were readily brought to our shores by immigrants. In short, the economic motivation toward establishing vocational education in the United States was missing for many years.[6]

Another important reason retarding the growth of vocational education involved the pattern of education itself during much of the 19th century. Much of the curricula of this era was tied to classical studies. The purpose of education, as seen by those involved in it, was to preserve and extend the general culture. They opposed other types of education.

But as much as this opposition from the prevailing power structure in-

---

[4] *Ibid.*, pp. 38–39.
[5] *Ibid.*, pp. 39–41.
[6] *Ibid.*, p. 43.

hibited the growth of vocational influences in the schools, it also produced another type of blockage from below to such a growth. The self-made man of the shop or farm had a distrust of any attempt to mix his practical ways with the prevailing pattern of education. Thus, despite the increasing frequency of calls for more useful and practical education, there was little support on his part for such education. The great majority of the vocational education institutions that were set up before the Civil War thus failed because there was a lack of both students and community acceptance.[7]

Given this general background, let us turn in the next sections of the chapter to a description of the principal legislation that was enacted from 1862 to the present time, a period of more than 100 years, which totally changed the picture we have sketched to this point.[8]

THE MORRILL ACT OF 1862

The slow evolution of vocational education which we have been discussing provides a backdrop for the enactment of one of the most revolutionary pieces of legislation enacted in the history of the United States. The Morrill Act was signed by President Abraham Lincoln in 1862. The Act provided grants of land to endow, support, and maintain state colleges devoted to the agricultural and mechanical arts "in order to promote the liberal and practical education of the industrial classes in the several pursuits and professions of life." The states also could not exclude other scientific and classical studies, including military tactics, from the curriculum. Under the terms of the Act, the states received a grant of 30,000 acres of federal land for each member of Congress. Income from the sale of the land was intended to provide an endowment to support colleges to teach agriculture and engineering subjects. However, toward the end of the 19th century the land grant colleges took positive action to establish special departments for training manpower for business and industry, the University of California at Berkeley being the first such land grant institution to acknowledge this new responsibility by founding a College of Commerce in 1898.[9]

The Morrill Act was passed neither on the crest of an inexorable wave of public opinion nor as a result of pressure from powerful interest groups. On the contrary, most farmers were ignorant of its meaning and even of its passage. No significant industrial support of the Act is recorded. Educators had almost no voice in its passage. Lincoln had no recorded opinions on the law. Historians agree that neither Senator Justin Morrill, the son of a

[7] *Ibid.*, pp. 43–44.
[8] For a more detailed analysis of this time period, see Fisher, *op. cit.*, pp. 3–228.
[9] Venn, *op. cit.*, pp. 43–44.

blacksmith and farmer who sponsored the bill, nor the influential Senator Benjamin Wade, who guided it through Congress, had any clear idea of the Act's educational implications. Apparently passage was sparked by a vaguely defined need to do something for the farmer, who had been over-looked in the legislative largesse of earlier Congresses, and to provide a framework within which officers and engineers could be trained for the war effort in the War Between the States.[10] There was clearly a social problem orientation present.

Despite the unpromising beginnings of the Morrill Act, it had many salutary long-range effects. It was the keystone in the development of about 70 institutions of higher learning in 50 states, many of which are today centers of great learning and prestige. These institutions provided the initial leadership, training, and research in fields that have since proven to be of great importance in the nation's growth. Beyond this, though, they induced a major redirection in the pattern of American education with at least five implications for subsequent vocational and technical education. First, a liberal and practical education was prescribed under the Act. Classical studies were integrated into curricula that were patently voca-tional, and both were to be accommodated without any sense of inferiority. Second, the Act opened the doors of higher education to a far wider public, removing forever the idea of a single classical-type education for a select few. Third, the Act gave important status to the mechanical arts and agriculture. The Act greatly changed the college-level teaching of these courses and of the other sciences, for now science was to be taught as an instrument for molding the social environment and not merely for its own sake. Fourth, the new form of education broke through the suspicions and fears of education held by both businessmen and farmers. Vocational edu-cation was accepted at the college level, which later had much significance in extending vocationalism into the public schools. Fifth, the role of the agricultural colleges in improving agriculture in the United States was so dramatic and so widely recognized that this new form of education came to be accepted as vital to the national welfare and as a spur to economic growth.[11]

The years between the end of the Civil War and the outbreak of World War I were ones of unprecedented growth for the United States and of spirited controversy concerning the role of vocationalism in education. The details of the story need not concern us here. However, a few of the more salient features must be pointed out in order to complete our analysis of public policy toward manpower, training, and vocational education.

[10] *Ibid.*
[11] *Ibid.*, pp. 44–45.

VOCATIONALISM BETWEEN THE CENTURIES

As we have seen, vocationalism reached into the colleges more than 100 years ago with the Morrill Act but took longer to be introduced at the high-school level. One reason is that American colleges from their earliest days through the 19th century enrolled a teen-age student body, students at a stage of the life cycle when they were most susceptible to learning the kinds of skills demanded by society at the time. Considering the age of the students, the content of the courses, and the level of instruction, the early land-grant colleges performed a function similar to that of a comprehensive high school today.[12]

It should be recalled that the high school of the 19th century was not necessarily a four-year institution and was quite different in social function from contemporary high schools. Many high-school graduates were young-sters from the grammar schools who had been rapidly moved through one or two years of the feeder schools that most colleges found necessary to maintain at the time. But, whether the high school was one or four years, its purpose was college preparatory. It was not terminal in function. It was simply the step in the educational ladder between the elementary school and higher education. For example, in 1870 eight out of ten high-school graduates entered college, where six of them ultimately received degrees. There were more than twice as many college graduates in the United States as there were people with high-school diplomas only.[13]

Between 1880 and 1920 this state of affairs was drastically changed. Beginning in 1880, more and more young people entered high school, and an increasing number remained in high school to graduate. After 1880 census figures show a doubling of both total enrollment and graduates for every decade that followed, up through 1930. On the other hand, college enrollments in this time period grew much more slowly.[14] In the period since 1930, and particularly since the end of World War II in 1945, we have seen the unprecedented growth of college enrollments. However, this is getting ahead of our main theme, namely, the growth of vocationalism.

Diffusion of High Schools

The growth and changing role of the high school had a profound effect on American higher education, and especially on land grant colleges. As the number of high-school graduates increased and as the colleges became

[12] *Ibid.*, pp. 45–46.
[13] *Ibid.*, p. 46.
[14] *Ibid.*

better established, they were able to require a four-year high-school course for admission. With a better prepared and more mature student body, colleges were able to upgrade their work substantially. Also, the growth of graduate study in the United States during the 1880s showed the land-grant colleges how much basic work needed to be done in agriculture- and industry-related studies. As a result, the new emphasis on research and graduate work exerted an upward pull on the undergraduate curricula. Thus, during the 1880s courses in farming became courses in agricultural science, and the mechanical arts evolved into engineering. In this way, the colleges blazed the vocational trail, but, as they advanced the level of their work into the highly skilled and professional areas, they left a vacuum in the field of middle-level vocational preparation.[15]

In retrospect, it was logical that this educational vacuum would be filled by the emerging new type of high school. If, indeed, vocational preparation for middle-level skills was a legitimate and necessary educational function, properly discharged during the terminal phases of the student's formal education and while he was in his late teens, then the high school should have taken up this societal function that the land-grant colleges had performed over the first two or three decades of their existence. But this transition did *not* take place because politics, pedagogy, and the pressures of tradition and status stood in the way. Over the span of the next three decades, however, the pressure to fill this middle-level skill vacuum was built up until finally society demanded that it be filled by the schools.[16] The emerging one- and two-year postsecondary technical institutes and community and junior colleges also were founded to fill the vacuum that had become obvious.

The Vocationalism Issue

During the decades from 1890 to 1910 vocationalism was one of the hottest issues in education. The failure of educators during that period to agree on the place of vocationalism in the schools was to leave a heavy mark on the kind of vocational education which ultimately was put in the schools. It was a problem to which John Dewey directed much penetrating thought. Sensing the inherent danger of a developing dualism in the educational system, Dewey strongly urged the integration of vocational education in the general school program. He stressed the benefits that would accrue to both forms of education, to the worker-citizen, and to the democratization of industry. His voice was not influential, and the more pragmatic vocationalists began to advocate a separate public vocational high-school system, one accommodating a separate kind of education in which work

[15] *Ibid.*, pp. 46–47.
[16] *Ibid.*, p. 47.

efficiency in an industrial democracy would be held more important than the cultural values of education. At the same time, management and organized labor divided sharply over vocational education. To management, vocational training in the schools was not only a valuable source of skilled manpower but also a way toward freeing itself from the growing control of apprenticeship by unions. Conversely, organized labor from its top leadership down to the rank and file saw such training in the schools as an attempt by management to break unions by using young people to undermine the hard-won gains achieved by adults. As a result, much of the history of the early vocational schools involved ticklish attempts to tread a line that would retain the support (both political and financial) of industry and organized labor (who controlled the needed instructors and the entry of graduates into the skilled-labor market).[17]

Similar kinds of related battles were also being fought on the farms. Although the total debate and actual educational accomplishment lagged a decade or two behind what was being done in the cities, some legislation was enacted to assist rural people by expanding the extension and demonstration programs of the land grant colleges. For example, the passage of the Hatch Act in 1887 and the Second Morrill Act in 1890 had important implications for the establishment of experiment stations, increased appropriations, and rural extension educational activities. Also, during the 1880s about two dozen states set up farmers' institutes at the high-school level, which became important forerunners of vocational education for rural America. In the following decades there were periods of still more growth and debate, with the land-grant colleges and farmers' institutes consolidating their footholds.[18] The Smith-Lever Act of 1914 established a system of cooperative extension services for adults. The Bankhead-Jones Act of 1935 greatly increased land-grant college appropriations.

Between 1900 and 1910 the population of the United States increased sharply from 76 million to more than 92 million people. The gross national product doubled. Industrial production increased dramatically. Along with these important social and economic changes came new demands from both the factory and the farm for skilled workers and managers. Up to 1900 much of this demand had been satisfied by the steady stream of skills provided by immigration; but the immigrants who entered the United States between 1900 and 1910 were largely people from Southern Europe, Russia, and Eastern Europe, few of whom possessed the skills demanded by the changing economy. Thus, by the early 1900s the need for skilled manpower became critical, and the country turned to its school system for an answer. Educational decisions had to be made during those years and

[17] *Ibid.*, pp. 51–52.
[18] *Ibid.*, pp. 52–53.

were made, not because of an educational consensus but because societal pressure was strong to get an educational job done. The traditional thinking on the goals and structure of high-school education was broken through by means of an extraordinary remedy for that time that had previously been used only on the colleges, namely, federal legislation.[19]

Management, organized labor, and agriculture all apparently stood to gain by the spread of vocational education. Yet, there was antipathy between these three blocs in American society which stifled the evolution of vocational education. For example, management and organized labor could not agree on urban programs and had little interest in rural programs. Rural-dominated state legislatures were not interested in voting money for vocational programs since most of the eligible schools would be in the cities. It took the work of a number of forward-looking educators, as well as several landmark studies, to influence public opinion sufficiently, as well as legislators, to open up state-level programs of vocational education. A score of states took action to develop vocationalism in the public schools, and the manual arts movement in education finally took hold.

By 1910 it was quite obvious that considerable progress had been made in gaining legislative recognition in the states but that more had to be done to establish educational plans and programs which held the key to coming to terms with the emerging new society. It was thought by some educators and by those active in the various movements in vocational education that federal aid was the answer to the perceived pressing national need. Some educators were stating that since the land-grant colleges had received their share of such federal assistance, why should not vocational education at the secondary level also obtain federal aid? This belief was an audacious conception at the time because almost the entire educational community was convinced that education was a state responsibility. Moreover, it was believed that, in any event, federal aid would mean federal control, an argument which has persisted since that time and has only recently been attenuated with the far-reaching programs of the 1960s.[20]

Vocational Commission Report

After 1910 there was considerable effort to obtain legislative support, and vocational education bills were introduced in Congress repeatedly (as they had been since 1906) until finally the Magna Carta of vocational education in the United States was stated. The latter is generally considered to be the Report of the Commission on National Aid to Vocational Education, which was authorized under a bill signed by President Woodrow Wilson prior to World War I. The report of the Commission outlined the

[19] *Ibid.*, p. 53.
[20] *Ibid.*, pp. 55–56.

need for a national program of support for vocational education in the United States and sharply showed the great need for farmers and industrial employees to obtain the skills required in their respective lines of work. Interesting comparisons were made with Germany to show that in Bavaria alone there were more trade schools than in the United States, a relevant precursor to the arguments made in the late 1950s that the United States had to catch up with Russia on scientific and technical education after the launching of Sputnik. The report of the Commission went on to describe the other economic needs for vocational education at the time. It suggested that by inadequate provision for vocational education the United States was despoiling the soil, wasting human resources in pools of underemployed and unemployed, hindering the growth of wage-earning power, restricting the quality and quantity of product output, raising prices with wasteful production techniques, holding down economic growth, and jeopardizing the nation's position in the world market. All these arguments were couched in bread-and-butter terms and were designed to attract the attention of industry, organized labor, farmers, consumers, conservationists, and nationalists.[21]

The Commission also felt that there was a need to democratize education, to recognize different tastes and abilities, to connect culture with utility through learning-by-doing and education with life through purposeful and useful training in the schools. It also recommended federal-state assistance to a cooperative program of vocational education on the secondary-school level (or, as it was stated, in schools "of less than college grade"). Teacher salary and training costs were to be federally supported. However, the cost of facilities and maintenance was to be borne by the states. A minimum of 50 percent of schoolday time was to be given to shop work on a useful or productive basis. Agricultural, industrial, trade, and home economics courses and offerings were to be supported.[22]

The Report of the National Commission on Aid to Vocational Education received a good press, and plans were laid to push passage of the recommended legislation when Congress convened in 1915. However, for reasons not entirely clear, the bill lay in Congressional pigeonholes for a couple of years and was finally not enacted until 1917 when talk became more frequent about the need to "catch up with the Germans" in the training of workers for the war effort. The vocational education bill was recognized as a factor in "national preparedness." Under this head of steam the bill was passed in February 1917 and signed by the President two months before the United States entered World War I.[23]

[21] *Ibid.*, pp. 57–58.
[22] *Ibid.*
[23] *Ibid.*, pp. 58–59.

THE SMITH-HUGHES ACT OF 1917 AND
SUBSEQUENT LEGISLATION

As we have seen, traditionally the American formal educational system has not sought to equip any large proportion of students with specific skills usable in the labor market. The emphasis has been essentially on a well-rounded general education and preparation for college. Interestingly, the final push for adoption of the most significant early piece of legislation in the field of vocational education at the secondary level was supplied by the United States Chamber of Commerce when its membership by referendum vote endorsed federal grants for vocational education.[24]

The Smith-Hughes Act of 1917, in addition to a series of measures passed in the succeeding years to reinforce and extend it, has been the initial basis for public secondary-level education in the United States. The Act provided a grant in perpetuity to the states of more than $7 million a year for the promotion of vocational education in agriculture, trade and industrial subjects, and home economics. Within three years enrollment of students in federally subsidized programs doubled, and total program expenditures, including state and local funds, had quadrupled.[25]

The passage of the Smith-Hughes Act was received with great joy by the proponents of vocational education in the United States, and the momentum of their efforts brought the provisions of the Act swiftly into reality. Because few states had had any experience with vocational education and the Smith-Hughes Act offered categorical aid only within narrowly defined limits, the subsequent federal influence in the development of state programs was very strong. Continued Congressional support seemed to assure continuing appropriations, and the passage of compulsory school attendance laws in each of the states by 1923 brought larger and larger numbers of students into the program. It was an exciting age of growth for vocational education, and the future promised nothing but better things to come.[26]

In 1929 the George-Reed Act was passed. This was the first amendment to the Smith-Hughes Act and added $1 million annually to expand vocational education in agriculture and home economics. When this act lapsed in 1934, the George-Ellzey Act was passed, which upped the supplemen-

[24] Sar A. Levitan, *Vocational Education and Federal Policy,* Upjohn Institute for Employment Research, Kalamazoo, 1963, pp. 1–3.

[25] Walter M. Arnold and Edgar E. Stahl, "Vocational and Technical Education," in Robert L. Craig and Lester R. Bittel, eds., *Training and Development Handbook,* McGraw-Hill, New York, 1967, pp. 397–398.

[26] Venn, *op. cit.,* pp. 59–60.

tary funds to $3 million and expanded support for trade and industrial training. This 1934 Act was succeeded in 1936 by the George-Dean Act which added $14 million to the basic $7 million Smith-Hughes appropriation. The funds were authorized on a continuing basis, and, for the first time, distributive occupations were to receive support. The increases in funds came, remarkably enough, during a period of great pressure for governmental economy. These were depression years when the United States Office of Education itself had its meager funds cut by 33 percent. Credit for securing the funding of this legislation is usually attributed to the American Vocational Association (AVA), which has maintained to this day the vocational education tradition of political activism that motivated the enactment of the Smith-Hughes Act in 1917.[27]

In 1937, the National Apprenticeship Act (also known as the Fitzgerald Act) authorized the Secretary of Labor to formulate labor standards for the welfare of apprentices and to cooperate with the United States Office of Education in providing related instruction. (This piece of legislation was consistent with the new Congressional interest in vocational education and was discussed in more detail in an earlier chapter where we reviewed the various facets of apprenticeship and technical training.)

In the three decades following the enactment of the Smith-Hughes Act, additional Congressional grants for vocational education were, in perspective, small. During World War II Congress put more than $100 million into a program called Vocational Education for National Defense (VEND) which, between 1940 and 1945, gave 7 million war production workers preemployment and supplementary training. The program received a great deal of justified praise, and vocational education received its reward in 1946 when Congress supplemented the $14 million George-Dean Act with the $29 million George-Barden Act. The latter act authorized funds for the same four vocational service fields (agriculture, home economics, trades and industry, and distributive occupations). Greater flexibility was allowed to the states in their programs.

Considerable sums of money also ultimately reached vocational education programs around the country through the provisions of the "G.I. Bill of Rights" or Public Law 346, 78th Congress, "The Servicemen's Readjustment Act of 1944"; and Public Law 16, 78th Congress, which provided vocational rehabilitation and training toward an employment objective for disabled veterans only.[28] Still other large amounts of money reached vocational education in subsequent extensions of modified ver-

---

[27] *Ibid.*, p. 60.

[28] *Ibid.*, pp. 60–61. For a review of the related field of vocational rehabilitation legislation, not covered in this chapter, see C. Esco Obermann, *A History of Vocational Rehabilitation in America*, Dennison, Minneapolis, 1965.

sions of the G.I. Bill to veterans of wars after World War II, such as the Korean conflict and the Vietnam War.

The early 1950s were undoubtedly years of beleaguerment for vocational education. As the war veterans completed their education, many inadequate programs foundered. At this time, the overall success of America's international political efforts and a rising economy of full employment were taken to vindicate the work of our educational system and, in particular, reinforced the position of those favoring its general or liberal arts orientation. The federal school aid controversy was at its height, and vocational education as a conspicuous instance of federal aid to secondary education was caught up in the argument. Heavy spending on the Korean conflict brought demands for cutbacks in domestic spending, and states' righters asserted that the Federal Government should get out of the program of support for vocational education altogether. The endorsement of business and organized labor was lukewarm. Against these forces the AVA rallied its legislative allies, and the vocational education program scraped through with no significant expansion except in 1956 when practical nursing and fishery trades were added to the George-Barden Act.[29]

THE NATIONAL DEFENSE EDUCATION ACT OF 1958

The contributions of science and invention in recent years have greatly increased the need for the systematic training of technicians and scientific manpower by creating great numbers of new jobs and at the same time modifying the requirements of old jobs. From a demand for manipulative skills to which vocational education could be addressed, the trend in occupational requirements has been toward a demand for technical knowledge and the ability to apply the acquired knowledge intelligently. Consistent with this trend, in 1958, Congress passed the National Defense Education Act which was another amendment of the George-Barden Act.[30]

This act brought the first significant addition to the American vocational education program since the passage of the Smith-Hughes Act some 40 years earlier. Under Title VIII of the National Defense Education Act (NDEA), federal funds were made available for the training of individuals designed to fit them for useful employment as highly skilled technicians in recognized occupations requiring scientific knowledge and in fields necessary for the national defense. The new title contemplated the support of area vocational education programs, that is, programs conducted by high-school and post-high-school institutions of less than college grade serving

[29] Venn, *op. cit.,* pp. 60–61.
[30] Bernard C. Nye, "A History of Vocational Education," *Delta Phi Epsilon Journal,* Vol. 8, No. 1, November 1965, p. 5.

more than one school district. Because of these restrictions, the program had considerable difficulty in getting under way; and, in fact, this title went out of existence with the passage of the Vocational Education Act of 1963. NDEA is notable today for the educational balls it started rolling more than a decade ago.

The program for area vocational education became Title III of the George-Barden Act of 1946, as later amended in the Vocational Education Act of 1963, and was intended to broaden and strengthen support for scientific and technical training and retraining for high school youths and adults. Other important titles in the NDEA are, however, still in existence, such as those pertaining to the student loan program, strengthening of elementary- and secondary-school instruction in a number of fields, graduate fellowships, efforts to improve counseling services for high-school youngsters, programs to strengthen language development, research into and demonstration of communications media for instructional use, and institutes for teachers and other school personnel.[31]

THE VOCATIONAL EDUCATION ACT OF 1963

In many respects 1963 was the most exciting and important year in the history of vocational education. After a one-year study by a special presidential panel (the first such study since the one which preceded the Smith-Hughes Act in 1914), Congress enacted new legislation which contained major departures in vocational education, major amendments to the Smith-Hughes and George-Barden Acts, and authority for a completely new program unfettered by the restrictions of the older legislation.[32]

The purpose of the Vocational Education Act of 1963 was to assist the states to maintain, extend, and improve existing programs of vocational education, to develop new programs of vocational education, and to provide part-time employment for youths who needed the earnings from such employment to continue their vocational training on a full-time basis. This act was the first legislation in the vocational-technical field that was people-oriented rather than occupation oriented. The emphasis in the Act was upon individual preparation for gainful employment and for continually keeping manpower abreast of the skills and knowledge needed to function in the world of work.[33]

The objectives of the new Act specified that: vocational and technical programs would be geared to the real needs of the labor market; training

[31] Wilbur J. Cohen, "National Defense Education Act: An Idea That Grew," *American Education,* Vol. 4, No. 8, September 1968, pp. 2–3. See also Joyce Rothschild, "The NDEA Decade," *American Education,* Vol. 4, No. 8, September 1968, pp. 4–7.

[32] Venn, *op. cit.,* p. 62.

[33] Arnold and Stahl, in Craig and Bittel, eds., *op. cit.,* p. 399.

would be provided across the whole range of occupations in the labor market, except for professional occupations that require a Bachelor's or higher degree; training programs would be provided at all levels of ability; vocational education would be offered in all kinds of institutions, public and private; evaluation could be required at every level of responsibility; and an allotment of 10 percent of each year's funds would be set aside for research and development.[34] Thus these programs would benefit students in high school; those who have dropped out of high school and are unemployed; those who have completed high school but seek specialized training; those who suffer from cultural and economic handicaps; employed adults who desire to upgrade their skills and technical knowledge; and people of all ages who must learn new skills to earn their living.

The programs were to be established in public school systems; nonprofit agencies and institutions; vocational education departments of high schools; specialized vocational high schools; vocational-technical schools, both secondary and postsecondary; junior and community colleges; and four-year colleges and universities, both public and private.

Training for any occupation, except the professions, that was realistic in terms of present and future employment opportunities could be given. There was to be close cooperation between management, organized labor, and the public employment services on both the state and local levels to make certain that the training was geared to economic reality and to prevent unemployment by offering training ahead of demand and for meeting the immediate needs of those unemployed.

The Act authorized grants of federal funds to help the states maintain, extend, and improve vocational education; to develop new programs; to promote research and experimentation; and to provide teacher training and the development of up-to-date instructional materials and curricula. The Act also authorized pilot programs for experimentation with residential vocational schools and for work-study programs for youths who needed money to stay in school on a full-time basis. The Smith-Hughes and George-Barden Acts were continued and amended by the VEA. Federal grants under these acts were in addition to funds provided in the Vocational Education Act of 1963, which was authorized to spend $225 million per year beginning in 1967 and the years thereafter.[35] The actual sums spent were considerably less due to cutbacks caused by the expense of the Vietnam War.

An important provision in the 1963 VEA is the authority to use federal funds for the construction of area vocational-technical school facilities.

[34] *Ibid.*
[35] U.S. Department of Health, Education, and Welfare, *The Vocational Education Act of 1963,* Government Printing Office, Washington, 1965, pp. 4–6.

This concept was earlier established in the NDEA, as we noted. Leaders in vocational education recognized that small independent school units, which usually operated on an extremely limited tax base, could not separately offer the varieties of curricula which were needed to serve both school-age youth and the adults in a community. Cooperative curriculum planning among adjoining area schools could result in programs to serve all age groups interested in education below the professional level. The Act specified that at least five occupational fields must be offered in each area school. The purpose was to assure that such schools would have offerings that would allow prospective students of varying interests a reasonably broad choice of the type of occupation for which they were to be trained.[36]

Although the Vocational Education Act of 1963 has been in operation now for quite a few years, a full-scale evaluation of its effectiveness has yet to be published. The increasing numbers of young people entering the labor market each year, the vast technological changes resulting in changing employment conditions, and the depletive migration of people from farms to urban areas are a few of the reasons that there is a need for modern vocational-technical education and for evaluating the effectiveness of present-day legislation. Vocational education has undoubtedly now arrived on the scene and is an integral part of our system for the development of human resources.

The Vocational Education Amendments of 1968 update and restructure existing legislation and authorize large resources which will be at the disposal of state and local education agencies. They also specify new categorical allotments to assure more adequate training opportunities for two types of students needing special help to reach their maximum occupational potential. One category comprises people in urban ghetto areas and others with special handicaps (mental, physical, social, and economic). The second includes individuals seeking post-high-school education.[37]

MANPOWER SPECIALISTS AND THE VOCATIONAL EDUCATION INTERFACE

Manpower specialists in organizations need to be aware of the scope and range of these vocational education programs in the United States. Their employing organizations stand to gain by the improvement of the development of skilled manpower through vocational programs available in the

---

[36] Arnold and Stahl, in Craig and Bittel, eds., *op. cit.*, pp. 399–400.

[37] *Manpower Report of the President, January 1969,* Government Printing Office, Washington, 1969, pp. 85–86. For background see Rupert N. Evans et al., *Education for Employment* (Policy Papers in Human Resources and Industrial Relations, No. 14), Institute of Labor and Industrial Relations, University of Michigan, Ann Arbor, 1969.

community and by reducing training expense. Manpower specialists should utilize the services of high schools and community colleges by encouraging employees to enroll in courses in those institutions which will assist them in their employment. In fact, manpower specialists in organizations can have a decided impact upon educational curriculum planning in vocational schools and reduce the training expense of their employers by encouraging vocational schools and community colleges to offer job-performance-related courses after working hours that assist employees in carrying out their present work and preparing for positions in prospect. The subsidization of vocational education by the federal government means that any courses which are developed in response to requests from manpower specialists and made available to employees are likely to be less costly than similar courses developed, staffed, and offered inside the employing organization.

Vocational education should also be of interest to training directors in all types of organizations because it supports training for an increasingly large number of positions except those that are specifically professional.

The manpower specialist and training director can also be expected in the future to be asked increasingly to serve on advisory committees composed of representatives from management, organized labor, and the government which meet to make certain that education and training programs offered under vocational education are geared to economic reality, can prevent unemployment by offering training ahead of demand, and do in fact meet the immediate needs of the unemployed. Obviously, in order to function effectively as an advisory committee member, the manpower specialist must be fully informed of the scope of vocational education and be able to provide advice on programming that is informed by the needs and requirements of the employer's occupational structure. Lastly, the manpower specialist as the linking pin between the private and public aspects of manpower policy cannot provide meaningful advice unless he is well steeped in the knowledge needed to make proposals on interface relations in vocational education. With projected vocational education enrollments rising from less than 400,000 in 1964 to 14 million by 1975 [38] the importance of this organizational linking-pin role cannot be minimized.

The manpower specialist should also take it upon himself to be aware of highlights if not the details of the vocational educational philosophy prevailing in the United States so that his thinking on policy matters in this area can be sharpened. For example, the philosophy of vocational education is characterized by uniformity. Until recently prevailing legislation prescribed what courses were to be supported and set the conditions under

---

[38] Michael Russo, "14 Million Vocational Students by 1975," *American Education*, Vol. 5, No. 3, March 1969, p. 10.

which they must be taught. This meant that vocational education tended to be uniform in character throughout the country and occupation oriented rather than people oriented. The very detailed nature of the prevailing legislation prevented federal support for a great deal of possible experimentation with new programs. Secondly, vocational education is characterized by duality. The historical antipathy of many general educators led the early vocationalists to set up separate vocational education school systems and these persist to the present time, many of which are obsolete, second-rate dumping grounds for disadvantaged minority youth or children who present "problems" to white middle-class teachers and are potential dropouts.[39] Thirdly, much vocational education is still oriented to the high-school or less-than-college grade level. The advent of area vocational schools may in the future shift the emphasis to a level beyond the high school. Fourthly, vocational education has always had a practical orientation. Fifthly, the vocational programs have typically been terminal in the sense that they are not designed for credit toward a baccalaureate degree. Sixthly, vocational education has tended to be on a track. The practical and terminal provisions of the various laws meant that the student electing the vocational program after the ninth grade was severely limiting his chances for continuing his education beyond the high school. Seventhly, farm-craft subjects have been heavily supported, primarily because of the efforts of the AVA. The emphasis upon vocational agriculture and home economics was also in part a need to boost secondary-school opportunities in rural America and partly a reflection of the power of rural interests in Congress. Eighthly, vocational education has stressed the need for fully equipped school shops operated under the guidance of a professional teacher with practical experience. In a period of comparatively slow technological change it was valid to assume that shop equipment and teachers would present few problems of obsolescence. In our era of rapid change this assumption is no longer valid. Lastly, vocational education has, as could be expected, stressed a narrow practical vocational outlook. It was implicitly assumed that the student's preparation for future retraining was not important and that the training he got was to be "vocational," that is, for life.[40]

Beginning in the 1960s there was an increasing awareness that vocational education could not be for life and that retraining was necessary to

[39] It should be noted not all vocational schools are of this type. See Benjamin C. Willis, "Education the Year Round," *Atlantic Monthly,* Vol. 215, No. 1, January 1965, pp. 83–86; John T. Shuman, "Educating for Industry," *Atlantic Monthly,* Vol. 214, No. 6, December 1964, pp. 90–93; and "Milwaukee: A Fair Deal," *Saturday Review,* Vol. 49, No. 2, January 8, 1966, pp. 54–60.

[40] Venn, *op. cit.,* pp. 58–66.

respond to some of the persistent problems of unemployment and under-employment which had been plaguing the nation for many years. The rapid pace of technological change could not be ignored any longer. Indeed, it was unconscionable that it had been ignored so long. The series of recessions in the post-World War II period, and particularly that of 1958, led to the contemporary emphasis upon the problems which characterize the manpower revolution and spawned many ideas in the realm of public policy on manpower, training, and industrial education.

THE EMPLOYMENT ACT OF 1946

Manpower specialists in organizations need to know thoroughly how another important stream of legislation developed which importantly effects the development of human resources in American society today and will have an increasing impact in the decade of the 1970s. This stream of legislation does not have its roots in vocational education legislation but rather in the Employment Act of 1946, which stresses the occupational structure of the nation in a different context.

Undoubtedly the first formal expression of a national manpower policy in the United States can be traced to the passage of the Employment Act in 1946. Congress, with the horrors of the Great Depression of the 1930s well in mind, and in anticipation of a return to high levels of unemployment at the end of World War II in 1945–46, established the postwar goal of maintaining high levels of employment in the American economy. In passing this legislation Congress committed the federal government to search for and establish policies conducive to economic stability and economic growth. The Employment Act of 1946, although it was originally designed to cope with the problem of minimizing unemployment, came, with the passage of time, to acquire something of the force of an economic institution. The President of the United States, his Council of Economic Advisors, the Congress, and in some degree the entire executive and administrative establishment of the federal government, including even the Federal Reserve Board, now function under this legislation when major economic policies are developed.[41]

To understand the Employment Act of 1946, it is beneficial, first, to review the principal provisions of the Act and then to examine briefly the legislative history behind the Act. Because the Employment Act of 1946 is closely related in subject matter to the Manpower Development and Training Act (MDTA) of 1962, we must review it to understand the MDTA. We subsequently analyze the MDTA together with a closely

[41] Arthur F. Burns, "Some Reflections on the Employment Act," *American Statistician*, Vol. 16, No. 5, December 1962, p. 10.

connected piece of legislation known as the Area Redevelopment Act of 1961 and draw the necessary points of comparison, contrast, and influence together. Our goal is to illuminate policy intent and direction as clearly as possible.

In introducing the Employment Act of 1946, Congress stated that it was the continuing policy and responsibility of the federal government to use all practical means to coordinate and utilize all resources for creating and maintaining conditions under which there will be afforded useful employment opportunities and to promote maximum employment, production, and purchasing power. Each January 20th the President is required by the Act to present his *Economic Report* to Congress setting forth, among other things, the levels of employment in the United States and the levels needed to carry out the policy of the Act, current and foreseeable trends in levels of employment, and his program and recommendations for additional legislation. A three-member Council of Economic Advisors was created to assist and advise the President, to gather and submit information, to appraise the various programs, to develop and recommend policies to foster and promote free competitive enterprise and to maintain employment, and to make and furnish studies and reports. A Joint Economic Committee, consisting of members of both houses of Congress, was also established to study and make recommendations.[42]

In the Senate version of the bill leading up to the Act, it was declared that it was the responsibility of the federal government to maintain *full* employment and *to assure* at all times sufficient opportunities to enable all men to exercise their right to continued full employment. The substitute bill of the House of Representatives, which was the bill finally adopted and made into law, rejected the term "full employment" and replaced it with "maximum employment." Thus, the goal was to be "maximum or high levels of employment." It was the theory of the House bill that employment was not the sole responsibility of the government and that industry, organized labor, and agriculture must share the burden. The role of the United States government was to promote employment by all practical means, including taxation, banking, credit and currency, foreign trade, public works, and loans.

It is rather interesting to note that not one single court case has been instituted to challenge the Employment Act of 1946 in any way and that no judicial action of any kind has ever arisen under the Act. This lack of activity can be construed to mean a number of things. Perhaps the Act is so altruistic and innocuous that no one would dare quarrel with it or even desire to attack it. Alternatively, perhaps the statute does not call for any

[42] Bertram M. Gross, "New Look for the Employment Act," *Challenge,* Vol. 11, No. 5, February 1963, pp. 10–11.

action of the type which would provoke controversy. It has been suggested that the wording of the Act is vague and that this very vagueness may be the reason that all parties are apparently satisfied.[43]

AREA REDEVELOPMENT ACT OF 1961

The Employment Act of 1946 had been on the books for 15 years before the formal expression of national manpower policy stated in it culminated in other legislation that was specifically responsive to the nagging problems of full employment and economic growth. In the post-World War II period there had been considerable unemployment (some of it episodic and some of it locally persistent) and displacement of workers attributable at least in part to automation. During this period unilateral and collectively bargained retraining plans and automation funds started to emerge on the industrial relations scene. In the presidential campaign of 1960 considerable stress was placed by presidential candidate John F. Kennedy on depressed areas and particularly West Virginia and a region surrounding it extending north-east and southwest which came to be called "Appalachia." [44]

Amidst this turmoil concerning the continued unemployment, the displacement threat of automation, and related social and economic problems, the realization grew that the National Defense Education Act and the traditional preemployment and extension programs of vocational and technical education previously discussed in the chapter were insufficient to meet the economic challenge of the new technology and the changing times. This realization led to the passage in 1961 of the Area Redevelopment Act (ARA) and, in 1962, of the Manpower Development and Training Act (MDTA). Both were enacted under the pressure of mounting technological job dislocation, both relate closely to the national-vocational-technical education effort.[45] Both are also tied back logically to the Employment Act of 1946.

The Area Redevelopment Act of 1961, essentially a program to alleviate unemployment in areas of chronic labor surplus, established a special program for the retraining of unemployed workers in depressed areas for occupations offering a reasonable expectation of employment. Among other things it authorized $4.5 million for the vocational training of unemployed and underemployed persons in designated "redevelopment areas." In its first 20 months of operation the ARA approved projects involving more

[43] "Economists Battle Past a Milestone," *Business Week*, No. 1904, February 26, 1966, p. 138. See also Burns, *op. cit.*, pp. 12–13.
[44] For background, see Harry M. Caudill, *Night Comes to the Cumberlands*, Little, Brown, Boston, 1963.
[45] Venn, *op. cit.*, p. 119.

than 15,000 trainees. Significantly, it recognized vocational training as an integral part of the attack on the problems facing distressed geographical areas.[46]

An interesting feature of both the ARA and later MDTA is the provision for payment of subsistence benefits to unemployed persons during training. Under the ARA Congress authorized annual expenditures of $5.4 million for training and $10 million for subsistence benefits, which were payable for a maximum of 16 weeks, in an amount equal to the average unemployment insurance paid in the state where the worker undertook training. Congress recognized that it would be unrealistic to expect an unemployed worker to undergo a training program without any means of subsistence. All the funds to defray ARA training came out of federal funds, and state and local government did not make any contributions to this program.[47]

Although the ARA training program had a limited impact in terms of the number of persons trained, the Act had other much broader implications. A major conceptual contribution of the ARA was that the program emphasized the relationship among existing but hitherto independent programs: employment services, including counseling and guidance, vocational education, and manpower projections. MDTA, which followed closely on the heels of ARA, further stressed the interdependence of these agencies and institutions and the need for closer cooperation if each were to succeed in carrying out its assigned mission.[48] Ever since then there has been a great debate over manpower services "delivery systems."

ARA and MDTA training programs stretched the meager public vocational-training facilities to the extreme. Programs established under these laws brought out the obvious relationship of problems among the employment service, vocational training, and job placement personnel and focused greater public attention on the inadequate scope and dubious quality of much of our public vocational education system at the time. It became obvious by the early 1960s that vocational education was a stepchild of our educational system and had often been given shabby facilities with old equipment, some of it consisting of leftovers from the National Youth Administration of the Depression of the 1930s. It is undoubtedly a tribute to vocational educators that they could adjust their programs on short notice to satisfy the increased burdens placed upon them by ARA and later MDTA.[49] Deficiencies in the vocational education system unearthed

---

[46] *Ibid.*

[47] Levitan, *Vocational Education and Federal Policy, op. cit.,* pp. 3–4.

[48] Sar Levitan, *Federal Aid to Depressed Areas,* Johns Hopkins Press, Baltimore, 1964, p. 186.

[49] *Ibid.,* pp. 186–187.

by the administration of the ARA and MDTA also influenced passage of the VEA of 1963.

ARA also tied training to economic growth and emphasized the harsh fact that American educational and vocational facilities had not kept pace in developing skills among our human resources so that they could take their places in our changing technology. As a result, significant sectors of the manpower in the United States had been left out of the mainstream of our changing economic life and needed to be reached and brought in.[50]

The limited ARA training experience also suggested the need for strengthening existing vocational education right away. It indicated that many presumably "unemployables" are salvageable when they are given the proper training opportunities. But it was also quite apparent that many, possibly most, communities in the early 1960s lacked adequate training facilities for the unemployed.[51]

Lastly, the ARA training experience indicated that some of the hard-core unemployed would not be absorbed by private industry in the immediate years ahead even assuming a higher rate of economic growth than that which prevailed in the decade before the enactment of the ARA.[52] Thus, it can be deduced that ARA served a useful purpose in pointing up some of the real problems that were preventing the development of human resources in the United States in the early 1960s and hinted that innovative programs would be necessary if these problems were to be seriously attacked and durable solutions found. ARA presaged much of the programming that came in the late 1960s after the ugly urban riots and culminated in the JOBS program of the National Alliance of Businessmen.

MANPOWER DEVELOPMENT AND TRAINING ACT OF 1962

MDTA expanded the ARA training concept by recognizing that the training needs of the new technology were nationwide and not confined solely to chronically depressed areas. The federal policy underlying MDTA was not new. The importance of a national balancing of people and jobs was, as we have seen, clearly recognized by Congress in the Employment Act of 1946. MDTA implemented the charge of the Employment Act with the commitment to improve the quality and adaptability of the manpower in the American labor force. For the first time, then, the national government's responsibility was clearly established for the full employment of manpower facing dislocation owing to technological change.[53] MDTA was

[50] *Ibid.*, p. 187.
[51] *Ibid.*
[52] *Ibid.*
[53] Venn, *op. cit.*, pp. 119–120.

undoubtedly a monumental act whose long-range value awaits careful assessment.

The provisions of MDTA are numerous, and amendments have been added to the basic legislation since 1962. In enacting the law, Congress found that there was a critical need for more and better trained manpower; that many employment opportunities remained unfilled because of a shortage of qualified personnel; and that it was in the national interest that persons be sought and trained. Congress also found that the skills of many persons had been rendered obsolete; that the problem of assuring sufficient employment would be compounded by a rapid growth of the labor force; and that many professional employees were in need of refresher courses or additional education. Based upon these premises, it was declared that the purpose of the MDTA was to require the federal government to appraise the nation's manpower requirements and resources and to develop and apply the information and methods needed to deal with the problems of unemployment resulting from automation and technological changes and other types of persistent unemployment.

In signing the Manpower Development and Training Bill in March 1962, President Kennedy stated the new law is "perhaps the most significant legislation in the area of employment" since the Employment Act was passed in 1946. The bill provided for $435 million over a three-year period which was to be used for a retraining program for the hard-core unemployed. It was expected 110,000 persons would be retrained the first year; 160,000, the second year; and 300,000, the third year. Under the program, retraining in selected skills, conducted in the states for a maximum of 52 weeks would be paid for by the Federal government for the first two years. In the third year the states would be required to match the federal grants. The unemployed who took the retraining would receive subsistence allowances approximately equal to their state unemployment insurance benefits but would be ineligible for receiving these benefits and the retraining subsistence allowances simultaneously.

The Secretary of Labor was charged with the duty of evaluating and studying programs, of assisting job development programs, and of carrying out pilot projects aimed to demonstrate the effectiveness of programs to increase the mobility of the unemployed and to place persons engaged in training. The Secretary of Labor was further required to provide the necessary programs for the selection of trainees. Agreements with the states were authorized covering payments to the trainees. The Secretary of Labor could also execute agreements with states, private agencies, employers, and unions to secure on-the-job training. A ten-man National Advisory Committee was to be appointed to make various manpower recommendations to the Secretary of Labor.

The Senate bill leading to the enactment of MDTA sought to deal with one major aspect of the problem of unemployment by enabling workers whose skills had became obsolete to receive training which would qualify them to obtain and hold jobs. The Act would also lead to the upgrading of persons already employed so that they could make a greater contribution to the national economy. Since a large part of the prevailing unemployment existed because idle workers could not be matched with available job vacancies, it was feared that structural unemployment would continue, even if the goal of maximum employment under the Employment Act of 1946 were achieved.

One of the main thrusts of the MDTA was, as previously suggested, to alleviate the problems brought about by automation and other technological changes. It was believed that it was not fair to allow the burdens of higher productivity to fall disproportionately on a few, namely, those whose jobs were eliminated. It was thought that the nation which benefits from increased productivity has the responsibility to provide the means by which displaced employees can acquire new jobs. Insofar as training which does not lead to employment is not only a waste of money but also a cause of frustration to the person trained, the bill leading to the enactment of the law was drawn to insure that the trainee would have a good chance of obtaining a job related to the training he had undertaken.

Manpower problems were viewed under MDTA as national problems, and the labor market was seen, by and large, as a national labor market. Therefore, if the nation's needs were to be met, national leadership was required. The MDTA was thought to be one method by which the federal government could meet its obligations under the Employment Act of 1946.

Under the Manpower Development and Training Act the President of the United States submits an annual *Manpower Report* to Congress in the spring of the year. This has been done annually since 1963. In addition the Secretary of Labor and the Secretary of Health, Education, and Welfare prepare separate reports covering related research and education and training activities carried out under the Act. These three documents contain interesting descriptive information as well as statistical data on program participation. The *Manpower Reports of the President,* particularly the most recent ones, constitute useful documents describing the rapidly changing panorama of programs for manpower planning and the development of human resources in the United States with emphasis upon the unemployed and the underemployed. (The earlier reports appear to be compilations of labor statistics routinely available from government agencies introduced by repetitious largely self-congratulatory progress appraisals and exhortations.) The *Manpower Report of the President* is probably now, however, the best single source of information pertaining to this subject-matter area. It should be read by every manpower specialist who desires to keep abreast of the field.

Amending MDTA

Unlike the situation of stability in respect to the Employment Act of 1946, there have been numerous changes in MDTA since its enactment. It would be well to review some of the main provisions of the law as it currently exists and then turn to the question of whether the Employment Act of 1946 and MDTA have served the purposes for which they were intended. Only a tentative answer is now possible, although, undoubtedly, manpower specialists in the future will want to analyze this matter more soberly. MDTA taken by itself is far from an answer to solving the nation's problems of manpower and work and indeed falls short of the stated goals of federal manpower policy. The reasons are several and all point to further responsibilities of the educational community for occupational and general education.[54]

As we previously suggested, MDTA expands the ARA training concept by recognizing that the training needs of the emerging technology are nationwide and not confined to chronically depressed areas. Yet, the federal policy underlying MDTA is not new. The importance of a national balancing of people and jobs was clearly recognized by Congress in the Employment Act of 1946, which charged the federal government with the responsibility of promoting maximum employment, production, and purchasing power. MDTA implements this charge with the commitment to improve the quality and adaptability of the American labor force. For the first time, the national government's responsibility is clearly established for the full employment of a labor force facing dislocation because of technological change.

MDTA was the second important piece of legislation of the Kennedy-Johnson New Frontier–Great Society antiunemployment programs and the first to survive the rigors of economic and political experience. MDTA is therefore important both for its own sake and because it established a pattern which influenced the other manpower and antipoverty programs which were enacted subsequently. The Act was passed primarily on the assumption that widespread job vacancies existed and that unemployment could be reduced by training the unemployed to fill these positions. Although MDTA has to its credit many accomplishments which more than justify their cost, its original goal is not among them. Still, tens of thousands of persons trained under the Act are employed today more steadily or have higher earnings than could have been expected had they not par-

---

[54] *Ibid.*, p. 120.

ticipated in the program. The annual *Manpower Report of the President,* required by the Act, has raised manpower policy to a level of visibility and a status second only to fiscal and monetary policy in national economic policy making. However, the *Manpower Report of the President* is unlikely to have the policy impact of the *Economic Report of the President* and has to date been given much less attention in the form of Congressional hearings. In the late 1960s the need for a *Social Report of the President* was stated by the outgoing Secretary of Health, Education, and Welfare to highlight still another facet of our progress in solving social problems.

Federal, state, and local governments are engaged in various types of manpower planning, partly as a consequence of passage of the Act. The experimental and demonstration projects completed under the Act have developed new tools for serving the disadvantaged, which have, in turn, become basic strategies in the war against poverty since the Sixties. These innovations and the earmarking of federal funds to such programs have provided leverage to pressure lethargic social welfare and associated institutions into serving population groups unfamiliar to them in new ways.[55]

MDTA was an important innovation, and the retraining concept embodied in it offered something attractive to everyone. To the economist who attributed unemployment to the changing structure of the American economy and to the fiscal conservative, MDTA was a frontal attack on the problem of unemployment. To the concerned legislator, MDTA represented direct aid to his constituents. To the economist interested in expanding demand, while convinced that training would not create jobs, MDTA provided the possibility that mismatches between available skills and job vacancies would be less likely and some expenditure on retraining as an addition to total demand would make a contribution to expanding the economy. Thus, for many reasons MDTA seemed a logical answer to some of the problems that were being experienced in the early 1960s.

It was also apparent that adult workers could not undertake training without financial support. The heart of the new legislation became full federal financing of the retraining effort for the first two years, followed by continued full federal support for on-the-job training but providing only 50 percent matching funds for institutional training of the unemployed in occupations for which there were reasonable expectations of employment. Under certain conditions heads of families could qualify for up to 52 weeks of training allowances at levels equal to the average unemployment compensation benefit in their state of residence. Limited numbers of youths aged 19 to 21 could receive training allowances of $20 per week.[56]

[55] Garth L. Mangum, *MDTA, Foundation of Federal Manpower Policy,* Johns Hopkins Press, Baltimore, 1968, pp. 1–2, 138–139.

[56] *Ibid.,* pp. 11–19.

The amendments to MDTA have been characterized by a kind of legislative "love-in": there has always been very little opposition to MDTA, and amendments have virtually sailed through Congress without opposition. Yet, its character changed importantly in the years between 1962 and 1970.

When conceived in the early 1960s, with general unemployment averaging above 6 percent and with 5 percent of married men seeking jobs, MDTA was apparently viewed by most members of Congress as a temporary recession expedient to aid the displaced experienced worker. The Act got off to a late start because of delays in appropriations, and this complication was accompanied by difficulty in identifying and enrolling a sufficient number of trainees. But rather than being a temporary phenomenon related to the initiation of the training program, securing trainees became a continuing source of concern and criticism which has still not been satisfactorily solved. One reason is that the major institutions involved in administering MDTA have had a tendency toward "creaming" built into their methodology, that is, placing persons on MDTA programs who are better qualified for work than other unemployed persons with less attractive qualifications for employers.

Creaming is well illustrated by considering the manpower activities of the state employment services. These organizations were accustomed to matching employer job orders with the most capable workers available, and they were quite capable of referring to MDTA projects only those who came seeking unemployment compensation or job referrals. The state and local employment services were neither provided with the resources nor the experience for "outreach" to ferret out those unemployed who needed such services worst but who tended to seek them least.[57] For example, substantial numbers of the hard-core unemployed in the ghettos were not reached.

In the mid-1960s the job market throughout the United States generally improved although reasonably attractive MDTA trainees were still available. But, with rising employment they were becoming a progressively smaller portion relative to the disadvantaged groups, who were becoming more visible and were a subject for increased concern because of the summer riots in many urban areas. Disturbed at the creaming propensity of the employment services and public schools, federal MDTA administrators launched their own experimental and demonstration projects. These bypassed the states, giving direct federal support primarily to private, nonprofit, community-based organizations serving various disadvantaged groups but primarily those interested in serving youth. Such programs were further endorsed by the 1965 amendments. All these youth-serving projects and the regular manpower development training projects were presenting the same message in respect to the need for literacy as a prerequisite

[57] *Ibid.,* pp. 20–21.

for known methods of occupational training. Basic education was consequently added to a number of MDTA courses. Training allowances were increased under certain conditions. The training period was ultimately expanded to 104 weeks to make possible the inclusion of the training of technicians. This provision made it possible to provide refresher training, particularly for professionals in employment where they were displaced by defense contract cancellations and military base closings. ARA training terminated in 1965, and MDTA of 1965 simply adopted the most generous provisions of ARA as well as anteceding MDTA legislation at that time.[58]

By the mid-1960s, MDTA was quite a different program in legislative direction, in administrative practice, and even in declared objectives, than it had been in 1962. In effect, an emergency recession measure designed to provide technologically displaced, experienced family heads with subsistence while they acquired new skills through either state operated vocational schools or private on-the-job training in order to fill existing job vacancies had become a permanent, wide-ranging, primarily federally financed and directed program, although one with less clearly defined objectives than the original bill. Clearly the emphasis had become that of assisting manpower with a wide variety of disadvantages to become effective competitors in the labor market. However, the provisions on professional manpower refresher, and part-time upgrading training, and the rhetoric of alleviating labor shortages indicated a trend toward a general purpose, remedial, out-of-school training program.[59]

The time span of the original MDTA was four years but for all intents and purposes the program is now permanent and will be operative in the 1970s with expiration dates providing no more than a convenient opportunity for Congressional review. The Congress has moved away from its original preference for state matching of financing toward a proposal for permanent federal funding with 10 percent "in kind" state matching requirement, which gives the Act an aura of state responsibility. However, Congress has in general given whatever authority for liberalization and expansion of MDTA which was requested but has never relinquished control over the purse strings. Requests for broadened authority under the Act have not been accompanied by corresponding requests for funding. The result has been Congressional authorization for enrichment of services but only at the price of reduction in the numbers served, leaving administrators with a difficult choice between a richer program for fewer or a leaner program for more.[60] This result also raises the question of what future public policy would be in respect to MDTA if once again large numbers of per-

[58] *Ibid.*, pp. 23–34.
[59] *Ibid.*, pp. 38–39.
[60] *Ibid.*, pp. 39–41.

sons were displaced or became unemployed for more than a limited time period. If unemployment levels in the United States were ever to again reach 5 or 6 percent, renewed attention might be given to the desirability of changing MDTA provisions so that the law would revert to its earlier purposes.

Evaluating MDTA

From the standpoint of public policy and that of private policy, linked by a common concern with manpower, it is relevant to consider the results in terms of human resources development obtained under MDTA. It can be said at the outset, however, that there have been no independent general evaluations of the act. But, there have been a number of studies of retrainees in such states as West Virginia, Tennessee, Connecticut, Massachusetts, and Michigan.[61] Most of these studies lead to the conclusion that retraining programs improve the labor market position of the trainees, trainees obtain employment in a larger proportion of cases than comparable groups of unemployed workers, and trainees believe that their training assisted them in securing employment. Among manpower experts there appears to be consensus that the overall contributions of MDTA have exceeded its costs by a margin which not only merits support but justifies its expansion.[62]

In order to evaluate MDTA in general terms, it is important to consider the goals as they have shifted over the years since 1962. The original act listed goals ranging from insuring against the burdens of automation to "staffing freedom." It is clear that the central concept was to retrain experienced adult heads of families displaced from established jobs by technological and economic change. As the employment picture brightened, the targets changed, first to youths and then to other groups, particularly minorities, facing disadvantages in competing for existing jobs. These changes had the effect of making MDTA an element in the antipoverty strategy which it still is.[63]

In addition to its primary objective of solving some of the problems of unemployment, tightening labor markets and inflationary pressures in 1965 and 1966 led to enunciation of an additional goal, namely, alleviation of labor shortages. MDTA also became a lever for changing traditional manpower and educational institutions. Although all these changing objectives can be justified by the original language of the Act, the shifting goals pres-

---

[61] See Gerald G. Somers, ed., *Retraining the Unemployed,* University of Wisconsin Press, Madison, 1968. This volume contains a number of empirical studies. See also the bibliography in the back of this book.

[62] Mangum, op. cit., pp. 77–78.

[63] *Ibid.,* p. 78.

ent problems in evaluating its general effectiveness.[64] Let us consider the extent to which the Act did achieve some of its objectives, turning first to the reduction of unemployment.

There are only two ways in which a retraining program can reduce the level of unemployment, as contrasted with facilitating the employment of particular individuals. First, the unemployed person can be trained for a job which would otherwise remain vacant. Second, employers can be motivated by the availability of trained manpower to undertake activities which they would otherwise have foregone. If the result of training is only to shift the burden of unemployment from the trainees to those who would otherwise obtain available jobs, obviously little has been accomplished.[65]

The responsiveness of employment in the United States to fiscal stimuli during and since 1964 indicates that inadequacy of demand rather than the availability of skills has been the effective restraint on economic activity. MDTA trainees who completed their training in 1963 experienced a level of placement success almost as high as that achieved in the tighter labor markets of 1966 and 1967. Had the program trained a million persons by mid-1965, the lack of job openings might have been a serious constraint. As it was, there were sufficient openings in the economy, which then had more than 70 million jobs, to absorb easily the little more than 200,000 persons who had actually completed training by the end of 1965. Regardless of these considerations, perhaps the best test of the program's success is its employment rates; and, therefore, it is worthwhile to consider the posttraining experience for institutional and on-the-job (OJT) training activities conducted under the Act because the characteristics of the trainees and their posttraining experience differ markedly in each type of program.[66]

For both institutional training and OJT there have been studies made which suggest that sizable proportions of trainees drop out before completing the training. For both types of programs it appears that those who completed the program obtained jobs and those who completed OJT remained with their contracting employers. However, these generalizations are very shaky because the studies which would support them are quite inadequate. Programs which "coupled" OJT with institutional training have also been operated but the results of these have been rather disappointing. Employers were reluctant to contract to accept particular trainees and specified numbers for OJT at the end of the institutional phase of the program.[67]

In respect to employing the disadvantaged employee, there is evidence

[64] *Ibid.*
[65] *Ibid.*, p. 79.
[66] *Ibid.*, pp. 80–81.
[67] *Ibid.*, pp. 83–93.

that the posttraining experience of some of the disadvantaged group has been improved as a consequence of the training. Specifically, OJT appears to be the least-cost means within MDTA of obtaining employment for the disadvantaged who complete OJT programs. For example, in the five years between 1962 and 1967 perhaps 250,000 low-income persons, one-half of whom were probably heads of families, were helped to raise their incomes by MDTA, most probably from below the poverty line to a little above it. However, with 9 million poor families in the United States, the dent made by MDTA programs on reducing poverty is hardly noticeable.[68]

Turning to the objective of MDTA in reducing labor shortages and combating inflation, several points should be brought out. MDTA was designed to serve the unemployed, not the labor market. Training has been provided not for occupations with manpower shortages but for those with a reasonable expectation of employment. The difference is philosophical in which ends and means are involved, but it has practical consequences. At one extreme, the occupations most likely to experience critical shortages of manpower are those requiring training time beyond the two-year legislative limit and the one-year practical limit of MDTA. Trainees can be paid for 52 weeks and in some circumstances be prevailed upon to take a two-year program, the second year of which would be without compensation. But few poor people could take such training. The new authority to provide refresher training for registered nurses and other professionals is the only significant potential contribution of the Act at the professional-technical level. Experience is insufficient to assess the results of MDTA for these kinds of manpower and womanpower.[69]

At the other extreme are occupations such as those of nurse's aid, hospital orderly, food service attendant, and custodian, which constantly suffer manpower shortages either because of low wages or poor working conditions. The turnover for such jobs is likely to be high and the demand continuous. Most of those for whom MDTA training was provided in these occupations could probably have obtained jobs without training, although the program probably served as a recruitment and placement mechanism.[70]

Every training effort adds to the total supply of skills available in the labor force of the nation. The contribution to human resources of this general upgrading process depends upon the degree to which the skills provided are relevant, durable, and transferable to other uses. MDTA has made its major contribution in being directly relevant to short-run labor market expectations and in training for jobs for which there was a current demand. The inclusion of basic education in institutional training was

[68] *Ibid.*, pp. 93–104.
[69] *Ibid.*, pp. 104–106.
[70] *Ibid.*, pp. 106–107.

probably the single most important contribution to upgrading the labor force, but it has been limited because this type of education lengthens courses and raises costs. Under these programs the individual, not the labor force, is still the focus. Thus, it could be said that the MDTA has resulted in upgrading only a relatively small proportion of the labor force involved and that this is a bonus not a primary objective.[71]

Future Perspectives on MDTA

In viewing MDTA in perspective, it is fair to say that it has placed increasing emphasis on training and jobs for the disadvantaged. In fact, many people at the national level and even more at the state and local levels complain that MDTA is simply another poverty program. They would be more pleased to see MDTA concentrating on manpower shortages and upgrading the labor force, serving the disadvantaged only as a part of the total operation. It was true when the Act was first made law that the persistence of a high unemployment rate and subsequent recognition of the plight of the disadvantagd, even with tight labor markets, kept policy makers' focus on employment as a source of income and status rather than upon manpower as an economic resource in the wealth of the nation. Further experience proved the effectiveness of broader economic policy measures, but it also introduced a certain modesty into expectations of forecasting ability and political wisdom. The complexities of labor markets are as great as those of any other economic or social phenomenon when examined beneath aggregate levels, such as at the level of the firm. Finally, there are no tools of aggregate manpower policy except general economic and educational policies. Below aggregate levels the complexities are too great to lend themselves to national policy determination.[72]

However, manpower specialists in organizations must be concerned with these policy questions at the level of the firm. There are a number of reasons for this and they can best be understood in the context of MDTA, vocational education, and in-company training programs.

While facilitating the employment of the unemployed and upgrading the quality of manpower in the labor force are justifiable social objectives implicit in MDTA, they raise two questions. The first is one concerning priorities. Training the disadvantaged upgrades the labor force but the opposite relationship is not necessarily true. Given the limited MDTA funds and the human and social costs and benefits involved, the goal of enabling the disadvantaged to share in the progress and prosperity of the American economy seems to merit priority.

The second question is one of means instead of ends. Preparing workers

[71] *Ibid.,* pp. 108–109.
[72] *Ibid.,* pp. 134–135, 165–166.

for employment is one purpose of the educational system and the specific goal of vocational education. As we have seen, offerings of the latter include both secondary and postsecondary training and evening courses for employed adults.[73]

Institutional training under MDTA is also a part of vocational education, but it has two differences. The first is that the MDTA enrollee is in the labor market and is in immediate need of a job and income. The typical vocational education student is preparing to enter the labor force or is pursuing a longer term goal of upgrading his skills. The significance of this difference is the MDTA allowance, received by five out of every six trainees. Vocational education students are expected to be self-supporting. MDTA trainees either require allowances for support or, in the case of youthful school dropouts, for motivation. Thus, the proper point of comparison for MDTA is the vocational education cooperative work-study programs in which students spend part of their time in school and part on the job. For these students, earnings are theoretically secondary to learning. By contrast, for MDTA enrollees, income is a primary consideration, particularly for the OJT enrollees who are full-time labor-force participants.[74]

The second difference between MDTA and vocational education is the willingness and ability of the former to serve those who have too often been ignored and left out of the mainstream of American social and economic life. Under MDTA, vocational educators have effectively served those with deficient educational preparation and have developed new remedial tools to do this. The Vocational Education Act of 1963 directed vocational education to move in the direction of serving persons with academic, socioeconomic, or other handicaps, but it provided no incentive for action. This may come with the 1968 amendments now in force. Only a very small percentage of persons enrolled in vocational education programs were the type contemplated by the term disadvantaged (in the sense of hard-core urban and rural unemployables). If vocational education can be moved to assume responsibilities for more such individuals, MDTA can and perhaps should be limited to remedial efforts on behalf of those already in the labor market who need special assistance.[75]

The social costs of failure to narrow the division between the prosperous many and the disadvantaged few in American society have become increasingly apparent. MDTA has to date not been a program for those who are alienated from society. It has been effective for those willing to learn and to work but who lack skills and opportunity. Members of low-income families have apparently predominated in MDTA programs but probably

[73] *Ibid.*, p. 166.
[74] *Ibid.*, pp. 166–167.
[75] *Ibid.*, p. 167.

654 Public Policy on Manpower, Training, and Vocational Education

only the most stable of those families have been served. It has reached Negroes, youths with more than elementary but less than high-school education, and the more employable poor. It has yet to involve in adequate numbers older workers, those with eight years or less of education, and the rural unemployed and underemployed. Also it has failed to penetrate the urban ghettoes to any substantial degree.[76] The Economic Opportunity Act of 1964 has most of these populations as its targets and to that extent these types of manpower are being served under the EOA.

MDTA administrators have been guilty of "creaming" yet this criticism can be modulated when we examine it closely. Given the pressures to demonstrate success, the relative accessability or inaccessability of various groups, and the tendency perhaps to follow lines of least resistance, it is doubtful that any program can avoid the tendency to select the best qualified from among eligible clients. About all that can be done is to set eligibility criteria so that the "cream" will be skimmed from the desired target groups rather than from those more favorably situated. It is by no means proven that the process of pushing over the dividing line between failure and success those for whom the distance between the two is shortest and the expense is least is undesirable as a manpower policy consideration.[77]

Turning, lastly, to the question of institutional and on-the-job training, there remains the problem of which of the two is better or whether the optimum educational and manpower result is obtained through coupling. Only longitudinal studies over an extended period will determine the relative long-term advantages of each of these approaches or their results when operated in concert (coupled). Until more evidence is in, a balance between these various methods is warranted and more experimentation is desirable.[78]

AN OVERVIEW OF RETRAINING PROGRAMS

Retraining through vocational education efforts stands high on the priority list of approaches to a comprehensive employment and manpower policy for America. Nevertheless, despite general acceptance of the idea that retraining will provide a means to more effective labor force participation, there has been limited substantive research to establish the kinds of programs in operation at present and what types of manpower can be reasonably expected to benefit from them. Acceptance of retraining as an important vehicle for improved labor force participation carries with it no assumption about its effects upon the overall unemployment rate. Specula-

[76] Ibid., pp. 168–169.
[77] Ibid., p. 169.
[78] Ibid., pp. 170–172.

tions of this kind are conjectural under almost any circumstances because we lack the tools to measure definitively the controlling variables. We lack adequate predictors of the extent and direction of technological and other changes that will affect production processes, consumer demand, and living patterns. Also, we need better tools for forecasting labor force requirements accurately and identifying future skill obsolescence. We need to know more about the job-making or job-displacing potential of automation. We need to know more about whether a better educated or more highly trained work force will necessarily lead to a lower rate of unemployment.[79]

Conflicting theories about the causes and cures of unemployment abound today. Debates as to what percentage rate is tolerable and even desirable, the extent to which tax cuts stimulate business activity and increase hiring, and whether structural adjustments will bridge the gap between people and jobs are indicative of the ideas that have been aired and argued. The economic aspects of unemployment may in some respects be unclear, but it is apparent that the serious social problems attending the phenomenon demand immediate solution. A vocational handicap is likely to be a self-perpetuating phenomenon, handed from generation to generation; and we recognize the urban hard-core unemployed and its ever-growing and crystalizing periphery as the makings of a caste alienated from the world of work. Retraining per se may not provide this emerging caste with jobs, but it can sometimes break the pattern of movement into a permanent state of unemployability by serving as leverage for entry into the work force.[80]

Unemployment as we have experienced it in the post-World War II period is a distinctly American complex of problems, perhaps generated by and certainly understood best in light of the particular economic, technological, and social influences of our time. In many respects, there seems to be little use in seeking guidelines to solutions for these problems through nostalgic references to other periods in our own history or by investigation of other countries. Indeed, if we were to rate the industrialized countries of the world on a scale of technological advance from the underdeveloped on the bottom, one could seriously hypothesize that America is overdeveloped.[81] The problems of unemployment which we are trying to cope with have yet to be faced by those lower down on the scale. Consequently, to study the apprenticeship system of a foreign country or to advocate that we emulate its vocational education practices can have only limited value.

[79] Ida R. Hoos, *Retraining the Work Force,* University of California Press, Berkeley, 1967, pp. 255–256.

[80] *Ibid.,* p. 256.

[81] Cf. Herbert Marcuse, *An Essay on Liberation,* Beacon, Boston, 1969.

The activities of labor organizations in America and the standard of living that prevails in this country make the apprentice systems of foreign countries inappropriate and anachronistic. Likewise, our democratic institutions of equal educational opportunity make the vocational programs of other countries an unsuitable model. Consequently, looking to other times and places for solutions to our problems of persistent unemployment, poverty, and race relations can do little more than provide us with data for a frame of reference.[82]

In the review of relevant legislation on manpower, retraining, and education covered to this point, it should be obvious from the context supplied that the first lesson to be derived from the investigation of *retraining* is that there is an overwhelming need for *training*. The American educational system in general and the vocational aspects of it in particular still require extensive overhauling. Since we lack a clear-cut generally endorsed educational philosophy, the entire approach to free public schooling is based upon an equalitarian assumption that by making a college-oriented curriculum accessible to all students we have fulfilled true democratic ideals. The fact is that only a relatively small percentage of our high-school graduates ever enter college and that the investment of nine to twelve years of their time has brought many of the others little appreciable return. As a result, retraining as a dynamic process is taking on new dimensions as a weapon in the attack on deprivation and poverty; new legislation has expanded the scope of the assault; new techniques for promoting it have been applied; and new public attitudes toward it have been generated.[83]

Yet, few citizens have probably asked themselves whether the Employment Act of 1946 and MDTA are serving the purposes for which they were intended, these kinds of questions being beyond their ken and left largely to the deliberations of economists, manpower specialists, and administrators in government agencies. It is apparent that there is still a critical shortage of strategic, high talent manpower and that the direction of employment demand is toward workers with higher skills and more education.[84]

For the future, the manpower solution to the problem of unemployment, if there is such a solution, will depend upon a number of factors. The first essential is that industry become aware of the fact that manpower is an indispensible economic asset so that out of this awareness appropriate manpower planning can begin to be implemented.[85] Continuous training

[82] Hoos, *op. cit.,* p. 256.

[83] *Ibid.,* p. 257.

[84] Frank H. Cassell, "Manpower Planning: The Basic Policies," *Personnel,* Vol. 42, No. 6, November-December 1965, pp. 55–56.

[85] *Ibid.,* p. 56.

is needed, and unions, together with industrial management, must recognize this need and become more flexible in administering hiring and seniority agreement provisions so that retrainees are retained by employers. Negotiated training benefits are taking hold in some parts of industry because unions have come to realize their stake in the worker's ability to obtain and hold a job.[86]

Thus it will be necessary that all interested parties including the government, industry, labor organizations, and manpower specialists work together so that the hardships resulting from unemployment can be mitigated, if not prevented. Each party must accept a responsible role, defined by a regard for the common good as well as its own immediate interests because with the advance of automation, the quantity and structure of jobs will continue to change. Skill obsolescence could realistically become a greater threat in the future as new processes and procedures permeate field, factory, and the office. The number of victims of "silent firing" (those who never are hired) could increase as machines replace people at the workbench.[87] All these possibilities point to the need for responsible collaboration between the aforementioned parties.

ECONOMIC OPPORTUNITY ACT OF 1964

The poor were apparently rediscovered by the intellectual community at large and the American people when John Kenneth Galbraith's phrase "the affluent society" from the book [88] of the same name became popular and Michael Harrington took up a similar phrase-making cudgel to show that there was "the other America." [89] In the 1960 presidential campaign President John F. Kennedy made West Virginia a focal point illustrating the assorted social ills of unemployment, industrial decline and migration, and poverty, and he proposed area redevelopment and retraining. After he was elected he appointed a Committee on Juvenile Delinquency and Youth Crime, many of whose ideas found their way into an omnibus antipoverty package.

The rediscovery of the poor came at a time when a generation or more of sociologists had been brought to intellectual maturity in an environment in which sociology was well on the way to doffing the mantle of being identified with social problems, amelioration, and reform movements. Dur-

[86] George Bennett, "Unemployment, Automation and Labor-Management Relations," *Personnel Administration*, Vol. 27, No. 5, September-October 1964, p. 23.
[87] Hoos, *op. cit.*, p. 272.
[88] John Kenneth Galbraith, *The Affluent Society*, Houghton Mifflin, Boston, 1958.
[89] Michael Harrington, *The Other America: Poverty in the United States*, Macmillan, New York, 1962.

ing the 1940s and 1950s budding sociologists in leading universities were well advised to eschew the "ideology of the social pathologists" [90] and adopt the outlook of the scientific sociologist who was concerned with building a science of society. There were strong critics of this view, too, such as Saul Alinsky, who has also rejected the "war on poverty." [91] Yet, the interest in social problems remained, particularly among students of social service administration and public welfare; and sociologists continued to maintain *Social Problems,* the journal of the Society for the Study of Social Problems (that, judging by *Social Problems,* seldom published articles on social problems!). During this period there were several studies of poverty in America, most notably by nonsociologists. [92]

Today, many sociologists, economists, and psychologists have become extremely interested in poverty; and the outpouring of journal articles, books, research reports, and other publications on poverty has been truly monumental—and very faddish, to boot. Never in recent memory has there been such a vast shifting of intellectual gears and a preoccupation with a previously ignored, if not belittled, problem. The entanglement of poverty with the civil rights revolution, urban renewal, Negro riots, education and training, unemployment, and technological change collectively has become the focal point of much attention, discussion, research, and writing which will continue well into the 1970s. The "war on poverty" launched in 1964 was clearly the opening campaign of a new era in an intermittent battle that had roots in the New Deal of the 1930s and early 1940s and the Fair Deal of the late 1940s. The battle, of course, has even deeper roots extending back through industrialization to the Elizabethan Poor Laws, if not indeed to the beginnings of recorded history. [93]

In many respects the war on poverty being waged in the United States contains some of the most challenging and responsive ideas regarding manpower planning and the development of human resources that have ever been stated and includes, as well, ideas on health, welfare, and re-habilitation programs. The war also is aimed at preventing the waste of human resources, to which we return in the next chapter.

The Manpower Development and Training Act of 1962 marked the beginning point of serious widespread interest in manpower planning at

[90] C. Wright Mills, "The Professional Ideology of Social Pathologists," *American Journal of Sociology,* Vol. 49, No. 2, September 1943, pp. 165–180.

[91] Saul D. Alinsky, "The War on Poverty—Political Pornography," *Journal of Social Issues,* Vol. 21, No. 1, January 1965, pp. 41–47.

[92] Such as Robert Bremner's *From the Depths,* New York University Press, New York, 1956.

[93] Sar A. Levitan, *The Design of Federal Antipoverty Strategy* (Policy Papers in Human Resources and Industrial Relations, No. 1), Institute of Labor and Industrial Relations, University of Michigan, Ann Arbor, pp. 2–17.

the national, regional, industrial, and firm levels. The Economic Opportunity Act of 1964, among other goals, marked the beginning point in launching a national program of new careers for the poor in which non-professional people living in poverty would be enabled to develop quasi-professional skills and, in time, acquire professional status. It should be noted that the means for developing these skills involved a variation on the apprenticeship model in which the more easily learned and routine aspects of the professional's job would be spun off and become the domain of the subprofessional. For example, many tasks in nursing can be carried out effectively by a nurse's aide. (In fact, when we consider the personality of certain nurses and specific nurse's aides the latter may be even more emotionally effective than the former in providing many types of patient care.) Similarly, it becomes possible to parcel out certain of the social worker's tasks to community aides and counselor aides; or certain of the classroom elementary and secondary teacher's duties to teacher's aides.

As the subprofessional becomes increasingly proficient in carrying out tasks, he can theoretically be given an ever-larger piece of the professional's job. If he ultimately acquires knowledge of the theory as well as the practice in the profession—and, importantly, can be formally certified as to this accomplishment—he can achieve full professional status.[94]

It may be hypothesized that in industry today there is very little interest in helping subprofessionals acquire professional employee status by sub-dividing jobs so that in the course of a career the subprofessional can move across the subprofessional (technical) and professional line. Industry appears to be primarily interested in recruiting college graduates for salaried technical, professional, and managerial positions. If anything, industry is probably upgrading jobs which genuinely do not require college education because of the increasing availability of college graduates for work in industry and the belief that while entry-level salaried positions may not require college training, subsequent higher-level positions do. Consequently, there is thought to be no harm in recruiting college graduates for the lower-level positions because if persons with lesser education filled them they would probably not possess the potential and qualifications for higher-level jobs. Inasmuch as most large-scale organizations like to promote-from-within as a matter of policy, they look to the qualifications input of manpower entering lower-level positions. If the educational qualifications of this manpower input is low, the potential for promotion is

[94] For more information on the new careers concept and promising but limited evidence on its value, see Arthur Pearl and Frank Riessman, *New Careers for the Poor*, Free Press, New York, 1965; Frank Riessman and Hermine I. Popper, *Up from Poverty*, Harper and Row, New York, 1968; and Frank Riessman, *Strategies Against Poverty*, Random House, New York, 1969.

assumed to be poor. As a result, industrial management believes it should take advantage of the rising general educational attainment of the American population by recruiting the best educated people available. This may often mean putting overqualified people to work in a way in which they are underutilized, if not malutilized. This approach is the exact opposite of the concept underlying new careers for the poor whereby jobs are redesigned so that subprofessionals can handle them and gradually move up to professional status.

Although industry's main interest in manpower has centered around the recruitment of college graduate trainees in the last several years, the National Alliance of Businessmen and other groups have been asked to undertake programs to recruit, select, train, and develop the hard-core unemployed, disadvantaged person typically found in the cities of America. It is a new type of responsibility which business has accepted as a challenge and constitutes a dimension of the war on poverty to which we return in the last chapter of the book. Our concern here is with the Economic Opportunity Act; and, although the concept of new careers for the poor has relevance for the industrial scene, we need first to consider the EOA from an overall point of view and then highlight a few of the programs which have as their goal enabling program participants to achieve economic independence: the Job Corps, Neighborhood Youth Corps, and Work Experience and Training.

The EOA recognized poverty as a national concern, directed attention to the hidden poor, and presented a coordinated approach to the causes of poverty. The approach used was to mobilize the human and financial resources of the nation to combat poverty in the United States. The Act dealt with the principal problems on a nationwide basis and identified the principal victims of poverty as: unemployed and untrained youth, members of blighted communities, the rural poor, migrant agricultural workers, and illiterate and unskilled adults who were dependent on public welfare. The various titles in the act are connected with those principal victims of poverty.

On another level, the EOA and poverty may be regarded largely as euphemisms to refer to legislation designed to help discriminated-against Negroes and other minority-priority target groups to muster their resources for movement out of the low-income backwaters of American society (poverty, in other words) into the mainstream of affluence. Antipoverty legislation thus has had an antidiscrimination or atonement connotation.

The opportunities available are largely educational and somewhat less "economic," although they are intended to foster long-run economic independence by building strong, well educated families that have incomes and by breaking the inheritance of poverty by intergenerational family cycles. Learning and earning are neatly combined in theory.

Defining the poverty group[95] and the so-called "culture of poverty"[96] has become quite an exercise in intellectual gamesmanship, although there probably is little doubt that almost 25 million Americans are still living at an economic level which could be reasonably regarded today as relative poverty.[97]

Provisions of the EOA

Title 1 of the act was concerned with youth programs and provided for establishing a Job Corps, a work-training program, and a work-study program. The Job Corps contained two types of projects, namely, rural and urban training centers catering to both young men and women in separate locations. In the rural centers activity was largely based upon conservation projects. Urban training centers concentrated on vocational training for young men or women aged 16 through 21. The work-training program enabled state or local governments or nonprofit organizations to sponsor full- or part-time employment. Full-time employment was provided through the Neighborhood Youth Corps for young men and women aged 16 through 21 to increase their employability. Part-time employment was made possible to enable young people to continue their education while developing good work habits and attitudes. The federal government paid a large part of the cost. The work provided was on public projects or on projects sponsored by private nonprofit organizations which would benefit the community and which would not otherwise have been performed. Under the work-study program, institutions of higher learning offered part-time employment to students from low-income families so that they could enter upon or continue higher education. Part of the cost was borne by the institution, but the major part, by the federal government.

Title 2 of the Economic Opportunity Act of 1964 was concerned with community action programs and authorized three types of activities: general community action, adult basic education, and voluntary assistance for needy children. A wide range of community organizations participated in coordinated programs involving employment, remedial reading, job training and counseling, health, vocational rehabilitation, housing, home

[95] See Earl Raab, "What War and Which Poverty?," *Public Interest,* Vol. 1, No. 3, Spring 1966, pp. 45–46; and John B. Parrish, "Is U.S. Really Filled with Poverty?," *U.S. News & World Report,* Vol. 63, No. 10, September 4, 1967, pp. 50–53.

[96] See Charles A. Valentine, *Culture and Poverty: Critique and Counterproposals,* University of Chicago Press, Chicago, 1968; and Jack L. Roach and Orville R. Gursslin, "An Evaluation of the Concept 'Culture of Poverty,'" *Social Forces,* Vol. 5, No. 3, March 1967, pp. 383–392.

[97] Mollie Orshansky, "The Shape of Poverty in 1966," *Social Security Bulletin,* Vol. 31, No. 3, March 1968, pp. 3–32. See also Lola M. Irelan, ed., *Low-Income Life Styles,* Government Printing Office, Washington, 1966.

management, and welfare. These programs were federally supported in full or in large part.[98]

The popular Head Start program for preschool children was financed and administered under Title 2 of the Act. This program was intended to help disadvantaged children between the ages of four and six obtain educational, medical, and environmental assistance so that they could avoid the spiral of failure that often occurs when children enter school inadequately prepared. (We do not discuss Head Start in the chapter because its bearing for manpower specialists in industry is remote, even though improvements in the socialization of children are obviously connected with human resources development.)

Title 3 was concerned with special programs to combat poverty in rural areas. It authorized loans up to $2500 to very low-income rural families for farm operations and nonagricultural producing enterprises, and loans to local cooperatives serving predominantly low-income families. It also authorized assistance to establish and operate housing, sanitation, education, and child-day-care programs for migrant farm workers and their families.

Title 4 was concerned with employment and investment incentives and authorized loans and loan guarantees to small businesses in amounts not exceeding $25,000 on more liberal terms than the regular loan provisions of the Federal Small Business Administration.

Title 5 of the Act was concerned with work experience programs and provided for funds to meet the costs of experimental, pilot, or demonstration work training programs to help unemployed fathers and other needy persons.

Title 6 of the Act authorized the director of the Office of Economic Opportunity (which, incidentally, was a newly established federal agency placed under the managership of R. Sargent Shriver, brother-in-law of President John F. Kennedy) to commence recruiting and training a corps of volunteers to serve in specified federal, state, and community programs. These volunteers were called VISTA—an acronym for Volunteers in Service to America. The program provided an opportunity for young people 18 and over to join the war on poverty. These volunteers were to work with migrant laborers, on Indian reservations, in urban and rural community action programs, in slum areas, hospitals, schools, and in institutions for the mentally ill and retarded. It was widely touted as the domestic Peace Corps. For this and other reasons the Peace Corps and VISTA had the effect of making Sargent Shriver in charge of two of the most attractive volunteer programs for youth in America. The period of service in VISTA

[98] For a tart evaluation of these, see Daniel Patrick Moynihan, *Maximum Feasible Misunderstanding,* Free Press, New York, 1969.

was one year. Volunteers received a living allowance and $50.00 a month.

Title 7 of the Act concerned the treatment of income for certain public assistance purposes. A policy declaration was made that an individual's opportunity to participate in programs under the EOA neither jeopardized nor was to be jeopardized by his receipt of public assistance.

There have been many other programs established to hitchhike on EOA or to augment it. The "Follow Through" programs have been essentially a continuation of "Head Start." [99] "Upward Bound" programs have been established to offer a taste of college during summer vacations to promising but disadvantaged youth. The goal is to spur them on in school and to motivate them toward higher education.[100]

In 1970 the Act will have been on the books for six years and commitments of probably around $9 to 10 billion will have been made. It is recognized that the impact of some of these antipoverty measures, no matter how successful they turn out to be, will not be discernible for years. Some may have no noticeable effect toward stimulating economic independence for almost a generation. For example, the economic benefits of Head Start may not be apparent for years because the senior members of this group are still young children.[101]

Fortunately, it is not necessary to delay a tentative assessment of the economic impact of the EOA for another decade. This is because in placing emphasis upon breaking the bonds of poverty, several programs inaugurated under the Act stressed job creation and training. An examination of these programs should be relevant to reaching some judgment about the extent to which the measures have led program participants to attain economic independence. The original act made explicit provision for three such manpower programs, namely, the Job Corps, Neighborhood Youth Corps, and Work and Training. The first two were limited to youths while the third served recipients of welfare as well as other needy adults.[102]

Similar to MDTA, the information available to estimate the contributions of these three poverty-oriented manpower programs to the economic

[99] Nolan Estes, "Follow Through," *American Education*, Vol. 3, No. 8, September 1967, pp. 12–14; and Harry Salsinger, "Following Up on Follow Through," *American Education*, Vol. 4, No. 5, May 1968, pp. 12–16.
[100] Paula Dranov, "A Taste of College," *American Education*, Vol. 3, No. 4, April 1967, pp. 25–27.
[101] Sar A. Levitan, *Antipoverty Work and Training Efforts: Goals and Reality*, Institute of Labor and Industrial Relations, University of Michigan, Ann Arbor, August 1967, p. 1.
[102] *Ibid.*, pp. 1–2. See also Sar Levitan, *Youth Employment Act*, W. E. Upjohn Institute for Employment Research, Kalamazoo, 1963.

independence of more than a million participants is difficult to obtain and when gotten is usually inadequate. As a result, any evaluation of the EOA is little more than a rough cut at what would be desirable. We turn our attention first to the Job Corps.

Job Corps

The Job Corps was created as part of the Act in order to prepare youths aged 16 through 21 for the responsibility of citizenship and to increase their employability by providing them in rural and urban residential centers with education, both vocational and other types, useful work directed toward the conservation of natural resources, and appropriate ancillary activities. The assumption underlying this set of goals was that many youths from impoverished homes must be removed from their home environments before they can be rehabilitated through training and education.[103]

Although the antecedents of the Job Corps may be traced back to the Civilian Conservation Corps of the 1930s, the contrasts between the two are greater than their similarities. The CCC was a product of the Great Depression, when deprivation and need were widespread. The 2.5 million CCC enrollees represented a broad cross section of the population.[104] The CCC had serious conservation goals as well as employment objectives whereas the Job Corps stressed the latter.

The CCC was terminated when the armed forces absorbed the bulk of its clients and acute wartime manpower shortages developed. The Job Corps, on the other hand, focused upon the special needs of a small minority of youths who because of educational deficiency and debilitating environment were at a competitive disadvantage in the labor market. The CCC was essentially a job-creation program which emphasized conservation work. The Job Corps stressed the needs of the individual corpsman, although the work experience of enrollees in conservation centers was also devoted to work that was useful to society.[105]

It is interesting and sardonic to note that the main opposition to the Job Corps was directed against the establishment of the conservation centers. It was argued that the work carried out there was not very relevant in preparing youths for the world of work, and the high cost of

---

[103] Levitan, *Antipoverty Work and Training Efforts: Goals and Reality, op. cit.,* p. 5.

[104] For a review of the origins of the CCC see Frances Perkins, *The Roosevelt I Knew,* Viking Press, New York, 1946, pp. 174–181; and Lewis Meriam, *Relief and Social Security,* Brookings Institution, Washington, 1946, pp. 428–459.

[105] Levitan, *Antipoverty Work and Training Efforts: Goals and Reality, op. cit.,* pp. 5–6.

maintaining a youth in a conservation center could not justify the work which they performed. However, the conservation lobbyists had their day and were successful in persuading Congress to specify that 40 percent of the male Job Corps enrollees be assigned to conservation centers.

Unlike MDTA, the Job Corps administrators were unable to attract the "cream" of the disadvantaged youths; and, because of the lack of creaming, the Job Corps enrollees tended to be the most poorly educated, most poorly motivated youths from disadvantaged groups in society. For example, two out of every five enrollees in May of 1967 had completed eight years of education or less. Reading and arithmetic comprehension for one-half of the enrollees was at about the fifth-grade level. Nearly one of every three was unable to read a simple sentence or to solve a second-grade arithmetic problem. Three out of every five came from a broken home and two of every five came from families on relief.[106] A large number had been convicted of felonies.

By June 1967 the Job Corps operated 122 centers with almost 40,000 enrollees. The urban centers were 28 in number, and 21 of these were operated by private industry, including such corporate giants as General Electric, IBM, Litton Industries, RCA, and Westinghouse. The remaining seven urban centers were administered by universities or nonprofit organizations. Corporate involvement was welcomed because it gave the Job Corps and the remainder of the war on poverty an image of respectability and acceptance by the business community.

Corporate involvement was caused by a mixture of a desire to display social responsibility and more traditional business interests, such as making profits and gaining experience in the newly emerging retraining "business." Profits were generally small but contractors had no financial risk at stake since they operated Job Corps centers on a cost-plus-fixed-fee basis. The opportunity to enter an expanding new market (the education and training of the disadvantaged) and to operate a laboratory for developing and testing new techniques and educational knowhow was probably at least as important, if not more important, than the social responsibility aspect of corporate involvement.

Corporations traditionally engaged in training manpower and the development of complex defense systems were expected to have little trouble developing new approaches and techniques for educating and training the disadvantaged. Yet, it does not appear that the corporations have lived up to these expectations. The high cost of running the centers forced the Job Corps to cut operating expenses and reduce budgets for research and development in educational and training activities. With such budget re-

[106] *Ibid.*, pp. 7–8.

strictions, corporate contractors attracted few proven top-level educators or administrators and frequently had to settle for ordinary garden-variety educators.[107]

Job Corps centers ranged in size from under 100 to more than 3000 enrollees. There were separate centers for men and women, and many of the centers for women immediately came under hostile attack. Many of the centers for men were located on abandoned military installations, and the Job Corps had to accept whatever sites were available. Some selections proved unfortunate because the communities did not welcome the corpsmen in their midst, thereby indirectly provoking community relations problems when corpsmen sought recreation in nearby cities.[108]

Underlying much of the discontent over the Job Corps was the high cost of the experiment itself. For example, the annual cost per enrollee was more than $8000 in fiscal 1967. The failure of Job Corps administrators to explain the reasons for the high costs added to the impression that the centers served as "country clubs for juvenile delinquents." The cost of supporting a student for a year at Harvard College was invidiously compared to that of a Job Corps enrollee. This was, of course, a rather irrelevant comparison but one which was nevertheless widely publicized by critics to show that the Job Corps was undeniably very expensive from the standpoint of training one individual. Costs were also complicated by the fact that more than 40 percent of all enrollees dropped out or were discharged from the program within three months of enrollment. Finally, during its first two years the Job Corps experienced considerable difficulty in filling its available capacity, and an ill-advised campaign to stimulate enrollments later did considerable damage because far more young people applied than could be served by the available spaces in the centers.[109]

The accomplishments of the Job Corps are nebulous, but at least several can be identified. The Job Corps experiment and experience showed that enrollment in a residential center helped youths improve their education and acquire training useful for securing and holding a job. Nine months of enrollment in a Job Corps center raised the average reading ability of corpsmen about 1.5 grades of schooling and improved their average arithmetic comprehension by 1.8 grades.

The quality of the vocational training received in Job Corps centers has never been adequately measured. Impressionistic evidence is that most corpsmen received satisfactory to excellent training.

There is a close correlation between the employment status of former corpsmen and the time they spent in the Job Corps. For example, those

[107] *Ibid.*, pp. 10–12.
[108] *Ibid.*, pp. 14–16.
[109] *Ibid.*, pp. 17–24.

who stayed for six months or longer (as contrasted with dropouts or youths discharged from the various centers) displayed advantages in securing employment immediately upon leaving the Job Corps—and the advantages were even more pronounced six months later. Yet when all the data are examined, it must be inferred that no conclusive case has as yet been established to justify the Job Corps on the basis of past performance. There may be alternative, more educationally effective, less costly programs.[110] For example, the vocational education programs under the VEA and related legislation reaches 9 million people and has nearly the same size budget as the Job Corps which trained about 60,000 annually but was down to about 25,000 about mid-1970.

Yet one cannot escape concluding that the Job Corps is at least one institution with potential for helping poor youths to bridge the gap between their aspirations and industrial reality. The harsh fact is that the Corps has helped only a minority of those who sought its aid despite the ample resources allocated to it. As a consequence, the future of the Job Corps remains in doubt. Its future will depend upon its ability to perform the Herculean tasks of operating residential centers efficiently where poor youths will remain sufficiently long to gain an experience meaningful to their future. It will also be important to persuade various groups in society that the effort is worth the investment.[111]

Overly optimistic expectations were largely responsible for much of the disappointment and disillusionment over the Job Corps. But these were hardly reasons for crossing the Corps off as a failure. It would be a bitter irony indeed if Congress were to shut down one of the programs most likely to produce new breakthroughs in social technology at precisely the time when our existing technologies for dealing with social problems simply do not measure up to our goals. In other words, the nation needs the Job Corps today not to solve the problem of teen-age poverty but to find a way to solve it through experimentation.[112]

President Richard M. Nixon in the 1968 presidential campaign pledged that he would eliminate Job Corps after being elected to the presidency. In 1969 he apparently changed his mind and decided to continue the Job Corps but to remove its administration from OEO to the Manpower Administration of the United States Department of Labor. Head Start would be assigned to the Department of Health, Education, and Welfare. President Nixon's concept of OEO was that it should be a "think tank" con-

[110] *Ibid.*, pp. 21–37.

[111] *Ibid.*, p. 43. See also "Job Corps Gets a Working Over," *Business Week*, No. 2068, April 19, 1969, p. 96.

[112] Christopher Weeks, *Job Corps, Dollars and Dropouts*, Little, Brown, Boston, 1967, pp. 237–241.

cerned with experimentation, community action programs, VISTA, and new programs aimed at human resources development rather than an agency which has a number of on-going programs to administer, such as the Job Corps. Thus the Job Corps today, while it does not exactly have a new lease on life, will be on the scene for at least another year or two. If the Job Corps staffs are properly trained, they may be able to perform effectively in the future.

Neighborhood Youth Corps

Turning to another program under EOA, namely, the Neighborhood Youth Corps, it should be noted that this program had as goals to put idle youth to work constructively and, in some cases, to help prevent high-school dropouts by providing part-time work. The program was intended to provide work experience and manpower for many needed community jobs.

NYC had two separate but related components: a part-time job creation program for youths attending school and a separate full-time work program for idle youths most of whom were high-school dropouts. As the program evolved, a third component was added, namely, the provision of summer employment opportunities in response to the need to quiet restive urban youth during the "long hot days" of the summers during which they might be prone to riot.[113]

Slightly less than 3 million youths were envisaged at first as the potential clientele for NYC. Given this large eligible population, it is not surprising to find that the financial resources allocated to the program were inadequate to meet total needs. The program has been funded at a high level and has become very popular. In fact, as many as 1 million youths may have benefited from the program, although the exact number is not known because the same youths may have been in several NYC programs. A youth enrolling in an NYC project normally received $1.25 an hour, the federal minimum wage at the time the EOA legislation was enacted. A few projects paid a somewhat higher rate but rarely more than $1.40 per hour. The number of hours for which a youth was paid depended upon the type of project on which he was employed. For in-school projects the maximum was 15 hours per week. For out-of-school projects, 32; and for summer programs, 28.[114]

The crucial test of the effectiveness of the in-school program is whether it provided sufficient incentives for enrollees to complete their high-school education. To date, no conclusive information has been developed to

[113] Levitan, *Antipoverty Work and Training Efforts: Goals and Reality, op. cit.,* p. 46.
[114] *Ibid.,* p. 47.

answer this query. Similarly, in evaluating the out-of-school program it appears that the longer a youth remained in NYC the better were his chances for getting full-time and part-time work. But the incidence of unemployment remained widespread among persons in the out-of-school programs. The proportion of unemployed among former NYC enrollees is no greater than for youths who completed MDTA institutional courses.

There is some evidence that NYC opened employment opportunities, especially for female enrollees. Fifteen percent of the women who worked after leaving NYC were employed in agencies where they had gotten their NYC work assignments. For males the comparable percentage was 5 percent. These data suggest that work assignments for women were to a large extent an integral part of agency operations and less of a "make-work" nature than was true for males.[115]

The goal of developing new careers and equipping disadvantaged youth who missed the opportunity at school to acquire a marketable skill is in line with our democratic traditions. The most pressing need of these youths is often to secure a job which will provide them with at least minimum support. The out-of-school program fulfilled for many enrollees this minimum and immediate need. NYC thus performed a useful function as an "ageing vat," helping youths when it was most difficult for them to find employment.

The rationale for viewing NYC as an "ageing vat" rests on the fact that unemployment rates among youth decline as they mature into adults. There is room, therefore, for a program which provides youth with income and work during their early years in the labor force, even if it does not provide them with education and training as traditionally conceived.[116]

Work Experience and Training Phases of the EOA

Turning now to the work experience and training phases of the Economic Opportunity Act, it should be noted that a major gap in the American Social Security System has historically been the lack of provision for persons subjected to long-term unemployment. In fact, much of the legislation enacted during the Kennedy-Johnson New Frontier and Great Society days was an attempt to fill in the interstitial areas of Social Security with imaginative new manpower and employment programs.

The work experience and training program under the EOA was an attempt to provide for the need of unemployed and underemployed adults who were handicapped in competition for jobs in the labor market. The work and training program was intended philosophically not to provide mere work relief but to enrich and expand these traditional programs and

[115] *Ibid.*, pp. 52–61.
[116] *Ibid.*, p. 64.

provide various services which would help rehabilitate the work recipients. But, as frequently happens with public programs, the actual implementation fell short of goals. The new programs did not differ greatly from the older work relief projects, and about 90 percent of the funds were dispersed for work payments, leaving very little for rehabilitative services.

The purpose of the work experience and training program was to expand the opportunities for constructive work experience and other needed training available to persons who were unable to support or care for themselves or their families. However, the hopes advanced for the program varied with the social philosophy of its proponents. Some hoped that malingerers on public assistance when faced with the choice of receiving relief and having to work for a living would leave the relief rolls and obtain employment. Others expected that participants would develop the "work habit" and that this combined with training and other services would help them secure jobs on the open market. Still others viewed the program as a means of expanding income maintainence to poor people who could not qualify under the stringent public assistance eligibility rules. (Unemployed parents in the majority of states are not qualified under the law to receive public assistance.) It was thus reasoned that the work experience and training program could circumvent some of the inadequacies of the federal-state public assistance programs by providing 100 percent federally funded income support to poor families.[117]

The program was riddled with difficulties from its beginning. The result of these difficulties was that the program turned out to be neither fish nor fowl. It provided little training, and much of the work experience was the old-fashioned work-relief type. It was a peculiar amalgamation of a welfare program and a manpower program.[118] In fact, the program assisted male family heads much less than female trainees. The trend was soon toward a declining male participation in the program, and it took stringent efforts to find a sufficient number of males interested in participating.[119]

Any final assessment of this program would depend upon the availability of data. There have been no meaningful national evaluations, although the press releases issued by officials responsible for the program have claimed achievements. The fairest thing to say seems to be that the program provided marginal training, which was a rather weak inducement to encourage trainees to complete their program. Moreover, in most cases, the wage that would be awaiting trainees at the termination of their training probably provided no more income than public assistance.[120]

In summary, the Job Corps, Neighborhood Youth Corps, and Work

[117] *Ibid.,* p. 72.
[118] *Ibid.,* p. 78.
[119] *Ibid.,* p. 86.
[120] *Ibid.,* pp. 94–100.

Experience and Training programs served overlapping populations. As far as their administration is concerned, the three programs were independent entities. There was no coordination between the Job Corps and the Neighborhood Youth Corps even though the two programs served essentially the same clientele. There was no mechanism for transferring NYC enrollees to the Job Corps or vice versa.

As a program, the Job Corps remains extremely controversial to this day. Even the basic educational premises of it have been challenged on the grounds that they are romantic and unrealistic because they expect to achieve the rehabilitation of youths from city slums or rural areas after a short stay of eight or nine months.[121] It is completely unrealistic to accomplish the resocialization of youth under these circumstances and particularly within those limited time periods.

NYC can be looked upon more as an assuaging political program than one which had clear-cut educational or training goals. In recent years more than one-half of the funds for it have been allocated to support in-school youth, and the various summer programs have had urban ghetto riot-control goals. The assumption that the income provided youth serves as an incentive for the enrollees to stay in school and to continue their education does not seem to be borne out by the limited data available concerning NYC. On the other hand, the out-of-school NYC program seems to be a mixture of work experience, income support, antiriot insurance, and the aforementioned "ageing vat." Thus far, NYC has failed to evaluate the effectiveness of these programs, which, to complicate evaluative matters further, are quite variable among communities in terms of programming ingenuity, resourcefulness, and the abilities of sponsoring organizations and administrators.[122]

In respect to the Work Experience and Training Program, available evidence raises questions as to whether the goals of this program were achieved. Although about one-third of former enrollees during the first two years secured jobs, it is doubtful whether participation in the program significantly contributed towards their securing employment. Indeed, the experience of the three programs mentioned indicated the difficulty of designing and administering mass projects which could lead to the economic self-sufficiency of the poor. It is not surprising, therefore, that much of the antipoverty funds have been expended on traditional relief measures to meet age-old problems rather than spent upon innovative educational and training programs. There remains the challenge to develop such effective programs in the future.[123] Steps have been taken in recent years to make changes.

[121] *Ibid.,* pp. 104–105.
[122] *Ibid.,* pp. 105–106.
[123] *Ibid.,* pp. 106–109.

In taking a broad look at the war on poverty and Great Society legislation analyzed to this point in the chapter, it appears that education and the democratic ideal have become tied together in a massive experimental effort to enable the disadvantaged to become employed. Table 2 provides some insight into the magnitude of these efforts. Equal employment opportunity, educational opportunity, and economic opportunity thus have found a kind of common meeting ground. The key to improved participation in the labor force and employment was thought to be in new approaches to vocational education and training. Let us turn next to some important changes in other educational legislation which has involved the federal government still more in the educational process and at the same time tried to enrich the development of human resources in contemporary American society. The continuing emphasis on helping the disadvantaged should be noted.

THE ELEMENTARY AND SECONDARY EDUCATION ACT OF 1965

The purpose of the Elementary and Secondary Education Act (ESEA) was to strengthen and improve educational quality and educational opportunities in the nation's elementary and secondary schools. The Act contained five titles, the first of which carried the vast bulk of the money and was directed toward financial assistance to local educational agencies for special educational programs in areas having high concentrations of children of low-income families. The amount each local school district would get depended upon two factors: the average annual current expenditure per schoolchild in the entire state; and, secondly, the number of school-age children in the district from families with annual incomes of less than $2000 and those in families receiving more than $2000 annually from the program of Aid to Families with Dependent Children. The President of the United States was required under the act to appoint a national advisory council on the education of disadvantaged children. This council was to review the administration and operation of Title 1 each year, particularly the Title's effectiveness in improving the educational attainment of deprived children.[124]

The many titles of the Act are of less interest to us in detail from a manpower standpoint. However, briefly they are the following. Title 2 provided grants for school libraries and other instructional resources and materials for both public and private schools. Title 3 was concerned with the establishment of local educational centers and services, particularly the

[124] "The First Work of These Times," *American Education,* Vol. 1, No. 4, April 1965, pp. 14–15.

creation of exemplary school programs. There was a realization that at the present time no systematic institutional format exists for translating educational research and innovation into practical, innovative school programs. An important thrust of this title was to provide a means for stimulating and assisting in the development of such model demonstration programs. Title 4 was directed at fostering educational research and training and covered the regional laboratories and research and development centers. Title 4 amended the Cooperative Research Act of 1954, which had supported much educational research. This effort was to be expanded through the availability of additional funds, both for programs of research and development and for the construction of national and regional research facilities. Lastly, Title 5, was concerned with strengthening state educational agencies. Funds could be used to improve educational planning; identify educational problems and needs; evaluate educational programs; analyze and report educational data; publish and distribute curriculum materials; conduct educational research; improve teacher preparation; train individuals to serve state and local educational agencies; and provide consultative and technical assistance in special areas of educational need.[125]

The Elementary and Secondary Education Act of 1965 had two characteristics which were carried forward from the past. First, it maintained the tradition that federal aid should be "categorical", that is, directed toward specifically stated goals, although the categories were fairly broad (such as "the educationally deprived"). Second, ESEA had sufficient latitude to provide benefits attractive to the various groups and persons concerned with elementary and secondary education.

Congress was clearly concerned at this time about poverty, unemployment, and similar ills; and, under the stimulation of President Johnson, concluded that education was the most likely available tool to solve the problem. Title 1 was thus an attack on educational deprivation. Yet, the task forces and others who initially plumped for the Act believed that the efforts of Title 1 were doomed if the administration of Title 1 was left solely to the existing educational bureaucracies. Title 3 was thus given to these moving forces as a source of innovation (and perhaps even revolution). Scholars of education, who doubted whether the state of the art was currently capable of achieving what Congress and the innovators wanted, were reassured by the provisions for basic research included under Title 4. In providing instructional materials for teachers and pupils (but not schools per se), Title 2 placated Catholics and other groups with parochial- and private-school interests. Finally, Title 5 was a bone thrown to state educational organizations which might have resented the strong local emphasis in Title 3 and the major role given to the United States Office of

[125] *Ibid.*, pp. 16–20.

Table 2 Estimated Number of Enrollments in Federally Aided Manpower and Vocational Education Programs, 1962–68

Program	Fiscal Year						
	1962	1963	1964	1965	1966	1967	1968
Manpower programs total [a]	11,900	66,600	108,500	481,400	1,079,000	1,434,900	1,287,000
Structured training:							
Redevelopment area (Area Redevelopment Act)	8,000	12,600	11,300	10,400	(b)		
Manpower Development and Training Act		34,100	77,600	156,900	235,800	265,000	265,000
On-the-job training		2,100	9,000	11,600	58,300	115,000	125,000
Institutional		32,000	68,600	145,300	177,500	150,000	140,000
Job Corps				12,400	47,100	70,700	64,600
New Careers						1,000	4,300
Manpower activities of Bureau of Indian Affairs	3,300	3,500	3,900	5,000	6,700	7,700	7,900
Work experience:							
Neighborhood Youth Corps				137,900	422,900	556,300	467,400
Operation Mainstream						11,000	12,600
Work-Study (College)				48,000 [c]	262,000	431,000	405,000
Work Experience (Title V, Economic Opportunity Act)				88,700	84,800	77,200	27,600 [d]
Community Work and Training (Title IV, Social Security Act)		16,400	15,700	22,100	19,700	15,000	14,000

Program support:

Concentrated Employment Program (special funds [e])					16,000
Special Impact					2,600
Vocational programs total [g]	4,566,000	5,431,000	6,070,000	7,048,000	7,534,000
Secondary	2,141,000	2,819,000	3,048,000	3,533,000	3,843,000
Postsecondary	171,000	207,000	442,000	500,000	593,000
Adult and special needs	2,255,000	2,404,000	2,580,000	3,015,000	3,098,000

([f]) appears in the fourth data column for Vocational programs total.

[a] Excludes regular placements by the public employment service; also the registration of apprenticeship programs by the U.S. Department of Labor's Bureau of Apprenticeship and Training. The JOBS and WIN programs do not appear because the first enrollees were not recorded until fiscal 1969. It should be noted that the figures may include some double counting of persons enrolled in more than one program.

[b] Merged with MDTA program.

[c] Program in operation only 5 months in fiscal 1965.

[d] Program phased out in fiscal 1968 and 1969. Clients to be served by the new WIN Program.

[e] Other participants in CEP are included in training or work-experience programs to which they were referred. These persons received some service but were not enrolled in any of the above.

[f] Not available.

[g] Covers data for available years since passage of the VEA of 1963.

Note. Detail may not add to totals due to rounding.

Source. Manpower Report of the President, January 1969, Government Printing Office, Washington, pp. 140, 252; and *Manpower Report . . . March 1970,* p. 322.

Education in the administration of the entire act.[126] At the present time about $1 billion of federal funds is sent annually to school districts under Title 1 alone.

Similar to much of the prior legislation enacted by recent Congresses concerned with the Great Society, the ESEA has not been evaluated definitively on a nationwide basis. Indeed, such an evaluation awaits more years of experience with its provisions so that its effectiveness can be judged.

HIGHER EDUCATION ACT OF 1965

As of several years ago only one American in eight had taken as much as one college course. Perhaps the higher tuition fees charged by colleges and universities in many instances placed these courses beyond the reach of the people who needed them most, such as displaced workers, women returning to the labor market, and individuals wishing to improve themselves. For these and other reasons the Higher Education Act of 1965 was passed into law. It was intended to strengthen the educational resources of American colleges and universities and to provide financial assistance for students in postsecondary and higher education. The act contains eight titles.[127]

Title 1 authorizes the appropriation of large sums of money for community service and continuing education programs. The programs were to be set up by the states and were intended to meet rural, urban, or suburban community needs. Special emphasis was to be placed on solving problems in urban and suburban areas.

Title 2 is concerned with college library assistance and library training and research. The desirable minimum standard for a library at a four-year college has been estimated by professionals to be 50,000 volumes, yet 50 percent of American colleges in the mid-1960s fell below this standard. The Act provided funds to improve libraries in various ways.

Title 3 had as its purpose the strengthening of developing educational institutions. For example, for every four American colleges there is one that cannot make the grade, that is, one that cannot obtain accreditation by some regional agency. This is particularly the case in smaller colleges. Funds would be provided under the Act to carry out cooperative programs

---

[126] Stephen K. Daily and Edith K. Mosher, *ESEA: The Office of Education Administers a Law,* Syracuse University Press, Syracuse, 1968. This book is an excellent summary of the evolution of the Act and should be consulted for more detail. See also *American Education,* Vol. 4, April 1968, pp. 2–29 for various articles.

[127] "A Fierce Commitment," *American Education,* Vol. 1, No. 10, November 1965, pp. 15–16.

and set up national teaching fellowships for developing institutions. Under a cooperative program, a developing institution could work in concert with similar institutions, with established colleges and universities, or with business organizations. The cooperation could take many forms and include such possibilities as exchanging faculty members and students, introducing new courses, sharing libraries or laboratories, bringing in visiting scholars, and offering cooperative work-study programs.

Title 4 was concerned with student financial assistance and provided for a college work-study program patterned after the NYC in-school youth program under the EOA. As we have seen, the average cost of attending a public college or university has risen rapidly in the past decade, and the relationship between family income and college attendance is well known. Title 4 was intended to start a program in education which would insure every American youth the fullest development of his mind and skills by establishing educational opportunity grants and by providing federally subsidized student loans. Colleges would administer the educational opportunity grants, including selecting the students eligible for help and making the decision as to how large a grant each student would get. Colleges were expected to search high schools for academic talent. Loan programs were to be administered either by a state, by a private nonprofit agency within a state, by a combination of both, or by the federal government.

Several provisions in the Act under Title 4 affected the college work-study program enacted as a part of the Economic Opportunity Act of 1964. In essence, the work-study program would be broadened making all needy students eligible for it instead of only those from low-income families, although preference would still be given to the latter.

Title 4 also amended the National Defense Education Act to allow colleges to use stronger procedures in collecting loans from students.[128]

Title 5 of the Act was concerned with programs for teachers and was directed toward improving the quality and number of teachers. This title established the National Teacher Corps and provided fellowships for graduate study. Members of the Teacher Corps could go by invitation to impoverished school districts to supplement the number of teachers employed there. Members of the Teacher Corps would be recruited, selected, and enrolled by the United States Commissioner of Education. They could be either experienced teachers or inexperienced teacher-interns having a bachelor's degree or its equivalent. Corpsmen would be employed, however, by the local school district; and the latter would have direct control over them, deciding where they were to be assigned or transferred and what they were to teach. Federal funds were to cover the corpsmen's

[128] *Ibid.*, pp. 16–19.

salaries, but the corpsmen would be on the local district's payroll and under local supervision. As indicated, Title 5 also authorized the Commissioner of Education to award two-year fellowships for graduate study leading to a master's degree or its equivalent to persons pursuing or intending to pursue a career in elementary or secondary education. As many as 4500 fellowships could be awarded in 1966 and 10,000 each in subsequent years.[129]

Title 6 provided for financial assistance for the improvement of undergraduate instruction. Since 1958, under the National Defense Education Act, high schools had been benefiting from new teaching methods, modern facilities, and up-to-date materials. But by 1965 it was thought that many of the freshmen enrolled in colleges were working with antiquated laboratories and other outdated equipment. Also, colleges had been training teachers for jobs in modernized high schools but were training them with instructional techniques that were out-of-date long before 1958, much less 1965. As a result, under Title 6 large sums of money were allocated to colleges and universities for teaching equipment and the minor remodeling of undergraduate facilities. Other funds were authorized for the purchase of television equipment and for related materials.

Title 7 amended the Higher Education Facilities Act of 1963 which had earlier provided for federal grants and loans for the construction of classrooms, laboratories, and libraries. However, grants for undergraduate use were restricted to the construction of libraries and facilities for the teaching of science, mathematics, modern foreign languages, and engineering subjects. These categorical restrictions were removed by the Higher Education Act of 1965, and a college could then begin to use its grant money as it chose within certain broad provisions, such as not using federal grants for buildings designed for events charging admission.

Lastly, under Title 8 certain general provisions were stated such as a stipulation concerning the responsibility for federal administration of the law while not exercising any direct supervision or control over the curriculum, program of instruction, administration, or manpower of any educational institution.[130] The latter provision of the law was consistent with the traditional democratic American belief that the federal government may have a role in education but it should not be one which results in a rigid control over local and state administration. This philosophy is somewhat of a movement away from the traditional idea that all education should be state and local and represents the most recent thinking concerning the role of the federal government in relationship to education.

[129] *Ibid.,* p. 20.
[130] *Ibid.,* pp. 18–22.

Again, we have no data which we can use to evaluate the Higher Education Act of 1965 and the more recent Higher Education Amendments of 1968.[131] Both pieces of legislation represent a long-range program that has significance for the nation and is important to manpower specialists in industry because it indicates the extent to which the federal government has stepped into another social problem area concerning education and taken action to improve the development of employees for professional positions. Like much prior legislation it has major provisions for the disadvantaged. Thus, whereas vocational education started in the United States a century ago in the colleges and worked down under federal government modeling and stimulation, professional education has been propped up about one hundred years later by improvements in the development of human resources at the primary- and secondary-school levels as well as by direct efforts to aid higher education to alleviate shortages of technical and professional manpower.[132]

EDUCATION PROFESSIONS DEVELOPMENT ACT OF 1967

The Education Professions Development Act (EPDA) of 1967 is concerned with bringing about another type of change in education. Under this act it is assumed that, if we want to alter the direction in which we are moving, educationally we as a nation must first bring about a change in people—in the attitudes, qualifications, and competencies of all the people who staff our schools and colleges. Early in its history American society preoccupied itself with school building and school programs while procrastinating over the preparation of people to work efficiently in those schools. The Elementary and Secondary Education Act, the Higher Education Act, the measures that explicitly stress vocational education (such as the Vocational Act of 1963 and the 1968 amendments), the Economic Opportunity Act of 1964 and others that have tackled adult illiteracy, and legislation that enabled financing the purchase of equipment and the construction of libraries and laboratories and other college facilities, all acknowledge that our society has now reached the point where it better understands the demands of schools and colleges. The Education Professions Development Act is a statement of our better understanding of how to meet those demands. In effect, this legislation endorses the concept that

[131] See Val Trimble, "Student Financial Aid: What, Where, How," *American Education*, Vol. 5, No. 2, February 1969, pp. 7–8.

[132] Relevant legislation not discussed in this chapter is: Nurse Training Act of 1964; Health Professions Educational Assistance Act of 1965; Allied Health Professions Personnel Training Act of 1966; and the Health Manpower Act of 1968.

none of the new educational programs, no matter how meticulously designed or expensively financed, can be effective without people prepared to make it educationally sound and operational.[133]

The EPDA is divided into six parts, each of which is worth a few words although any comments on the law itself would be premature since it has been on the books such a short period of time. First, the Act establishes an independent National Advisory Council on Education Professions Development which reports to the President and Congress the Commissioner of Education's annual assessment of educational manpower needs and a national education professions recruitment program. Second, the Teacher Corps is transferred from the Higher Education Act to inclusion in the Act. Third, there is a state grants program to meet immediate critical shortages of classroom manpower. Fourth, there are provisions for fellowships and training projects for prospective and experienced manpower of all kinds at the elementary and secondary level. There are, lastly, two provisions for training higher-education personnel and vocational educational personnel respectively.[134] The seeds for a national educational-planning report to take its place with the *Economic Report* and *Manpower Report* may be in EDPA.

CONCLUSIONS

In this chapter we have been discussing the evolution of legislation concerned with manpower, training, and industrial education. One of the most striking themes is the change in the nature of vocational education in the United States as it has evolved out of the public schools into a variety of imaginative new uses for developing manpower at all levels in American society. Certainly no one would argue any longer that vocational education should be confined to the secondary-school level. Indeed, it has always had implications for college-level instruction and the preparation of people for a variety of professional occupations. Now more than ever its applicability has been extended.

In a way we can say that the old three R's of education now center around race, revolt, and religion each of which is intimately tied to the emphasis upon, barriers to expansion of, and basis for building the American society of the future. Such recent innovations as the Model Cities Program, Special Impact Program, New Careers Program, Operation Mainstream, the Concentrated Employment Program (CEP), and

[133] Don Davies, "Education Professions Development," *American Education,* Vol. 5, No. 2, February 1969, p. 9.
[134] *Ibid.,* pp. 9–10. See also John Chaffee, Jr., "First Manpower Assessment," *American Education,* Vol. 5, No. 2, February 1969, pp. 11–12.

Work Incentive Program (WIN)[135] are still other aspects of contemporary human resources development and poverty fighting which may assume importance in the future.

If one were to summarize the vast and almost bewildering amount of legislation and programming pertaining to the development of manpower in American society today, there is little doubt that this undertaking would justify a fat book in itself. In panoramic view, we can see the integration of manpower planning, training programs, and opportunities for learning in industry with the evolving and virtually all-encompassing legislation in force in American society. The classroom and the factory are more than ever interconnected, and the same is true for the office and for the professional occupations.

Manpower and educational planning have rapidly become the concern of the Federal government; and, as the latter has realized that it cannot solve all of the complicated social problems involved, it has increasingly asked industry to intervene. Industry, in turn, has shown its willingness to participate widely in administering Job Corps centers, in accepting on-the-job trainees under MDTA, and in making proposals for the expansion of curricula in junior colleges and in high schools where funds from the Vocational Education Act of 1963 and 1968 amendments are being expended. We may or may not have a military-industrial complex in this country that acts as a power elite, but there is little doubt that we have an emerging industrial-governmental-educational complex of institutions which interpenetrate one another and show continuing signs of growth and integration for manpower development.

In broad perspective, the New Frontier and Great Society legislation may be viewed as the contemporary effort to complete the earlier New Deal of Franklin Delano Roosevelt. The Social Security legislation of the New Deal left many gaps that had to be closed in time because its basic approach to welfare and education was in terms of categories. Many people fell through the eligibility slats and drifted out of the mainstream of American society. Specifically, as the post-World War II period unfolded, it became obvious that not all persons in American society could be serviced by a categorical approach and, as a result, people in need both of jobs and education were not being serviced. The proliferation of new manpower, vocational education, and employment programs were an attempt to provide the necessary services.

As we look into the 1970s, there is no doubt that the manpower revolution of the 1960s and the legislation enacted during that decade will remain on the books and will not be discarded. The emphasis upon federal

[135] See *Manpower Report of the President, January, 1969, op. cit.,* pp. 7–9 for the details of some of these programs.

government programs in education and manpower will cause state and local school administration and manpower specialists in organizations to reassess their needs in the light of using and contributing to the conduct of government programs.

The Nixon administration will undoubtedly in time have some impact upon the manpower and education legislation, but it will certainly not be in the direction of extirpating the legislation from the books. There may be a greater emphasis than has existed in the past in encouraging private industry to participate more in solving manpower, employment, and educational problems. If this is to be the case, it suggests even more that manpower specialists in industrial and other organizations must be thoroughly acquainted with existing legislation and reassess the needs of their employers in the light of using and contributing to the conduct of government programs. In other words, the industrially employed specialist in manpower matters must think through organizational policies, plans, programs, and procedures and make a linkage with existing legislation. He must prepare himself to become organizational spokesman and the source of internal expertise on the direction public policy on manpower, employment, and education should take in the future. This new role certainly means that the limited-view training director of the past has become outmoded. In his place the manpower specialist must have a new outlook and a new sophistication in respect to public policy on manpower, training, and vocational education. It is quite true to say that vocational education will never be the same again. Whether it will become maximally useful, relevant, and effective will depend in major part upon what manpower specialists know about it and do about it.

CHAPTER 14

Manpower Planning and the Future: Conclusions and Prospects

Who today believes in static conceptions or pat answers to complex problems? The great new truth about society is *change,* movement. The unprecedented worldwide ferment we are experiencing is not a temporary disturbance that will go away in a few years. The causes that have set off change in American and world society are deep; and they are forever gathering strength. Individuals and nations today are volatile, restless, and increasingly motivated by a belief that they can radically alter their lives and their characters. They can and they do.[1] This dynamism is seen in the manpower field as well.

CHANGE AND THE TEMPORARY SOCIETY

In reality, American society may best be viewed as temporary and change as the constant. Ours is a society of temporary systems, nonpermanent relationships, turbulence, uprootedness, unconnectedness, mobility, and, above all, unexampled social change. Whereas it is too late to slow down the pace of temporary societies, it is not too late to examine ways that may be more adaptive in coping with temporary systems, ways that could both realize our full human potentialities and extract the benefits of change.[2] How can we do this?

To attain these planned changes we must continually confront and test our humanness and strive to become more fully human. In our society, we typically operate on a narrow range of the full spectrum of human potential. For the most part, our lives in large-scale organizations tend to com-

[1] Max Ways, "Gearing U.S. Policy to the World's Great Trends," *Fortune,* Vol. 79, No. 5, May 1, 1969, p. 65.

[2] Warren G. Bennis and Philip E. Slater, *The Temporary Society,* Harper and Row, New York, 1968, pp. 124–125.

press the possibilities even more. To be more fully human means that we must work hard at coming to terms with unfamiliar aspects of the human personality. It means we have to work equally hard to get other people to widen their responses so that they can understand and accept unfamiliarity and uncertainty. It means we must perceive our common humanness without fear of absorption or nothingness.[3]

There are many social forces operating today which conspire against our becoming fully human. For example, interpersonal relations and organizational life are both predicated upon the assumption of shared and stable expectations, making our very humanness difficult to preserve and project on the job.[4] For these reasons and others, manpower planning has become all the more essential in moving toward the accommodation of change and the socialization and growth of the individual in work organizations.

However, our society, and particularly our formal educational systems, must also become involved to help people develop the necessary competencies rather than, as tends to be true of most contemporary education, work against our full human development. Our educational systems should (1) help us to identify with the adaptive process without fear of losing our identity, (2) increase our tolerance of ambiguity without fear of losing our intellectual mastery, (3) increase our ability to collaborate without fear of losing our individuality, and (4) develop a willingness to participate in social change while recognizing the implacable forces operating to cause change. In short, we need an educational system that can help us make a virtue out of contingency rather than one which induces hesitancy or expediency.[5] We need to become more irreverent about bureaucracy and more humble about what we really know about management and the good life for people. We need to put some of the alternatives to bureaucratic styles into operation.[6]

We need also to develop some permanent or abiding commitments that can be widely held in our society. In the past, the economic, cultural, social, and political characteristics of a nation could remain fixed for generations. Policy makers, by knowing some history, knew a great deal about the present human material with which they dealt. But today, when nations and all other institutions are in motion, the policy maker needs to know where each is going rather than where it has been.[7] Possibly those

[3] *Ibid.*, pp. 125–126.
[4] *Ibid.*, pp. 126–127.
[5] *Ibid.*, p. 127.
[6] *Ibid.*, pp. 74–76.
[7] Ways, *op. cit.*, p. 65.

who do not know history are doomed to repeat it. But we cannot direct our future lives by a backward-looking orientation; and those who ignore the future may be doomed to destruction by it.

Without a clear formulation of national purpose and widespread commitment to it, our society can become prey to ongoing technology, such as trying a new weapons system merely because "it's there," and letting the instruments of policy become the determinants of policy. This is the essence of President Dwight D. Eisenhower's farewell address admonishing against the military-industrial complex, which we have yet to learn.[8]

Yet, we should avoid oversystematized formulas and strive for open adaptive policies that will prepare American society for dangers ahead that may be quite different from the dangers of the recent past. Without trying to forecast tomorrow's crises, we can be certain that world peace and domestic tranquility are not going to take the form of a stable equilibrium among nations or groups that are fixed and known quantities.[9] As in dominant-minority group relations, the most pacific mode will probably be an unstable, rolling equilibrium.

We are not able today to construct a very meaningful model of what the world ought to be. In fact, we cannot imagine with much precision what our own nation ought to be 20 years from now. In both domestic and foreign policy we are groping. But we are moving toward the realization of values that are deeply implanted in American society and also, it now seems, in mankind.[10] These values center upon human resources.

EDUCATION AND INDIVIDUALITY

The causes of social change in today's world are ascribed to science and technology. They have made manpower planning a necessity. But these are encompassed in a more fundamental cause: the rapid rise of education. Mass literacy and prolonged schooling are already established in many countries. Nobody doubts that these trends are spreading and accelerating. The educated man has replaced the strong man, the rich man, and the sacerdotal man as the characteristic leader of society.[11] The net change runs from muscle to mind, from power based upon the legalities of office

---

[8] *Ibid.*, p. 150. See also John Kenneth Galbraith, "How to Control the Military," *Harpers*, Vol. 238, No. 1429, June 1969, pp. 31–45.

[9] Ways, *op. cit.*, p. 153.

[10] *Ibid.*

[11] For an excellent analysis of this point, see Peter F. Drucker, *The Age of Discontinuity,* Harper & Row, New York, 1969, pp. 263–310.

and ownership to influence derived from knowledge and the arts of communication.[12]

Therefore, we see a rise in human self-awareness, self-respect, and self-expression. These are a great complex of patterns and values, often formulated as "rights," which amount to a new sense of personhood or individuality. Today education, especially at the higher levels, stimulates individuality. Specialized knowledge is internal and personal in a way that no property right can ever be internal and personal. As an asset, education is thus literally "inalienable." The person who brings such an asset into cooperation with the specialized skills of other men deals from a strong bargaining position that will increasingly protect not only his material income but also his self-concept and self-expression.[13] The person lacking knowledge is widely identified in American society as "disadvantaged" and must struggle vigorously to express his individuality, if, indeed, he can. Such people are regarded today as incompletely socialized or in need of resocialization. Their very existence is our prime contemporary social problem.

This change to a society requiring men-of-knowledge, a dominant salariat of managerial, professional, and technical manpower, is most visible in the United States, but it is starting to appear elsewhere in the world, too. In the last 30 years, and especially the last five, the internal character of American business organizations has begun a basic transformation reflecting the enhanced position of the individual. Increasingly, the assembly line in the factory is becoming automated, signifying it is the way machines, not men, work. The undifferentiated blue-collar proletariat is slowly disappearing, and its destiny is not of a great deal of interest to top management in large-scale organizations, except when its future survival is brought up and bargained for by unions or aspirants for political power.

Impersonal routine is being replaced by imaginative innovation; command, by persuasion and participative techniques; and hierarchical decision making, by a broader, subtler process in which many more people become involved democratically in an organization's direction.[14] Increasingly, the emergence of an awareness of our humanness and the need for its preservation and expression are calling to mind that there are such realizable human resource development goals as joy [15] and ecstasy.[16]

[12] Ways, *op. cit.*, p. 66.
[13] *Ibid.*
[14] *Ibid.*
[15] William C. Schutz, *Joy*, Grove Press, New York, 1967.
[16] George B. Leonard, *Education and Ecstasy*, Delacorte Press, New York, 1968.

Indeed, nothing short of self-actualization [17] may become our eventual goal in respect to the development of human resources in society. Conversely, the cardinal sins would become malutilization and underachievement.

The achievement of individuality through self-actualizing experience truly presents a challenge that will tantalize the manpower specialist in the remaining decades of the 20th century, *1970–2000* A.D. Not only must he conceive of his role in terms of behavior change leading to skill development but also growth toward self-actualization.[18] The latter may be viewed as simply another way of looking at the practical side of an active manpower policy, which is already touted by the Secretary of Labor as a national goal: to enable every American to realize his full potential and to utilize it fully in his own and the nation's interest.

These manpower concerns as they relate to the future are the subject matter of this chapter. Our approach is to set in this context such apparently diverse manpower problems as: the future of the federal-state employment service as a national manpower service coordinator; the National Alliance of Businessmen and its implications for the social responsibility of business today; the Urban Coalition, ghetto plants, and black capitalism; the New Federalism of the Nixon Administration; new views on the interrelationship of public and private manpower planning; industry and change; and the conclusion.

There are, as would be expected, several enigmas concerning policy, practice, problems and organizational structure which are examined in this concluding chapter. There is little doubt that we have much to learn about manpower planning and human resources development. Practice will probably run ahead of theory and research because the latter two tend to lag behind the fast-moving world of everyday life.

Problems in manpower planning and human resource development confront organizations daily, and absent viable theories or research findings, actions will be taken to surmount these problems. These actions will not be unguided by theory because all human actions are based upon some assumptions, beliefs, or rules-of-thumb. It would, of course, be preferable to act on carefully thought-out bases, consistent with some objectives. We try here in the last chapter of the book to establish guideposts for policy and practice by considering actions already underway or advocated in proposed legislation. As has been stated by two prominent observers of the manpower scene: "In the end, the manpower problems of the past few years cannot be blamed upon the lack of information concerning the

---

[17] Everett L. Shostrom, *Man, The Manipulator,* Bantam, New York, 1968.
[18] See also Bennis and Slater, *op. cit.,* pp. 127–128.

manpower future. Action, not information, has been the absent factor." [19]
Guideposts for action by manpower specialists in firms are our concern.

THE FEDERAL-STATE EMPLOYMENT SERVICE

Inasmuch as 90 percent of the American people make their living through having a job (as opposed to others "working for themselves" as farmers, physicians, lawyers, and the like), the existence of jobs and the persons having them are central concerns. Preparing for a job, getting a job, holding a job, separating from a job, and finding another job to replace it are crucial matters for large numbers of persons. The institution which assists the individual in this process (the employment service) is therefore vital to the welfare of the nation, the efficiency of the economy, and the maximum utilization of human resources.[20] Yet this institution remains quite defective in the United States.

Public responsibility for assisting in the employment process has an extensive history. Much of the American educational system is related to it, such as skilled-trades apprenticeship and vocational training of all types. Many years ago, there were municipal labor exchanges where workers and employees could meet one another. Later the federal and state governments became aware of the need for job-finding services, which in time were expanded to include counseling, guidance, testing, job referral, job placement, and labor market and job information. The public institution now supplying these services is the United States Employment Service (USES— or ES, for short).[21]

The ES is a federal-state system of public employment offices. In partnership with the states, the ES operates a nationwide system under which the federal partner provides general policies, overall direction, technical service to the states; and also develops tools, techniques, and operating procedures. The individual states operate and staff the local offices and pay their employees with federal funds according to each state's salary schedule.[22] In recent years, there have been 2400 full-time local offices and 1900 itinerant points served by the ES.[23]

[19] Garth L. Mangum and Arnold L. Nemore, "The Nature and Function of Manpower Projections," *Industrial Relations,* Vol. 5, No. 3, May 1966, p. 15.

[20] William Haber and Daniel H. Kruger, *The Role of the United States Employment Service in a Changing Economy,* Upjohn Institute for Employment Research, Kalamazoo, 1964, p. 1.

[21] *Ibid.,* pp. 1–2.

[22] *Ibid.,* p. 2.

[23] Leonard P. Adams, *The Public Employment Service in Transition, 1933–1968* (Cornell Studies in Industrial and Labor Relations, Volume XVI), New York State School of Industrial and Labor Relations, Cornell University, Ithaca, 1969, pp. 68–73.

The ES goes back to the Wagner-Peyser Act of 1933 which, among other things, provided for the federal grant-in-aid plan for funding the state employment offices and for the provision of a few selected services, such as counseling and placement help for the handicapped and special assistance for veterans and farmers.[24] Its subsequent historical evolution as a social invention has been aptly described as the search to find a more rational approach to improving labor market organization and to bring about a more effective utilization of human resources.[25] Yet, it has suffered severely from a bad image and the dumping of other complex machinery on it almost from the day of its birth. For example, in 1935 after the passage of the Social Security Act the local ES offices were given the task of administering the work test for unemployment insurance benefit claims. Taking claims and paying benefits tended to overshadow and obscure the basic worker-finding and job-finding activities of the ES. Consequently, the "employment office" became the "unemployment office" or the "social security office" in the public mind, and with the advent of publicly known "chiseling" [26] the new institution came to be regarded in some quarters as a big boondoggle.

The ES has had its friendly, objective critics over the years, all of whom have carefully examined its problems, shortfalls, and accomplishments.[27] All have made proposals for its improvement. Yet, among the public, there still exists much of this reasoning about the desirability of a public employment service: when times are good and the business cycle is on the upswing, anyone who really wants to work can find a job either on his own, through the help of friends or relatives, through newspaper advertisements, or by direct application; when times are bad, there are not any jobs to be found; therefore, the ES cannot do anything for anyone anyhow.

Criticism of the Employment Service

Since the mid-1960s, the ES has served (or tried to serve) the hard-to-place worker and the employer with the hard-to-fill job. In fact, few institutions have been asked to change so much in so brief a period as has the ES in recent years. New functions have been assigned to it; new and often inconsistent goals have been set; and profound shifts have been

[24] *Ibid.*, pp. 23–24.

[25] Haber and Kruger, *op. cit.*, p. 40.

[26] See Erwin O. Smigel, "Public Attitudes Toward 'Chiseling' with Reference to Unemployment Compensation," *American Sociological Review,* Vol. 18, No. 1, February, 1953, pp. 59–67.

[27] See Haber and Kruger, *op. cit.;* Adams, *op. cit.;* Richard A. Lester, *Manpower Planning in a Free Society,* Princeton University Press, Princeton, 1966; and E. Wight Bakke, *A Positive Labor Market Policy,* Merrill, Cincinnati, 1963.

underway in the distribution of power within the system.[28] Almost overnight the disdained agency became the chosen instrument of the manpower revolution. In many respects it appeared that the ES was trying to become all things to all men. Fuzzy thinking was rife. It is therefore worthwhile to analyze nine reasons why some of the major expectations of the ES have appeared to be exaggerated if not unrealizable.[29]

First, the ES cannot get a job for everyone who is seeking one. Many people are not directly employable. In other cases, the demand for manpower is weak.

Second, it may not even be possible for the ES to provide a meaningful service for every person who seeks its help. If a job cannot be provided, there may be nothing else that a registrant wants or can use.

Third, the ES will not always be able to meet all employers' demands, even for unskilled labor, because the effective manpower supply is inadequate.

Fourth, it is not the province of the ES to be sole provider of service to potential employees and potential employers. In some communities, employer opposition to the ES runs deeply and has been of long standing. For certain types of employees, such as recent college graduate trainees, new institutional channels have arisen in the form of college placement offices which have now virtually preempted the ES from access to this high-talent manpower.[30]

Fifth, the detailed record-keeping and reporting demands made of the ES probably can never be relaxed because unemployment insurance monies are involved. Yet, these requirements are likely to maintain the clerically oriented image of the ES, which is out of step with the concept of the ES as a one-stop community manpower center with a smooth-honed services delivery system.

Sixth, much stress has been placed upon the desirability of attracting and retaining higher caliber staff personnel in the ES. Yet, this same exhortation is made of every large-scale organization, public and private, and does not really provide a solution unless more is known about a staff member's education and personality and his job performance.

Seventh, it is argued that the ES should spend more time appraising those who seek its help. Yet, more time spent with clients would require corresponding adjustments of staff and budgets. There is evidence that

---

[28] Sar A. Levitan, *Federal Training and Work Programs in the Sixties,* Institute of Labor and Industrial Relations, University of Michigan, Ann Arbor, 1969, p. 335.

[29] Eli Ginzberg, "Employment Service—Chosen Instrument of the Manpower Revolution," *Employment Service Review,* Vol. 4, Nos. 3–4, March-April 1967, pp. 7–8.

[30] See Haber and Kruger, *op. cit.,* pp. 61–64.

when time, staff, and budget are made available that employability can be enhanced.[31]

Eighth, the ES has been criticized for placing people, particularly young people, in low-level jobs. But what realistic employment alternative is there for an unskilled man or woman, especially one not interested in additional training?

Lastly, the ES has been accused of not doing all that it can and should do to implement the manpower programs legislated into existence in the 1960s. Yet, with the very modest adjustments in budgets and staff given it, the service cannot be expected to work miracles.[32] In many respects the ES has had a serious problem of digestion of new manpower responsibilities for which it was neither prepared nor aided.

In short, the ES has been advised to do too much with too little. Its critics have often had no real understanding of the complexities involved in providing effective services to the hard-to-place individual. Also, the critics have further underestimated the lack of public acceptance, if not outright hostility, that the ES faces in many communities.[33] The employer with the hard-to-fill lower-level job has sought applicants from the ES, but the source for managerial, technical, and professional manpower is seldom seen to be the local bad-image "social security office."

CAMPS, HRD, and the New USTES

The CAMPS Program (Cooperative Area Manpower Planning System) announced in 1966 by the federal Manpower Administration has tried to tie together various levels of government involved in the ES in administering all federally aided manpower programs. The CAMPS structure is based upon local planning committees in 400 labor markets across the country. Local governmental agencies closely linked with participating federal agencies have formed the nucleus of these committees. Information, advice, and assistance are sought from community leaders, employers, and unions. These local organizations are complemented by a state system of CAMPS committees. The state committee is responsible for developing a comprehensive state plan which allocates all federal manpower programs available to the state. The state plan is reviewed by a federal regional CAMPS committee chaired by the regional manpower administrator, which has approval authority. CAMPS is thus the most ambitious and far-reaching attempt to regularize manpower planning that has ever been

---

[31] Thomas H. Patten, Jr., and J. Douglas Foley, "The Hard-to-Place Professional," *Management of Personnel Quarterly*, Vol. 8, No. 2, Summer 1969, pp. 24–30.

[32] These nine essential points are Ginzberg's, *op. cit.*, p. 8.

[33] *Ibid.*

undertaken. It has already produced information never before available and has made strides toward the coordination of manpower plans. The extent to which CAMPS should become a funding system has not been resolved. The extent to which it can become flexible and adaptable to redirecting programs to meet emergency needs remains untested.[34] Whether the ES can make CAMPS all that it could be remains to be seen. The same may be said of other important new departures of the ES, to which we turn next.

In 1965 the Secretary of Labor announced a "Human Resources Development Program (HRD)" to combine the resources of a number of agencies in an intensive effort to solve the employment problems of ghetto residents. The HRD concept was adopted as a major new thrust involving a large share of ES resources and staff. The national office moved to install the HRD concept as operating policy at all levels of the ES.[35]

The HRD concept proposes to screen in rather than screen out the disadvantaged, and involves outreach into urban slums and rural pockets of poverty with an accent on youth, referral to supportive services to improve the employability of those not ready for training or a job, counseling and interviewing, training, job development, and placement geared to the special needs of the disadvantaged. Its implementation has been fostered by shifts in funding, by the push for localized plans of service, and by the adoption of a new budget system which departs from the emphasis upon the number of ES placements as in the past and concentrates instead on new programs and goals.[36]

Considering the shifts in emphasis in the ES in recent years, it is not surprising that the HRD concept has yet to achieve general acceptance throughout the ES. Some evidence suggests the state, local, and even federal ES staff members still prefer the more traditional roles. However, others who have sought to implement the community manpower service agency concept of the ES, but who lacked the resources and support for it, welcome the new thrust with fewer reservations. Many staff people are bothered because they are expected to add the new HRD emphasis to existing work loads with no clear designation or priorities. Presently, ambivalence exists between those eager to serve the disadvantaged and those who believe that doing so will hamper their ability to serve· other groups and will damage their image in the eyes of employers and their communities by becoming another welfare agency.[37]

---

[34] *Manpower Report of the President, January, 1969*, Government Printing Office, Washington, 1969, pp. 129–131.

[35] Levitan and Mangum, *op. cit.*, pp. 350–351.

[36] *Ibid.*, p. 351.

[37] *Ibid.*, pp. 351–352. For insights into HRD and the transition of the ES, see Frank

It is probably too early to appraise the efforts made in recent years to redirect the tradition-bound administrative system of the ES. While it can be argued that the ES should be the chosen instrument for the nation's manpower programs in the inner city where minorities are concentrated, in many cities the ES has been forced to yield, often after bitter fights, to new programs and agencies funded in part by the federal government. Despite HRD and similar efforts, the inability of the men at the top of the ES to make these new concepts and policies stick suggests far-reaching personnel and organizational changes are required.[38]

To a large extent, the ES services consist of working with minority-group clientele and filling entry-level, unskilled jobs. It is therefore regrettable that many state employment services lack a vigorous equal opportunity stance and a record which corresponds. Despite efforts to change it, the orientation of ES officials too often remains that of serving the employer rather than the client. Furthermore, the complex administrative structure of the ES provides strategic advantages to those with older and more traditional outlooks and to those who have a vested interest in undercutting new civil rights policy objectives.[39]

Among the significant innovations started in the last few years to improve the Employment Service is the Experimental Training Center for Employment Security administered by the School of Labor and Industrial Relations at Michigan State University. This experimental program has been used to train ES managerial and professional employees in management skills, communications, and in other technical tools and skills needed to improve ES operations.

Also of importance are the changes initiated in the Nixon administration which build upon suggestions for improving the ES made by various task forces and friendly critics and are also addressed to the overlap and loose administration of manpower programs, caused by their proliferation from $3 million to $2.5 billion in the last five years of the 1960s. The essential changes are establishing an Assistant Secretary of Labor for Manpower who is responsible for policy matters and a redefinition of the work of the federal Manpower Administrator, who would carry out day-to-day administration in the newly created United States Training and Employment Service. This service would be a new central manpower clearinghouse and

---

H. Cassell, *The Public Employment Service: Organization in Change,* Academic Publications, Ann Arbor, 1968.

[38] Richard P. Nathan, *Jobs & Civil Rights,* Government Printing Office, Washington, 1969, pp. 170–171, 207.

[39] *Ibid.,* pp. 206–207. For an overview of employment services in other countries, see Alfred L. Green, *Manpower and the Public Employment Service in Europe,* New York State Department of Labor, Albany, 1966.

would handle all employment, work-experience, and training programs (except apprenticeship), including certain functions of the former United States Employment Service and about a dozen other agencies. The USTES would be, in effect, a new superbureau. Eight regional administrators, consolidating all the manpower functions with their regions, will report directly to the federal Manpower Administrator.[40]

The USTES should save time and money and reduce the effort needed to make things happen. For example, formerly a program that might have required approving action in five or more bureaus now may be handled in one national and one regional office. This streamlining also offers a benefit potentially even more important for manpower specialists in organizations: improved governmental cooperation with industrial and community groups. It is well known that some companies and organizations with the desire and ability to help solve manpower problems have hesitated to enter the labyrinth of technical requirements (or have been frustrated when they tried).[41]

The reorganization may mean greater decentralization of authority in manpower and training to the state and local level. This shift will probably mean more direct involvement of the governors and mayors in manpower programs. Although such a shift promises to heighten political pressures, it should also put far more thrust behind job programs.[42]

In the past few years, new hopes have been attached to the states to solve various urban and manpower problems. The cities lack the resources to cope with their most serious problems. The federal government, even if it were not beset by competing military and economic pressures, has proved in three decades of stabbing involvement that it is too awkward a bureaucratic giant to respond intelligently to the needs of cities with diverse problems. Private enterprise and the great foundations are entering the fray, but by themselves they have neither the funds nor the legal authority to achieve more than piecemeal solutions. The states remain, and they are the legal creators of the cities. They possess the legal powers required to repair most of the urban weaknesses, but they usually lack the financial capacity and political will to take on the job.[43]

The federal government has now virtually gotten its manpower house

---

[40] "Straightening Out the 'Useful Mess,' " *Business Week,* No. 2067, April 12, 1969, p. 164.

[41] *Ibid.*

[42] *Ibid.*

[43] A. James Reichley, "The States Hold the Keys to the Cities," *Fortune,* Vol. 79, No. 7, June 1969, p. 134. For views stressing the centrality of the cities, see Fred Powledge, "The Flight from City Hall," *Harper's,* Vol. 239, No. 1434, November 1969, pp. 69–86.

in order as it enters the 1970s and is better prepared to play its proper leadership role. It is delegating operating responsibility to the regions, states, and cities. It is bringing manpower programs closer to the business- man and to the men and women who want decent jobs, not a handout.[44] These shifts should make it easier for manpower specialists in organiza- tions to work collaboratively with governments. They also mean they will need to become increasingly involved in urban affairs. Already more and more employers are becoming heavily involved, which we examine next.

THE NATIONAL ALLIANCE OF BUSINESSMEN AND SOCIAL RESPONSIBILITY

Despite all the reports and evaluations made of the Employment Service in recent years, the fact remains that it failed to fulfill the central purpose of its existence, at least historically viewed, *viz.,* placing people on jobs. There may be many good reasons for the failures but the consequences have meant that other organizations have arisen to accomplish results or have been forced into existence to solve problems which the ES could not. For example, voluntary placement agencies have been set up in urban areas to place minority youth not served by the YOC's (i.e., Youth Op- portunity Centers of the ES). The JOBS (Job Opportunities in the Busi- ness Sector) program of the NAB (National Alliance of Businessmen) has carried out an effective campaign of job development where the Employ- ment Service probably never could. College placement offices have proven more convenient and effective for employers than the Employment Ser- vice's handful of professional placement centers. The examples could be multiplied, but all suggest that the late 1960s were spawning years for new solutions to social problems and innovations in the manpower field.

Beginning with the black rebellion in Watts in 1964 and culminating in the Detroit riots of 1967, the more prominent socioeconomic malaises of America exploded in violence which influential observers thought could reach epidemic dimensions.[45]

Ever since the enactment of the Area Redevelopment Act in 1961 and the Manpower Development and Training Act in 1962, the need for more relevant, timely, and comprehensive programs for manpower development, training, jobs, and civil rights in employment was obvious. The cities were

[44] "Straightening Out the 'Useful Mess,' " *op. cit.,* p. 164. See also John Fischer, "Can the Nixon Administration Be Doing Something Right?," *Harper's,* Vol. 241, No. 1446, November 1970, pp. 22–37.

[45] Alfonso J. Cervantes, "To Prevent a Chain of Super-Watts," *Harvard Business Review,* Vol. 45, No. 5, September-October 1967, pp. 55–65.

seething with restive hard-core unemployed ethnic and racial minorities, and the rural backwaters and hollows contained large numbers of poverty-stricken people whom life had passed by. The American legal system and tardy but rational approach through legislation for solving problems was under attack. In at least some corners, it was being said that for 35 years government had failed to solve social problems; all that was really needed was the knowhow of the free enterprise system, business. This type of generalization is often made these days when the subject under discussion is business and the urban crisis.[46]

However, it is as foolish to think business has all the answers to social problems as it is to assume that government does. The cliche that "business has the answer" could come back to plague the business community because, when the problems are still with us a few years hence, business could become the whipping boy.[47] However, it is surely true in the language of the ghetto: they (business) are the cats that have the bread.

On the other hand, there is a certain inherent logic in looking toward business for solutions. Governments have made limited headway, are top-heavy in bureaucracy, and lack the money. Government may be the largest of growth "industries" today, but its performance lacks clout. Moreover, there are probably greater job-creation possibilities in business than in government. If business is asked to tackle the problems, accepts the challenge, and fails to solve them, public administrators will feel more confident about trying again through legislation and ameliorative programs, perhaps taking some pleasure in seeing business fail. If business solves the problems, any credit it gets will be attenuated by the expectation that it should have succeeded anyhow. Thus, in either event, shifting the burden for solving social problems to industry probably will not do harm to governments unless industry takes a continuing interest in the new business (at a profit) of social problem solving, such as building ghetto housing or restoring slum neighborhoods. The needs to rebuild urban America and to respond to the doubling of our urban population have obvious implications for profit opportunity. It may be that we are on the threshold of a new era of government-industry relations.

The role of business in solving social problems must be viewed practically and clearly because the full potential of business in this area is unknown. Hopefully, business can do more than seems possible now. But a proper perspective on this issue cannot be obtained without reference to one cardinal consideration: in major undertakings requiring the substantial

[46] Robert D. Stuart, Jr., "Business and the Urban Crisis," *Manpower,* Vol. 1, No. 4, May 1969, p. 6.
[47] *Ibid.*

investment of funds, the profit potential must be sufficient to attract business interest on an economic basis. To justify the full energy and strength
of the corporation, there must be a chance for profit; it is a disservice to
all concerned when this consideration is ignored.[48]

Yet, stressing the need for profits when business attacks social problems
does not mean that business must show a profitable return on everything
it does to improve society.[49] Inasmuch as most large firms operate in urban
areas, it is pragmatic for them to help solve the manpower, employment,
and training problems of ghetto residents as a *quid pro quo* for not having
their factories burned down.

The traditional role of business as a socially responsible corporate
citizen—while it is not enough in today's environment—is undoubtedly
more important than it ever has been. There are a multitude of governmental and civic affairs that are related to the profit motive and that
reflect directly on the company and contribute to a better environment for
everyone, including the business community. Three criteria apply to
whether an organization should involve itself in a program designed to
solve social problems. The program should: (1) perform a genuine service;
(2) be innovative and ultimately capable of multiplying its effect by being
adopted by other organizations; and (3) reflect creditably on the sponsoring firm.[50]

The JOBS program of NAB meets these criteria and is worth at least
brief elaboration here because it holds the greatest promise for achieving
practical results.

Both NAB and JOBS were called for by President Lyndon B. Johnson
in his Manpower Message to Congress on January 23, 1968. The National
Alliance of Businessmen is a panel of 15 of the nation's most prominent
business executives; Henry Ford II was the original chairman of the NAB,
serving for one year, and he has since been succeeded by other prominent
business leaders. Initially, NAB's goal was to put 500,000 severely disadvantaged workers on business payrolls by June, 1971, with the first
100,000 to be on the job by July, 1969. According to the NAB, this
interim target of 100,000 has already been exceeded; and the three-year
target of 500,000 has been raised to 614,000. The NAB has also announced plans to take the JOBS program into 75 more cities, bringing the
total number of cities involved to 125.[51] Whether NAB can deliver jobs

[48] *Ibid.,* pp. 6–7.
[49] *Ibid.,* p. 7.
[50] *Ibid.*
[51] Emil Michael Aun, "JOBS Is Putting People to Work," *Manpower,* Vol. 1, No.
4, May 1969, pp. 14–17.

and provide continuing employment for the hard core in the long run depends upon the installation of reverse seniority or functionally equivalent plans intended to improve the hard-core individual's toehold to jobs.

Under the JOBS program the company provides employment and training for the disadvantaged and bears as much of the cost as would be experienced if the new trainees were not disadvantaged. The cost of the additional training and supportive service (i.e., remedial education, medical services, supervisory training, and the like) necessary to bring the disadvantaged to a satisfactory level of performance and to retain them are borne by the federal government. These supportive services are intended to facilitate the assimilation of the hard-core unemployed and to make them permanent and productive members of the labor force—thereby bringing them into the mainstream of American society. Recent revisions of the JOBS program not only provide for hiring and training the disadvantaged but also the upgrading of present employees. Not-for-profit organizations—such as hospitals and health and welfare agencies—can now participate together with profit-making enterprises. Government officials and businessmen have found that locating and hiring the disadvantaged is much easier than keeping and motivating them. They recognize that the use of special, supportive services is necessary for the long-range success of any manpower program aimed at the hard-core unemployed.

The evidence available to date suggests that JOBS does perform a genuine service, that it is an innovation that can be multiplied in its effects in times of prosperity and full employment by being spread to many organizations, and that it reflects creditably on the NAB members. However, not all efforts made by large-scale organizations to solve social problems have been as successful in their respective realms, and we turn to these next.

THE URBAN COALITION, GHETTO PLANTS, AND BLACK CAPITALISM

It is important to remember that the United States was founded, built, populated, and sustained by individuals whose characteristic response to social problems was flight, escape, and avoidance.[52] Suburbia and exurbia are also a result of these impulses. These phenomena explain how it was possible for an entire generation of corporate executives to drive their Cadillacs to work daily through the freeways adjacent to (if not in) the slums of America and not realize that someday these ghetto poor would

---

[52] Bennis and Slater, op. cit., p. 50, citing K. Erikson, Wayward Puritans, Wiley, New York, 1966, p. 39.

rise to threaten both the corporate balance sheet and the whole fabric of American life.[53]

A number of businessmen, aware that civic chaos was not in their best interest, formed the Urban Coalition in 1966 to mobilize a broad base of support for jobs, housing, and school programs for minority groups. The Detroit Riot of 1967 hardened the Coalition's resolve and accelerated its sense of urgency, for Detroit was home base for the nation's greatest industry, a progressive union (The United Automobile Workers), and a mayor who was perceived as dynamic and *au courant* with all the manpower and other problems of urban areas.

The Urban Coalition

The Urban Coalition provides an umbrella for leaders from five major segments of American society: management, organized labor, religion, minority groups, and local government. It also provides a forum for an exchange of ideas in our era of change and violence. The Coalition commits a businessman to a first-hand confrontation of ghetto problems and gives him a chance to hammer out programs with Negro and church leaders.[54]

One of the Coalition's early goals was to create counterpart coalitions in the nation's major cities with the same leadership elements that make up the national coalition, and with each locally financed. Similar to the national, the local coalitions have task forces working to mobilize community consensus on manpower issues and urban problems. The Coalition has tried to avoid the image of being an organization that merely conducts meetings, holds press conferences, and issues position-paper handouts. It has, in fact, had some legislative clout under its distinguished head, John W. Gardner.[55] Yet, there is still much doubt as to how effective it has actually been in galvanizing into action at the local level the various segments of society seeking solutions to pressing urban problems.[56] With Gardner's resignation in 1970 the future of the coalition was clouded.

Ghetto Plants

Meanwhile, in the ghettos themselves, the task of training the unemployed and bringing them into the mainstream of American life has been

---

[53] "Employing the Unemployable," *Fortune*, Vol. 78, No. 1, July 1968, p. 29.

[54] "Business Joins the War on Urban Ills," *Business Week*, No. 2017, April 27, 1968, pp. 84–86.

[55] *Ibid.*, pp. 86–90.

[56] "Coalition Acts as Critics Talk," *Business Week*, No. 2078, June 28, 1969, pp. 54–56. See also, Grace J. Finley, "An Assessment of the Urban Coalition," *Conference Board Record*, Vol. 7, No. 2, February 1970, pp. 48–52.

taken on by minority group members, well-known corporations, and programs of black capitalism.

One of the most frequently mentioned success stories of efforts made by minority group members is the program begun in 1964 by Reverend Leon H. Sullivan, founder and chairman of the board of Opportunities Industrialization Center (OIC) in Philadelphia. His work with OIC is notable as the first massive, grass-roots, manpower training program in the United States. His program is intended to train the unskilled and pays no training allowances, although every person who stays on the program until completion is guaranteed there will be a job at the end—and, importantly, a job with a future.[57]

Two other innovations of the OIC programs are attempts made at resocialization of trainees. The OIC concept provides for a Feeder School, a free vocational school (with courses lasting from two weeks to three months, depending upon the student) that includes in its curriculum courses in self-confidence and grooming along with basic reading, writing, and arithmetic. The objective, according to Reverend Sullivan, is ". . . to unwash the brainwashed mind of enrollees who have come to OIC with poor opinions of themselves and who, for 100 years, have been brainwashed into inferiority." Trainees are also taught Negro history so that they can obtain some perspective on their historical roots. After completing the Feeder School, the trainee is assigned to a technical training center where he learns a skill.[58]

The OIC programs are considered very successful. Ninety-seven percent of the trainees are in poverty income brackets, and more than 35 percent are from the relief rolls. Of the first 10,000 trainees who were enrolled, 5000 were placed in meaningful jobs with a future.[59] OIC now operates centers in 80 cities and has trained about 50,000 people. Many business leaders have asked President Nixon to make OIC a major element in his manpower programs. They believe that Reverend Sullivan's methods of motivating trainees are unsurpassed and that OIC can be an effective companion to NAB, which has been less than successful in involving small- and medium-sized companies in its volunteer effort.[60] Other Negro bootstrapping programs could also be cited, but none has succeeded like OIC.

Corporations had also stepped up to solving the problems of ghetto employment before NAB was founded. Some of these companies which,

---

[57] *Mobilizing for Urban Action,* American Management Association, New York, 1968, pp. 16–17.

[58] *Ibid.*

[59] *Ibid.,* p. 17.

[60] "Business Lobbies for Ghetto Program," *Business Week,* No. 2078, June 28, 1969, pp. 56–57.

either on their own or under government prodding, put up plants in slum areas are: Avco Corporation (which built a commercial printing plant in the predominantly Negro Roxbury area of Boston); Control Data Corporation of Minneapolis; Aerojet-General (which set up a factory at Watts to carry out manufacturing work in heavy fabrics, metal, and wood); and Lockheed Aircraft Corporation (which attracted Negroes from Atlanta to its plant fifteen miles away in Marietta and lured Mexican-American farm laborers from outside San Jose to the Sunnyvale, California, plant).[61] Other companies and their programs could also be mentioned.[62]

Black Capitalism

Black capitalism is a third approach to solving manpower problems in the ghetto, although possibly it is turning out to be more of a catchy phrase and canard than a workable, programmable idea. In the 1968 Presidential election the phrase cropped up many times.

The concept of black capitalism is based upon the fact that the Negro has been largely excluded from the economic control of his own destiny. The situation in New York's Harlem is illustrative of the economic conditions in other large urban ghettoes. Harlem has 500,000 black people who spend $500 million each year on consumer goods. Eighty percent of Harlem's 6000 retail and manufacturing businesses are owned and managed by whites who show little interest in the welfare of the community itself. Harlem's central problem is the huge leakage of its capital. Profits made in Harlem are drained off the Harlem community and never find their way back. The root difficulty is that almost no one who lives in Harlem owns anything. The solution often proposed is black capitalism or programs directed toward giving Negroes increasing control over their own economic interests. This could be done by creating and implementing new business ventures for black entrepreneurs. In turn, this suggestion raises questions about how Negro entreprises can finance and establish new businesses, subcontracting to minority vendors, franchising, and getting corporations to deposit corporate funds in banks controlled by blacks.[63]

Black capitalism so construed would never be more than a partial solution to the manpower and training problems of Negroes, anymore than

[61] For details see "Bringing New Jobs into the Ghettoes," *Business Week*, No. 1996, December 2, 1967, pp. 84–86; and James D. Hodgson and Marshall H. Brenner, "Successful Experience: Training the Hard-Core Unemployed," *Harvard Business Review*, Vol. 46, No. 5, September-October 1968, pp. 148–156.

[62] For more negative views on ghetto plant programs and the extent they would be economically justifiable without government manpower training subsidies, see John T. Garrity, "Red Ink for Ghetto Industries?," *Harvard Business Review*, Vol. 46, No. 2, May-June 1968, pp. 4–16, 158–171.

[63] *Mobilizing for Urban Action, op. cit.*, pp. 32–33.

white capitalism would solve the same problems for disadvantaged whites (who, of course, are not subjected to the discriminations suffered by minorities). The idea of black capitalism smacks of segregation and withdrawal rather than integration and democracy. Yet, there is evidence that Negro ghetto residents can be transformed into entrepreneurs,[64] if, indeed, this needed to be proven in the light of long-standing evidence of successful Negro entrepreneurship, tens of thousands existing as long ago at 1910.[65] Legitimate questions should be raised about the public policy aspects of black capitalism that amounts to black separatism.[66] It is quite possible that the concept will prove faddish or be reinterpreted to mean: equal opportunity for blacks as well as whites in order to become independent businessmen or industrial managers and professional employees in organizations of all kinds.

In summary, the new ideas evolving for the solution of manpower problems in urban areas under the umbrella of a concerted urban coalition, the establishment of plants in ghettos, efforts made by blacks to lift themselves up by their own bootstraps or with some government funding, and the stimulation of new black industrial enterprise are examples of private-public partnerships or at least acts of institutional interpenetration. It can be confidently predicted that we shall see more of these interpenetrations in the 1970s as well as a continuation of the NAB programs. Let us turn next to the concepts the stream of new legislation is likely to encapsulate.

MOVING AHEAD IN THE 1970S: THE NIXON NEW FEDERALISM

President Richard M. Nixon announced his concepts of a "new federalism" and "full opportunity" in the continuing war on poverty during the summer of 1969. His major proposals were: assigning the Office of Economic Opportunity the role of developing and testing new approaches to the solving of social problems (with the spinning off of operating programs—such as the Job Corps—to old-line government agencies); abolishing the present aid to families with dependent children program (AFDC) and replacing it with a program of family-assistance supplements; overhauling the Manpower Development and Training Act with a new Manpower Training Act intended to overcome the confusion, arbitrariness,

[64] Robert B. McKersie, "Vitalize Black Enterprise," *Harvard Business Review,* Vol. 46, No. 5, September-October 1968, pp. 88–99; and Louis L. Allen, "Making Capitalism Work in the Ghetto," *Harvard Business Review,* Vol. 47, No. 3, May-June 1969, pp. 83–92.

[65] Gunnar Myrdal, *An American Dilemma,* Harper, New York, 1944, pp. 304–332 and particularly p. 309.

[66] Frederick D. Sturdivant, "The Limits of Black Capitalism," *Harvard Business Review,* Vol. 47, No. 1, January-February 1969, pp. 122–128.

and rigidity of many of the federal government's job-training programs; and sharing revenue with the states to achieve a new type of federalism, with the states obtaining a larger measure of decentralized power.[67] With the exception of the revamping of OEO, the other innovations are worth some elaboration here because they have important implications on the policy and operational sides for manpower specialists.

The abolition of AFDC, or what in the public mind is often perceived as "welfare," would eliminate what has been termed by Nixon "a colossal failure." AFDC was one of the forms of categorical assistance created in the United States in the 1930s which acted as conduits for income to people in certain categories (the aged, blind, and disabled) who were in need of financial assistance. The states and cities found AFDC to be a welfare quagmire in which case loads increased, benefit levels fluctuated widely from state to state, costs escalated, and recipients became increasingly dependent and detached from the world of work. AFDC not only brought states and cities to the brink of disaster but also failed to meet the elementary human, social, and financial needs of the poor. In effect, because of administrative provisions, AFDC broke up homes, penalized the person with enough incentive to work, and robbed the recipients of their dignity. Homes were broken up because in most states a family was denied payments if the father were present—even though he was unable to support his family. Thus, the father would desert so that his family would obtain the financial benefits of AFDC at the expense often of family social disorganization. This system often made it possible for a welfare recipient to get more money through AFDC than he would on a low-paying job. This situation created a nonincentive to work and was unfair to the working poor.[68] The system robbed people of their dignity because they had to live on handouts and apply for aid often under conditions of humiliation and harassment rather than earn their own living.

The Family Assistance Plan (FAP)

The proposed new family-assistance system was intended to correct the conditions that gave rise to AFDC and would thus lessen the long-range burden even though it would cost more initially than the system it replaced. Under the total welfare tent, the so-called "adult" categories of aid (to the aged, blind, and disabled) would be continued, but a national minimum standard for benefits would be set with the federal government contributing to its cost and also sharing the cost of additional state payments above that amount. The new family-allowance system would rest on three

---

[67] "Nixon's 4-Front War on Poverty," *U.S. News & World Report,* Vol. 67, No. 7, August 18, 1969, pp. 78–80.

[68] *Ibid.,* p. 78.

principles: equality of treatment, a work requirement, and a work incentive. The new system would provide benefits to the working and non-working poor and to families with dependent children, whether headed by a father or mother; and a basic federal minimum level of benefit would apply to all states.[69]

The idea behind the new family-assistance system can be traced back to much contemporary thinking in the field that is coming to be known as "income maintenance," although many of its ideas are rather old.[70] Undoubtedly, the economic thought and philosophy of Professor Milton Friedman was extremely influential.[71] He has advocated negative income taxation for many years, that is, that the income tax rates be extended beyond zero to negative levels in order to pay negative taxes (or transfer payments) to low-income families. The family-assistance idea is also closely associated with the New Frontier–Great Society guru and urbanologist, Daniel Patrick Moynihan, who caused a national sensation in the mid-1960s with his popularization of the long-known problem of Negro family disorganization.[72] The subject has also been discussed under the general name of a "guaranteed income"[73] not to be confused with the guaranteed annual wage concept in use in the field of industrial relations. The family-assistance concept thus is being built into the archway of manpower and employment policy in the United States.

With family assistance, the federal government would build a foundation under the income of every family with dependent children (anywhere in the United States) that cannot care for itself. Under the initially proposed formula, the basic federal payment would be $1600 per year for a family of four on welfare with no outside income. States would normally add to that floor. Outside earnings would be encouraged so that a worker would keep the first $60 a month of outside earnings with no reduction in his benefits, and, beyond that, benefits would be reduced by only 50 cents for each dollar earned.[74]

A family head already employed at low wages, the so-called "working

---

[69] *Ibid.*

[70] The best background studies are James C. Vadakin, *Children, Poverty, and Family Allowances,* Basic Books, New York, 1968; and Christopher Green, ed., *Negative Taxes and the Poverty Program,* Brookings Institution, Washington, 1967.

[71] Milton Friedman, *Capitalism and Freedom,* University of Chicago Press, Chicago, 1962.

[72] See Lee Rainwater and William L. Yancey, *The Moynihan Report and the Politics of Controversy,* MIT Press, Cambridge, 1967.

[73] Most notable here is social economist Robert Theobald. See Theobald, ed., *The Guaranteed Income: Next Step in Economic Evolution?,* Doubleday, Garden City, 1966.

[74] "Nixon's 4-Front War on Poverty," *op. cit.,* p. 78.

poor," would get a family-assistance supplement. For example, a family of five in which the father earns $2000 a year would get family-assistance payments of $1260 for a total income of $3260. Thus, for the first time, the federal government would recognize that it has no less of an obligation to the working poor than to the nonworking poor; and, for the first time, benefits would be scaled so that there would always be an incentive to work.[75]

The Nixon family-assistance proposal is coupled in other ways with employment and training. Every person who accepts benefits must also accept work or training, provided suitable jobs are available either locally or at some distance if transportation is provided. The only exceptions would be people unable to work and mothers of preschool children. Even such mothers would have the opportunity to work because Nixon proposed simultaneously a major expansion and improvement of day-care centers to make it possible for mothers to take jobs by which they can support themselves and their children.[76]

In summary, the new family assistance would provide aid for needy families, a work requirement, and a work incentive. These would be linked to effective programs of job training and job placement, particularly for preparation for jobs that provide self-respect and self-support. To accomplish this linkage, MDTA would be sweepingly overhauled.

Retraining and the Computerized Job Bank

President Nixon's Manpower Training Act is intended to accomplish three goals: (1) to pull together the array of programs that currently exist and equalize standards of eligibility for MDTA, the Job Corps, and the Community Work and Training Program for the Economic Opportunity Act; (2) to provide flexible program funding so that federal money will follow the demands of labor and industry and flow into those programs that people most want and need; and (3) to decentralize program administration gradually from Washington to the states and localities, leaving the United States Department of Labor in general charge. If the states and localities declined to pick up the responsibility, the federal government would continue to manage the programs. If they tried and failed, the federal government could resume the responsibility.[77]

The Manpower Training Act had other provisions specifically designed to help move people off the welfare rolls and on to payrolls, to become a "workfare" program, as Vice-President Spiro T. Agnew put it. A career development plan would be created for trainees tailored to their individual

[75] *Ibid.*
[76] *Ibid.*, p. 79.
[77] *Ibid.*

capabilities and ambitions. A "National Computerized Job Bank" would be set up to match unemployed workers with job vacancies that call for their skills. For persons on welfare, a $30 a month bonus would be offered as an incentive to go into job training. Uniform standards for living allowances would be granted trainees under various instruction programs where in the past allowances varied widely. Funds for training would automatically be increased by 10 percent if the national unemployment rate rose to 4.5 percent for three consecutive months. Lastly, the proposal would add about 150,000 persons to the training rolls, boosting costs by $400 million a year. Most of these people would be heads of families now on AFDC.[78]

Revenue Sharing

Perhaps the most profound of all the changes proposed is the concept of revenue sharing. Looking ahead to the 1970s and 1980s, President Nixon wanted to insure that the states and localities could continue to do their part in solving social problems. Thus, whenever we discuss poverty, jobs, or opportunity, or making government more effective or getting it closer to the people, we immediately get into the financial plight of states and cities. The cities lack the wherewithal to solve their own problems, but neither the states nor the federal government can solve their problems for them. Yet, in Nixon's view, for a third of a century, power and responsibility have flowed toward Washington—and the federal government has taken for its own the best sources of revenue. He advocated reversing the tide, that is, turning back to the states a greater amount of responsibility for solving their problems; and with this, an enlarged share of federal revenues. Accordingly, he proposed that a set portion of the revenues from federal income taxes be remitted directly to the states. There would be a minimum of federal restrictions on how those dollars were to be used, and there would be a requirement that a percentage of them be channeled for the use of local governments. Finally, the funds to be shared would not be great the first year ($1 billion), but the principal would have been established and the amounts subsequently increased as the federal budgetary situation improved.[79]

Evaluation of the New Federalism

There is little doubt among manpower specialists, political leaders, businessmen, social scientists, and pundits representing the gamut of ideo-

[78] "Nixon's Job-Training Plan: How It Will Work," *U.S. News & World Report,* Vol. 67, No. 8, August 25, 1969, p. 62.
[79] "Nixon's 4-Front War on Poverty," *op. cit.,* p. 80.

logical views that President Nixon's welfare, manpower training, and revenue-sharing proposals have cleared the air and offered some real solutions to pressing problems worthy of experimentation. In fact, his proposals for reforming welfare (particularly AFDC) could easily turn out to be one of the major achievements of his administration, although Congress will undoubtedly take considerable time in mulling things over. His welfare plan is far more than merely an ingenious compromise of opposing points of view. Indeed, it is a new and promising approach to a problem that never could be solved within the framework of the old system.[80] All his measures should make change possible.

Nixon's proposal for sharing federal tax revenues with the states and cities has a beguiling look of simplicity. Moreover, it is implicitly based upon the so-called "peace dividend," the amount of money that will be available for new domestic programs when spending for the Vietnam War ends. There may not be a dividend, depending upon the behavior of the economy. Moreover, even if the funds are appropriated—and winning over Congress will be difficult—it may be faulty to assume that local governments would use their appropriation to solve their most urgent problems. Some local governments would probably spend the money on the handiest political project, leaving such high-priority problems as the schools, the slums, and the collapsing urban transit systems exactly where they were before.[81]

There is also doubt that the no-strings approach to revenue sharing really is the best way of attacking social problems financially. An alternative would be to consolidate and streamline the present system of categorical grants. This approach would give local authorities more latitude but would assure that the money was applied to the major problems.[82]

It is also arguable that it would be better for the federal government to cut its taxes or renounce certain taxes, leaving the local authorities to levy their own imposts. The status quo in tax procedures preserves the link between spending and revenue raising, which historically has been the taxpayer's best protection against irresponsibility and extravagance.[83]

It is largely true that local and state governments are coping with social and economic problems of their own making. At present, these problems certainly are beyond the financial powers of the local government units. But it does not follow from this that the federal government will help matters by starting in with $1 billion and making annual expenditures of $5 billion by 1975. On the contrary, this addition to the federal tax load

[80] *Business Week,* No. 2085, August 16, 1969, p. 130.
[81] *Business Week,* No. 2086, August 23, 1969, p. 108.
[82] *Ibid.*
[83] *Ibid.*

could make it impossible for local and state governments ever to become self-sufficient.[84]

In respect to the job-training plans, the administrative changes proposed are praiseworthy. In fact, in the late 1960s, much planning under MDTA and CAMPS was increasingly state and local in origin, as we have seen; and serious students of manpower advocated greater decentralization and integration of federal-state-local efforts in program delivery systems.[85] Probably the real issues are whether Congress will go along with the "countercyclical automatic trigger" or boosting of training allowances if heavier rates of unemployment came in the 1970s and whether the computerized job-bank projects will bear fruit in time. The automaticity of training funds can be justified as can the computerization of information on job seekers and job vacancies based upon results attained. Such will never be known without social experimentation. The remaining changes in job-training seem largely administrative in character and desirable for the purpose intended: to provide incentives and means for individuals to become self-sustaining.

In the final analysis, this superstructure of manpower policy change in the economy should benefit employers and society. Ranging from improved day-care through strengthened training programs, these changes should make the socialization of young people and adults more effective in terms of ability to prepare for and perform in work organizations. These changes should mean that a larger step can be taken toward self-actualization for many people and that the individual who appears at the factory gate, sales office, bureau, or agency is a more capable human being than he would otherwise be. For these reasons, manpower specialists in organizations will need to follow federal legislation closely in the 1970s as it unfolds. The major alternatives are giving up on people, which is probably intolerable in a tension-ridden society such as ours, or falling back to a concept of the government as an employer of last resort, where the unemployed are put to work indefinitely on worthwhile jobs in the public sector which seem never to get done, such as reforestation, conservation, and highway beautification, or possibly on low-level jobs in the new careers hierarchy.

On the other hand, with the concentration on the disadvantaged, manpower policies and human resource development programs for high-talent people will probably be given less attention and remain unchanged in the early 1970s, although the laws pertaining to them will be gradually liberalized and extended if imbalances between manpower supply and demand in certain of the professional occupations persist.

---

[84] *Ibid.*

[85] Sar A. Levitan and Garth L. Mangum, *Federal Training and Work Programs in the Sixties,* University of Michigan, Ann Arbor, 1969, pp. 335–451, *passim.*

PUBLIC AND PRIVATE MANPOWER PLANNING

In American society, equivocal values have historically prevailed on the desirability of public planning of almost any kind until the problems under consideration were widely regarded as intolerable. As a result, public policy on a particular issue usually evolves piecemeal; so that, in time, the result is a quilt rather than a blanket. The patchwork sometimes results in a sight that offends the problem solver and induces him to start over again with a fresh approach, such as is the case in President Nixon's new federalism, at least in AFDC.

We have seen that investments in man and his development have reflected the public-private approaches so typical of the resolution of social problems in the United States. Government has played a role whenever private initiative seemed inadequate or inefficient, much as government took legislative action for the same reasons in union-management relations and in providing social security in the 1930s.

The manpower, training, and educational legislation now on the statute books is a strong beginning toward human resource development objectives which are unclear. Will ours be the first society of self-actualized people?

Legislation leads to the establishment of administrative agencies. In the United States, there has been an historical tendency to start new programs and agencies and layer them on top of or beside the old to provide a counter-bureaucratic stimulus when existing structures were unresponsive or inadequate. This tendency, in time, has led to bureaucratic mergers and other actions to allay the fears of the government's intervening too deeply in social life and threatening cherished values. People have feared governmental control of education, manpower development, and job selection; but they have approved governmental policies designed to improve human resources, develop individual potential without discrimination, make it easier to choose careers and change jobs, and acquire a greater understanding of organizational manpower needs and supplying individuals to meet them. People in America fear automation if it is perceived as leading toward job displacement and unemployment, but they will accept public and private policies which bring about technological change if it is cushioned by mechanisms for areal, social, and personal adjustment. People will fear the enlargement of employment opportunities for anyone if these are disguises for costly make-work programs devoid of value, yet they will support public and private policies if they lead to bona fide jobs caused by an expanding economy or changing occupational structure. In general, people will support legislation that democratically promotes the welfare of the individual by enlarging opportunities for self-development or of the industrial firm by helping it to earn a profit and serve the public and the nation by conserving and properly utilizing its people.

IMPOSSIBLE DREAMS AND IMPOSSIBLE TASKS

Considerable doubt exists today about the administrative agencies that have been charged with duties concerning manpower, training, and employment. In the 1960s, much effort went into changing the reputation and range and quality of services offered by the federal-state employment service. Broadly, the image was to be changed from that of a routine agency concerned with aspects of unemployment insurance administration and the placement of factory blue-collar labor to a dynamic planner and optimizer of manpower mobility. In a way, the ES was asked to become all things to all men from a service standpoint—an impossible task.

In addition, the ES had to cope with a continuing set of complications to achieve change, such as: increases in the size of the labor force, particularly youths; recurrence of creeping prosperity unemployment and its uneven incidence; shifts in the major types of employment in the economy; coping with the barriers to mobility; the problem of the geographical size of the nation, despite the improvements in mass communications; and the increasing complexity of federal-state-local relations. It had to address itself to such sticky problems as: facilitating the transition from school to work for youth through better guidance and counseling and occupational preparation; creating a more effective employment service for white-collar office professional, technical, and managerial personnel; devising new ways for the interstate matching of people and jobs; conducting more sophisticated research and analytical work as well as timely information; waging a campaign with employees to relax soaring hiring standards and to avoid thereby separating American society into high-hiring-standard and low-living-standard sections; and improving the coordination of employment policy (affecting demand, and dealt with under the Employment Act) with manpower policy (affecting supply, and dealt with by much of the legislation on manpower, training, and education).[86] There may be solid reasons for bringing all the federal manpower programs into a single agency[87] as has been done in part in the new United States Training and Employment Service since the Nixon Administration took office.

[86] Lester, *op. cit.,* pp. 209–212 and *passim.*
[87] Levitan and Mangum, *op. cit.,* pp. 446–449.

Educational Policy and Planning

In respect to formal education per se, the knowledge explosion and requirements for survival of a complex society point to the need for educational policies that are appropriate for the era in which we are living. Presently, formal education is in turmoil, and the student rebellion in colleges may be matched in the future at the secondary level. The rebellion may even be carried into industry by college graduates. A comprehensive evaluation of formal education at all levels is warranted as a prelude to identifying desirable future policies and long-range objectives. Then a basis may be established for establishing educational and training policy in firms to tie in with public policy.

National policies and plans should consider as a beginning: financing education at all levels; designing master plans for university-level education throughout the nation; innovating in the administration of education so that bureaucratization will be controlled and true professionalization fostered; heading off educational obsolescense in all occupations; removing the many vestiges of poor quality that bear greatest on the education, training, and unemployment of Negroes; experimenting with new methods of evaluating manpower planning, human resource development, and the results of educational efforts; continuing and expanding actions that allow human potential to seek its own level and contribute across institutional or group lines (as reflected in such devices as the Peace Corps, Executive Service Corps, and industrial sabbatical leaves); and establishing new ways in which industrial and educational institutions can assist one another in achieving the goals of a democratic society.[88] There may be solid reasons for elevating the United States Office of Education to cabinet-level status as a means for making things happen.[89] Certainly, much work remains to be done to straighten out the twists, shapes, and incongruities that exist in education at all levels today.

The manpower specialist can do much to identify the main topics with which policy should be concerned and approaches to the solution of problems in manpower and educational planning.

He can also cooperate with governmental agencies in providing meaningful data for regional and manpower planning so that the whole of national manpower planning will be equal to the sum of the parts, a problem

---

[88] Wilbur B. Brookover and David Gottlieb, *A Sociology of Education,* Second Edition, American Books, New York, 1964, pp. 69–127. See also Grant Venn, *Man, Education, and Manpower,* American Association of School Administrators, Washington, 1970, pp. 233–259.

[89] Rufus E. Miles, Jr., "The Case for a Federal Department of Education," *Public Administration Review,* Vol. 27, No. 1, March 1967, pp. 1–9.

which we explored in an earlier chapter in reference to congruency in overall corporate manpower planning.

No one has pat answers to the planning policy issues raised in this section of the chapter. Yet they are key ones which deserve deliberation and experimentation if we are to solve today's and tomorrow's problems.

INDUSTRY AND CHANGE

There has been a growing interest since the mid-1960s in encouraging industry to take an expanded part in planning and executing change, both internally and externally. Looking ahead, it has been predicted that of all the institutions of present-day American life, industry is perhaps best prepared to meet the year 2000 A.D. Industry has had renowned technical knowhow. It is acquiring vision in the importance of persons, of interpersonal relationships, and of open communication. Industry will increasingly come to value persons as persons at all organizational levels and to recognize that only out of the communicated knowledge of all members of the organization can innovation and progress come.[90]

The old hierarchical system of authoritarian boss and compliant employee is already obsolete in many organizations. The only road to true efficiency seems to be that of persons communicating freely with persons through an individually initiated network which permits the flow of essential information throughout the organization.[91] The bureaucratic form of organization is increasingly becoming obsolete because it has been incapable of managing the tension between individual and managerial goals and the need to adapt to the scientific and technological revolution. The failure of the bureaucratic form to adapt to the new environment has led to the predicted demise of bureaucracy and to the collapse of management as we know it now.[92] The characteristics of industrial organizations of the future have already been set forth.[93] The manpower specialist will have a key role to play in the transition to the new organizational types and managerial styles.

More than two decades ago, at a conference of personnel managers who shared a mutual interest in establishing specific standards for attaining the objectives of personnel management, no mention was made of the need for manpower planning. Yet, it was agreed that the objectives of

---

[90] Carl R. Rogers, "Interpersonal Relationships: U.S.A. 2000," *Journal of Applied Behavioral Science,* Vol. 4, No. 4, July-August-September 1968, pp. 275–276.

[91] *Ibid.*

[92] Warren G. Bennis, *Changing Organizations,* McGraw-Hill, New York, 1966, p. 10.

[93] Jay W. Forrester, "A New Corporate Design," *Industrial Management Review,* Vol. 7, No. 1, Fall 1965, pp. 5–17.

personnel management were: (1) effective utilization of human resources; (2) desirable working relationships among all members of the organization; and (3) maximum individual development.[94] The missing ingredients at the level of the firm were the manpower specialist and planning techniques that could help him make things happen developmentally.[95] There was even little implicit thought given to how manpower utilization and development would take place. Today the picture is quite different. Tomorrow it will be vastly changed, and these future dimensions and conclusions on the state of the art at the present time should be food for thought for the reflective manager and manpower specialist of today.

CONCLUSION

As a last word in this book, we might say that all of what has been set forth amounts to a dynamic new concept of what used to be called "staffing," a rather passive-appearing organizational function in traditional personnel work. Manpower planning, when followed up by the systematic development of human resources, will bring us closer to the achievement of democracy and the solution of at least some of our social problems. To this extent, we shall have accomplished more than the staffing of our organizations; we shall have enhanced and enlarged the quality of our manpower through the intelligent management of our most precious resource.

[94] Twenty Personnel Executives, "The Function and Scope of Personnel Administration," in Paul Pigors et al., eds., *Management of Human Resources,* Second Edition, McGraw-Hill, New York, 1969, p. 58.
[95] Suggested by Frank H. Cassell at a conference, "Manpower Planning in the Firm," Michigan State University, May 15, 1969.

Selected Bibliography

Adams, Leonard P., *The Public Employment Service in Transition, 1933–1968.* Ithaca: New York State School of Industrial and Labor Relations, Cornell University, 1969. 264 pp.

Allen, Charles R., *The Foreman and His Job.* Philadelphia: Lippincott, 1922. 526 pp.

Allen, Louis A., *The Management Profession.* New York: McGraw-Hill, 1964. 375 pp.

Andrews, Kenneth R., *The Effectiveness of University Management Development Programs.* Cambridge: Graduate School of Business Administration, Harvard University, 1966. 340 pp.

Andrews, Kenneth R., *The Case Method of Teaching Human Relations and Administration.* Cambridge: Harvard University Press, 1953. 271 pp.

Argyris, Chris, *Integrating the Individual and the Organization.* New York: Wiley, 1964. 330 pp.

Atherton, J. C. and Anthony Mumphrey, *Essential Aspects of Career Planning and Development.* Danville: Interstate, 1969. 307 pp.

Bailey, S. K., *Congress Makes a Law: The Story Behind the Employment Act.* New York: Columbia University Press, 1950. 282 pp.

Baker, Richard M., Jr., and Gregg Phifer, eds., *Salesmanship: Communication, Persuasion, Perception.* Boston: Allyn and Bacon, 1966. 422 pp.

Bakke, E. Wight, *A Positive Labor Market Policy.* Columbus: Merrill, 1963. 221 pp.

Barnard, Chester I., *The Functions of the Executive.* Cambridge: Harvard University Press, 1938. 334 pp.

Barry, Ruth, and Beverly Wolf, *An Epitaph for Vocational Guidance.* New York: Bureau of Publications, Teachers College, Columbia University, 1922. 241 pp.

Bass, Bernard M., and James A. Vaughan, *Training in Industry: The Management of Learning.* Belmont: Wadsworth, 1966. 149 pp.

715

Beal, Edwin F., and Edward D. Wickersham, *The Practice of Collective Bargaining* (rev. ed.). Homewood: Irwin, 1967. 809 pp.

Bearden, James H., ed., *Personal Selling: Behavioral Science Readings and Cases.* New York: Wiley, 1967. 353 pp.

Belitsky, A. Harvey, *Private Vocational Schools and Their Students.* Cambridge: Schenkman, 1969. 186 pp.

Bennett, Willard E., *Manager Selection, Education and Training.* New York: McGraw-Hill, 1959. 210 pp.

Bennis, Warren G., *Changing Organizations.* New York: McGraw-Hill, 1966. 223 pp.

Bennis, Warren G., *Organization Development.* Reading: Addison-Wesley, 1969. 87 pp.

Bennis, Warren G., and Edgar H. Schein, eds., *Leadership and Motivation.* Cambridge: MIT Press, 1966. 286 pp.

Bennis, Warren G., et al., eds., *The Planning of Change* (2nd ed.). New York: Holt, Rinehart and Winston, 1969. 627 pp.

Bernstein, Marvin H., *The Job of the Federal Executive.* Washington: Brookings Institution, 1958. 241 pp.

Berg, Ivar, *Education and Jobs: The Great Training Robbery.* New York: Praeger Press, 1970. 200 pp.

Bienvenu, Bernard J., *New Priorities in Training.* New York: American Management Association, 1969. 207 pp.

Blake, Robert R., and Jane S. Mouton, *The Managerial Grid.* Houston: Gulf Publishing Company, 1964. 340 pp.

Blake, Robert R., et al., *Managing Intergroup Conflict in Industry.* Houston: Gulf Publishing Company, 1964. 210 pp.

Bolino, August C., *Manpower and the City.* Cambridge: Schenkman, 1969. 282 pp.

Bradford, Leland P., *et al.*, eds., *T-Group Theory and Laboratory Method.* New York: Wiley, 1964. 498 pp.

Bradshaw, T. F., *Developing Men for Controllership.* Boston: Graduate School of Business Administration, Harvard University, 1950. 231 pp.

Bremner, Robert H., *From the Depths.* New York: New York University Press, 1956. 364 pp.

Brookover, Wilbur B., and David Gottlieb. *A Sociology of Education* (2nd ed.). New York: American Books, 1964. 488 pp.

Bruner, Jerome S., *Toward a Theory of Instruction.* Cambridge: Belknap Press, 1966. 176 pp.

Burt, Samuel M., *Industry and Vocational-Technical Education.* New York: McGraw-Hill, 1967. 525 pp.

Coombs, Philip H., *The World Educational Crisis.* New York: Oxford University Press, 1968. 241 pp.

Corwin, Ronald G., *A Sociology of Education.* New York: Appleton-Century-Crofts, 1965. 450 pp.

Craig, Robert L., and Lester R. Bittel, eds., *Training and Development Handbook.* New York: McGraw-Hill, 1967. 650 pp.

Dale, Ernest, *Management: Theory and Practice.* New York: McGraw-Hill, 1965. 743 pp.

Davis, Russell G., *Planning Human Resource Development: Educational Models and Schemata.* Chicago: Rand McNally, 1966. 334 pp.

De Phillips, Frank A., et al., *Management of Training Programs.* Homewood: Irwin, 1960. 481 pp.

Dickson, William J., and F. J. Roethlisberger, *Counseling in an Organization.* Boston: Graduate School of Business Administration, Harvard University, 1966. 480 pp.

Dill, William R., et al., *The New Managers: Patterns of Behavior and Development.* Englewood Cliffs: Prentice-Hall, 1962. 258 pp.

Doeringer, Peter B., ed., *Programs to Employ the Disadvantaged.* Englewood Cliffs: Prentice-Hall, 1969. 261 pp.

Douglas, Paul H., *American Apprenticeship and Industrial Education.* New York: Columbia University Press, 1921. 348 pp.

Drucker, Peter F., *The Age of Discontinuity.* New York: Harper & Row, 1969. 394 pp.

Drucker, Peter F., *The Practice of Management.* New York: Harper, 1954. 404 pp.

Dubin, Robert, ed., *Leadership and Productivity.* San Francisco: Chandler, 1965. 138 pp.

Executive Study Conference, *The Selection and Training of Negroes for Managerial Positions.* Princeton: Educational Testing Service, 1964. 167 pp.

Ferman, Louis A., et al., eds., *Negroes and Jobs.* Ann Arbor: University of Michigan Press, 1968. 591 pp.

Ferman, Louis A., et al., eds., *Poverty in America.* Ann Arbor: University of Michigan Press, 1965. 560 pp.

Fisch, Gerald G., *Organization for Profit.* New York: McGraw-Hill, 1964. 321 pp.

Fisher, Berenice M., *Industrial Education.* Madison: University of Wisconsin Press, 1967. 267 pp.

French, Wendell, *The Personnel Management Process: Human Resources Administration.* Boston: Houghton Mifflin, 1964. 624 pp.

Fryer, Douglas H., et al., *Developing People in Industry*. New York: Harper and Row, 1956. 210 pp.

Gardner, John W., *Excellence*. New York: Harper and Row, 1961. 171 pp.

Gardner, John W., *Self-Renewal*. New York: Harper and Row, 1964. 141 pp.

Ghiselin, Brewster, ed., *The Creative Process*. New York: New American Library (Mentor Book), 1952. 251 pp.

Ginzberg, Eli, *The Development of Human Resources*. New York: McGraw-Hill, 1966. 299 pp.

Ginzberg, Eli, *Human Resources: The Wealth of a Nation*. New York: Simon and Schuster, 1958. 183 pp.

Ginzberg, Eli, *Manpower Agenda for America*. New York: McGraw-Hill, 1968. 250 pp.

Ginzberg, Eli, and Alfred S. Eichner, *The Troublesome Presence: American Democracy and the Negro*. New York: Free Press of Glencoe, 1964. 339 pp.

Ginzberg, Eli, and Ewing W. Reilley, *Effecting Change in Large Organizations*. New York: Columbia University Press, 1957. 155 pp.

Ginzberg, Eli, et al., *The Negro Potential*. New York: Columbia University Press, 1956. 144 pp.

Glaser, Robert, ed., *Training Research and Education*. Pittsburgh: University of Pittsburgh Press, 1962. 596 pp.

Goldwin, Robert A., and Charles A. Nelson, eds., *Toward the Liberally Educated Executive*. New York: New American Library (Mentor Book), 1960. 142 pp.

Golembiewski, Robert T. and Arthur Blumberg, eds., *Sensitivity Training and the Laboratory Approach*. Itasca: Peacock, 1970. 515 pp.

Gordon, Robert A., ed., *Toward a Manpower Policy*. New York: Wiley, 1967. 372 pp.

Gordon, Robert A., and James E. Howell, *Higher Education for Business*. New York: Columbia University, 1959. 491 pp.

Gordon, William J. J., *Synectics*. New York: Harper, 1961. 180 pp.

Goslin, David A., *The School in Contemporary Society*. Chicago: Scott, Foresman, 1965. 173 pp.

Grant, Nigel, *Soviet Education*. Baltimore: Penguin Books, 1964. 190 pp.

Green, Alfred L., *Manpower and the Public Employment Service in Europe*. Albany: New York State Department of Labor, 1966. 204 pp.

Greenlaw, Paul S., et al., *Business Simulation in Industrial and University Education*. Englewood Cliffs: Prentice-Hall, 1962. 356 pp.

Gross, Neal, and Robert E. Herriott, *Staff Leadership in Public Schools*. New York: Wiley, 1965. 247 pp.

Gunning, Robert, *New Guide to More Effective Writing in Business and Industry*. Boston: Industrial Education Institute, 1962. 1 vol. (various pagings).

Gunning, Robert, *The Technique of Clear Writing*. New York: McGraw-Hill, 1952. 289 pp.

Haber, William, and Daniel H. Kruger, *The Role of the United States Employment Service in a Changing Economy*. Kalamazoo: W. E. Upjohn Institute for Employment Research, 1964. 122 pp.

Haber, William, et al., eds., *Manpower in the United States*. New York: Harper, 1954. 225 pp.

Harbison, Frederick H., and Charles A. Myers, *Management in the Industrial World*. New York: McGraw-Hill, 1959. 391 pp.

Harbison, Frederick, and Charles A. Myers, *Manpower and Education*. New York: McGraw-Hill, 1965. 343 pp.

Harrington, Michael, *The Other America: Poverty in the United States*. New York: Macmillan, 1962. 191 pp.

Head, Robert V., *Real-Time Business Systems*. New York: Holt, Rinehart and Winston, 1964. 368 pp.

Herzberg, Frederick, *Work and the Nature of Man*. Cleveland: World, 1966. 203 pp.

Heyel, Carl, ed., *The Foreman's Handbook* (4th ed.). New York: McGraw-Hill, 1967. 591 pp.

Hinrichs, John R., *High-Talent Personnel*. New York: American Management Association, 1966. 288 pp.

Hook, Sidney, *Education for Modern Man* (new enlarged edition). New York: Knopf, 1963. 235 pp.

Hoos, Ida Russakoff, *Retraining the Work Force*. Berkeley: University of California Press, 1967. 281 pp.

House, Robert J., *Management Development: Design, Evaluation, and Implementation*. Ann Arbor: Bureau of Industrial Relations, University of Michigan, 1967. 138 pp.

Houston, George C., *Manager Development, Principles and Perspectives*. Homewood: Irwin, 1961. 299 pp.

Hutchins, Robert M., *The Learning Society*. New York: Praeger, 1968. 154 pp.

International Labour Organization, *European Apprenticeship: Effects of Educational, Social and Technical Development on Apprenticeship Training Practices for Eight Countries*. Geneva: International Labour Organization. 1966. 276 pp.

Jakubauskas, Edward B., and C. Philip Baumel, eds., *Human Resources Development*. Ames: Iowa State University Press, 1967. 163 pp.

Jencks, Christopher, and David Riesman, *The Academic Revolution*. Garden City: Doubleday, 1968. 580 pp.

Kahler, Alfred, and Ernest Hamberger, *Education for an Industrial Age*. Ithaca: Cornell University Press, 1948. 334 pp.

Kellogg, Marion S., *What to Do about Performance Appraisal*. New York: American Management Association, 1965. 221 pp.

Kelly, Joe, *Organizational Behaviour*. Homewood: Irwin, 1969. 666 pp.

Kepner, Charles H., and Benjamin B. Tregoe, *The Rational Manager*. New York: McGraw-Hill, 1965. 275 pp.

King, David, *Training Within the Organization*. London: Tavistock, 1964. 274 pp.

Korol, Alexander G., *Soviet Education for Science and Technology*. New York: Wiley, 1957. 513 pp.

Kuriloff, Arthur H., *Reality in Management*. New York: McGraw-Hill, 1966. 300 pp.

Kursh, Harry, *Apprenticeship in America*. New York: Norton, 1965. 200 pp.

Landsberger, Henry A., *Hawthorne Revisited*. Ithaca: Cornell University Press, 1958. 119 pp.

Le Breton, Preston P., and Dale A. Henning, *Planning Theory*. Englewood Cliffs: Prentice-Hall, 1961. 357 pp.

Lee, Irving J., ed., *The Language of Wisdom and Folly*. New York: Harper, 1949. 361 pp.

Leiter, Robert D., *The Foreman in Industrial Relations*. New York: Columbia University Press, 1948. 200 pp.

Leonard, George B., *Education and Ecstasy*. New York: Delacorte Press, 1968. 239 pp.

Lester, Richard A., *Manpower Planning in a Free Society*. Princeton: Princeton University Press, 1966. 232 pp.

Levitan, Sar A., *Federal Aid to Depressed Areas*. Baltimore: Johns Hopkins Press, 1964. 268 pp.

Levitan, Sar A., *The Great Society's Poor Law*. Baltimore: Johns Hopkins Press, 1969. 348 pp.

Levitan, Sar A., and Garth L. Mangum, *Federal Training and Work Programs in the Sixties*. Ann Arbor: Institute of Labor and Industrial Relations, University of Michigan, 1969. 465 pp.

Levitan, Sar A., et al., *Towards Freedom from Want*. Madison: Industrial Relations Research Association, 1968. 243 pp.

Lewis, Roy, and Rosemary Stewart, *The Managers: A New Examination of the English, German, and American Executive*. New York: New American Library, 1961. 256 pp.

Likert, Rensis, *New Patterns of Management*. New York: McGraw-Hill, 1961. 279 pp.

Likert, Rensis, *The Human Organization*. New York: McGraw-Hill, 1967. 224 pp.

Ling, Cyril Curtis, *The Management of Personnel Relations*. Homewood: Irwin, 1965. 554 pp.

Lippitt, Gordon L., *Organizational Renewal*. New York: Appleton-Century-Crofts, 1969. 321 pp.

Lippitt, Ronald, et al., *The Dynamics of Planned Change*. New York: Harcourt, Brace, 1958. 312 pp.

Luft, Joseph, *Group Processes*. Palo Alto: National Press, 1963. 57 pp.

Lumsdaine, A. A., and Robert Glaser, *Teaching Machines and Programmed Learning*. Washington: National Education Association, 1960. 736 pp.

Lynton, Rolf, and Udai Pareek, *Training for Development*. Homewood: Irwin, 1967. 408 pp.

Mace, Myles L., *The Growth and Development of Executives*. Boston: Graduate School of Business Administration, Harvard University, 1950. 200 pp.

Mager, Robert F., *Preparing Objectives for Programmed Instruction*. San Francisco: Fearon, 1961. 62 pp.

Mahler, Walter R., and W. H. Monroe, *How Industry Determines the Need for Effective Training*. New York: Psychological Corporation, 1952. 152 pp.

Mahoney, Thomas A., et al., *Development of Managerial Performance*. Cincinnati: South-Western, 1963. 67 pp.

Mangum, Garth L., *MDTA, Foundation of Federal Manpower Policy*. Baltimore: Johns Hopkins Press, 1968. 184 pp.

Mangum, Garth L., ed., *The Manpower Revolution*. Garden City: Doubleday, 1966. 580 pp.

Marrow, Alfred J., *Behind the Executive Mask*. New York: American Management Association, 1964. 143 pp.

Marrow, Alfred J., *Making Management Human*. New York: McGraw-Hill, 1957. 241 pp.

Marshall, F. Ray, *The Negro and Organized Labor*. New York: Wiley, 1965. 327 pp.

Marshall, F. Ray, and Vernon M. Briggs, Jr., *The Negro and Apprenticeship*. Baltimore: Johns Hopkins Press, 1967. 283 pp.

Maslow, Abraham H., *Eupsychian Management: A Journal*. Homewood: Irwin, 1965. 277 pp.

Maslow, Abraham H., *Motivation and Personality*. New York: Harper and Row, 1954. 411 pp.

Meriam, Lewis, *Relief and Social Security*. Washington: Brookings Institution, 1946. 912 pp.

Merton, Robert K., and Robert A. Nisbet, eds., *Contemporary Social Problems*. New York: Harcourt, Brace & World, 1961. 754 pp.

Michael, Donald N., *Cybernation: The Silent Conquest*. Santa Barbara: Center for the Study of Democratic Institutions, 1962. 47 pp.

Miller, E. J., and A. K. Rice, *Systems of Organization*. New York: Tavistock, 1967. 286 pp.

Miller, Herman P., *Poverty American Style*. Belmont: Wadsworth, 1966. 304 pp.

Morgan, Howard K., *Industrial Training and Testing*. New York: McGraw-Hill, 1945. 225 pp.

Moynihan, Daniel P., *Maximum Feasible Misunderstanding*. New York: Free Press, 1969. 218 pp.

Moynihan, Daniel P., ed., *On Understanding Poverty*. New York: Basic Books, 1969. 425 pp.

McBeath, Gordon, *Organization and Manpower Planning* (rev. ed.). London: Business Books, 1969. 262 pp.

McCarthy, E. Jerome, *Basic Marketing* (rev. ed.). Homewood: Irwin, 1964. 978 pp.

McGehee, William, and Paul W. Thayer, *Training in Business and Industry*. New York: Wiley, 1961. 305 pp.

McGregor, Douglas, *The Human Side of Enterprise*. New York: McGraw-Hill, 1960. 246 pp.

McGregor, Douglas, *The Professional Manager*. New York: McGraw-Hill, 1967. 224 pp.

McLarney, William J., and William M. Berliner, *Management Training* (5th ed.). Homewood: Irwin, 1970. 732 pp.

McNair, Malcolm P., ed., *The Case Method at the Harvard Business School*. New York: McGraw-Hill, 1954. 292 pp.

McNulty, Nancy G., *Training Managers, The International Guide*. New York: Harper and Row, 1969. 572 pp.

Nathan, Richard P., *Jobs and Civil Rights*. Washington: Government Printing Office, 1969. 318 pp.

National Bureau of Economic Research, *The Measurement and Interpretation of Job Vacancies*. New York: Columbia University Press, 1966. 593 pp.

National Manpower Council, *A Policy for Skilled Manpower*. New York: Columbia University Press, 1954. 299 pp.

National Manpower Council, *Education and Manpower*. New York: Columbia University Press, 1960. 326 pp.

National Manpower Council, *Womanpower*. New York: Columbia University Press, 1957. 371 pp.

Nosow, Sigmund, and William H. Form, eds., *Man, Work, and Society: A Reader in the Sociology of Occupations*. New York: Basic Books, 1962. 612 pp.

Odiorne, George S., *Management by Objectives*. New York: Pitman, 1965. 204 pp.

Odiorne, George S., and Arthur S. Hann, *Effective College Recruiting*. Ann Arbor: Bureau of Industrial Relations, University of Michigan, 1961. 288 pp.

Orth, Charles D., III, *Social Structure and Learning Climate*. Boston: Graduate School of Business Administration, Harvard University, 1963. 236 pp.

Osborn, Alex F., *Applied Imagination* (3rd rev. ed.). New York: Scribner's, 1963. 417 pp.

Otto, Calvin P. and Rollin O. Glaser, *The Management of Training: A Handbook for Training and Development Personnel*. Reading: Addison-Wesley, 1970. 410 pp.

Parnes, Herbert S., *Forecasting Educational Needs for Economic and Social Development*. Paris: Organization for Economic and Social Development, 1962. 113 pp.

Patten, Thomas H., Jr., *The Foreman: Forgotten Man of Management*. New York: American Management Association, 1968. 191 pp.

Pearl, Arthur, and Frank Riessman, *New Careers for the Poor*. New York: Free Press, 1965. 273 pp.

Perrucci, Robert, and Marc Pilisuk, eds., *The Triple Revolution*. Boston: Little, Brown, 1968. 640 pp.

Perry, Ronald, *Apprenticeship—Past and Present* (rev. ed.). Washington: Government Printing Office, 1962. 31 pp.

Pigors, Paul and Faith, *Case Method in Human Relations: The Incident Process*. New York: McGraw-Hill, 1961. 413 pp.

Planty, Earl G., and J. Thomas Freeston, *Developing Management Ability*. New York: Ronald, 1954. 447 pp.

Planty, Earl G., et al., *Training Employees and Managers for Production and Teamwork*. New York: Ronald, 1948. 278 pp.

Porter, Elias H., *Manpower Development*. New York: Harper & Row, 1964. 138 pp.

Pound, Arthur, *The Turning Wheel*. Garden City: Doubleday, Doran, 1934. 517 pp.

Prince, George M., *The Practice of Creativity*. New York: Harper and Row, 1970. 197 pp.

Proctor, John H., and William M. Thornton, *Training: A Handbook for Line Managers*. New York: American Management Association, 1961. 224 pp.

Prosser, Charles A., and Charles Allen, *Vocational Education in a Democracy*. New York: Appleton-Century, 1925. 580 pp.

Rainwater, Lee, and William L. Yancey, *The Moynihan Report and the Politics of Controversy*. Cambridge: MIT Press, 1967. 493 pp.

Reeves, Elton T., *Management Development for the Line Manager*. New York: American Management Asosciation, 1969. 240 pp.

Rice, A. K., *Learning for Leadership*. London: Tavistock, 1965. 200 pp.

Richman, Barry M., *Management Development and Education in the Soviet Union*. East Lansing: Graduate School of Business Administration, Michigan State University, 1967. 308 pp.

Ross, Arthur M., ed., *Employment Policy and the Labor Market*. Berkeley: University of California Press, 1965. 406 pp.

Ross, Arthur M., and Herbert Hill, eds. *Employment, Race, and Poverty*. New York: Harcourt, Brace & World, 1967. 598 pp.

Rourke, Francis E., and Glenn E. Brooks, *The Managerial Revolution in Higher Education*. Baltimore: Johns Hopkins Press, 1966. 184 pp.

Rummler, Geary A., et al., eds., *Managing the Instructional Programming Effort*. Ann Arbor: Bureau of Industrial Relations, University of Michigan, 1967. 294 pp.

Schein, Edgar H., and Warren G. Bennis, *Personal and Organizational Change through Group Methods: The Laboratory Approach*. New York: Wiley, 1965. 376 pp.

Schneider, Herman, *Education for Industrial Workers*. New York: World Book, 1915. 98 pp.

Schultz, Theodore W., *The Economic Value of Education*. New York: Columbia University Press, 1963. 92 pp.

Schutz, William C., *Joy*. New York: Grove, 1967. 223 pp.

Selznick, Philip, *Leadership in Administration*. New York: Harper and Row, 1957. 162 pp.

Sharp, Laure M., *Education and Employment*. Baltimore: Johns Hopkins Press, 1970. 162 pp.

Shostrom, Everett L., *Man, the Manipulator*. New York: Bantam Books, 1968. 189 pp.

Slichter, Sumner H., *Union Policies and Industrial Management*. Washington: Brookings Institution, 1941. 597 pp.

Slichter, Sumner H., et al., *The Impact of Collective Bargaining on Management*. Washington: Brookings Institution, 1960. 982 pp.

Somers, Gerald G., ed., *Retraining the Unemployed*. Madison: University of Wisconsin Press, 1968. 351 pp.

Staton, Thomas F., *How to Instruct Successfully*. New York: McGraw-Hill, 1960. 304 pp.

Steiner, George A., ed., *Managerial Long-Range Planning*. New York: McGraw-Hill, 1963. 334 pp.

Stokes, Paul M., *Total Job Training: A Manual for the Working Manager.* New York: American Management Association, 1966. 158 pp.

Sufrin, Sidney, C., *Administering the National Defense Education Act.* Syracuse: University of Syracuse Press, 1963. 76 pp.

Tead, Ordway, *The Art of Leadership.* New York: McGraw-Hill, 1935. 303 pp.

Tead, Ordway, *Human Nature and Management.* New York: McGraw-Hill, 1929. 312 pp.

Theobald, Robert, *The Challenge of Abundance.* New York: Potter, 1961. 235 pp.

Theobald, Robert, *Free Men and Free Markets.* New York: Potter, 1963. 203 pp.

Theobald, Robert, *The Guaranteed Income.* Garden City: Doubleday, 1966. 233 pp.

Thompson, Joseph W., *Selling: A Behavioral Science Approach.* New York: McGraw-Hill, 1966. 384 pp.

Tracey, William R., *Evaluating Training and Development Systems.* New York: American Management Association, 1968. 304 pp.

Tyler, Ralph W., and Annice L. Mills, *Report on Cooperative Education.* New York: Thomas Alva Edison Foundation, 1961. 32 pp.

Vaizey, John, *The Economics of Education.* New York: St. Martin's Press, 1966. 781 pp.

Venables, P. F. R., *Sandwich Courses.* London: M. Parish, 1959. 160 pp.

Venn, Grant, *Man, Education, and Manpower.* Washington: American Association of School Administrators, 1970. 281 pp.

Venn, Grant, *Man, Education, and Work.* Washington: American Council on Education, 1964. 184 pp.

Vetter, Eric W., *Manpower Planning for High Talent Personnel.* Ann Arbor: Bureau of Industrial Relations, University of Michigan, 1967. 222 pp.

Walker, Charles R., et al., *The Foreman on the Assembly Line.* Cambridge: Harvard University Press, 1956. 197 pp.

War Manpower Commission, *The Training Within Industry Report.* Washington: Government Printing Office, 1945. 195 pp.

Weber, Arnold R., et al., eds., *Public-Private Manpower Policies.* Madison: Industrial Relations Research Association, 1969. 210 pp.

Weeks, Christopher, *Job Corps.* Boston: Little, Brown, 1967. 241 pp.

Weinberg, Ian, *The English Public Schools.* New York: Atheling Books, 1966. 250 pp.

Weschler, Irving R., and Jerome Reisel, *Inside a Sensitivity Training Group.* Los Angeles: Institute of Industrial Relaitons, University of California, 1960. 127 pp.

Wickert, Frederic R., and Dalton E. McFarland, eds., *Measuring Executive Effectiveness*. New York: Appleton-Century-Crofts, 1967. 242 pp.

Williams, Gertrude, *Apprenticeship in Europe*. London: Chapman and Hull, 1963. 208 pp.

Wilson, James W., and Edward H. Lyons, *Work-Study College Programs*. New York: Harper, 1961. 232 pp.

Wolfbein, Seymour L., *Employment, Unemployment, and Public Policy*. New York: Random House, 1965. 210 pp.

Woodward, Joan, *Industrial Organization*. New York: Oxford University Press, 1965. 281 pp.

Wooldridge, Roy L., *Cooperative Education and the Community Colleges in New Jersey*. New York: National Commission for Cooperative Education, 1966. 26 pp.

Young, Michael, *The Rise of Meritocracy, 1870–2033: An Essay on Education and Equality*. Baltimore: Penguin Books, 1962. 189 pp.

Zaleznik, Abraham, *Foreman Training in a Growing Enterprise*. Boston: Graduate School of Business Administration, Harvard University, 1951. 232 pp.

Zelko, Harold, and Frank E. X. Dance, *Business and Professional Speech Communication*. New York: Holt, Rinehart and Winston, 1965. 244 pp.

Index

Acton Society Trust, 410

Administrative Staff College, Henley-on-Thames, 145–146, 434–435, 475, 476

Advanced Management Program (of Graduate School of Business Administration Harvard University, 398, 439, 446–448, 483

Aerojet-General Corporation, 701

Agency for International Development (AID), 470

Agnew, Spiro T., 705

Agreements, collectively bargained, 284, 289, 657

Aid to Families with Dependent Children (AFDC), 672, 702–705, 706, 707, 709

Air Force, United States, 333

Akron, University of, 457

Alfred P. Sloan Foundation, 448

Alinsky, Saul, 658

Allen, Louis A., 465, 466, 467

Allied Health Professions Personnel Training Act of 1966, 620, fn 679

Aluminum Company of Canada, Ltd., 180

American Airlines, Incorporated, 135

American Federation of Labor and Congress of Industrial Organizations (AFL–CIO), 290

American Machine and Foundry Company (AMF), 247

American Management Association, 359, 394, 483, 559

Management Internship Program, 559

American Society for Engineering Education (ASEE), 454, 500, 501, 509

American Society for Training and Development (ASTD), 208

American Telephone and Telegraph Company (AT&T), 135, 430, 455–458, 459, 467, 534

American Tobacco Company, 586

American Vocational Association (AVA), 631, 632, 637

Andrews, Kenneth R., 441, 442, 445, 446

Antioch College, 499, 514–515

Apollo Moon Project, 247

Appalachia, 640

Apprenticeship, 172, 278–341, 204, 301–303, 602, 605, 622–623, 659–660; see also Vocational education

apprentice-journeyman ratio, 90–104, 325

Bureau of Apprenticeship and Training, 287–289, 302, 313–314, 324, 340

discrimination against Negroes, 290, 303, 308–311, 312

Europe, 334–338

history of, 278, 284–289, 333–338

indenture, as a concept, 282, 293, 294–295

Joe McGees, 299–304

Joint Apprenticeship Committees, 314, 315, 320–321, 324

journeyman, as a concept, 293

pre-apprenticeship, 310–311, 327–328

programs, registration of, 286, 313–314

related instruction, 293, 296, 318–323, 325

role of unions, 284, 289–290, 300, 301, 308–311, 315, 320–321, 627, 628

selection, 304–307, 310–311, 324

standards, 324–325

training program, 83–104, 227

Area Redevelopment Act of 1961, 620, 639, 640–642, 648, 674, 695

Area skill surveys, 47, 50

Area vocational schools, 330–331, 632–633

727